Applying AUTOCAD®
A Step-By-Step Approach
for AutoCAD Release 12

by
Terry T. Wohlers
Wohlers Associates

GLENCOE
Macmillan/McGraw-Hill

New York, New York
Columbus, Ohio
Mission Hills, California
Peoria, Illinois

Send all inquiries to:
GLENCOE DIVISION
Macmillan/McGraw-Hill
3008 W. Willow Knolls Drive
Peoria, IL 61614-1083

Sixth Edition
ISBN 0-02-677130-6 (Work-text)
ISBN 0-02-677131-4 (Instructor's Guide)
ISBN 0-02-677132-2 (Diskette)
ISBN 0-02-677133-0 (Guide to AME)

Printed in the United States of America.

1 2 3 4 5 6 7 8 9 10   CUS   99 98 97 96 95 94 93 92

Except where otherwise credited, all CAD drawings within this book were developed with AutoCAD by the author and plotted using a Houston Instrument pen plotter or Apple LaserWriter IIg. The AutoCAD image on the front cover was produced with the Bell & Howell Color Digital Imager (CDI) IV film recorder. The drawing was created by Riley Clark of Hicks & Hartwick, Inc.

Applying AutoCAD is a work-text for those who wish to learn how to use the AutoCAD® software. AutoCAD® is a computer-aided drafting and design package produced by Autodesk, Inc. For information on how to obtain the AutoCAD® software, contact Autodesk at (415) 332-2344.

AutoCAD and AutoLISP are registered trademarks of Autodesk, Inc.
AME and ADS are trademarks of Autodesk, Inc.

5-2-94 - 199 - UNIT QUESTIONS
5-2-94 - 150 - UNIT PROBLEMS

Dedication

To the newest addition to my family, Heather Briana, born April 1992; and to her brother, Chad Ryan, born a decade earlier; and to their mother and my wife, Diane, for her support and encouragement.

Acknowledgments

A very special thanks to Jody James for helping to make this edition the best ever. Her knowledge, professionalism, and incredible efficiency contributed more than she will ever know. Jody is an editorial consultant from Oviedo, Florida.

The author sincerely thanks the editorial, marketing, and production staff at Glencoe for their continued commitment to this book. A special thanks to Debie Baxter, Wes Coulter, Jean Gardner, Mike Kenny, Trudy Muller, and Arvella Utley for their assistance.

Thanks to all of the people at Autodesk, especially Duff Kurland, Carl Bethea, and Neele Johnston. The author thanks Professor Gordon Wormsbecker of the University of Alberta for his many suggestions, and Chad Wohlers for reproducing reams of manuscript pages.

Finally, the author wishes to thank the following people and organizations for their support of this book: Rob Hohman of Media Marketing Associates; Richard Stehr of CalComp; Ariel Communications; Artist Graphics; Apple Computer; Bell & Howell Quintar Division; Houston Instrument; Radius Inc.; and Toshiba.

Glencoe wishes to thank the Calcomp Digitizer Products Group of CalComp Inc. for supplying a *DrawingBoard II* digitizing tablet for use in editing this work-text.

Advisory Board

The author and publisher gratefully acknowledge the contributions of the Advisory Board members, who reviewed *Applying AutoCAD* and provided valuable input for its revision.

David B. Cox, CPA
Computer Consultant
Vienna, WV

Patrick H. DePass
AT&T Bell Laboratories
Holmdel, NJ

Wayne J. Elinger
Dean of Manufacturing
  and Engineering
Spokane Community College
Spokane, WA

(continued next page)

Jerry T. Hagmeier
Coordinator, Computer-Aided
    Design Instruction
John Wood Community College
Quincy, IL

Gary J. Hordemann
SPOCAD Centers of Gonzaga
    University
Spokane, WA

Steve Huycke
Instructor/CAD
Lake Michigan College
Benton Harbor, MI

John F. Kirk
Technical Bridge Services
Ceres, CA

Stephen Manlove
University of Minnesota
Minneapolis, MN

Jackie McAninch
Manager, AutoCAD Training Center
Mesa State College
Grand Junction, CO

Dr. Jack Michie
Professor Retired
Arizona State University
Scottsdale, AZ

Dan Myers, President
Informance Computer Services
Highlands Ranch, CO

Kent Parkinson
Parkinson & Associates
West Lafayette, IN

Donald Sanborn
Unique Solutions
Colorado Springs, CO

Donnia M. Tabor-Hanson
CAD by Designing Trends
Oak Ridge, TN

Ronald W. Weseloh
Red Bud High School
Red Bud, IL

William H. Work, AIA
KPF Interior Architects, PC
New York, NY

Gordon T. Wormsbecker
University of Alberta,
    Edmonton
Alberta, Canada

Joseph K. Yabu, Ph.D.
Associate Professor
Division of Technology
San Jose State University
San Jose, CA

Table of Contents

(continued next page)

(continued next page)

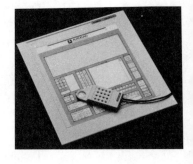

(continued next page)

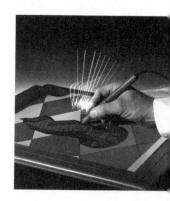

(continued next page)

xvi

AutoCAD at Work Stories

Illustrations in front matter provided by the following:

Mitsubishi Electronics America, Inc. (pp. v and vii); Digital Equipment Corporation (p. vi); Ron Shea (p. vii); IBM Corporation (p. ix); Houston Instrument (p. x); CalComp (pp. xi, xiii, and xvii); Apple Computer Inc. (p. xv).

Introduction

Applying AutoCAD®: A Step-By-Step Approach is a work-text based on the AutoCAD® Release 12 computer-aided drafting and design package. It is designed primarily for new users of AutoCAD, though experienced users also will find it to be a helpful aid for reference and review. Through step-by-step instruction, the book takes students from the beginning to the advanced level. Along the way, they are encouraged to experiment, to create, and to learn firsthand the power and versatility of AutoCAD.

Applying AutoCAD is not restricted to one discipline. Rather, it serves all areas which require methods of drafting, design, and engineering, such as architecture, civil engineering, mapping, landscaping, mechanical and structural engineering, electricity/electronics, facilities planning, and interior design. Less common but potentially very productive areas include theater set and lighting design, museum display design, graphic arts, and even archaeology.

Operating System

Applying AutoCAD: A Step-By-Step Approach is fully compatible with personal computers running the MS-DOS operating system. AutoCAD is available for other types of systems, such as the Macintosh and several UNIX workstations, although AutoCAD is installed on more MS-DOS computers than all others combined. Therefore, this book has been written for users of the MS-DOS version of AutoCAD. Appendices A-D offer special assistance in using MS-DOS with AutoCAD.

The AutoCAD commands presented in *Applying AutoCAD* are the same as those for the Macintosh and UNIX versions of AutoCAD. However, users of these versions can select menu items that differ from one AutoCAD version to the next. While most of the instructions in *Applying AutoCAD* apply to all versions of AutoCAD, some of them do not.

Format

The contents of this book are formatted in a straightforward, simple-to-use manner so that instructors, regardless of their background, can easily adapt the book to their existing courses. The book's structure in fact lends itself to picking and choosing units and problems as instructors see fit. Therefore instructors should by no means feel obligated to use the entire work-text to accomplish their course objectives.

For educators beginning a new course using AutoCAD, the book provides an excellent foundation for developing the course. The units are sequenced in the best order for learning AutoCAD, so instructors are encouraged to use the book's outline as their course outline.

The book contains enough exercises for an entire semester course. Some instructors have used the earlier editions for introductory, intermediate, and advanced courses spread over several semesters. The instructor can adjust the pace and assignments according to the level of the learner group and to the number of hours the students receive on the AutoCAD stations.

What's New in This Edition

This edition of *Applying AutoCAD* includes the new and enhanced commands and features of AutoCAD Release 12. The following is a sampling of what's new:

- Noun/Verb syntax, simplifying and speeding object selection and command entry for individuals that prefer this technique
- Advanced object selection and editing using grips, reducing the steps necessary to select and edit objects

- Dialogue boxes for opening drawing files, obtaining help, selecting text fonts, reviewing and changing dimensioning variables, renaming objects, plotting, and a host of other AutoCAD functions
- Cascading pull-down menus, allowing you to review relevant menu choices at once
- Automatic timed saves, helping you avoid the possibility of losing data

The new edition also includes:
- New dimensioning capabilities, such as dimensioning variables and dimension dragging and editing
- Improved 3D viewpoint selection, dynamic viewing, and 3D object editing
- Basic shading and advanced rendering, entirely within AutoCAD
- Two-dimensional region modeling, involving the same union, subtraction, and intersection Boolean operations used in the Advanced Modeling Extension™ (AME™)
- What-you-see-is-what-you-get (WYSIWYG) plot previews and multiple output device configuration

Features

- Fifty-nine clearly-defined units guide students in their progress from basic to advanced levels. Progress is easy to see and review is simple.
- In addition to the fundamentals of AutoCAD, the book presents advanced topics of special interest, including
  - symbol libraries
  - attributes and bills of materials
  - isometric drawing
  - 3D wireframe modeling using surfaces of revolution, ruled surfaces, tabulated surfaces, Coons surface patches, and basic 3D polygon meshes
  - X/Y/Z point filters, User Coordinate Systems (UCSs), and dynamic view facility
  - external references (Xrefs)
  - viewports in paper space and multiple-view plotting
  - screen, tablet, pull-down, and icon menu development and customization
  - AutoLISP applications and programming
  - DXF and IGES translations
  - slide shows and slide libraries
  - digitizing and plotting
  - hard disk organization, use of batch files, and system management
- To help students locate additional information, notations in margins correlate topics to AutoCAD's eleven reference manuals. These publications are included with the AutoCAD software.
- Hint sections throughout the units help students effectively tap the full power of AutoCAD.
- Questions and problems at the end of each unit ensure mastery of AutoCAD.
- Optional problems section challenges and motivates advanced students.
- Useful appendices on topics such as disk formatting, producing backup copies, and configuring AutoCAD help students organize AutoCAD.
- "AutoCAD at Work" stories help students understand how AutoCAD is used in business and industry.

Guide to AME™

Guide to AME™ is a supplement for individuals and organizations that own the optional Advanced Modeling Extension™ (AME™) software for AutoCAD. AME enables you to create moderately complex solid models entirely within AutoCAD using the union, subtraction, and intersection Boolean operations. The guide follows the same step-by-step format used in the *Applying AutoCAD* work-text. For purchasing information, phone 1-800-334-7344.

Instructor's Guide

An instructor's guide is available as a companion to the *Applying AutoCAD* work-text. It provides instructors with a range of helpful teaching supplements, such as a sample course syllabus, instructional tips and advice, optional group activities, and transparency masters. For purchasing information, phone 1-800-334-7344.

Applying AutoCAD Diskette

An optional companion diskette is available for use with *Applying AutoCAD*. The diskette contains more than 50 useful files. For example, AutoLISP® routines (including a special parametric program) and menu files presented in this book are contained on the diskette, saving you the time and effort of accurately entering them manually.

If you want to experiment with DXF and IGES files created by other CAD systems, several are contained on the diskette so that you can see how they import to AutoCAD. Also available on the diskette are several drawing files, including prototype drawings, for use with many of the exercises presented throughout *Applying AutoCAD*. These files save you drawing preparation time when completing the exercises.

The diskette also contains a sample slide show as well as a program that enables you to create a bill of materials. For additional information, phone 1-800-334-7344.

To the Student

By following the step-by-step exercises in this book, you will learn to use AutoCAD to create, modify, store, retrieve, and manage AutoCAD drawings and related files. For review and practice, questions and problems have been provided at the end of each unit. In addition, there is a section of more challenging problems following Unit 59.

In order to derive the full benefit of this book, you should be aware of the following:

- *Notational conventions.* Computer keyboards differ. In this book, you will find many references to the RETURN key. On your keyboard, this key may be marked ENTER, NEXT, etc. Likewise, you will find references to the CTRL (control) key. On some keyboards this key is labeled with a different name.

  In the step-by-step instructions, user input is in **boldface** type. For example, the instruction "enter the **LINE** command" means that you should type the LINE command on the keyboard and press RETURN. Command names are usually shown in uppercase letters, but you can type them in either upper or lower case letters.

  On the computer screen, AutoCAD default values are displayed within < >. You can select the default value by simply pressing the RETURN key or the space bar.

- *ACAD.DWG prototype drawing.* As you work with AutoCAD, you will learn of the AutoCAD defaults and how these modes and settings are stored in AutoCAD's default prototype drawing called ACAD.DWG.

- *End-of-unit questions.* The questions at the end of each unit are intended to help you review the material in the unit and to expand your knowledge. Therefore, in order to answer some of the questions, you may need to work on the computer or refer to the manuals that accompany the AutoCAD software.

About the Author

Terry Wohlers is the principal consultant and president of Wohlers Associates, an engineering and manufacturing consulting firm located near Denver, Colorado. Most recently, Terry has counseled organizations on how to effectively select and manage technologies for CAD/CAM/CAE, rapid prototyping, and reverse engineering.

Terry is the author of 180 books, articles, and technical papers on engineering and manufacturing automation. His articles have appeared in *Manufacturing Engineering, Computer-Aided Engineering, Rapid Prototyping Report, PC Magazine, InfoWorld, CADalyst, DesignNet, Architectural & Engineering Systems, CAD/CAM Journal,* and *T.H.E. Journal.* Terry is a contributing editor of *Computer Graphics World* and one of the longest regular contributors to *CADENCE*, a publication dedicated to AutoCAD.

Terry has become a highly sought-after speaker at industry events around the globe. He has given keynote presentations at many conferences, including the First European Rapid Prototyping Convention in Paris, France, the Sixth International CAD Forum in Nottingham, England, and the Fifth International Patternmaking Congress in Toronto, Canada. Terry's 1986 award-winning presentation in London, England, accurately predicted the explosive growth of desktop systems for computer-aided design and drafting.

Terry is an elected member of the National Computer Graphics Association's (NCGA) Board of Directors. He is also a founder and chairman of the NCGA CAD Society, the only independent CAD member organization of its kind. Formerly, Terry developed and taught undergraduate and graduate courses on CAD at Colorado State University, including one of the nation's first university courses on AutoCAD. Terry holds M.S. and B.A. degrees from Colorado State University and the University of Nebraska, respectively.

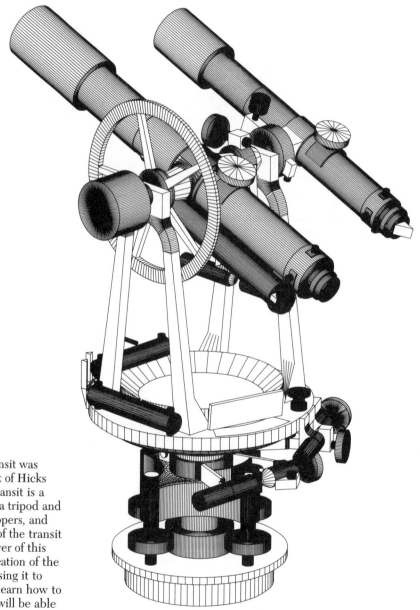

This three-dimensional model of a transit was created with AutoCAD by Riley Clark of Hicks & Hartwick, Inc. (Redlands, CA). A transit is a surveying instrument that mounts on a tripod and is used by civil engineers, land developers, and building contractors. A zoomed view of the transit is spread across the front and back cover of this book. The model reflects the sophistication of the AutoCAD software and the value of using it to communicate new designs. After you learn how to apply AutoCAD using this book, you will be able to complete similar work.

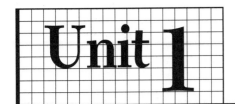 **Unit 1** Straight to AutoCAD

Reference *

REF 52

■ **OBJECTIVE:**

To understand the purpose of the components found in the AutoCAD graphics screen and to learn the purpose of the NEW, OPEN, SAVE, SAVEAS, QSAVE, END, and QUIT commands

The AutoCAD graphics screen is where most AutoCAD users spend most of their time. It allows you to create, open, change, view, and plot drawings. It is therefore necessary for you to understand the purpose of each component found in the AutoCAD graphics screen.

Taking a Look Around ─────────────

1 Start AutoCAD, and you will find yourself in the AutoCAD graphics screen, as shown on the following page.

HINT: AutoCAD is usually started by entering ACAD386.BAT or a similar batch file. If you need assistance with logging onto the proper drive or directory and starting AutoCAD, see Appendices C and D at the back of this book.

*The numbers in this column correspond to pages in AutoCAD's reference manuals. Refer to these pages if you would like additional information about topics covered in *Applying AutoCAD*. The letters before each page number refer to the individual manuals, as follows:

REF   Reference Manual
TUT   Tutorial
REND   Render Reference Manual
EXTR   Extras Manual
CUST   Customization Manual
SQL   SQL Extension Manual
ADS   AutoCAD Development System Programmer's Reference Manual
LISP   AutoLISP Programmer's Reference Manual
INST   Interface, Installation, and Performance Guide
AME   Advanced Modeling Extension Reference Manual
IGES   AutoCAD IGES Interface Specifications

For example, if you would like to learn more about the AutoCAD graphics screen, turn to page 52 of the *Reference Manual.*

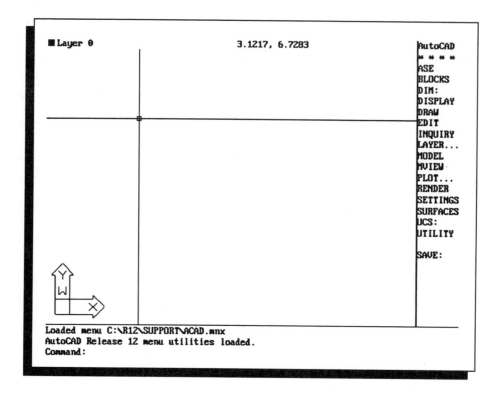

```
■ Layer 0                    3.1217, 6.7283            AutoCAD
                                                       ** ** ** **
                                                       ASE
                                                       BLOCKS
                                                       DIM:
                                                       DISPLAY
                                                       DRAW
                                                       EDIT
                                                       INQUIRY
                                                       LAYER...
                                                       MODEL
                                                       MVIEW·
                                                       PLOT...
                                                       RENDER
                                                       SETTINGS
                                                       SURFACES
                                                       UCS:
                                                       UTILITY

                                                       SAVE:




 Loaded menu C:\R12\SUPPORT\ACAD.mnx
 AutoCAD Release 12 menu utilities loaded.
 Command:
```

The path listed by "Loaded menu" may differ, depending on your individual installation of AutoCAD.

2 With your pointing device (mouse or cursor control), move the graphics cursor (crosshairs) to the top of the screen.

The words *File, Assist, Draw,* etc., should appear. These words make up the menu bar.

3 Move to the left and select **File**, causing a pull-down menu to appear.

HINT: Push the first button on your pointing device. This is called the pick button.

The File pull-down menu contains items that enable you to open, save, and plot AutoCAD drawings.

4 Select **New...** found at the top of the File menu.

The Create New Drawing dialogue box should appear as shown here.

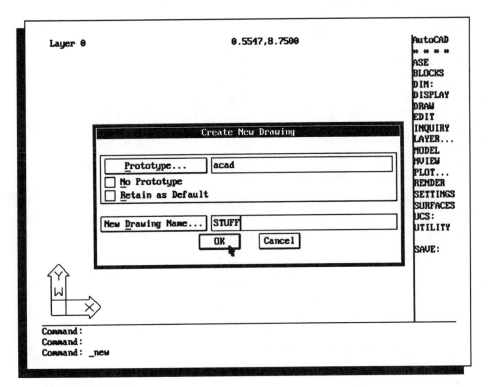

5 Type **STUFF** (in upper or lower case letters) for the name of the drawing and press **RETURN** or select the **OK** button.

You have just created an AutoCAD drawing file named STUFF.DWG.

NOTE:

Naming the drawing at this time and in this way is optional. In the future, it is okay to name and save your work using the Save... or Save As... menu options. In addition, you can enter commands at the "Command:" prompt to save your work.

CAUTION:

If you are storing your drawing on a floppy diskette, NEVER REMOVE THE DISKETTE FROM THE DRIVE WHILE YOU ARE IN AUTO-CAD. If you do, you will damage your drawing file. It is recommended that you store drawing files on the hard disk.

At the right of the screen, you'll find the root page of the standard screen menu. Note each of the items found in this menu.

Notice the "Command:" prompt line at the bottom of the screen. Keep your eye on this area. This is where you enter commands and receive messages from AutoCAD.

At the top of the screen is the status line. The status line tells you the name of the current layer, the status of various AutoCAD modes, and the coordinates of the screen crosshairs.

The rest of the screen is the work area.

Let's see how the screen changes when we enter information.

1　Using your pointing device, select **DRAW** from the root page of the standard screen menu and watch what happens.

4

2   Next, select one of the Draw commands, such as **LINE**. Notice that the prompt line has changed:

```
Command:  _LINE From point:
```

You have just entered the LINE command. AutoCAD is asking you to tell it where you want the line to start. In Unit 2, you'll actually draw some lines.

3   For now, cancel by pressing **CTRL** (control key) and **C** simultaneously.

4   Select the **LAST** option and notice where it takes you.

5   Next, select the **AutoCAD** option found at the top of the standard screen menu.

6   Now select another item from the root page of the standard screen menu and step through the submenus as you did above. If you accidentally enter a command, press the **CTRL** and **C** keys.

HINT:

Selecting a menu item which ends with a colon (as in DIM:) will enter this command as well as display a submenu.

Selecting a menu item whose name is all UPPER CASE, but *without* a colon, will display only a submenu.

A menu item with three trailing periods (as in LAYER...) displays a dialogue box.

Subcommands and command options are generally lower case or mixed case (as in "color" or "Color") and work properly only when picked in response to the appropriate prompts.

Maneuvering AutoCAD Files _____

There are various commands for opening a drawing file, storing your drawing to disk, and exiting AutoCAD. They are described below.

NEW — allows you to specify a new file name for your drawing.

OPEN — opens an existing drawing; automatically converts older AutoCAD drawings to Release 12.

SAVE — requests a file name and saves the drawing.

SAVEAS — identical to SAVE, but also renames the current drawing.

QSAVE — saves a named drawing without requesting a file name.

END — saves your drawing and exits AutoCAD.

QUIT — exits AutoCAD but does not save your work.

You will have many opportunities to practice these commands throughout this book.

 ## *What If I Enter the Wrong Command?* _____

As you work with AutoCAD, you will be entering commands either by selecting them from menus or typing them at the keyboard. Occasionally you might accidentally select the wrong command or make a typing error. It's easy to correct such mistakes.

If you catch a typing error *before* you press RETURN . . .	use the backspace key to delete the incorrect character(s). Then continue typing.
If you select the wrong command from the standard screen menu . . .	you can usually get back to the "Command:" prompt if you press the space bar once or twice;

OR

enter CTRL C (press the control and C keys at the same time).

If you type the wrong command . . .	enter CTRL C to return to the "Command:" prompt.
If you select a command and a text screen appears . . .	press the F1 function key to return to the AutoCAD graphics screen.

1 Enter the **END** command when you are finished. ("Enter" means to type the command and press **RETURN**.)

The END command will store your changes on the disk and return you to the operating system. (In this case, you are storing an empty file named STUFF.)

Questions

1. Explain the overall purpose of the AutoCAD graphics screen.

   Its where you create, change, edit, plot drawings

2. Explain the purpose of the "New..." item contained in the File pull-down menu.

   New starts a new drawing

3. Briefly describe the function of the following standard screen menu options:

   LAST *goes to the last command you activated*

   DRAW *gives you items to draw ie: circle, line, hatch*

   AutoCAD *is root menu for working with AutoCAD*

   LINE: *draws lines where you tell it to*

4. Briefly explain the basic function of the AutoCAD "Command:" prompt line.

   You type commands here and receive messages from AutoCADE

5. Explain the purpose of the following AutoCAD commands:

   OPEN *opens a drawing that was already created*

   SAVE *saves your drawing to file or floppy*

   SAVEAS *saves to where you want & renames*

   QSAVE *saves without asking for filename*

   END *saves & exits AutoCAD*

   QUIT *exits but does not save*

6. With regard to standard screen menu items, what does a colon (:) after the menu item indicate?

   Contain sub commands under it

Problems

Select the following submenus from the root page of the screen menu. Then select the commands indicated and list the options available under each command. The first problem has been completed as an example.

ROOT PAGE MENU ITEM	COMMAND	AVAILABLE OPTIONS
1. EDIT ⟶	CHAMFER ⟶	distance
		dist = 0
		polyline
2. DRAW ⟶	CIRCLE ⟶	Center, Radiu
		Center, Diameter
		2 Point
		3 Point
		TAN, TAN, RADIUS
3. EDIT ⟶	ERASE ⟶	Select Objects
		E LASt
		E Pick
		E Previous
		OOPS:
4. DISPLAY ⟶	SHADE ⟶	SHADEdif
		SHADEDGE
		256 - Col
		256 - EDG
		Hidden
		Filled
		REGEN:
		SHADE:

Unit 2   The Line Forms Here

■ OBJECTIVE:

To apply the LINE, MULTIPLE, POLYGON, and RECTANG commands, cascading pull-down menus, command aliases, and the Open Drawing dialogue box

The LINE command is the most often used AutoCAD command. There are a number of ways to produce lines. Some ways are simple; others can be a bit confusing. The following exercise uses the simplest approach to producing lines.

Opening Files

REF 11, 76

1   Start AutoCAD.

2   Select **Open...** from the **File** pull-down menu.

Notice that this selection issues the OPEN command. Also, the following dialogue box should appear.

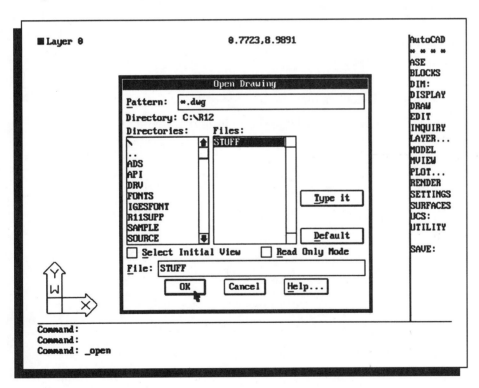

The same dialogue box appears when you enter OPEN at the keyboard. The left list box contains a list of directories. If you choose one of these directories, drawing files contained in it will appear in the right list box. In the case above, the current drive and directory is C:\R12. The drawing STUFF is contained in it, as well as the list of directories.

③ Select **STUFF** from the Files list box or type **STUFF** at the blinking cursor.

④ Pick the **OK** button or press **RETURN**.

HINT:

If you choose to select STUFF from the list box, you can double click on STUFF. This is the same as clicking on it once and then picking OK or pressing RETURN, but faster.

You have just opened the drawing file you created in Unit 1.

Cascading Pull-Down Menus

REF 55-56
TUT 10-12

Cascading pull-down menus allow you to select a series of pull-down menus that are linked to one another.

① Select the **Draw** pull-down menu and highlight the **Line** menu item.

REF 129-132

② Move your pointing device (slowly) to the right until a submenu appears.

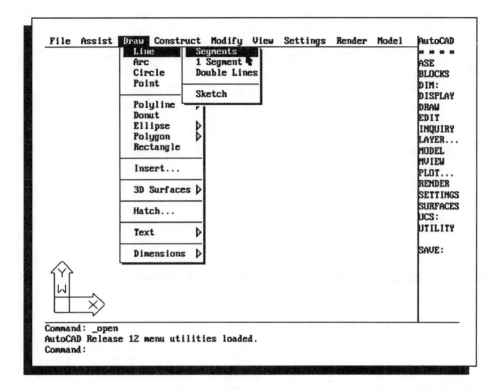

These are called cascading pull-down menus. Menu items containing a small arrow to the right offer cascading pull-downs.

NOTE:

When you use cascading menus, AutoCAD "remembers" the items you pick. The next time you need to choose the same sequence, just double click the top of the pull-down menu.

Any one of the first three selections, when picked, enters the LINE command. The fourth option enters the SKETCH command.

③ Pick **Segments**.

Notice that AutoCAD entered the LINE command at the "Command:" prompt and is now requesting the first point. Also notice that the standard screen menu changed. It now shows the LINE command options.

④ With your pointing device, draw two of the polygons shown here. (See the following hint.)

HINT:

After you've completed one polygon, press RETURN or the space bar to end the LINE command. To construct the next polygon, bring up the LINE command again by pressing RETURN or the space bar. This will enter the previously used command—a real shortcut and timesaver.

REF xxiv

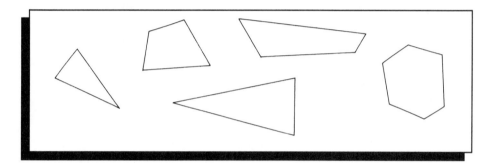

5 Create more polygons using the LINE command. (See the following hint.)

HINT:

To automatically close a polygon and terminate the LINE command, type the letter C and press RETURN (or select "close" from the screen menu) prior to constructing the last line segment of the polygon. Press RETURN or the space bar to reenter the LINE command.

REF 130-131

Abbreviated Command Entry

TUT 235

AutoCAD permits you to issue commands by entering the first one or two characters of the command. Command abbreviations, such as these, are called *command aliases*.

1 Type **L** and press **RETURN**.

The LINE command should have entered. You are able to enter other frequently used commands such as those listed here.

Command	Enter	Command	Enter
ARC	A	MOVE	M
CIRCLE	C	MSPACE	MS
COPY	CP	PAN	P
DVIEW	DV	PSPACE	PS
ERASE	E	PLINE	PL
LINE	L	REDRAW	R
LAYER	LA	ZOOM	Z

② Enter the above commands using the abbreviated method, but do not enter MS and PS. Enter **CTRL C** to cancel each command.

Command aliases are defined in the AutoCAD file ACAD.PGP, contained in the SUPPORT directory. Additional command aliases can be created by modifying this file using a text editor or word processor.

MULTIPLE Command _____

The MULTIPLE command is available to achieve multiple entries of a command. For example, "Command: MULTIPLE LINE" will cause AutoCAD to automatically repeat the LINE command until a cancel (CTRL C) is issued.

① Type **MULTIPLE L** and press **RETURN**.

② Create several polygons.

Notice that the LINE command remains entered.

③ Enter **CTRL C** to cancel the LINE command.

④ Practice drawing additional polygons using the automatic close feature as well as the other shortcuts just described.

LINE Undo Option _____

From time to time, it's necessary to back up or undo one or more of the line segments. Suppose you have drawn three lines in creating a polygon, and you're about to enter your fourth point when you realize the third line you drew is incorrect. The easiest and fastest way of correcting this is to select the Undo option from the screen menu or type U (short for Undo) and press RETURN.

① Enter the **LINE** command. ("Enter" means to type the command or command alias and press **RETURN**.)

② Create three connecting line segments of any length and orientation.

③ Type **U** and press **RETURN**.

Your last line segment should disappear.

4 Continue to enter **U** until all the line segments are gone and then draw new line segments.

5 Press **RETURN** to terminate the LINE command.

POLYGON Command

REF 147-148

The POLYGON command enables you to create regular polygons with 3 to 1024 sides. A regular polygon is one with sides of equal length. Let's try a pentagon.

1 Select the **Draw** pull-down menu.

2 Highlight the **Polygon** menu item and its cascading menu.

3 Select **Inscribed** from the menu.

NOTE:

Typing the POLYGON command at the "Command:" prompt is an alternative to the preceding three steps. If you are a fast typist, you may prefer to do this. If you use this method, you should also select I-scribe from the standard screen menu or type I and press RETURN.

4 Type **5** in reply to "Number of sides:" and press **RETURN**.

AutoCAD now needs to know if you want to define an edge of the polygon or select a center point. Let's use the default, "Center of polygon."

5 With your pointing device, pick a point in an open area on the screen. This will be the center of your polygon.

AutoCAD now wants to know the radius of the circle within which the polygon will appear.

6 With your pointing device, move the screen crosshairs from the center of the polygon.

7 Pick a point, or enter a numeric value, such as **0.5**, at the keyboard.

8 Draw several more regular polygons using the remaining options provided by the POLYGON command. Enter **POLYGON** at the keyboard and also try selecting it from the standard screen menu.

RECTANG Command _____

You can quickly create basic rectangles using the RECTANG command.

1 Enter the **RECTANG** command at the keyboard.

As you can see at the "Command:" prompt, AutoCAD is asking for the first corner of the rectangle.

2 In reply to "First corner:" pick a point at any location on the screen.

3 Move your pointing device in any direction and notice that a rectangle begins to form.

4 Pick a second point at any location to create the rectangle.

You can also enter the RECTANG command using a pull-down menu.

5 Select the **Draw** pull-down menu.

Notice that an arrow is not located at the right of the Rectangle menu item. A cascading menu, therefore, will not appear when you select it.

6 Pick **Rectangle**, and create a second rectangle.

7 Since the RECTANG command was just entered, reenter it by pressing the space bar.

8 Create a third rectangle.

As you experiment with the different methods of entering commands (i.e., the keyboard, standard screen menus, pull-down menus, and eventually tablet menus), you may prefer one method over another. For example, entering L at the keyboard is faster than selecting it from one of the menus, if you know the keyboard. Bear in mind, however, that there is no right or wrong method of entering commands. Experienced users of AutoCAD ordinarily use a combination of methods.

9 Last, select the **File** pull-down menu and pick **SAVE** to save your work.

10 Select **Exit AutoCAD** from the same menu to exit AutoCAD.

Questions

1. Describe the purpose of the "Open..." item contained in the File pull-down menu.

   OPENS A EXISTING DRAWING

2. Explain the relationship between your pointing device and the screen crosshairs.

   SHOWS WHAT YOU ARE DOING AS YOU DO THE COMMANDS

3. What is the fastest and simplest method of reentering the previously entered command?

   USING THE ENTER KEY

4. What is the fastest method of closing a polygon when using the LINE command?

   TYPE C THEN ENTER

5. Describe the purpose of the MULTIPLE command.

   LETS YOU CONTINUE DRAWING NEW OBJECTS

6. Explain the use of the LINE Undo option.

   UNDOES PREVIOUS LINE(S)

7. Explain the use of the LINE Continue option.

   LETS YOU ADD to EXISTING LINE

8. How are commands such as LINE, ERASE, and ZOOM entered quickly at the keyboard?

   using First LETTER only

9. Explain each of the following POLYGON command options.

   Edge *SHOWS PICKS WHERE EDGE OF POLYGON IS*

   I-scribe (Inscribed) *DRAWS INSIDE IMAGINARY CIRCLE*

   C-scribe (Circumscribed) *DRAWS OUTSIDE IMAGINARY CIRCLE*

10. Name two ways of entering the RECTANG command.

    Typing OR PULL DOWN MENU

16

How to Save Your Problems

Most units of this work-text conclude with some problems for you to complete. You'll probably want to save your problems, so start a new file for each one. Code the file by unit and problem number. For example, for the problems in this unit:

1. Begin a new drawing by entering the **NEW** command.
2. For the first problem, call the file **PRB2-1**.
3. When you are finished with that problem, enter **END** to save it and exit AutoCAD.

When you are ready to start PRB2-2, repeat Steps 1 through 3.

Problems

Using the LINE, POLYGON, and RECTANG commands, draw each of the following objects. Don't worry about exact sizes, but do try to make them look as much like the ones below as possible. Practice the shortcuts and various options covered in this unit.

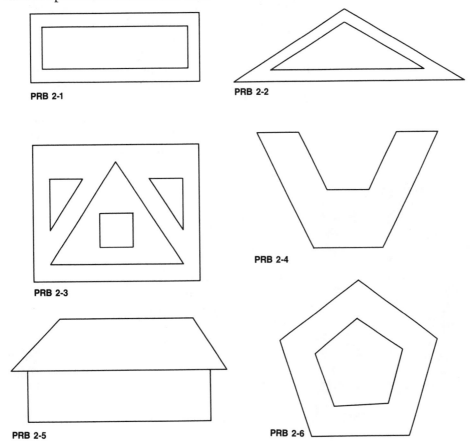

PRB 2-1

PRB 2-2

PRB 2-3

PRB 2-4

PRB 2-5

PRB 2-6

PRB 2-7

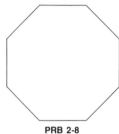

PRB 2-8

AUTOCAD® AT WORK

CAM (Computer-Aided Monster)*

New York City lies in ruins, destroyed by an earthquake. Even worse, the temblor has awakened a giant beast. Eyes flashing, lips snarling, he roars with anger as smoke and flames surround him. King Kong is on the rampage.

The scene is witnessed by a group of visitors who have come to view the wreckage. Fortunately, they are safe in their specially built tour trams—or are they? As the trams cross a suspension bridge, the thirty-foot ape shakes the bridge's cables. Kong's huge jaws open, showing the visitors menacing yellow fangs and enveloping them in his steamy breath.

The visitors, however, manage to escape. They always do, for the ruined city is actually a set on the Universal Studio lot in Hollywood, and Kong is a mechanical and electronic marvel designed and built by Sequoia Creative Inc. to terrify and delight tourists.

To create the monster, the special-effects company used metal, plastic, fur, paint—and AutoCAD. Using the Auto-CAD computer drafting package saved time and money. After the designer finished drawing a main part, a detail drafter used that drawing as the basis for his work. This avoided having to start a new drawing for each piece. Also, the ability to draw plans quickly and accurately reduced the number of revisions needed during construction.

AutoCAD's accuracy and the skills of Sequoia Creative's staff paid off. Originally, an audience distance of eighty feet was planned so that imperfections in the monster would not be seen. The final result, however, was so realistic that the tour trams now pass within six feet of Kong, almost close enough to shake hands with this furry celebrity!

*Based on a story in *CADalyst* magazine, Vol. 3, No. 5.

Courtesy of Sequoia Creative, Inc.

Unit 3   And Around We Go

■ OBJECTIVE:

To apply the CIRCLE, ARC, ELLIPSE, DONUT, and DRAGMODE commands

The purpose of this unit is to experiment with the AutoCAD commands that allow you to produce arcs and circular objects.

The following race car is typical of the extent to which drawings utilize round and curved lines. Later, you may wish to create a simplified version of this car.

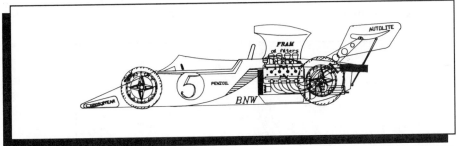

AutoCAD Drawing Courtesy of BNW, Inc.

■ *CIRCLE Command* ———————————

AutoCAD makes it easy to draw round and curved lines. For example, to draw wheels, follow these steps.

1   Start AutoCAD and create a new drawing named **CAR**.

HINT: Enter the NEW command at the keyboard or select "New..." from the File pull-down menu.

2   Select the **CIRCLE** command from the **DRAW** submenu contained in the standard screen menu at the right of the screen.

3   Select the **CEN,RAD** option. (This stands for center and radius.)

4   Draw the larger (outer) circle of the wheel first. Use your pointing device to pick the center point and then the radius. AutoCAD will complete the circle. Don't worry about exact location or size.

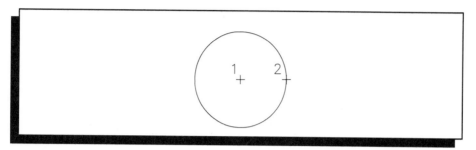

5 Next, draw the smaller circle, again by selecting **CEN,RAD** from the standard screen menu and picking the center point and the radius.

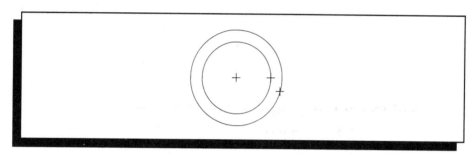

6 Now enter **DRAGMODE**. Select it from the SETTINGS submenu in the standard screen menu or enter it at the keyboard.

REF 311

Note the prompt line that appears on the screen. If DRAGMODE is <On> or <Auto>, type **OFF** to turn it off. If DRAGMODE is <Off>, enter either **ON** or **Auto**.

7 Now draw the second wheel, again using the CIRCLE **CEN,RAD** option.

What is the difference between drawing circles with DRAGMODE ON (or Auto) and drawing them with DRAGMODE OFF?

As you have seen, dragging allows you to visually drag an object into place. It also applies when you move, rotate, or scale an object. Not every command supports dragging.

NOTE:

DRAGMODE ON enables dragging for every command that supports it. To initiate dragging within a command, enter DRAG. If the DRAG request is embedded in the menu item—as is the case with the CEN,RAD option— you do not need to enter DRAG.

DRAGMODE Auto enables dragging for every command that supports it, without having to enter DRAG.

When DRAGMODE is OFF, no dragging of objects can occur, even when DRAG is embedded in menu items.

To learn more about how dragging works, try the following.

8 With DRAGMODE **ON**, draw a circle as before. (Be sure to select **CEN,RAD** from the standard screen menu.)

Now, let's draw another circle, but this time . . .

9 . . . instead of selecting CEN,RAD from the standard screen menu, press the space bar to enter the **CIRCLE** command.

10 Pick a center point for the circle. Note what happens when you move the crosshairs. The circle does not drag because DRAGMODE is ON instead of set to Auto. Therefore, you must enter DRAG to initiate dragging.

11 Enter **DRAG** to initiate dragging.

12 Pick the radius of the circle, or enter a numerical value, such as **0.75**.

13 Experiment with other ways of drawing circles, *i.e.*, 2 POINT, 3 POINT, CEN,DIA, and TTR. Try them with and without dragging.

REF 133-134

Can you drag when using the CEN,DIA option?

ARC Command

REF 136-139

Now let's focus on the ARC command. (If you need to clear the screen, see Unit 4 for instructions on how to use the ERASE command.)

1 Enter the **DRAGMODE** command and the **Auto** option.

2 Select the **ARC** command from the **DRAW** submenu contained in the standard screen menu at the right of your screen. (See the following hint.)

HINT: If you see DRAW at the bottom of the standard screen menu, select it to make the DRAW submenu appear.

3 Select the **3-point** option and pick three consecutive points. Produce several different arcs.

REF 136

Let's experiment with other methods of creating arcs.

1 Select the **S,C,E** (start point, center, endpoint) option from the menu.

REF 137

2 Specify three consecutive points: start, center, and end.

3 Select the **S,C,A** (start point, center, included angle) option.

REF 137

4 Specify a start point and center point.

5 Then enter a number (positive or negative) up to 360. The number specifies the angle in degrees.

6 Try the **S,E,R** (start point, endpoint, radius) option.

REF 138

7 Enter two points and a numerical value for the radius.

8 Experiment with the remaining ARC options. What do the following options specify?

S,C,E = _____ Start, Center, End _____

S,C,A = _*START CENTER ANGLE*_

S,C,L = _*"   "   LENGTH*_

S,E,A = _*Start END ANGLE*_

S,E,R = _*"   "   RADIUS*_

S,E,D = _*START END DIRECTION*_

C,S,E = _*Center Start END*_

C,S,A = _*"   "   ANGLE*_

C,S,L = _*"   "   LENGTH*_

Next, let's produce the following curved line, which is really a series of arcs.

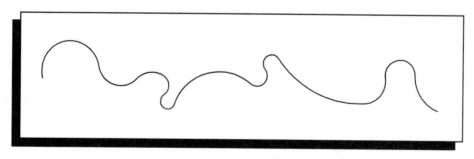

1 Make sure DRAGMODE is set to **Auto** or **ON**.

2 Enter the **ARC 3-point** option and draw an arc.

HINT:
Enter "A" for ARC. The 3-point option is the ARC command's default setting.

③ Pick the **CONTIN:** option (short for continue) found in the ARC submenu.

④ Create the next arc segment.

Notice it is tangent to the first.

⑤ Repeat Steps 3 and 4 until you are finished.

ELLIPSE Command _____

① Make sure DRAGMODE is set to Auto.

② Select the Draw pull-down menu.

③ Highlight the **Ellipse** menu item and its cascading submenu and pick **Axis, Eccentricity**.

Notice that AutoCAD entered the ELLIPSE command.

④ Pick the first point as shown in the following illustration.

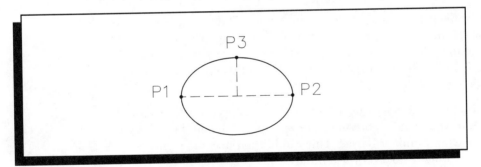

⑤ Specify the second point directly to the right of the first point.

⑥ Move the crosshairs and watch the ellipse develop. Pick a point, or enter a numeric value, and the ellipse will appear.

⑦ Experiment with the **Center, Axis, Axis** option.

DONUT Command _____

Solid-filled donuts can be created using AutoCAD's DONUT command.

① Enter the **DONUT** command at the keyboard or select it from one of the two menus.

2 Specify an inside diameter of **0.75** . . .

3 . . . and an outside diameter of **1.3**.

Your crosshairs should now be locked onto an outline of a donut ready to be dragged and placed by its center.

4 Place the donut anywhere on the screen by picking a point.

5 Move your crosshairs away from the new solid-filled donut and notice the prompt line at the bottom of the screen.

6 Place several donuts on the screen.

7 Press **RETURN** when you're finished.

That's all there is to the DONUT command.

8 Save your work and exit AutoCAD by entering the **END** command at the keyboard.

Time Out for a Discussion on Storing Your Drawings

Until now, you may have been storing your AutoCAD drawing files in the main AutoCAD directory. This directory will eventually grow large and too cumbersome to review your files. Also, disk access becomes slow. Therefore, it is not a good practice to continue storing files in this fashion. Another, much better, alternative is explained here.

Create a directory under your main AutoCAD directory. Its name should reflect the files you plan to store in it. For example, you could call it by your first name, such as Frank or RaNae. This would then become your personal directory for storing AutoCAD-related files.

NOTE:

Refer to Appendix C for steps in creating and using hard disk directories.

If you choose this option, you must create a new directory and specify it when you name the drawing file, using the NEW command, as shown in the following illustration.

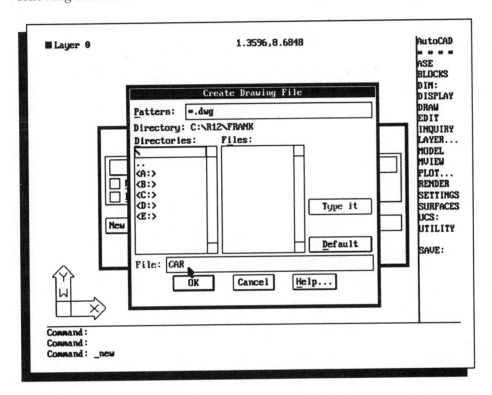

In the example above, AutoCAD will store the drawing file named CAR in the directory named FRANK.

Another, less desirable, option is to store your AutoCAD drawings on a formatted floppy diskette. This is easy to do, and it keeps your main AutoCAD directory clean of user files. Disadvantages, though, are that floppy drives operate more slowly than hard disk drives, and floppy diskettes have less capacity than hard disks. Also, floppy diskettes are not as reliable. Defects develop and files can become damaged or lost. If you use this option, you must specify the drive when you name the drawing.

The units in this book are *not* written specifically to either of these storage options. This leaves it up to you to choose the option best for you. Once you have decided, use this option to override the way drawings are created and retrieved in this book. If you don't, they will be stored in the main AutoCAD directory.

Whichever method you choose, back up your files regularly. The few seconds required to make a backup copy may save you hours of work. Experienced users back up faithfully because they have experienced the consequences of ignoring it.

Questions

1. When drawing circles, arcs, and ellipses, what happens when the DRAGMODE command is set to Auto?

   You see the form of the object as you move it

2. What happens when the DRAGMODE command is OFF?

   You do not see the form of the object

3. Briefly describe the following methods of producing circles.

   2-point *uses both points for diameter*

   3-point *uses all points for diameter*

   CEN,DIA *uses center & diam for total size*

4. In what AutoCAD submenu are the ARC and CIRCLE commands found?

   DRAW

5. What function does the ARC CONTIN option serve?

   Continues the arc in different angles lengths,

6. When specifying an angle in degrees, what direction does a negative number specify: clockwise or counterclockwise?

   Clockwise

7. Explain the purpose of the DONUT command.

   Puts solid filled donuts on screen

8. Describe the recommended procedure for storing AutoCAD files.

   In a directory you make

Problems

Using the commands you've just learned, complete the following drawings. Don't worry about text matter or exact shapes, sizes, or locations, but do try to make your drawings look similar to the ones below. You do not need to enter the text for "Lake AutoCAD."

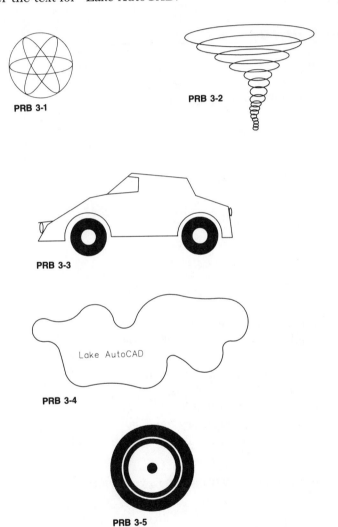

PRB 3-1

PRB 3-2

PRB 3-3

Lake AutoCAD

PRB 3-4

PRB 3-5

 **Unit 4** Now You See It . . .

■ OBJECTIVE:

To apply the ERASE, REDRAW, and OOPS commands, transparent commands, and object selection options

This unit shows you how to delete and restore all or part of a drawing. Also, the unit will introduce you to AutoCAD objects, called entities, and the different ways you can select them.

■ *First, a Word about Entities* ─────────

REF 44-45

An entity is a predefined element placed in a drawing. AutoCAD treats each entity as an individual element. For example, the smallest object that can be erased from a drawing using the ERASE command is an entity.

AutoCAD uses 16 types of entities:
> Lines
> Points
> Circles and Arcs
> Dimensions
> Traces (2D solid lines of a specified width)
> Polylines (2D connected series of line and arc segments of a specified width)
> Solids (2D solid filled areas)
> Text (words, numbers, etc.)
> Shapes (small objects that can be filed separately and then added to drawings; shapes are seldom used)
> Blocks (objects formed from groups of other entities)
> Attributes (text information stored in Blocks for later extraction and reporting purposes)
> 3D Polylines (3D objects composed of straight line segments)
> 3D Faces (3D triangular or quadrilateral plane sections)
> 3D Meshes (3D polygon meshes of rectangular topology)
> Polyface Meshes (general polygon meshes of arbitrary topology)
> Viewports (rectangular areas in paper space that contain a view of model space)

You'll learn more about these entities and how to use them as you complete the exercises in this book.

■ *Erasing and Restoring Entities* ─────────

1 Start AutoCAD and create a new drawing named **MISTAKES**.

NOTE:

As explained near the end of the previous unit, you may choose to store your files in a personal directory or on a diskette. In either case, enter the NEW command and type MISTAKES for the name of the drawing, but do not press RETURN or pick the OK button. Select the "New Drawing Name..." button in the dialogue box. When the Create Drawing File dialogue box appears, find the name of the directory in which you want to store the MISTAKES file and select it. If the directory does not exist, you must create it. (See Appendix C for information on how to create directories.)

If you choose to store MISTAKES on a floppy diskette (not recommended), select drive A or B in the Directories list box. Place a floppy diskette into the disk drive before you select the drive letter.

2 Using the LINE and CIRCLE commands, draw the following triangle and circle at any convenient size and location.

3 Enter the **ERASE** command by entering **E** at the keyboard.

AutoCAD asks you to "Select objects:". Notice that your crosshairs have changed to a small box.

REF 200-201

4 Type **W** for Window and press **RETURN**.

5 Place a window around the triangle you created.

REF 31

HINT:

To do this, imagine a box or rectangle surrounding the entire figure. Move the crosshairs to any corner of the imaginary box and pick a point. Then move the crosshairs to the opposite corner and pick a point. The object must lie entirely within the window.

Notice what happens. The object to be erased is highlighted with broken lines as shown in the following illustration.

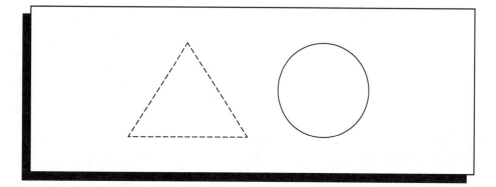

⑥ Press **RETURN** to make it disappear.

Now the lines are gone, but the "blips" (construction points) remain.

⑦ To clear the screen of these, enter the **REDRAW** command by entering **R**.

HINT:
If you pick the * * * * at the top of the screen menu, you will find REDRAW toward the bottom of the submenu. Redraw is also contained in the View pull-down menu.

REF 308-309

NOTE:

AutoCAD allows you to issue REDRAW while another command is entered. You just enter 'R. (Notice the apostrophe.) Here is an example:

> Command: LINE
> From point: 'R

After REDRAW is performed, the following appears:

> Resuming LINE command.
> From point:

This operation is called the *transparent* use of a command. Try it.

You can perform the same transparent entry by selecting the command from one of the menus. Try it.

REF 123-125

Reference

What if you erased an object by mistake and you want to restore it?

8 Enter the **OOPS** command.

REF 201

What if you want to select single entities, such as individual line segments?

1 Enter **E** at the keyboard.

AutoCAD will ask you to "Select objects:".

2 Use your pointing device to pick two of the line segments in the triangle.

3 Press **RETURN** and the objects highlighted will disappear.

HINT: If you are using a pointing device with more than one button, pressing one of them, usually the second or third, is the same as pressing the RETURN key.

Now let's try the Last option.

1 Issue **OOPS** to restore the line segments.

2 Enter the **ERASE** command. (Reminder: Just enter **E**.)

3 Type **L** (for Last) and press **RETURN**.

REF 33

The last object you drew should be highlighted.

4 Press **RETURN**.

If you reenter ERASE and Last, entities will be erased in the reverse order from which they were created.

Now let's try a new object selection procedure.

1 Enter **OOPS** to restore the entities, or if necessary, recreate the objects.

2 Enter the **ERASE** command.

③ Place a window around the triangle, but do not press RETURN yet. (See the following hint.)

HINT:
You can select an object using a window without entering W (for Window). Try it.

④ Type **R** (for Remove) and press **RETURN**.

Notice that the prompt line changes to "Remove objects:". You can now remove a line or lines from your erase window. The line(s) you remove will *not* be erased.

⑤ Remove one of the lines by picking one with your pointing device.

Note that the line you picked is no longer broken.

To restore the "Select objects:" prompt . . .

⑥ . . . type **A** for Add and press **RETURN**.

Notice that your prompt line changes back to "Select objects:".

——— NOTE: ———
Rather than entering A for Add and R for Remove at the keyboard, you can select them from the pull-down menu. They appear when you pick "Select Objects" from the menu.

⑦ Now use your pointing device to select the circle or one of the lines in the square.

⑧ Press **RETURN** to make the broken lines disappear.

So you see, you can select and remove objects as you wish until you are ready to perform the operation. The objects selected are indicated by broken lines. These selection procedures work not only with the ERASE command but also with all commands that require object selection, such as MOVE, COPY, MIRROR, ARRAY, and many others.

⑨ Enter **OOPS** to restore the figures to the screen.

Let's try another way of backing up or undoing objects you have selected.

① Enter the **ERASE** command.

② Pick two lines from the triangle, but do not press RETURN.

Two lines should now be broken.

③ Type **U** and press **RETURN**, or select the **Undo** option from the standard screen menu. (You must first pick "Select Objects" from the menu.)

Notice what happened to the last line you selected.

④ Select the **Undo** option again and press **RETURN**.

So you see, you can back up one step at a time with the Undo option.

Crossing Option

The Crossing option is similar to the Window option, but it selects all objects within and crossing the window boundary.

① Enter the **ERASE** command.

② Type **C** and press **RETURN**, or select **Crossing** from the standard screen menu, and pick a point in the center of the screen.

③ Move your crosshairs to form a box and notice that it is made up of broken lines.

④ Form the box so that it crosses over at least one entity on the screen and press the pick button in reply to "Other corner:".

Notice that AutoCAD selected those entities which cross over the box.

⑤ Press **RETURN**.

Single Option

① Select the **Erase Single** item from the **Modify** pull-down menu.

The Single (SI) object selection option is embedded in this menu item.

② Select one of the lines on the screen.

The Single option causes the command to execute immediately, without pause for further interaction, and restores the "Command:" prompt.

③ Enter **ERASE** again.

④ In reply to "Select objects:" enter **SI** and select a single entity.

This is equivalent to selecting "Erase Single" from the pull-down menu or "E Pick:" from the standard screen menu.

⑤ Enter **OOPS** to restore the last erasure. If necessary, recreate the other object.

Box Option _____

The Box option enables you to apply the Window and Crossing options without the need to enter them.

① Enter **ERASE** at the keyboard, or press the space bar if it was the last command you entered.

② Enter **box** and pick a point in the center of the screen in reply to "First corner:".

③ Move your pointing device to the right, and then up or down to form a box, but do not pick a point.

If you were to pick a second point, you would erase all objects that lie entirely within this box. This is equivalent to the "Window" option.

④ Move your pointing device to the left of the first point, and then up or down to form another box.

Notice the box is made up of broken lines. If you were to pick a second point, you would erase all objects that lie within or cross the box. This is equivalent to the "Crossing" option.

⑤ Pick a point and press **RETURN**.

⑥ Experiment further with the Box object selection option.

WPolygon, CPolygon, and Fence Options _____

The WPolygon, CPolygon, and Fence options are similar to the Window and Crossing options. However, they offer more flexibility.

① Fill the screen with several entities, such as lines, circles, arcs, rectangles, polygons, ellipses, and donuts.

② Enter **E** for the ERASE command.

③ In reply to "Select objects:" enter **WP** for WPolygon. (W is for Window.)

④ Pick a series of points that form a polygon of any shape around one or more entities and press **RETURN**.

NOTE: _____

When forming the polygon, AutoCAD automatically connects the last point with the first point.

5️⃣ Press **RETURN** to erase the entities.

The CPolygon option is similar to WPolygon.

REF 32

1️⃣ Enter **E** for ERASE.

2️⃣ In reply to "Select objects:" enter **CP** for CPolygon. (C is for Crossing.)

3️⃣ Pick a series of points to form a polygon. Make part of the polygon cross over at least one entity and press **RETURN**. (As you create the polygon, notice that it is made up of broken lines, indicating that the Crossing option is in effect.)

As you can see, CPolygon is similar to the Crossing option, whereas WPolygon is similar to the Window option.

4️⃣ Enter **RETURN** to complete the erasure.

The Fence option is similar to the CPolygon option except that you do not close a Polygon. When you select objects using the Fence option, AutoCAD looks for objects that touch the fence.

REF 32

1️⃣ Enter **ERASE**.

2️⃣ Enter **F** for Fence.

3️⃣ Draw a line that crosses over one or more entities and press **RETURN**.

4️⃣ Press **RETURN** to complete the erasure.

All Option

REF 33

The All object selection option permits you to select all entities on the screen quickly.

1️⃣ Create several objects.

2️⃣ Enter **E** (for ERASE).

3️⃣ In reply to "Select objects:" enter **All**.

AutoCAD will select all entities on the screen.

4️⃣ If you want to erase them all, press **RETURN**.

5 Select the **File** pull-down menu and pick **Save...** to save your work.

6 Select **Exit AutoCAD** from the same menu if you want to return to the operating system.

In the upcoming units, you will have the opportunity to apply these object selection techniques to all commands that ask you to select objects. In Unit 15, you will experiment with advanced object selection and editing techniques. That unit uncovers the useful Grips feature and the noun/verb selection method.

Questions

1. After you enter the ERASE command, what does AutoCAD ask you to do?

   SELECT OBJECTS

2. What command is used to delete the construction points?

   REDRAW

3. How do you place a window around a figure during object selection?

   USE ~~ERASE~~, DOUBLE CLICK

   _____

4. If you erased an object by mistake, how could you restore it?

   OOPS

   Will this method work if you drew something else after erasing the object?

   NO

5. How can you retain part of what has been selected for erasure while remaining in the ERASE command?

   USE REMOVE

6. What is the fastest way of erasing the last object you drew?

   USE ERASE & LAST

7. Describe each of these object selection options. (See Unit 2 for the Multiple Option and the *AutoCAD Reference Manual* for the Auto option.)

   Multiple = DRAW MULTIPLE OBJECT W/1 COMMAND

   Last   = LAST ITEM DRAWN

   Previous = GOES TO LAST VIEW FOR ZOOM

   Window   = BOX OR RECTANGLE FOR SELECTING

Crossing	=	*MAKES DOTTED BOX*
Box	=	*MAKES WINDOW BOX*
AUto	=	*AUTOMATICALLY DOES THINGS WITH CERTAIN COMMANDS*
SIngle	=	*ONLY AFECTS SINGLE ITEM*
Add	=	*ADDS to the ITEMS AFFECTED*
Remove	=	*DOES NOT LET COMAND AFECT WHAT IS PICKED*
Undo	=	*UNDOES LAST COMMAND*
WPolygon	=	*WINDOW POLYGON*
CPolygon	=	*CROSSING POLYGON*
Fence	=	*ERASE WHATEVER it TOUCHES*
All	=	*EVERY thing ON SCREEN*

Problem

To gain skill in using the object selection options and the ERASE command, try the following exercise. **Do not** select Erase from the pull-down menu for this particular problem.

1. Load the drawing called **STUFF**.

2. Enter the **ERASE** command and use the various object selection options to accomplish the following *without* pressing RETURN.

   • Place a window around polygon *a*.
   • Pick two of polygon *b*'s lines for erasure.
   • Use the Crossing option to select polygons *c* and *d*.
   • "Remove" one line selection from polygon *c* and one from polygon *d*.
   • Pick two lines from polygon *e* for erasure but then "Remove" one of the lines so it won't be erased.

3. Now press **RETURN**.

4. Enter **REDRAW**.

You should have nine entities (line segments) left on the screen.

5. Enter **OOPS** to restore your drawing to its original form.

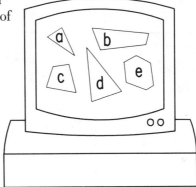

AUTOCAD® AT WORK

*Using CAD to Design a Computer Center**

The Center for Computer-Integrated Engineering and Manufacturing (CCIEM) at the University of Tennessee's College of Engineering provides students, faculty, and staff with access to several state-of-the-art computer-aided design/computer-aided engineering (CAD/CAE) systems. In addition, the Center provides local industries with technical assistance in CAD/CAE, CIM (computer-integrated manufacturing), robotics, and artificial intelligence research and development.

In June of 1984, the process of specifying the design and layout of this multi-vendor computational facility was initiated. The proposed facility was to occupy space previously designated for classrooms and consisted of about 2,800 sq. ft. The design had to maximize the space available and provide for future growth of the facilities. Steven R. Foster, manager and coordinator of CCIEM, recognized that the task could best be handled on a CAD system, and AutoCAD was selected for its features and moderate cost.

The design of the CCIEM facility included a number of steps, each step providing information to the next to build up the database. Information required to design the facility included specifications for hardware, a raised floor, workstations, air conditioning, lighting, power, fire protection, and security. As bid data were prepared, the requirements for the equipment were captured from the specifications and entered into the graphics database.

The first step in the renovation process was to make a 3D drawing of the existing layout to serve as a background drawing. Using the background drawing as a base, a composite drawing was created containing the raised floor system and the location of access doors and ramps.

Symbols were developed for each item of computer equipment to be used in the facility. Additional information for power requirements and device description was included in the attribute data assigned to each symbol. It was a simple task to insert the equipment symbols into the background drawing. Symbols were also used for the furniture, simplifying layout.

Now completed, the CCIEM represents one of the most advanced computer facilities on the University of Tennessee campus. It offers a pleasant, comfortable environment in which to conduct research and development. Additionally, as the Center grows it will be possible to utilize an up-to-date set of plans maintained in the CCIEM centralized database to change the configuration of the Center.

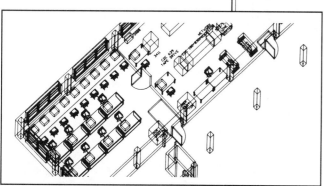

*Based on a story in *CADENCE* magazine, Vol 2, No. 1.

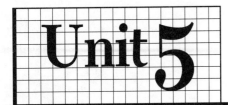

Reference

■ OBJECTIVE:

To obtain help when using AutoCAD commands

Working with AutoCAD is easy as long as everything goes smoothly, but sometimes you get stuck on how to use a certain command. Help is available, and this unit shows you how to get it.

HELP Command ───────────────────────

REF 71-73

1 Start AutoCAD and open the **STUFF** drawing.

2 After the drawing appears, enter **HELP** or **?** at the keyboard or select **Help** from the **Assist** pull-down menu.

The following Help dialogue box will appear.

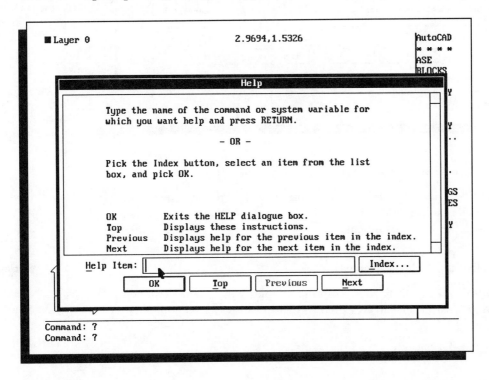

At this point you can type in the name of a command to obtain instructions on how to use that command. Or you can obtain an alphabetical list of AutoCAD commands. Let's try both.

3 Type **MOVE**. (Don't forget to press **RETURN**.)

You should get a screen that looks like this:

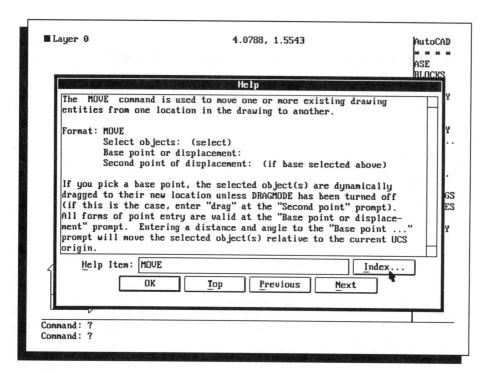

```
■Layer 0                      4.0788, 1.5543          AutoCAD
                                                      * * * *
                                                      ASE
                                                      BLOCKS
┌──────────────────────────── Help ─────────────────────────┐ Y
│The  MOVE  command is used to move one or more existing drawing│
│entities from one location in the drawing to another.         │
│                                                             │ Y
│Format: MOVE                                                 │
│        Select objects:  (select)                            │ ..
│        Base point or displacement:                          │
│        Second point of displacement:  (if base selected above)│
│                                                             │ .
│If you pick a base point, the selected object(s) are dynamically│
│dragged to their new location unless DRAGMODE has been turned off│ GS
│(if this is the case, enter "drag" at the "Second point" prompt).│ ES
│All forms of point entry are valid at the "Base point or displace-│
│ment" prompt.  Entering a distance and angle to the "Base point ..."│ Y
│prompt will move the selected object(s) relative to the current UCS│
│origin.                                                      │
│   Help Item: MOVE                        [ Index... ]        │
│   [   OK   ]  [   Top   ]  [ Previous ]  [   Next   ]        │
└─────────────────────────────────────────────────────────────┘
Command: ?
Command: ?
```

4 Turn to Chapter 6 of the *AutoCAD Reference Manual.*

This section describes Edit and Inquiry commands. Note that this chapter includes detailed information on the MOVE command that is not provided when you use the HELP command.

5 Select the **Index...** button.

A list of AutoCAD commands and system variables will appear, as shown in the following illustration. This is called the Help Index subdialogue box.

6 Using the scroll bar, scan the list.

7 Find the SNAP command, select it and pick the **OK** button.

40

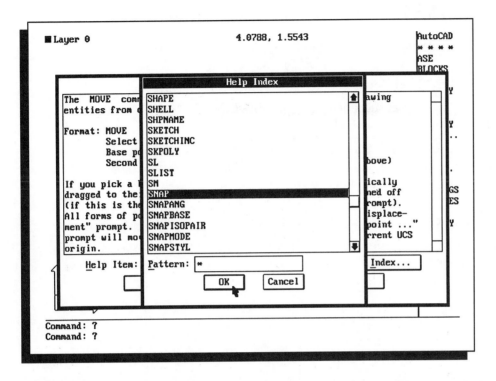

```
■ Layer 0                    4.0788, 1.5543           AutoCAD
                                                      * * * *
                                                      ASE
                                                      BLOCKS
        ┌─────────────────── Help Index ───────────────────┐
  The MOVE com│SHAPE                          │▲│awing
  entities from │SHELL                         │ │
              │SHPNAME                       │ │
  Format: MOVE  │SKETCH                        │ │        Y
         Select│SKETCHINC                     │ │        ..
         Base po│SKPOLY                        │ │
         Second│SL                            │ │bove)
              │SLIST                         │ │        .
  If you pick a │SM                            │ │ically
  dragged to the│SNAP                          │ │ned off    GS
  (if this is the│SNAPANG                       │ │rompt).   ES
  All forms of p│SNAPBASE                      │ │isplace-
  ment" prompt. │SNAPISOPAIR                   │ │point ..." Y
  prompt will mo│SNAPMODE                      │ │rrent UCS
  origin.       │SNAPSTYL                      │▼│
              └──────────────────────────────┘        Index...
    Help Item: │Pattern: │*              │
              ┌─────────┐   ┌────────┐
              │   OK    │   │ Cancel │
              └─────────┘   └────────┘
Command: ?
Command: ?
```

HINT:

Instead of picking the OK button, you can select the SNAP command by double clicking on it. Double clicking means to select it twice very fast.

8 Using the scroll bar, review the help information on the SNAP command.

9 Pick the **Index...** button again.

10 Place the blinking cursor in front of the asterisk (*), type **DD** and press **RETURN**.

AutoCAD finds all commands that begin with DD and creates a list of them. A command that begins with DD displays a dialogue box when entered. Commands such as SAVEAS and PLOT also cause a dialogue box to appear.

11 Select **DDOSNAP** and read the help information on it.

12 Pick the **OK** button to make the dialogue box disappear.

Obtaining Help After Entering a Command _____

There is another very useful way of obtaining help.

1 Enter the **OSNAP** command.

2 In reply to "Object snap modes:" type **'HELP** or **'?** (note the leading apostrophe) and press **RETURN**.

As you can see, this transparent HELP command entry allows you to obtain help in the middle of a command, when you're most likely to need it. When you pick the "OK" button, the command resumes.

3 Press the **CTRL** and **C** keys to cancel the OSNAP command.

4 Exit AutoCAD by entering **QUIT**. (Obtain HELP if you're unsure how to use QUIT.)

Questions

1. After you enter HELP or ? at the "Command:" prompt, what does AutoCAD display?

   HELP DIALOGUE BOX

2. How do you obtain a listing of all AutoCAD commands?

   PICK INDEX BOX

3. How is the information in the *AutoCAD Reference Manual* different from the screen help information?

   DETAILED INFO ABOUT MOVE IS NOT IN ACAD HELP

4. Suppose you have entered the MIRROR command. At this point, what is the fastest way of obtaining AutoCAD screen help on the MIRROR command?

   TYPE 'HELP OR ?

5. In the Help Index subdialogue box, how do you generate a list of all commands that being with "DIM"?

   TYPE DIM *

Problems

1. Obtain AutoCAD help on each of the following commands and state their basic purpose.

   REDRAW *REFRESHES DRAW and RIDS ERRORS*
   QUIT *ENDS AutoCAD*
   GRID *Control GRID Alignment Dots*
   TIME *Auto Current status of TIME VARIABLES*
   SAVETIME *Auto SAVE TIME iN minutes*
   ORTHO *Controls ORThogonal Drawing*

2. Locate each of the above commands in the *AutoCAD Reference Manual* and read what it says about each of them.

AUTOCAD® AT WORK

An Exemplary CAD Vocational Program

Eight years ago, Red Bud High School's drafting program was in need of a revision. We were offering strictly board drafting, and we used no computers. Although industry had been supportive of our program in the past, we found that we were placing fewer students because they lacked entry level computer skills.

We sent several proposals to the board for purchasing computers, but costs were prohibitive. As we researched our options, we discovered that working hand in hand with the private sector and promoting economic links with other educational and governmental agencies are two very important approaches to promoting our educational program.

Our goal was to begin instructing drafting students using the latest technology so that they could obtain good jobs in related fields. Our first big break came when V.I.P. (Vocational Instructional Practicum) provided the opportunity for Ron Weseloh, a faculty member, to work in industry during a summer period. As he worked at Snyder General Corporation and Red Bud Industries, a relationship formed. These companies agreed to match our funds to purchase the needed CAD equipment. The VICA (Vocational Industrial Clubs of America) raised funds for the project. Since industry would match these funds, the board agreed to provide the balance needed to purchase the first station.

After the equipment was purchased and the first year's training took place, the computer, along with the CAD student who had trained on it, was placed in industry for summer employment. The first placement was very successful, and the results that followed were quite positive. Local industry responded with financial support as well as equipment and software donations.

It has been seven years since the first system was obtained. We now have ten complete stations and three plotters. Over the years, students have competed in various CAD contests, including the VICA Skill Olympics in which they have won more than $32,000 worth of CAD software for the school.

Because of increased student interest in the program, more students are seeking post-secondary training in CAD-related fields. Our high school CAD lab is also being used for a night class through Belleville Area College. The software materials and equipment are adaptable to all levels of student abilities and community need.

Red Bud High School's approach to obtaining financial support from industry and other outside agencies is easily adoptable by other schools. The first requirement is a strong commitment by the school and its staff to the goal of developing a full CAD program. The other major requirements are flexibility, perseverance, and the desire to equip drafting students with highly marketable job skills.

This story was contributed by Ron Weseloh, instructor in Industrial Technology at Red Bud High School in Red Bud, Illinois. Mr. Weseloh also teaches part-time in the Drafting Technology Department at Belleville Area College.

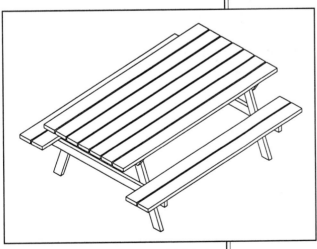

Drawing by Dan Cowell of Red Bud High School.

Unit 6 — Becoming a Keyboard Artist

Reference

REF 16-17

■ OBJECTIVE:

To enter coordinates using the absolute, relative, and polar methods

So far, you have used only the pointing device to enter coordinates. Another method is to use the keyboard to specify coordinates. This method allows you to draw lines of any specific length and angle.

AutoCAD uses a Cartesian coordinate system. (See the illustration below.) The *origin* is the point where the values of X and Y are both zero. On the computer screen, the origin usually is located at the lower left corner. AutoCAD calls this system the *World Coordinate System* (WCS). Temporary coordinate systems whose origins are specified by the user are also available in AutoCAD. They are called *User Coordinate Systems* (UCS) and are explained fully in Unit 39.

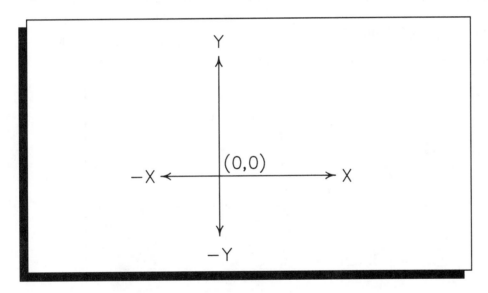

A point is expressed as an (*x,y*) coordinate pair. For two-dimensional (2D) drafting, all work can be done using (*x,y*) coordinates. If your work involves three-dimensional (3D) modeling, the Z-axis can be added to locate 3D points using an (*x,y,z*) coordinate triple. The Z-axis is perpendicular to the plane defined by the X and Y axes. Refer to Units 37-45 for details on how to apply AutoCAD's 3D capabilities.

Methods of Entering Points

Consider the following three ways to specify coordinates when using the LINE command.

Absolute Method

REF 16-17

Example: LINE From point: 2,3
 To point: 5,8

This will begin the line at absolute point 2,3 and end it at 5,8.

Relative Method

Example: LINE From point: 2,3
       To point: @2,0

This will draw a line 2 units in the positive X direction and 0 units in the Y direction from point 2,3. In other words, the distances 2,0 are relative to the location of the first point.

Polar Method

Example: LINE From point: 2,3
       To point: @4<60

This will produce a line segment 4 units long at a 60-degree angle. The line will begin at point 2,3.

The polar method is useful for producing lines at a precise angle. Note the following illustration. If you specify an angle of 90 degrees, the line will extend upward vertically from the last point.

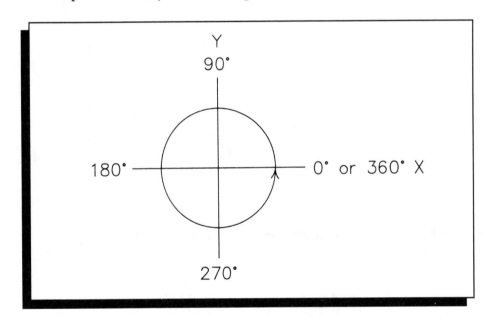

1 Start AutoCAD and begin a new drawing named **GASKET**.

2 Enter the **LINE** command (just enter **L**) and input the following sequence to produce a drawing. Don't forget to press **RETURN** after each entry.

LINE From point: **4,3**
To point: **@3,0**
To point: **@2.5<90**
To point: **C**

These entries should have produced a triangle, as shown in the following illustration.

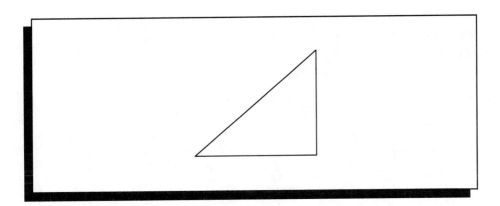

NOTE:

In Unit 12, you will learn to use editing commands such as MOVE, COPY, and MIRROR. Absolute, relative, and polar coordinate specification can be combined with these commands and others. As an example, consider the last step in the following sequence.

Command: MOVE
Select objects: (select a line)
Select objects: (press RETURN to complete the selection set)
Base point or displacement: (pick end of line)
Second point of displacement: @3.25<45

If you enter the @ character without anything else at the "Command:" prompt, you will specify the last point entered. Try it.

Creating a Gasket

1 Erase the object you just created so that the screen is blank.

2 Enter the **LINE** command again.

3 Using the keyboard, create the following drawing of a gasket. Don't worry about the exact location of the holes. Do not try to place the dimensions on the drawing at this time. However, do make your drawing exactly this size and place it near the bottom of the screen.

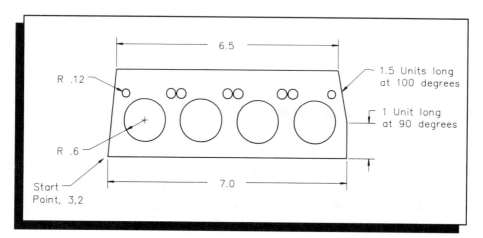

4 Enter **R** (for REDRAW) to delete the construction "blips."

5 Enter **END** to save your drawing and return to the operating system.

NOTE:

You can enter negative values for line lengths and angles, as shown here.

LINE From point: 5,5
To point: @2<–90

This polar point specification would produce a line segment 2 units long downward vertically from absolute point 5,5. This is the same as entering @2<270.

Questions

1. Briefly describe the differences between the absolute, relative, and polar methods of point specification.

   ABSOLUTE USES KNOWN Points

   RELATIVE USES DISTANCE with X & Y AXIS

   POLAR USES DISTANCE & Compass Direction

2. Is there an advantage to specifying endpoints from the keyboard rather than with the pointing device? Explain.

   YES if DRAWING BY MEASUREMENTS

3. What is the advantage of specifying endpoints with the pointing device rather than the keyboard?

   ON UNMEASURED DRAWINGS it iS QUICKER

4. Why may entering absolute points be impractical much of the time when completing drawings?

   It MAY TAKE LONGER LocAting All Points for the DRAWING

5. How can you back up one step if you make a mistake in specifying LINE endpoints?

   Typing A U or Clicking oN UnDO

Problems

For each of the following drawings, list exactly what you would enter when using the LINE command to produce the drawings. Try to incorporate all three methods—absolute, relative, and polar—to enter the points. After completing all of the blanks, step through the sequence in AutoCAD.

1. Command: LINE From point: *3, 2*
   To point: *@ 3.20 < 0*
   To point: *@ 3.04 < 63*
   To point: *@ 2.50 < 180*
   To point: *@ 1.20 < 270*
   To point: *@ 2.60 < 180*
   To point: *3, 2*

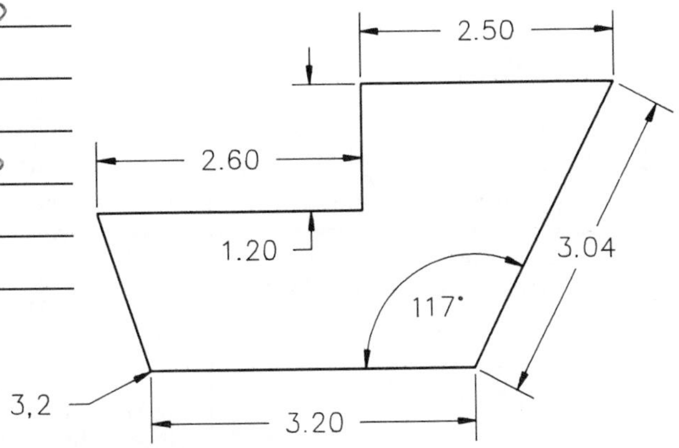

   2.50

   2.60

   1.20

   3.04

   117°

   3,2

   3.20

   PRB 6-1

49

2. Command: LINE From Point: _4,3_
   To point: _@ 4.27 ∠ 339_
   To point: _@ 3.04 ∠ 81_
   To point: _@ 2.50 ∠ 180_
   To point: _@ 1.30 ∠ 90_
   To point: _@ 1.20 ∠ 180_
   To point: _4,3_

PRB 6-2

Courtesy of SPOCAD

 **Unit 7** Snagging Points

Reference

REF 368-370
TUT 16-19

■ OBJECTIVE:

To apply the object snap feature and the APERTURE and DDOSNAP commands

This unit uncovers the powerful object snap capability and shows how to size the target box for use with object snap.

Using Object Snap ─────────────

There will be times when you will want to automatically "grab" a specific point in your drawing, such as an endpoint of a line or the center of a circle. With AutoCAD's object snap feature, you can do both, and more.

1 Start AutoCAD and begin a new drawing named **OBJSNP**.

2 In preparation for using the object snap feature, draw the following object. Omit all numbers and, at this point, ignore the words. Don't worry about exact sizes and locations.

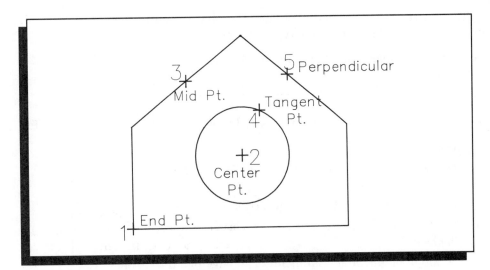

When you are finished with the above drawing, let's practice using the object snap feature.

1 Enter the **LINE** command.

Notice that the standard pickbox disappears from the center of the crosshairs.

2 In reply to "From point:" type the object snap mode **END** and press **RETURN**.

The word "of" should appear in the prompt area of the screen. Also, notice that a larger box, called a target box, is now a part of the crosshairs.

51

③ Move your crosshairs/target box so that it touches the horizontal or vertical line near point 1, and pick it. (See note below.)

NOTE:

The center of the crosshairs do not have to lie exactly on point 1. The crosshairs can be away from point 1 as long as the target box touches the line and is closer to point 1 than to the other endpoint of the line.

This begins to illustrate the power and accuracy of object snap. Let's experiment with another object snap mode.

④ In response to the "To point:" prompt on the screen, type **CEN** (for "center") and press **RETURN**.

⑤ Move the crosshairs/target box and pick the line that makes up the circle.

The line should have snapped to the center of the circle.

HINT:

The Assist pull-down menu contains the object snap modes. This allows you to select them instead of typing them.

Also, you can access the object snap modes by selecting the **** item from the top of the standard screen menu.

The following is a list of all the object snap modes and their meaning.

CENter	center of arc or circle
ENDpoint	closest endpoint of line or arc; corner of trace, solid, or 3D face
INSert	insertion point of text, block, or attribute
INTersection	intersection of lines, arcs, or circles; corner of trace, solid, or 3D face
MIDpoint	midpoint of line or arc; midpoint of an edge of a trace, solid, or 3D face
NEArest	nearest point on a line, arc, circle, or point
NODe	nearest point entity or dimension definition point
PERpend	perpendicular to line, arc, or circle
QUAdrant	quadrant point of arc or circle
QUICK	quickly selects the first point it sees
TANgent	tangent to arc or circle
NONE	turns off object snap

REF 368-370

During the following steps, pick the modes from one of the menus.

6 Snap to point 3 using **MIDpoint**.

7 Snap to point 4 using **TANgent**.

8 Snap to point 5 using **PERpend** and press **RETURN**.

Your drawing should now look like the following. If it doesn't, try it again.

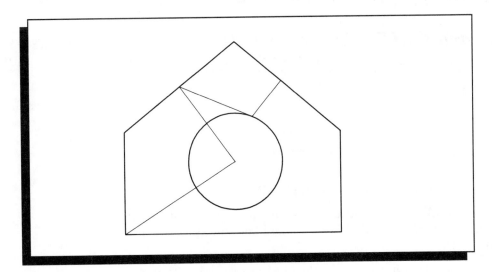

9 Experiment with each of the remaining object snap modes.

——— NOTE: ———

Even though the object snap submenu may seem convenient, you may choose to type the modes as you need them. Additionally, if you are using AutoCAD's tablet menu, consider picking the object snap modes from it. See Unit 52 for details on using the standard AutoCAD tablet menu.

APERTURE Command ———————————

REF 372

In the future, you may need to adjust the size of the target box, depending on the complexity of the drawing.

1 Enter the **APERTURE** command.

You can choose any size from 1 to 50 pixels. A pixel is a picture element on a screen. All images you see on the computer screen are made up of these tiny dots called pixels.

2   Enter **18** for the aperture size.

3   Use one of the object snap modes to see the new size of the target box. It should now be almost twice its original (10-pixel) size.

4   Change the target box size to **3** pixels. The smaller size may help you be more precise when drawings are dense.

5   View the new size by using an object snap mode. The target box should now be six times smaller.

6   Change the target box back to **10**.

OSNAP and DDOSNAP Commands

REF 371-372
TUT 19

The OSNAP and DDOSNAP commands permit you to set one or more running object snap modes.

1   Enter the **OSNAP** command.

AutoCAD prompts you to enter one or more modes.

2   Type **END,CEN,INT** and press **RETURN**.

3   Enter the **LINE** command and select an endpoint, a center point and an intersection point (where two or more lines intersect) and press **RETURN**.

As you can see, you don't need to enter the object snap modes. They are preset.

4   Enter the **DDOSNAP** command.

This displays a dialogue box (see the following illustration) that enables you to set running object snap modes more easily. Notice that Endpoint, Center, and Intersection are checked. Also, observe the slider bar.

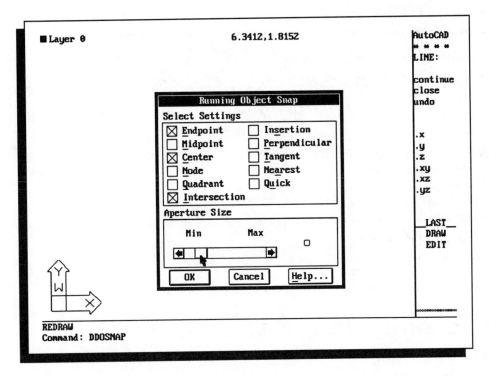

5 Move the slider bar and notice how the pickbox changes in size.

6 Pick the **Help...** button, read the help information, and pick the **OK** button.

7 Pick the **OK** button to make the Running Object Snap dialogue box disappear.

8 Select the **Settings** pull-down menu and pick the **Object Snap...** menu item.

This is another way to access the Running Object Snap dialogue box.

9 Pick the **Cancel** button.

10 Enter **END** to save your drawing and return to the operating system.

Questions

1. Explain the purpose of the object snap modes.

   LETS YOU GRAB SPECIFIC POINTS ON OBJECTS OF DRAWING

2. In order to snap a line to the center of a circle, what part of the circle does the target box need to touch?

   ANY PART OF CIRCLE LINE

3. Explain one of two ways of changing the size of the target box.

   TYPE APERATURE
   OR PULL DOWN FROM SETTINGS

4. Describe a situation in which you would want to change the target box size.

   TO PICK AREA OBJ IN SMALL AREA

5. Briefly describe the use of each of the following object snap modes.

   CEN *SNAPS to CENTER OF LINE*
   END *" to END POINT OF LINE*
   INS *BLOCK INSERT POINT, OR TEXT, OR ATTRIB*
   INT *" to CLOSEST INTERSECTION*
   MID *" to MIDDLE OF LINE*
   NEA *" to NEAREST PART OF LINE*
   NOD *NEAREST POINT*
   PER *SNAPS PERPENDICULAR FROM START*
   QUA *SNAPS to QUADRANT OF CIRC, ELIPS*
   QUICK *SELECTS FIRST POINT IT SEES*
   TAN *TANGENT to ARC, CIRC*
   NONE *TURNS OFF SNAP*

6. Name one of two ways of accessing the Running Object Snap dialogue box.

   TYPE OBJSNAP
   PULL DOWN MENU

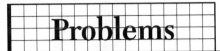

Problems

1. Draw this square.

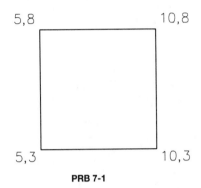

PRB 7-1

Use object snap to make these additions.

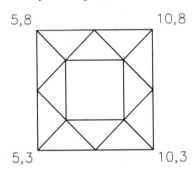

2. Using object snap, construct the following object. Don't worry about exact sizes and locations.

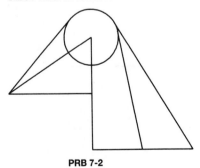

PRB 7-2

Five Favorable Features

Reference

REF 257

■ OBJECTIVE:

To control certain AutoCAD features including Printer Echoing, Coordinate Display, Ortho, the TIME command, and the SAVETIME system variable

This unit describes several special AutoCAD features. You will have an opportunity to practice these features and learn how you can apply them in an AutoCAD work environment.

Printer Echoing

Simultaneously pressing CTRL (control) and Q on the keyboard will cause AutoCAD to print everything you type. The printing actually occurs after the text appears on the screen. This procedure is called printer echoing.

NOTE:

Before you begin, make sure a printer is properly connected to your computer, is turned on, and is loaded with paper.

1 Start AutoCAD, but it is not necessary that you open or begin a new drawing.

2 Press the **CTRL** and **Q** keys at the same time.

"<Printer echo on>" should appear on your screen. If "<printer not responding>" appears, check the printer connection and press CTRL Q again.

3 Now enter an AutoCAD command of your choice and complete the entire command.

Did the text echo to the printer?

4 Practice by echoing other information to the printer.

5 Press **CTRL Q** to turn off the printer echo.

You should receive the message "<printer echo off>".

NOTE:

As you've just seen, CTRL Q serves to turn the printer echo both on and off. Thus it acts like a toggle switch. Using keys in this manner is referred to as toggling.

Printer echoing is useful when you want to record your steps with AutoCAD. Later, you will discover more applications for it as you learn to use commands such as LAYER, STATUS, and LIST.

Reference

REF 375

Coordinate Display

Another useful feature is the display of coordinate information. This information, displayed in digital form, is found in the upper portion of the graphics screen and is part of what AutoCAD calls the *status line*. The coordinate display reveals the current position (or coordinate position) of your crosshairs as you move the pointing device. It also gives the length and angle of line segments as you use the LINE command.

1 Move the crosshairs on the screen by moving your pointing device.

Note how the coordinate display changes with the movement of the crosshairs.

2 Enter the **LINE** command and draw the first line segment of a polygon. Note the coordinate display as you draw the line segment.

NOTE:

> Most personal computer keyboards have function keys called F1, F2, F3, and so on. AutoCAD has assigned many of these function keys to specific functions, such as the coordinate display and the Ortho feature.

3 Press the **F6** function key once, draw another line segment, and notice the coordinate display.

It should now be off.

4 Press **F6** again, draw another line segment or two, and watch the coordinate display.

As you can see, this information is similar to specifying line endpoints using the polar method of specifying coordinates. How could this information be useful when drawing?

5 While in the LINE command, press the **CTRL** and **D** keys and note the change in the coordinate display as you pick points.

6 Create additional line segments, pressing **CTRL D** between each.

As you can see, CTRL D serves the same function as F6.

The Ortho Mode

REF 354-355
TUT 15

Now let's focus on an AutoCAD feature called Ortho. Ortho is a useful feature that allows you to quickly and easily draw lines either horizontally or vertically.

1 Enter the **ORTHO** command and specify **on**. Or, press **CTRL O**. (They perform the same function.)

Ortho is on whenever the word "Ortho" is displayed on the status line at the top of the screen.

2 Experiment by drawing lines with Ortho turned on and then with Ortho off. Note the difference. (See the following hint.)

HINT:

Like the coordinate display feature, Ortho can be toggled on and off at any time, even while you're in the middle of a command such as LINE. Simply press CRTL O, or, easier yet, press the function key F8.

3 Attempt to draw an angular line with Ortho on.

Can it be done?

4 Now, draw the following object, first with Ortho off and then with Ortho on. Don't worry about exact sizes and locations.

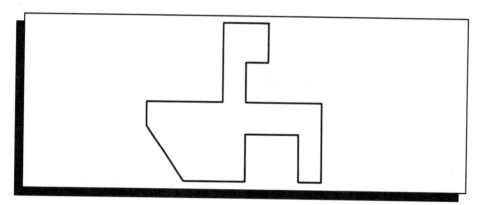

Was it faster with Ortho on?

TIME Command _____

REF 111-113

While you are in AutoCAD, AutoCAD is keeping track of time. With the TIME command, you can review this information.

1 Enter the **TIME** command.

The following should look similar to what you see on your screen. Dates and times will of course be different.

```
Current time:            24 Jul 1992 at 10:26:12.550
Times for this drawing:
  Created:               24 Jul 1992 at 09:52:19.760
  Last updated:          24 Jul 1992 at 09:52:19.760
  Total editing time:    0 days 00:33:52.790
  Elapsed timer (on):    0 days 00:33:52.790
  Next automatic save in: 0 days 00:14:14.020

Display/ON/OFF/Reset:        [HOURS] [MINUTES] [SECONDS] [MILLISECONDS]
```

Here's what this information means.

Current time:	Current date and time
Created:	Date and time drawing was created
Last updated:	Date and time drawing was last updated
Total editing time:	Total time spent editing the current drawing
Elapsed timer:	A timer you can reset or turn on or off
Next automatic save in:	Time before the next automatic save occurs

If the current date and time are not displayed on your screen, they were not entered after the computer was turned on. If the date and time are displayed even though you did not enter them, your computer has a built-in clock/calendar, and it enters the date and time automatically.

2 If the date and time are incorrect, exit AutoCAD and enter the **DATE** and **TIME** DOS commands at the DOS prompt (*e.g.*, C:\>).

3 If you exited AutoCAD, restart AutoCAD and enter the **TIME** command.

What information is different? Check the current time, total editing time, and elapsed time.

___ NOTE: ___

The times, found after the day, month, and year, are displayed to the nearest millisecond using 24-hour "military" format. For example, 14:15:00.000 means 2:15 P.M.

4 With the TIME command entered, type **D** for Display, and notice what comes up on your screen.

This is updated time information.

5 Next, select the **OFF** option, and **D**isplay the time information again.

The "Elapsed timer" should now be off.

NOTE:

You would probably specify OFF if you wanted to leave your computer to get a cup of coffee, for instance. When you returned, you would turn the timer ON. This would keep an accurate record of the actual time (elapsed time) you spent working on the drawing.

6 Reset the timer by entering **R**, and **D**isplay the time information once again.

The "Elapsed timer" should show 0 days 00:00:00.000.

7 Last, turn **ON** the timer and **D**isplay the time information.

Notice the elapsed timer has kept track of the time since the timer was turned ON.

Why is all of this time information important? In a work/production environment, the TIME command will track specific times spent on each project or job.

SAVETIME

SAVETIME allows you to preset AutoCAD to save your drawing automatically. This helps to prevent a loss of work due to a power failure, system crash, or some other event that causes your software or hardware to fail. For example, if AutoCAD saves your drawing every 10 minutes, the most you could lose is 10 minutes of work.

1 Press **RETURN** to terminate the TIME command and **F1** to return to the graphic screen.

2 Enter **SAVETIME** and enter **2** for the new value.

3 Draw an object on the screen.

4 Draw additional objects or sit idle for at least two minutes.

5 After two minutes has elapsed, add another object or make a change to the existing one.

AutoCAD will automatically save your work in a file named AUTO.SV$. If you lose your work in the future and need to resort to the AUTO.SV$ file, rename it to a drawing file. For example, you could rename it HEATHER.DWG. (See Appendix B for instructions on how to rename files.)

6 Select **Exit AutoCAD** from the **File** pull-down menu.

7 Pick the **Discard Changes** button.

Questions

1. What two keys activate the printer echo feature?

   Ctrl Q

2. Why would you want to echo your text to the printer while entering and responding to AutoCAD commands?

   To BE ABIE to CHECK COMMANDS WhiIe DRAWING

3. How do you turn off the printer echo?

   ENTER Ctrl Q AGAIN

4. What key, in conjunction with CTRL, allows you to turn on the coordinate display feature?

   D

5. Of what value is the coordinate display?

   METRIC

6. What's the name of the feature that forces all lines to be drawn only vertically or horizontally?

   ORTHO MODE

7. What key, used with CTRL, controls this feature?

   O

8. Of what value is the TIME command?

   TO CHECK WHEN YOU STARTED DRAWING & HOW LONG YOU HAVE EDITED

9. Briefly explain each of the components contained in the TIME command.

   Current time: NOW'S TIME & DATE

   Created: WHEN DRAWING WAS CREATED

   Last updated: LAST UPDATE FOR DRAWING

   Total editing time: TIME SPENT EDITING

   Elapsed timer: TIMER YOU CAN TURN OFF OR ON

   Next automatic save in: NEXT AUTO SAVE OCCURS

10. Explain the purpose of SAVETIME.

    AUTO SAVES IN CASE OF POWER FAILURES AT TIME YOU SET IT

Problems

1. Practice using Ortho by drawing the following shapes. Utilize Ortho when appropriate. Don't worry about exact sizes and locations. Preset AutoCAD to save your work automatically every 5 minutes. Turn on the coordinate display, and note the display as you construct each of the shapes. Last, when you construct one (just pick one) of the objects, echo everything you enter on the keyboard to the printer.

PRB 8-1

PRB 8-2

PRB 8-3

PRB 8-4

PRB 8-5

PRB 8-6

2. With the TIME command, review the time you spent completing PRB8-1 through PRB8-6. Echo this information to the printer or record it below.

All   6.29 min

64

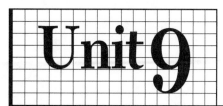 **Unit 9**   Helpful Drawing Aids

■ OBJECTIVE:

To apply the GRID and SNAP commands

This unit focuses on two very helpful construction aids. They are related to one another because each of them assists the AutoCAD user during the layout and placement of objects.

GRID Command _____

The GRID command allows you to set an alignment grid of dots of any desired spacing, making it easier to visualize distances and drawing size. The Grid feature is nothing more than a visual aid.

Let's work with this feature.

1 Start AutoCAD and begin a new drawing named **SNAPPY**.

2 Toggle on the Grid feature by pressing **CTRL G**.

There should now be a grid of dots on the screen. (If not, continue anyway.)

3 Enter the **GRID** command and change the grid spacing to 0.5 unit by entering **0.5**.

4 Enter the **GRID** command again and change the spacing to **1** unit. (Remember, just press the space bar to reissue the last command.)

5 Next, turn the grid off by pressing **CTRL G** . . .

6 . . . and then turn it back on.

7 Press the **F7** function key to toggle the Grid feature off and on.

_____ NOTE: _____

As you can see, AutoCAD has assigned functions to your keyboard's function keys. They serve as on/off toggle switches. Press each of them to see what they do. Keys F2 - F5 have not been assigned a function. Use the "Quick Reference" page at the end of the book to record the function of each key.

Reference

REF 349-352

SNAP Command _____

The Snap feature is similar to the Grid feature because it is also a grid, but it is an invisible one. You cannot see the Snap feature, but you can see the effects of Snap as you move the crosshairs across the screen.

1   Press **CTRL B** to turn on the Snap feature. The word Snap should appear on the status line when Snap is on. If it is not there, press **CTRL B** again.

2   Slowly move your pointing device and watch closely the movement of the crosshairs.

3   Enter the **SNAP** command.

4   Enter **0.25** to specify the snap resolution.

5   Move your pointing device and note the crosshair movement.

HINT:
If the grid is not on, turn it on to see better the movement of the crosshairs. Notice the spacing relationship between the snap resolution and the grid. They are independent of one another.

So you see, the Snap feature is like a set of invisible magnetic points. The crosshairs jump from point to point as you move the pointing device. This allows you to lay out drawings quickly, yet you have the freedom to toggle Snap off at any time. Object snap, on the other hand, permits you to snap to points on objects, such as the midpoint of a line.

There may be times when you want the crosshairs to snap one distance vertically and a different distance horizontally. Here's how to do it:

1   Enter the **SNAP** command.

```
Snap spacing or ON/OFF/Aspect/Rotate/Style <0.2500>:
```

2   Enter the Aspect option by typing **A** and pressing **RETURN**.
AutoCAD will ask for the horizontal spacing.

REF 350

3   Enter **0.5**.

Next you will be asked for the vertical spacing.

4 For now, enter **1**.

5 Move the crosshairs up and down and back and forth. Note the difference between the amount of vertical and horizontal movement.

Let's experiment with the Rotate option.

REF 350-351

1 Enter the **SNAP** command again, and this time enter the **Rotate** option.

2 Leave the base point at 0,0 by giving a null response. (Simply press the space bar or **RETURN**.)

3 Enter a rotation angle of **30** (degrees).

The Grid, Snap, and crosshairs should rotate 30 degrees.

4 Draw a small object at this rotation angle near the top of your screen.

5 Return to the original rotation of 0.

Now, let's try drawing another object.

1 Draw the following figure with the Snap set at 0.5 unit both horizontally and vertically. Use only your pointing device to specify all points.

HINT: Turn on Ortho to speed the drawing of the horizontal and vertical lines. Also, use the coordinate display when specifying endpoints.

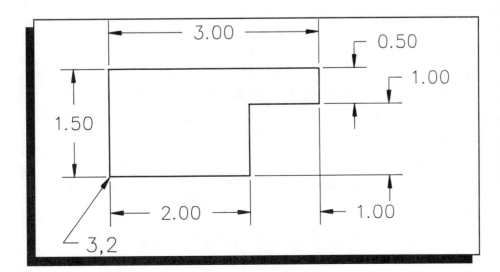

Drawing Aids Dialogue Box

The Drawing Aids selection found in the Settings pull-down menu assists you in reviewing and changing the Snap, Grid, and other settings. The Drawing Aids dialogue box is shown here.

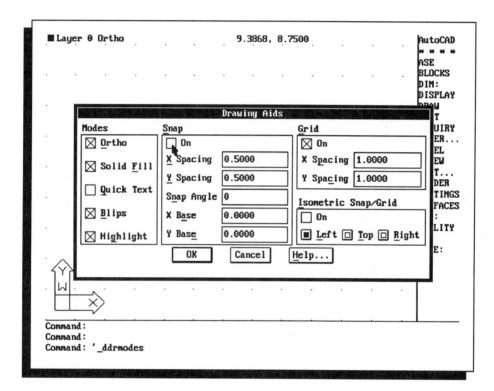

1 Choose the **Settings** pull-down menu.

2 Select the "**Drawing Aids...**" item found in the Settings menu.

The Drawing Aids dialogue box should appear.

NOTE:

You can also make this dialogue box appear by entering the DDRMODES command.

3 Examine the items in the dialogue box.

As you can see, it permits you to change many different settings by checking boxes and filling in new values. The check boxes serve as on/off toggle switches.

You will learn and use the solid fill, quick text, isometric, and highlight features in future units.

When the Blips item is checked, temporary construction points, called blips, appear on the screen. They do not appear when the Blips item is not checked.

4 Make several changes to the current settings and pick **OK** to save the changes.

— NOTE: —

AutoCAD saves your changes with the drawing. Therefore, if you or someone else begins a new drawing, the old settings return.

5 Draw several objects and notice how the new settings have changed the behavior of AutoCAD.

6 Enter **END** to save your work and exit AutoCAD.

Questions

1. What is the purpose of the GRID command? How can it quickly be toggled on and off?

   Put Dots on Screen   Use Ctrl
   6 or F7

2. When would you use the Snap feature? When would you toggle off the Snap feature?

   To SNAP to Points on Screen
   When Need to Go Between Points
   if Not the Set Distance

3. How can you set the Snap feature so that the crosshairs move a different distance horizontally than vertically?

   Use Rotate Option

4. Explain how to rotate the Grid, Snap, and crosshairs 45 degrees.

   Enter "SNAP" Type "R" Enter
   & Again Past Base Point Type 45
   At Angle Prompt Enter Again.

5. How do you make the Drawing Aids dialogue box appear?

Setting in Pull Down then Drawing Aids

6. What is the benefit of using the Drawing Aids dialogue box?

To make Changes to Blips, Snap Modes, Grid, Isometric

Problems

Draw the following objects using the Grid and Snap settings provided beside each object.

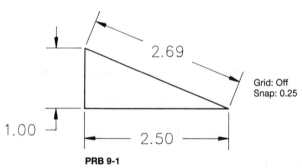

2.69

Grid: Off
Snap: 0.25

1.00

2.50

PRB 9-1

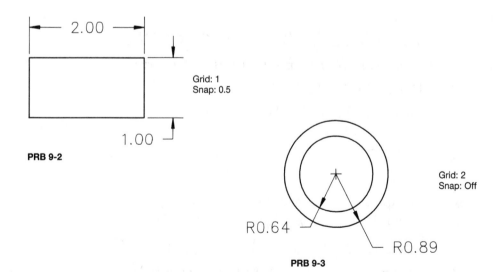

2.00

Grid: 1
Snap: 0.5

1.00

PRB 9-2

Grid: 2
Snap: Off

R0.64

R0.89

PRB 9-3

AUTOCAD® AT WORK

*AutoCAD Becomes Fashionable**

With the advent of low-cost CAD packages like AutoCAD, fashion designers are discovering the benefits and possibilities that computer-aided design can offer. Eleanor London, a CAD/CAM/CIM consultant, has helped fashion designers make the transition to CAD.

She points out the similarities between manual tools and CAD tools. Students are given charts that list traditional tools and their CAD equivalents: Tailor's square = Ortho; French curve = Arcs; Transparent rule = Units and snap; Cutting table = Limits; Pattern paper = Grid or layers; Pivot = Rotate; Seam allowance = Offset; Slopers = Blocks; Notches/punch hole = Attributes.

Students then use the computer to explore their new drafting tools with simple exercises like fitting curves between points, drawing various line widths, and drawing continuous line shapes. Next, students draft front and back bodice sloper patterns, which are based on dress form size measurements. The slopers are drafted by connecting a series of points established by the dress form measurements. The completed slopers are saved as a Block for future use in development of construction patterns.

Pattern symbols, such as center front folds, punch holes, grain-lines, and notches, are drawn and stored in a symbol library.

The sloper patterns and the pattern symbols are used in creating the final patterns. The patterns are plotted actual size. The students cut the patterns in muslin and tie them on dress forms. Corrections are made and translated to the patterns on the CAD system. After all corrections are made, the patterns are plotted again and cut in the chosen fabric.

Using AutoCAD for pattern design increases productivity by reducing duplication time and lets the designer work on complicated designs. The final payoff is that AutoCAD provides a competitive edge and a quality product for domestic manufacturers in the world marketplace.

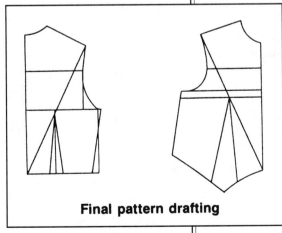

Final pattern drafting

Based on a story in *CADENCE* magazine, Vol. 2, No. 3.

 **Unit 10** Undoing What You've Done

■ **OBJECTIVE:**

To apply the U, REDO, and UNDO commands

AutoCAD allows you to back up to any earlier point in an editing session using the commands U, REDO, and UNDO. Additionally, you can reverse the effect of one Undo if you went one step too far. Let's work with these commands.

U Command

REF 251-252

1 Start AutoCAD.

2 Enter the **DONUT** command and place a half dozen donuts on your screen at any size and location.

3 With the **GRID** and **SNAP** commands, set the grid and snap spacings.

4 At the "Command:" prompt, enter the U command by typing **U** and pressing **RETURN**.

What happened? AutoCAD should have undone your last operation.

5 Enter the **U** command again, and then again.

So you see, the U command simply backs up one step at a time. With it, you can actually back up to the beginning of your editing session.

REDO Command

REF 252

1 Enter the **REDO** command and watch what happens.

REDO undoes the last Undo. In other words, it reverses the effect of the last Undo.

HINT: Both U and REDO are found in the screen menu which is displayed as a result of picking the * * * * screen menu item. They are also located in the Assist pull-down menu.

UNDO Command _____

Reference

REF 252-256

The UNDO command is similar to the U command, but UNDO provides several options. Let's try a few.

1 Draw the following objects at any size and location using the POLYGON, ELLIPSE, and CIRCLE commands.

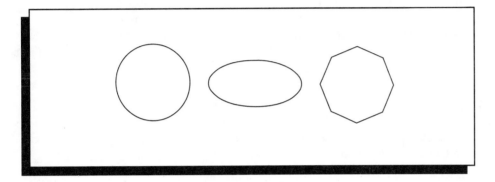

2 Enter the **UNDO** command.

The following subcommands should appear on your screen:

```
Auto/Back/Control/End/Group/Mark/<number>:
```

3 Respond to "<number>" by typing the number **2** and pressing **RETURN**.

By entering 2, you told AutoCAD to back up two steps. UNDO 1 is equivalent to the U command.

Now let's try the Mark and Back subcommands.

REF 252-253

1 Enter the **RECTANG** command and draw a small rectangle at any size and location.

Let's say, for instance, that you want to proceed with drawing and editing, but you would like the option of returning to this point in your session at a later time. This is what you must do.

2 Enter the **UNDO** command.

3 Enter the Mark subcommand by typing **M** and pressing **RETURN**.

AutoCAD has (internally) marked this point in your session.

4 Perform several operations, such as drawing and erasing objects and changing mode settings such as Ortho, Snap, and Grid.

Now suppose you decide to back up to the point where you drew the rectangle in Step 1.

5 Enter the **UNDO** command and then the **B**ack subcommand.

You have just practiced two of the most powerful and common uses of the UNDO command. Other UNDO subcommands exist, such as Group and End. Refer to AutoCAD's Help facility or the *Reference Manual* for more information on these options.

REF 253-254

———— NOTE: ————

The Undo feature can use a large amount of disk space and can cause a "disk full" situation when only a small amount of disk space is available. If so, you may want to disable the U and UNDO commands, partially or entirely, by using the UNDO Control option.

Let's experiment with UNDO Control.

REF 255

1 Enter the **UNDO** command and then the Control option.

2 Enter the **O**ne option.

3 Draw one item on your screen, such as an arc.

4 Enter the **UNDO** command.

Notice that UNDO now allows you to undo only a single operation.

5 Press **RETURN**.

With UNDO Control set at One, AutoCAD stores only a small amount of Undo information. This minimizes the risk of a "disk full" situation, especially when storing on a floppy diskette.

6 Enter the **UNDO C**ontrol option again.

7 This time, enter **N**one.

8 Perform a couple of AutoCAD draw or edit functions.

9 Now enter **UNDO**.

Reference

Since UNDO Control is set at None, AutoCAD does not give you the option of undoing, only the option of changing UNDO Control.

10 Enter **CTRL C** and try the U command by typing **U** and pressing **RETURN**.

The U command is also disabled.

11 With **UNDO**, enter the Control **All** option.

Now the AutoCAD Undo feature is once again fully enabled.

12 Enter **UNDO** again and note the complete list of subcommands.

13 Further experiment with AutoCAD's Undo feature.

14 Enter **QUIT** to exit AutoCAD. Discard changes.

AUTOCAD® AT WORK

CAD Helps Steam Engines Keep Chugging

At one time, all locomotives were powered by steam. Today, however, most locomotives are diesel-electric. What, then, would CAD have to do with old-fashioned steam engines? In Lomita, California, there's a shop that sells kits for miniature working steam trains, and the design drawings for those kits are being produced with AutoCAD.

When Moodie Braun, a former Lieutenant Colonel in the U.S. Air Force Space and Missile System Division, bought the Little Engines shop eight years ago, he found an archive of about 3,000 drawings. The drawings—for sixteen different models of trains in three scales—dated back to the 1930s. Each kit typically included drawings with details for machining, drilling, filing, soldering, and painting.

As materials ceased to be available or if errors were discovered, the drawings had to be revised. It was a tedious job. Braun and his staff were making erasable photocopies, revising the copies, and having new sepias (brown prints) made.

Recently, the shop began using AutoCAD. Drawing time has been cut in half, and it's much easier to update drawings. Instead of altering photocopies, Braun and his staff simply revise on the computer and plot out new drawings. Considering the complexity of some kits (the largest train can carry 75 people), the improvements in the accuracy and quality of the drawings are a benefit to the customers as well as the shop.

Courtesy of Little Engines and Autodesk, Inc.

Questions

1. Explain the differences between the U and UNDO commands.

   THE U COMMAND ONLY GOES BACK 1 STEP while UNDO GIVE SEVERAL other options

2. What is the purpose of the REDO command?

   UNDOES the LAST UNDO CMND

3. Explain how you would quickly back up or undo your last five operations.

   TYPE UNDO & ENTER
   TYPE 5 & ENTER

4. Explain the use of the UNDO Mark and Back subcommands.

   MARK LETS YOU DESIGNATE A POINT to RETURN to FOR EDITING LATER / BACK UNDOES to THE MARK

5. Describe the three UNDO Control options.

   All *LETS YOU GO BACK to BEGIN OF SESSION*
   None *WILL NOT LET YOU UNDO*
   One *ONLY DOES ONE AT A TIME*

6. Is the U command enabled or disabled when UNDO Control is set at One? Why?

   ENABLED BUT ONLY lets you GO BACK 1 STEP

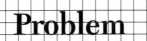

Draw this simple house elevation at any convenient size. Prior to drawing the roof, use UNDO to mark your current location in the drawing. Then draw the roof.

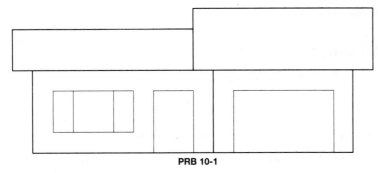

PRB 10-1

With UNDO Back, return to the point prior to drawing the roof. Draw the following roof in place of the old roof. Use the U and UNDO commands as necessary as you complete the drawing.

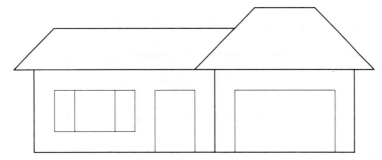

Unit 11   Altering and Adding Entities

■ OBJECTIVE:

To practice the CHAMFER, BREAK, FILLET, and OFFSET commands and the double line feature

These commands allow you to make chamfered or rounded corners and to break a line. Also, they enable you to produce double lines, such as those used in architectural floor plans.

■ *CHAMFER Command* ——————————

The CHAMFER command enables you to place a chamfer at the corner formed by two lines.

REF 230-233

1 Start AutoCAD and open the drawing called **GASKET**.

2 Enter the **CHAMFER** command. (**Chamfer** is contained in the **Construct** pull-down menu.)

You will receive the following:

```
Polyline/Distances/<Select first line>:
```

3 Type **D** for Distance. (You can also select **distance** from the standard screen menu.)

REF 232

4 Specify a chamfer distance of **0.25** unit for both the first and second distances.

5 Enter the **CHAMFER** command again (press the space bar) and place a chamfer at each of the corners of the gasket by picking the two lines which make up each corner. (Reenter **CHAMFER** by pressing the space bar before selecting each pair of lines.)

When you're finished, your drawing should look similar to the one below.

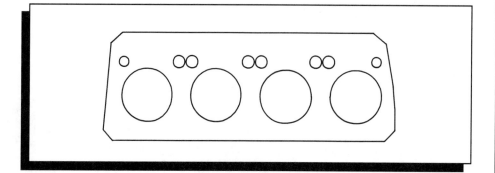

BREAK Command _____

Now let's remove (break out) sections of the gasket so that it looks like the drawing below.

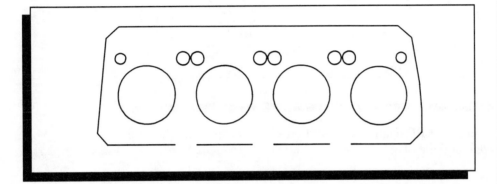

As you know, the bottom edge of the gasket was drawn as a single, continuous line. Therefore, if we were to use the ERASE command to break the line, it would erase the entire line since the line is an entity. The BREAK command, however, allows us to "break" certain entities such as lines, arcs, and circles.

1 Enter the **BREAK** command.

2 Pick a point where you'd like the break to begin. Since the locations of the above breaks are not dimensioned, approximate the location of the start point.

3 Pick the point where you'd like the break to end.

Did a piece disappear?

Let's break out two more sections of approximately equal size as shown in the above gasket drawing.

4 This time, select the **Modify** pull-down menu, select the **Break** item, and pick **Select Object, 2nd point**.

5 Repeat steps 2 and 3.

As you can see, this option is the same as entering the BREAK command at the keyboard.

When you're finished breaking out the small sections, let's place arcs in the broken sections as on the following illustration.

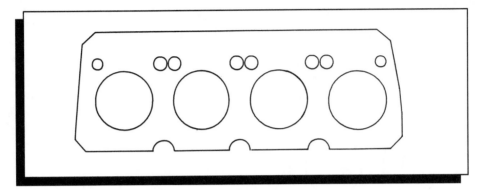

6 Using the **ARC** command, insert arc-shaped ribs along the broken edge of the gasket.

HINT:
Use the ENDpoint object snap mode to accurately place the arcs.

Let's break out a section of one of the holes in the gasket.

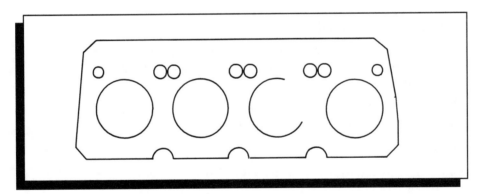

1 Select **EDIT** from the standard screen menu and pick **BREAK**.

2 Pick the first break point on the circle.

3 Working counterclockwise, pick the second point.

4 Enter **OOPS**.

The broken piece of the circle does not return. Why not? OOPS works only in conjunction with the ERASE command and not BREAK.

Reference

REF 226-230

⑤ Enter **U**.

The broken piece should have returned. If not, enter U again.

⑥ Experiment with the remaining BREAK options.

FILLET Command

Now let's change the chamfered corners on the gasket to rounded corners.

① Erase each of the chamfered corners using the **ERASE** command.

② Enter the **FILLET** command and set the radius at **0.3** unit.

HINT: The fastest way to do this is to enter FILLET, then R, and then 0.3. Be sure to press RETURN after each entry.

③ Reenter the **FILLET** command (press the space bar) and produce fillets at each of the four corners of the gasket by picking each pair of lines.

Your gasket drawing should now look similar to the following.

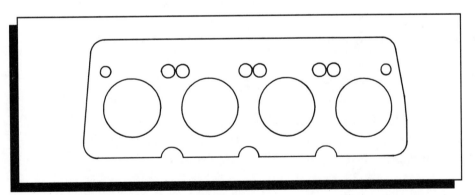

NOTE:

You can also fillet any combination of two lines, arcs, or circles.

④ Enter **QSAVE** to save your work.

Let's move away from the gasket and try something new.

① Draw lines similar to the ones on the next page. Omit the numbers.

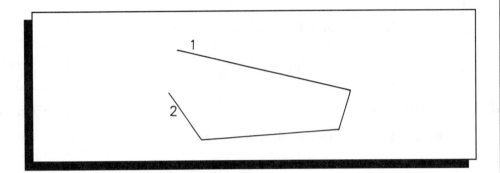

2 Set your fillet radius at **0**.

3 Reenter the **FILLET** command and select lines 1 and 2.

The two lines should have extended to form a corner.

This technique works with the CHAMFER command, too.

OFFSET Command

REF 223-235

The OFFSET command provides a means for producing double lines similar to those used in architectural floor plan drawings. Let's practice using the OFFSET command.

1 Enter the **OFFSET** command.

2 For the offset distance, enter **0.2**.

3 Select one of the circles in the gasket drawing.

4 Pick a point inside the circle in reply to "Side to offset?".

Did another circle appear?

5 Select another circle and pick a side to offset.

This time, let's use the Through option of OFFSET.

1 Draw a triangle of any size.

2 Enter **OFFSET** and select the **Through** option from the standard screen menu or enter **T**.

3 Pick any one of the three lines that make up the triangle.

4 Pick a point a short distance from the line and outside the triangle.

5 Do the same with the remaining two lines in the triangle so that you have an object similar to the following.

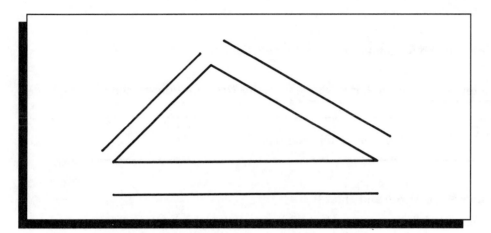

6 Enter **CHAMFER** and set the first and second chamfer distances at **0**. (Note that "dist = 0" is an item contained in the CHAMFER submenu in the standard screen menu.)

7 Enter **CHAMFER** again (press the space bar) and pick two of the new offset lines.

8 Do this again at the remaining two corners to complete the second triangle.

9 Clean up your drawing so that only the gasket remains and save your work using **QSAVE**.

Double Lines

EXTR 23-26

The OFFSET command is useful for adding offset lines to existing lines, arcs and circles. If you want to produce two parallel lines simultaneously, you can do so with the DLINE command.

1 Start a new drawing named **DOUBLE**.

2 Enter **DL**, short for DLINE.

Since DLINE is technically an AutoLISP application and not a standard command, AutoCAD must initialize and load it. AutoLISP is an implementation of the LISP programming language and is embedded in AutoCAD.

3 Create a triangle by picking three points. Enter **CL** (for CLose) to close the triangle.

4 Enter **R** for REDRAW.

Notice how the corners of the triangle meet perfectly.

5 Erase the triangle or repeat the **U** command until the triangle is gone.

6 Enter the **SNAP** command and set it at **0.25** unit.

7 Enter **DLINE** again, but this time from the **Draw** pull-down menu.

HINT:
Select the Line menu item and pick Double Lines.

8 Enter **W** for Width and enter **0.2**.

9 Create the following at any size and location. Pick the points as if you were drawing a single line using the LINE command.

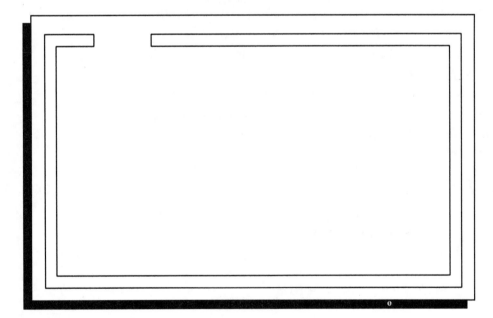

10 Press **RETURN** to terminate DLINE and enter **R** for REDRAW.

Let's add the interior wall, as shown in the following illustration.

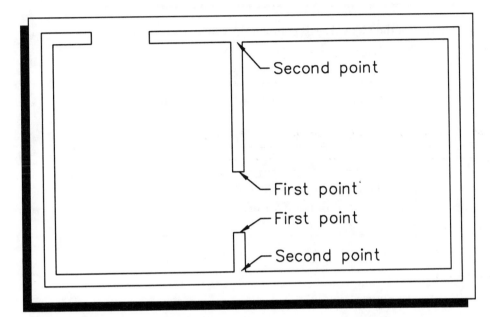

11 Enter **DL** and, with Snap on, pick the first point of one of the interior wall segments.

12 With Snap off, pick the second point.

13 Repeat steps 10 and 11 for the interior wall segment, and enter **R** to remove the construction points.

AutoCAD should have constructed the wall intersections as shown in the previous drawing. If not, repeat the U command until the wall segment disappears and try it again.

14 Enter **END** to save your work and exit AutoCAD.

You will have the opportunity to apply other DLINE options in upcoming units. In the meantime, if you are interested in learning more about DLINE, refer to pages 23-26 in the *AutoCAD Extras Manual*.

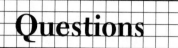

Questions

1. What is the function of the CHAMFER command?

   Allows you to CHAMFER At Junction of 2 LINES

2. How is using the BREAK command different from using the ERASE command?

   BREAK ERASES only SMAll Portion
   ERASE ERASES All of Item

3. If you want to break a circle or arc, in which direction do you move when specifying points: clockwise or counterclockwise?

   Counter Clockwise

4. In what pull-down menu is the FILLET command found?

   Construct

5. How do you set the FILLET radius?

   TYPE R to FIllet PROMPT & ENTER than TYPE iN RADiUS & ENTER

6. Will the FILLET radius change or stay the same after you END and exit AutoCAD?

   ONLy IN THAt DRAWiNG

7. What can be accomplished by setting either FILLET or CHAMFER to 0?

   THEY will EXtEND to MAKE A CORNER iNstEAD OF A RADiUS

8. Explain the purpose of the OFFSET command.

   Allows DRAWiNG of Dbl LiNES

9. Describe an application for the DLINE command.

   MAKES DBl LiNES At SAME TiME PARAlell

Problems

1. Create the first drawing shown below left. Don't worry about exact sizes and locations, but do use SNAP and ORTHO. Then use FILLET to change it to the second drawing. Set the fillet radius at 0.2 unit.

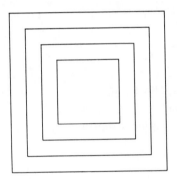 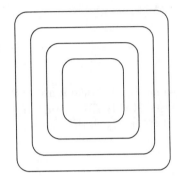

PRB 11-1

2. Create the triangle shown below. Then use CHAMFER to change it into a hexagon. Set the chamfer distance at 0.66 unit.

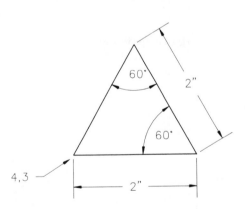 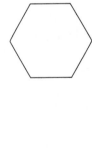

PRB 11-2

3. Draw the following object; don't worry about specific sizes. Use the FILLET command to place fillets in the corners as indicated.

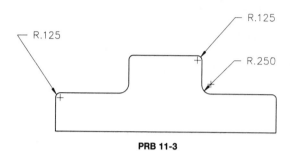

PRB 11-3

4. Draw the following object. Make it about 2 units long by 1 unit in diameter. Use the CHAMFER command to place a chamfer at each corner. Specify 0.125 for both the first and second chamfer distances.

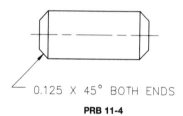

0.125 X 45° BOTH ENDS

PRB 11-4

5. Using the ARC and CHAMFER commands, construct the following object.

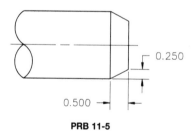

PRB 11-5

6. Using AutoCAD's double line feature, create a basic floor plan of a garage or shed. Be creative.

AUTOCAD® AT WORK

Ready to Work

The Boeing Commercial Airplane Scientific and Computing Training Group, managed by Paul D. Berg, uses AutoCAD to prepare high school students for the job market. Ron Shea, an instructor from the group, teaches a course at New Market Vocational Skills Center, in Tumwater, Washington. New Market offers a variety of vocational programs at the high school level, where students can take classes for credit. Its instructors are provided by several area businesses, including the Boeing group.

Boeing uses AutoCAD for many things, including airplane interior layout and facilities design. Employees take courses in CAD that last eight hours a day for three days. Ron Shea teaches these courses, which provide employees a working knowledge of AutoCAD and other drafting programs. He has incorporated the employee programs into the course he teaches at New Market.

Rather than the intense three-day program, the course at New Market is spread out over one semester, or about four months. Students learn how to use AutoCAD and how to compare and contrast it with other drafting programs. Ron encourages their creativity as they become more comfortable with the software. They are allowed to design their own products using AutoCAD.

Ron Shea feels that it is important for students to know how to operate AutoCAD and other CAD systems in order to be prepared for the job market. His course helps to prepare students for careers in drafting, design, engineering, and architecture.

The Boeing group sends Ron Shea to New Market because it feels that quality education is important. By taking part in education, they are helping to raise the quality of future workers in the industry. These students won't necessarily be hired by Boeing upon graduation, but they might work for a company that serves or works with Boeing. This type of education encourages students to pursue quality careers that use these skills. When they begin to look for jobs, they will already be trained and therefore more desirable to employers.

A comprehensive knowledge of CAD, especially Auto-CAD, is valuable in the job market. Through hands-on experience with AutoCAD, high school students in the state of Washington graduate better prepared to become drafters and engineers.

Unit 12   Moving and Duplicating Objects

■ OBJECTIVE:

To apply CHANGE, MOVE, COPY, and MIRROR

When drawing, there are times when you need to move or duplicate an object. With AutoCAD, it's a simple process.

■ *CHANGE Command* _____

The CHANGE command is used for a number of purposes, such as fixing the placement of lines. Let's experiment with it.

REF 214-218

1 Start AutoCAD and open the drawing called **GASKET**.

2 Above the gasket, draw a line segment of any length.

3 Select the **Modify** pull-down menu, highlight **Change**, and pick the **Points** option.

4 In reply to "Select objects:" pick the line near one of its ends and press **RETURN**.

5 In reply to "Properties/<Change point>" pick a point a short distance from the end of the line.

AutoCAD will redraw the line so it passes through the new point.

1 Erase the line.

2 Draw three intersecting lines like the ones below. Omit the letters.

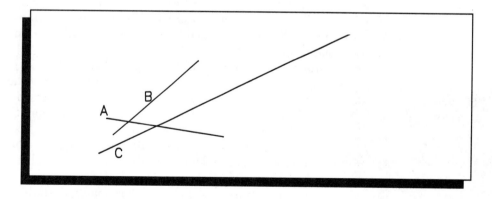

Using the CHANGE command, let's fix these lines to form a perfect arrow as shown in the illustration below.

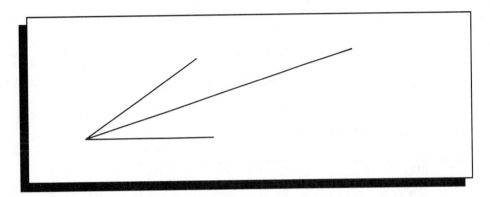

3. Enter the **CHANGE** command, this time at the keyboard.

4. In response to "Select objects:" pick lines A and B and press **RETURN**.

5. In reply to "Properties/<Change point>" pick the leftmost endpoint of line C. Use the object snap ENDpoint mode to accurately select the point.

Did the lines change into the shape of an arrow? If not, try it again.

HINT: AutoCAD provides help on each of its commands, including the CHANGE command. If CHANGE is entered, you can get immediate help on this command by entering 'HELP. (Note the apostrophe.)

6. Experiment with the CHANGE command by creating and fixing other intersecting lines.

You can also use the CHANGE command to change the radius of a circle. Let's do it.

1. Draw a small circle of any radius.

2. Enter the **CHANGE** command, pick the circle, and press **RETURN**.

3. In reply to "Properties/<Change point>" pick a point near the circle. The circle's radius should change through that point.

Drag can be invoked by pressing RETURN just prior to specifying a change point. The new radius can then be dragged into place. Drag mode must be set at "Auto." Try it.

We'll explore other ways of using the CHANGE command at a later time.

4 For now, erase the line, arrow, and circle so that you'll have room for the next operation.

MOVE Command _____

Let's move the entire gasket to the top of the screen using the MOVE command.

REF 201-202

1 Enter the command called **MOVE**.

HINT: _____
M is the command alias for MOVE.

AutoCAD should now be showing the "Select objects:" prompt.

2 Type **W** and press **RETURN**.

3 Place a window around the entire gasket drawing and press **RETURN**.

4 In reply to "Base point or Displacement," place a base point somewhere on or near the gasket drawing as shown in the following illustration.

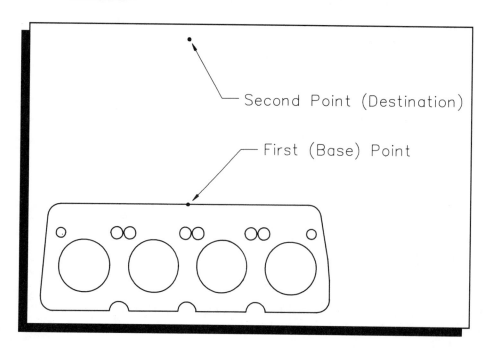

Second Point (Destination)

First (Base) Point

5 Move your pointing device in the direction of the second point (destination). If the gasket does not dynamically drag as you move to the second point, type **drag** and press **RETURN**.

6 Pick the second point.

Did the drawing move as illustrated below?

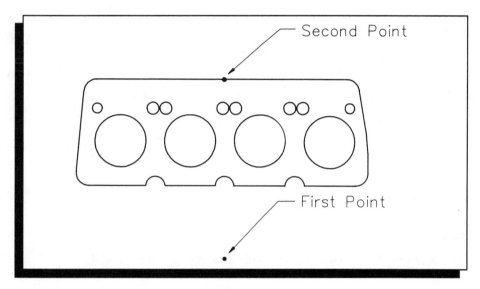

7 Practice using the MOVE command by moving the drawing to the bottom of the screen.

Now let's drag two of the holes in the gasket to a new location.

1 Select **Move** from the **Modify** pull-down menu.

2 In response to the prompt "Select objects:" pick two of the four holes (circles) and press **RETURN**.

3 Specify the first point (base point). Place the point anywhere on or near either of the two circles.

4 In reply to "Second point of displacement:" move your pointing device.

5 After you decide on a location for the circles, pick that location with your pointing device.

6 Drag the circles back into the gasket as they were before.

▮ COPY Command _____

The COPY command is almost identical to the MOVE command.
The only difference is that the COPY command does not move the object;
it copies it.

REF 202-203

1 Erase all of the large holes in the gasket except for one.

2 Enter the **COPY** command, select the remaining circle, and press **RETURN**.

3 Specify the Multiple option by entering **M**, and select the center of the circle for the base point.

HINT: _____
Use the CENter object snap mode. Also, turn Ortho on before completing the following step.

4 Move your crosshairs and place the circle in the proper location.

5 Repeat Step 4 until all four large circles are in place; then press **RETURN**.

6 Practice using the COPY command by erasing and copying the small circles.

▮ MIRROR Command _____

There are times when it is necessary to produce a mirror image of a drawing, detail, or part. A simple COPY of the object is not adequate because the object being copied must be reversed, as was done with the butterfly in the following drawing. One side of the butterfly was drawn and then mirrored to produce the other side.

REF 206-207

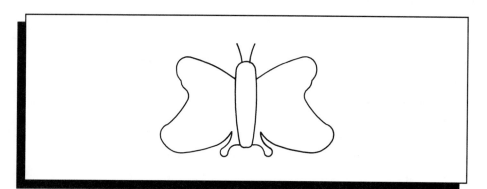

The same is true if the engine head gasket we developed is to be reproduced to represent the opposite side of the engine; that is, if the gasket we are producing is for an eight-cylinder engine.

1 Move the gasket either to the top or bottom of the screen to allow space for another gasket of the same size.

2 Enter the **MIRROR** command, select the gasket by placing a window around it, and press **RETURN**.

3 Create a horizontal mirror line near the gasket by selecting two points on a horizontal plane as shown below. Ortho should be on.

4 The prompt line will ask if you want to delete old objects. Enter **N** for "no," or press **RETURN** since the default is No.

The gasket should have mirrored as shown below.

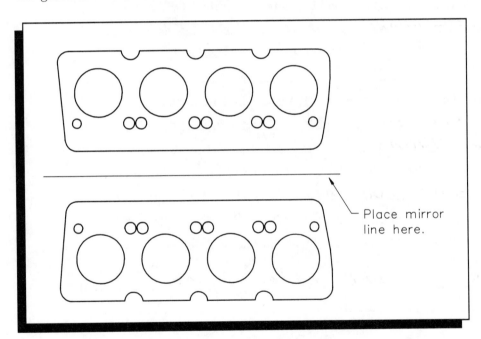

Place mirror line here.

Mirrored images can also be created around an axis (mirror line) other than horizontal or vertical.

5 Draw a small triangle and mirror it with an angular (*e.g.*, 45°) mirror line.

6 Erase the triangles and enter **END** to save your work and exit AutoCAD.

Questions

1. In what pull-down menu is the CHANGE command found?

   MODIFY

2. Describe a situation where CHANGE would be used for changing endpoints of lines.

   IF PLACEMENT OF LINES IS WRONG AND YOU NEED them AT A INTERSECTION

3. In what pull-down menu is MOVE located?

   MODIFY

4. Explain how the MOVE command is different from the COPY command.

   MOVE - CHANGES POSISTION OF Item While COPY DUPLICATES ITEM

5. How does DRAGMODE affect the MOVE and COPY commands?

   YOU SEE the GOHST LINES OF THE Item

6. Describe a situation in which the MIRROR command would be helpful.

   IF BOTH SIDE ARE SAME AND YOU HAVE DRAWN ONLY ONE SIDE OR HALF

7. During a MIRROR operation, can the mirror line be specified at any angle? Explain.

   YES IF the ORtho is OFF

Problems

In problems 1 and 2, follow each step to create the objects. Use the ARC Continue option at Step 2 of problem 1. Use the MIRROR and COPY commands to complete Steps 3 and 4. Your final work should show all four steps. Use the COPY command to copy your work from one step to the next.

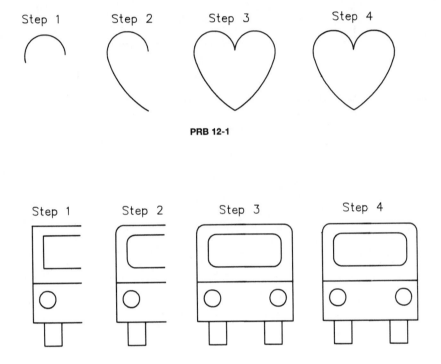

Step 1 Step 2 Step 3 Step 4

PRB 12-1

Step 1 Step 2 Step 3 Step 4

PRB 12-2

In problem 3, draw the objects and room as shown. Then use the MOVE and COPY commands to move the office furniture into the room. Omit the lettering on the drawings.

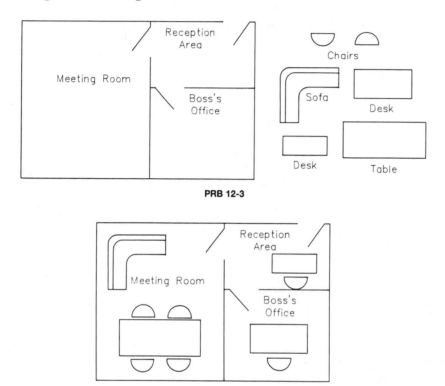

PRB 12-3

HINT: In certain situations, MOVE and COPY may work better with the Ortho and Snap modes off.

In the drawing made for problem 3, use the OFFSET command to produce double-line walls for the office. Set the Offset distance at 0.2 and use other AutoCAD commands, such as CHAMFER and BREAK, to complete and clean up the wall constructions. If necessary make the drawing larger for easier editing.

Start a new drawing named PRB12-4. Recreate the floor plan using AutoCAD's double line feature. Set the width at 0.15 unit.

The Powerful ARRAY Command

■ OBJECTIVE:

To create rectangular and polar arrays

This unit uses the ARRAY command to construct two drawings: (1) a schematic of computer chip sockets and (2) a bicycle wheel with spokes.

REF 209-213

Producing Rectangular Arrays _____

1 Start AutoCAD and begin a new drawing named **CHIPS**.

2 In the lower left corner of the screen, draw the following and make it small (approximately 1 unit wide by 1 unit tall).

REF 209-211
TUT 79-80

HINT:
Use the COPY command to duplicate the small circle. Then use the MIRROR command to make the bottom half identical to the top half.

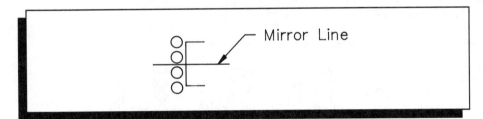

3 Using the MIRROR command, mirror the object to complete the opposite side as shown below. If your drawing does not look exactly like the one here, that's okay.

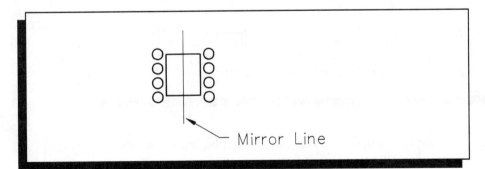

The object you have just drawn represents a computer chip socket. It resembles a schematic of the sockets found inside your computer. The sockets house the RAM chips that are currently holding the information you see on the screen.

4 Enter the **ARRAY** command. (Snap should be off.)

5 In reply to the "Select objects:" prompt, select the chip socket by placing a window around it, and press **RETURN**.

6 Enter the Rectangular array option by typing **R** and pressing **RETURN**, or by selecting it from the standard screen menu.

7 Specify **3** rows and **5** columns.

8 Specify that you want **1.5** units between the rows and **1.75** units between the columns. (The distances specify the center of one object to the center of the next.)

You should now have 15 chip sockets on the screen, arranged in a 3 × 5 array as shown in the following illustration.

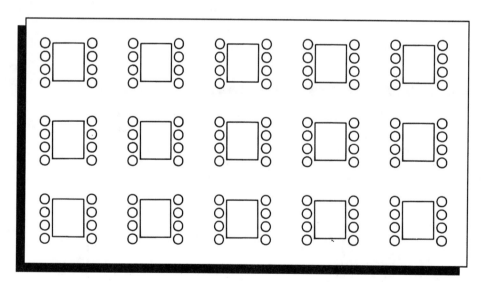

If your array does not look like the above, erase everything except for the chip socket in the lower left corner of your screen and try again.

If it does look like the figure above, good job!

NOTE:

Rectangular arrays can be produced at any angle by changing the Snap rotation angle prior to the ARRAY command. Also, you can specify the distances between rows and columns by picking the opposite corners of a rectangle with your pointing device.

⑨ Save your array by entering the **QSAVE** command.

Producing Polar (Circular) Arrays

Next, we're going to produce a bicycle wheel using the Polar array option.

REF 211-213

① Begin a new drawing named **WHEEL**.

② Draw a tire/wheel similar to the one in the following drawing. Don't worry about the exact sizes of the circles, but do make the wheel large enough to fill most of your screen.

HINT:

Use the CENter object snap mode to make the circles concentric.

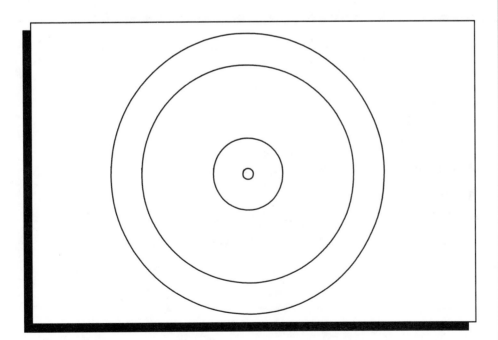

③ Using the **LINE** command, draw two crossing lines similar to the ones on the next page.

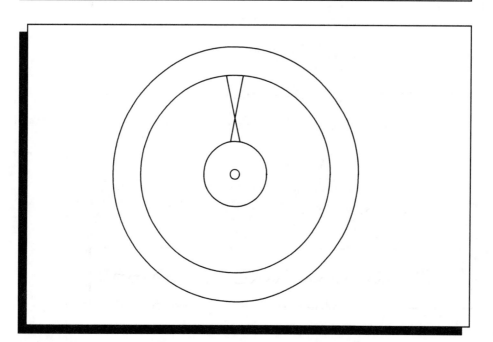

4 Enter the **ARRAY** command and use the following information when responding to each step. (Snap should be off.)

(a) Select each of the two crossing lines for the array and press **RETURN**.

(b) Choose the **P**olar array option.

(c) Make the center of the wheel the center point for the array. (Use object snap to locate the center point precisely.)

(d) Specify **18** for "Number of items."

(e) Enter **360** for "Angle to fill" by pressing **RETURN**.

(f) . . . and yes, you want to rotate the spokes as they are copied.

If you were not successful, try again. The wheel should be similar to the following.

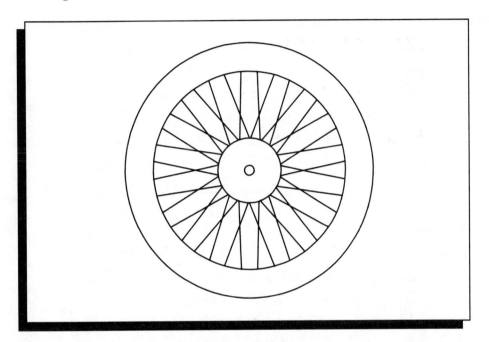

5 Practice using the ARRAY Polar option by arraying other objects. At least once, specify less than 360 degrees when replying to "Angle to fill."

NOTE:

During the ARRAY Polar sequence, the prompt "Angle to fill (+ = ccw, -= cw)" appears. AutoCAD is asking for the angle (in degrees) to fill the array. "+ = ccw" means that a positive number will produce an array in a counterclockwise direction, and "-= cw" means that a negative number will produce an array in a clockwise direction.

6 Enter **END** to save your work and exit AutoCAD.

Questions

1. In what pull-down menu is the ARRAY command found?

   ~~Draw~~ Construct

2. Name the two types of arrays.

   POLAR & RECTANUlAR

3. State one practical application for each type of array.

   RECt - FENCE POStS FOR YARD

   Polar - SPOKES ON TIRES

4. When creating a polar array, do you have the option of specifying less than 360 degrees? Explain.

   Y All you DO At the DEGREE PROmPt is tyPE iN DEGREES you WANt

5. Explain how a rectangular array can be created at any angle.

   By CHANGing SNAP Rotation AGlE PRiOR to ARRAy

Problems

1. Using the ARRAY command and the Polar option, draw the following figure.

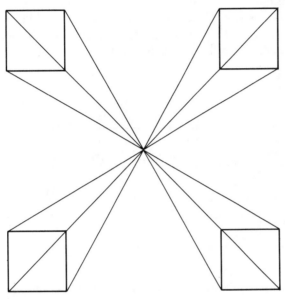

PRB 13-1

2. Use ARRAY again to create the following figure. (Start by drawing an ellipse and then array it.) Experiment to see how changing the shape of the ellipse, the number of ellipses, and the center of the polar array changes the outcome of the array.

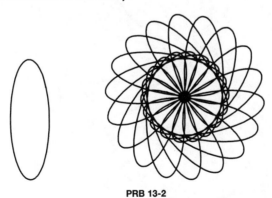

PRB 13-2

3. Develop an auditorium with rows and columns of seats using the **ARRAY** command. Design the room any way you'd like.

4. Identify another practical application for using an array. Draw the first object and then array it.

5. Load your drawing called **GASKET**. Erase each of the circles. Replace the large ones according to the locations shown below, this time using the **ARRAY** command. Also reproduce the small circles using the **ARRAY** command, but don't worry about their exact locations. The radius of the large circles is 0.6; the small circles have a radius of 0.12.

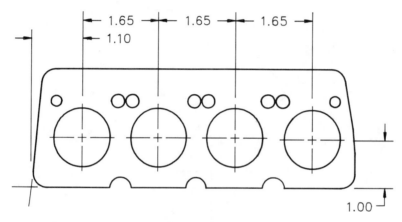

6. Using the **ARRAY** command (you decide how), draw the following figure.

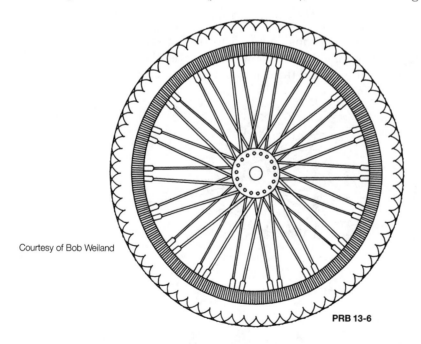

Courtesy of Bob Weiland

PRB 13-6

7. Array text, such as "Goodyear," on a tire. Begin by arraying a single letter. Then, using the **CHANGE** command, change each letter to the correct letter. Refer to Unit 20 for instructions on how to place text.

106

Unit 14 — Modifying and Maneuvering

■ OBJECTIVE:

To apply the STRETCH, SCALE, ROTATE, TRIM, and EXTEND commands

AutoCAD offers numerous editing commands for changing the appearance of drawings. For instance, you can stretch the end of a house to make it longer, scale it down if it is too large, rotate it to better position it on a lot, trim sidewalk lines that extend too far, and extend driveway lines which are too short. We will do all of this, and more, in the following steps.

1 Begin a new drawing named **SITE**.

2 Draw the following site plan according to the dimensions shown. With Snap on, place the lower left corner of the property line at absolute point 1,1. Omit dimensions. All points in the drawing should fall on the Snap grid.

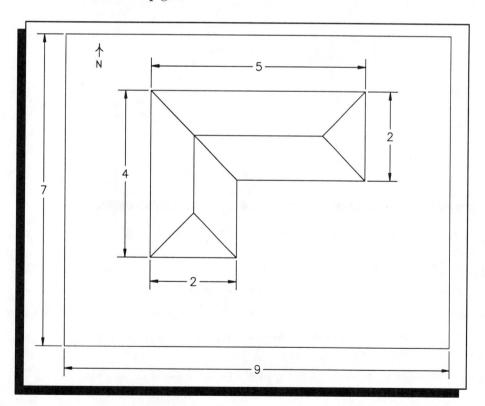

STRETCH Command _____

1 Enter the **STRETCH** command and select the east end of the house as shown in the next drawing, and press **RETURN**. Use the Crossing object selection procedure. (See the following hint.)

HINT:

In reply to "select objects:" enter C for Crossing. If you select Stretch from the Modify pull-down menu, the Crossing option is embedded in the command sequence and therefore is entered for you automatically.

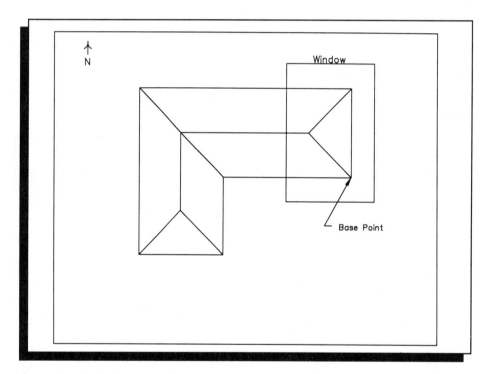

② Pick the lower right corner of the house for the base point as shown above.

③ In reply to "Second point of displacement" stretch the house 1 unit to the right. (Snap should be on.) The house stretches dynamically.

The house should now be longer.

④ Stretch the south portion of the house so that it looks similar to the house on the next page.

Remember, if you make a mistake, use the U or UNDO command to back up.

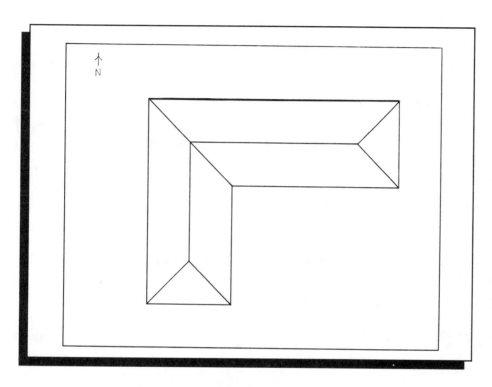

NOTE:

You can also use STRETCH to alter dimensions. This is part of the associative dimensioning feature covered in the section titled "Associative Dimensioning" in Unit 24.

SCALE Command

REF 204-205

Since the house is now slightly too large, let's scale it down to fit the lot.

1 Enter the **SCALE** command, select the object by placing a window around the entire house, and press **RETURN**.

HINT:

Scale, Rotate, Trim, and Extend are located in the Modify pull-down menu.

2 Pick the lower left corner of the house as the base point.

At this point, the house can be dynamically dragged into place or a scale factor can be entered.

3 Move the crosshairs and notice the dynamic scaling.

4 Enter **0.5** in reply to "<Scale factor>/Reference."

Suppose the house is now too small. Let's scale it up using the SCALE Reference option.

1 Enter **SCALE** (press the space bar) and select the house as before.

2 Pick the lower left corner of the house again for the base point.

3 Enter the **Reference** option.

4 For the reference length, pick the lower left corner of the house, and then pick the corner just to the right of it as the second point.

5 In response to the "New length:" prompt, move the crosshairs about 1/2 unit to the right of the second point (Ortho should be on) and pick a point.

Did the house enlarge according to the specified length?

ROTATE Command

REF 203-204

Let's rotate the house.

1 Enter the **ROTATE** command, select the entire house, and press **RETURN**.

2 Pick the lower left corner of the house for the base point.

3 As you move the crosshairs, notice that the object rotates dynamically. (Ortho should be off.)

NOTE:

Drag is embedded in the command sequence and therefore is entered for you automatically.

4 For the Rotation angle, enter **25** (degrees).

Did the house rotate 25 degrees counterclockwise?

Let's rotate the house again, but this time with the Drag option.

1 Enter **ROTATE**, select the house, and press **RETURN** after you have made the selection.

2 Pick the lower left corner of the house for the base point.

3 At the "<Rotation angle>/Reference:" prompt, drag the house in a clockwise direction a few degrees so that it is positioned similarly to the one on the next page.

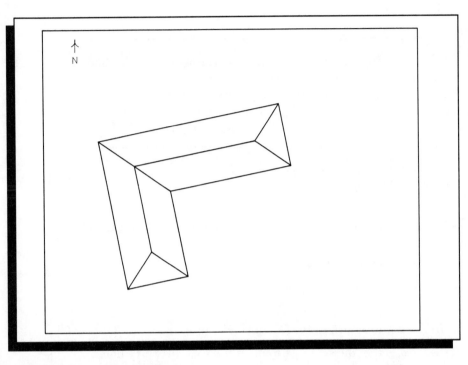

TRIM Command

REF 222-224

1. With Ortho on and Snap off, draw two lines near the bottom of the site plan to represent a sidewalk. Extend the sidewalk beyond the east and west property lines as shown here.

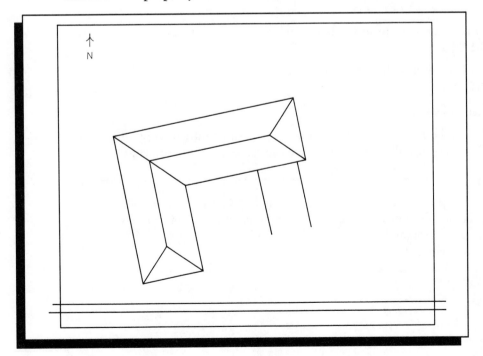

② With Ortho off, draw a partial driveway as shown in the preceding drawing.

HINT: When drawing the first line of the driveway, notice the line angle found in the coordinate display. (Turn on the coordinate display if it is off.) Use this angle when drawing the second line so that the lines are approximately parallel. Also, use the object snap NEArest mode so that the endpoints of the driveway fall exactly on the edge of the house.

③ Enter the **TRIM** command.

④ Select the east property line as the cutting edge and press **RETURN**.

⑤ Select the far right ends of the sidewalk lines.

Does the sidewalk now end at the property line?

⑥ Press **RETURN** to return to the "Command:" prompt.

⑦ Trim the west end of the sidewalk to meet the west property line using the **TRIM** command.

EXTEND Command

REF 224-225

① Enter the **EXTEND** command.

② Select the south property line as the boundary edge and press **RETURN**.

③ Pick the ends of the two lines which make up the driveway and press **RETURN**.

Did the driveway extend?

④ Using the BREAK command, remove the short intersecting lines so that the sidewalk and driveway look like the following drawing.

HINT: After selecting the line you want to break, use the BREAK First option. Then, when picking the Break points, use the object snap INTersection mode. Remember, if you make a mistake, use the U or UNDO command to correct it.

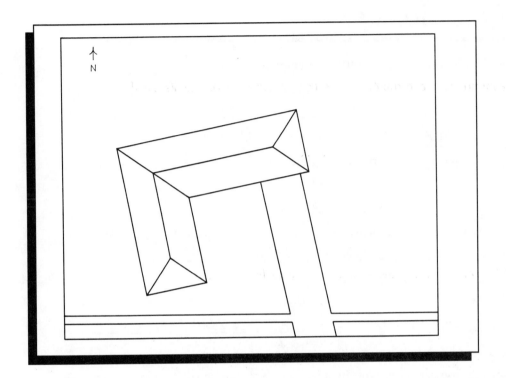

Questions

1. Explain the purpose of the STRETCH command.

   CHANGES LENGTHS OF lines or Items

2. Using the SCALE command, what number would you enter to

   enlarge an object by 50 percent? *50*

   enlarge it to 3 times its present size? *3*

   reduce it to 1/2 its present size? *.5*

3. Explain how you would dynamically scale an object up or down.

   SELECt A BASE Point and DRAGing It to where you want

4. Can you dynamically rotate an object? Explain.

   yES By turning the ortho off AND moving the Puck

5. How would you accurately specify a 90-degree clockwise rotation of an object?

   TYPE 90 At ANGLE PromPt

6. Explain the purpose of the TRIM command.

   Trims/removes Excess BEyoND A Point you Pick

7. Describe a situation in which the EXTEND command would be useful.

   WHEN A line, OR ARC NEED to BE LONGER

Problem

Bring up the SITE drawing you created in this unit. Perform each of the following operations on the drawing.

- Stretch the driveway by placing a (Crossing) window around the house and across the driveway. Stretch the driveway to the north so that the house is sitting farther to the rear of the lot.

- Add a sidewalk parallel to the east property line. Use the TRIM and BREAK commands to clean up the sidewalk corner and the north end of the new sidewalk.

- Reduce the entire site plan by 20 percent using the SCALE command.

- Stretch the right side of the site plan to the east 1 unit.

- Rotate the entire site plan 10 degrees in a counterclockwise direction.

- Place trees and shrubs to complete the site plan drawing. Use the ARRAY command to create one tree and one shrub. Use the COPY command to duplicate them.

The site plan should now look similar to the one below.

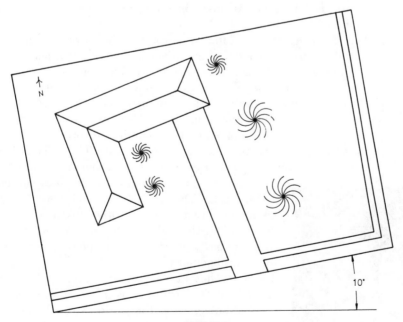

PRB 14-1

AUTOCAD® AT WORK

You're Expecting How Many?

Have you ever planned a party or meeting and needed to figure out how many chairs or tables were required? Did you have to decide whether or not there would be room for all the people you wanted to invite? Imagine what would happen if that party included thousands of people, and you discovered at the last minute that they would not fit into the space.

That was the problem frequently faced by the Pine Bluff Convention Center in Pine Bluff, Arkansas, before the introduction of AutoCAD. The staff would be setting up the tables and chairs and then learn, to their horror, that the room set aside for the event would not hold even half the people who would be arriving in a few hours. It was a planner's nightmare.

Then, in 1984, the convention center created a computer graphics department for the purpose of drawing convention setups to scale and calculating the correct amount of space and equipment needed. Using AutoCAD, the department currently turns out about 25 drawings per week, the same number that formerly took about three months to complete. Most important, the seating and floor space estimates are accurate. The staff can draw setups within setups and keep closer control over equipment inventories.

Says the Center's computer graphics director, John David Rauls, "The application of AutoCAD has given us a greater ability to show creativeness in our setups, has reduced part-time labor costs due to incorrect hand drawings, and has provided us with a powerful advertising tool for securing clients."

The center hosts 1,500 events each year and accommodates around 350,000 visitors. It is the most fully computerized convention center in the world. Not only are floor plans done by computer, but heating and cooling, accounting, payroll, and scheduling, and booking of events are also handled by the Center's mainframe. Computerization has proved so successful that the Center has begun offering its services to other convention centers across the country.

Unit 15

Advanced Object Selection and Editing

■ OBJECTIVE:

To introduce alternative, advanced, and in some instances, faster methods of selecting and editing entities

The quickest way to edit an object is to click and drag. This is true whether you are using a $100 drawing program on a $1,000 computer or a $4,000 CAD program on a $40,000 computer. AutoCAD offers a "click 'n drag" editing feature called Grips. This feature permits you to pick an object and immediately stretch, move, rotate, or mirror it, *without* entering a command.

AutoCAD also offers a noun/verb selection technique. It allows you to select an object first and then enter a command. Prior to Release 12, AutoCAD users were required to enter a command, such as MOVE, and then select the object.

■ *Grips* ———————————————————

REF 188-200

1 Start AutoCAD.

2 Enter the **RECTANG** command and draw a rectangle of any size and at any location.

3 Select any point on the rectangle. (A command should not be entered at the "Command:" prompt.)

Notice that small boxes, called grips, appear at each corner of the rectangle.

4 Pick any one of the four grips. (As you pick the grip, notice how the pickbox locks onto the selected grip.)

The grip should turn red, showing that you've selected it. Notice that the command line has changed and indicates that AutoCAD is in stretch mode as shown below.

REF 193-194

```
** STRETCH **
<Stretch to point>/Base point/Copy/Undo/eXit:
```

5 Move your pointing device and notice that you can stretch the rectangle. (Do not pick a point.)

——— NOTE: ———

Turn off Ortho and Snap if either is on.

6 Press the space bar and note the change in the "Command:" prompt area, as shown below.

```
** MOVE **
<Move to point>/Base point/Copy/Undo/eXit:
```

You are now in Move mode.

REF 194

7 Move your pointing device and notice that you can move the rectangle. (Do not pick a point.)

8 Press the space bar and again note the change in the "Command:" prompt area.

You are now in Rotate mode.

REF 195

9 Move your pointing device and notice that you can rotate the rectangle. (Do not pick a point.)

10 Press the space bar and note the change in the "Command:" prompt area.

You are now in Scale mode.

REF 196-198

11 Move your pointing device and notice that you can scale the rectangle. (Do not pick a point.)

12 Press the space bar and note the change in the "Command:" prompt area.

You are now in Mirror mode.

REF 198

13 Move your pointing device and notice that you are able to mirror the rectangle. (Do not pick a point.)

14 Press the space bar again.

You've returned to the Stretch mode.

15 Now you can pick a point.

The "Command:" prompt is now available to you for keyboard command entry. The object will remain selected until you enter a command, select certain menu items, or press CTRL C twice.

As you can see, the Grips feature offers a faster way of editing objects.

16 Practice the Grips feature by stretching, moving, rotating, scaling, and mirroring the rectangle.

Copying with Grips

You can also copy objects using Grips.

1 Draw a circle of any size and at any location.

2 Select the circle and pick one of the four grips that lie on it.

3 Move your pointing device and notice how you can adjust the circle's radius.

4 Press the space bar so the Move mode is active.

5 Enter **C** for Copy.

HINT: You can also select Copy from the standard screen menu. Note, also, that you can select a Grips mode from the same submenu.

6 Copy the circle three times by picking three points anywhere on the screen.

7 Enter **X** to exit the Grips mode or select **eXit** from the standard screen menu.

8 Press **CTRL C** twice to clear the grips from the circle.

You can also copy objects by pressing the shift key as you pick a new location.

1 Select the rectangle, select one of its corners, and press the space bar.

2 Press the shift key as you move the rectangle and pick a point.

AutoCAD should have copied the rectangle.

3 Enter **X** to exit the Grips mode and enter **CRTL C** twice.

Grips Dialogue Box

REF 189-190

You can make changes to the Grips feature using the Grips dialogue box.

1 Enter **DDGRIPS** or select **Grips...** from the **Settings** pull-down menu.

DDGRIPS is an AutoLISP application, not a standard command, so AutoCAD must initialize and load it. After doing so, the following will appear.

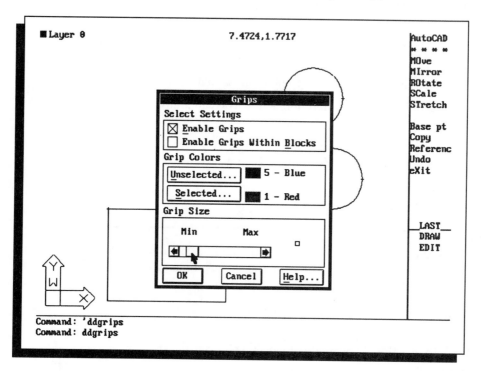

② Move the slider bar and watch how it changes the size of the box to the right of it.

This adjusts the size of the grips box.

③ Increase the size of the grips box and pick the **OK** button.

④ Select one of the objects and notice the notice the increased size of the grips.

⑤ Pick one of the grips and perform an editing operation.

⑥ Display the Grips dialogue box again and adjust the size of the grips box.

The Grips dialogue box also permits you to enable/disable the Grips feature, as well as control the assignment of grips within Blocks. You will learn about Blocks in Unit 29. You can also make changes to the color of selected and unselected grips. For now, do not change these settings.

⑦ Pick the **Help...** button if you are interested in learning more.

⑧ Pick the **OK** button to make the dialogue box disappear.

Reference

REF 26-27

Noun/Verb Selection Technique

As mentioned at the beginning of this unit, AutoCAD lets you select one or more objects and then execute an editing command, such as ERASE, on the object(s) you selected. This is called a noun/verb technique because you first select the object, such as a *line* (the noun) and then the function, such as *erase* (the verb). You may find it convenient to use, especially if you are familiar with other graphics programs that use this technique. Before Release 12, AutoCAD users were limited to a verb/noun syntax, the technique used prior to this unit.

1 Select one of the circles.

2 Enter **E** for ERASE.

As you can see, AutoCAD erased the circle without first asking you to select objects. You have just used the noun/verb technique.

1 Select the rectangle and another circle.

2 Enter the **ARRAY** command.

AutoCAD does not ask you to select objects because it knows you've already selected them.

3 Enter **CTRL C** to cancel the ARRAY command.

The noun/verb technique applies to AutoCAD commands that require object selection. Practice this technique in the future.

Entity Selection Settings Dialogue Box

REF 26-28

You can change entity selection modes using the Entity Selection Settings dialogue box.

1 Enter **DDSELECT** or select **Selection Settings...** from the **Settings** pull-down menu.

The following dialogue box will appear.

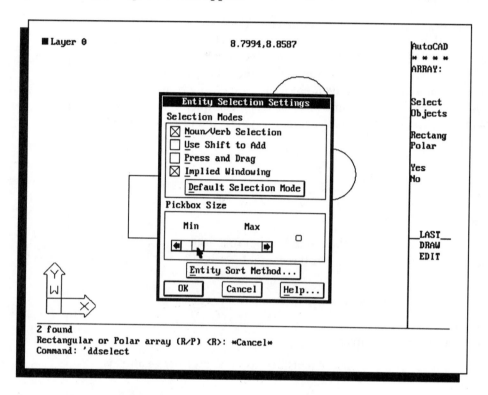

The selection modes area in the dialogue box allows you to select from four entity selection methods. The settings as you see them here are adequate for most AutoCAD work and usually do not require changes.

2 Pick the **Help...** button and read the information on DDSELECT.

3 Pick the **OK** button to exit the help facility.

4 Pick the **OK** button to exit the Entity Selection Settings dialogue box.

5 Enter **QUIT** to exit AutoCAD. Do not save your changes.

Questions

1. When you use a graphics program, such as AutoCAD, what is the quickest way to edit an object?

   CLICK & DRAG

2. Explain the primary benefit of using the Grips feature.

   It Allows you to Pick, move stretch Rotate, scale & mirror Items without CMNDS

3. What editing functions become available to you when you use grips?

   MOVE stretch Rotate mirror scale

4. What do you press on the keyboard to change from one Grips mode to the next?

   SPACE BAR

5. Explain how you copy an object using grips.

   Select move mode then ENter C

6. What is the purpose of the slider bar contained in the Grips dialogue box?

   CHANGE sizes of GRip BOXES

7. Explain the difference between the noun/verb and verb/noun selection techniques.

   NOUN/VERB is ACtion then SELECTION VERB/NOUN is selection then Action

Problem

Start AutoCAD and open the drawing named PSGLOBE, which is contained in the SAMPLES directory. This file and directory come with AutoCAD and are usually installed with it. Be certain you have a backup copy of this file before you proceed with this problem.

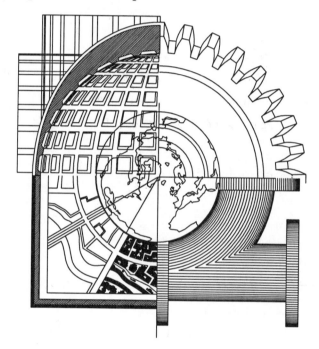

Save the file as PSGLOBE2 using the SAVEAS command. Using Grips and the noun/verb technique you learned in this unit, change the drawing to look like the following.

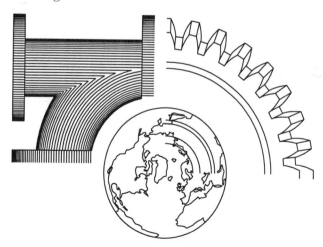

Unit 16 AutoCAD's Magnifying Glass

■ OBJECTIVE:

To practice the ZOOM, REGEN, and VIEWRES commands

The ZOOM command allows you to increase and decrease the apparent size of drawings on the screen. ZOOM can magnify objects as much as ten trillion times! This unit utilizes the ZOOM command to practice this process, and it covers the effects of screen regenerations and redraws.

■ *ZOOM Command* _____

REF 271-279

Let's apply the ZOOM command.

1   Start AutoCAD and begin a new drawing named **ZOOM**.

2   Draw the following room, including the table and chair. Don't worry about exact sizes and locations of the objects, but do fill most of the screen.

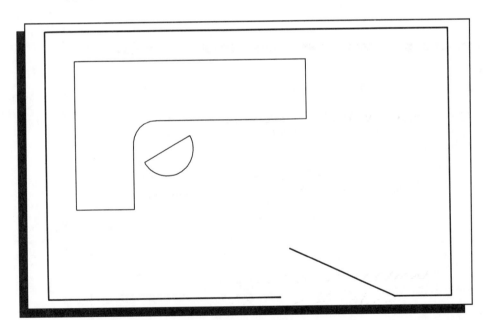

3   Enter **Z**, the command alias for the ZOOM command. Note each of the **ZOOM** options, as shown below.

```
All/Center/Dynamic/Extents/Left/Previous/Vmax/Window/<Scale(X/XP)>:
```

4 Place a window around the table and chair as shown below.

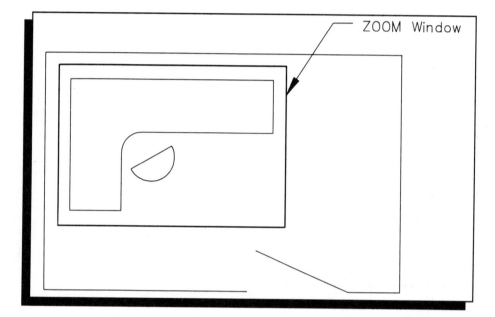

Did the table and chair magnify to fill most of your screen? It should have.

5 Next, draw schematic representations of several components which make up a CAD system as shown below. Approximate their sizes and omit the text.

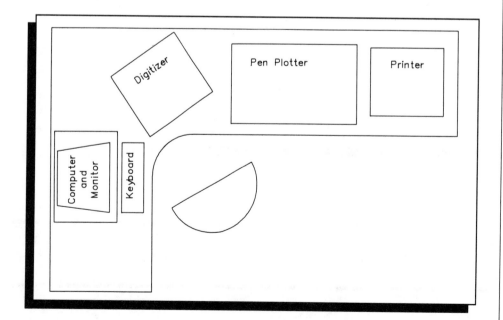

Reference

Now let's zoom in on the keyboard. This can be done using ZOOM L.

6 Enter **Z** (for ZOOM) and then enter the **L** (Left) option. REF 277

The prompt line will ask for a lower left corner point.

7 With your pointing device, pick a point near the lower left corner of the keyboard. (If you pick a point *within* the keyboard, you may lose the borders of the keyboard.)

The prompt line will now ask for magnification or height.

8 Use the pointing device to pick a point just above the keyboard.

You may have to zoom again so that the keyboard fills most of your screen.

9 In the lower left corner of the keyboard, draw a small square to represent a key, as shown below.

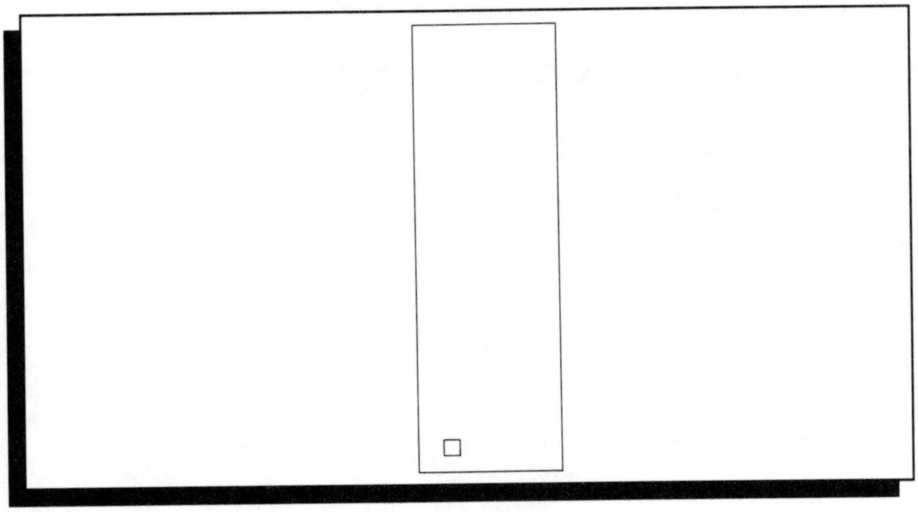

10 Zoom in on the key, this time using **ZOOM C** (Center). Pick a center point by picking the center of the key and then specify the height by picking points below and above the key. REF 273-274

11 Using the **POLYGON** command, draw a small trademark on the key as shown in the following drawing.

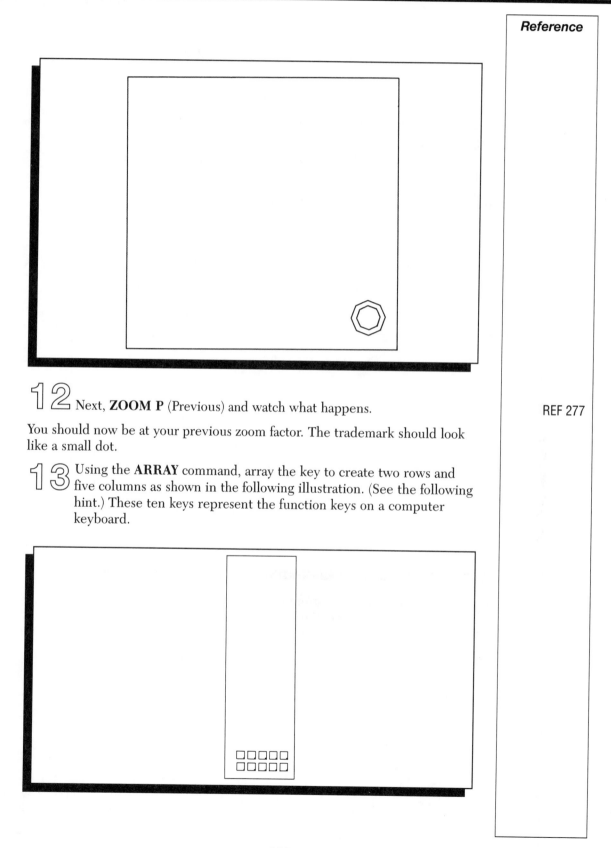

12 Next, **ZOOM P** (Previous) and watch what happens.

You should now be at your previous zoom factor. The trademark should look like a small dot.

13 Using the **ARRAY** command, array the key to create two rows and five columns as shown in the following illustration. (See the following hint.) These ten keys represent the function keys on a computer keyboard.

REF 277

HINT:
You can use your pointing device to indicate the row/column distances. The format is:

Unit cell or distance between rows (---): *Pick point 1.*
Other corner: *Pick point 2.*

The following illustrates this operation.

Point 2

Point 1

Original key. Others will appear
after second point is picked.

14 Next, **ZOOM A** (All).

REF 273

AutoCAD zoomed the drawing to its original size.

15 **ZOOM E** (Extents) and watch what happens.

REF 276

AutoCAD zoomed the drawing as large as possible while still showing the entire drawing on the screen.

16 Enter **Z** (or press the space bar) and enter **2**.

This causes AutoCAD to magnify the screen by 2 times relative to the ZOOM All display (All = 1).

17 Enter **ZOOM** and **0.5**.

This causes AutoCAD to shrink the screen by one half relative to the ZOOM All display.

18 Enter **ZOOM** and **Extents**.

19 Enter **ZOOM** and **0.9x**.

This reduces the screen to 9/10ths its current size.

20 Continue to practice using the ZOOM command by zooming in on the different CAD components of the drawing and including detail on each.

REF 269-270

NOTE:

The ZOOM Dynamic option is discussed fully in the following unit.

Screen Regenerations

A screen regeneration, unlike a screen redraw, requires the recalculation of each vector (line segment) in the drawing. All AutoCAD entities (including arcs, text, and other curved shapes) are made up of vectors stored in a high-precision, floating-point format. As a result, the regeneration of large, complex drawings can take considerable time.

Let's force a screen regeneration with the ZOOM command.

1 Enter **ZOOM All**.

"Regenerating drawing" will appear at the bottom of the screen.

Since your current drawing is not large and complex, it does not take long to regenerate.

HINT:

To save time when drawing with AutoCAD, you should avoid screen regenerations as much as possible. The ZOOM command will cause a regeneration when ZOOM All is issued, or if the ZOOM magnification goes beyond the virtual screen. This is unlikely because AutoCAD maintains a virtual screen of 4,294,967,296 pixels in each axis. See the discussion on virtual screens in Chapter 7 of the *AutoCAD Reference Manual*.

Screen regenerations can also be caused by using other AutoCAD commands, including the REGEN command.

2 Enter **REGEN**.

Did your screen regenerate as it did when you entered ZOOM All? As you work with AutoCAD commands such as QTEXT and FILL, you will use the REGEN command.

3 Zoom in on one of the keys on the keyboard. Zoom repeatedly until AutoCAD performs a screen regeneration.

As you see, AutoCAD performs a regeneration whenever the screen magnification exceeds a certain point, the point being the 4,294,967,296-pixel by 4,294,967,296-pixel virtual screen described in the previous hint.

4 Enter **Z** and **V** for ZOOM Vmax.

Reference

The Vmax option causes AutoCAD to zoom out as far as possible without forcing a screen regeneration. The Vmax option is used to avoid unnecessary screen regenerations.

5 **Zoom All**.

VIEWRES Command _____

REF 312-313

The VIEWRES command controls the "fast zoom" mode and sets the resolution for arcs and circles.

1 Enter the **VIEWRES** command.

2 In reply to "Do you want fast zooms?" enter **Yes**.

This causes all ZOOMs, PANs, and VIEW Restores to avoid regenerations and will perform at Redraw speed whenever possible. You will apply the PAN and VIEW commands in the following unit.

3 Enter **20** for the circle zoom percent.

The "circle zoom percent" enables you to control the appearance of circles and arcs. A high number will make circles and arcs appear smooth but at the expense of regeneration speed.

4 Construct an arc or circle and notice its "coarse" appearance.

As you can see, arc and circle entities now contain fewer vectors and therefore will generate more quickly on the screen.

5 Enter **VIEWRES** again; enter Yes; enter **150**.

6 Notice the smooth appearance of arcs and circles on the screen.

Transparent ZOOM _____

REF 282

With AutoCAD, you can perform transparent zooms. This means you can use ZOOM while another command is in progress. To do this, enter 'ZOOM (notice the apostrophe) at any prompt that is not asking for a text string. Let's try it.

1 Enter the **LINE** command and pick a point on the screen.

2 At the "To point:" prompt, enter **'Z**.

③ Zoom in on any portion of the screen.

Notice the prompt at the bottom of the screen.

④ Pick an endpoint for the line and press **RETURN**.

Transparent zooms give you great zoom magnification flexibility while using other commands. For instance, if your line endpoints require greater accuracy than your present display will allow, the transparent zoom provides you with a solution.

——— NOTE: ———

Some restrictions and operational hints are noted here.

- Fast ZOOM mode (set by the VIEWRES command) must be ON in order for ZOOM to operate transparently.
- Transparent operations can be done only if a screen regeneration is not required.
- ZOOM All and ZOOM Extents cannot be used transparently since they always require a screen regeneration.

These items also apply to the PAN and VIEW commands, which are covered in the next unit.

⑤ When you are finished working with REGEN and ZOOM, enter **END** to save your work and to exit AutoCAD.

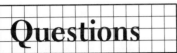

Questions

1. Explain why the ZOOM command is useful.

It lets you get in, out, and around your drawing at different magnifications

2. Cite one example of when it would be necessary to use the ZOOM command for completing a technical drawing and explain why.

To zoom in for detail work

3. In which pull-down menu is the ZOOM command found?

View

4. Describe each of the following ZOOM options.

All *Goes (zooms) to original size*

Center *Pick center of object to view*

Extents *Goes as large as possible keeping whole drawing visible*

Left *Pick lower left of an object*

Previous *Goes to the previous view before last zoom*

Vmax *Goes as far as possible without regeneration*

Window *Goes to area you pick with within drawing*

Scale *Alters size of existing object*

5. Explain a screen regeneration.

A recalculation of all line segments of drawing

6. How is REGEN different from REDRAW?

It requires a recalculation of all vectors in the drawing

Problems

1. Create a drawing such as an elevation plan of a building, a site plan of a land development, or a view of a mechanical part. Using the ZOOM command, zoom in on your drawing and include detail. Zoom in and out on your drawing as necessary using the different ZOOM options.
2. Refer to the file named LAND.DWG and instructions contained on the optional *Applying AutoCAD* Diskette.

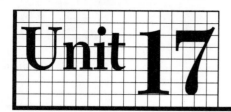

Unit 17

Getting from Here to There

■ **OBJECTIVE:**

To apply the PAN and VIEW commands and perform dynamic zooms and pans

Like most CAD systems, AutoCAD provides a means for moving around on large drawings so that you can add details. This unit illustrates and applies this method and offers suggestions for doing it the most efficient way possible.

Note the degree of detail in the following architectural floor plan.

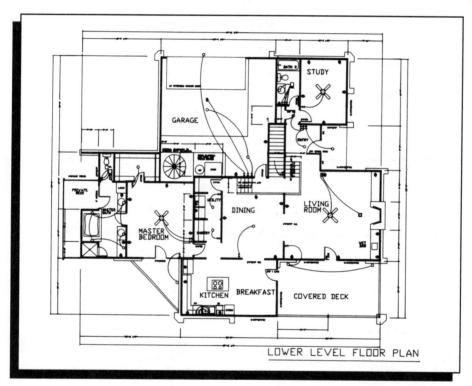

LOWER LEVEL FLOOR PLAN

AutoCAD Drawing Courtesy of Lansing Pugh, Architect

The drafter who completed this CAD drawing zoomed in on portions of the floor plan in order to include detail. For example, the drafter zoomed in on the kitchen to place the kitchen cabinets and appliances.

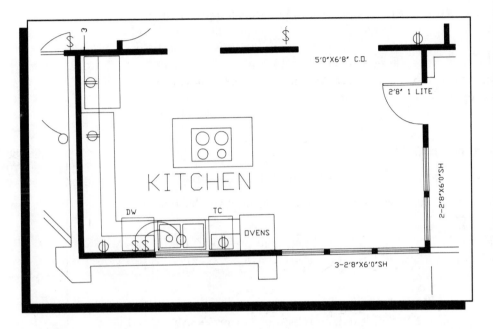

Suppose the drafter wants to include detail in an adjacent room but wants to maintain the present zoom magnification. In other words, the drafter wants to simply "move over" to the adjacent room. This operation is accomplished using the PAN command.

PAN Command ————————————————————

REF 279

1. Open the drawing called **ZOOM**.

2. Using the **ZOOM** command, zoom in on the right third of the drawing.

Let's pan (move) to the left side of the drawing.

3. Enter the **PAN** command. (Just enter **P**.)

4. For Displacement, specify two points: the first point in the left portion of your screen, the second point in the right portion of your screen.

The drawing should have moved to the right the distance you specified. If it did not, try it again.

5. Experiment further with the PAN command until you feel comfortable with it. Pan in different directions and at different zoom magnifications.

Imagine you are working on an architectural floor plan like the one shown previously. You've zoomed in on the kitchen to include details such as the appliances, and now you're ready to pan over to the utility room. Before leaving the kitchen, you foresee a need to return to the kitchen for final touches or revision. But, by the time you're ready to do this final work on the kitchen, you may be at a different ZOOM magnification and/or at the other end of your drawing. The VIEW command solves the problem.

VIEW Command

REF 280-281
TUT 67

Let's apply the VIEW command with the ZOOM drawing.

1 **ZOOM** in on a small portion of the drawing, if you have not done so already.

2 Enter the **VIEW** command and save your present ZOOM window by entering **S** for Save. Give it a one-word name.

3 Now **PAN** to a new location.

4 Enter the **VIEW** command, and restore your previously named view by entering **R** (or **restore**) and the name of the view.

If it did not work, try again.

5 Enter the **VIEW** command once again and this time issue the Window option.

6 Type another view name and press **RETURN**.

7 Define a view window by specifying two corner points.

8 Restore the new view.

9 Practice using the VIEW command by zooming and panning to different locations on your drawing and saving views. Also define new views using the VIEW Window option. Then restore those named views.

After storing several views, it is possible to forget their names. Therefore there is a way of listing all named views.

1 Enter the **VIEW** command and then enter a question mark (**?**) or select it from the standard screen menu.

2 Press **RETURN** in reply to "views to list<*>".

You should receive a listing of all named views.

Reference

③ Return to the drawing by pressing the flip screen function key (usually **F1**).

④ Use the **VIEW D**elete option to delete one of your saved views.

⑤ **ZOOM A**ll to restore your original zoom magnification.

■ *Transparent PAN and VIEW* ————————

REF 282

The PAN and VIEW commands can be used transparently. Transparent PAN and VIEW are particularly useful for reaching line endpoints that are located off the current display. Certain transparent pans and "view restore" operations may cause a screen regeneration, although this seldom happens. As a consequence, the transparent pan or view is not allowed. To help avoid this potential problem, use transparent pans and views only within the virtual screen boundary. For more information on the virtual screen and on screen regenerations, see the section titled "Screen Regenerations" in Unit 16.

Here is an example of the transparent use of PAN.

```
Command: LINE
From point: (Pick an endpoint)
To point: 'PAN (Notice the leading apostrophe.)
>>Displacement: (Pick a point)
>>Second point: (Pick a point)
Resuming LINE command.
To point: (Pick an endpoint)
```

See Unit 16 for some restrictions and operational hints on transparent use of commands.

■ *Dynamic Zooms and Pans* ————————

REF 274-275

The ZOOM Dynamic option avoids the possibility of a screen regeneration. It displays the area you should stay within during zooms and pans to avoid time-consuming screen regenerations.

Let's take a closer look.

① Enter **ZOOM A**ll and then issue the **ZOOM D**ynamic option.

You should see something similar to the following on the screen. You should also see a large box on the screen with an "X" in the center. This is called the "view box."

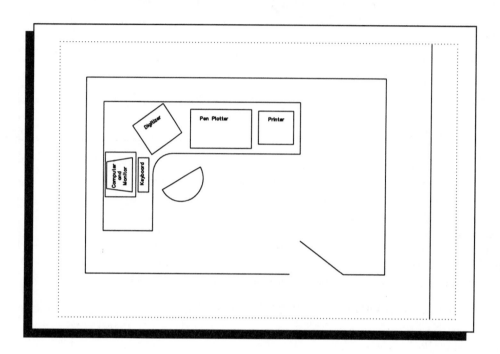

The four corners represent a large area, so they may not be visible. The corners are very important because they represent the virtual screen. It is the portion of the drawing AutoCAD has previously generated and stored in memory. Sections in this area can be viewed at redraw speed using the ZOOM and PAN commands. The current zoom magnification is depicted by a dotted green box.

② Press the pick button on your pointing device, and move it to the left to decrease the size of the box to about 1/2 its original size. (Do not press RETURN. See the following note.)

An arrow at the right side of the view box should have appeared. This indicates "zoom" mode.

NOTE:

If you were to press the RETURN key at this time, AutoCAD would perform a zoom on the area defined by the view box. If the view box extends outside the four corners (generated area), AutoCAD will force a regeneration of the screen. A small hourglass may appear in the lower left corner of the display to remind you that a lengthy regeneration will be required if that view is chosen.

③ Press the pick button again and move the view box around the screen.

You should again have an "X" in the center of the view box. This means you are presently in the "pan" mode.

The pick button toggles the way the view box appears. When you are able to increase and decrease the size of the view box, the "zoom" mode is active. When you are able to move the entire box at a fixed size about your screen, you are in the "pan" mode. By pressing RETURN in either mode, your drawing changes to fill the area defined by the view box.

4 Press **RETURN**.

The drawing should have appeared on the screen—at redraw speed.

5 Enter **ZOOM D**ynamic again.

Notice the box on the screen defined by dotted lines (green, if you have color). This represents the current zoom magnification.

6 Change the size of the view box with the pick button, reposition the view box, and press **RETURN**.

So you see, this can be a very useful and time-effective way of moving about your drawing.

7 Practice using the dynamic zoom and pan, and avoid time-consuming screen regenerations.

8 Enter **END** to save your work and exit AutoCAD.

Questions

1. Explain why the PAN command is useful.

   PAN LETS YOU MOVE TO ALL SIDES WITHOUT USING ZOOM COMMAND

2. Explain why the VIEW command is useful.

   YOU CAN SAVE DIFFERENT ZOOM VIEWS FOR USE lATER WHEN YOU NEED TO RETURN TU it.

3. How do you list all named views?

   ENTER ? then * At VIEWPROMPT

4. Within the ZOOM Dynamic screen, what does the dotted line represent?

   THE AREA TO which YOU will ZOOM TO UPON Clicking it.

5. Explain the difference between the dynamic zoom and pan modes while in the ZOOM Dynamic screen.

   ZOOM DYNAMIC ADVOID SCREEN REGENERATIONS

Problems

1. Draw each of the following shapes. Don't worry about their exact sizes and locations. Zoom in on one of the shapes and store it as a View. Then pan to each of the other shapes and store each as a View. Restore each named View and alter each shape by adding and erasing lines. Be as creative as you wish.

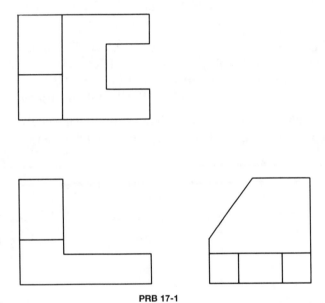

PRB 17-1

2. Perform dynamic pans and zooms on the above drawing. Avoid time-consuming screen regenerations.

3. Refer to the file named LAND.DWG and instructions contained on the optional *Applying AutoCAD* Diskette.

Unit 18   Viewports in Model Space

Reference

■ OBJECTIVE:

To learn how to use AutoCAD's viewport facility in model space

Viewports allow you to see one, two, three, four, or more views of a drawing at once. By default, AutoCAD begins a new drawing using a single viewport that fills the entire graphics area. The drawing information in each of the viewports can be viewed at any magnification, and you are able to draw and edit from one viewport to the next. For instance, you can begin a line in one view and complete it in another.

REF 264-269,
303-307
TUT 131-138

AutoCAD permits you to work in *model space* or *paper space*. Most AutoCAD drafting and design work is done in model space. Paper space is used to lay out, annotate, and plot two or more views of your work.

REF 263, 308

Viewports can be applied to both model space and paper space. This unit focuses on the use of viewports in model space only. Unit 47 concentrates on the use of viewports in paper space and covers the MVIEW, PSPACE, MSPACE, and VPLAYER commands and the TILEMODE system variable.

The following illustration gives an example of applying multiple viewports. Notice that each viewport is different both in content and magnification.

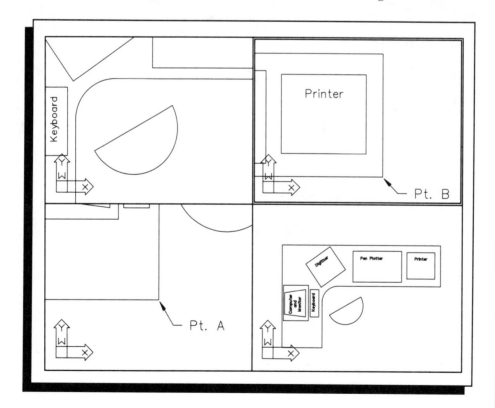

Reference

REF 302-303

Creating Additional Viewports _____

Viewports are controlled with the VPORTS (also called VIEWPORTS) command.

Use the keyboard to enter the VPORTS command in the following steps.

1 Open the drawing file named **ZOOM**.

2 Using the **ZOOM** command, make the drawing fill most of the screen.

3 Enter the **VPORTS** command. (See the following note.)

——— NOTE: ———

The VPORTS command is disabled when TILEMODE is set to 0 (Off). If so, enter TILEMODE and 1, and then reenter VPORTS. You will learn more about TILEMODE in Unit 47.

The following options should appear.

```
Save/Restore/Delete/Join/SIngle/?/2/<3>/4:
```

4 Enter **4**.

You should now have four identical drawings on the screen.

5 Move your pointing device to each of the four viewports.

As you can see, the standard crosshairs appear only in the viewport with the bold border. This is the current (active) viewport.

REF 266

6 Move to one of the three nonactive viewports.

An arrow should appear in place of the crosshairs.

7 Press the pick button on your pointing device.

Now which is the current viewport?

Using Viewports

Let's modify the ZOOM drawing using the viewport facilities.

1 Refer to the preceding illustration and create four similar viewports using the **ZOOM** and **PAN** commands.

2 Save this viewport configuration by entering the **VPORTS** **S**ave option and name it **WORKPLACE**.

3 Make the lower left viewport current.

4 Enter the **LINE** command and pick point A. Refer to the preceding illustration for Point A.

HINT:

Use the object snap feature to accurately locate the point.

5 Move to the upper right viewport and make it current.

Notice that the LINE command is now active in this viewport.

6 Pick point B and press **RETURN**.

The line represents the hard surface on which the chair can roll.

So you see, you can easily begin an operation in one viewport and continue it in another. And, the change is reflected in all viewports. This is especially useful when working on large drawings with lots of detail.

Let's move the printer from one viewport to another.

NOTE:

You may need to shrink the printer a small amount, so that it will fit its new location. Use the Grips Scale mode to scale the printer.

7 With the upper right viewport current, enter the **MOVE** command and select the printer. (Just enter **M**.)

8 Pick a base point at any convenient location on or near the printer.

9 Move to the lower left viewport and make it current. (Make sure Ortho is off.)

10 Place the printer in the open area on the table by picking a second point at the appropriate location.

Did the printer location change in the other viewports? It should.

Reference

REF 303-307

VPORTS Command Options _____

Let's combine two viewports into one.

1 Enter the **VPORTS** command and select the Join option.

2 Choose the upper left viewport in reply to "Select dominant viewport <current>:".

3 Now choose the upper right viewport in reply to "Select viewport to join:".

As you can see, the Join option enables you to expand—in this case, double—the size of the viewport.

4 Enter the **VPORTS SI**ngle option.

As you can see, the screen changed to single viewport viewing. This single viewport is inherited from the current viewport at the time VPORTS SIngle is issued.

5 Enter the **VPORTS ?** option and press **RETURN**.

Notice that AutoCAD stores information about the active viewports as well as the stored viewport configurations, such as WORKPLACE.

6 Enter the **VPORTS R**estore option and enter **WORKPLACE**.

As you can see, the viewports restored as they were stored under the name WORKPLACE. But the drawing does not restore to its earlier form. The printer remains next to the monitor, for example. In short, saving viewport configurations stores only the viewports themselves, not the drawing information.

7 Enter **VPORTS** and then enter **4**.

As you can see, AutoCAD allows you to create additional viewports in the current viewport.

8 Make one of the four small viewports the current viewport by selecting it.

9 Enter **VPORTS** and 3.

The following should appear.

```
Horizontal/Vertical/Above/Below/Left/<Right>:
```

10 Enter the **Above** option.

11 Step through the remaining options on your own. Draw and edit using the different viewport configurations.

—— NOTE: ——

The REDRAW and REGEN commands affect only the current viewport. If multiple viewports are active and you want to redraw or regenerate all of them, you can use the REDRAWALL or REGENALL command. REDRAWALL can be used transparently.

12 Enter **END** to save your work and exit AutoCAD.

Questions

1. How can multiple viewports help you to construct drawings?

   YOU CAN DRAW AT DIFFENT MAGNIFICATIONS & VIEWS

2. How is a viewport made the current viewport?

   BY CLICKING IN THE VIEWPORT YOU WANT

3. Briefly describe each of the following VPORTS options.

   Save *KEEPS THAT VIEW UNDER CHOSEN NAME*

   Restore *BRINGS BACK ANY SAVED VIEW*

   Delete *REMOVES DESIGNATED VIEW PORT*

   Join *COMBINES 2 VIEWS INTO 1*

   SIngle *SWITCHES TO VIEWING ONLY ACTIVE VIEWPORT*

   ? *LIST OF VIEWPORT CONFIGS*

   2 *GIVES 2 VIEWPORTS H/V*

   3 *VIEWPORTS H/V/A/B*

   4 *VIEWPORTS*

4. What do you enter to obtain two viewports in the top half of the screen and one viewport in the bottom half of the screen?

   3   Option B

146

Problems

1. Create each of the following viewport configurations and save each under a name of your choice.

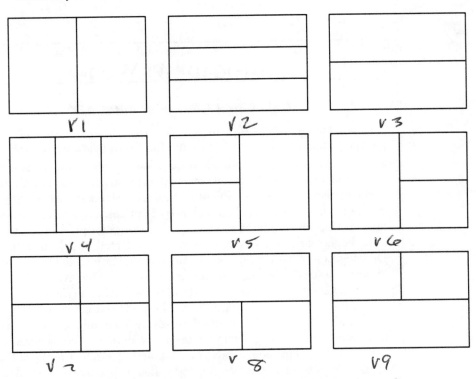

V 1   V 2   V 3

V 4   V 5   V 6

V 7   V 8   V 9

2. Select one of the viewport configurations from Problem 1. Complete a drawing entirely using the different viewports.

V 5

AUTOCAD® AT WORK

*Going First Class with AutoCAD**

Reese Design of Austin, Texas, specializes in the design of aircraft interiors—but not for ordinary aircraft. This design firm creates state-of-the-art showcase aircraft that provide unparalleled luxury, comfort, and entertainment for their clients. It's all done with skill, imagination, and AutoCAD.

When planning a project, Reese Design creates conceptual drawings that can be modified to suit a client's choice of options. Final selections evolve into working specifications and technical drawings for product fabrication.

To begin with, a prototype drawing is selected and loaded into the Drawing Editor. Next, a block drawing is created or inserted from a symbol library. The designers then modify the item—whether it's furniture or a coffee maker—to create the look and feel preferred by the client. The design is saved as a Block so that options can be reviewed using the slide show commands. This is an ideal method for reviewing a number of alternatives that cannot be fully described with their alphanumeric file names alone.

Just as slide show commands review different product options, the dynamic ZOOM command is manipulated so floor plans can be checked closely for tolerances and overall balance and continuity.

Once the floor plan is finalized, the designer prepares cross section views of each aircraft bulkhead and compartment. These cross sections detail the overhead space. When these views are generated, the designer references them with the floor plans to develop elevations.

Once the space planning is complete, interior design embellishments are added. For instance, a sculpture or accessory item can be designed using the SKETCH command and later actually produced by an artist.

When asked if AutoCAD suits his corporate needs, Michael Reese, president of Reese Design, said, "Since our international clientele require design services for a wide range of projects, the scope of our corporate abilities and innovative processes is continually expanding. With quality and professionalism being our foremost objectives, we are creatively participating in the development of our clients' futures. The capabilities of AutoCAD have been very useful."

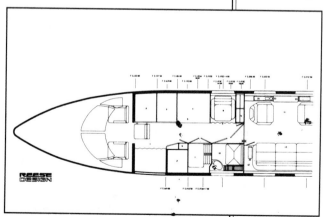

*Based on a story in CADENCE magazine, Vol. 2, No. 1.

Unit 19 AutoCAD File Maintenance

■ OBJECTIVE:

To practice the FILES, SHELL, SH, AUDIT, and RECOVER commands

When working with AutoCAD, there may be times when you'd like to list a disk directory, or delete, rename, copy, or unlock files. This unit gives you practice in using these functions, as well as facilities that attempt to repair drawing files containing errors. Refer to Appendices B and C for additional information on AutoCAD file maintenance.

File Utilities Dialogue Box

REF 102-109

By now, you may have several drawing files. AutoCAD's File Utilities dialogue box helps you organize these files.

1 Start AutoCAD.

2 Enter the **FILES** command.

AutoCAD will display the following.

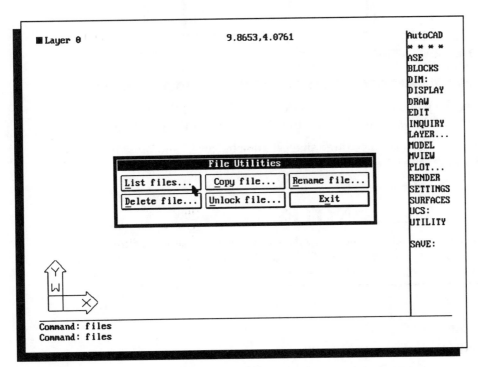

3 Pick the **List files...** button.

AutoCAD will display the Standard File dialogue box. You can use it to review your files and directories. Let's generate a list of all files in the current directory.

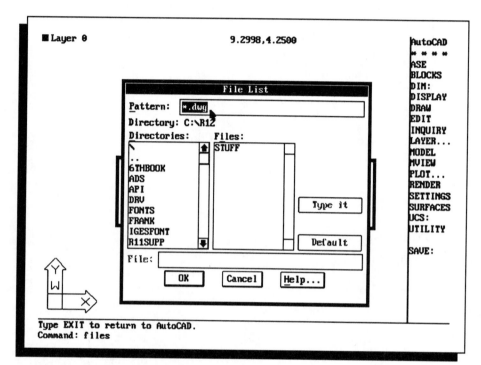

4   Move the pointer to the Pattern edit box at the top of the screen, exactly as shown in the previous drawing, and press the pick button.

5   Press the backspace key three times (to delete "dwg") and press the asterisk (*) key once.

You should now see *.* after "Pattern:".

NOTE:

The Pattern edit box allows you to specify a search pattern for files, either explicitly or by entering wild-cards. The following offers several examples using the * and ? wild-card characters.

Search Pattern	*Lists*
.	All files in the current directory
*.dwg	AutoCAD DWG (drawing) files
acad.*	Files that contain "acad" to the left of the file extension
acad??.*	Files with names that contain "acad" and up to two additional characters to the left of the file extension.

⑥ Press **RETURN**.

AutoCAD will list all files in the current directory.

⑦ Using the scroll bar, review the list of files.

⑧ Find and double click **SUPPORT** from the Directories list box and review the files contained in it.

⑨ List all AutoLISP files by entering ***.LSP** for the search pattern and review the files. (Be sure to press **RETURN**.)

⑩ List all files that begin with DDATT by entering **DDATT???.*** for the search pattern.

⑪ Pick the **OK** button.

Copying Files _____

REF 105

Now let's copy a file.

① Pick the **Copy file...** button.

② In the Directories list box, double click on the .. symbol (the two periods).

———— NOTE: ————

The .. symbol represents the current directory's parent directory. When you select it, you move up one directory. The \ symbol represents the root directory. When you select it, you move to the root directory.

③ Enter ***.dwg** for the search pattern. (Be sure to press RETURN.)

Notice that "Source File" is at the top of the dialogue box.

④ If the drawing named STUFF is present, double click on it. (If it is not present, select another drawing file you've created.)

"Destination File" should now appear at the top of the dialogue box.

⑤ At the blinking cursor, type **STUFFED.DWG** in upper or lower case letters and pick the **OK** button or press **RETURN**.

You have just created a duplicate copy of the STUFF drawing file.

⑥ Pick the **List files...** button.

The new STUFFED file should appear in the Files list box.

⑦ Pick the **OK** button.

Deleting Files

Let's delete the STUFFED.DWG file.

1   Select the **Delete file...** button.

2   Scroll to the bottom of the list, find the **STUFFED.DWG** file, and select it.

3   Pick the **OK** button.

4   If you are certain you selected the STUFFED.DWG file, pick the **Yes** button.

AutoCAD then deletes the file.

Renaming and Unlocking Files

You can also use the File Utilities dialogue box to rename and unlock files.

1   Rename a file, such as STUFF.DWG, on your own.

> **HINT:**
> Renaming files is very similar to copying files. Follow the same steps. Don't forget to include the file extension ("DWG" for AutoCAD drawing files) when you enter the new name.

2   Rename the same file back to its original name.

AutoCAD locks files to prevent more than one person from accessing the same file at the same time. Occasionally, files become locked inadvertently. If so, it is necessary to unlock the file before you can open it. Before you unlock the file, you should be certain that no one else is using it. This applies only if your AutoCAD station is part of a network.

1   Pick the **Unlock file...** button to unlock a file.

2   Pick **STUFF.DWG** even though it may not be locked.

3   Pick the **OK** button.

If the file you chose was not locked, AutoCAD displays the message "0 files unlocked."

4   Pick the **Exit** button to exit the File Utilities dialogue box.

Reference

REF 116-118

SHELL and SH Commands _____

The SHELL and SH commands allow you to access operating system (OS) commands directly and also let you execute utility programs while remaining in AutoCAD. For example, you can load a word processor and create or edit a text file. Later, you may find this very useful when creating and editing screen and tablet menus and script files.

1 First, obtain help on the SHELL or SH command.

HINT:
See Unit 5 if you are unsure how to obtain help.

2 Enter **SH**.

The SH command performs the same functions as SHELL.

NOTE: _____
If you receive an error message, your computer may not contain sufficient free memory to run SH.

You should see "OS Command:" on the screen.

3 Try the DOS DIRectory command by typing **DIR** and pressing **RETURN**.

Notice that you are able to execute one OS command. AutoCAD then returns automatically to the AutoCAD "Command:" prompt. It is possible to remain in OS if you need to execute a series of OS functions.

4 Enter the **SH** command. Press **RETURN** a second time.

You should now see a DOS prompt such as "C:\R12>>." Note the second ">." This is present to remind you that you are operating DOS from AutoCAD's shell.

Also notice the note "Type EXIT to return to AutoCAD."

5 Enter the DOS **DIR** command, and notice that at the end, you return to the DOS "C>>" prompt rather than the AutoCAD "Command:" prompt.

6 If you have access to another program such as a word processor like WordPerfect® or Microsoft® Word or a spreadsheet like LOTUS 1-2-3™ or Microsoft® Excel on your hard disk drive, try loading one of them.

The program will run only if your computer contains sufficient memory.

NOTE:

If you change your current drive or directory, be sure to change back to your original AutoCAD directory before returning to AutoCAD's "Command:" prompt. If you do not, you may obtain unpredictable results while in AutoCAD.

7 Type **EXIT** and press **RETURN**.

The "Command:" prompt should now be on your screen.

Entering OS Commands at "Command:" Prompt

REF 106, 110

AutoCAD also permits you to enter certain OS commands directly at the "Command:" prompt.

1 Enter **DIR**.

AutoCAD will ask for a file specification. This is the same as a search pattern.

2 Enter ***.exe**.

3 Enter **TYPE**.

4 In reply to "File to list:" enter **README.DOC** in upper or lower case letters.

HINT:

Press the CTRL and S keys to stop scrolling. Press any key to resume scrolling. Press the CTRL and C keys to cancel the operation.

5 Enter **DEL**ete.

6 In reply to "File to delete:" press **CTRL C**.

AUDIT Command

REF 109-110

The AUDIT command is available as a diagnostic tool. It examines the database of drawing files to check their validity and correct errors.

1 Enter the **AUDIT** command.

2 In reply to "Fix any errors detected?" press **RETURN**.

Information similar to the following should appear.

```
Fix any errors detected? <N>
  Ø         Blocks audited
Pass 1 Ø           entities audited
Pass 2 Ø           entities audited

Total errors found Ø fixed Ø


Command:
```

In the above example, if you would have entered Yes in reply to "Fix any errors detected?" the report would have been the same. If a drawing file contains errors and AUDIT can't fix them, use the RECOVER command explained in the following section.

The AUDIT command automatically creates an audit report file containing an .ADT file extension when the AUDITCTL system variable is set to 1. The default setting is 0.

RECOVER Command

REF 110

You can attempt to recover damaged files using the RECOVER command.

1   Enter **RECOVER** and pick the **Discard Changes** button.

2   Select one of your drawing files, such as STUFF or ZOOM, even though it may not be damaged. (The drawing recovery process is the same regardless.)

AutoCAD performs an automatic audit of the drawing. If the audit is successful, AutoCAD displays an AutoCAD Alert box saying that no errors were detected and loads the drawing. An audit report file (containing an .ADT file extension) is created when AUDITCTL is set to 1.

NOTE:

Listed here are probable causes of damaged files.

- An AutoCAD system crash
- A power surge or disk error while AutoCAD is writing the file to disk
- Removal of a floppy diskette containing the drawing file prior to exiting AutoCAD

Listed here are typical effects of damaged files.

- AutoCAD may refuse to edit or plot a drawing file
- A damaged file may cause an AutoCAD internal error or fatal error

A drawing file may be damaged beyond repair. If so, the drawing recovery process will not be successful.

3 Enter **QUIT** to exit AutoCAD unless the file was damaged and recovered. In that case, enter **END**.

Questions

1. What is the purpose of the FILES command?

   GIVES List of All Files & for MAINTAINANCE OF FILES

2. Explain the purpose of the SHELL or SH command.

   To TEMPORAIRLY LEAVE AUTO CAD to DOS

3. Explain the difference between the SHELL and SH commands.

   SH Allows ACCESS INTERNAL Sys ComDS SHELL Allows ACCESS to other PROGRAMS

4. Identify a practical application for using the SH command.

   CREATE / EDIT Files

5. Can a sequence of DOS functions be executed without reentering the SH command for each function? Explain.

   YES AFTER SH ENTER ↵ aGAIN

6. What is the primary purpose of the AUDIT command?

   CHECKS DB FILES & CORRECTS ERRORS

7. How may AutoCAD's RECOVER command be useful?

   IT RECOVERS DAMAGED FILES

Problems

Using the commands described in this unit, complete the following.

1. Generate a list of drawing files from one or more of AutoCAD's directories and print the list(s).

2. Generate a list of menu files found on one or more of AutoCAD's directories and print the list(s).

HINT: AutoCAD menu files have an extension of .MNU. Therefore enter *.MNU for the search pattern.

3. Generate a list of all AutoCAD drawing BAK files.

4. Rename one of your drawing files. Then change it back to its original name.

5. Delete the BAK file from one of your drawing files.

6. While in AutoCAD, load another program such as a word processor, create a text file, and then return to AutoCAD.

7. Diagnose one of your drawing files and fix any errors that may be detected.

AUTOCAD® AT WORK

Who's Manufacturing with AutoCAD?*

CADENCE magazine conducted a survey to learn the answer to that question. The staff found that many manufacturers are using AutoCAD, in ways that are almost as varied as the products produced.

At BIMBA Manufacturing in Monee, Illinois, AutoCAD is used for tooling and fixture design and, in some cases, for the design of NC machines used to manufacture pneumatic cylinder components. Additionally, the company uses the system for facilities planning and project management.

At McDonnell Douglas in St. Louis, AutoCAD plays a part in design of systems for nondestructive testing. It provides a cost effective 2-D capacity and complements the company's current Unigraphics system, which is used for analysis and 3-D design.

Ford Motor Company in Dearborn uses AutoCAD for conceptual design of manufacturing systems, specifically for systems which produce engine parts. Basically, the Advanced Manufacturing Development group uses AutoCAD for generating concept sheets. A typical drawing incorporates notes describing specific manufacturing phases—how a part should be produced, how it should be folded and fixtured, how much metal should be removed, etc. These drawings are transferred to a Computervision mainframe system for further analysis and for the actual design work.

Custom Tool & Manufacturing in Lexington, Kentucky, makes automated assembly equipment, including robotic tool changers. AutoCAD is used to design equipment, add marketing touches to the drawings, and incorporate these drawings in the company's product literature. Additionally, mechanical and electrical drawings, as well as printed circuit board layouts, are produced.

Another interesting application is the use of AutoCAD for design of walk-in coolers for such fast food giants as McDonalds and Burger King. Vollrath in Sheboygan, Wisconsin, generates a design and sends a disk with the drawings to the client for incorporation into the restaurant drawings. The disk is then returned to Vollrath with the appropriate dimensions for manufacturing.

The list goes on, including such well-known companies as General Foods, General Electric, and AT&T Bell Laboratories. The question "Who's manufacturing with AutoCAD?" can be answered in many ways since manufacturing integrates so many different functions in a production environment. AutoCAD is used in many aspects of manufacturing—from plant design to packaging design. As a productivity tool in a production environment, AutoCAD is clearly a leader.

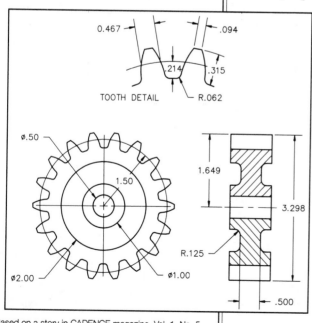

Based on a story in CADENCE magazine, Vol. 1, No. 5.

Placing Notes and Specifications

■ OBJECTIVE:

To practice the use of TEXT, STYLE, DDEDIT, DTEXT, and QTEXT

This unit focuses on the placement of text using the TEXT and DTEXT commands and on the creation of new text styles using the STYLE command. The QTEXT command is practiced as a time-saving device.

The following drawing shows the number of notes and specifications typical in many drawings. Some drawings, of course, contain more.

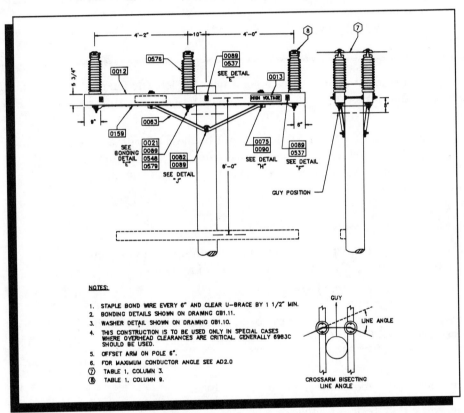

AutoCAD Drawing Courtesy of Russ Burns, Sacramento Municipal Utility District

As you can see, the text information is an important component in describing the drawing. With traditional drafting, the text would be placed by hand, consuming numerous hours of tedious work. With CAD, the words are placed on the screen almost as fast as you can type them.

TEXT Command _____

Start AutoCAD and begin a new drawing named **TEXT**.

Enter the **TEXT** command.

You should now have the following information on the screen.

_____

```
Justify/Style/<Start point>:
```

_____

In response to <Start point> place a point near the left portion of the screen. Your text will be left justified (aligned) beginning at this point.

With Ortho on, reply to the "Height" prompt by moving your pointing device up a short distance (approximately 0.25 unit) from your starting point. Pick that point. (You could type in the height instead.)

Enter **0** (degrees) in reply to "Rotation angle."

At the "Text:" prompt, type your name using both upper and lower case letters and press **RETURN**. (See the following note.)

_____ NOTE: _____

> If you make a mistake when typing, use the backspace key to correct it. If that doesn't work, press CTRL C to cancel and start over.

After entering the above, press the space bar twice.

You should again see the "Text:" prompt.

Type your P.O. Box, rural route, or street address and press **RETURN**.

Where was it placed?

Press the space bar twice again and enter your city, state, and zip code.

Now let's enter the same information you entered above, but this time in a different format.

1 Enter the **TEXT** command (press the space bar once) and **J** for the Justify option.

The following should appear.

```
Align/Fit/Center/Middle/Right/TL/TC/TR/ML/MC/MR/BL/BC/BR:
```

2 Enter the **C** (Center) option or select **center** from the standard screen menu.

3 Place the center point near the top, center of the screen and set the text height at **0.2** unit. Do not insert the text at an angle.

4 Repeat steps 6-9 on the preceeding page.

When you're finished, your text should have a format like the one below. If it doesn't, try again.

> Mr. John Doe
> 601 West 29th Street
> Caddsville, CA   09876

AutoCAD has another **TEXT** option very similar to Center called Middle.

1 Enter **TEXT** again and **J**ustify.

2 This time select the **M**iddle option.

3 Place another string of text such as "Vance and Shirley."

How is the Middle option different from Center? If you're not sure, try the Center option again.

AutoCAD also allows for placement of text between two specified points. The options Align and Fit have similarities, but there is a difference. Let's experiment.

1 Enter **TEXT**, **J**ustify, and **A**lign.

2 Pick a point at the left of the screen.

③ Pick a second point near the right of the screen. (See the following hint.)

HINT:
If you want the text to appear perfectly horizontal, turn on Ortho.

④ Enter the following: **This sentence will be aligned between two points.**

Let's use the Fit option and try to determine the difference between Fit and Align.

① Enter **TEXT**, **J**ustify, and **Fit**.

REF 176

② Pick two points approximately 4 units apart.

③ Specify a height of **0.25** unit.

As you may recall, "height" was not part of the Align option.

④ Enter the following text: **Check this out!**

Do you recognize the difference between Fit and Align? Fit adjusts the width of the text only, at a specified height. Align adjusts both the width and the height.

⑤ Experiment with each of the following TEXT Justify options on your own.

TL — Starts the top-left portion of text at a given start point
TC — Centers the top of text at a given point
TR — Ends the top of text at a given point
ML — Starts the middle of text at a given start point
MC — Centers the middle of text at a given point
MR — Ends the middle of text at a given point
BL — Starts the bottom-left portion of text at a given start point
BC — Centers the bottom of text at a given point
BR — Ends the bottom of text at a given point

STYLE Command

REF 184-185
TUT 88-89

New text styles are created using the STYLE command. During their creation, you are able to expand, condense, slant, and even draw them upside down and backwards.

① Enter the **STYLE** command.

2 Enter **COMP1** for the text style name.

The Select Font File dialogue box should appear.

3 Use the scroll bar in the Files list box to find the file named **COMPLEX.SHX** and double click on it.

4 Reply to each of the remaining prompts using the following information.

Height: **0** (This means the height is not fixed; it can be varied.)
Width factor: **1**
Obliquing angle: **0**
Backwards: **N**
Upside-down: **N**
Vertical: **N**

When you're finished, you are ready to use the new COMP1 text style with the TEXT command. Notice the statement on your screen: "COMP1 is now the current text style."

——— NOTE: ———

COMP1 is now the current text style for dimensions too.

1 Enter the **TEXT** command and **J**ustify option.

2 Right-justify the text by selecting **R** (Right) from the list of options.

3 Place the endpoint near the right side of the screen.

4 Set the height at **0.3** unit.

5 Set the rotation angle at **0**.

6 For the text, type the following three lines. Be sure to press the space bar twice after each line of text.

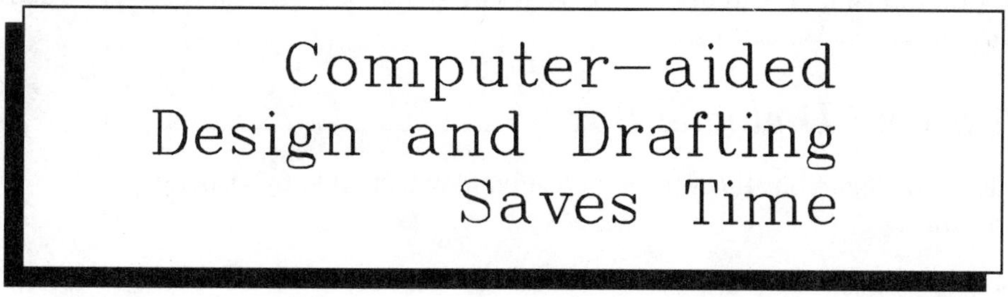

Computer—aided
Design and Drafting
Saves Time

Your text should look like the text in the illustration above.

HINT: If you've made a spelling error, erase the entity (line of text) which contains the error and enter the correct text. You can also change the text using the CHANGE and DDEDIT commands. These commands are discussed on the following pages.

With the STYLE command, you can develop an infinite number of text styles. Therefore, try creating other styles of your own design. You can give them any name, up to thirty-one characters. The ROMANS text font is recommended for most applications.

NOTE: The text styles you create remain within the current drawing file. They cannot be transported into other drawings unless the *entire* drawing containing the styles is inserted into the other drawings.

As you create more text styles within a drawing file, you may occasionally want to check their names.

1 Enter the **STYLE** command.

2 In response to "Text style name (or ?):" enter **?** and press **RETURN** a second time.

You should receive a listing of all the text styles available for the current drawing. What information is included about each style? Notice that the STANDARD style was developed using the TXT font. This is the default text style.

NOTE: The MONOTXT font is identical to the TXT font, but it is mono-spaced, whereas TXT is proportionally spaced.

AutoCAD provides many individual text fonts. For samples of these fonts, see Appendix H. (Additional fonts can be created as described in Chapter 5 of the *AutoCAD Customization Manual*.)

REF 181-183
CUST 49-66

Select Text Font Dialogue Box

AutoCAD offers a dialogue box that lets you create a new text style by visually selecting a text font.

1 Select the **Draw** pull-down menu.

2 Highlight the **Text** item and then select **Set Style...** from its cascading menu.

The following dialogue box should appear.

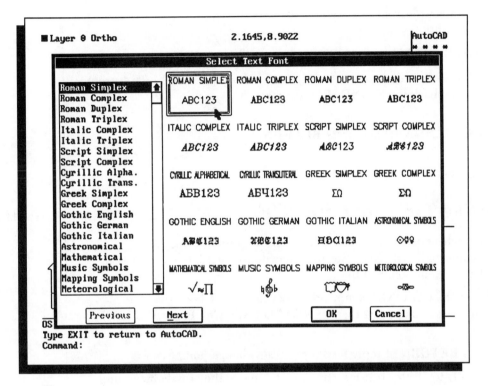

③ Pick the **Next** button.

④ Pick the **Previous** button.

⑤ Move the pointer to the ROMAN SIMPLEX font, as shown in the previous illustration, and double click on it.

⑥ Press **RETURN** six times to accept each of the six default settings.

Notice that ROMANS is now the current text style. "ROMANS" is the name that AutoCAD automatically gave to the new style.

⑦ Enter the **STYLE** command and ?.

⑧ Press **RETURN** to list the text styles defined in this drawing.

The ROMANS style should be one of three in the list of text styles.

Changing the Current Text Style

Reference
REF 175
TUT 85-86

Next, let's set a new current text style.

1 Enter the **TEXT** command and select the Style option.

At this point, you can generate a list of styles as before or select a new current style. Let's bring back the STANDARD text style.

2 Type **STANDARD** and press **RETURN**.

3 Place some new text on the screen.

Correcting Text with CHANGE

REF 216

You can make changes to text you've placed on the screen using the CHANGE command. CHANGE was introduced in Unit 12, where it was used for changing endpoints of lines.

1 Enter the **CHANGE** command, select the text "Check this out!" (which was done using the STANDARD text style). Press **RETURN**.

2 Press **RETURN** in reply to "Properties/<change point>:".

3 In reply to "Enter text insertion point:," move the crosshairs around the screen and watch what happens (Ortho and Snap should be off); then press **RETURN**.

4 Enter **COMP1** for the new style and move the crosshairs up and down.

5 Enter **0.3** for the new height.

6 Enter **Check out this text!** in reply to "New text:".

DDEDIT Command

REF 219-220
TUT 91-92

The CHANGE command is useful for changing the text height, position, or style. If only text editing is required (such as in the case of a misspelled word), the DDEDIT command is faster.

1 Enter **DDEDIT** and select **"Check out this text!"**

A dialogue-oriented edit box should appear.

2 Move the pointer to the area containing the text and pick a point between the words "out" and "this."

166

③ Press the backspace key until the words "Check out" are gone.

④ Type the words **Look at** and pick the **OK** button.

The line should now read "Look at this text!"

⑤ Press **RETURN** to terminate the command.

Special Characters and Control Codes

REF 179-180

AutoCAD also allows you to underscore (underline) words, place degree or circle diameter symbols within your text, and much more.

Let's underscore a word.

① Enter the **TEXT** command and make ROMANS the current text style.

② Pick a start point at the left of the screen.

③ Set the text height at **0.25** and leave the insertion angle at 0.

④ Type the following exactly as it appears and press **RETURN**.

AutoCAD is a %%upowerful%%u tool.

Is the word "powerful" underlined?

The AutoCAD control codes are:

%%o — Toggle overscore mode on/off
%%u — Toggle underscore mode on/off
%%d — Draw "degree" symbol
%%p — Draw "plus/minus" tolerance symbol
%%c — Draw "circle diameter" dimensioning symbol
%%% — Force a single percent sign
%%nnn — Draw special character number "nnn"

⑤ Experiment with each of them.

DTEXT Command

REF 180-181
TUT 83-84

DTEXT, short for Dynamic TEXT, lets you see the text develop on the screen as you type it. With this command, you can see whether or not the new text you are entering will fit as you would like it to. This is especially important in tight areas of the drawing.

① Enter the **DTEXT** command or select the **Text Dynamic** option from the **Draw** pull-down menu.

Your options are the same as with the TEXT command.

② Pick a start point near the left of your screen, give a height of **.3**, and do not specify an insertion angle.

Notice the small box at the start point.

③ Type the following and watch the text appear on your screen.

Dynamic Text!

④ Press **RETURN**.

⑤ Experiment further with DTEXT. When you're finished, press **RETURN** in reply to the "Text:" prompt.

QTEXT Command _____

The QTEXT command saves screen redraw and regeneration time, especially when drawings contain large amounts of text.

① Enter **QTEXT** and **On**.

② Enter **REGEN**.

Rectangles, containing only four vectors each, should have replaced each line of text.

③ Place additional text on the screen using the TEXT command.

Notice that it appears as text — not as rectangles.

④ Force another regeneration of the screen by entering **REGEN**.

QTEXT (short for Quick TEXT) replaces text with lines which form rectangles where the text once was. The purpose of this is to speed up screen regenerations and redraws. As you may know, each text character is made up of many short lines. The greater the number of lines on your screen, the longer it takes to regenerate the screen. QTEXT temporarily reduces the total number of lines and consequently saves time, especially with heavy use of text.

⑤ Enter **QTEXT** again and enter **Off**.

⑥ Force another regeneration of the screen.

Your text should reappear.

⑦ Enter **END** to save your work and exit AutoCAD.

Questions

1. In connection with the TEXT command, describe the following:

   Align *Puts Text Between 2 Points w/ Width option*

   Fit *Puts Text Btwn 2 Points w/ Height option*

   Center *~~Puts~~ Centers Text Horizontally*

   Middle *Centers text Horiz/Vert*

   Right *Right Justifies Text*

2. What is the purpose of the TEXT Style option?

   Create Text Styles, Angles, Direction

3. Name at least six text fonts provided by AutoCAD.

   Roman, Crylic, Italic, Gothic, Greek, Script

4. What command do you enter at the keyboard to create a new text style?

   "Style"

5. What does AutoCAD display when you pick the Text "Set Style..." option from the Draw pull-down menu?

   Text Dialogue Box

6. How does turning on QTEXT speed screen regenerations?

   It Replaces Text Lines with Rectangle Decreasing Lines so Regens Are Faster

7. Briefly describe how you would create a tall and thin text style.

   By Adjusting Height and Width in "Style" mode

8. If you entered the text 72%%d, what would the result be?

   72°

9. Explain the changes that can be made to text using the CHANGE command.

   Text Height Posistion ori style or Layer

10. What is the purpose of the DDEDIT command?

   EDit SElected TExt

11. How is DTEXT different from the TEXT command?

   DTExt is DyNAmic
   TExt isN't

Problems

In problems 1 and 2, create new Text styles using the information provided.

1. Style name: **CITYBLUEPRINT**
   Font file: **CITY BLUEPRINT (CIBT.PFB)**
   Height: **0.25** (fixed)
   Width factor: **1**
   Obliquing angle: **15**
   Backwards: **N**
   Upside-down: **N**

2. Style name: **ITAL**
   Font file: **ITALIC**
   Height: **0** (not fixed)
   Width factor: **0.75**
   Obliquing angle: **0**
   Backwards: **N**
   Upside-down: **N**
   Vertical: **N**

In problems 3 and 4, place text on your screen using the information provided. Use the DTEXT command.

3. Use the CITYBLUEPRINT text style you created in problem 1.
   Right-justify the text.
   Do not rotate the text.
   The text should read:

> Someday,
> perhaps in the near future,
> drafting boards will
> be obsolete.
>
> **PRB 20-1**

4. Use the ITAL text style you created in problem 2.
   Center the text.
   Set the text height at 0.3 unit.
   Rotate the text 90 degrees.
   The text should read:

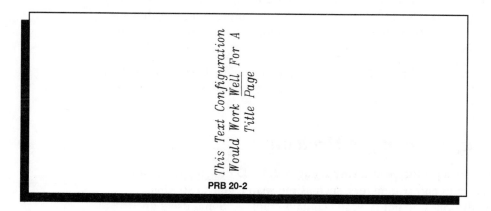

PRB 20-2

Notice the word "Well" is underscored.

5. Use the CHANGE command to change the style to CITYBLUEPRINT
   and the height to 0.2 unit.

Unit 21 Preparing for a New Drawing

Reference

■ OBJECTIVE:

To apply and practice the use of DDUNITS, UNITS, LIMITS, STATUS, and prototype drawings

The purpose of this unit is to focus on the process of creating the foundation for new drawings. Considerations include: identifying the type of drawing you are about to create, the scale, and the sheet size; determining the drawing units and limits; setting the grid and snap resolution; and checking settings and parameters with the STATUS command.

The first several steps necessary for setting up a new drawing are important and deserve special attention. Once you have set up a prototype drawing, subsequent drawing setups are fast.

Creating a Prototype Drawing ———————————

REF 39-46

Simply stated, a prototype drawing is any AutoCAD drawing file that contains drawing settings and parameters, such as the snap and grid spacings. Prototype drawings do not typically contain graphics. Some users do, however, choose to include a border and title block in the prototype drawing.

The purpose of a prototype drawing is to minimize the need to establish new drawing settings each time you begin a new drawing. When you use a prototype drawing, its contents are automatically loaded into the new drawing at the beginning. The prototype's settings thus become the new drawing's settings.

Prototype drawing development includes the following steps. Note that the first three steps are common to traditional means of planning drawings using drafting boards.

1) Determine what you are going to draw (*e.g.*, mechanical detail, house elevation, etc.).
2) Determine the drawing scale.
3) Determine the sheet size. (Steps 2 and 3 normally are done simultaneously.)
4) Set the drawing units.
5) Set the drawing limits.
6) ZOOM All. (This will zoom the entire limits.)
7) Set the grid.
8) Set the snap resolution.
9) Enter STATUS to review your settings.
10) Establish several new layers with colors, linetypes, etc.
11) Set linetype scale (LTSCALE).
12) Create new text styles.
13) Set DIMSCALE, dimension text size, arrow size, etc.
14) Store as a prototype drawing.

Reference

This unit and the next three will provide an opportunity to practice these steps in detail as well as introduce you to new commands and features.

DDUNITS Command

Let's begin.

1 Start AutoCAD and begin a new drawing named **PROTO1**.

——— NOTE: ———

PROTO1 will be our first prototype drawing. Prototype drawings are stored with a .DWG file extension, like any other AutoCAD drawing file. Prototype drawings can also be edited and updated like any other Auto-CAD drawing file.

A standard prototype drawing comes with AutoCAD and contains all the default settings you have been using up to this point. Details on this prototype drawing, named ACAD.DWG, can be found in Appendix A in the *AutoCAD Reference Manual*.

REF 553-556

Let's identify a specific drawing, such as a stair detail for a house or commercial building, on which to base our new prototype drawing.

Next, we must determine the drawing scale for the stair detail. This information will give us a basis for setting our limits, linetype scale, and DIMSCALE later. Let's use a scale of $1/2'' = 1'$.

We also need to decide on the sheet size for our drawing. Let's use $11'' \times 17''$ paper.

It's time now to enter information into the computer.

2 Enter the **DDUNITS** command or select **Units Control...** from the **Settings** pull-down menu.

REF 85-87

AutoCAD will display the following Units Control dialogue box.

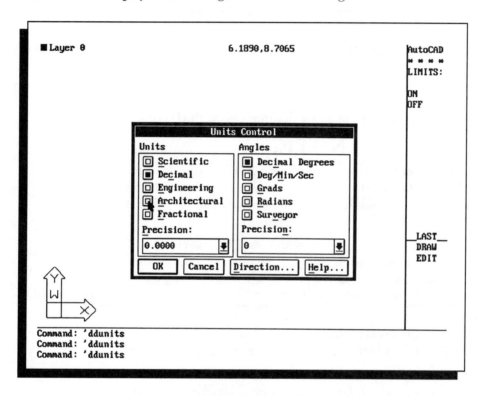

NOTE:

It is possible to use the UNITS command to perform the following unit settings.

REF 88-91
TUT 35

③ Under Units, pick the **Architectural** radio button.

REF 85

④ Underneath it, pick the down arrow to review the precision list of options.

⑤ Accept the 1/16″ default setting by picking it.

This means that 1/16″ is the smallest fraction that AutoCAD will display.

As you can see, Decimal Degrees is the default setting under Angles. This is the setting we want to use for the prototype drawing, so no selection is required from you. "Decimal Degrees" means that when AutoCAD displays angle measurements, it will present them using decimals.

REF 85-86

⑥ Underneath it, select the down arrow to adjust the angle precision.

⑦ Pick **0.0**.

This means AutoCAD will carry out angle measurements one decimal place (*i.e.,* in tenths).

8 Select the **Direction...** button.

REF 86-87

The Direction Control subdialogue box will appear. It permits you to control the direction for angle measurements. As discussed in Unit 6, AutoCAD assumes that 0 degrees is to the right (east) and angles increase in the counterclockwise direction.

9 Pick the **OK** button to accept the default settings.

10 Pick the **OK** button to make the Units Control dialogue box disappear.

NOTE:

To see how the new units affect the coordinate display, move the pointing device and note how the coordinate display changes.

Scaling Your Drawing

REF 43

The next step is to set the drawing limits. The limits are a sized boundary for constructing the drawing, and they should correspond to both the drawing scale and sheet size. (See Appendix G for a chart showing the relationships among sheet size, drawing scale, and drawing limits.)

NOTE:

Actual scaling does not occur until you plot the drawing, but you should set the limits to correspond with the scale and sheet size. The limits and sheet size can be increased or decreased up to the time you plot the drawing. The plot scale can also be adjusted prior to plotting. For example, if a drawing will not fit on the sheet at $1/4'' = 1'$, enter new drawing limits to reflect a scale of $1/8'' = 1'$. Likewise, enter $1/8'' = 1'$ instead of $1/4'' = 1'$ when you plot.

1 Enter the **LIMITS** command or select **Drawing Limits** from the **Settings** pull-down menu.

REF 83-84
TUT 35

2 Leave the lower left limit at 0,0 by pressing **RETURN**.

As mentioned above, the limits—specifically, the upper right limit—should reflect the drawing scale and sheet size. Let's look at an example.

If the sheet size is 17″ × 11″, the active plotting (and drawing) area is approximately 15″ × 10″. This is the area on 17″ × 11″ sheets in which most plotters are able to plot. If your drawing scale is 1″ = 1′, then the upper right limit would be set at 15′,10′. Why? Because 15 inches horizontally on the sheet will occupy 15 scaled feet, and 10 inches vertically on the sheet will occupy 10 scaled feet.

Let's consider another one. If the drawing scale is 1/4″ = 1′, what should be the upper right limit, given that the lower left remains at 0,0? Since each plotted inch on the sheet will occupy 4 scaled feet, it's a simple multiplication problem: 15 × 4 = 60 and 10 × 4 = 40. The upper right limit should be set at 60′,40′ because each plotted inch will represent 4′.

Since *our* scale is 1/2″ = 1′, what would be the upper right limit?

HINT:

How many 1/2″ units will 15″ include? How many 1/2″ units will 10″ include?

③ Enter **30′,20′** for the upper right limit. (See the following note.)

NOTE:

When entering 30′,20′ type it exactly as you see it here; use an apostrophe for the foot mark. If you do not use a foot mark, the numbers will be assumed to represent inches. Inches can be specified using ″ or no mark at all.

④ **ZOOM All.**

This zooms the limits to fill the display. The screen will then reflect the sheet size, which corresponds to the limits. To realize this . . .

⑤ . . . move the crosshairs to the upper right portion of the screen and review the coordinate display. (If the coordinate display is not on, turn it on.)

⑥ Enter **GRID**, and set it at 1′. (Be sure to enter the apostrophe.)

The purpose of setting the grid is to give you a visual sense of the size of the units and limits. The grid fills the entire limits, with a distance of 1′ between the grid dots.

⑦ Enter **SNAP**, and set it at 6″.

Use the quote key for the inch mark if you wish. As stated earlier, if no mark is used, AutoCAD assumes inches.

Reference

REF 82-83

_ NOTE: _

SNAP will provide for a 6″ modular layout of your drawing components.

⑧ Move the crosshairs to the upper right corner of the grid.

The coordinate display should read exactly 30′-0″, 20′-0″.

Status of Prototype Drawing

1 To review your settings up to this point, enter the **STATUS** command.

You should receive a screen similar to the following. Note each of the components found in STATUS.

```
Ø entities in PROTO1
Model space limits are X:      Ø'-Ø"    Y:       Ø'-Ø"   (Off)
                       X:     3Ø'-Ø"    Y:      2Ø'-Ø"
Model space uses       *Nothing*
Display shows          X:      Ø'-Ø"    Y:       Ø'-Ø"
                       X:     3Ø'-Ø"    Y: 21'-7 1/2"        Z:        Ø'-Ø"
Insertion base is      X:      Ø'-Ø"    Y:       Ø'-Ø"   Z:       Ø'-Ø"
Snap resolution is     X:      Ø'-6"    Y:       Ø'-6"
Grid spacing is        X:      1'-Ø"    Y:       1'-Ø"

Current space:         Model space
Current layer:         Ø
Current color:         BYLAYER -- 7 (white)
Current linetype:      BYLAYER -- CONTINUOUS
Current elevation:      Ø'-Ø"  thickness:       Ø'-Ø"
Fill on  Grid on  Ortho off  Qtext off  Snap on  Tablet off
Object snap modes:     None
Free disk: 13756416 bytes
Virtual memory allocated to program: 3592 KB
Amount of program in physical memory/Total (virtual) program size: 1ØØ%
Total conventional memory: 444 KB      Total extended memory: 9ØØ4 KB
-- Press RETURN for more --
Swap file size: Ø KB
Command:
```

Several of the above numbers, such as "Display shows," "Free disk," and "Total extended memory," will differ. Our prototype drawing, PROTO1, now contains several settings and parameters specific to creating architectural drawings at a scale of 1/2″ = 1′. It will work well for beginning the stairway detail mentioned earlier.

The next steps in creating a prototype drawing deal with establishing layers. Use of the LAYER command will be practiced in the next unit, and the remaining steps for creating a prototype drawing will be covered in Unit 24.

② For now, enter **END** to save all you have entered to this point and exit AutoCAD.

③ Produce a backup copy of the prototype drawing named PROTO1.DWG.

For details on producing copies of files, see Appendix B, "Commonly Used DOS Commands" or refer to Unit 19.

Backup copies are important because if you accidentally lose the original (and you may, sooner or later), you will have a backup. A backup can be produced in just a few seconds, and it can save you hours of lost work. An entire day's work can be lost in a few seconds, so be prepared!

Questions

1. Explain the purpose and value of prototype drawings.

   Allows you to set up a drawing with all scales, layers, limits, units etc to use as master copy for all your dwgs.

2. What is the purpose of the DDUNITS command?

   Sets coordinates, angles, formats & precision

3. What function does the LIMITS command serve?

   Changes & checks drawing area boundry

4. What determines the upper right limit?

   Scale of drawing & paper size & units

(continued)

5. Describe the information displayed as a result of entering the STATUS command.

Limits, model space use, Insertion Base, snap, Grid, Cur space, Cur layer, Cur Color, Cur Linetype, Cur Elevation, Free Disk space;

Problems

In problems PRB21-1 and PRB21-2, establish the settings for a new drawing based on the information provided. Set each of the commands as indicated.

PRB21-1. Drawing type: Mechanical drawing of a machine part

Scale: 1″ = 2″

Sheet size: 17″ × 11″   30, 20

UNITS: Engineering (You choose the appropriate options)   15 × 10

LIMITS: Lower left corner 0,0
    Upper right corner 30″,20″

(Reminder: Be sure to ZOOM All)

GRID value: 0.5″

SNAP resolution: 0.25″

(Review settings with STATUS command.)

PRB21-2. Drawing type: Architectural drawing of a house and plot plan

Scale: 1/8″ = 1′

Sheet size: 24″ × 18″

UNITS: Architectural (You choose the appropriate options)   22 × 16

LIMITS: Lower left corner 0,0
    Upper right corner 184′,136′ (Based on plotting area of 23″ × 17″.)

(Reminder: Be sure to ZOOM All)

GRID value: 4′

SNAP resolution: 2′

(Review settings with STATUS command.)

In PRB21-3 and PRB21-4, fill in the missing data, based on the information provided. More than one answer exists in both problems.

PRB21-3. Drawing type: Architectural drawing of a detached garage

Approximate dimensions of garage: 32' × 20'

Other considerations: Space around the garage for dimensions, notes, specs., border, and title block

Scale? _1/4" ~ 1'_   88 × 64

Paper size? _C 24×18   Act 22×16_

UNITS? _ARCH_

LIMITS? _88' × 64'_

GRID value? _1'_

SNAP resolution? _1'_

PRB21-4. Drawing type: Mechanical drawing of a bicycle pedal

Approximate dimensions of pedal: 4" × 2.75"

Other considerations: Space around pedal for dimensions, notes, specs., border, and title block

Scale? _1" × 1"_

Paper size? _C 22×17   Act 20×15_

UNITS? _MENG_

LIMITS? _22" × 17"_

GRID value? _1"_

SNAP resolution? _1"_

AUTOCAD® AT WORK

Pillsbury Turns to CAD for High-Tech Designing

Few of us give much thought to cardboard cartons. They're just the containers that other things come in—wrappings to be torn apart so we can get at the goodies inside. But every carton, whether we notice or not, has to be carefully designed with precisely symmetrical folds so that corners fit together, end flaps lock, and contents are kept safe and secure. Every new carton design, however simple, requires at least several drawings: a template (a drawing that can be used as a full-size model by the keyliner, plate maker, and carton manufacturer) and specification drawings (scale drawings that give precise dimensions and other important information).

Paul Mueller is the computer technologist in the packaging group of the Research and Development Laboratories at The Pillsbury Company in Minneapolis, Minnesota. The group designs hundreds of cartons to hold the food products available under the Pillsbury banner, including such brands as Green Giant, Jeno's, French's Potatoes, and Azteca, among others.

Traditionally, all of Pillsbury's design work has been done by hand, with the final specification drawings and templates carefully drawn in pencil on a drafting board. But it takes skill and concentration to create a final drawing accurate to 1/32″ or better by hand. It also takes time, especially when alterations must be made to a complicated drawing. Creating drawings with a consistent look to them, even in minor matters, is no easy task either.

With a CAD program such as AutoCAD, drawings can be done more quickly, and with greater precision and consistency, than is possible with hand drafting. Furthermore, the drawings can be edited electronically and the modified drawings reproduced quickly.

To build a carton on the computer screen, Mueller and his coworkers use layering. By putting the basic outline of the carton in one layer, the score lines (along which the carton will be folded) in another layer, the dimensions in yet another, and any text in still another, designers can easily view a drawing in different ways—just the outline and the score lines, for example, or just the outline and the dimensions. In addition, they can now make both template and specification drawings from one electronic original, printing the outline and score layers full-size for the template and then including the text and dimensions in a scale drawing for the specifications.

Another benefit of using the CAD system has been increased precision in the drawings. Because the templates that are sent to the carton manufacturers are used as full-size models, it's important that all their measurements be absolutely accurate and consistent. Says Mueller, "After our drawings are done, we sit down with a ruler—and we still do this with AutoCAD, by the way—and measure it all up. We've found we get far fewer errors using AutoCAD than we did before when our work was done by hand."

Courtesy of The Pillsbury Company

Unit 22 Layering Your Drawings

■ OBJECTIVE:

To apply the LAYER, COLOR, LINETYPE, and LTSCALE commands and further the prototype drawing development

This unit focuses on AutoCAD's layering capability. It covers creating layers; setting the current layer; assigning colors and linetypes to layers; turning layers on and off; freezing and thawing layers; and setting the linetype scale.

This unit will enable you to create and set the following layers, colors, and linetypes.

Layer name	State	Color	Linetype
Ø	On	7 (white)	CONTINUOUS
BORD	On	4 (cyan)	CONTINUOUS
CEN	On	2 (yellow)	CENTER
DIM	On	3 (green)	CONTINUOUS
HID	On	2 (yellow)	HIDDEN
NOTES	On	6 (magenta)	CONTINUOUS
OBJ	On	1 (red)	CONTINUOUS
PHANT	On	5 (blue)	PHANTOM

Creating New Layers

REF 322-323

It may be helpful to think of layers as transparent overlays. Certain components can be drawn on these layers, the layers can be visible or invisible, and specific colors and linetypes can be assigned to each layer.

For example, a house floor plan could be drawn on a layer called FLOOR and displayed in red. The dimensions of the floor plan could be drawn on a layer called DIM and displayed in yellow. Furthermore, a layer called CEN could contain blue center lines.

Layers and their colors are also very important when plotting since plotter colors are assigned to AutoCAD colors. You'll gain a much better feel for all of this after you have stepped through the following.

1 Start AutoCAD and open the drawing called **PROTO1**.

─── NOTE: ───

Be sure to make a backup copy of PROTO1.DWG if you have not already done so. Instructions for making backup copies are in Appendix B.

2 Enter the **DDLMODES** command or select **Layer Control...** from the **Settings** pull-down menu.

REF 322-327

182

The following Layer Control dialogue box will appear.

```
■ Layer 0 Snap          16'-0",3'-6"              AutoCAD
                                                  * * * *
                                                  SNAP:
. . . . . . . . . . . . . . . . . . . . . . . . .

┌─────────────────── Layer Control ──────────────────┐
│                                                      │
│  Current Layer: 0                    ┌────┐ ┌────┐  │
│  Layer Name    State  Color  Linetype│ On │ │Off │  │
│ ┌──────────────────────────────────┐ └────┘ └────┘  │
│ │0             On . .  white  CONTINUOUS┌────┐┌──────┐│
│ │                                   │   │Thaw││Freeze│││
│ │                                   │   └────┘└──────┘│
│ │                                   │  ┌──────┐┌────┐ │
│ │                                   │  │Unlock││Lock│ │
│ │                                   │  └──────┘└────┘ │
│ │                                   │ Cur VP: Thw Frz │rd
│ │                                   │                 │
│ │                                   │ New VP: Thw Frz │le
│ │                                   │                 │ue
│ │                                   │  ┌───────────┐  │
│ │                                   │  │Set Color..│  │
│ │                                   │  └───────────┘  │
│ │                                   │  ┌───────────┐  │
│ │                                   │  │Set Ltype..│  │
│ │                                   │  └───────────┘  │
│ ┌────────┐ ┌───┐ ┌───────┐ ┌──────┐ Filters          │
│ │Select All│ │New│ │Current│ │Rename│ ┌─┐ ┌────┐      │
│ └────────┘ └───┘ └───────┘ └──────┘ │ │On│Set..│      │
│ ┌────────┐ ┌──────────────────────┐ └─┘ └────┘      │
│ │Clear All│ │                      │                  │
│ └────────┘ └──────────────────────┘                  │
│         ┌──┐  ┌──────┐  ┌─────┐                       │
│         │OK│  │Cancel│  │Help..│                      │
│         └──┘  └──────┘  └─────┘                       │
└──────────────────────────────────────────────────────┘

Command: DDLMODES
Command:  DDLMODES
Command:  DDLMODES
```

NOTE:

You can also use the LAYER command to create and control the layers presented in this unit.

First, let's create layer OBJ, short for "objects."

3 At the blinking cursor, type **OBJ** in upper or lower case letters and pick the **New** button located directly above it.   REF 324

You have just created a new layer, as indicated in the Layer Name list box.

4 Create the layers **BORD, CEN, DIM, HID, NOTES,** and **PHANT** on your own, as listed at the beginning of this unit.

Changing the Current Layer ───────────   REF 324

Let's change the current layer from layer 0 to layer OBJ.

1 In the Layer Name list box, pick **OBJ**.

2 Pick the **Current** button.

The upper left corner of the dialogue box should read "Current Layer: OBJ."

③ Pick the **OK** button and notice that the status line now reads "Layer OBJ."

Assigning Colors _____

The Layer Control dialogue box also permits you to assign screen colors to the layers.

① Press the space bar to bring back the Layer Control dialogue box.

② Pick **OBJ** in the list of layers and pick the **Set Color...** button.

The Set Color subdialogue box will appear. It contains a palette of colors available to you.

③ Pick the color red from the "Standard Colors" and pick the **OK** button.

The color red should now be assigned to OBJ.

_____ NOTE: _____

If you are using a monochrome monitor, exit out of the dialogue boxes by picking the Cancel buttons. Enter the LAYER command and enter C for Color. In reply to "Color:" type RED and press RETURN. In reply to "Layer name(s) for color 1 (red):" type OBJ and press RETURN twice. Skip Step 5.

Even though you may be using a computer with a monochrome (single-color) monitor, it is important to practice assigning colors to layers. AutoCAD's colors are directly associated with plotter colors. The colors, therefore, define the relationship between the layer and the plotter colors.

④ Assign colors to the other layers as indicated in the layer listing at the beginning of this unit. (Cyan is light blue and magenta is purple.)

HINT: _____

Pick the Clear All button to clear layer selections.

⑤ Pick the **OK** button.

NOTE:

AutoCAD also contains a command called COLOR. The COLOR command allows you to set the color for subsequently drawn entities. Therefore you can control the color of each entity individually.

The ability to set the color of objects either individually, using the COLOR command, or by layer gives you a great deal of flexibility, but it can become confusing. It is recommended that you avoid use of the COLOR command and that its setting remain at BYLAYER. The BYLAYER setting means that the color is specified by layer.

Drawing on Layers

1 Draw a circle of any size on this layer.

It should appear in the color red.

2 Set **HID** as the current layer and draw a large triangle on it.

It should appear in the color yellow.

Turning Layers On and Off

REF 324

1 Bring back the Layer Control dialogue box.

2 Select (highlight) layer **OBJ** and pick the **Off** button located in the upper right corner.

3 Pick the **OK** button and notice that the circle disappears.

4 Press the space bar to bring back the Layer Control dialogue box.

5 Select layer **OBJ** again and pick the **On** button located in the upper right corner.

6 Pick the **OK** button and notice that the circle reappears.

Assigning Linetypes

Next, let's take a look at the different linetypes AutoCAD makes available to you.

1 To obtain a listing of linetypes, enter the **LINETYPE** command and then enter the **?** option.

REF 339-340

2 Press **RETURN** or pick the **OK** box. (ACAD should be the default setting.)

This should list the linetypes contained in the ACAD.LIN library file. Your screen should look similar to the following.

```
Linetypes defined in file D:\R11\ACAD.lin:

        Name            Description
----------------   --------------------
BORDER             __ __  .  __ __  .  __ __  .  __ __  .  __ __  .  __ __
BORDER2            _ . _ . _ . _ . _ . _ . _ . _ . _ . _ . _ . _ . _ . _
BORDERX2           ____  ____  .  ____  ____  .  ____  ____  .  ____
CENTER             ____  _  ____  _  ____  _  ____  _  ____  _  ____
CENTER2            ___  _  ___  _  ___  _  ___  _  ___  _  ___  _  ___

CENTERX2           ____   __   ____   __   ____   __   ____   __
DASHDOT            _ . _ . _ . _ . _ . _ . _ . _ . _ . _ . _ . _ . _ .
DASHDOT2           _._.._.._.._.._.._.._.._.._.._.._.._.._.._.._.._
DASHDOTX2          __  .  __  .  __  .  __  .  __  .  __  .  __  .
DASHED             __  __  __  __  __  __  __  __  __  __  __  __  __

DASHED2            - - - - - - - - - - - - - - - - - - - - - - - - -
DASHEDX2           ____  ____  ____  ____  ____  ____  ____  ____
DIVIDE             ____ . . ____ . . ____ . . ____ . . ____ . . ____
DIVIDE2            _ .. _ .. _ .. _ .. _ .. _ .. _ .. _ .. _ .. _ .. _
DIVIDEX2           ____ . . ____ . . ____ . . ____ . . ____ . . ____
-- Press RETURN for more --

DOT                .  .  .  .  .  .  .  .  .  .  .  .  .  .  .  .  .  .
DOT2               . . . . . . . . . . . . . . . . . . . . . . . . . . .
DOTX2              .     .     .     .     .     .     .     .     .
HIDDEN             __  __  __  __  __  __  __  __  __  __  __  __  __
HIDDEN2            - - - - - - - - - - - - - - - - - - - - - - - - -

HIDDENX2           ____  ____  ____  ____  ____  ____  ____  ____
PHANTOM            ____  __  __  ____  __  __  ____  __  __  ____
PHANTOM2           ___  _ _  ___  _ _  ___  _ _  ___  _ _  ___  _ _
PHANTOMX2          ____  ___  ___  ____  ___  ___  ____  ___  ___

?/Create/Load/Set:
```

③ Enter the **Load** option.

④ Enter ***** in reply to "Linetype(s) to load:".

⑤ Select **OK** or press **RETURN** in reply to the dialogue box. (ACAD should be the default setting.)

The list of linetypes should load.

⑥ Press **RETURN** to terminate the command.

⑦ Bring back the Layer Control dialogue box.

⑧ Select layer **HID** and pick the **Set Ltype...** button.

⑨ Pick the **Next** button, pick the **HIDDEN** linetype, and pick the **OK** button.

186

You should see HIDDEN in the Linetype column in the Name Layer list box.

10 Pick the **OK** button.

Did the triangle on layer HID change from a continuous line to a hidden line? It probably did, but don't be surprised if you don't see it.

If it appears as though the triangle linetype did not change, the linetype scale (LTSCALE) needs to be set.

LTSCALE Command

REF 343-344
TUT 150

1 Enter the **LTSCALE** command.

Let's scale your linetypes to correspond to the scale of the prototype. This is done by setting the linetype scale at 1/2 the reciprocal of the plot scale. By doing this, your broken lines, such as hidden and center lines, will be plotted similar to ANSI standards.

HINT:

As you recall, we are creating a prototype drawing based on a scale of 1/2″ = 1′. Another way to express this is 1″ = 2′ or 1″ = 24″. This can be written as 1/24. The reciprocal of 1/24 is 24, and half of 24 is 12. Therefore, in this particular case, you would set the LTSCALE at 12.

2 In reply to "New scale factor:" enter **12**.

3 Now view the triangle. Is it made up of hidden lines?

4 If you're not sure, zoom in on it.

5 Next, assign the center linetype to layer CEN and the phantom linetype to layer PHANT.

6 Pick the **OK** button to terminate the dialogue box.

NOTE:

REF 340-341

The LINETYPE command contains a Set option, which allows you to set the linetype for subsequently drawn entities. All new entities would be drawn with this linetype, regardless of the current layer. This gives you a great deal of flexibility, but it can become confusing. Therefore it is recommended that you avoid using the LINETYPE Set option and that its setting remain at BYLAYER. The BYLAYER setting means the linetype is specified by layer.

Freezing and Thawing Layers ———————————

1 Press the space bar to make the Layer Control dialogue box reappear.

2 Select layer **OBJ** and pick the **Freeze** button.

The letter F, for "Freeze," should appear under the State column.

3 Pick the **OK** button and notice what happens to the circle.

The circle should disappear.

4 Make the Layer Control dialogue box reappear.

5 Select layer **OBJ**, pick the **Thaw** button, and pick **OK**.

Did the circle reappear? As you can see, freezing and thawing layers is similar to turning them off and on. The difference is that AutoCAD will regenerate a drawing faster if the unneeded layers are frozen rather than turned off. Therefore, in most cases Freeze is recommended over the Off option. Note that you cannot freeze the current layer.

Locking Layers ———————————

AutoCAD permits you to lock layers as a safety mechanism. This prevents you from accidentally editing entities in complex drawings.

1 Make the Layer Control dialogue box reappear.

2 Select layer **OBJ** and pick the **Lock** button.

The letter L, for "Lock," should be listed in the State column.

3 Pick the **OK** button and try to edit the circle.

AutoCAD will not let you edit it because it is on a locked layer.

4 In the Layer Control dialogue box, select layer **OBJ** and pick the **Unlock** button.

5 Pick the **OK** button.

REF 325-326

REF 326

Other Features

The Layer Control dialogue box offers a few additional features.

1 If any layers are selected (highlighted), pick the **Clear All** button.

2 Select layer **BORD**.

3 Pick a point in the Layer Name edit box, as shown in the following illustration.

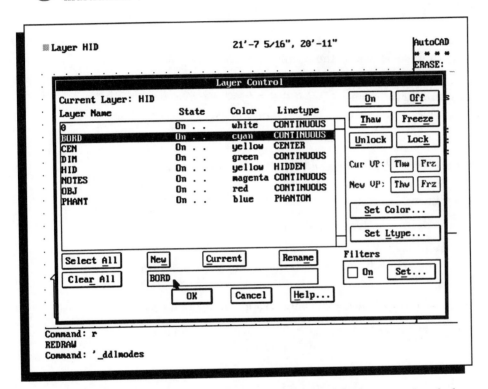

4 Add the letters **ER** to BORD so that it spells BORDER, and pick the **Rename** button.

AutoCAD should have renamed BORD to BORDER.

The Filters area, located in the lower right corner of the dialogue box, permits you to filter layers.

5 Pick the **Set...** button.

With the Set Layer Filters subdialogue box, you can show layer names in the Layer Name list box according to their names, colors, linetypes, whether they are frozen or thawed, on or off, and locked or unlocked. You can use wild-card search characters to filter layer names, colors, and linetypes.

REF 324

REF 327

6 Pick the **OK** button.

REF 325

The items "Cur VP:" and "New VP:" stand for "current viewport" and "new viewport," respectively. You can use the Thw and Frz buttons to control the visibility of layers within individual viewports. These items become available when TILEMODE is Off (0). The default setting is On (1). Unit 47 introduces you to TILEMODE.

7 Pick the **OK** button to terminate the dialogue box.

Moving Entities from Layer to Layer ───────────

Occasionally, you may draw an object on the wrong layer. If this happens, AutoCAD offers commands that fix the problem.

1 Enter **DDCHPROP** or pick the **Change Properties** option from the **Modify** pull-down menu.

REF 218-219

2 Select the circle, and press **RETURN**.

The Change Properties dialogue box should appear.

3 Pick the **Layer...** button.

The Select Layer subdialogue box should appear.

4 Select layer **NOTES** from the list box and pick the **OK** button.

5 Pick the **OK** button from the Change Properties dialogue box.

The circle should now be magenta because you assigned this color to layer NOTES.

6 Move the circle back to layer **OBJ** on your own.

────────── NOTE: ──────────

You can also move entities from layer to layer using either the CHPROP or the CHANGE command.

7 Erase both the circle and the triangle and make layer **OBJ** the current layer.

8 Enter **QSAVE** to save your work in PROTO1.

Reference

Applying Our (Nearly Complete) Prototype Drawing

The prototype drawing preparation is nearly complete. The last few steps (12, 13, and 14 from p. 172) typically involve creation of new text styles and setting the dimensioning variables and DIMSCALE. All of this is covered in Units 23 and 24.

The prototype drawing concept may lack full meaning to you until you have actually applied it. Therefore let's begin a new drawing using our prototype drawing PROTO1.

1 Start AutoCAD and enter the **NEW** command or select **New...** from the **File** pull-down menu.

2 Type **STAIRD** for the new drawing name, but *do not* press RETURN.

3 Pick the **Prototype...** button located in the upper left corner.

REF 74

4 Find and select **PROTO1** from the Files list box.

HINT: You may need to double click the .. symbol from the Directories list box.

5 Pick **OK**; pick **OK** again.

Notice the status line at the top of the graphic screen.

6 Review the list of layers.

Look familiar? Do you now see why prototype drawings are of value?

7 Enter **END** to save the STAIRD drawing file and exit AutoCAD.

NOTE:

The contents of PROTO1 were loaded into STAIRD at the beginning, so there is no need to specify PROTO1 when editing STAIRD. In other words, prototype drawings are used only when you begin a new drawing. Furthermore, you are not locked into the prototype drawing environment. When you open STAIRD in the future, you can add more layers and change all the settings according to your needs.

PROTO1 is also available for the creation of other new drawings, saving you time when starting new drawings.

Questions

1. Explain at least two purposes of layers.

   To ASSigN LiNetype & Colors to OBJ

2. Using the Layer Control dialogue box, how do you change the current layer?

   SElect Item Click Current Click OK

3. Describe the purpose of the LTSCALE command and explain how it is set.

   SEts SCAle FActor of All LiNES iN DRAWiNg, TYPE LTSCALE GivE NEW SCALE SizE ENtER

4. Why/when would you want to freeze a layer?

   To SEE other ENtities with out it and For REGENS its FASter

5. Name five of the linetypes AutoCAD makes available.

   ContiN, CEN, PHAN, DASHED, HiDDEN

6. What is the purpose of the COLOR command?

   Allows you to SEt Colors for SubSEqUENt DRAW ENtities

7. What is the purpose of locking layers?

   KEEPS you FRom EDiting the locKED LAYErs unintentionAlly

8. If you accidentally draw on the wrong layer, how can you correct your mistake without erasing and redrawing?

   USE CHANGE CmD OR DD moDiFy OR moDify FROm Pull DOWN

192

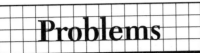

Problems

1. Create the following layers with corresponding settings.

PRB 22-1

Layer name	State	Color	Linetype
Ø	Frozen	7 (white)	CONTINUOUS
BORD	On	4 (cyan)	CONTINUOUS
CEN	On	2 (yellow)	CENTER
DIM	On	3 (green)	CONTINUOUS
HID	On	2 (yellow)	HIDDEN
OBJ	On	1 (red)	CONTINUOUS
PHANT	On	5 (blue)	PHANTOM
TEXT	Frozen	8	CONTINUOUS

Current layer: OBJ

PRB 22-2

Layer name	State	Color	Linetype
Ø	On	7 (white)	CONTINUOUS
CEN	Frozen	5 (blue)	CENTER
DIM	On	2 (yellow)	CONTINUOUS
ELECT	On	4 (cyan)	CONTINUOUS
FOUND	On	6 (magenta)	DASHED
HID	On	5 (blue)	HIDDEN
NOTES	On	2 (yellow)	CONTINUOUS
PLUMB	Frozen	7 (white)	CONTINUOUS
TITLE	Frozen	3 (green)	CONTINUOUS
WALLS	On	1 (red)	CONTINUOUS

Current layer: Ø

2. Refer to the file named LAYERS.DWG and instructions contained on the optional *Applying AutoCAD* Diskette. The drawing shows examples of layers, colors, and linetypes, and the instructions give suggestions for its use.

AUTOCAD® AT WORK

CAD Gives Small Business Its Competitive Edge

When you're a relatively small business, you need whatever edge you can get. For Trusco Industries Ltd., a family business with 20 employees located in Prince George, Canada, that edge is CAD.

Trusco manufactures roof and floor trusses for housing and commercial projects, generally building wood web trusses with steel connector plates. All its design work is done with AutoCAD. One of the company's biggest projects was designing and manufacturing trusses for temporary wooden structures at Vancouver's Expo '86.

Another large job was the married personnel quarters at a Canadian Armed Forces base. "It was entirely in metric," notes Bruce Richards, Trusco's CAD operator, "but with CAD you don't have to worry about units, since the computer doesn't care. Because the footings were offset, dimensions had to be taken from the footings and transferred to the bearing walls and beams above. I used AutoCAD's layering capability to isolate footings, beams, and bearing walls. Then, using AutoCAD's copy and change commands, I was able to transfer lines within drawings to other layers, and thus arrive at final dimensions."

"Typically, I'd use about thirty layers on a drawing like that. I'd have a different layer for each floor of an apartment building, for example, with each floor having its own sublayers for truss layout and beams. Once you've got all those layers, though, how do you remember which ones to turn on and off? I've designed a macro (a customized command that initiates a series of steps with a single keystroke) that turns layers on and off according to what part of a building I'm working on. I play with the program to get CAD doing what I want."

One aspect of his CAD system that Richards particularly likes is that it can be customized. "I had an engineering student from the University of British Columbia working with me one summer," he notes. "He caught on to AutoCAD very quickly and was able to write AutoLISP programs. Now, AutoLISP programs can generate cross sections of buildings for us. For example, we'll ask for the span and slope of a given truss and its depth. Automatically, the program creates a totally dimensioned building cross section."

In a further customization, Richards' brother Bryan has written a DXF (drawing interchange file) program that automatically draws flat trusses (used for flat roofs and floors) and converts them to a file that can be read by AutoCAD.

Trusco has found CAD to be a sound investment. Says Richards, "It's fast and it's accurate. I like the fact that everything you draw consistently fits together and that you don't have to draw objects more than once. Those capabilities are worth a lot of money in manufacturing."

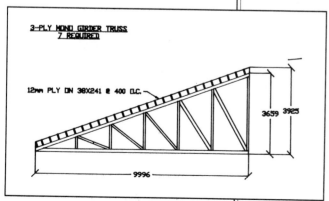

Courtesy of Trusco Industries Ltd. and Autodesk, Inc.

Basic Dimensioning

OBJECTIVE:

To apply AutoCAD's basic dimensioning capabilities

One of AutoCAD's powerful features is its semiautomatic dimensioning. This unit covers the different types of dimensioning, including linear, angular, diameter, and radial dimensioning.

Preparing to Dimension

Before we can dimension the following object, we need to prepare a few drawing settings and parameters.

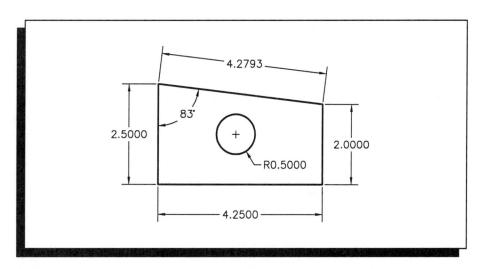

1 Start AutoCAD and begin a new drawing named **DIMEN**.

2 Create two new layers. Call one of them **OBJ** and the other **DIM**.

3 Assign the color green to OBJ and the color yellow to DIM. Set layer **OBJ** as the current layer.

_____ NOTE: _____

When you draw the object, place the object lines on layer OBJ and the dimensions on layer DIM.

4 Set your Snap at **0.25** unit.

5 Draw the object, shown on the previous page, and omit dimensions at this point. Don't worry about the exact location of the circle. (See the following hint.)

HINT: Begin in the upper left corner and work counterclockwise as you specify the line endpoints.

Dimension Text Style

The current text style is what AutoCAD uses for the dimension text. Therefore, let's create a new text style.

1 Using the Roman Simplex (ROMANS.SHX) text font, create a new text style. Accept each of the default settings for the new style.

HINT: Refer to Unit 20 for instructions on how to create new text styles.

Dimensioning Horizontal Lines

1 Set layer **DIM** as the current layer.

2 Select the **Draw** pull-down menu.

3 Highlight the **Dimensions** item and its **Linear** cascading menu.

4 Pick the **Horizontal** option, as shown in the following.

REF 450-457

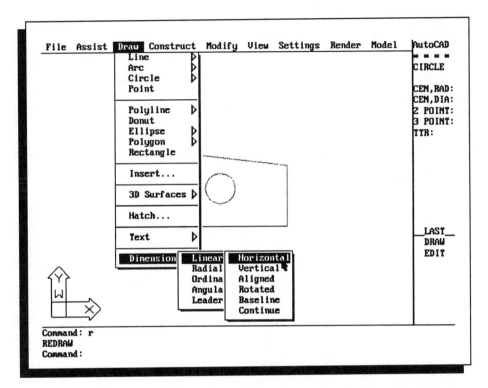

5　In reply to "First extension line origin or RETURN to select:" pick one of the endpoints of the object's horizontal line.

6　Then pick the second extension line origin (the other end of the horizontal line).

7　Move your pointing device downward to locate the dimension line approximately 1 unit away from the object and pick a point.

8　Press **RETURN** to accept the default dimension text.

Did the dimension appear correctly? If not, use the U command to undo the last operation and try it again.

9　**ZOOM** in on the dimension to examine it, and then **ZOOM** Previous.

Dimensioning Vertical Lines

Now, let's dimension the vertical lines in the object. Start with either line.

1　This time, enter the **DIM** command at the keyboard or pick **DIM:** from the root page of the standard screen menu.

The dimensioning submenu should appear on the screen. Also, you should see the "Dim:" prompt at the bottom rather than the usual "Command:".

NOTE:

The "Dim:" prompt must be present when you select dimensioning subcommands from the standard screen menu or enter them at the keyboard.

2 Enter the **VERTICAL** subcommand at the keyboard or select **Vertical** from the standard screen menu.

3 Select the first and second extension line origins as you did before.

4 Place the dimension line as you did before, and press **RETURN** at the "Dimension text:" prompt.

Let's dimension the other vertical line, but this time let's do it a faster way.

1 Enter **VERTICAL** or select it from the standard screen menu.

2 This time when AutoCAD asks for the first extension line origin, press **RETURN**.

The crosshairs should change to a pickbox.

3 Pick any point on the vertical line.

4 Proceed at the next two prompts as you did before until the dimension appears on the screen.

5 Enter the REDRAW command by entering **R** at the "Dim:" prompt.

As you can see, the "Dim:" prompt accepts the REDRAW command.

Dimensioning Inclined Lines

Let's dimension the inclined line by "aligning" the dimension to the line.

1 Enter **ALIGNED** or pick **Aligned** from the submenu.

2 Proceed exactly as you did with the last dimension until the aligned dimension appears on the screen.

If it appears to be correct on your screen, then you did it right.

Dimensioning Circles and Arcs

Now let's dimension the circle.

1 Select **Radius** from the dimensioning submenu or enter it at the keyboard.

TUT 188

REF 463-464
TUT 170-171

2 Pick the circle at the point where the arrow touches it in the drawing on page 195. (You may need to turn off snap.)

3 Press **RETURN** in response to "Dimension text."

4 Move the crosshairs and watch what happens.

5 Pick a point a short distance down and to the right as shown in the drawing.

The radial dimension should appear.

Dimensioning Angles ─────────────

Last, let's dimension the angle as shown in the drawing.

1 Select **Angular** from the dimensioning submenu.

2 Pick both lines which make up the angle.

3 Move the crosshairs outside the object and watch the different possibilities that AutoCAD presents.

4 Pick a convenient location for the dimension arc.

5 Press **RETURN** in response to "Dimension text."

6 Specify where you'd like the text to appear.

The angular dimension should appear similar to the one on page 195.

7 If the angular dimension did not appear correctly, enter the UNDO subcommand by entering **U** and repeat Steps 1-6.

REF 457-461
TUT 179-180

──── NOTE: ────

In addition to the DIM command, the DIM1 command is available. The only difference between them is that DIM1 allows you to execute only one dimensioning subcommand and then returns to the normal "Command:" prompt. Use DIM if you plan to execute a series of dimensioning subcommands.

Moving Dimensions _____

Using AutoCAD's Grips feature, you can change the location of dimension lines and dimension text.

1 Obtain the "Command:" prompt by pressing **CTRL C** or by entering **EXIT**.

2 Pick one of the linear dimensions.

Five grips should appear.

3 Pick one of the two grips near the arrows.

4 Move your pointing device and notice that the dimension moves back and forth from the object.

5 Pick a new location for the dimension.

6 Pick the grip located at the center of the dimension text.

7 Move the text and pick a new location for it.

8 Enter **END** to save your drawing and exit AutoCAD.

Questions

1. Describe the alternative to specifying both endpoints of a line when dimensioning a line.

   PuSHing ENter to Select LiNES

2. Explain the difference between the DIM and DIM1 commands.

   Dim CoNtinuES Dim CommAD
   Dim1 Puts you At CmD PROmPt AFter 1 DimeNsioN

3. What prompt must be present in order to enter or select dimensioning subcommands?

   Dim!

4. In which pull-down menu can you find dimensioning items, such as Linear and Horizontal?

   DRAW

5. Which dimensioning subcommand is used to dimension inclined lines? Angles?

   ALIGNED   ANGLES

6. Which dimensioning subcommand do you use to dimension arcs and circles?

   RADIUS

Problems

Begin a new drawing for each of the following problems. Place object lines on a layer named OBJ and place dimensions on a layer named DIM. Approximate the locations of the circles and create a new text style using the ROMANS text font. If you have the optional *Applying AutoCAD* Diskette, refer to files PRB23-1.DWG and PRB23-2.DWG, as well as the instructions that apply.

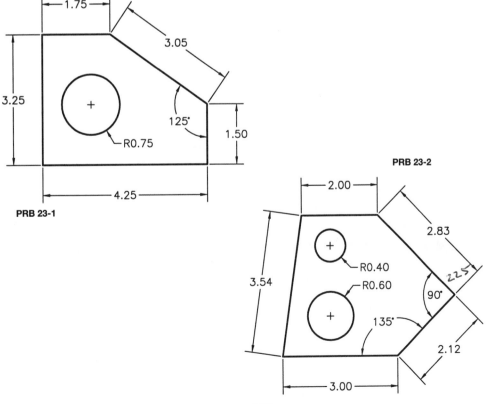

PRB 23-1

PRB 23-2

Unit 24 — Advanced Dimensioning

■ OBJECTIVE:

To apply AutoCAD's advanced dimensioning capabilities, including associative dimensioning, and basic dimensioning variables

This unit introduces additional semiautomatic dimensioning techniques and allows you to practice them. With this knowledge, you will step through the completion of the PROTO1 prototype drawing. First, let's focus on AutoCAD's dimensioning variables so that we can properly dimension the following drawing.

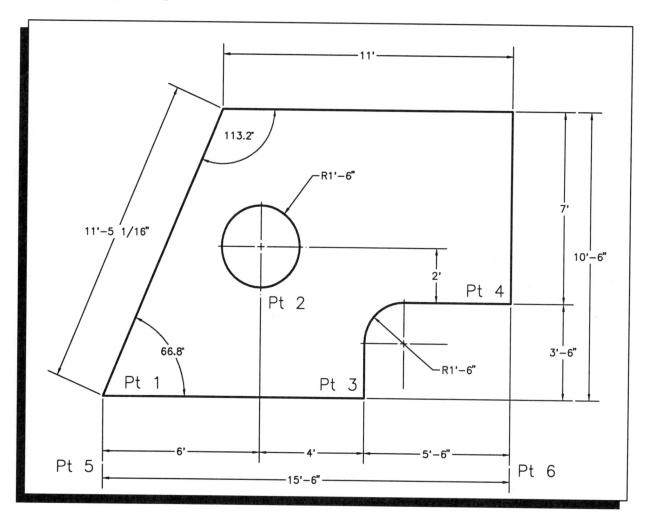

Reference

REF 435-450

REF 472

Dimensioning Variables

AutoCAD permits you to change the appearance of dimensions with dimensioning variables. For example, you can adjust the size of the dimension text and arrows.

1 Start AutoCAD.

2 Enter the **DIM** command.

3 At the "DIM:" prompt, enter the **STATUS** subcommand or select **next** and then **Status** from the standard screen menu.

The list of dimensioning variables should appear. The following table contains these variables. In addition, it includes a column showing the variable type.

Variable Name	Description	Variable Type	Default Setting
DIMALT	Alternate Units	Switch	Off
DIMALTD	Alternate Units Decimal Places	Integer	2
DIMALTF	Alternate Units Scale Factor	Scale	25.4
DIMAPOST	Alternate Units Text Suffix	String	None
DIMASO	Associative Dimensioning	Switch	On
DIMASZ	Arrow Size	Distance	0.18
DIMBLK	Arrow Block	String	None
DIMBLK1	Separate Arrow Block 1	String	None
DIMBLK2	Separate Arrow Block 2	String	None
DIMCEN	Center Mark Size	Distance	0.09
DIMCLRD	Dimension Line Color	Color number	BYBLOCK
DIMCLRE	Extension Line Color	Color number	BYBLOCK
DIMCLRT	Dimension Text Color	Color number	BYBLOCK
DIMDLE	Dimension Line Extension	Distance	0.0
DIMDLI	Dimension Line Increment	Distance	0.38
DIMEXE	Extension Line Extension	Distance	0.18
DIMEXO	Extension Line Offset	Distance	0.0625
DIMGAP	Dimension Line Gap and Reference Dimensioning	Distance	0.09
DIMLFAC	Length Factor	Scale	1.0
DIMLIM	Limits Dimensioning	Switch	Off
DIMPOST	Dimension Text Prefix, Suffix or both	String	None
DIMRND	Rounding Value	Scaled distance	0.0
DIMSAH	Separate Arrow Blocks	Switch	Off
DIMSCALE	Dimension Feature Scale Factor	Scale	1.0
DIMSE1	Suppress Extension Line 1	Switch	Off
DIMSE2	Suppress Extension Line 2	Switch	Off
DIMSHO	Show Dragged Dimensions	Switch	On
DIMSOXD	Suppress Outside Dimension Lines	Switch	Off

(continued)

Variable Name	Description	Variable Type	Default Setting
DIMSTYLE	Dimension Style	Name	*UNNAMED
DIMTAD	Text Above Dimension Line	Switch	Off
DIMTFAC	Tolerance Text Scale Factor	Scale	1.0
DIMTIH	Text Inside Horizontal	Switch	On
DIMTIX	Text Inside Extension Lines	Switch	Off
DIMTM	Minus Tolerance Value	Scaled distance	0.0
DIMTP	Plus Tolerance Value	Scaled distance	0.0
DIMTOFL	Text Outside, Force Line Inside	Switch	Off
DIMTOH	Text Outside Horizontal	Switch	On
DIMTOL	Tolerance Dimensioning	Switch	Off
DIMTSZ	Tick Size	Distance	0.0
DIMTVP	Text Vertical Position	Scale	0.0
DIMTXT	Text Size	Distance	0.18
DIMZIN	Zero Suppression	Integer	0

We will need to change some of the dimensioning variables before we dimension the drawing. For example, we will use DIMSCALE to fit the dimensions to the drawing scale properly. If we don't, the dimensions will be much too small.

Let's begin.

1 Use the PROTO1 prototype drawing to create a new drawing named **DIMEN2**. (See the following hint.)

PROTO1 is not entirely complete, but it will work for this exercise.

HINT:
Refer to the end of Unit 22 if you need help with applying prototype drawings.

2 Enter the **DIM** command and enter **STATUS** to list the dimensioning variables in DIMEN2.

Note how the settings are different from the default settings you saw before. For example, you should see fractional inches instead of decimal inches. This is because we specified architectural units in the prototype drawing.

3 At the "Dim:" prompt, enter the dimensioning variable **DIMASZ** (for dimension arrow size).

REF 475

NOTE:
You can also select "Dim Vars" from the standard screen menu and pick "dimasz" from the list of variables.

4 In reply to "Current value (3/16″) New value:" enter **1/8″**.

204

	Reference

The inch (double quote) mark is optional because AutoCAD assumes you are working in inches.

> **5** Enter **DIMTXT** (for dimension text) or select **dimtxt** from the standard screen menu, and enter **1/8″** for the new value.

REF 480

This will make the dimension text 1/8″ tall.

> **6** Enter **DIMCEN** or select **dimcen** from the menu, and enter **–1/16″**.

REF 475

DIMCEN controls the drawing of center marks and center lines at the center of arcs and circles. A positive value specifies center marks only. A negative value, such as –1/16″, specifies full center lines with 1/16″ center marks.

DIMSCALE

REF 478

DIMSCALE lets you enter a scale factor for all dimensions in the drawing.

> **1** Determine the DIMSCALE setting by calculating the reciprocal of the drawing's plot scale.

HINT: Your plot scale is 1/2″ = 1′, which is the same as 1/24, as discussed in the section on LTSCALE in Unit 22. The reciprocal, therefore, is 24.

> **2** Select **dimscale** from the list of dimensioning variables (or enter **DIMSCALE**) and enter **24**.

Dimension Styles

REF 434-435

A dimension style is a group of dimensioning variable settings saved under a name. Restoring a saved dimension style can save time because fine-tuning a set of variables can require a considerable amount of time.

> **1** Enter the **SAVE** subcommand at the "Dim:" prompt and enter **STYLE1**.

This will save the current dimensioning variable settings under the dimension style name STYLE1.

> **2** Enter the **RESTORE** subcommand, enter **?** and press **RETURN** to obtain a list of all named dimension styles.

Do you see the style named STYLE1? So you see, the SAVE and RESTORE dimensioning subcommands allow you to store and retrieve a group of dimensioning variables.

> **3** Enter **CTRL C**.

4 Enter the **VARIABLES** subcommand and enter **STYLE1**.

This should produce a list of the STYLE1 dimensioning variables.

5 Enter the **EXIT** subcommand.

Completing the Drawing

1 Create a new text style named **ROMANS** using the Roman Simplex (ROMANS.SHX) text font. Accept each of the default settings.

ROMANS should now be the current text style.

2 On layer OBJ, create the drawing shown on the first page of this unit, but omit dimensions at this point. (Read the following hint.)

HINT:

For best results, begin at the lower left corner of the object and draw the object in a counterclockwise direction. Add the arc using the FILLET command.

Finally, we will dimension the object.

Let's begin by dimensioning the circle.

1 Make layer **DIM** the current layer.

2 Enter the **DIM** command and enter **RADIUS** or select **Radius** from the standard screen menu.

3 Dimension the circle as shown in the drawing.

Full center lines should appear with the dimension.

4 Enter the **CENTER** subcommand and pick the arc.

Full center lines should appear at the center of the arc.

Next, let's dimension the horizontal string of dimensions.

5 Enter **HORIZONTAL** or select **Horizntl** from the menu.

6 Pick the lower left corner of the object (point 1) for the first extension line origin.

7 Pick the end of the vertical center line (point 2) for the second extension line origin.

8 Place the dimension line 2′ from the object.

Reference

REF 456-457

9 Enter the **CONTINUE** subcommand or pick **Continue** from the standard screen menu.

10 In reply to "Second extension line origin," pick point 3 and press **RETURN**.

11 Enter **CONTINUE** again, pick point 4, and press **RETURN**.

NOTE:

You can also issue "continue" from the Draw pull-down menu. Pick Dimension, then Linear, and then Continue.

12 Using the **HORIZONTAL** subcommand, add the 15'-6" dimension. Pick points 5 and 6. Place the dimension 1' away from the string of dimensions.

HINT:
Use the END object snap mode to snap to points 5 and 6.

13 Complete the remaining dimensions on your own.

14 If you have access to a pen plotter and know how to operate it, plot the drawing using a thick pen (*e.g.*, 0.7 mm) for color 1 and a thin pen (*e.g.*, 0.3 mm) for color 3.

15 Enter **SAVE** at the "Command:" prompt to save your work.

Associative Dimensioning

REF 423-432

Associative dimensions are created whenever the variable DIMASO is On. The default setting for DIMASO is On (1). When DIMASO is Off, the lines, arcs, arrows, and text are drawn as separate entities.

Associative dimensioning provides for automatic updating of dimensions when the dimensioned object is altered using the commands SCALE, STRETCH, ROTATE, EXTEND, TRIM, MIRROR, and ARRAY.

1 Enter the **SCALE** command, enter **All** to select the entire object, and press **RETURN**.

2 Enter **0,0** for the base point.

3 In reply to "Scale factor," enter **1.1**.

Notice the dimensions changed to reflect the new sizes.

4 Enter the **STRETCH** command and stretch the rightmost portion of the object a short distance to the right. (When selecting the portion to be stretched, be sure to use the Crossing option.)

The dimensions should again change to reflect the new size.

5 Use the **U** command to undo steps 1 through 4.

6 Enter **QSAVE** to save your work.

Completing the Prototype Drawing _____

Now that we know how to perform the remaining steps (12-14, page 172) in creating a prototype drawing, let's finish PROTO1.DWG.

1 Open **PROTO1**.

2 Create a new text style using the Roman Simplex (ROMANS.SHX) text font, and accept the default settings.

_____ NOTE: _____

If you'd like your prototype drawing to contain more text styles, create them at this time. The last style you create will be the current style in the prototype drawing. The Roman Simplex font is recommended for most applications.

Now let's set a few dimensioning variables.

1 Enter **DIM**.

2 Enter **STATUS** and review the variable **DIMASZ**.

3 Enter **DIMASZ** and 1/8″.

4 Set **DIMTXT** at 1/8″.

5 Change **DIMCEN** to –1/8″.

6 Using **DIMSCALE**, scale all of the dimensioning variables to correspond with your prototype drawing scale: enter **24** as discussed on page 205.

Other changes in the dimensioning variables could be made at this time, but let's stop here.

7 Enter **EXIT** to return to the "Command:" prompt, and **END** to save your changes in PROTO1 and exit AutoCAD.

Your prototype drawing is now complete and ready for use with a host of new drawings.

As you continue to use this prototype drawing, as well as others you may create, feel free to modify them further to tailor them to your specific needs.

Documenting Your Prototype Drawings

It is important that you be able to use your prototype drawings effectively in the future. To know what is contained in each prototype drawing, you must document the contents of each by printing certain information, such as your DIM status. You and others will then be able to review the settings of each prototype drawing prior to choosing the one you need. At the top of the printout, write the name of the prototype drawing, the directory on which it resides, and the drawing scale and paper size.

Questions

1. Why is it important to place dimensions on one layer and object lines on another layer?

   Plots of Dimen are thiner & you can freeze

2. Explain how to specify a text style to appear in the dimensions.

   Type Dimstyle Save then "Style" & enter

3. What is the purpose of the dimensioning variables?

   To Tailor them to your Requirements

4. How do you determine the DIMSCALE setting?

   By your Drawing Scale

5. Explain the difference between AutoCAD's center marks and center lines, and describe how to generate each.

   Marks are small Crosses Locating Center Lines Locate Center & Go thru

6. Explain the use of the CONTINUE dimensioning subcommand.

Quickly Place Dimen Along same side

7. Describe the purpose of each of the following dimensioning variables.

DIMASZ _ARROW SIZE_

DIMTXT _Dim Text Size_

DIMCEN _Center marks & lines_

DIMSCALE _Dim scale factor_

Problems

Begin a new drawing and establish the following drawing settings and parameters. Store as a prototype drawing. (You could name it PROTO2.) Then complete the following dimensioning problems using this prototype drawing.

UNITS: Engineering

Scale: 1″ = 10′ (or 1″ = 120″)

Paper Size: 17″ × 11″

LIMITS: Lower left corner 0,0

LIMITS: Upper right corner ___?___ (You determine the upper right limit based on the scale and paper size.)

GRID: 10′

(Reminder: Be sure to ZOOM All)

SNAP resolution: 2′

LAYERs:
Name	Color
Thick	1
Thin	2

Text: Create a new text style using the Roman Simplex (ROMANS.SHX) font. Do not make the style height fixed; leave it at 0.

DIMASZ: 0.125

DIMTXT: 0.125

DIMSCALE: 120

DIMCEN: –0.0625

Create a new arrow block and enter it using the DIMBLK dimensioning variable. (Refer to pages 441 and 475 of the *AutoCAD Reference Manual* for directions on how to create and use an arrow block.)

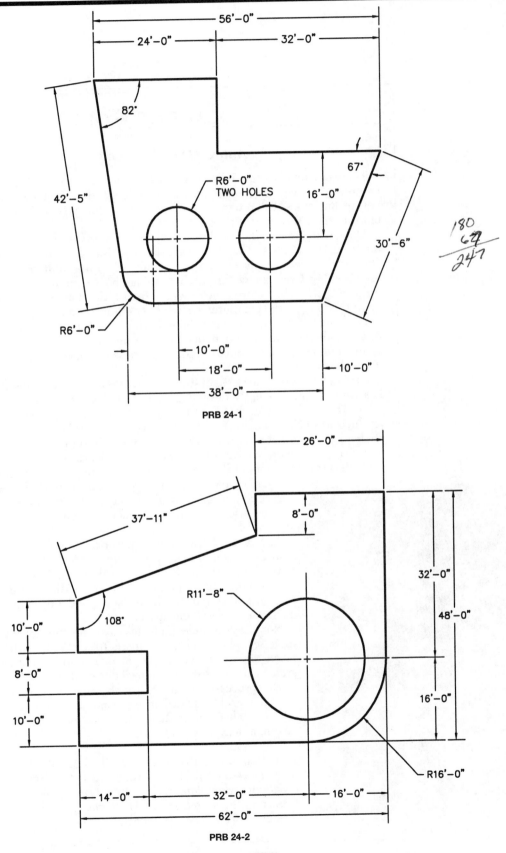

PRB 24-1

PRB 24-2

AUTOCAD® AT WORK

AutoCAD and Beyond

Three or four years ago, Ben Crow, a teacher at Casa Grande High School, entered a summer program designed to instruct and excite teachers about new technologies. The program was supported by the Arizona Department of Education, Vocational Education Division, and Arizona State University.

Along with other high school teachers, Mr. Crow underwent an intensive three weeks of study and hands-on experience with a variety of technologies. One of the areas of instruction was AutoCAD. Like most of the other teachers, Mr. Crow knew absolutely nothing about computers, much less AutoCAD, when he entered the program. In fact, the state provided a small grant that bought the computer system to get him started.

The program was an enormous help to Mr. Crow and the other teachers that attended, but the real benefits soon became evident in the classrooms around the state. The secondary students in these teachers' classrooms were the real winners.

For Ben Crow, the successes in student outcomes have been phenomenal. His students are currently designing parts and then precision-machining them. They are using AutoCAD and similar software to design and engineer products as small as mechanical linkages and as large as horse trailers! The students then market their products. Their sales help support the program.

Perhaps even more important, the students are learning about the basic skills necessary to compete in the marketplace. They are learning how

economics, conservation of resources, math skills, reading and communication skills, problem solving, and teamwork can be used together to make a product or business successful.

As a result of the summer program, Ben Crow has used AutoCAD and related programs in areas that reach far beyond a substitute for mechanical drafting. His students have become more proficient in basic skills, the dropout rate has declined to almost zero, and enrollment has outstripped classroom space.

Now, Casa Grande graduates have a distinct advantage in their schooling and in the marketplace. Those who have taken Mr. Crow's classes begin their post-secondary programs with a substantial knowledge of CAD and CAM.

The process is ongoing. By the time this is in print, student use of CAD will have expanded even more. Exploration of what can be done with CAD programs has only begun, at least at Casa Grande.

This story was contributed by Dr. Jack Michie. Dr. Michie recently retired from a distinguished 42-year career in vocational education, ranging from teaching in classrooms to serving as a college president and professor. He now resides in Scottsdale, Arizona.

Unit 25 — Fine-Tuning Your Dimensions

Reference

■ OBJECTIVE:

To alter dimensions using dimensioning subcommands and dialogue boxes

This unit covers special dimension editing techniques that help you fine-tune your dimensions. In addition, the unit steps you through the many dialogue boxes that adjust the appearance of dimensions.

■ *Editing Dimensions*

As presented in Unit 23, you can move dimensions using grips. In addition, you can edit dimensions using the ERASE and EXPLODE commands.

1　Start AutoCAD.

2　Use **DIMEN2** as a prototype drawing to begin a new drawing named **DIMEN3**.

3　Attempt to erase a single element of any dimension, such as the dimension text or extension line.

AutoCAD selects the entire dimension because AutoCAD treats an associative dimension as a single entity.

4　Enter **CTRL C** to cancel the ERASE command.

5　Enter the **EXPLODE** command, select any dimension, and press **RETURN**.

REF 249-250

The dimension is no longer an associative dimension, so its color will change. You can now edit individual elements of the dimension.

6　Erase part of the dimension.

■ *TEDIT Subcommand*

REF 468-469

The TEDIT subcommand allows you to move the dimension text of an associative dimension.

1　Enter the **DIM** command.

2　Enter the **TEDIT** subcommand and select one of the associative dimensions.

3　Move the crosshairs and notice that the dimension text moves too. (Ortho and Snap affect the movement.)

4　Pick a new location for the dimension text.

HOMETEXT Subcommand

Reference
REF 467

HOMETEXT restores the text of an associative dimension to its default (home) location if it was moved.

1 Enter **HOMETEXT**.

2 Select the dimension you edited with the TEDIT subcommand and press **RETURN**.

The dimension text should return to its original location.

TROTATE Subcommand

REF 469-470

TROTATE permits you to adjust the orientation of dimension text of one or more associative dimensions.

1 Enter **TROTATE** at the "Dim:" prompt, and enter **20** (degrees) for the new text angle.

2 Select any associative dimension and press **RETURN**.

The dimension text should rotate 20 degrees counterclockwise.

NEWTEXT Subcommand

REF 467-468

Use NEWTEXT to change the content of the dimension text.

1 Enter **NEWTEXT**.

2 Enter an arbitrary number, such as **25.5**.

3 Select any dimension and press **RETURN**.

The dimension text should change to 25.5.

UPDATE Subcommand

REF 470

Use UPDATE to change existing associative dimensions to the current dimension variables, dimension style, text style, and units.

1 Restore the "Command:" prompt by entering **EXIT** or by pressing **CTRL C**.

2 Enter **DDUNITS**, change the units to **Decimal**, and pick **OK**.

3 Enter **DIM** and the **UPDATE** subcommand.

4 In reply to "Select objects:" enter **All** and press **RETURN**.

All associative dimensions should change to decimal units.

LEADER Subcommand

Use LEADER to create a leader, followed by a note or dimension.

1 After restoring the "Command:" prompt, explode the circle dimension and erase the leader and text.

2 Enter **DIM** and **LEADER**.

3 In reply to "Leader start:" pick a point on the circle where you would like AutoCAD to place the arrow of the leader.

HINT:

Use the NEArest object snap mode to ensure that the point of the arrow touches the circle.

4 Move the crosshairs away from the circle and pick a point. (The leader line should point at the center of the circle.)

5 Press **RETURN**.

6 In reply to "Dimension text < >:" enter **R0.50**.

OBLIQUE Subcommand

Use OBLIQUE to set an oblique angle for the extension lines of one or more associative dimensions.

1 Enter **OBLIQUE**.

2 Select a linear dimension and press **RETURN**.

3 Enter **15** for the obliquing angle.

The dimension's extension lines should rotate 15 degrees counterclockwise.

OBLIQUE is especially useful when you are dimensioning isometric drawings, such as those that follow. The right drawing is the result of applying OBLIQUE to the left drawing.

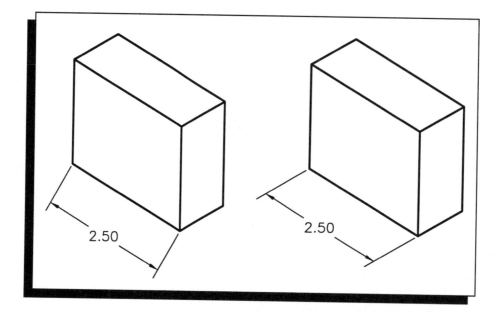

2.50   2.50

Other dimensioning subcommands are available. OVERRIDE updates an associative dimension by modifying one or more of the dimensioning variables on a one-time basis. The ORDINATE subcommand permits you to dimension an X or Y coordinate of a feature.

 Experiment with these subcommands on your own.

Dimension Styles and Variables Dialogue Box

REF 433-450

In the last unit, you named a dimension style and changed four dimension variables. You can use the Dimension Styles and Variables dialogue box to create new dimension styles and change dimensioning variables.

1   Enter **DDIM** or pick **Dimension Style...** from the **Settings** pull-down menu.

HINT:
You can enter DDIM from either the "Dim:" or the "Command:" prompt.

The following dialogue box will appear.

```
■ Layer DIM Snap          240.0000,240.0000              AutoCAD
                                                         * * * *
                       132.8000                          DIM:
                                                         Aligned
                                                         Angular
          ┌─────────────────────────────────────┐       Diameter
          │   Dimension Styles and Variables     │       Horizntl
          │  Dimension Styles    Dimension Variables      Leader
          │  ┌─────────────┐    ┌──────────────────┐     Ordinate
          │  │ STYLE1      │    │  Dimension Line...│     Radius
   137.0830│  │             │    ├──────────────────┤     Rotated
          │  │             │    │ Extension Lines...│     Vertical
          │  │             │    ├──────────────────┤     Edit
          │  │             │    │    Arrows...      │     Dim Styl
          │  │             │    ├──────────────────┤     Dim Vars
          │  │             │    │  Text Location... │     next
          │  │             │    ├──────────────────┤     Exit
          │  │             │    │   Text Format...  │      LAST
          │  │             │    ├──────────────────┤      DRAW
          │  │             │    │    Features...    │      EDIT
          │  └─────────────┘    ├──────────────────┤
          │                     │    Colors...      │
          │  Dimension Style: ┌─────────┐
          │                   │ STYLE1  │
          │     ┌────┐  ┌────────┐  ┌───────┐
          │     │ OK │  │ Cancel │  │ Help..│
          │     └────┘  └────────┘  └───────┘
          └─────────────────────────────────────┘

Command:
Command:
Command: ddim
```

② Pick **STYLE1** from the Dimension Styles list box if it is not already selected.

③ Pick a point in the Dimension Style edit box, as shown.

④ Erase "1" by pressing the backspace key once.

⑤ Type **2** and press **RETURN**.

You have just created a new dimension style named STYLE2 which is identical to STYLE1. Changes you make to AutoCAD's dimensioning variables will now become a part of STYLE2 because it's the current style.

⑥ Pick the **OK** button.

Text Format Subdialogue Box

REF 445

Let's change the settings in STYLE2 using the Text Format subdialogue box.

① Enter **DDUNITS**, change the unit precision to tenths (0.0), and pick **OK**.

AutoCAD will not store this change in STYLE2.

② At the "Dim:" prompt, enter **UPDATE**.

③ In reply to "Select objects:" enter **All** and press **RETURN**.

④ Enter **DDIM** and pick the **Text Format...** button to display the Text Format subdialogue box.

You should see the following.

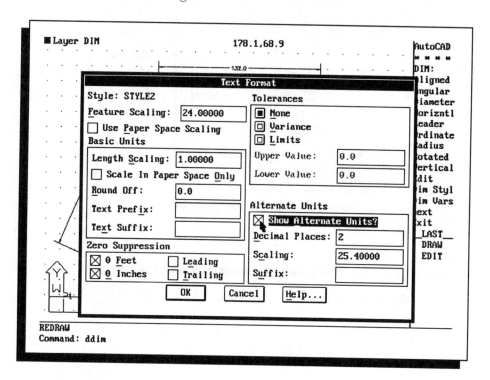

The settings in this dialogue box are tied directly to the settings in the following dimensioning variables.

DIMSCALE	DIMLFAC	DIMRND
DIMPOST	DIMZIN	DIMTOL
DIMLIM	DIMTM	DIMTP
DIMALT	DIMALTF	DIMALTD
DIMAPOST		

Therefore, if you make a change in the dialogue box, you will affect one or more of these dimensioning variables.

———— NOTE: ————

See the previous unit for a brief description of dimensioning variables.

⑤ In the Alternate Units area, check the box beside **Show Alternate Units?** as shown above.

Reference

Checking this box is equivalent to changing the DIMALT dimensioning variable from Off to On.

Note that "Scaling:" is set at 25.4. This is the multiplier used to change inches to millimeters. Changing this number is equivalent to changing the DIMALTF dimensioning variable.

6 Pick **OK**; pick **OK** again.

The dimension text should change to include both inches and millimeters. AutoCAD stores this setting in the STYLE2 dimension style.

7 Enter **DDIM**, select **STYLE1**, and pick **OK**.

8 Enter **UPDATE**, **All**, and press **RETURN**.

AutoCAD will change the dimensions to conform to the STYLE1 settings.

9 Change the dimensions back to the STYLE2 settings. (Don't forget to issue the **UPDATE** command.)

Specifying Tolerances

REF 447-448

You can also define tolerances using the Text Format subdialogue box.

1 Bring back the Text Format subdialogue box and disable "Show Alternate Units?" by picking the check box.

2 In the Tolerances area, pick the **Limits** radio button, and enter **0.5** for both the upper and lower values.

NOTE:

Picking the Limits radio button is equivalent to turning On the DIMLIM variable and turning Off DIMTOL. AutoCAD stores the upper and lower values in variables DIMTP and DIMTM, respectively.

3 Pick **OK**; pick **OK** again.

AutoCAD will change all dimensions to reflect the upper and lower values.

4 Bring back the Text Format subdialogue box and pick the **Variance** radio button in the Tolerances area.

Picking the Variance radio button is equivalent to turning On the DIMTOL variable and turning Off the DIMLIM variable.

5 Pick **OK**; pick **OK** again.

AutoCAD will change the dimensions to plus and minus tolerances.

1 Bring back the Text Format subdialogue box.

As you can see, it includes other settings. "Feature Scaling" is equivalent to DIMSCALE. As you may recall, we set it at 24 in the PROTO1 prototype drawing.

The "Use Paper Space Scaling" relates to the use of paper space. You will learn about paper space in Unit 47. Changing the "Length Scaling" edit box is equivalent to changing the DIMLFAC dimension variable.

2 Explore the remaining settings on your own.

Other Subdialogue Boxes

Once you know how to use one dimensioning subdialogue box, other dimensioning subdialogue boxes are straightforward. Let's review the remaining ones.

1 Display the Dimension Styles and Variables dialogue box and pick the **Dimension Line...** button.

REF 437-438

The settings in the Dimension Line subdialogue box affect the following dimension variables.

DIMSCALE	DIMCLRD	DIMOXD
DIMTOFL	DIMGAP	DIMDLI

2 Pick the **Basic Dimension** check box and pick **OK**; pick **OK** again.

3 Bring back the Dimension Line subdialogue box and disable the Basic Dimension setting.

4 Enter **0.3** in the Text Gap edit box and pick **OK**; pick **OK** again.

This causes AutoCAD to widen the gap between the dimension text and the dimension line. Review the other Dimension Line settings on your own.

5 Enter **DDIM** and pick the **Extension Line...** button.

REF 438-439

The settings in this subdialogue box affect the following variables.

DIMSCALE	DIMCLRE	DIMEXE
DIMEXO	DIMSE1	DIMSE2
DIMCEN		

6 Make one or two changes in the Extension Lines area of the subdialogue box and see how they affect the dimensions.

7 Pick the remaining subdialogue boxes on your own and experiment with each of them.

Listed here are the system variables that are affected by the remaining subdialogue boxes.

REF 440-441

Arrows Subdialogue Box

DIMSCALE	DIMCLRD	DIMASZ
DIMTSZ	DIMBLK	DIMBLK1
DIMBLK2	DIMSAH	DIMDLE

REF 442-445

Text Location Subdialogue Box

DIMSCALE	DIMCLRT	DIMTXT
DIMTFAC	DIMTIX	DIMSOXD
DIMTAD	DIMTVP	DIMTIH
DIMTOH		

REF 450

Colors Subdialogue Box

DIMSCALE	DIMCLRD	DIMCLRE
DIMCLRT		

——— NOTE: ———

If you change a dimensioning variable by entering it at the "Dim:" prompt, the current dimension style becomes a new *UNNAMED style.

REF 449-450

8 Display the Dimension Styles and Variables dialogue box and pick the **Features...** button.

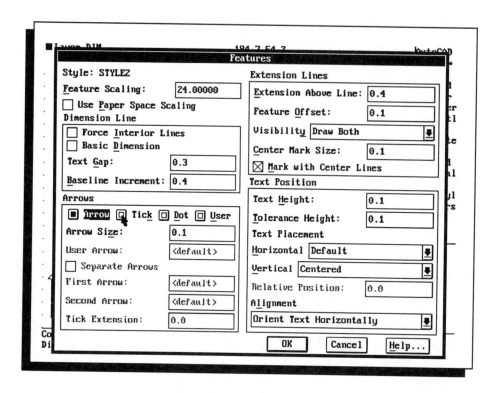

The Features subdialogue box displays a summary of several subdialogue boxes, including the Dimension Line, Extension Lines, Arrows, Text Location, and Text Format subdialogue boxes.

⑨ Pick the **OK** button twice to return to the "Dim:" prompt, and enter **EXIT** to return to the "Command:" prompt.

⑩ Enter **END** to save your work and exit AutoCAD.

Questions

1. How would you erase a piece of an associative dimension?

   EXPLODE it then ERASE ITEM YOU WANT

2. What part of an associative dimension does the TEDIT subcommand allow you to move?

   DIMEN TEXT

3. Will HOMETEXT work with a dimension that is not an associative dimension? Explain.

   NO ONCE EXPLODED its NO LONGER PART OF DIMEN

4. With which dimensioning subcommand can you rotate dimension text?

   TROTATE

5. What is the purpose of the NEWTEXT subcommand?

   CHANGE Context OF Dim TEXT

6. Which settings are considered when you issue the UPDATE subcommand?

   Dim VAR, Dim STYle, TEXT & Units

7. With which subcommand can you adjust the angle of a dimension's extension lines?

   OBLIQUE

8. Is it possible to change the dimensioning variable settings using dialogue boxes? Explain.

   YES USing Dim STYLES & VARIBLES DiALOg BOX

9. Explain how you would specify plus and minus tolerances using the Text Format subdialogue box.

   CliCK Limits RADIO BUtton & Put IN VALUES

10. Which dimensioning subdialogue box offers a summary of the other subdialogue boxes?

    FEATURES SUb DiALOg

Problems

1. Create a new drawing named PRB25-1. Plan for a drawing scale of 1″ = 1″ and sheet size of 11″ × 17″. After you apply the following settings, create and dimension the following drawing. Use the dimension dialogue boxes to set the dimensioning variables.

LIMITS: Upper right corner 16,10

SNAP resolution: 0.25

GRID: 1

Layers: Create layers to accommodate multiple colors and linetypes.

LTSCALE: 0.5

Text font: Roman Simplex (ROMANS.SHX)

Dimension style name: HEATHER

Feature scaling (DIMSCALE): 1

Dimension text height (DIMTXT): 0.16

Arrow size (DIMASZ): 0.16

Center mark size: 0.08

Mark with center lines? Yes

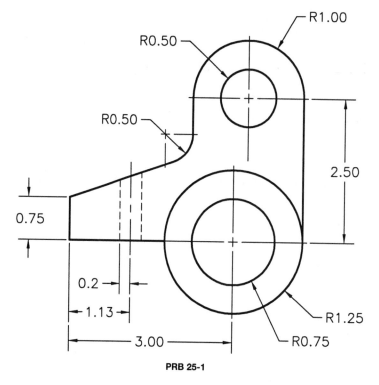

PRB 25-1

2. Create a new drawing named PRB25-2 using PRB25-1 as a prototype drawing. Use AutoCAD's commands, such as EXPLODE and STRETCH, and dimensioning subcommands, such as TEDIT and NEWTEXT, to make the following changes. Note that the 2.25 dimension is now 2.50. Stretch the top part of the object upward 0.25 unit and let the associative dimension text change on its own.

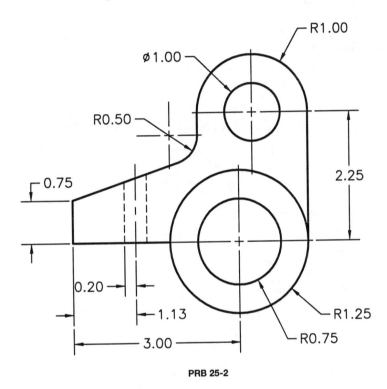

PRB 25-2

3. Create a new drawing named PRB25-3 using PRB25-1 as a prototype drawing. Using AutoCAD's dimensioning dialogue boxes, make the following changes.

- Save the settings in a new dimension style named FRESH.
- Change the dimension text height to 0.13.
- Change the center marks to 0.07.
- Change the dimension arrows to 0.08 dots.
- All dimensions, except the smallest hole, should show a tolerance of +/– 0.03. Use a leader to show that this hole does not require a tolerance. Specify 0.08 for the extension line feature offset.
- Change the dimension text color to green.

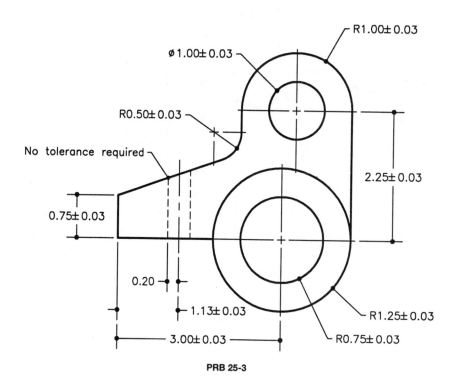

PRB 25-3

Unit 26 Heavy Lines and Solid Objects

Reference

■ OBJECTIVE:

To apply the TRACE, SOLID, and FILL commands

This unit focuses on thick lines and solid objects and how they are produced in drawings such as house elevations.

Note the heavy lines in the following drawing.

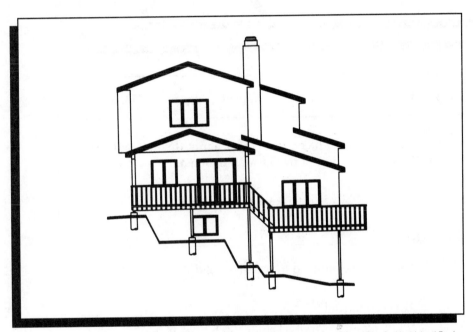

AutoCAD Drawing Courtesy of Tim Smith, Hyland Design

The AutoCAD SOLID and TRACE commands were used to create the thick lines and solid filled areas. Let's draw similar lines and solid objects.

■ *TRACE Command* _____

REF 140
*See also
the optional
Applying
AutoCAD
Diskette*

1 Load AutoCAD and begin a new drawing named **TRACE**. Use PROTO1 to create the drawing.

2 Enter the **TRACE** command.

The TRACE command is used very much like the LINE command, except TRACE requires you to enter a trace width in units.

3 Specify a TRACE width of **4** inches and draw the figures on the next page. Don't worry about exact sizes.

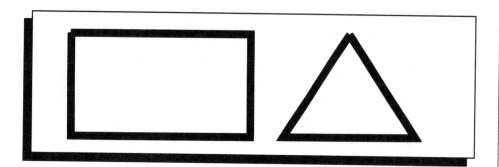

HINT:

To get the last line of the object to appear, just press RETURN.

You'll notice that it is difficult to produce a perfect corner at the first and last points of a polygon. This is the nature of the TRACE command.

4 Practice using TRACE by creating several more objects.

SOLID Command

Now let's work with the SOLID command to produce solid-filled objects.

1 Enter the **SOLID** command.

2 Produce a solid filled object similar to the one below. Pick the points in the exact order shown, and press **RETURN** when you are finished.

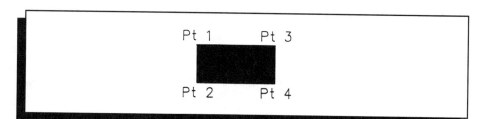

Pt 1   Pt 3

Pt 2   Pt 4

3 Pick a fifth and sixth point.

4 Experiment with the SOLID command. If you pick the points in the wrong order, AutoCAD creates an hourglass-shaped object.

Leave your objects on the screen so you can practice the FILL command.

FILL Command

The FILL command works in conjunction with the TRACE, SOLID, and PLINE commands. You will work with PLINE (which produces polylines) in the following unit. FILL is either on or off. When FILL is off, only the outline of a Trace, Solid, or Polyline is represented. This saves time whenever the screen is redrawn or regenerated.

1 Enter the **FILL** command, and turn it off by entering **OFF**.

──── NOTE: ────

After turning FILL on or off, a regeneration of the screen must occur before the change will take place. . .

2 . . . therefore enter the **REGEN** command.

The objects should no longer be solid-filled.

3 Reenter the **FILL** command and turn it on.

4 Enter **REGEN** to force a screen regeneration.

5 Enter **END** to save the drawing and exit AutoCAD.

1. The FILL command is used in conjunction with both TRACE and SOLID. What is its purpose and how is it used?

   Controls solid fill on or off

2. What might be a limitation of using the TRACE command?

   No perfect corner closing polygons

3. How would you draw a solid-filled triangle using the SOLID command?

   By making point 4 same as 3

4. Can you draw curved objects using the SOLID command?

   No

Problems

1. Construct PRB26-1 using the TRACE and SOLID commands. Specify a TRACE width of 0.05 unit. Don't worry about the exact size and shape of the roof.

PRB 26-1

2. After you have completed PRB26-1, place the solid shapes as indicated below. Don't worry about their exact sizes and locations.

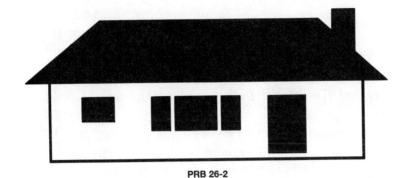

PRB 26-2

3. Are the Trace and Solid entities like the Line, Circle, and Arc entities? To find out, try removing a small piece of the roof. What is your conclusion?

NO THEY ARE 1 PIECE YOU CAN
NOT ERASE ONLY A little

4. Construct the elevation drawing shown on the first page of this unit. You may choose to use a prototype drawing when you begin the drawing.

26 - 4

AUTOCAD® AT WORK

*Mixing CAD and Traditional Tools for Boat Design**

In the CAD industry, success stories are usually accompanied with the claim, "We are totally committed to CAD." Ed Fry of FRYCO, a custom yacht design firm in Houston, Texas, has a surprisingly different approach; FRYCO has automated only what needed to be automated and left the rest of the work to be done on drawing boards. The computer is used for things that cannot be easily accomplished on the boards. Repetitive work such as fairing and framing of the hulls and panels is an example.

Boat design is a balancing act. The hull design is a critical part of the balance because there are two centers of gravity: one stationary and one in flux, and the balance is in water. The difficulties in hull design are compounded when the skin is put on the frames of the boat. If the boat has not been properly faired, the skin will come out wrinkled and the boat will not only lose aesthetic appeal but will also require more horsepower to meet the speed specifications.

Before computers, a boat's hull was laid out on the drawing board and fairing was hand calculated. "That used to take us at least two days," Fry says. If a customer changed his mind about the length, girth, or overall design of a hull designed on the boards, the whole process would start over and most of the previous work would have to be scrapped.

Today FRYCO uses a combination of AutoYacht (from Coast Design) and AutoCAD. AutoYacht is a stand-alone package that includes many of the sophisticated features a boat designer needs, most importantly, the creation of master curves that can be imported into other CAD packages for finishing. The master curves are used to construct the hull to specifications. Some of the other features of AutoYacht include hydrostatic and intact stability analysis, sail plan analysis, spar design, a velocity prediction program, and weight estimating.

Fry transfers the work done in AutoYacht to AutoCAD for further manipulation and plotting. The work from AutoYacht is imported with a simple DXFIN command, and most of the drawing is done full size and scaled when it's plotted out. FRYCO also uses AutoCAD alone to draw mechanical details, electrical schematics, and other mechanical drawings to insure accuracy during construction. The majority of the AutoYacht/AutoCAD output is sent directly to the boat builder as just another page in the set of plans.

While Fry is conservative in the CAD field, he is a pioneer in the boat design field. No matter what the future holds for the rest of the boating industry, FRYCO has a promising future with its carefully blended mix of modern technology and old fashioned design skill.

*Based on a story in CADENCE magazine, Vol. 3, No. 10.

Joining Straight and Curved Objects

■ OBJECTIVE:

To apply Polylines using the PLINE, 3DPOLY and PEDIT commands

This unit deals mostly with Polylines. A Polyline is a connected sequence of line and arc segments. It is treated by AutoCAD as a single entity. Polylines are often used in lieu of conventional lines and arcs because they are more versatile. The examples below illustrate some uses of Polylines.

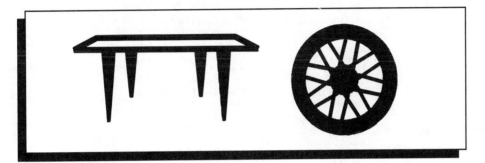

■ *PLINE Command* ———————————

Reference

REF 142-146

Let's create the following Polyline using the PLINE command.

1 Start AutoCAD and begin a new drawing named **POLY**. Do *not* use a custom prototype drawing.

2 Set the snap resolution at **0.5**.

3 Enter **PL**, the PLINE command alias.

HINT: You can also select Polyline from the Draw pull-down menu. Pick the 2D option from the cascading submenu.

4 Pick a point in the left portion of the screen.

You should see the following PLINE options on your screen.

```
Current line-width is 0.0000
Arc/Close/Halfwidth/Length/Undo/Width/<Endpoint of line>:
```

5. Enter **W** (for Width) and enter a starting and ending width of **0.15** unit. Notice that the ending width value defaults to the starting width value.

6. Draw the object by approximating the endpoints, and don't worry about exact sizes. If you make a mistake, enter **U** to undo the segment. Press **RETURN** when you have finished the object.

7. Move the Polyline a short distance.

Notice that the entire object is treated as a single entity.

PEDIT Command _____

REF 237-249

Now let's edit the Polyline using PEDIT.

1. Enter the **PEDIT** command at the keyboard and pick the Polyline.

The Polyline will not highlight as it does during a normal object selection. The following options will appear when you select the Polyline.

```
Close/Join/Width/Edit vertex/Fit/Spline/Decurve/Ltype gen/Undo/eXit <X>:
```

You can also pick PolyEdit from the Modify pull-down menu to obtain the same list of options.

2. Press **RETURN** to exit the PLINE command.

3. Pick **PolyEdit** from the **Modify** pull-down menu and pick the polyline.

The selection caused the polyline to highlight. Also, notice that the list of options did not appear after you selected the object.

4. Press **RETURN** to obtain the list of options.

A similar list of options should appear in the standard screen menu.

	Reference

Let's change the Polyline width.

5 Enter **W** and specify a new width of **0.1** unit.

REF 240

As you can see, PEDIT is useful in changing the width of a series of thick lines.

Now let's close the Polyline as shown on the next page.

6 Enter **C** for Close.

REF 239

AutoCAD will close the object.

Let's do a simple curve fitting operation.

7 Enter the **F** for Fit.

REF 240-241

How did the drawing change?

8 Enter **D** (for Decurve) to return it to its previous form.

REF 243

Next, let's move one of the object's vertices as shown below.

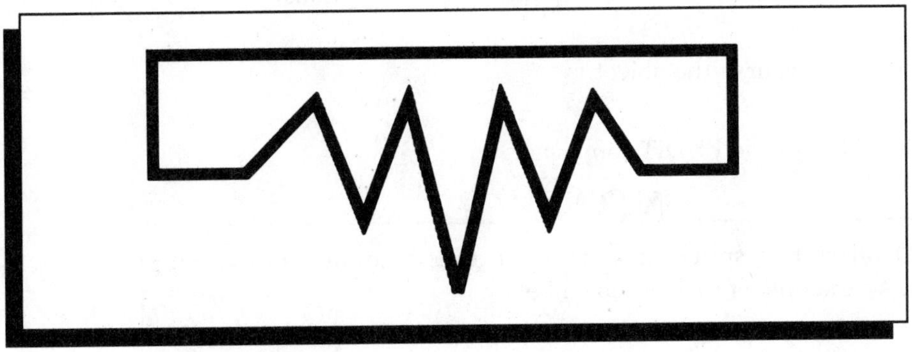

9 Enter **E** for Edit.

REF 240

Notice a new set of choices, shown below, become available. Also notice the "X" in one of the corners of the Polyline.

```
Next/Previous/Break/Insert/Move/Regen/Straighten/Tangent/Width/eXit <N>:
```

10 Move the "X" to the vertex you want to change by pressing **RETURN** several times.

11 Enter **M** for Move and pick a new point for the vertex.

REF 245

Try it again if it did not work.

12 To exit the PEDIT command, enter **X** (short for exit) twice.

REF 244

Note that there are many more editing features contained within PEDIT. Experiment with each of these on your own.

Spline Curves

REF 241-243
TUT 208-209

With AutoCAD, you can create spline curves, also referred to as B-splines.

The PEDIT "Spline" option uses the vertices of the selected Polyline as the control points of the curve. The curve passes through the first and last control points and is "pulled" toward the other points but does not necessarily pass through them. The more control points you specify, the more "pull" they exert on the curve.

1 Enter the **PEDIT** command and select the Polyline.

2 Enter **S** for Spline.

Do you see the difference between the "Spline" and "Fit" options?

3 Enter **D** to decurve the object.

4 Enter **X** to exit the PEDIT command.

___ NOTE: ___

AutoCAD offers two spline options: quadratic B-splines and cubic B-splines. An example of each is shown below.

| Original | Fit Curve | Quadratic B-spline | Cubic B-spline |

The system variable SPLINETYPE controls the type of spline curve to be generated. Set the value of SPLINETYPE at 5 to generate quadratic B-splines. Set its value at 6 to generate cubic B-splines.

REF 242

The PEDIT Decurve option enables you to turn a spline back into its frame, as illustrated in Step 3 above. In addition, you can view both the spline curve and its frame, by setting the system variable SPLFRAME to 1.

	Reference

Breaking Polylines _____

REF 244-245

You can remove small pieces from Polylines using the BREAK command. Let's try it.

1   Enter the **BREAK** command.

2   Pick a point on the Polyline where you'd like the break to begin.

3   Pick a second point a short distance from your first point.

A piece of the Polyline should have disappeared.

4   Undo the break by entering **U**.

Exploding Polylines _____

REF 249-250

The EXPLODE command gives you the ability to break up a Polyline into individual line/arc segments.

1   Enter the **EXPLODE** command.

2   Pick the Polyline and press **RETURN**.

Notice the message "Exploding this polyline has lost width information."

This is the nature of applying **EXPLODE** to a Polyline that contains a width greater than 0. You now have an object that contains numerous entities for easier editing, but you have lost your line thickness. If you need the thickness, you can restore the Polyline using the UNDO command.

3   To illustrate that the object is now made up of numerous entities, edit one of them.

PLINE's Arc Option _____

REF 142, 143-144

In some drafting applications, there is a need to draw a series of continuous arcs to represent, for example, a river on a map. If the line requires thickness, the ARC Continue option will not work. But the PLINE Arc option can handle this task.

1   Enter the **PLINE** command and pick a point in any convenient location on your screen.

2   Enter **A** for Arc.

The following list of options should appear.

```
Angle/CEnter/CLose/Direction/Halfwidth/Line/Radius/Second pt/Undo/Width/
<Endpoint of arc>:
```

3 Move the crosshairs and notice that an arc begins to develop.

4 Enter the **Width** option and enter a starting and ending width of **0.1** unit.

5 Pick a point a short distance from the first point. . .

6 . . . then pick a second point, and a third. . .

7 Press **RETURN** when you're finished.

3DPOLY Command

The 3DPOLY command enables you to create Polylines consisting of x, y, and z vertices. 3D Polylines are made up of straight line segments only and they cannot take on a specified thickness.

You can edit 3D Polylines with the PEDIT command, and you can fit a 3D B-spline curve to the vertices of a 3D Polyline.

1 Enter the **3DPOLY** command or pick **Polyline** and **3D** from the **Draw** pull-down menu.

2 Pick a point.

Notice fewer Polyline options are given.

3 Pick a series of points and press **RETURN** when you are finished.

4 Enter the **PEDIT** command and select the new Polyline.

Here again fewer options are provided.

5 Enter the **Spline** option and enter **X** to exit the command.

The Polyline is now a fully three-dimensional spline curve.

Refer to Units 37-45 to learn about AutoCAD's 3D environment and how you can apply the 3DPOLY command.

6 Enter **END** to save your work and exit AutoCAD.

Questions

1. Briefly define a Polyline.

   CONNECTED LINES & ARC TREATED AS 1

2. Briefly describe each of the following PLINE options.

   Arc *SWITCHES PLINE to ARC MODE*

   Close *DRAWS LINE FROM LAST to START*

   Halfwidth *WIDTH FROM CENTER to EDGE*

   Length *DRAWS SAME ANGLE but YOU tell LENGTH*

   Undo *REMOVES MOST RECENT ITEM*

   Width *YOU tell HOW WIDE*

3. Briefly describe each of the PEDIT command options.

   Close *JOINS LAST AND FIRST*

   Join *WILL ADD TOUCHING items to PLINE*

   Width *CHANGES WIDTH*

   Edit vertex *MOVE LOCATIONS ON VERTEX'S*

   Fit *PUTS CURVES ON ITEM*

   Spline *USES VERTEX FOR CURVES*

   Decurve *TAKES CURVES OUT*

   Ltype gen *TOGGLE FOR CONTINUOUS PATTERN OR DASHED*

   Undo *REMOVES 1 EDIT FUNCTION*

   eXit *EXITS P EDIT COMAND*

4. Describe one application for the PLINE Arc option.

   DRAW HIGHWAYS

5. Of what importance is the EXPLODE command to Polylines?

   LETS YOU BREAK PLINE INTO SEGMENTS

6. What effect does EXPLODE have on Polylines that contain a width?

   YOU LOSE WIDTH INFO

7. Is it possible to remove a small piece (smaller than an entity) of a Polyline? Explain.

   YES WITH BREAK

8. Describe the system variable SPLINETYPE.

   YOU CONTROL B-SPLINE CURVE to BE MADE

1. Create the approximate shape of the following racetrack using PLINE. Specify 0.4 unit for both the starting and ending widths. Select the Arc option for drawing the figure.

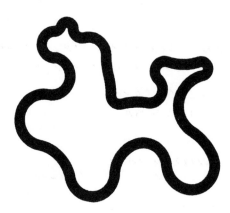

PRB 27-1

2-6. Draw each of the following objects using the PLINE and PEDIT commands.

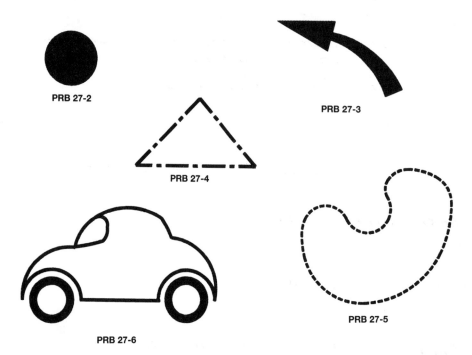

PRB 27-2

PRB 27-3

PRB 27-4

PRB 27-5

PRB 27-6

AUTOCAD® AT WORK

AutoCAD, the Ultimate Furniture Mover

As might be expected, AutoCAD makes room design easier. Moving a chair or even a wall here or there and then printing the different results helps designers plan the most efficient use of space. However, what about really *big* areas? What about a facility comprising a *million square feet*?

Well, for big areas, AutoCAD is almost indispensable. The Indiana Convention Center and Hoosier Dome in Indianapolis makes available to its clients one million square feet of exhibit space, banquet halls, ballrooms, and meeting rooms. The center uses AutoCAD to make floor plans for upcoming events. The plans show seating arrangements, stage and riser locations, rows of booths, even positions of indoor tracks and basketball courts.

Every meeting room, convention hall, ballroom, and even the 61,000-seat Hoosier Dome is stored in the computer as a Block and appears on a customized screen menu. Another customized menu lists the different sizes of stages, risers, curtains, podiums, chairs, and tables used. Many of the Blocks are drawn as generic rectangles so that a Block representing a stage, for instance, might also be used to represent a dance floor. More specialized items, such as pianos, are included on the tablet menu.

Working from specifications set by clients, the Center's event coordinators start with a room from the screen menu and insert major features needed, such as a dance floor or basketball courts. Then, the coordinator adds any standard seating arrangements, such as bleacher sections, that are of a uniform size. If rows of tables or seating are required, the coordinator inserts one item of that type from the existing Block, then uses the ARRAY command to generate the required number of units. Afterwards, the arrays can be moved, in whole or in part, allowing for staggered table arrangements or aisles between seating sections. An array can be copied or mirrored to avoid doing the same array over and over. Notes, arrows, and other details, such as distance between sections of seats, are then added. The floor plan is then ready for the plotter.

One of the major benefits of using AutoCAD to plan events is that many events are rescheduled year after year. Only minor changes need to be made to the previous year's diagram, saving hours of planning time.

Some of the events that have been planned using Auto-CAD include the 1987 Pan American Games, Indiana's Black Expo, Indianapolis Colts football, the Rolling Stones' Steel Wheels concert tour, Farm Aid IV, NCAA Indoor Track and Field Championships, and in 1991, the NCAA Basketball "Final Four" Championships.

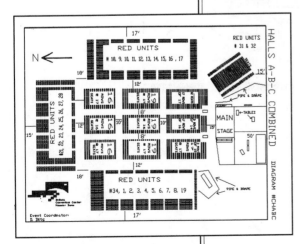

Unit 28 A Calculating Strategy

■ OBJECTIVE:

To apply the ID, DIST, AREA, LIST, DBLIST, DIVIDE, SETVAR, and MEASURE commands

This unit focuses on the commands that allow you to perform a variety of calculations on your drawings. In addition, it covers the AutoCAD commands that reveal hidden (but important) data about specific components within your drawing.

The drawing below shows an apartment complex with parking lots, streets, and trees. It is possible to perform certain calculations on the drawing, such as determining the square footage of the parking lot or the distance between the parking stalls.

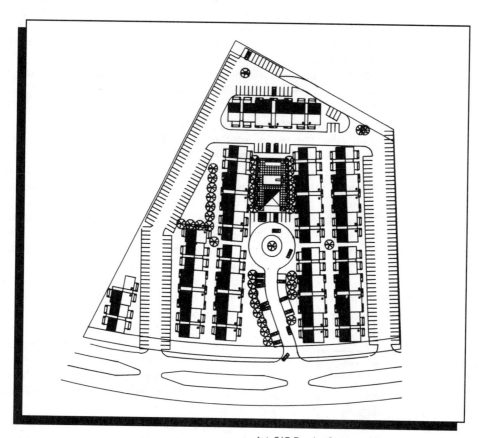

AutoCAD Drawing Courtesy of Buday-Wells, Architects

Let's bring up AutoCAD and practice these functions.

242

ID and DIST Commands

1 Load AutoCAD and begin a new drawing named **CALC**.

2 Draw a rectangle (Polyline) with a circle around it at the sizes shown below. Omit the numbers and dimensions, and don't worry about the exact placement of the circle in relation to the polyline.

See also the optional Applying AutoCAD Diskette

HINT: Set your snap resolution at 0.25 before drawing the object, and use the coordinate display as you construct it.

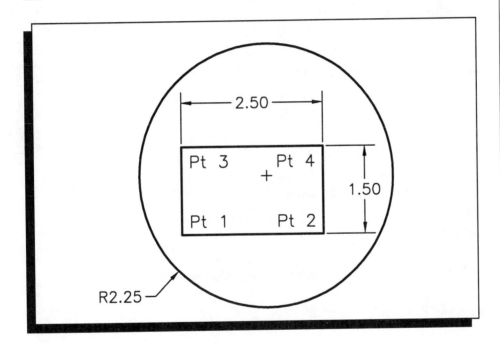

Now we're ready to perform a few simple calculations. First, let's find the absolute coordinates of point 1.

3 Enter the **ID** command and pick point 1. (ID stands for "identify.")

REF 258

HINT: Use the object snap feature to obtain accurate locations (unless your points are located on your snap resolution and Snap is on).

The absolute coordinates of point 1 should appear.

4 Try it again with point **2**.

The DIST command allows you to calculate the distance between two points.

5 Enter **DIST** and pick points 1 and 4.

REF 258

In addition to the distance, what other information does DIST produce?

AREA Command

REF 259-261

Use the AREA command to calculate the area of circles and polygons.

1 Enter **AREA** and **E** for Entity.

REF 259-260

2 Pick the rectangle.

The area of the rectangle is 3.75 square units; the perimeter is 8 units.

The AREA command will also calculate areas with holes. Suppose we want to know the area of the circle minus the rectangle.

3 Reenter **AREA** and enter **A** for "Add."

REF 260

4 Enter **E** for Entity and pick the circle.

AutoCAD will display the area (15.9 square units) and the circumference (14.14 units) of the circle.

5 In reply to "(ADD mode) Select circle or polyline:" press **RETURN**.

6 Enter **S** for "Subtract."

7 Enter **E** for "Entity" and pick the polyline (rectangle).

AutoCAD will subtract the area of the rectangle from the area of the circle and display the result (12.15 square units).

CAL Command

EXTR 104-123

AutoCAD offers an on-line geometry calculator that evaluates vector, real, and integer expressions.

1 Enter **CAL**.

2 Enter (3*2)+(10/5).

EXTR 105-106

AutoCAD should calculate the answer as 8.

CAL also recognizes object snap modes and you can use the command transparently.

EXTR 104

③ Enter **PL**.

④ Enter **'CAL**. (Note the leading apostrophe.)

⑤ Enter **(cen + end)/2**.

⑥ Pick any point on the circle.

⑦ Pick either line near point 1.

AutoCAD calculated the midpoint between the circle's center and point 1.

⑧ Press **RETURN** to terminate the PLINE command.

LIST and DBLIST Commands

These commands display database information on selected entities.

① Enter the **LIST** command, pick any point on the circle, and press **RETURN**.

REF 256-257

The entity type, layer, space center point, radius, circumference, and area should appear. You will learn more about AutoCAD's model space and paper space in Unit 47.

② Enter **LIST** again, but this time pick the rectangle.

What information did you receive?

③ Last, enter **DBLIST** and watch what you get.

REF 258

You should receive information on all entities in the drawing database.

DIVIDE Command

REF 235-236

The DIVIDE command is used to divide an entity into a specified number of equal parts.

① Enter the **DIVIDE** command.

② Select any point on the circle.

③ In reply to "<Number of segments>/Block:," enter **20**.

It may appear as though nothing happened. Something did happen: the DIVIDE command divided the circle into 20 equal parts using 20 point entities; you just can't see them. Here's how to use them.

4 Enter the **LINE** command.

5 Enter the **NOD**e object snap mode. (Node is used to snap to the nearest point entity.)

6 Pick any place on the circle.

AutoCAD should snap to the nearest of the 20 point entities. If it doesn't, move your pointing device slightly and try again. Make sure Ortho is off.

7 Snap to the center of the circle using the object snap mode **CEN**ter. (Remember, you have to pick a point on the circle.)

8 Enter the **NOD**e mode again and snap to another point entity on the circle.

You should now have an object that looks similar to the following.

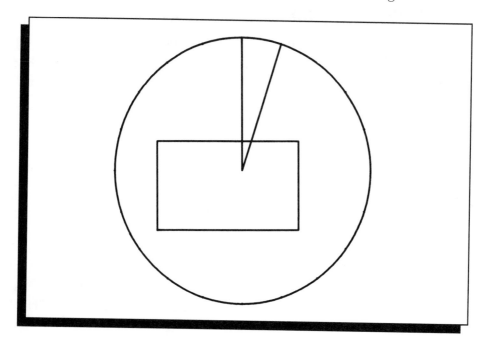

9 Press **RETURN** to terminate the LINE command.

Reference

REF 113-114

Making the Points Visible with SETVAR

SETVAR, short for "set system variables," allows you to change a number of pre-established modes, sizes, and limits. One of the variables, called PDMODE, is used to control the appearance of point entities. Let's use the SETVAR command and PDMODE to make the points on our circle visible.

1. Enter the **SETVAR** command.

2. Enter **?** and press **RETURN** to obtain a listing of all the system variables and to look for the PDMODE.

As you can see, the dimensioning variables are a part of the system variables. What is the value of PDMODE?

3. Enter **SETVAR** again, and then enter **PDMODE**.

HINT: You can enter system variables, such as PDMODE, directly at the "Command:" prompt without first entering SETVAR.

4. Enter **32** for the new value, and enter the **REGEN** command.

Did 20 equally spaced circles appear on the circle as shown on the next illustration?

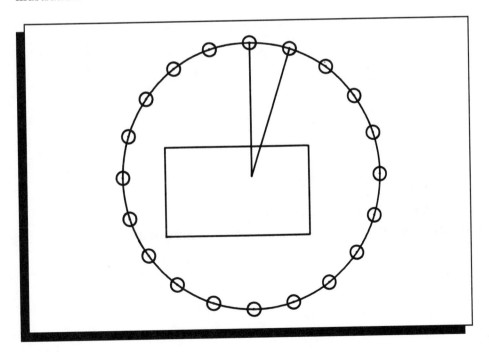

The following list and the illustration show how other values control the appearance of point entities.

Value	Draws
0	a dot at the point (default setting)
1	nothing
2	a cross through the point (like a "blip")
3	an X through the point
4	a vertical line upward from the point

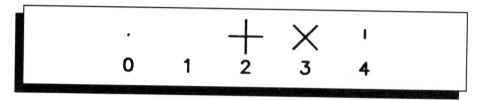

To each of the values shown above, you can add 32, 64, or 96 to select a figure to be drawn around the point in addition to the figure drawn through it, as shown on the next illustration. For example, 2 + 32 = 34, and 34 represents a cross with a circle on it.

Value	Draws
32	a circle around the point
64	a square around the point
96	both a circle and a square

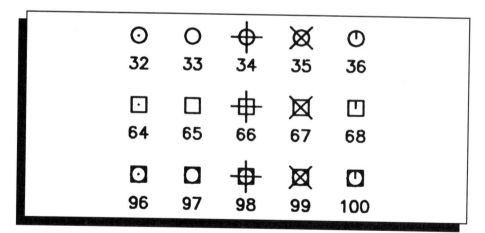

5 Experiment with several of these values, and remember to regenerate the screen each time.

MEASURE Command

The MEASURE command is similar to DIVIDE except that MEASURE does not divide the entity into a given number of equal parts like DIVIDE. Instead, MEASURE allows you to place markers along the object at specified intervals.

1 Enter the **MEASURE** command and select one of the two lines.

2 In reply to "<Segment length>/Block:" enter **0.4** unit.

AutoCAD should space point entities 0.4 unit apart.

3 Further experiment with MEASURE.

4 When you're finished, enter **END** to save your work and exit AutoCAD.

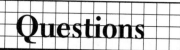

Questions

1. What AutoCAD command is used to find coordinate points?

   ID

2. What information is produced with the AREA command?

   SQ units

3. What information is produced with the LIST command?

   LAYER, RADIUS, CIRCUM, AREA ETC

4. Describe the difference between LIST and DBLIST.

   LIST is FOR 1 ENTITY
   DBLIST is FOR ALL

5. How do you calculate the perimeter of a polygon?

   WITH AREA CMND

6. How do you find the circumference of a circle?

   WITH LIST CMND

7. Explain the difference between the DIVIDE and MEASURE commands.

   MEASURE PLACES MARKERS AT INTERVALS
   DIVIDE SEPERATES INTO INDIV PARTS

8. Explain how you control the appearance of point entities.

   TYPE IN PD MODE THEN
   POINT STYLE

Problems

Draw the objects found in the following problems at any convenient size, omitting all letters. Then perform the inquiry commands listed above the objects. Write their values in the blanks provided.

If you have the optional *Applying AutoCAD* Diskette, refer to files PRB28-1.DWG, PRB28-2.DWG, and PRB28-3.DWG.

1. ID of point A? _X=0'-3¼"   Y=0'-2¾"   Z=0'-0"_

    DIST between points A and B? _Y=1-3/8"_

    AREA of the polygon? _Not Circle or 2D/3D Polyline_ 2.18 Sq in

    Perimeter of the polygon? _8 3/4"_

PRB 28-1

2. DIST between A and B? _X= 1-¼"   Y= 3/4"   Z=0"_

    DIST between B and C? _Y=1¼4"_

    AREA of circle? _1.13 Sq in_

    Circumference of circle? _3 3/4" Circ_

    AREA of polygon? _5 Sq in._

    Perimeter of polygon? _8 5/16"_

    Area of polygon minus the circle? _3.87 Sq in_

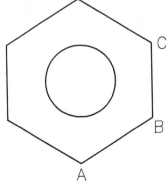

PRB 28-2

3. LIST information on arc A?

LAYER   OBJ2   SPACE   MODEL SPACE

CEN X= 4 3/8" Y = 3/2"   RADIUS 1"

START ANGLE   30

END ANGLE   150

LIST information on line B?

LAY = OBJ2   SPACE : MODEL

FROM X= 3 1/2" Y= 4"   Z= 0"

to   X= 3 1/2" Y= 2 1/4" Z= 0"

LENGth = 1 3/4" ANGle XY PLANE = 270

DELTA X= 0"   Y= 1 3/4" Z= 0"

DBLIST information for entire screen?

TO MUCH to RECORD HERE

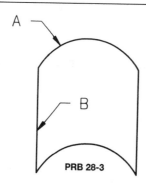

PRB 28-3

4. On the above object, divide line B into 5 equal parts. Make the point
   entities visible.

5. On arc A above, place markers along the arc at intervals of 0.25 unit. If the
   markers are invisible, make them visible.

Unit 29 Building Blocks

■ OBJECTIVE:

To apply the BLOCK, INSERT, MINSERT, EXPLODE, RENAME, DDRENAME, PURGE, DDINSERT, and WBLOCK commands

If CAD systems are managed properly, their users should never have to draw the same objects twice. This is a primary reason why CAD is beneficial. Success, however, depends on the techniques by which the drawings are created, stored, documented, and retrieved.

This unit focuses on the commands that enable you to create, store, and reuse the symbols, drawings, and details that you need repeatedly.

■ *BLOCK Command* _____

REF 377-382

The BLOCK command allows you to combine several entities into one, store it, and retrieve it at a later time. Let's work with the BLOCK command.

1 Start AutoCAD and begin a new drawing named **BLKS**.

2 Obtain help on the BLOCK command.

Now that you know what a Block is, let's create one.

3 On layer 0, draw the following object using the **LINE** and **CIRCLE** commands. Approximate its size, but make it small.

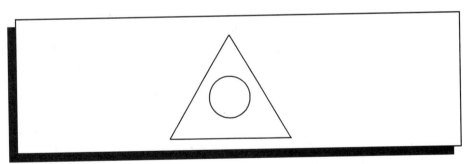

4 Enter the **BLOCK** command.

5 Create the Block based on the following information.

    — Name the Block **MENTAL**.
    — Specify the lower left corner of the object as the insertion base
      point.
    — Select all four entities.
    — Press **RETURN**.

After completing the above, the object should disappear. If it did, then you have successfully created a Block.

Your MENTAL Block is now stored in the current drawing file for subsequent insertion.

————————— **NOTE:** —————————
| You can enter OOPS to make the individual entities reappear. |

INSERT Command

REF 382, 386-390

Let's insert the Block.

1 Enter the **INSERT** command and specify the Block name **MENTAL**.

It should appear on the screen.

2 Insert the MENTAL Block using the following information.

— Insert near the lower left corner of your screen.
— Specify the scale at **0.75** on both the X and Y axes.
— Rotate the Block 45 degrees counterclockwise by entering **45**.

It should appear in the position you indicated. If it didn't, try again.

3 Attempt to erase the circle from the Block.

The entire object, including the circle, is now treated as a single element called a Block, so you cannot erase or edit any single element within it.

4 If you completed the ERASE command, enter **OOPS** to recover the object.

In the future, you may want to edit a Block.

1 Enter **INSERT** once again.

2 This time, when typing the Block name, place an asterisk (*) before it: ***MENTAL**.

3 Step through the entire INSERT command and enter whatever scale and rotation factor you wish.

4 After it appears on the screen, try to erase the circle from the Block.

Did it work? What can you conclude about the * option?

MINSERT Command

REF 392-393

MINSERT, short for Multiple Insert, allows you to insert a rectangular array of Blocks. The MINSERT command is sort of a combination of the INSERT and ARRAY commands. Let's apply it.

1 Enter **MINSERT** and then enter **MENTAL**.

2 For the insertion point, pick an open space near the lower left corner of the screen.

3 Enter **0.25** for both the X and Y scale factors and **0** for the rotation angle.

4 In reply to "Number of rows," enter **3**, and enter **5** for the "Number of columns."

5 Enter **1** for the distance between rows and **1** for the distance between columns.

Fifteen MENTAL Blocks should appear on the screen.

Reviewing Block Names

After creating several Blocks, it's easy to forget their names. This is especially true when you edit the drawing file weeks after you have created the Blocks.

1 Enter the **INSERT** command.

2 Type **?** and press **RETURN** twice.

NOTE:

You can also obtain a listing of Blocks by entering the BLOCK command and entering ? in response to "Block name (or ?):".

Exploding Blocks

REF 249-250

Often, you will insert Blocks without the "*" option because you want to manipulate those Blocks as a single element. Examples are doors and windows in a house elevation drawing or components on an electrical schematic.

1 Insert the **MENTAL** Block without the "*" option.

Reference

2. Enter the **EXPLODE** command, pick any point on the Block, and press **RETURN**.

The EXPLODE command reverses the effect of the BLOCK command. The object is no longer a Block entity.

RENAME Command

REF 120-121

The RENAME command lets you rename previously created Blocks. Let's do one.

1. Enter the **RENAME** command.

You should receive the following on the screen.

```
Block/Dimstyle/LAyer/LType/Style/Ucs/VIew/VPort:
```

NOTE:

> As you can see by the list, RENAME can be used to rename not only Blocks, but also dimension styles, Layers, linetypes, Text styles, User Coordinate Systems, Views, and viewports.

2. Select **B**lock from the list of options.
3. In reply to "Old block name:" enter **MENTAL**.
4. Enter **SQUARE** for the new Block name.
5. Enter **INSERT** and ? to obtain a listing of Blocks.

Rename Dialogue Box

REF 119-120

Let's rename the Block back to MENTAL.

1. Enter **DDRENAME**.

The Rename dialogue box should appear, similar to the one in the following illustration.

2. Pick **Block** in the "Named Objects" list box and pick **SQUARE** in the "Items" list box.

SQUARE should now appear in the "Old Name" edit box.

③ Pick the edit box to the right of the "Rename To" button and type **MENTAL**.

④ Pick the **Rename To** button, as shown in the following illustration, to perform the rename.

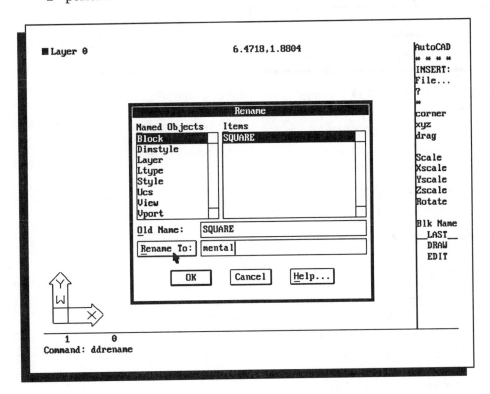

```
■ Layer 0                    6.4718,1.8804           AutoCAD
                                                     * * *
                                                     INSERT:
                                                     File...
                                                     ?
                                                     *
                              Rename                  corner
     Named Objects    Items                          xyz
     Block            SQUARE                          drag
     Dimstyle
     Layer                                           Scale
     Ltype                                           Xscale
     Style                                           Yscale
     Ucs                                             Zscale
     View                                            Rotate
     Vport
                                                     Blk Name
     Old Name:     SQUARE                             _LAST_
                                                       DRAW
     Rename To:    mental                              EDIT

          [  OK  ]   [ Cancel ]   [ Help... ]

    1        0
Command: ddrename
```

AutoCAD should have renamed SQUARE to MENTAL in the "Items" list box.

⑤ Pick the **OK** button.

PURGE Command

REF 121-123

The PURGE command enables you to selectively delete any unused, named objects, including Blocks. Named objects may be purged as long as the purge is the first operation you perform after you open the drawing.

① Enter the **PURGE** command.

② If you receive the message "The PURGE command cannot be used now," enter **QSAVE** to save your work.

③ Open the same **BLKS** drawing file.

④ Enter the **PURGE** command.

The following should appear.

```
Purge unused Blocks/Dimstyles/LAyers/LTypes/SHapes/STyles/All:
```

---

⑤ Select one type of object to purge or reply **All** to purge all named object types.

If you have any unused objects of the specified type, AutoCAD prompts you with the name of each object and asks whether you want to purge it.

Inserting Drawing Files _____

REF 384-386

You can also insert drawing files into your existing drawing using the INSERT and DDINSERT commands.

① Enter **INSERT**.

In addition to inserting Blocks at this point, AutoCAD permits you to enter a drawing file name, if you know the name of the file and its location. File and directory names are often difficult to remember and they're cumbersome to enter. AutoCAD, therefore, offers an alternative.

② Press **CTRL C** to cancel the INSERT command.

③ Enter **DDINSERT** or select **Insert...** from the **Draw** pull-down menu.

The Insert dialogue box should appear as shown in the following illustration.

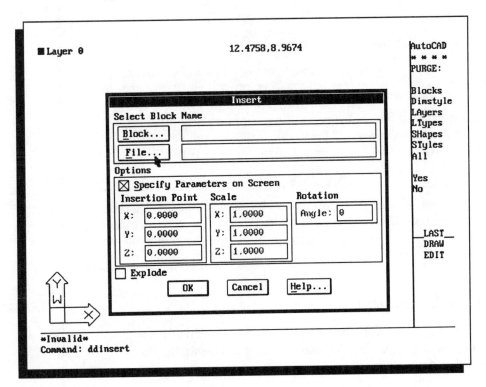

4 Pick the **Block...** button.

This selection causes a subdialogue box to appear with a list of the Blocks available for insertion in the current drawing. Let's not insert a Block at this time.

5 Pick the **Cancel** button.

6 Pick the **File...** button and locate a drawing, such as CALC, to insert.

7 After selecting the drawing, pick **OK**.

Notice that the "Specify Parameters on Screen" check box is checked. If you were to leave it checked, AutoCAD would require you to enter the insertion point and the scale and rotation values at the "Command:" prompt.

8 Pick the **Specify Parameters on Screen** check box so it is no longer checked.

⑨ Change the x, y, and z scale values to **0.5** and the rotation value to **10**.

⑩ Pick the **Explode** check box and pick **OK**.

Checking Explode has the same effect as exploding a Block after inserting it.

If this procedure did not work, try it again with another drawing file.

So you see, any drawing file contained on the computer's disk drive can be inserted into the current drawing. This enables you to combine any of your drawings and create highly sophisticated drawings in a short time.

NOTE:

The BASE command may be useful for establishing a drawing insertion base point other than 0,0 (which is the default). For instance, if your current drawing is of a part that you expect to insert into other drawings, you can specify the base point for such insertions using the BASE command.

REF 391

WBLOCK Command

REF 393-394

You understand that all drawing files are accessible for insertion in any drawing. But what about Blocks? Is there a method of making the Block(s) available to other drawings?

① Enter **WBLOCK**.

The Create Drawing File dialogue box should appear.

② Enter **MENT** for the file name and pick **OK**.

③ Enter **MENTAL** for the Block name.

Note the light on the computer's disk drive as you complete the command. The computer created a new file called MENT with the contents of MENTAL.

Let's review the MENT.DWG file.

④ Enter the **FILES** command and list all drawing files.

You should see MENT.

Now that the MENTAL Block is in a drawing file format, you can insert it into any other drawing file. If you keep track of it, you'll never need to draw it again.

⑤ For practice, create another Block and store it as a drawing file using WBLOCK.

NOTE:

The * option, when used with the WBLOCK command, creates a new drawing file of the current drawing, similarly to the SAVE command. However, any unreferenced Block definitions, layers, linetypes, text styles, and dimension styles are not written. Consider the following.

Command: WBLOCK

File Name: BK

Block Name: *

⑥ When you're finished, enter **END** to save your work and exit AutoCAD.

AUTOCAD® AT WORK

Landscaping with AutoCAD

For 150 years, a typical landscape designer's work tools—a drafting table, pen and pencil, paper, and templates—remained virtually the same. But the introduction of CAD changed the profession. Nowadays landscape architects who don't use CAD are at a serious disadvantage. Layouts that traditionally took two days to prepare by hand can now be completed by CAD in a few hours.

Landscape architecture focuses on everything above the ground and outside a building, including vegetation, fountains, sculptures, and roads. In working with their clients, landscape architects must draw up detailed plans that can be adapted quickly and easily, and the special features of CAD programs such as AutoCAD complement the professional nicely.

By using the layering feature, the architect can plot buildings, roads, boundaries, irrigation systems, and recreation areas on separate layers. Or the architect can combine any of the layers to use for presentations to clients or for construction plans for engineers and work crews.

AutoCAD's symbol library capability is especially useful. It can be utilized to store symbols, such as a tree, and data about materials and costs. Use of symbols increases drawing speed, and the data can be used to generate reports.

By using a telecommunications link, a landscape architect in one city and a client in another can view a proposed drawing and make immediate modifications. Also, the architect can exchange information with other professionals working on the project, and field personnel—such as surveyors—can make on-site suggestions.

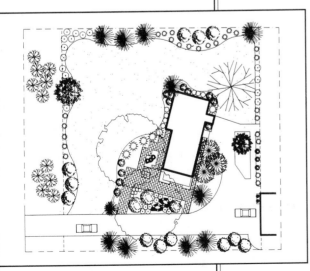

Courtesy of Mill Brothers Landscape and Nursery, Inc.

Questions

1. Briefly describe the purpose of Blocks.

   YOU CAN MAKE ITEM & STORE THEM AS ONE AND INSERT INTO DRAWING

2. Explain how the INSERT command is used.

   YOU INSERT BLOCKS & SCALE/ROTATE AS NEEDED

3. How can you list all defined Blocks contained within a drawing file?

   BY TYPING ? OPTION

4. A Block can be inserted with or without an asterisk preceding the name. Describe the difference between the two.

   WITH * YOU CAN EDIT
   WITHOUT YOU NEED TO EXPLODE TO EDIT

5. Explain how WBLOCK works.

   CHANGES it TO A DRAWING FILE ON DISK WITH FILE NAM

6. When would WBLOCK be useful?

   TO PUT IN ITEM YOU HAVE DRAWN IN OTHER DRAWINGS

7. What is "exploding a Block," and what is its purpose?

   TURNS ITEM INTO SEPERATE ENTITIES FOR EDITING

8. How are Blocks renamed?

   RENAME w/ BLOCK OPTION

9. Explain the function of the MINSERT command.

   INSERTS MULTIPLE COPIES IN RECT PATTERN

10. Explain the PURGE command.

    REMOVES UNUSED BLOCKS, LTYPES, LAYERS ETC.

Problems

1. Begin a new drawing named LIVROOM. Draw the furniture representations and store each as a separate Block. Then draw the living room outline. Don't worry about exact sizes or locations, and omit the text. Insert each piece of furniture into the living room at the appropriate size and rotation angle. Feel free to create additional furniture and to use each piece of furniture more than once.

   If you have the optional *Applying AutoCAD* Diskette, refer to LIVROOM.DWG.

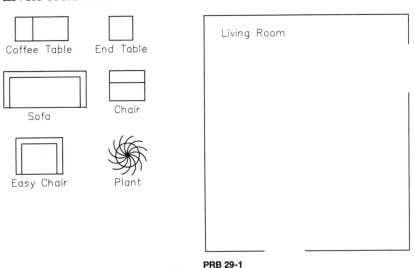

PRB 29-1

2. After creating the Blocks, write two of them (of your choice) to disk using WBLOCK.

3. Using MINSERT, create a lecture room full of chairs arranged in a rectangular pattern.

4. Explode the PLANT Block and erase every fourth arc contained in it. Then store the PLANT again as a Block.

5. Rename two of your furniture Blocks.

6. Purge unused objects.

AUTOCAD® AT WORK

Computer-Aided Drafting at John Wood

John Wood Community College's building was not originally designed to house a community college. It was built to house an "Individually Paced Learning" environment for grade-school students. When this environment was no longer needed due to a changing local population, the building was vacated. Since the college needed a permanent location, the college purchased the building from the school district.

As a grade school, the building was designed into separate areas, or pods, as they are called. There was a central pod and four other pods located around the periphery of the center area. To add to this confusion, additional classrooms, in other buildings, have been added as the college has grown.

As you might imagine, room locations and directions within the building are a nightmare for new students and visitors from our community. The simplest solution was to furnish a layout of the building to provide directions, coordinate internal space allocations, and so on. The CAD department developed the new layout using AutoSketch (V2.0).

Before the new layout was developed, the college handed out a hand-sketched layout of the building to help people find their way around the building. When we realized the potential of the AutoSketch layout, we loaded the file into AutoCAD using the "DXF OUT" feature of AutoSketch and the "DXF IN" feature of AutoCAD.

Once the drawing was loaded into AutoCAD, a CAD student enhanced the drawing to show not only the room locations, but also locations of various departments and services, such as Student Services, Financial Aid, Instructional Services, the cafeteria, and so on. As departments were added to the drawing, the need for "outbuildings" on campus also became evident. As the buildings were added, the drawing was updated to reflect the current campus configuration. Other changes have been required because of new government regulations and laws, but these changes, too, are easily accomplished using AutoCAD.

By now, the building layout drawing has been changed many times by both students and the instructor to keep it current. Some of the changes and additions have enabled us to use it as a handout to first-time users of the building as well as an "Emergency Shelter" indicator and a chemical storage areas locator.

We accomplished many of these changes using AutoCAD Release 10. However, we are now using Release 11, and we hope to incorporate Release 12 in the near future.

This story was contributed by Jerry Hagmeier. Mr. Hagmeier is currently the CAD Coordinator/Instructor at John Wood Community College. Previously, he spent 25 years working in industry.

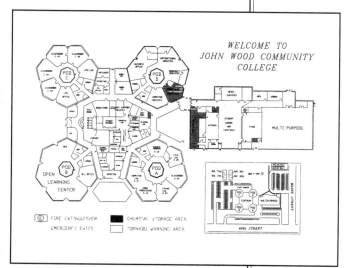

Unit 30 Symbol Library Creation

Reference

See also
the optional
Applying
AutoCAD
Diskette.

■ OBJECTIVE:

To create and use a library of symbols and details

The purpose of this unit is to create a group of symbols and details and to store them in a library. The library will then be applied in a new drawing.

The following is a collection of electrical substation schematic symbols contained within an AutoCAD drawing file that was named LIBRARY1. Each of the symbols was stored as a single Block and given a Block name. (In this particular case, numbers were used for Block names rather than words.) The crosses, which show the Blocks' insertion base points, and the numbers were drawn on a separate layer and frozen when the Blocks were created. They are not part of the Blocks; they are used for reference and retrieval purposes only.

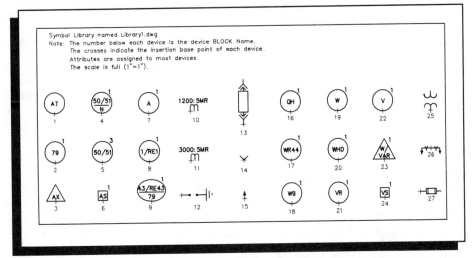

Courtesy of City of Fort Collins, Light & Power Utility

After the symbols were developed and stored in LIBRARY1, the LIBRARY1 file was inserted into a new drawing for creation of the electrical schematic shown on the following page.

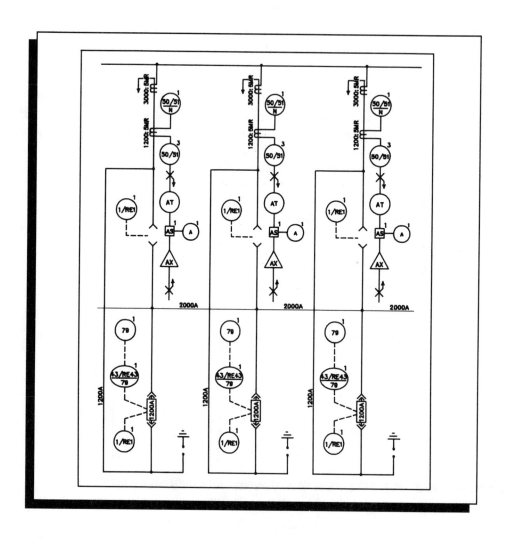

The Blocks were inserted into the new drawing along with other LIBRARY1 elements. They were then inserted into their proper locations, and lines were used to connect them. Hence, approximately 80 percent of the work was completed before the drawing was started. This is the primary advantage of grouping Blocks in symbol libraries.

Creating a Library _____

Let's step through a simple version of the procedures just described.

1 Start AutoCAD and begin a new drawing named **LIB1** (short for LIBRARY1).

NOTE:

As described in earlier units, you should use a prototype drawing to save time when creating a new drawing. But for the purpose of this exercise, do not specify a prototype drawing since you have not created one specifically for this application.

2 Create the following simplified representations of tools. Construct each relatively small on layer 0, and omit the text.

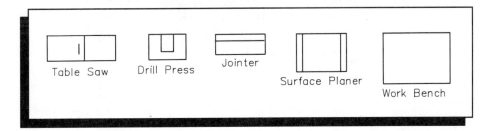

3 Create a new layer called **TEXT**, and make this the current layer.

4 On the layer named TEXT, create the reference information (*i.e.*, Block names and insertion base points) shown below. Do this now even though the Block names and insertion points technically do not yet exist.

HINT:

Create a small cross (+) and store it as a Block. Make the center of the cross its insertion point. Insert the cross at each of the components' insertion points as indicated below. Use the INSERT command instead of DDINSERT to insert the crosses. For this job, it is faster.

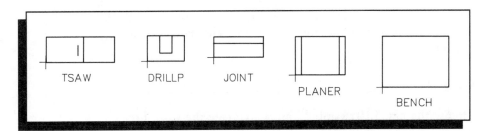

5 After you have placed the crosses and text on the layer called TEXT, make layer 0 the current layer and freeze layer TEXT.

The Block names and crosses (insertion points) should have disappeared.

6 Store each of the tool representations as a Block using the same Block names and insertion points you used earlier.

NOTE:

A Block can be made up of entities from different layers, with different colors and linetypes. The layer, color, and linetype information of each entity is preserved in the Block. When the Block is inserted, each entity is drawn on its original layer, with its original color and linetype, no matter what the *current* drawing layer, entity color, and entity linetype are.

A Block created on layer 0 and inserted onto another layer will inherit the color and linetype of the layer on which it is inserted and will reside on this layer. This is why it was important to create the tools on layer 0. Other options exist, but they can cause confusion. Therefore Block creation on layer 0 is generally recommended if you want the Block to take on the characteristics of the layer on which it was inserted.

The screen should now be empty.

7 Thaw the layer called TEXT.

The Block names and crosses (insertion points) should have reappeared.

8 To restore each of the tools, insert the Blocks into their exact locations according to their insertion points.

HINT:

Use DDINSERT. For this job, it is faster.

9 Assign color number 1 (red) to layer 0 and color number 2 (yellow) to layer TEXT.

10 Enter **QSAVE** to save your work.

Your symbol library is now complete.

11 If you know how to plot drawings, plot LIB1. You could use a thick line for color 1 and a thin line for color 2. Save the hard copy for future reference.

Using the Library

We're going to use the new LIB1 symbol library to create the workshop drawing on the following page.

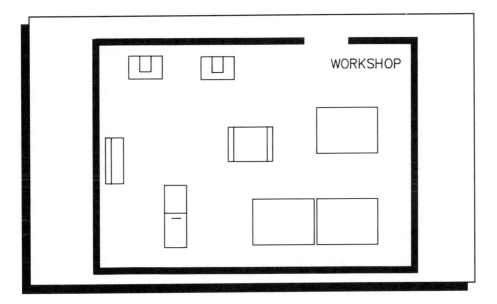

1   Begin a new drawing named **WORKSHOP**.

2   Using **PLINE**, create the outline of the workshop as shown above. Make the starting and ending width **0.1** unit, and make the workshop outline large enough to fill most of your screen.

Let's load and use the symbol library named LIB1.

3   Enter the **DDINSERT** command and pick the **File...** button.

4   Find and select the drawing file named **LIB1**.

5   Pick **OK**; pick **OK** again, but then stop.

6   IMPORTANT: When AutoCAD asks for the insertion point, cancel (press **CTRL C**). Continue, and you'll see why.

7   Enter the **DDINSERT** command again and look at the list of Blocks.

All Blocks from LIB1 should be present.

So now you see why we inserted LIB1 and why we canceled the insertion before LIB1 was drawn on the screen. What we wanted from LIB1 were the Block definitions contained in LIB1, not the graphics themselves. Now that the Block definitions are present in the current drawing (WORKSHOP), we can insert each as we wish.

Insert each of the symbols in an arrangement similar to the one in the drawing shown on the preceding page. Rotate each as necessary.

Because you had access to a previously created symbol library, you have just created a drawing in a fraction of the time it would otherwise have taken. Now that you know how to do it, the next time will be even faster.

HINT:

It is good practice to add to the library file continuously by storing new symbols, shapes, and details in it. Plot the library file and place it in a notebook or on the wall near the CAD system. Eventually, you will want to create new libraries for other specialized applications.

⑨ Enter **END** to save your work and exit AutoCAD.

NOTE:

If you are using AutoCAD's tablet menu, notice the empty portion at the top of the overlay. This area is available for items such as your library of symbols. Unit 52 will discuss the steps involved in adding new menu items to this area of the tablet menu.

Questions

1. What is the primary purpose of creating a library of symbols and details?

   So you Don't DRAW SAME thing OVER

2. When creating a library, what layer is recommended for creating and storing the Blocks? Why?

   LAYER Ø BECAUSE they CAN BE PUt ON other LAYERS

3. In the symbol libraries discussed in this unit, Block names and insertion points are stored on another layer. Why is this information important, and why store it on a separate layer?

   Viewing, Plotting when inserting

4. When inserting a symbol library, at what point do you cancel and why?

   when ASKED for insertion Point

5. Identify one application for creating and using a library of symbols and details.

   Toilets, CHAirs

Problems

1. Based on steps described in this unit, create an entirely new symbol library specific to your discipline. For example, if you practice architectural drawing, create a library of doors and windows. First create and/or specify a prototype drawing (such as the prototype drawing outlined in Unit 21, if it's appropriate).

2. After you have completed the library symbols and details, begin a new drawing and insert the new library file as you did before. Then, create a drawing using the symbols and details.

3. If you have the optional *Applying AutoCAD* Diskette, refer to the file LIBRARY1.DWG.

AUTOCAD® AT WORK

Computer-Aided Drafting Plays in Peoria

For 30 years, the Central Illinois Light Company (CILCO) of Peoria, Illinois, struggled to keep its electric construction standards book up to date. . .and lost. This book, containing 250 pages of important drawings and specifications for use by design engineers and field construction people, had been drafted by hand in the 1950s and maintained by hand ever since. It had become obsolete, but according to Senior Electric Engineer Craig D. Frommelt, "It would take so many man-hours to redo that it simply never was redone."

Frommelt and others at CILCO felt that updating the standards book was a AutoCAD as their drafting program. Now CILCO is experiencing a productivity gain of about 2:1 in creating new drawings for the standards book and expects gains of 4:1 or 5:1 when it comes to maintaining the book in the future.

CILCO achieved these gains by using AutoCAD to create custom libraries of symbols for commonly used parts such as transformers. Using these libraries, an engineer can rapidly create a new drawing by selecting the proper symbols and indicating where on the new drawing they should be placed.

The power to customize features of the CAD program, such as the symbol libraries, also pays off in another project now beginning—the drafting and design of electric utility substations. Frommelt expects CAD to be a great timesaver on this project because CILCO must keep many drawings for each substation: site layouts, architectural drawings of buildings, electrical schematics, and mechanical drawings used to verify clearances when replacing machines.

CILCO chose to begin the project with electrical schematics because those drawings use the same symbols repeatedly. Starting with the symbols used in the standards book, CILCO's engineers created a custom CAD library of close to 1000 schematic symbols. They then created custom menus showing those symbols, in order to make the cut-and-paste process as simple as possible. "We are able to get anywhere from a 5:1 to 10:1 productivity advantage in making schematic diagrams," says Frommelt.

CILCO is considering other applications for its newfound CAD power. One is facilities mapping, which involves first digitizing the map of a service area (converting it into a computer-readable form) and then superimposing symbols for poles, transformers, and other equipment to make a complete geographic inventory. Using the CAD system, a person could assign attributes, such as model numbers and descriptions, to each symbol on a map. Then if it appeared that a particular model of transformer, for example, was likely to fail after ten years, an engineer could have the program identify all transformers of that model and age and highlight them in red. Those transformers could then be replaced quickly for better schedule maintenance.

Courtesy of CILCO

272

Unit 31   Remarkable Attributes

Reference

■ OBJECTIVE:

To create and display Attributes with the ATTDEF, DDATTDEF, ATTDISP, ATTEDIT, and DDATTE commands and the ATTDIA system variable

The purpose of this unit is to experiment with AutoCAD's powerful Attribute feature.

REF 394-412

Attributes are text information stored within Blocks. The information describes certain aspects of a Block, such as size, material, model number, cost, etc., depending upon the nature of the Block. The Attribute information can be made visible, but in most cases, you do not want the information to appear on the drawing. Therefore it usually remains invisible, particularly during plotting. Later, the Attribute information can be extracted to form a report such as a bill of materials.

The following electrical schematic contains Attribute information, even though you cannot see it. It's invisible. (The numbers you see in the components are not the Attributes.)

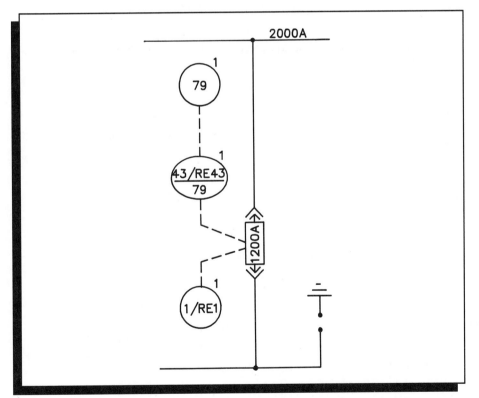

Courtesy of City of Fort Collins, Light & Power Utility

The following example shows a zoomed view of one of the schematic components. Notice that in this example the Attribute information is displayed near the top of the component.

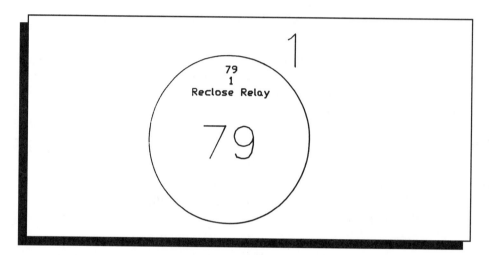

All of the Attributes contained in this schematic were compiled into a file and placed into a program for report generation. The following report (bill of materials) was generated directly from the electrical schematic drawing.

DESCRIPTION	DEVICE	QUANTITY/UNIT
Recloser Cut-out Switch	43/RE43/79	1
Reclose Relay	79	1
Lightning Arrestor	--	3
Breaker Control Switch	1/RE1	1
1200 Amp Circuit Breaker	52	1

Creating Attributes

Attributes can be extracted, and reports produced, from any type of drawing, not just electrical.

1   Start AutoCAD and open the library drawing called **LIB1**. It should look somewhat like the one on the next page.

NOTE:

If, for some reason, you do not have LIB1 on file, quickly create it using the steps outlined in the previous unit.

2 Explode each of the five Blocks.

Exploding an inserted Block reverses the effect of the BLOCK command. Exploding is necessary so that we can redefine the Blocks with Attributes.

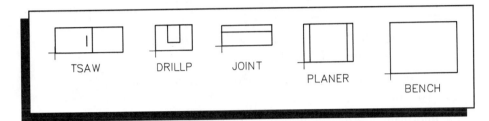

Let's assign Attribute information to each of the tools so that we can later insert them and then generate a bill of materials. We'll design the Attributes so that the report will contain a brief description of the component, its model, and the cost.

3 Zoom in on the first component (table saw). It should fill most of the screen.

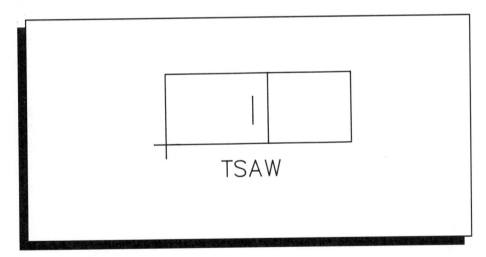

Now you're ready to assign Attributes to the table saw.

4 Enter the **ATTDEF** (Attribute Definition) command or select it from the BLOCKS submenu of the standard screen menu.

5 Set the Attribute modes as follows, and press **RETURN** when you're finished setting them.

Invisible: Y
Constant: Y
Verify: Y
Preset: N

REF 399-400

The modes can be changed from Yes to No or from No to Yes by simply typing the first letter of each mode. For example, if you want to change Invisible to Yes, type the letter I and press RETURN.

6 Type the word **DESCRIPTION** (in upper or lower case letters) for the Attribute tag and press **RETURN**.

7 Type **Table Saw** (exactly as you see it here) for the Attribute value and press **RETURN**.

8 Place the information inside the tool, near the top. Be sure to make it small. When placing the information, use the same technique used with the TEXT command.

The word DESCRIPTION should appear. If it extends outside the table saw representation, that's okay.

9 Press the space bar to repeat the ATTDEF command.

10 The Attribute modes should remain the same, so press **RETURN**.

11 This time, enter **MODEL** for the Attribute tag and **1A2B** for the Attribute value. Press **RETURN** in reply to "Justify/Style/<Start point>:."

The word MODEL should now appear on the screen.

12 Repeat Steps 8, 9, and 10, but enter **COST** for the tag and **$625.00** for the value.

You are now finished entering the table saw Attributes. That's all there is to it.

Storing Attributes

Now let's store the Attributes in the Block.

1 Using the **BLOCK** command, redefine the TSAW Block using the same **TSAW** name.

HINT:
AutoCAD will display the message "Block TSAW already exists. Redefine it? <N>." Enter Y for Yes, because you want to redefine it. When selecting the Block, be sure to select the Attributes also, but do not select the cross and text reference information.

Reference

The Attribute information should now be stored within the TSAW Block.

2 Insert the Block in the same location where the table saw was before. The Attribute tags should not appear.

Displaying Attributes

Let's display the Attribute values using the ATTDISP (Attribute Display) command.

1 Enter **ATTDISP** and specify **On**.

REF 402

You should see the Attribute values, similar to the drawing below.

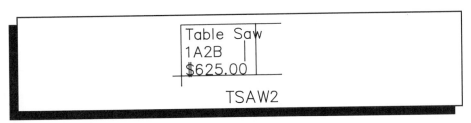

```
Table Saw
1A2B
$625.00
        TSAW2
```

2 Enter **ATTDISP** again and enter **N** for **Normal**.

The Attribute values should again be invisible.

Applying What You've Learned

Now, let's assign Attributes to the rest of the power tools and components.

1 Using the **ATTDEF** command, assign Attributes to the drill press and jointer using the following information. Then redefine the Blocks and insert them in the same locations as their predecessors.

Description	Model	Cost
Drill Press	7C-234	$590.00
Jointer	902-42A	$750.00

DDATTDEF Command

REF 397-399
TUT 101-104

Let's use DDATTDEF to assign Attributes to the surface planer and work bench.

1 Enter **DDATTDEF** or select **Text**, **Attributes**, and **Define...** from the **Draw** pull-down menu.

The Attribute Definition dialogue box should appear.

2 After the dialogue box appears, enter **DESCRIPTION** (in upper or lower case) for the tag and **Surface Planer** for the value.

Notice that the remaining options default to the options you selected when you last used the ATTDEF command.

3 Select the **Pick Point** button, pick a start point for the Attribute text, and pick the **OK** button.

"DESCRIPTION" should appear.

4 Press the space bar to repeat the **DDATTDEF** command.

5 Check the **Align below previous attribute** check box.

This will cause AutoCAD to place the Attribute tag below the previously defined Attribute.

6 Insert the remaining Attributes for the surface planer: **MODEL 789453, COST $2070.00.**

7 Use **DDATTDEF** to assign the following Attributes to the work bench.

Description	Model	Cost
Work Bench	31-1982	$825.00

8 Use the **BLOCK** command to redefine the PLANER and BENCH blocks.

9 When you're finished assigning Attributes, redefining the Blocks, and inserting them, display the Attribute values to make sure they are complete.

10 Enter **QSAVE** to save your work.

Your symbol library, LIB1, now contains Attributes. When LIB1 is inserted into a new drawing and tools are inserted, the Attributes will be contained in the Blocks.

The following unit will involve the extraction of the Attributes and the generation of a bill of materials.

Variable Attributes _____

Thus far, you have experienced the use of fixed Attribute values. With variable Attributes, you have the freedom of changing the Attribute values as you insert the Block. Let's step through the process.

1 Using the PROTO1 prototype drawing, begin a new drawing and name it **WINDOW**.

2 Zoom in on the lower ¼ of the display, make layer **0** the current layer, and set your snap resolution to **2″**.

3 Draw the following architectural window symbol and approximate the dimensions that are not given. Do not place dimensions on the drawing. (The symbol represents a double-hung window for use in architectural floor plans.)

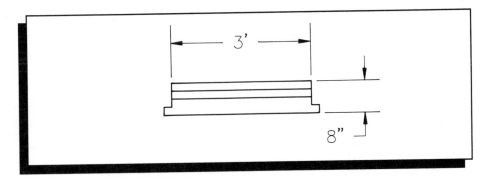

4 Enter the **ATTDEF** command, set the following modes, and press RETURN when you're finished.

Invisible: Y
Constant: N
Verify: N
Preset: N

Notice that, unlike before, the Constant and Verify modes are set at "No." Attribute values that are not Constant, called variable Attributes, can be edited. In the following section titled "Attribute Editing," we will practice editing variable Attributes. But for now, let's continue.

5 Enter **TYPE** for the Attribute tag.

You should now have "Attribute prompt:" on the screen. As you may recall, you did not receive this statement before when the Constant mode was set to "Yes."

6 In reply to "Attribute prompt:", enter **What type of window?** and press **RETURN**.

You will see what this is for when we insert the Block.

7 Enter **Double Hung** for the default Attribute value.

8 Center the Attribute over the top of the window and leave space for two more Attributes. (Make the Attribute text small.)

The word TYPE should appear on the screen.

9 Press the space bar to reenter **ATTDEF** and leave the Attribute modes as they are.

10 Enter **SIZE** for the Attribute tag, **What size?** for the Attribute prompt, and **3′ × 4′** for the default Attribute value.

11 At the "Justify/Style/<Start>:" prompt, press **RETURN**.

The word SIZE should appear on the screen below the word TYPE.

12 Repeat Steps 9, 10, and 11, using the following information.

Attribute tag: **MANUFACTURER**
Attribute prompt: **What manufacturer?**
Default Attribute value: **Andersen**

13 Store the window symbol and Attributes using the **BLOCK** command. Name it **DH** (short for Double Hung) and pick the lower left corner for the insertion base point.

Inserting Variable Attributes _____

1 Insert the Block **DH**. Accept the default insertion settings.

What's different about this Block insertion?

2 Press **RETURN** to use the default manufacturer, Andersen.

3 Enter **3′ × 5′** for the size.

4 Press **RETURN** in reply to "What type of window?"

The window should appear.

5 Enter **ATTDISP** and specify **On**.

Did the correct Attribute values appear?

_____ NOTE: _____

You also have the option of using the Attribute mode "Preset." It allows creation of Attributes that are variable but are not requested during Block insertion. In other words, when you insert a Block containing a preset Attribute, the Attribute value is not requested but rather is set automatically to its default value. The primary purpose of the preset mode is to limit the number of prompts to which you must respond.

Enter Attributes Dialogue Box _____

AutoCAD offers a special dialogue box for entering variable attributes.

1 Enter the **ATTDIA** system variable and enter a value of **1**.

2 **INSERT** the Block named **DH**.

The Enter Attributes dialogue box should appear as shown in the following illustration.

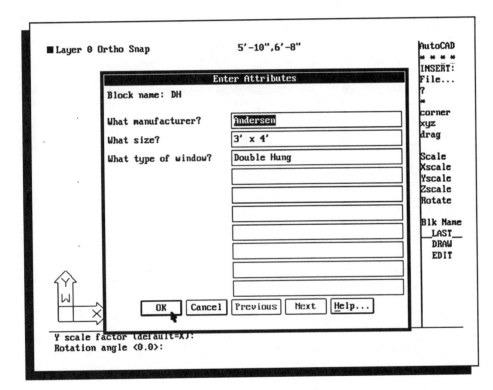

3 Change one of the Attribute values or leave the values as they are.

4 Pick the **OK** button when you are finished.

Attribute Editing _____

One very simple way of editing Attributes is to first insert the Block using the "*" option. As you know, this brings in the object as individual pieces and not as a Block. The Attributes contained in the object are also pieces (entities) and any of them can be erased. Using ATTDEF, new Attributes can be added, and using the BLOCK command, the object can be redefined as a Block.

Use of ATTEDIT, short for Attribute Edit, is a more powerful, but more involved, method of editing Attributes. It allows you either to edit Attributes one at a time, changing any or all of their properties, or to do a global edit on a selected set of Attributes, changing only their value strings.

You should currently have something similar to the following on the screen.

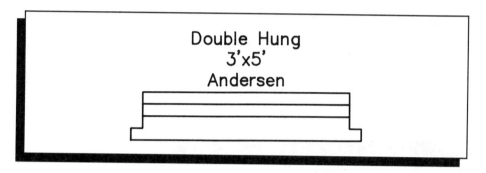

Make sure ATTDISP is On.

1   Enter the **ATTEDIT** command.

2   Accept each of the following default settings. Stop at "Select Attributes:".

Edit attributes one at a time? <Y>
Block name specification <*>:
Attribute tag specification <*>:
Attribute value specification <*>:

3   Pick the Attribute value **Andersen**. It will appear as though nothing happened. Then press **RETURN**.

The following list of options should appear on the screen. Also notice the "X" at the word Andersen.

```
1 attributes selected.
Value/Position/Height/Angle/Style/Layer/Color/Next <N>:
```

4   Enter **V** for **Value**.

5   Enter the **Replace** option.

6   In reply to "New attribute value:" enter **Pella** and press **RETURN** again.

Now Pella is contained in the DH Block definition in place of Andersen.

7   Practice editing other Attribute values contained in the window symbol.

Edit Attributes Dialogue Box _____

The DDATTE command is provided for dialogue-oriented Attribute editing.

1   Enter the **DDATTE** command or pick **Text, Attributes,** and **Edit...** from the **Draw** pull-down menu.

2   Pick one of the Blocks contained on the screen.

The dialogue box pictured in the previous illustration should appear. Its name, however, will be different.

3   Edit one of the Attribute values and pick **OK**.

4   When you're finished, enter **END** to save your work and exit AutoCAD.

Questions

1. Explain the purpose of creating and storing Attributes.

   DATABASE INFO, X + Y VALUES, COORDINATE, FOR CREATING REPORTS OF A DWG, SUCH AS A BILL OF MATERIALS

2. Briefly define each of the following commands.

   ATTDEF *ASSIGNS ATTRIBUTES to DRAWING*

   DDATTDEF *DIALOG BOX ASSIGNS Attrib to DRWG*

   ATTDISP *CHANGE visibility*

   DDATTE *to EDit ATTRIBUTES*

   ATTEDIT *EDits Attributes*

3. What are Attribute tags?

   CATAGORIES UNDER which ATTRIBS GO

4. What are Attribute values?

   SPECIFICS STORED IN BLOCKS

5. Explain the Attribute modes Invisible, Constant, Verify, and Preset.

   HINT: See pages 397-398 of the *Reference Manual*.

   INVISIBLE - LETS BLOCK BE SEEN OR NOT
   CONSTANT - GIVES FIXED VALUE
   VERIFY - LETS YOU DBICHECK to SEE if CORRECT
   PRESET - to CREAT VARIABLE Attribs

6. What advantage do variable Attribute values have over fixed Attribute values?

   YOU CAN CHANGE them AS YOU INSERT

Problems

1. Load the drawing containing the furniture representations you created in Unit 29. If this file is not available, create a similar drawing. Outline a simple plan for assigning Attributes to each of the components contained in the drawing. Create the Attributes and redefine each of the Blocks so the Attributes are stored within the Blocks.

2. Refer to SCHEM.DWG and SCHEM2.DWG and instructions contained on the optional *Applying AutoCAD* Diskette. Display and edit the attributes contained in the drawing files.

AUTOCAD® AT WORK

MIT Biology Building

The new headquarters for the Massachusetts Institute of Technology biology department will contain 250,000 sq. ft. of research laboratories and associated teaching and administrative facilities. In developing the design for this dramatic structure, the architectural firm, Goody, Clancy, & Associates, chose to take full advantage of the 3D capabilities of AutoCAD—working in a 3D format throughout the architectural process, rather than using traditional 2D design. As a result, the designers and consulting engineers were able to gain a reliable, practical understanding of every part of the building as it was developed. They could quickly make design changes and construct a variety of views of not only the broad aesthetic effects but also the relationships between building materials. The result is an exceptional new laboratory design and mechanical system that is expected to be completed in late 1993.

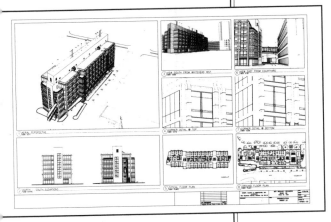

Courtesy of Goody, Clancy, & Associates, Architects, Inc.

Based on a story provided by Autodesk, Inc.

Unit 32 Bill of Materials Generation

■ OBJECTIVE:

To practice report generation using ATTEXT, DDATTEXT, BASIC, and ATTEXT.BAS

After finishing the Attribute assignment process (Unit 31), you are ready to create a report such as a bill of materials. The first step in this process involves extracting the Attribute information and storing it in a file that can be read by another computer program.

Attribute Extraction

1 Start AutoCAD and begin a new drawing named **EXTRACT**.

2 Insert the latest version of the LIB1 library containing the Attributes. (See the following hint.)

HINT:

Use the DDINSERT command. At the "Insertion point:" prompt, cancel by pressing CTRL C.

3 Reenter the **DDINSERT** command and list the Blocks available in the drawing.

Block names of the tools should be present.

4 Insert each of the Blocks in a comparable arrangement to what you see in the drawing below.

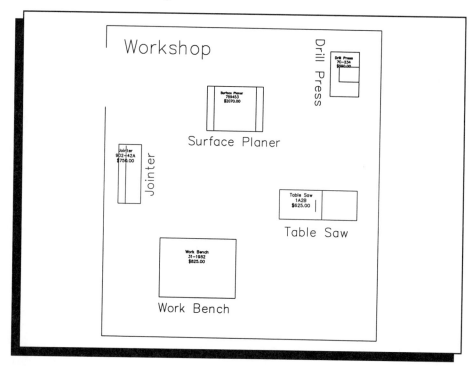

Each of the tools should contain Attributes as shown in the drawing. ATTDISP can be On so that you can see the Attributes. You may need to zoom in order to read them.

⑤ Enter the **ATTEXT** (short for Attribute Extraction) command.

REF 408-412
REF 407

CDF and SDF are similar file formats that allow you to write Attribute information to an ASCII text file. Both formats are compatible with the dBASE III software, as well as common text editors. CDF creates a comma delimited file, while SDF creates a space delimited file.

The DXF option is a variant of AutoCAD's popular Drawing Interchange File format used to import and export AutoCAD drawing files from one CAD system to another. The variant creates a DXX file extension to distinguish it from normal DXF files.

⑥ Enter **D** for DXF.

A Create Extract File dialogue box should appear, giving you the opportunity to name and store the new file.

⑦ Pick the **OK** button or press **RETURN** to accept the EXTRACT file name—the same name as the drawing file (but with a DXX file extension).

AutoCAD has stored the Attributes in a format that other programs can read.

DDATTEXT Command

REF 407-408
TUT 116-118

DDATTEXT is an alternative to the ATTEXT command.

① Enter **DDATTEXT** or pick **Text, Attributes,** and **Extract...** from the **Draw** pull-down menu.

The Attribute Extraction dialogue box should appear as shown in the following illustration. This dialogue box also enables you to extract Attributes and create CDF, SDF, and DXF files.

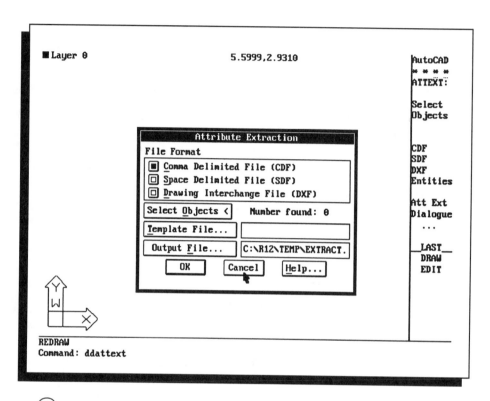

2 Since we've already created the file we need, pick the **Cancel** button.

Attribute Reporting _____

Now let's load the new extract file into the BASIC program called
ATTEXT.BAS. This will require exiting AutoCAD.

1 Enter **END** to save your work and exit AutoCAD.

You should now have the DOS prompt (such as C:\>) on the screen.

The next few steps will involve the preparation of files. This preparation is
necessary before you can proceed with the bill of materials generation.

2 Locate your DOS directory or diskette containing the BASIC
Program Editor called BASIC.COM.

HINT: _____
BASIC.COM is usually contained in a directory named DOS
with the other DOS files (such as FORMAT.COM and CHKDSK.COM) or
on the DOS diskette.

288

3 Locate the AutoCAD file ATTEXT.BAS. (See the following note.)

NOTE:

Your Release 12 package may not contain the ATTEXT.BAS file. However, this file was shipped on the Sample Drawings diskette with AutoCAD 9, 2.6x, 2.5x, and 2.1x. Therefore you can obtain ATTEXT.BAS from one of these earlier versions if you have access to one of them. Or, ATTEXT.BAS can be obtained by purchasing the optional *Applying AutoCAD* companion diskette from the Glencoe Division of Macmillan/McGraw-Hill. Call 1-800-334-7344 for Customer Service.

4 Copy ATTEXT.BAS, BASIC.COM, and EXTRACT.DXX (your new extract file) to a single directory. Combining these three files is not mandatory, but having them together will simplify your work.

Now you're ready to create a bill of materials.

NOTE:

The steps listed after this note box are for the original BASIC language. However, several different versions of BASIC are currently available (QBASIC, GWBASIC, etc.) Each version may require different steps to create the bill of materials. For example, in QBASIC you would:

1 Enter QBASIC to enter the program.

2 Select Open from the File pull-down menu.

3 Double-click on ATTEXT.BAS from the list of files.

4 Select Start from the Run pull-down menu, or press the shift key and F5 simultaneously.

5 At the "Enter extract file name:" prompt, enter EXTRACT. (Do not enter the .DXX extension.)

If you own a different version of BASIC, consult your owner's manual for the proper procedure.

1 At the DOS prompt, type **BASIC** and press **RETURN**.

This will load the BASIC Program Editor.

2 Then type **LOAD"ATTEXT** and press **RETURN** to load the ATTEXT.BAS program.

The message "OK" will appear if the program loads properly.

3 Type **RUN** and press **RETURN** to run the ATTEXT program.

4 When the program asks you for the extract file name, type **EXTRACT** and press **RETURN**.

——————— NOTE: ———————

Be sure to indicate the directory and drive (such as C:\R12\CHAD) if the extract file EXTRACT.DXX is located in another location.

The BASIC program should have generated the bill of materials. Your report should look very similar to the one below.

```
COST            DESCRIPTION       MODEL
--------        ---------------   -------

$750.00         Jointer           902-42A
$590.00         Drill Press       7C-234
$2070.00        Surface Planer    789453
$825.00         Work Bench        31-1982
$625.00         Table Saw         1A2B
```

5 To print the report, use the computer's keyboard print-screen feature.

6 To return to the DOS prompt (*e.g.*, C:\>), type **SYSTEM** and press **RETURN**.

NOTE:

You can list the contents of EXTRACT.DXX with the DOS TYPE command. Consider the following example:

C>TYPE EXTRACT.DXX

The following gives a sampling of what should appear. This is the raw data read by the ATTEXT.BAS program.

```
        0
INSERT
        8
        0
       66
            1
        2
BENCH2
       10
2.248004
       20
0.967268
       30
0.0
        0
ATTRIB
        8
        0
        1
$825.00
        2
COST
       70
            7
```

Questions

1. Describe the purpose of AutoCAD's ATTEXT and DDATTEXT commands.

   THEY SHOW attRib DAtA

2. What type of AutoCAD files can be read and manipulated by other computer programs?

   DFX Files

3. Explain the process of loading the BASIC Program Editor when generating a report.

   MAKE BASIC . Com AVAilAble Then TYPE BASIC After PROMPt

4. Explain the process of loading and running the BASIC program called ATTEXT.BAS.

   TYPE LOAD ATTEXt anD REtuRN THEN TYPE RUn anD REtuRN

5. What command is used to exit the BASIC Program Editor and return to the DOS prompt?

   System

Problems

1. Load the drawing that contains furniture representations. Using the steps outlined in this unit, create a bill of materials.

2. Refer to SCHEM.DWG and SCHEM2.DWG and instructions contained on the optional *Applying AutoCAD* Diskette. Using the ATTEXT command, DXF option, and ATTEXT.BAS program, create bills of materials from the two drawing files.

Unit 33 Dressing Your Drawings

■ OBJECTIVE:

To apply the HATCH, BHATCH, and SKETCH commands

This unit covers the application of hatching using the many patterns made available by AutoCAD. Sketching is also practiced using the SKETCH command and subcommands.

Some drawings make use of hatching and sketching to communicate accurately and correctly the intent of the design, as illustrated in the drawing below.

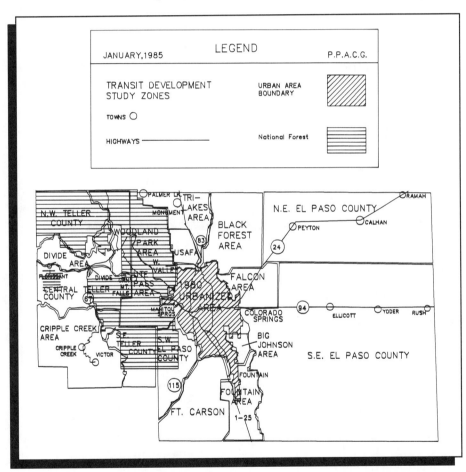

Courtesy of David Salamon, Pikes Peak Area Council of Governments

Both hatching and sketching can enhance the quality of drawings greatly, but both consume lots of disk space. Therefore both hatching and sketching should be used only when necessary. Be aware of their disk space requirements to avoid a system crash when storing drawings on floppy diskettes.

293

HATCH Command

Let's see what AutoCAD's HATCH command can do.

1 Start AutoCAD and begin a new drawing named **HATCH**.

2 Draw the following, but don't worry about exact sizes and locations. Include the text and outside rectangle as well.

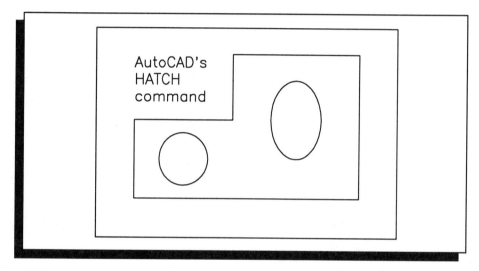

AutoCAD's
HATCH
command

3 Enter the **HATCH** command.

You should see the following at the bottom of the screen.

```
Pattern (? or name/U,style):
```

4 Create a listing of all hatch patterns by entering **?**. Press **RETURN** again.

As you can see, AutoCAD provides many hatch patterns—more than fifty, in fact. Let's use one of them on our drawing.

5 Enter the **HATCH** command again, and this time enter the hatch pattern **ANSI31** (the standard cross-hatch pattern).

6 Specify a scale of **1**.

_____ NOTE: _____

Like DIMSCALE, the "Scale for pattern" should be set at the reciprocal of the plot scale so that the hatch pattern size corresponds with the drawing scale.

7 Specify an angle of **0**.

8 To define the hatch boundary, place a window around the entire drawing, including the rectangle, and press **RETURN**.

Does your drawing look like the one below? If not, try again.

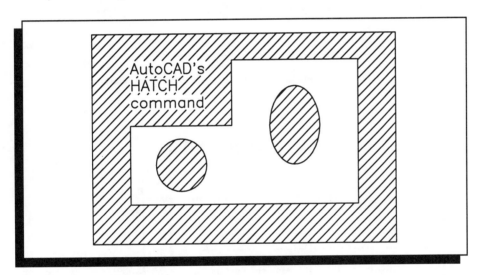

Note the areas which received hatching.

9 Erase the hatching by picking any one of the hatch lines.

HINT: _____
The entire hatch pattern is treated as a single entity. If you want the freedom to edit small pieces from the hatch pattern, precede the hatch pattern name with an asterisk (*). This is similar to inserting Blocks with an asterisk (see Unit 29).

10 Hatch the outermost area only using the **O** option. (When you enter the name of a pattern, follow it with a comma and O, as in EARTH,O.)

Did it work?

11 Undo the last operation and then use the **I** option (as in HONEY,I) to Ignore the internal structures.

The hatch pattern should cover the internal areas.

12 Erase the hatching.

BHATCH Command _____

REF 490-503
TUT 68-78

BHATCH, an expanded version of the HATCH command, takes advantage of dialogue boxes.

1 Enter the **BHATCH** command or pick **Hatch...** from the **Draw** pull-down menu.

The Boundary Hatch dialogue box should appear as shown in the following illustration.

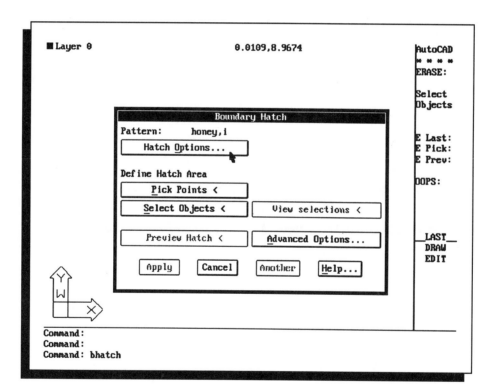

The last hatch pattern you used and any conditions you may have set will appear at the top of the dialogue box.

2 Pick the **Hatch Options...** button.

The Hatch Options subdialogue box should appear as shown in the following illustration.

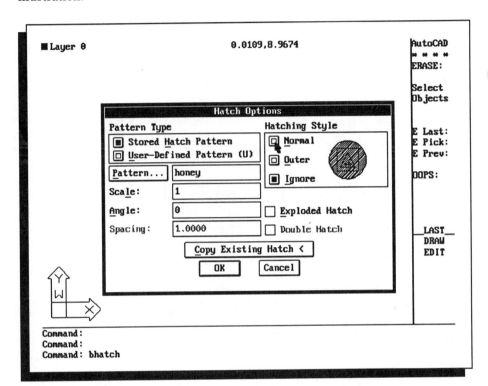

It shows the settings that were entered when either the HATCH or BHATCH command was last issued.

3 Select the **Normal** radio button contained in the upper right corner.

Selecting "Normal" is equivalent to omitting "Outer" and "Ignore" with the HATCH command.

Notice the Exploded Hatch check box. Checking it is equivalent to preceding the hatch pattern name with an asterisk (*) when using the HATCH command.

4 Pick the **Pattern...** button.

The Choose Hatch Pattern subdialogue box should appear.

5 Using the **Next** button repeatedly, find and select the **STARS** pattern.

HINT:

Use the "Previous" button if necessary to review previously displayed hatch patterns. Once you've found STARS, pick a point inside the STARS hatch pattern, as shown in the following illustration, to select it.

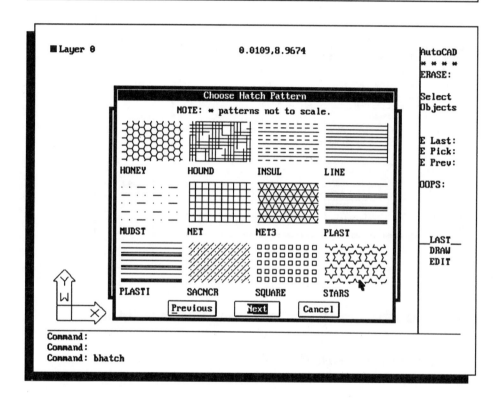

STARS should appear as the current pattern in the Hatch Options subdialogue box.

⑥ Pick the **OK** button.

⑦ Select the **Pick Points** button.

⑧ In reply to "Select internal point" pick a point inside the rectangle, but outside the six-sided polygon.

NOTE:

If you receive a "Boundary Definition Error," pick the OK button and pick another point inside the rectangle.

⑨ After AutoCAD accepts the point, press **RETURN** and pick the **Select Objects** button.

10 Select each of the three lines of text and press **RETURN**.

This causes AutoCAD to refrain from hatching over the text.

11 Select the **Pick Points** button again and pick a point inside the six-sided polygon, but outside the circle and ellipse.

—— NOTE: ——

If you receive a "Boundary Definition Error," pick the OK button and pick another point.

12 Pick points inside the circle and ellipse and press **RETURN**.

13 Pick the Preview Hatch button to preview the hatching and press **RETURN** after you've previewed it.

14 If the hatch locations are the same as those shown in the illustration on page 295, pick the **Apply** button. If not, cancel and repeat the previous 13 steps.

15 Experiment further with BHATCH on your own.

SKETCH Command ————

REF 154-160

Now let's try some freehand sketching.

1 If necessary, clear a small area on the screen so that you'll have room for the sketch.

2 Enter the **SKETCH** command.

3 Specify **0.1** unit for the Record increment.

You should now see the following at the bottom of the screen.

```
Sketch.  Pen eXit Quit Record Erase Connect .
```

The following is a brief description of each of the SKETCH subcommands.

Pen	Raise/lower pen (or toggle with pick button)
eXit	Record all temporary lines and exit
Quit	Discard all temporary lines and exit
Record	Record all temporary lines
Erase	Selectively erase temporary lines
Connect	Connect to a line endpoint
. (period)	Line to point

4 To begin sketching, simply pick a point where you'd like the sketch to begin. The pick specifies (toggles) "pen down."

5 Move the pointing device to sketch a short line.

6 Pick a point.

This specifies (toggles) "pen up."

7 Move to a clear location on the screen and sketch the following lake.

NOTE:

If you make a mistake or need to back up, toggle "pen up" and select Erase from the SKETCH submenu (or type E). Then reverse the direction of the crosshairs until you have erased that which needed to be removed; press the pick button to terminate the Erase mode; press it again to toggle "pen down."

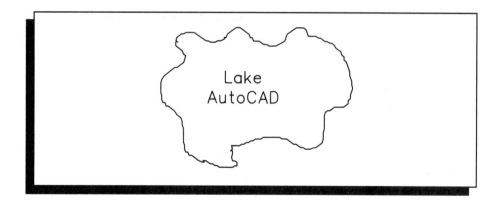

It's okay if your sketch doesn't look exactly like the one above.

8 When you're finished sketching the lake, enter either **R**ecord or e**X**it to record and finalize the temporary lines.

NOTE:

If you select Record, you have the option to sketch additional lines or to Quit.

9 Practice sketching by using the remaining SKETCH subcommands. Draw anything you'd like.

CAUTION:

If you are storing the drawing on a floppy diskette, you may want to erase some of the sketching to avoid a system crash.

10 When you're finished, enter **END** to save and exit.

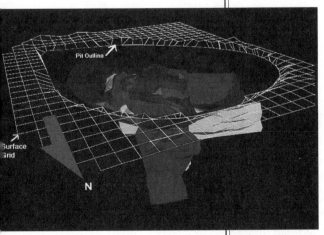

AUTOCAD® AT WORK

Mining Industry Uses 3D AutoCAD

Modern-day mining operations take advantage of the power of computer technology to define potential deposits of copper, gold, and other minerals. Working with Auto-CAD and Autodesk 3D Studio, geologists at Noranda, Inc., build 3D computer models of potential ore zones based on data obtained from test drilling. These models provide accurate representations of ore bodies hundreds of feet below ground and serve as a tool for guiding efficient, productive mining operations. The image shown here is a geological interpretation of one mining site and shows the layers of ore zones hidden underground. When information is needed about a specific section, the geologist can quickly generate a 2D slice through the model for use in ore reserve calculations or in the design of underground workings.

Based on a story provided by Autodesk, Inc.

1. Explain why hatch patterns are useful.

   Fill in OBJ/AREAS with PATTERNS

2. How is the scale of a hatch pattern determined?

   By Plot SCALE

3. Briefly describe the following HATCH style options.

   O *Fills Outer AREAS*

   I *IGNORES INTERNAL STRUCTURE*

4. Briefly describe the purpose of each of the following SKETCH subcommands.

   Pen *RAISE/Lower PEN*

   eXit *RECORD TEMP LINES AND EXIT*

   Quit *DISCARDS All and EXITS*

   Record *KEEPS All TEMP lines*

   Erase *Selectively ERASES TEMP lines*

   Connect *Connects line to END Point*

   . (period) *LINE to A point*

5. SKETCH requires a Record increment. What does it determine?

   How long EACH Portion of Line will be

HINT:

Specify a coarse increment such as 0.5 or 1 and notice the appearance of the sketch lines.

Problems

Construct each of the following drawings. Use the HATCH, BHATCH, and SKETCH commands where appropriate, and don't worry about specific sizes. The hatch patterns to be used are indicated below each of the drawings.

In PRB33-2 and PRB33-3, use the SKETCH and LINE commands to define temporary boundaries for the hatch patterns. Place the boundaries on a separate layer and freeze that layer after you are finished hatching.

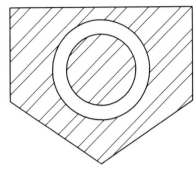

ANSI32

PRB 33-1

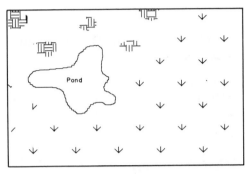

EARTH AND GRASS

PRB 33-2

Pond

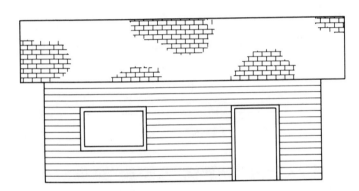

BRICK AND LINE

PRB 33-3

PRB 33-4

Unit 34   From Display to Paper

■ OBJECTIVE:

To practice plotting and printing AutoCAD drawings using the PLOT command

This unit steps you through the plotting/printing process. Plotting typically refers to the use of a plotter, such as a pen or electrostatic plotter. AutoCAD printing refers to the same procedure, even though the output device may be a laser, ink jet, or thermal printer.

Plot Previewing _____

AutoCAD allows you to preview a plot.

1   Start AutoCAD and open the drawing named **HATCH**.

2   Enter the **PLOT** command or pick **Plot...** from the **File** pull-down menu.

REF 510-538

The Plot Configuration dialogue box will appear.

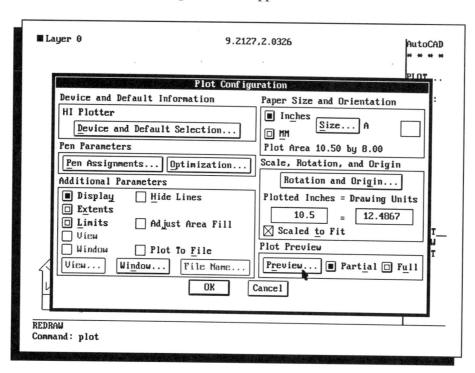

Notice that "HI Plotter" appears in the upper left corner of the dialogue box in the illustration. This means a device named "HI Plotter" was configured previously. In this case, a Houston Instrument DMP-61 MP pen plotter was chosen. The device you see in this area will probably be different. AutoCAD stores plotter settings in the configuration file ACAD.CFG, so other settings may also differ depending on how they were last set.

REF 511

NOTE:

If the name of a specific plotter device (such as "HI Plotter") does not appear in the upper left corner, you must configure one before you proceed with the following steps. Refer to Appendix E and the following unit for information on how to configure plotter devices.

Note the Plot Preview area located in the lower right area of the dialogue box.

REF 523-527

③ If the **Partial** radio button is not selected (darkened), as shown in the previous illustration, pick it.

④ Pick the **Preview...** button.

This feature gives you a quick preview of the effective plotting area on the sheet, as shown in the following illustration.

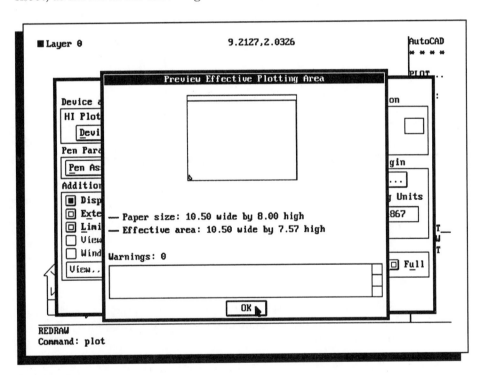

The effective plotting area, represented by the smaller rectangle (in blue), is the area the configured plotter will plot. The larger rectangle (in red) represents the sheet.

⑤ Pick the **OK** button.

⑥ Pick the **Full** radio button and pick the **Preview...** button again.

In the lower right corner, a "percentage done" meter appears, indicating that AutoCAD is regenerating the drawing. AutoCAD then displays the drawing as it will appear on the sheet (shown in the following illustration).

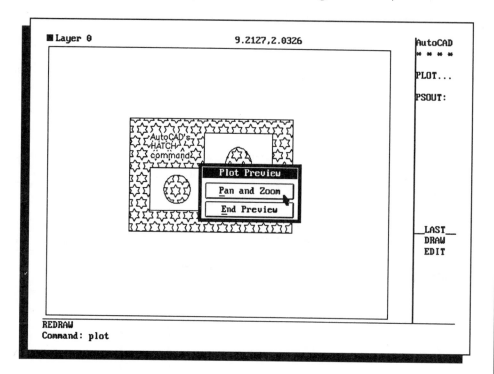

7 Pick the **Pan and Zoom** button located in the middle of the screen.

REF 526-527

This feature is very similar to the Dynamic Pan and Zoom capability that is part of the ZOOM Dynamic option.

8 Use the pick button to change the size of the zoom window and press **RETURN** to perform the zoom.

This enables you to examine the drawing closely before you plot it. Large drawings can take considerable time to plot, so spotting errors before you plot can save time as well as plotting supplies.

9 Pick the **End Preview** button.

10 Pick **OK**.

NOTE:

If your computer is connected to the configured plotter or printer and it is turned on and ready, continue with step 12. If it is not, enter S (for Stop) and prepare the device. If you do not have access to an output device, cancel by pressing CTRL C and skip to the next section, titled "Tailoring the Plot."

11 Press **RETURN** to initiate plotting.

When AutoCAD has finished processing the drawing data, it will display the message "Plot complete." However, since we did not make changes to the plot settings before plotting, the plot may be incorrect.

Tailoring the Plot

The following steps consider sheet size, drawing scale, and other plotter settings and parameters.

1 Open the drawing named **DIMEN2** (created in Unit 24) and review the drawing limits and layers stored in this drawing.

As you may recall, PROTO1 was used to create this drawing, and you considered the following criteria when you created it.

Scale: $1/2'' = 1'$
Sheet size: $17'' \times 11''$
Effective plotting area: $15'' \times 10''$
Drawing limits: $30' \times 20'$

2 Enter the **PLOT** command.

3 In the upper right corner of the dialogue box, pick the **Inches** radio button if it has not already been picked (darkened).

Specifying Sheet Size

REF 535-536

1 Pick the **Size** button to display the Paper Size dialogue box.

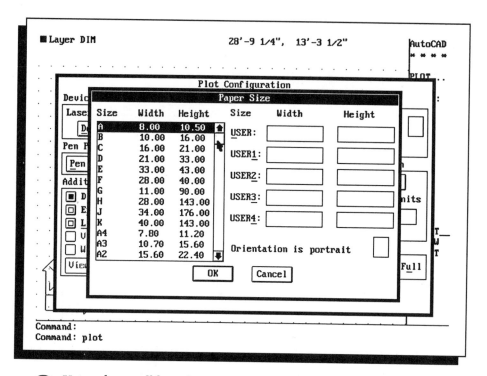

2 Using the scroll bar, if necessary, review the entire list of sizes available for the configured plotter.

AutoCAD may not offer a "17 width × 11 height" B-size sheet for your configured plotter. While a "16 × 10" may be available and would be acceptable for this exercise, let's define a sheet size.

3 Enter **17** in the edit box provided to the right of "USER:" in the Width column.

AutoCAD knows that you mean inches because the Inches radio button was selected.

4 Enter **11** in the Height column and press **RETURN**.

This new user-defined size should appear in the list box, allowing you to select it in the future.

5 Pick the **OK** button.

"USER" should appear to the right of the "Size..." button.

Reference

REF 521-522

Rotation and Origin

1 Pick the **Rotation and Origin...** button.

This permits you to rotate the drawing and specify the plot origin.

2 If the **0** radio button is not selected, pick it.

Both X and Y origins should be set at 0′0″. If not, . . .

3 . . . change the X and Y origins to **0′0″**.

4 Pick the **OK** button.

Additional Parameters

REF 516-520

1 Select the **Limits** radio button contained in the Additional Parameters area.

We selected "Limits" because we want to plot the entire drawing area as defined by the 30′ × 20′ drawing limits. You may choose to select one of the other options in the future. If so, here's what they mean.

Display	Plots current view
Extents	Similar to ZOOM Extents; plots the portion of the drawing that contains entities
Limits	Plots the entire drawing area as defined by drawing limits
View	Plots a saved view
Window	Plots a window whose corners you specify; use the Window button to specify the window to plot
Hide Lines	Plots 3D objects with hidden lines removed
Adjust Area Fill	Specifies pen width; uses width information when plotting solid-filled Traces, Polylines, and Solids
Plot to File	Sends plot output to a file rather than to a device

NOTE:

In the future, you may choose to create a plot (PLT) file. After creating the file, you can plot it using the DOS COPY command, as shown in this example:

COPY DIMEN2.PLT COM1:

This would send DIMEN2.PLT to a device connected to the computer's COM1 serial port. Many third-party software products also accept PLT files.

"Hide Lines" and "Plot to File" should not be checked. If they are, . . .

2 . . . deselect them.

It doesn't matter whether "Adjust Area Fill" has been checked.

Drawing Scale

REF 522-523

Focus your attention on the "Scale, Rotation, and Origin" area of the dialogue box. Notice the values contained in the edit boxes under "Plotted Inches = Drawing Units." These values represent the drawing scale. When "Scale to Fit" is checked, these values will reflect the actual scale used to fit the drawing on the sheet.

1 If "Scaled to Fit" is checked, deselect it.

2 Enter ½ (or **0.5**) in the first edit box and **1′** in the second edit box.

Plotting the Drawing

Let's preview and plot the drawing.

1 Pick the **Full** radio button and pick **Preview....**

2 Pick the **End Preview** button.

3 If your output device accepts B-size (17″ × 11″) sheets, prepare the device for plotting.

___ **NOTE:** ___

If your device does not accept B-size (17″ × 11″) media, pick the "Size..." button, select or define a size the device will accept, and pick the OK button. Preview the plot to make certain it fits properly on the sheet. If it doesn't, make any necessary adjustments.

4 Pick **OK** again, check the connection between the computer and output device, and press **RETURN** to initiate plotting.

After plotting is complete, examine the output carefully. The dimensions on the drawing should measure correctly using a ½″ = 1′ scale. For instance, the 6′ dimension should measure 3″. Text and dimension sizes, such as dimension text, arrows, and center marks, should measure ⅛″ on the sheet.

___ **NOTE:** ___

Pen assignments, optimization, and device and default selection are covered in the following unit.

5 Enter **END** to save any changes you may have made to the drawing and exit AutoCAD.

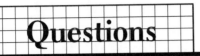
Questions

1. Explain the difference between the Partial and Full plot preview options.

   PARTIAL SHOW PLOT AREA ON SHEET
   FULL SHOWS DRAWING ON SHEET

2. Is it possible to specify a unique sheet size? Explain.

   YES USING USER

3. Briefly describe each of the following plot options.

   Display *PLOTS CURRENT VIEW*
   Extents *PLOTS PORTION with ENTITIES*
   Limits *PLOT ENTIRE DRWG AREA*
   View *PLOTS SAVED VIEW*
   Window *WINDOW AREA YOU PICK*
   Hide Lines *REMOVES HIDDEN LINES FROM 3D PLOTS*
   Adjust Area Fill *SPECIFIES PEN WIDTH FOR TRACES, SOLIDS*
   Plot to File *SENDS PLOT OUTPUT to FILE INSTEAD OF PLOTTER*

4. Why is it important that you draw using colors if you intend to plot a drawing?

   PENS GO to LAYER COLOR

5. What would you enter at the DOS prompt to send a plot file named PART.PLT to an output device connected to the computer's COM2 serial port?

   Copy PART.Plt Com2:

6. The drawing plot scale for a particular drawing is 1 = 4″. What does the 1 represent and what does the 4″ represent?

   1 PLOTTED iNCH = 4″ SCALED

311

Problems

In problems 1 and 2, prepare to plot a drawing using the information provided. Choose any drawing to plot—it doesn't matter because you won't actually plot it.

1. Unit of measure: Inches
   Sheet size: 24″ × 18″
   Rotate plot 90 degrees
   Plot origin: 0,0 on both X and Y
   Plot Limits
   Do not Hide Lines
   Adjust Area Fill
   Do not Plot to File
   Scale: 1″ = 10′
   Perform Partial and Full Previews

2. Unit of measure: Millimeters
   Sheet size: 285 × 198
   Do not rotate the plot
   Plot origin: 0,0 on both X and Y
   Plot Display
   Hide Lines
   Do not Adjust Area Fill
   Plot to File (using the drawing file name)
   Scale: Scaled to Fit
   Perform a Full Preview

3. Plot the PLT file you created in problem 2 to a plotter or printer.

4. Choose and plot a drawing that you created in an earlier unit. Consider scale and drawing limits so that dimensions measure correctly on the plotted sheet. Text, linetypes, and dimension sizes (such as text and arrows) should also measure correctly on the sheet. For example, 1/8″ tall text should measure 1/8″ in height. Ignore colors and pen assignments. They are covered in the following unit.

AUTOCAD® AT WORK

CAD Brings Unexpected Benefits

An improvement in one area can sometimes result in a host of unexpected benefits in other areas. Consider the case of Advanced Micro Devices (AMD), which recently incorporated micro-based CAD into its design process.

The Manufacturing Services Division of AMD, a semiconductor manufacturer in San Jose, California, designs and produces packages for all of AMD's semiconductor devices. The packages protect fragile electronic circuits from contamination. The strategic planning manager for the division, Mark Brodsky, realized AMD engineers needed a quicker way to modify piece-part drawings used in package assembly.

The division already had—and intended to keep—a dedicated drafting system called Pegasys. But AMD still needed a way for its engineering staff to modify documentation quickly and accurately as it shuttled between the engineers and the vendor. To accomplish this goal, AMD purchased the AutoCAD software package plus a file server and network to run with the program. In addition to serving a front-end function for the existing drafting stations, the system also could allow the Manufacturing Services Division to integrate their office automation procedures. These rewards greatly exceeded those commonly associated with a CAD system.

In looking for micro-based software, Brodsky had sought a program that featured simplicity and ease of use, as well as the ability to work with all the other constraints. "We found AutoCAD to be the most applicable for general-purpose drawings, and the simplest to use," Brodsky said. "We also found that AutoCAD's DXF (Drawing Interchange File) was becoming the major format standard." The company that originated Pegasys was preparing translation software that would convert Pegasys to DXF. Thus choosing AutoCAD meant that all the work done by the drafters on Pegasys would be compatible with the new system, and vice versa.

As soon as the division's staff had satisfied their drafting needs, they were able to explore other benefits of their new system. Brodsky describes one of them: "We've asked vendors of our piece parts to provide us with electronic copies of our drawings. This eliminates the tedious task of our vendors having to redraw an AMD drawing in order to set up their photo plot equipment. Two major vendors will begin transferring drawings to AMD in AutoCAD's DXF format. DXF, we now realize, is the most widely used translator for all of our vendors' inhouse CAD systems." When the vendors' work is complete, they provide AMD with a disk of the finished product. "We can load the disk on AutoCAD, send it through our network to the Pegasys system, and, with very little modification, offer translation into Pegasys format and then print out an official AMD drawing ready for signoff." explains Brodsky. "It's a good sign that we are already using CAD for purposes beyond our original goals," he adds. "We anticipate that, over time, we'll find still other uses."

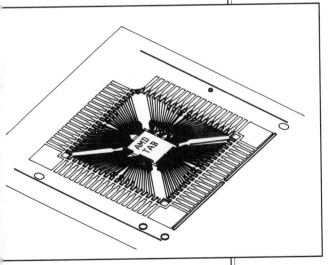

Courtesy of Advanced Micro Devices and Autodesk, Inc.

 **Advanced Plotting**

Reference

■ OBJECTIVE:

To configure multiple output devices, adjust pen parameters, and store plot settings

Whether you are using a pen plotter or a raster output device, you will need to change the pen settings occasionally. (Laser, ink jet, thermal, and electrostatic printers are examples of raster devices.) In the future, you may want to experiment with AutoCAD's pen optimization feature. When set properly, it can reduce plot time.

As you make changes to these plot settings, you may want to store them in a file so you don't have to enter them over and over again. AutoCAD's support of multiple output devices allows you to configure more than one device.

Configuring Plotter Devices _____

INST 43 *

AutoCAD allows you to configure more than one output device. Multiple device configuration conveniently permits you to select one of them from the Device and Default Selection dialogue box.

1 Start AutoCAD and open the drawing named **DIMEN2**.

2 Enter the **CONFIG** command or select **Configure** from the **File** pull-down menu.

AutoCAD will display the current AutoCAD configuration. The information will not appear in a dialogue box.

3 Press **RETURN** until you come to the "Configuration menu" options.

4 Enter **5** for "Configure plotter," and read the list of options.

In addition to adding a plotter configuration, notice that you can also delete, change, or rename a plotter configuration.

5 Enter **1** to add a plotter configuration.

This entry will produce a long list of plotter device options.

6 Select **Houston Instrument ADI 4.2 - by Autodesk** and opt for the **DMP-61MP**.

7 Step through the remaining options (which are unique to the selected device) and enter **DMP-61MP** for the plotter description.

*Page numbers given for the *Interface, Installation, and Performance Guide* refer to the DOS 386 version. If you are running AutoCAD on a different platform, check the index for the appropriate page numbers.

NOTE:

If you are not sure what to enter for each of the device options, press RETURN to accept the default setting.

⑧ Keep the configuration changes and return to the AutoCAD graphics screen.

⑨ Enter the **PLOT** command or select **Plot...** from the **File** pull-down menu.

⑩ Pick the **Device and Default Selection...** button located in the upper left corner of the Plot Configuration dialogue box.

The DMP-61MP device you just configured and named should be included in the list of devices. The actual list of devices will probably be different from those shown here.

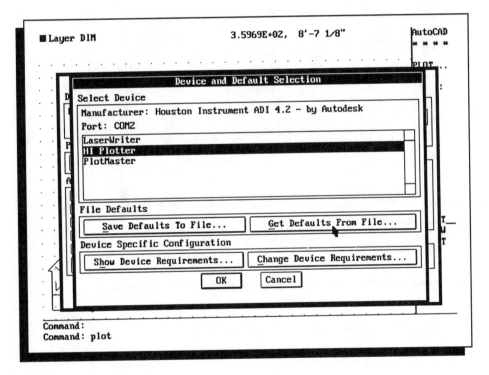

⑪ Select the **DMP-61MP** device and press **OK**.

⑫ If this device is connected and ready, pick **OK** and press **RETURN** to initiate plotting. If not, pick **OK** and press **CTRL C** to cancel.

Pen Parameters

AutoCAD allows you to control the color and thickness of plotted lines using the Pen Assignments subdialogue box. This applies to both pen plotters and raster devices.

1 Enter the **PLOT** command or select **Plot...** from the **File** pull-down menu.

2 In the Pen Parameters area, pick the **Pen Assignments...** button.

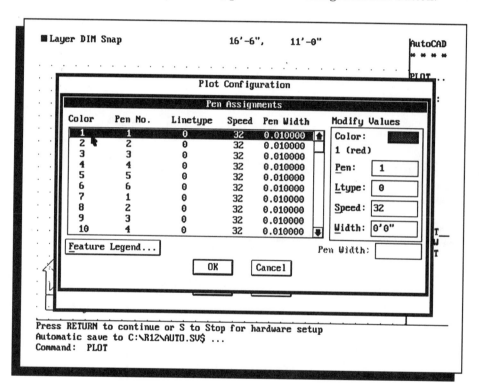

3 Pick color **1**, as shown in the previous illustration.

NOTE:

Color 1 refers to the red color 1 in the AutoCAD graphics screen, not the color produced by the output device.

AutoCAD shows the values associated with color 1 in the Modify Values area. We want pen number 1 assigned to color 1, so do not change this value. As you may recall, linetypes are set "bylayer," so don't change the Ltype value either. Certain output devices will not permit you to make changes to values, such as the Ltype and Speed.

The Speed and Width values may require changes for each of the colors used in the DIMEN2 drawing. The values you enter vary depending on the requirements of the output device. Consider the following two types of output devices.

Laser Printers. Suppose you are using a laser printer. For the DIMEN2 drawing, you would only need to change the Width value for color 1. For example, setting a width of 0.03 would cause AutoCAD to plot relatively thick object lines. If a width of 0.01 were assigned to all remaining colors, the laser printer would plot the rest of the drawing, including text and dimensions, using a thin 0.01 line. AutoCAD would not permit you to change the Speed value because this refers to the speed of the pens, and laser devices do not use pens.

Pen Plotters. If you're using a pen plotter, pay attention to the Pen and Speed values for each of the colors. You can ignore the Width value because the size of the pen tip controls the width of the plotted line. In the future, you will need to enter the width of each pen if you pick the "Adjust Area Fill" check box. You may choose to change the Speed value to a lower number, such as 12. Liquid ink pens may require a value as low as 4.

The Speed value refers to inches per second. Therefore, a value of 12 means 12 inches/second. If you select "MM" (for millimeters) instead of "Inches," the Speed value refers to centimeters/second.

4 Pick the **Feature Legend...** button and review its contents.

REF 515

```
■ Layer DIM Snap              16'-6",    11'-0"             AutoCAD
                                                            * * * *
  .  .  .  .  .  .  .  .  .  .  .  .  .  .  .  .  .  .  . PLOT . .
 ┌──────────────────── Plot Configuration ──────────────────┐
 │ ┌────────────────────── Feature Legend ─────────────────┐ │
 │ │ Linetypes: 0 = continuous line      Pen speed :       │ │
 │ │            1 = ...................                     │ │
 │ │            2 = . . . . . . . . . .  Inches/Second:     │ │
 │ │            3 = -------------------  1, 2,  4,  8, 16, 24, 32 │
 │ │            4 = - - - - - - - - - -                    │ │
 │ │            5 = -- -- -- -- -- -- -  Cm/Second:        │ │
 │ │            6 = --- --- --- --- ---  3, 5, 10, 20, 40, 60, 80 │
 │ │            7 = -- - -- - -- - -- -                    │ │
 │ │            8 = __--__--__--__--_                      │ │
 │ │                                                       │ │
 │ │                  ┌──────┐                             │ │
 │ │                  │  OK  │                             │ │
 │ │                  └──────┘                             │ │
 │ └───────────────────────────────────────────────────────┘ │
 └───────────────────────────────────────────────────────────┘
 Press RETURN to continue or S to Stop for hardware setup
 Automatic save to C:\R12\AUTO.SV$ ...
 Command: PLOT
```

The Feature Legend subdialogue box may show a legend of linetypes and pen speeds. However, the legend will vary from device to device. It is not applicable to some devices. For these devices, the legend is not available to you.

5 Pick the **OK** button.

If you are using a multi-pen plotter, you can assign multiple pens to the colors used in DIMEN2. Normally, you would use a thick, dark pen for color 1 so that object lines stand out. Use pens that produce thin lines for the other colors. Pen colors are your choice, yet it is a good practice to standardize the pens you use for pen 1, pen 2, pen 3, etc. Likewise, it is best to standardize the pens you assign to color 1, color 2, color 3, etc.

6 Using the previous discussion as a guide, change the values in the **Modify Values** area for each color used in the DIMEN2 drawing. Do not change Ltype values.

7 Pick the **OK** button; pick **OK** again.

8 Prepare your output device and press **RETURN**.

9 Compare the plotted drawing with the values you set in the Pen Assignments subdialogue box.

10 If DIMEN2 did not plot correctly, make adjustments in the Pen Assignments subdialogue box and plot the drawing again.

Pen Optimization

INST 45

Pen optimization can minimize pen motion and can reduce plot time.

1 Enter the **PLOT** command.

2 Pick the **Optimization...** button.

REF 516

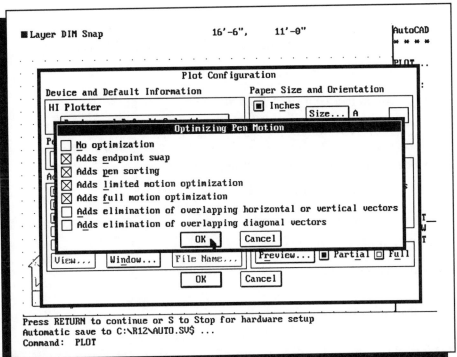

The Optimizing Pen Motion subdialogue box permits you to change and potentially optimize the motion of the plotter pens. The content provided in the subdialogue box will vary from one configured device to another.

3 Pick the **OK** button—*do not* make any changes to these settings at this time.

Device and Default Selection _____

The Device and Default Selection subdialogue box enables you to review up to 29 previously configured output devices.

1 Pick the **Device and Default Selection...** button to display the Device and Default Selection dialogue box.

REF 511-513

2 Pick the **Get Defaults From File...** button.

A standard File dialogue box should appear. It enables you to select an ASCII Plot Configuration Parameters (PCP) file if one is available. PCP files contain default settings, such as pen assignments, drawing scale, and all of the other options made available in the Plot Configuration dialogue box.

3 Pick the **Cancel** button.

④ Pick the **Save Defaults To File...** button.

The standard File dialogue box should reappear. AutoCAD suggests that you use the drawing file name for the PCP file name. Therefore, "DIMEN2" will appear in the "File:" edit box.

⑤ Pick the **OK** button to accept the DIMEN2 name.

This will save the current plot settings in a file named DIMEN2.PCP.

⑥ Pick the **Get Defaults From File...** button again.

You should now see DIMEN2 in the Files list box. Notice the directory within which it is stored.

⑦ Pick the **OK** button.

This will retrieve the settings contained in DIMEN2.PCP.

⑧ Pick **OK**; pick **OK** again.

⑨ Press **CTRL C** to cancel the plot.

Viewing the Contents of PCP Files

PCP files store plot information using standard ASCII text.

① Enter the **SH** command to shell out to the operating system and press **RETURN**.

② Use the DOS **DIR** and **CD** commands to locate **DIMEN2.PCP**. Use either the DOS **TYPE** or **MORE** command to view the contents of **DIMEN2.PCP**.

HINT:
Refer to Appendix B for information on how to use the DIR, CD, TYPE, and MORE commands.

As you can see, the file contains a long list of plot settings.

③ Enter **EXIT** to return to AutoCAD. (See the following note.)

NOTE:
If you used the CD command, be sure to change back to the original directory before entering EXIT.

320

Companies that use AutoCAD exchange drawing files frequently. If you give a drawing file to another person, you may want to include a PCP file with it so they don't have to guess what plot settings you intended to use.

4   Enter **END** to save any changes you may have made to the drawing and exit AutoCAD.

Multiple Viewport Plotting

Until now, you have been plotting a single viewport only. In the future, you may want to plot multiple viewports. Multiple viewport plotting is especially useful when you create AutoCAD drawings in three dimensions.

Multiple viewport plotting is covered in Unit 47: "Multiple Viewports in Paperspace." Several units leading to Unit 47 cover AutoCAD's 3D capabilities. Unit 47 focuses on the TILEMODE system variable and the MVIEW, PSPACE, MSPACE, and VPLAYER commands. You should be familiar with these commands and features before you attempt to plot multiple viewports.

Questions

1. The Pen Assignments subdialogue box allows you to make plotter changes related to the colors used in the AutoCAD graphics screen. Relative to these screen colors, describe the purpose of entering values for each of the following.

   Pen number _ASSIGN PEN to specific Color_

   Linetype _ASSIGN LINETYPE to SPEC Color_

   Speed _ASSIGN PEN SPEED to SPEC Color_

   Pen Width _ASSIGN PEN WIDTH to SPEC Colon_

2. Suppose you are using a raster device that does not use pens. Are any of the previous settings applicable? Explain.

   YES But other PERAMETERS ARE NOT APPLIC.

3. Is it recommended that you change the Linetype values in the Pen Assignments subdialogue box? Explain.

  NO LiNETYPES ARE BY lAYER ChANGing OveRRiDES BY lAYER

4. Explain the purpose of pen optimization.

  REDUCE Plot time by REDUCing PEN motioN

5. What is the purpose of creating and using PCP files?

  To EXChANGE DRWG fileS with other Co or PEOple

6. Is it possible to configure more than one output device? Explain.

  YES up to 29 DEVICES

7. How do you select a configured output device?

  USE DEVICE & DEFAUlt selectioN

Problems

1. Open a drawing (any drawing will work) and set the following values. Certain output devices will not allow you to enter values (for Linetype and Speed, for instance) in the Modify Values area. If this applies to you, select another configured device. If another device is not configured, configure one.

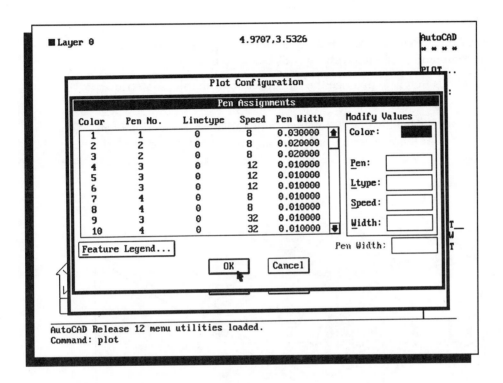

2. Retrieve the DIMEN2.PCP file created in this unit and review the plot settings contained in it. Change the sheet size and a few pen assignments and create a new PCP file named DIMEN3.

3. Configure each of the following output devices. Unless a specific setting is given below, accept the default setting suggested by AutoCAD.

PostScript device ADI 4.2
300 dpi
COM2
Description: LaserWriter

CalComp ColorMaster Plotters ADI 4.2
PlotMaster 5902A, A/A4 Sheet
Port: Parallel
Connected to: LPT2
Description: PlotMaster

Houston Instrument ADI 4.2
Model: DMP-51MP
COM1
Default scale: 1 = 1
Description: HI Plotter

4. Review the devices you configured (in problem 3) in the Device and Default Selection subdialogue box. Select the "HI Plotter" device. When you make the selection, your screen should match the illustration on page 315.

Unit 36 — Isometrics: Creating Objects from a New Angle

■ OBJECTIVE:

To apply AutoCAD's isometric drawing capabilities using the SNAP and ISOPLANE commands and the Drawing Aids dialogue box

The purpose of this unit is to practice the construction of simple isometric drawings.

Isometric drawing is one of two ways to obtain a pictorial representation of an object using AutoCAD. Below is an example of an isometric drawing created with AutoCAD.

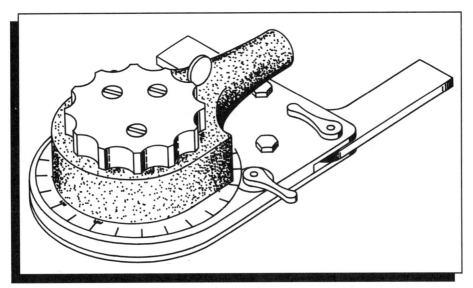

AutoCAD Drawing Courtesy of CAD Northwest, Inc.

■ *Isometric Mode* _____

REF 347-348

Let's do some simple isometric drawing.

1 Start AutoCAD and begin a new drawing named **ISO**.

2 Set the grid at **1** unit and the snap resolution at **0.5** unit.

AutoCAD isometric drawing is accomplished by changing the SNAP Style to Isometric mode.

REF 349-352

3 Enter the **SNAP** command.

4 Enter **S** for Style or select **Style** from the standard screen menu.

5 Enter **I** for Isometric or select **Iso** from the standard screen menu.

Reference

REF 348

6 Enter **0.5** for the vertical spacing. (This should be the default value.)

You should now be in Isometric drawing mode, with the crosshairs shifted to one of the three (Left, Top, or Right) isometric planes.

7 Move the crosshairs and notice that they run parallel to the isometric grid.

Drawing Aids Dialogue Box

You can also use the Drawing Aids dialogue box to change to the Isometric drawing mode.

1 Pick **Drawing Aids...** from the **Settings** pull-down menu.

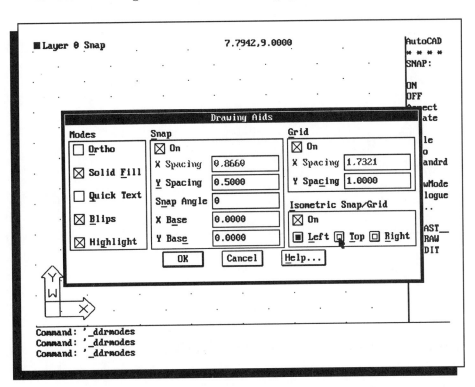

As you can see, the "Isometric Snap/Grid" is turned on. We did this in Steps 3-6. In the future, you can check the "On" check box instead.

2 Pick the **Top** radio button.

This shifts the crosshairs to the top isometric plane.

3 Pick **OK**.

ISOPLANE Command

The ISOPLANE command also allows you to change from one isometric plane to another.

1 Enter **ISOPLANE**.

2 Enter **L, T,** or **R** to change to the Left, Top, or Right plane. (Experiment with each.)

3 Enter **ISOPLANE** and press **RETURN**.

This toggles you to the next isometric plane.

Another method of toggling the crosshairs is to enter CTRL E. You may find this the fastest and most practical method.

4 Enter **CTRL E**; enter **CTRL E** again.

5 Experiment further with each of the methods of changing the crosshairs.

Isometric Drawing

Let's construct a simple isometric drawing.

1 Enter the **LINE** command and draw the following box. Don't worry about specific sizes.

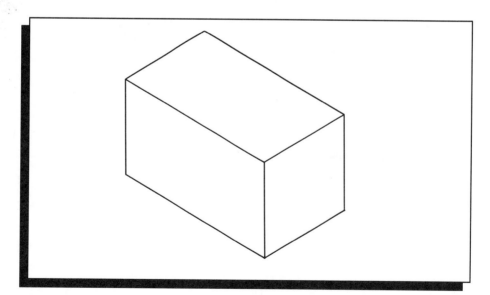

2 Alter the box so that it looks similar to the one on the next page, using the **LINE**, **BREAK**, and **ERASE** commands.

HINT: You can use all of the AutoCAD commands while constructing isometric drawings.

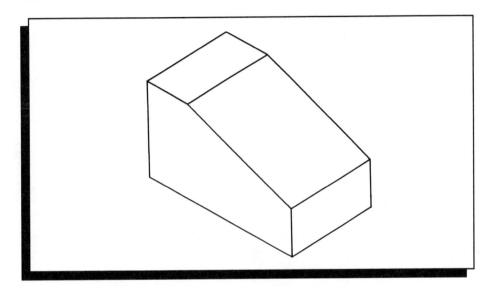

3 Further alter the object so that it looks similar to the following. Use the **ELLIPSE** command to draw the isometric circle.

HINT: Since the ellipse is to be drawn on the top isometric plane, toggle (change) the crosshairs to reflect this plane. Then choose the ELLIPSE command's Isocircle option.

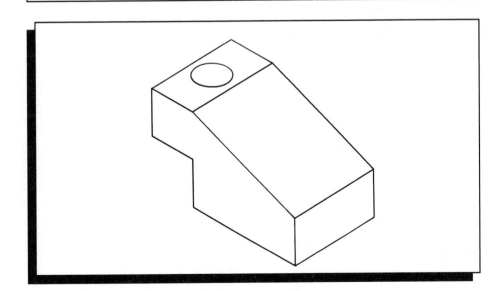

4 Add dimensions to the object.

HINT:

Refer to the section on the OBLIQUE subcommand in Unit 25.

5 Further experiment with AutoCAD's isometric drawing capability by constructing other isometric objects.

NOTE:

To change back to AutoCAD's standard drawing format, enter the SNAP, Style, Standard sequence, or use the Drawing Aids dialogue box.

6 Enter **END** to save your work and exit AutoCAD.

AUTOCAD® AT WORK

*It Fits Like a Glove**

Glovemaker Wells Lamont had a vexing problem. Glove styles change annually, which means each year Wells Lamont had to draw new styles mechanically, cut the patterns out of tin, and refine them in a painfully slow way.

In its quest to modernize both design and manufacturing, Wells Lamont turned to Conversion Graphics, Inc., a Chicago-area scanning and data conversion service bureau. CGI used CAD Overlay software to scan the glove patterns and convert them for use in AutoCAD. CAD Overlay (developed by Image Systems Technology, Inc., Troy, NY) combines raster and vector technologies within AutoCAD to provide low-cost drawing conversion with complete CAD capabilities.

Every few weeks, CGI receives a batch of tin patterns that are reproduced photographically, several to a page, and then scanned into AutoCAD as a single image. The working file information is then translated and supplied in Wells Lamont's working file format. Wells Lamont can open these files on its computer system and manipulate the graphic information to restyle the glove and numerically cut a new pattern.

Use of CAD Overlay has resulted in several significant savings, according to Randy Worozaken, Vice President of Sales and Marketing at CGI. "It has streamlined our operation by eliminating the vectorizing process, a 2-6 hour step, and enhancing editing time by about 25 percent. It also eliminates the guesswork involved in drawing conversion by giving us a true image."

In addition to assisting glovemakers and other manufacturers requiring CAD/CAM pattern manipulation, CAD Overlay is well suited to other applications. In fact, CGI is using it to enter drawings for projects involving illustrations, schematics, mapping, architecture, shop floor display, logo design, red lining, and archiving. CGI can output data to most mainframe and micro CAD packages.

*Based on a story in *CADENCE* magazine, Vol. 3, No. 6.

Questions

1. Describe two methods of changing from AutoCAD's standard drawing format to isometric drawing.

   ENTER SNAP then STYLE THEN ISO opt.

2. Describe the purpose of the ISOPLANE command.

   SELECT CURRENT PLANE

3. Describe two methods of changing the isometric crosshairs from one plane to another.

   Ctrl E, ISOplane At Cmd Line

4. Explain how to create accurate isometric circles.

   Ellipse w/ ISO Circle opt. USE Cen opt Give Radius, or Drag

5. How do you change from isometric drawing to AutoCAD's standard drawing format?

   ENtr SNAP, STYle, and STANDARD

Create each object in PRB36-1 through PRB36-4 using AutoCAD's isometric capability. Don't worry about their exact sizes.

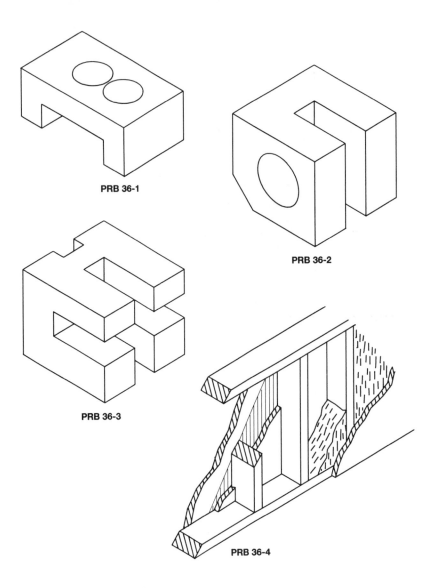

PRB 36-1

PRB 36-2

PRB 36-3

PRB 36-4

AutoCAD Drawing Courtesy of Autodesk, Inc.

(continued on next page)

In PRB36-5 accurately draw an isometric representation of the orthographic views. Draw and dimension the isometric according to the dimensions provided.

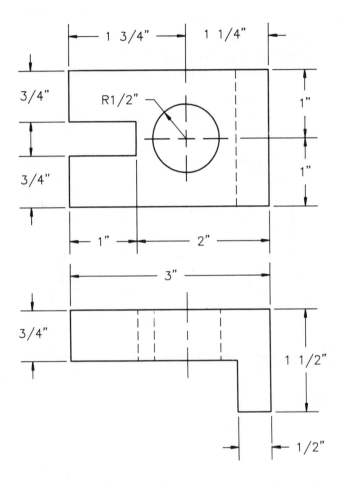

PRB 36-5

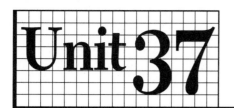

Unit 37 — The Third Dimension

■ OBJECTIVE:

To apply AutoCAD's 3D modeling capability using the ELEV, VPOINT, DDVPOINT, and HIDE commands, and the THICKNESS system variable

This unit introduces AutoCAD's three-dimensional capability with four easy-to-use commands. They permit you to create simple 3D models (boxes, cylinders, etc.) and view them from any point in space. An example of an AutoCAD-generated 3D model is shown below, left. The model on the right is the same object viewed from the top.

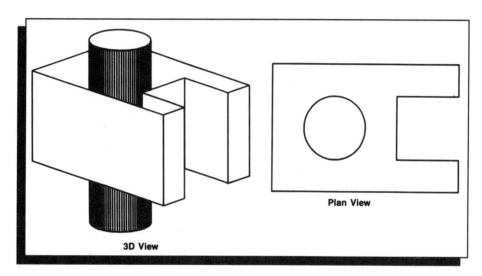

3D View

Plan View

Let's draw a simple 3D model like the one here.

ELEV Command _____

REF 344-345

1　Start AutoCAD and begin a new drawing named **THREE-D**.

2　Enter the **ELEV** command and set the new current elevation at **1** and the new current thickness at **3**.

_____ NOTE: _____

An elevation of 1 means the base of the object will be located 1 unit above a base plane of 0 on the Z-axis. The thickness of 3 means the object will have a thickness on the Z-axis of 3 units upward from the elevation plane. This is called the extrusion thickness. The THICKNESS system variable also permits you to specify the extrusion thickness.

3　Draw the top (plan) view of the object using the **LINE** command. Construct the object as shown above, right, but omit the circle (cylinder) at this time. Don't worry about exact sizes. Turn on snap, ortho, and grid.

VPOINT and HIDE Commands _____

Now let's view the object in 3D.

1 Pick **Set View, Viewpoint,** and **Axes** from the **View** pull-down menu.

HINT: _____

Instead, you may choose to type the VPOINT command and press RETURN twice. You may find this to be faster than picking items from the pull-down menu.

2 Move the pointing device and watch what happens.

3 Place the small crosshairs inside the globe representation, also referred to as the compass, as shown in the following illustration and pick that approximate point.

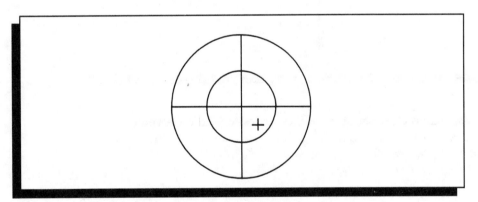

A 3D model of the object should appear on the screen.

Study the following globe representation carefully. The placement of the crosshairs on the globe indicates the exact position of the viewpoint. Placement of the crosshairs inside the inner ring (called the equator) will result in viewing the object from above. Placing the crosshairs outside the inner ring will result in a look underneath the object.

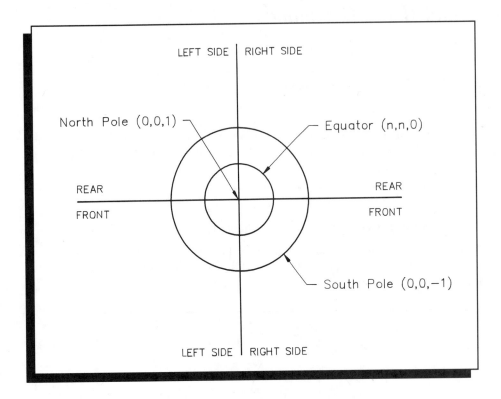

If the crosshairs are on the right side of the vertical line, the viewpoint will be on the right side of the object. Similarly, if the crosshairs are in front of the horizontal line, the viewpoint will be in front of the object.

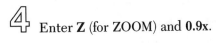 Enter **Z** (for ZOOM) and **0.9x**.

The object should look somewhat like the one below.

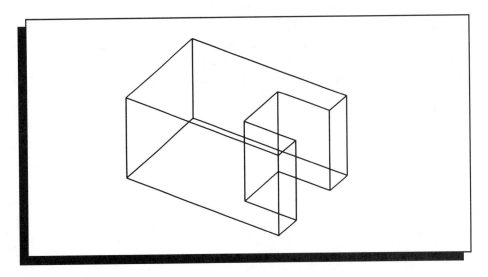

5 Enter the **HIDE** command to remove the hidden lines.

The object should now look similar to the following.

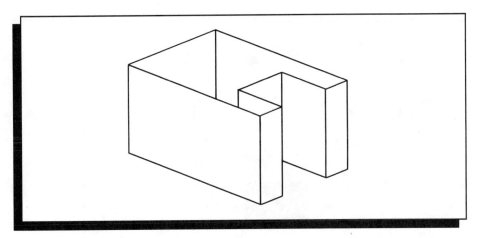

6 Return to the plan view (0,0,1) of the object by entering **VPOINT** and then selecting **plan** from the screen menu. You may instead enter **0,0,1**.

7 **ZOOM All** to obtain the original plan view of the model.

Adding Objects of Different Elevation and Thickness

Let's add the cylinder to the model at a new elevation and thickness.

1 Enter the **ELEV** command and set the elevation at **–1** and the thickness at **6**.

2 Draw a circle in the center of the model as shown on the first page of this unit.

Visualize how the cylinder will appear in relation to the existing object.

3 Enter **VPOINT** and **axes** from the standard screen menu (or use whatever VPOINT method you prefer). Place the crosshairs in approximately the same location as before and pick a point.

Does the model appear as you had visualized it?

4 Remove the hidden lines by entering the **HIDE** command.

Does the model now look similar to the one shown at the beginning of this unit? It should.

5 Experiment with VPOINT to obtain viewpoints from different points in space, and create a 3D view of the model as shown in the following illustration.

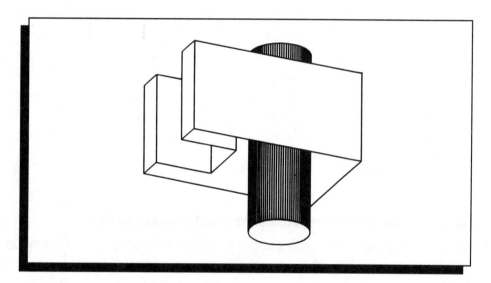

HINT:
Type VPOINT and press RETURN twice. Select a point in the globe. Press the space bar (or RETURN) to reissue the VPOINT command, and press RETURN to display the globe. Repeating this is a quick way to view the object from several different viewpoints.

Viewpoint Presets Dialogue Box

The Viewpoint Presets dialogue box offers another way to choose viewpoints.

1 Enter the **DDVPOINT** command or pick **Set View, Viewpoint,** and **Presets...** from the **View** pull-down menu.

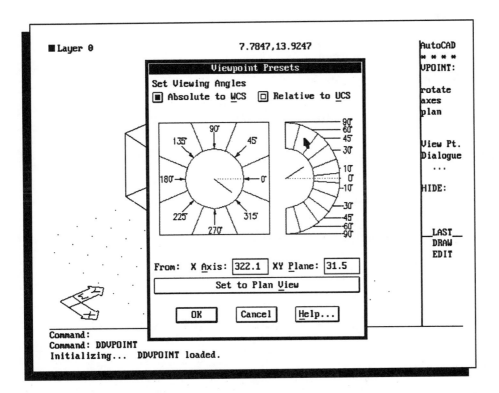

NOTE:

You can also display this dialogue box by picking the "View Pt. Dialogue" from the VIEWPOINT submenu in the standard screen menu.

For now, ignore the radio buttons at the top of the dialogue box. Unit 39 covers user coordinate systems, including WCS and UCS.

The half-circle located at the right allows you to set the viewpoint height.

② Pick a point (as shown in the previous illustration) so that you view the object from above at a 60-degree angle and pick the **OK** button.

You should now be viewing the object from above at a 60-degree angle.

③ Display the dialogue box again by pressing the space bar.

The full circle (located in the left part of the dialogue box) allows you to set the viewpoint rotation.

④ Pick a point so that you will view the object at a 135-degree angle and pick **OK**.

5 Enter **HIDE**.

6 Display the dialogue box again.

The two edit boxes enable you to enter values for the rotation and height.

7 Pick the **Set to Plan View** button and pick **OK**.

8 **ZOOM** All.

9 Experiment further with the Viewpoint Presets dialogue box.

10 Enter **END** to save your work and exit AutoCAD.

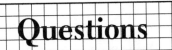

Questions

1. Describe the purpose of the VPOINT command.

   lets you spec any view point

2. What is the viewpoint (*i.e.*, the X, Y, and Z coordinates) when viewing the plan view of a 3D model?

   0, 0, 1

3. The extrusion thickness of an object is specified with which command? System variable?

   ELEV. Thickness

4. Briefly explain the process by which you create objects (within the same model) at different elevations and thicknesses.

   USE ELEV CMDD, spec ELEV & Thickness THEN DRAW Item. Repeat to Change FOR Diff Items

5. When the small crosshairs are in the exact center of the globe, what is the location of the viewpoint in relation to the object?

   ABOVE

6. With what command are hidden lines removed from 3D objects?

   HIDE

7. Indicate on the globe below where you must position the small crosshairs to view an object from the rear and underneath.

   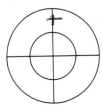

8. Match the following globe representations with the objects. The first one has been completed to give you a starting point.

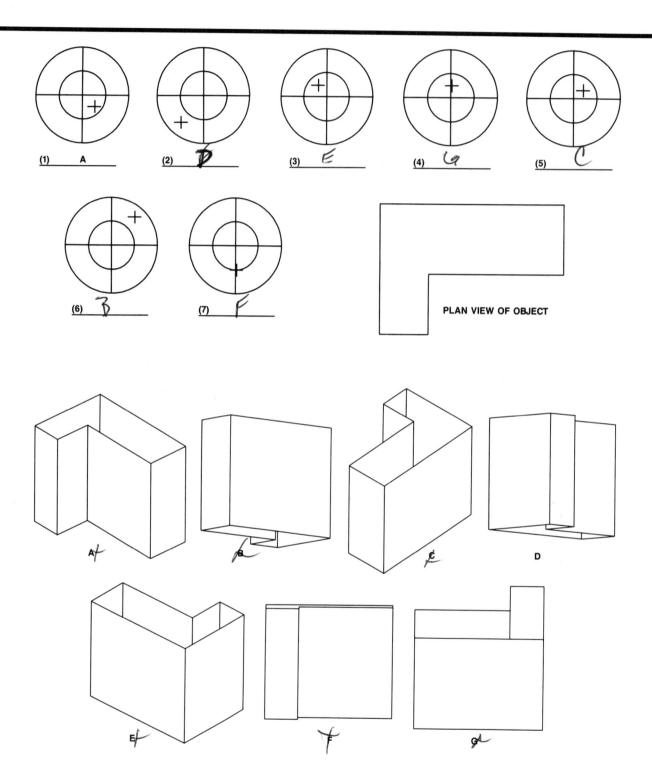

(1)   A

(2)   D

(3)   E

(4)   G

(5)   C

(6)   B

(7)   F

PLAN VIEW OF OBJECT

A

B

C

D

E

F

G

Problems

Draw the following objects and generate a 3D model of each.

1. In PRB37-1 set the elevation at 1 inch.

2. In PRB37-2 set the elevation for the inner cylinder at 0. Set the snap resolution prior to picking the center point of the first circle. Do not use object snap to select the center point of the second circle.

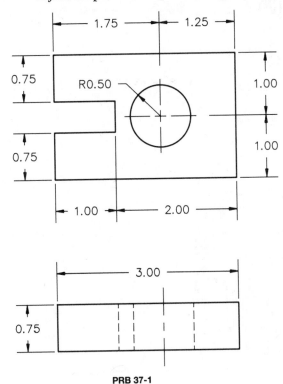

PRB 37-1

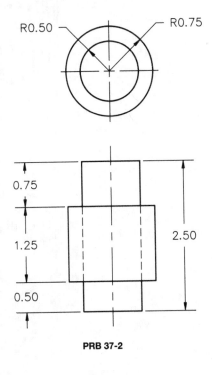

PRB 37-2

3. In PRB37-3 try as best you can to draw a similar object.

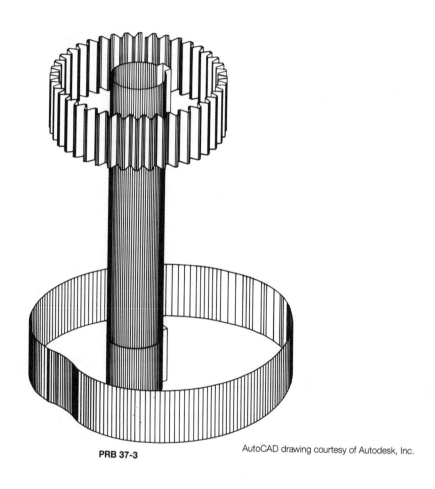

PRB 37-3

AutoCAD drawing courtesy of Autodesk, Inc.

AUTOCAD® AT WORK

Designing the Right Stuff with AutoCAD

Engineers at the Electromechanical Branch of NASA's Goodard Space Flight Center (Greenbelt, MD) are using AutoCAD to develop a completely new type of robot hand. Unlike previous robot hands, the five-finger anthrobot (anthropomorphic robot) hand resembles the basic skeletal structure of the human hand and incorporates its dexterity. Instead of relying on elaborate computer architecture for this dexterity, the anthrobot hand mirrors the natural, intuitive hand movements of a human operator. The operator wears a special glove that records and transmits hand movements to the anthrobot hand, which then repeats each movement. Eventually, the anthrobot hand may be used in space by NASA mission specialists to work remotely on projects requiring human dexterity.

The anthrobot hand research project is one of four that Chuck Engler, a mechanical engineer at NASA's Goodard Space Flight Center (GSFC), is working on simultaneously. Because his time is so valuable, Engler says "I can't afford to spend a lot of time on design iterations, even though design iterations are a basic part of research and development. What's nice about using AutoCAD is that I don't have to start over from scratch every time I make a design change." He estimates that his design time has been cut by more than 50 percent.

At the GSFC, quality is the watchword. Before prototypes can be built, design drawings must be created to extremely high standards. "If you want to send a drawing down to the shop, they will not look at it unless it meets certain Goodard specifications," Engler explains. "I can use AutoCAD to set up my format parameters so every drawing meets these specifications. With AutoCAD, along with decreased design time, I get high-quality drawings."

Already, there are three space-flight hardware designers and five engineers using AutoCAD for their projects. "Now, all I have to do is put my drawing on a floppy disk, take it to a designer and ask him for his opinion," Engler says.

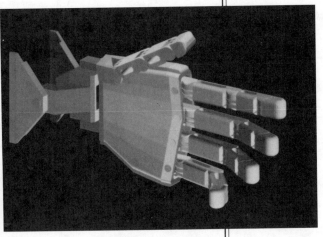

Courtesy of Autodesk, Inc.

Unit 38 — X/Y/Z Point Filters

Reference

■ OBJECTIVE:

To apply AutoCAD's 3D X/Y/Z point filters using the 3DFACE command

This unit continues with AutoCAD's 3D wireframe modeling facility. X/Y/Z filters enable you to enter coordinates using both the pointing device and the keyboard. With the LINE and 3DFACE commands, you can create lines and surfaces in three-dimensional space using X, Y, *and* Z coordinates. For instance, you can create inclined and oblique surfaces, such as a roof on a building. AutoCAD is also capable of creating 3D wireframe cones, domes, spheres, and other 3D objects with commands presented in the following units.

■ *3DFACE Command*

REF 161-163

The 3DFACE command creates a three-dimensional object similar in many respects to a two-dimensional Solid entity. The 3DFACE prompt sequence is identical to that of the SOLID command. However, unlike the SOLID command, points are entered in a natural clockwise or counterclockwise order to create a normal 3D face. Z coordinates are specified for the corner points of a 3D Face, forming a section of a plane in space.

1 Start AutoCAD and begin a new drawing named **THREE-D2**, using THREE-D as a prototype drawing.

2 If you don't already have the plan view on the screen, obtain it by entering **VPOINT** and **0,0,1** or pick **plan** from the standard screen menu; then **ZOOM All**.

3 Erase the cylinder (circle) from the 3D model.

4 Set the Snap at **0.25** unit and Grid at **0.5** unit.

5 Enter **3DFACE** or pick **3D Surfaces** from the **Draw** pull-down menu and pick **3D Face**.

6 Select **.xy** from the standard screen menu because you are about to pick an x,y point.

HINT:

You can also enter .xy—as you see it here—at the keyboard. Be sure to include the period before the letters.

7 In reply to ".xy of," approximate the x,y position of point 1 in the following illustration and pick that point. (Point 1 is about ½ unit from the corner of the object.)

Reference

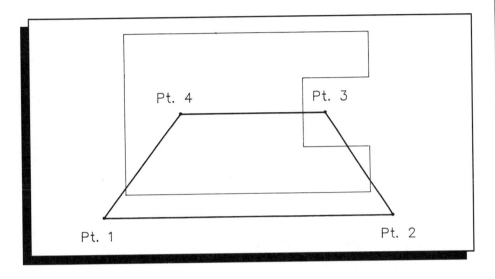

As shown on the prompt line, the first point also requires a Z coordinate. Therefore . . .

8 . . . enter a Z coordinate of **3.5**.

This method of entering 3D points is referred to as X/Y/Z filtering.

9 In reply to "Second point:" select **.xy** from the screen menu or enter **.xy** at the keyboard and pick point 2 as shown in the illustration.

10 Enter **3.5** for the Z coordinate.

11 Repeat these steps for points 3 and 4, but enter **7** for the Z coordinate of these points. (Be sure to enter or select **.xy** *before* picking the point.)

12 Press **RETURN** to terminate the 3DFACE command.

Do you know what you've just created? If not, try to visualize its position in relation to the object. It's an inclined surface resembling a portion of a roof. Let's make the opposite portion.

1 Enter the **MIRROR** command, select the 3D Face entity you just created, and press **RETURN**.

2 Place the mirror line so the two sections of the roof meet at the middle of the object. Do not delete the "old object."

Now let's view the object in 3D.

3 Enter the **VPOINT** command and obtain the globe representation.

REF 374-375

4 Pick a point on the globe so that you view the object from above, front, and right side.

HINT:

See pages 333 and 334 for assistance.

5 Enter the **HIDE** command.

Does your model look similar to the one here? It should.

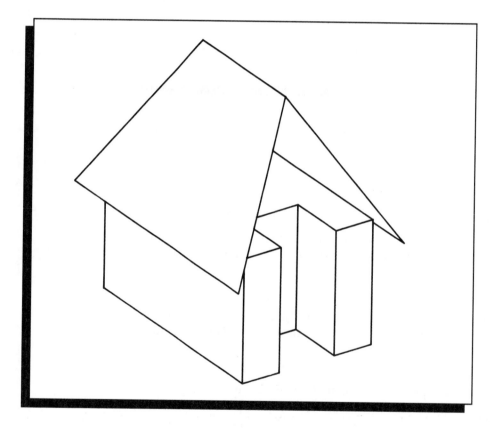

Let's finish the roof so that it looks similar to the following.

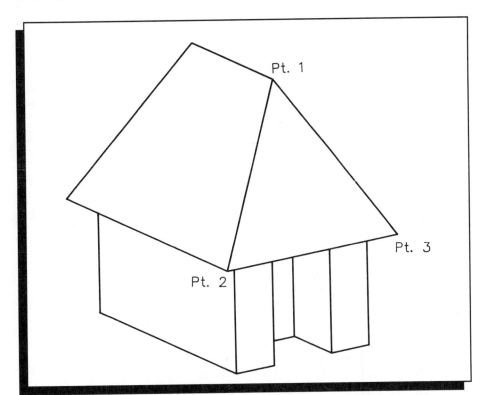

1 With the current 3D view remaining on the screen, enter the **3DFACE** command and then enter the **END**point object snap mode.

2 Snap to point 1, shown in the preceding illustration.

3 Enter the **END**point mode again and snap to point 2.

4 Enter **END**point and snap to point 3.

5 Enter **END**point once more and snap to point 1 to complete the surface boundary.

6 Press **RETURN** to terminate the 3DFACE command.

7 Enter the **HIDE** command.

8 View the object from above, front, and left side using either **VPOINT** or **DDVPOINT**, and enter **HIDE**.

9 Create the remaining portion of the roof using the 3DFACE command and object snap.

10 Generate a view similar to the one following.

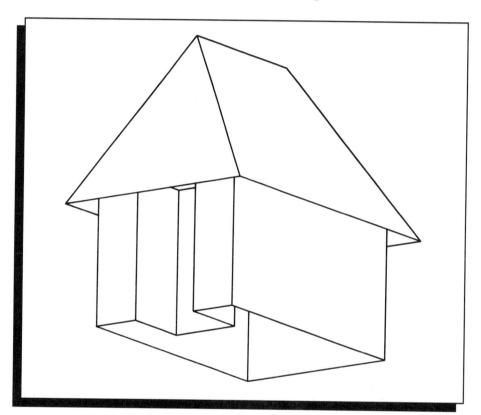

Invisible Option

3D Faces can define visible and invisible edges.

1 Generate the plan view.

2 Enter **ZOOM** and **0.5x**.

3 Using **3DFACE**, create the following pentagon anywhere on the screen and at any size.

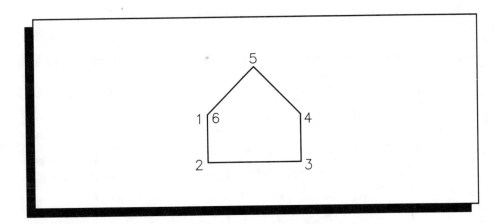

HINT:

Consider the following.

Command: 3DFACE
First point: (pick point 1)
Second point: (pick point 2)
Third point: (pick point 3)
Fourth point (enter I and pick point 4)
Third point: (pick point 5)
Fourth point: (enter I and pick point 6)
Third point: (press RETURN)

The invisible option is useful when connecting two or more 3D faces together to create a 3D model.

The system variable SPLFRAME controls the display of invisible edges in 3D Faces. When set to a nonzero value, invisible edges are displayed. This allows you to edit them as you would a visible 3D Face.

The following illustration shows the same pentagon with SPLFRAME set at a nonzero value.

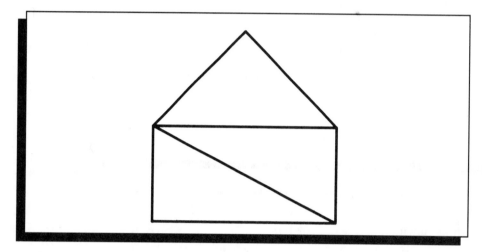

 Enter **SPLFRAME** and enter **1**.

 Enter **REGEN**.

Your pentagon should now look similar to the preceding illustration.

 Set **SPLFRAME** back to **0** and enter **REGEN**.

 Erase the pentagon 3D Face entity.

Creating 3D Lines

REF 129-132

The LINE command creates full 3D lines in space. Therefore, all lines you have created with AutoCAD are three-dimensional. Their endpoints are made up of X, Y, and Z coordinates. Let's create a 3D property line around the building using LINE.

 ZOOM All.

Enter the **ELEV** command and change the elevation to **1** and the thickness to **0**.

Enter the **LINE** command and pick one of the four corners of the property line shown in the following illustration. (Approximate its location.)

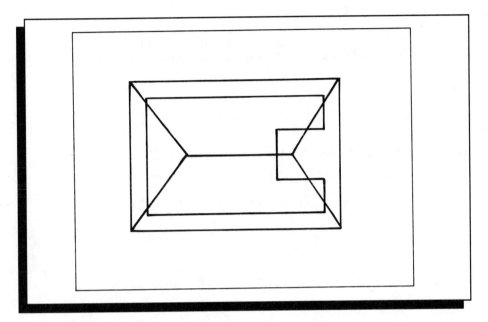

4 Approximate the location of the remaining corners and press **RETURN** when you are finished.

5 Obtain a view similar to the following using either **VPOINT** or **DDVPOINT**.

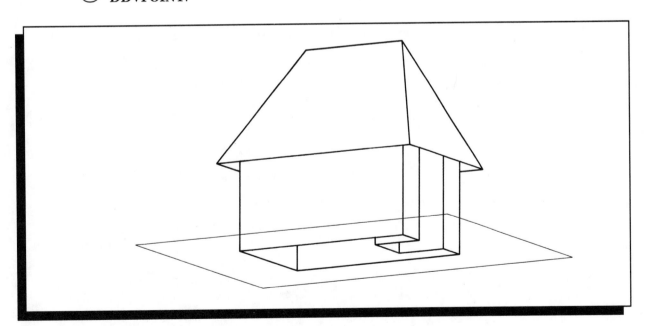

6 Further experiment with the LINE and 3DFACE commands.

VPOINT *Rotate Option* _____

The VPOINT Rotate option lets you specify a viewpoint in terms of two angles: one with respect to the X-axis (in the X-Y plane) and another "up" from the X-Y plane.

1 Enter the **VPOINT** command and **Rotate** option.

2 Enter **0** for the first angle and **0** for the second angle.

An end view (right side) of the building should appear.

An easier way to take full advantage of the Rotate option is with DDVPOINT.

1 Enter **DDVPOINT**.

2 Select **270** degrees for the rotation and **0** degrees for the height.

A front elevation view of the building should appear.

3 Remove hidden lines.

4 Create other elevation views on your own.

5 Enter **END** to save your work and exit AutoCAD.

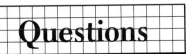

Questions

1. Describe a 3D Face entity.

   OBJ DEFINED BY X, Y & Z COORDS

2. What basic AutoCAD command is the 3DFACE command most like?

   SOLID

3. What can be created with the 3DFACE command that cannot be created with the LINE command? Be specific.

   A ROOF OF Bldg

4. Describe the X/Y/Z filtering process of entering 3D points.

   USE .XY At Point Prompt Click At Point Type iN Z COORDS

5. Describe the purpose of the VPOINT Rotate option.

   SPEC VIEW with Z AXES

6. What is the primary benefit of using X/Y/Z point filters?

   Combine Key BOARD & Pointing DEVICE

Problems

1. Using AutoCAD's 3D modeling facilities, add a door, window, and fireplace chimney to the object you created earlier. When finished, your drawing should look similar to the one here.

HINT: Use the 3DFACE command and X/Y/Z point filters when creating the door and window.

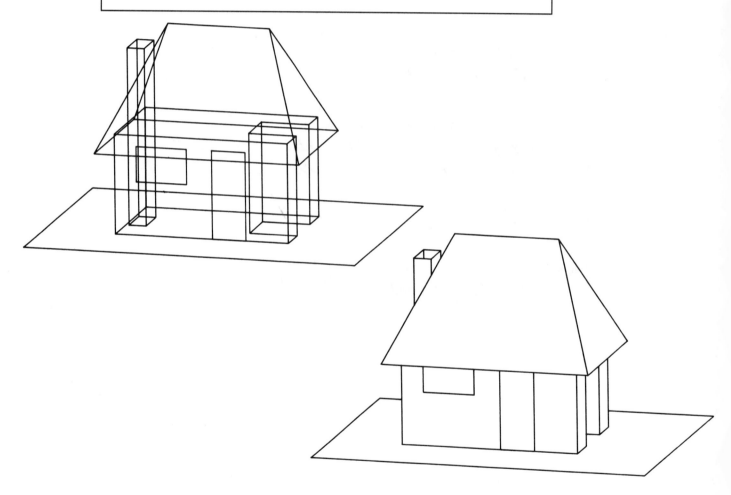

2. Embellish the drawing further by adding other details to the building. Save the finished drawing as PRB38-1.

Unit 39

User Coordinate Systems

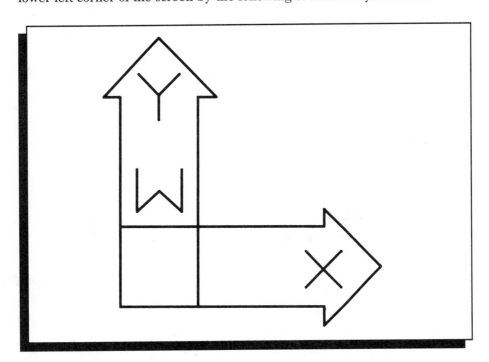

■ OBJECTIVE:

To understand the user-definable User Coordinate System (UCS) and apply it to the construction of 3D wireframe models

As you know, AutoCAD uses a coordinate system; points in a drawing are located by their X,Y,Z coordinates. AutoCAD's default coordinate system is the World Coordinate System (WCS). In this system, the X-axis is horizontal on the screen, the Y-axis is vertical, and the Z-axis is perpendicular to the XY plane (the plane defined by the X and Y axes). The WCS is indicated in the lower left corner of the screen by the following coordinate system icon.

REF 40

You may create drawings in the World Coordinate System, or you may define your own User Coordinate System (UCS). The advantage of a UCS is that its origin is not fixed. You can specify it to be located anywhere within the world coordinate system. Thus the axes of the UCS can be rotated or tilted in relation to the axes of the WCS. This is a useful feature when you're drawing a three-dimensional model.

REF 41-42,
356-357

Consider the following 3D model. A UCS was defined to match the inclined plane of the roof as indicated by the arrows. Once established, all new objects constructed lie in the same plane as the roof.

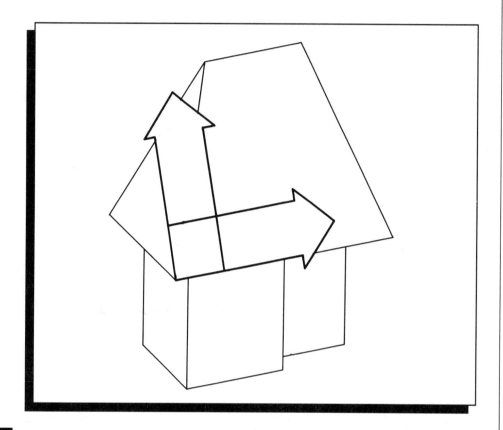

UCS Command

REF 357-364

The UCS command enables you to create a new current UCS. Let's try it.

1 Start AutoCAD and open **THREE-D2**.

2 Alter the plan view so that it resembles the illustration on the next page. Remove the property line around the model.

HINT:

Be sure to set the elevation at 1 and the thickness at 3 before drawing new lines.

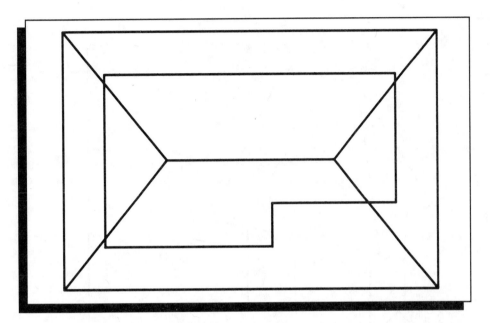

③ Obtain a view similar to the one shown on the preceding page.

HINT: With reference to the globe (see page 334), place the viewpoint in front, above, and to the left.

④ Enter the **UCS** command.

You should see the following list of options.

```
Origin/ZAxis/3point/Entity/View/X/Y/Z/Prev/Restore/Save/Del/?/<World>:
```

⑤ Enter **3** for the 3point option.

This option allows you to specify the origin, orientation, and rotation of the XY plane in a UCS. It is one of the most useful options of the UCS command.

⑥ In reply to "Origin point <0,0,0>:" pick point 1 (shown on the following page) using the **END**point object snap mode.

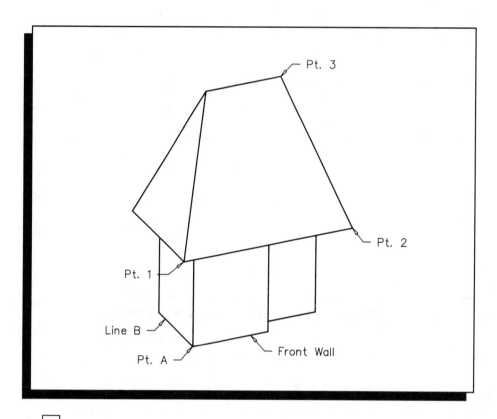

7 In reply to the next prompt, snap to point 2.

This defines the positive X direction from the first point.

8 In reply to the next prompt, snap to point 3. Point 3 lies in the new XY plane and has a positive Y coordinate.

Note that the drawing does not change. However, the crosshairs, grid, and coordinate system icon shift to reflect the new UCS.

9 With the coordinate display on, notice the X and Y values in the status line as you move the crosshairs to each of the three points you selected.

10 Save the current UCS by entering the **UCS S**ave option. Name it **FRTROOF**.

UCSICON Command

REF 366-367

REF 41

The coordinate system icon indicates the positive directions of the X and Y axes. A "W" appears in the icon if the current UCS is the World Coordinate System. If the icon is located at the origin of the current UCS, a " + " is displayed at the base of the icon. A box is formed at the base of the icon if you're viewing the UCS from above. The box is absent if you are viewing the UCS from below.

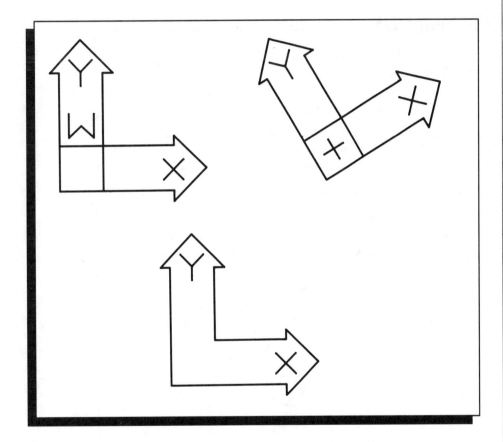

The UCSICON command permits you to control the visibility and position of the coordinate system icon.

1 Enter **UCSICON** and **OR**igin option.

The coordinate system icon should move to the origin of the current UCS.

2 Enter **UCSICON** and **N**oorigin option.

The coordinate system icon should return to its original location.

3 Enter **UCSICON** and **Off**.

The coordinate system icon should disappear.

4 Enter **UCSICON** and **On**.

The coordinate system icon should reappear.

The UCSICON All option applies changes to the coordinate system icons in all active viewports.

Using the New UCS

Suppose you want to construct the line of intersection between the roof and a chimney passing through the roof.

1 Change both the elevation and thickness values to **0**.

2 With the **LINE** command, draw the line of intersection (where a chimney would pass through as shown in the following illustration) by creating a rectangle at any convenient location on the roof.

HINT:
Turn on Ortho and Snap.

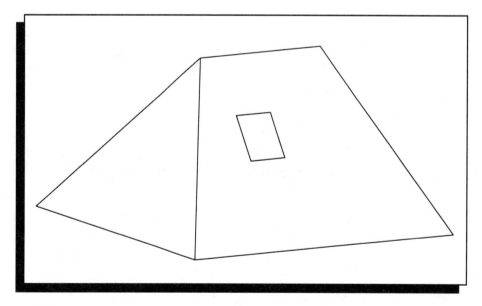

3 Return to the WCS (World) using the **UCS** command.

4 To prove that the rectangle lies on the same plane as the roof, view the 3D model from different points in space.

HINT:

The viewpoint 4,–0.1,1 illustrates it well. (Notice the position of the coordinate system icon.)

Let's create a second UCS, this time using a different UCS option.

1   View the model from an orientation similar to the one used before (as shown on page 358).

2   Enter the **UCS** command and select the **Entity** option.

3   Select the bottom edge of the roof. (Use the same section of the roof as before.)

4   With the coordinate display on, move the crosshairs to the same three corners you chose when applying the 3point option.

Notice that the Entity option created an identical UCS.

You are likely to use the 3point and Entity options for most applications, at least at first. However, other UCS creation options are available.

1   Enter the **UCS** command and choose the **ZA**xis option. (Turn off Ortho).

2   Snap to point A (see the illustration on page 358) in reply to "Origin point <0,0,0>:".

3   In reply to the next prompt, pick any point on line B.

This point specifies the positive Z direction of the UCS. AutoCAD then determines the directions of the X and Y axes using an arbitrary but consistent method.

The new UCS should be on the same vertical plane as the front wall of the building. In relation to the wall, notice the positive X, Y, and Z directions that make up the UCS, and notice the coordinate system icon.

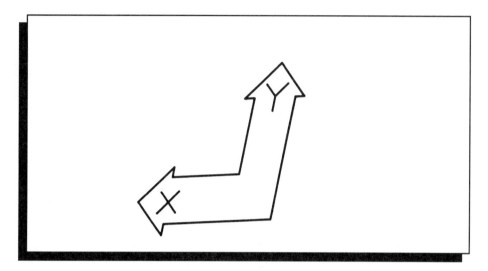

4 Enter **UCS** and **Prev.**

This restores the previous UCS. AutoCAD saves the last ten User Coordinate Systems in a stack, so you can step back through these systems with repeated UCS Previous operations.

5 Enter **UCS** and **Restore.**

This will restore a previously saved UCS, but first let's review previously stored UCSs.

6 Enter **?** and press **RETURN** twice.

The screen should display data about the FRTROOF user coordinate system, which you saved earlier.

7 Enter **FRTROOF** to restore that UCS.

8 Enter **UCS** and **World**—the default action of the UCS command.

This restores the World Coordinate System. Notice that W (for World) appears in the coordinate system icon.

NOTE:

If you want to place a point in the WCS while you are in another UCS, do so by entering an asterisk prior to the coordinates (*e.g.*, *7.5,4). During line construction, for example, you can also place relative coordinates (*e.g.*, @*5,3) and polar coordinates (*e.g.*, @*3.5<90) in the WCS regardless of the current UCS.

REF 19-20

⑨ Enter **UCS** and **View**.

This option creates a new UCS perpendicular to the viewing direction; that is, parallel to the screen. This is helpful when you want to annotate (add notes to) the 3D model.

⑩ Using the **TEXT** command, place your name near the model at any convenient location.

⑪ Enter **UCS** and **Z**.

⑫ Enter **30**.

The current UCS should rotate 30 degrees about the Z axis.

⑬ Use the X and Y options to rotate the current UCS about the X and Y axes. (See the following hint.)

HINT:
You may choose to draw basic entities on the current UCS and view them from different viewpoints before experimenting with the X and Y options so you can more easily see their effects.

UCS Del lets you delete one or more saved User Coordinate Systems. UCS Origin defines a new UCS by moving the origin of the current UCS, leaving the orientation of its axis unchanged.

REF 363

UCS Control Dialogue Box _____

REF 365

The UCS Control dialogue box enables you to name, rename, restore, and list existing User Coordinate Systems.

① Enter **DDUCS** or select the **Settings** pull-down menu and pick **UCS** and **Named UCS...**.

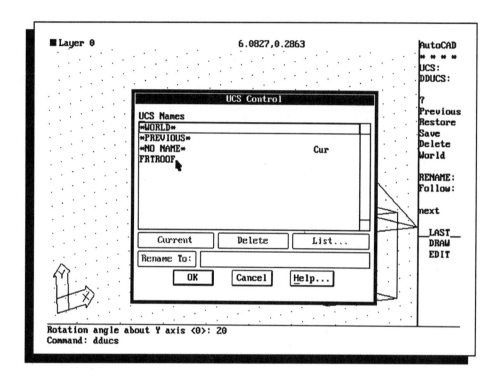

The current UCS (indicated by "Cur") has no name. Therefore, AutoCAD calls it *NO NAME*.

2 Select **FRTROOF** and pick the **List...** button.

This lists the points that define the FRTROOF UCS.

3 Pick **OK**.

Notice the "Delete" and "Rename To" buttons. They allow you to delete and rename existing User Coordinate Systems.

4 Pick the **Current** button and pick **OK**.

FRTROOF is now the current UCS.

UCS Orientation Dialogue Box _____

This dialogue box enables you to select predefined User Coordinate Systems.

1 Enter the **DDUCSP** command or select the **Settings** pull-down menu and pick **UCS** and **Presets...**.

364

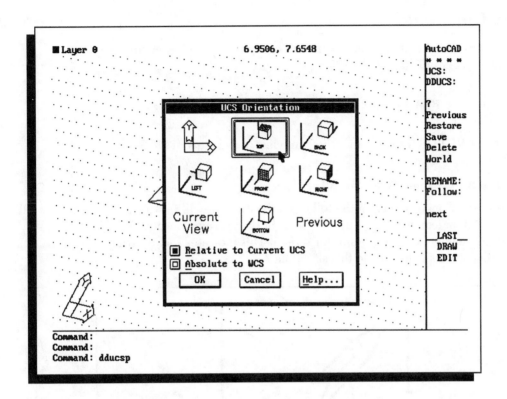

You can now select a new UCS that is at right angles to the current UCS or WCS.

2 Pick the **RIGHT** image tile and pick **OK**.

The position of the user coordinate icon should reflect the new UCS.

3 Bring back the UCS Orientation dialogue box and pick the **Absolute to WCS** radio button.

4 Select the image tile of the coordinate system icon located in the upper left corner and pick **OK**.

The WCS should now be the current coordinate system.

5 Bring back the dialogue box, select the **FRONT** image tile, and pick **OK**.

This should produce a new UCS that is perpendicular to the WCS and parallel to the front of the building.

6 Experiment with the other options on your own.

PLAN Command REF 294-295

The PLAN command enables you to generate easily the plan view of any User Coordinate System, including the WCS.

1 Enter the **PLAN** command.

2 Press **RETURN** to generate the plan view of the current UCS.

3 Enter **PLAN** and **W** for World.

A "broken pencil" icon, shown in the following illustration, will replace the coordinate system icon whenever the XY plane of the current coordinate system is perpendicular to the computer screen. This indicates that drawing and selecting objects is limited in this situation.

REF 366

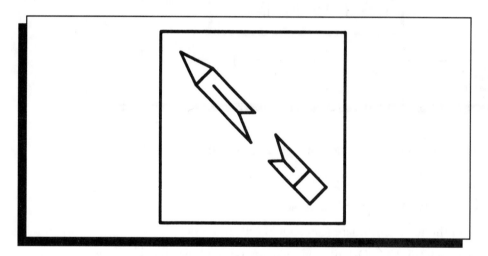

4 Enter the **UCS** command and enter the **World** option.

If you want to display the plan view of previously saved User Coordinate Systems, enter the PLAN UCS option.

___ NOTE: ___

If you want AutoCAD to generate a plan view automatically whenever you change from one UCS to another, set the system variable UCSFOLLOW to 1 (on).

REF 364

5 **ZOOM** All.

6 Enter **END** to save your work and exit AutoCAD.

Questions

1. What is the purpose and benefit of User Coordinate Systems (UCSs)?

   CREATE ONE OR MORE DRAWING PLANES

2. Describe the UCS command's 3point option.

   PICK ORIGIN, ORIENTATION AND ROTATION

3. What purpose does the coordinate system icon serve?

   INDICATES POS DIR IN X & Y AXIS

4. What does the "W" represent in the coordinate system icon?

   MEANS WORLD COORD SYS IS ACTIVE

5. If a box is present at the base of the coordinate system icon, what does this mean?

   YOU ARE VIEWING FROM ABOVE

6. What is the purpose of the UCS Control dialogue box?

   LETS YOU NAME, RENAME & STORE UCS'S

7. Describe, briefly, the UCS command's View option.

   CREATES UCS PERP TO YOUR VIEW

Problems

1. With the UCS 3point option, create a UCS using one of the walls that make up the building found in this unit. Save the UCS using a name of your choice. With this as the current UCS, add a door and window to the building. Save this drawing as PRB39-1.

2. Using VPOINT or DDVPOINT, obtain a 3D view of the building contained in this unit. With the UCS View option, create a UCS. At any convenient location and size, create a border and title block for the 3D model. Include your name, date, file name, etc., in the title block. Save your work as PRB39-2.

Unit 40   Dynamic View Facility

■ OBJECTIVE:

To practice using AutoCAD's powerful dynamic view facility in connection with 3D wireframe modeling

The VPOINT and DDVPOINT commands let you view 3D models from any angle in space. The DVIEW command also lets you view models from various angles in space, but in a dynamic way. It provides a range of 3D viewing features and enables you to generate 3D perspective projections—as opposed to parallel projections—of your 3D work.

Other benefits of the dynamic view facility are its exceptionally fast dynamic zooming and panning capability and fast hidden line removal. Plus, you are able to create front and back *clipping planes* of your 3D models.

Consider the following two views of the building from the previous unit. Both views are from the same point in space. However, the one on the left is shown in standard parallel projection. The lines are parallel and do not converge toward one or more vanishing points. The right view is a true perspective projection. Parts of the building that are farther away appear smaller—the same as in a real-life photograph.

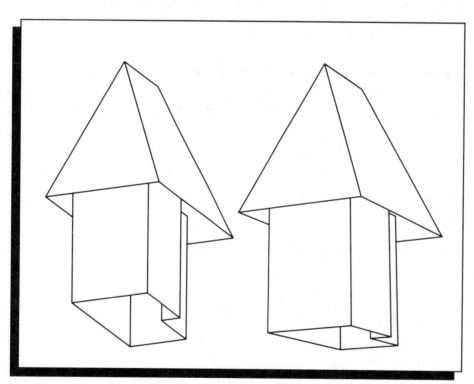

Reference

Perspective Projections

Using the dynamic view facility, let's generate a 3D perspective projection.

1 Start AutoCAD and open **THREE-D2**.

2 Using either **VPOINT** or **DDVPOINT**, create a view similar to the parallel projection shown in the preceding illustration and remove hidden lines.

3 Enter **DV** (for DVIEW) at the keyboard or select the **View** pull-down menu and pick **Set View** and **Dview**.

REF 285-294

4 In response to "Select objects:" select the entire model and press **RETURN**.

___ NOTE: ___

The entities you select will be those you preview as you perform the DVIEW options. If you select too many entities, dragging and updating of the image will be slow. However, choosing too few entities may not provide an adequate preview.

The following options should appear.

```
CAmera/TArget/Distance/POints/PAn/Zoom/TWist/CLip/Hide/Off/Undo/<eXit>:
```

5 Enter the **Distance** option.

REF 289-290

REF 286-287

A *slider bar* should appear at the top of the screen.

The DVIEW command uses a camera and target metaphor. The slider bar is labeled from 0x to 16x, with 1x representing the current distance. Moving the slider to the right increases the distance between the camera and the target. Moving the slider to the left moves the camera closer to the target.

6 With the pointing device, slowly move the slider bar cursor to the right and then to the left and notice the changes in the drawing.

7 Position the slider bar cursor so the model fills the screen and press the pick button on the pointing device.

The model is now in perspective projection as indicated by the perspective icon found at the lower left corner of the screen.

8 Enter the **DVIEW Hide** option.

REF 294

Notice that hidden lines are removed the same as when the HIDE command is applied. But, two things are different. First, you are currently in the DVIEW command. Second, you are viewing the model in perspective projection—not parallel projection—with hidden lines removed.

9 Enter the **DVIEW Z**oom option.

REF 291-292

A similar slider bar should appear. You can zoom dynamically by moving the slider back and forth.

10 Move the slider so the building fills about one-third of the screen and press the pick button.

11 Enter the **D**istance option again, and change the distance between the camera and target.

12 Enter the **H**ide option and press **RETURN** to terminate the DVIEW command.

Notice that the hidden lines reappear but the perspective view remains.

13 Enter **DVIEW**, select the model (and press **RETURN**), and select the **Off** option to turn off the perspective projection.

REF 294

14 Experiment further with the **DVIEW D**istance, **Z**oom, and **H**ide options and press **RETURN** when you are finished.

Other DVIEW Options

Use of the camera/target metaphor helps you view the 3D model as it appears from any point in space. The line of sight (also referred to as the viewing direction) is the line between the camera and the target.

1 Enter the **DVIEW** command, select the model once again, and press **RETURN**.

2 Enter the **Off** option and then the **CA**mera option.

REF 288-289

3 Slowly move the crosshairs up and down and back and forth.

Notice that the movement of the crosshairs rotates the model. Technically, you are moving the camera—the point you are looking from—around the target.

4 Position the 3D model at any orientation, pick a point, and enter the **H**ide option.

5 Enter the **CA**mera option again and pick a new point.

6 Enter the **U**ndo option to undo the last operation.

	Reference

REF 289

7 Enter the **DVIEW TA**rget option and pick a point.

The Target option is similar to the Camera option, but it rotates the target point—the point you are looking *at*—around the camera.

8 Experiment further with the DVIEW **TA**rget option on your own.

——— NOTE: ———

REF 290-291

The DVIEW Points option is available if you want to define new camera and target points using X, Y, and Z coordinates.

As a result of using the Target option, the model may appear partially off the screen.

REF 291

9 Enter the DVIEW **PA**n option to dynamically shift the model to a new location. (See the following hint.)

HINT:

Place the first point (that is, the displacement base point) on or near the model. Drag the model to the second point.

REF 292

10 Enter the DVIEW **TW**ist option, move the crosshairs, and pick a point at any location.

The Twist option lets you rotate the model around the line of sight. It is similar to using the ROTATE command in a 2D environment.

Clipping Planes

REF 292-293

The DVIEW Clip option enables you to create front and back *clipping planes*. It lets you view the interior of your model in a manner similar to using conventional sectional views.

1 Using the various DVIEW options, position the model so it is similar to the ones at the beginning of this unit.

2 Enter the **DVIEW CL**ip option and then choose the **F**ront option.

3 Slowly move the slider and pay particular attention to how the model changes.

4 Attempt to display only half of the model and pick a point.

5 Enter the **DVIEW H**ide option.

The Clip Front option should remove the front portion of the model—the portion between you and the clipping plane—and produce a drawing similar to the following.

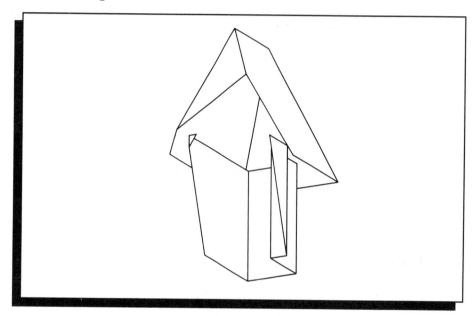

6 Experiment with the **DVIEW CL**ip **B**ack option on your own.

7 Enter the **DVIEW H**ide option to realize the effect of the Clip Back option.

Does your view look similar to the following? Notice that both front and back clipping planes are in effect.

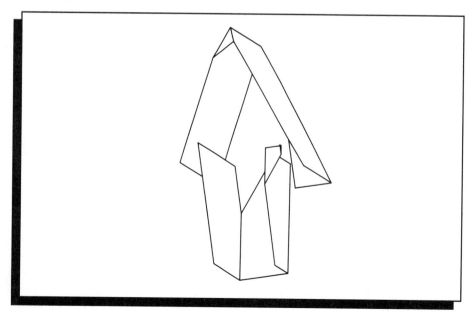

⑧ Enter the **DVIEW CLip Off** option.

The model should return to its previous form.

⑨ Terminate DVIEW by pressing **RETURN**.

10 Enter **DVIEW** and give a null response (press **RETURN**) in reply to "Select objects:".

A new building model should appear.

11 Use the **DVIEW Z**oom option to resize it.

The edges of the model are aligned with the X, Y, and Z axes of the current UCS. The model is updated to reflect the changes you make while in the DVIEW command and is meant for experimentation purposes. When you exit the DVIEW command, the current drawing regenerates, based on the view you selected.

12 Press **RETURN**.

Notice that the drawing regenerates based on the view you selected.

13 Enter **END** to save your work and exit AutoCAD.

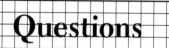

Questions

1. How are 3D perspective projections generated?

   Using DVIEW & DISTANCE

2. What does the DVIEW Camera option enable you to do?

   VIEW FROM ANY POINT IN SPACE

3. What is the purpose of the DVIEW Twist option?

   ROTATE AROUND LINE OF SIGHT

4. Of what benefit are front and back clipping planes?

   LETS YOU VIEW INTERIOR

5. Describe at least two additional features of the dynamic view (DVIEW) facility.

   PAN to SHIFT MODEL

   ZOOM to GET CLOSER OR FARTHER

Problems

1. While in the WCS plan view, create an array of lines. Create them in both the X and Y directions and place them approximately one unit apart. View the grid of lines at an arbitrary point in space using the VPOINT command. Create a perspective projection of the view using the DVIEW command. Use other dynamic view options to view the grid at various orientations and sizes in space. Save your grid as PRB40-1.

2. Obtain a left view of the building using the DVIEW command. Use a front clipping plane to create a full cross section of the model. Save this drawing as PRB40-2.

AUTOCAD® AT WORK

AutoCAD Puts KBJ Architects on the Fast Track

When KBJ Architects undertook the Orlando Airport expansion project three years ago, everybody knew they would have to work fast. Because it was a fast track project, some of the structures had to be designed at the same time that others were being built.

"On any fast track job, as you're designing and as you're building, there is always a lot of rethinking," says KBJ vice president Kim Goos. "As the design changes, the documents have to be changed in a hurry before things get built out there. AutoCAD certainly helped us adjust quickly to changing conditions. That was a big plus."

When you consider the scope of the Orlando Airport project, it's easy to appreciate the need for fast design work. The $700 million project entails erecting an automated ground transportation (AGT) tram system, building a seven-story hotel and seven story parking garage, and expanding the airport's landside passenger terminal building by 130 percent.

For KBJ Architects, expanding the landside building alone meant creating floor plans and ceiling plans for one million square feet of space. But this was by no means their only concern. Specifying the scope and placement of the AGT people mover system presented another formidable challenge. Completing the specifications for the system required the architects to lay out the entire airport site, including gates and plane locations. This was no small task, according to Goos.

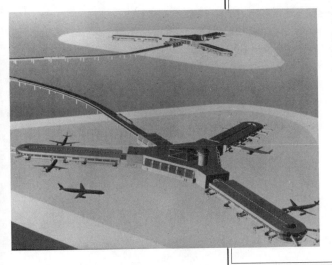

"There are a lot of rules and regulations as far as plane spacing and which planes can park where," he explains. "AutoCAD was really beneficial at that stage because we were able to simulate the different planes and rotate jetways about their pivot points, and that greatly speeded up the process."

The Orlando Airport project may have been the first project for which KBJ Architects used AutoCAD, but, according to Goos, it definitely won't be the last. "Since then, we've standardized with AutoCAD," he says. "Now we have a lot of other projects going out with AutoCAD."

Based on a story provided by Autodesk, Inc.

◼ OBJECTIVE:

To apply REVSURF and RULESURF commands to the construction of curved surfaces in 3D space

The REVSURF command enables you to create a surface of revolution by rotating a path curve (or profile) around a selected axis. The RULESURF command lets you create a polygon mesh representing a ruled surface between two curves.

The following 3D model represents a table lamp. The lamp's base was created with the REVSURF command, while the lamp shade was created with the RULESURF command.

3D Prototype Drawing _____

In preparation for creating a lamp similar to the one shown above, let's create a prototype drawing. The prototype drawing will apply to subsequent 3D exercises in this unit and following units. Its purpose is to help you orient yourself as you create 3D models.

1 Start AutoCAD and begin a new drawing named **3DPROTO**.

2 Set the Grid at **1** unit and Snap at **0.5** unit.

3 Create the following three layers:

Layer name	Layer Color
BOX	**White**
3DOBJ	**Yellow**
OBJ2	**Blue**

NOTE:

Create the above layers and specify each color as indicated even if you are using a monochrome monitor.

4 Set the layer named **BOX** as the current layer.

5 Enter the **ELEV** command; enter **0** for the elevation and **2** for the thickness.

6 In the center of the screen, construct a rectangular box using a Polyline. Make it 4 units on the X-axis by 3 units on the Y-axis.

7 Specify a viewpoint in front, above, and to the right of the rectangular 3D box.

8 If necessary, use the **PAN** command to center the box on the screen.

9 Enter **ZOOM** and **0.9x**.

10 Using the **UCS** command and 3point option, create and save each of the six User Coordinate Systems as indicated in the following illustration. Remember, the 3point option lets you specify the origin, orientation, and rotation of the XY plane.

HINT:

On the following illustration, each UCS name lies on its respective UCS. Likewise, each leader points to its respective UCS origin (0,0,0). Do not include the leaders and text.

11 List the new User Coordinate Systems.

You should have six of them.

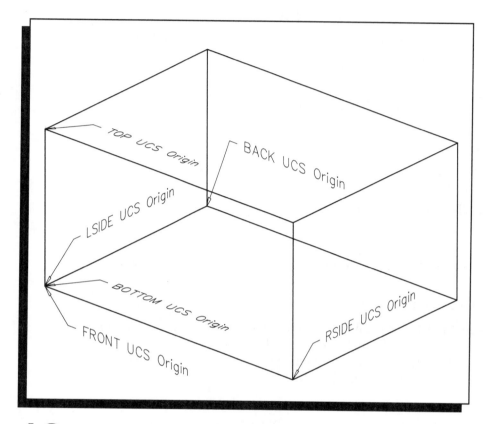

TOP UCS Origin

BACK UCS Origin

LSIDE UCS Origin

BOTTOM UCS Origin

RSIDE UCS Origin

FRONT UCS Origin

12 Make **3DOBJ** the current layer.

SURFTAB1 and SURFTAB2

The system variables SURFTAB1 and SURFTAB2 control the density (resolution) of 3D meshes created by 3D commands such as RULESURF and REVSURF.

1 Enter the **SURFTAB1** system variable.

2 Enter **20** for its value.

3 Enter the **SURFTAB2** variable.

4 Enter **8** for its value.

_____ NOTE: _____

See the section titled "3D Polygon Meshes," later in this unit, for more information on SURFTAB1 and SURFTAB2.

REF 163
TUT 199

REF 169-170

REF 171

Reference

REF 170-171
TUT 205

*See also
the optional
Applying
AutoCAD
Diskette*

5 Enter **ELEV** and set both elevation and thickness to **0**.

6 Enter **QSAVE** to save your work.

REVSURF Command

1 Using the 3DPROTO drawing, begin a new drawing and name it **LAMP**.

2 Enter the **DDUCS** command and make **FRONT** the current UCS.

3 Enter the **HIDE** command to remove hidden lines.

4 Using the front, right corner of the rectangular 3D model as the starting point, approximate the following shape with the **PLINE** command and the **Arc** option. (See the following hint.)

HINT:
Begin at the bottom corner and use PLINE's Undo option if you need to redo segments of the Polyline.

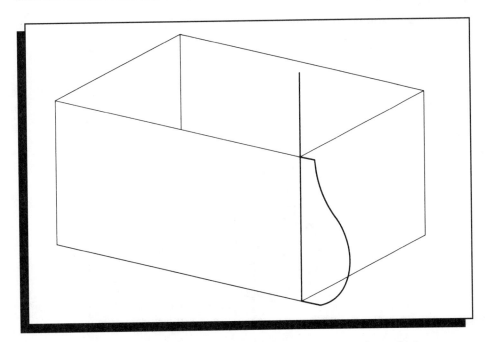

5 With the **LINE** command, draw a line that passes through the corner of the rectangular model and extends upward as indicated.

6 Enter the **REVSURF** command or pick the **Draw** pull-down menu and pick **3D Surfaces** and **Surface of Revolution**.

7 Pick the Polyline in reply to "Select path curve:".

8 Pick the line in reply to "Select axis of revolution:".

9 Enter **0** (the default) in reply to "Start angle:".

10 Enter **360** (the default, "Full circle") in reply to "Included angle:".

A 3D model of the lamp base should appear.

11 Freeze the layer named **BOX**.

12 Enter the **HIDE** command to remove hidden lines.

——— NOTE: ———

The HIDE operation could take several seconds if you are working on a relatively slow computer.

13 Thaw the layer named **BOX**.

Your lamp base should be similar to the one here.

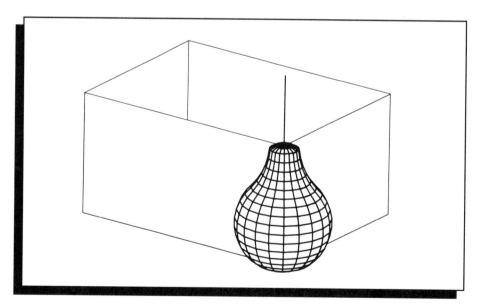

RULESURF Command ————————————————

Reference

REF 168-169
TUT 200-205

Now let's create the lamp shade.

1 Make **OBJ2** the current layer.

2 Enter the **DDUCS** command and make **TOP** the current UCS.

3 Enter the **CIRCLE** command.

4 Pick the upper, front, right corner of the rectangular model for the circle's center point. (Refer to the following illustration.)

5 Enter **1.25** units for the radius of the circle.

This circle lies in the TOP UCS, and it will remain on this plane.

6 Create another circle using the same center but enter a radius of **0.75**.

This circle also lies in the TOP UCS, but you will move it upward in Step 8.

7 Make **FRONT** the current UCS.

This will allow you to move the circle upward in the next step.

8 With the Ortho and Snap modes on, use the **MOVE** command to move the smaller circle up **1.5** units.

HINT: ————————————————
Turn on the coordinate display and watch it as you move the circle upward.

This circle is now 1.5 units above the TOP UCS.

Your 3D model should now look similar to this one.

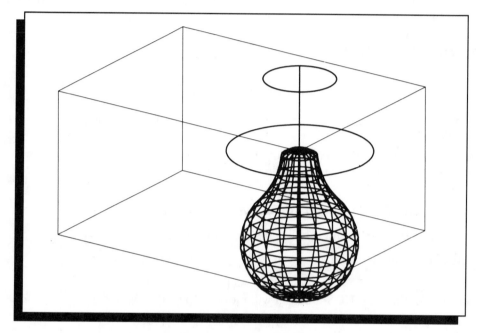

9 Enter the **RULESURF** command or pick the **Draw** pull-down menu and pick **3D Surfaces** and **Ruled Surface**.

10 Pick one of the two circles in reply to "Select first defining curve:".

HINT:
You may need to turn Snap off.

11 Pick the other circle in reply to "Select second defining curve:".

Did the lamp shade appear as you envisioned it?

12 Freeze layer **BOX**.

13 Enter the **HIDE** command.

Your 3D model should look similar to the one found at the beginning of this unit.

14 Enter the **DVIEW** command and view the lamp from various orientations in space.

15 Enter **END** to save your work and exit AutoCAD.

HINT: When constructing 3D models, consider using multiple viewports. The following provides an example.

3D Polygon Meshes

REF 163-164

A polygon mesh is defined in terms of $M \times N$ vertices. Envision the vertices as a grid consisting of columns and rows, with M and N specifying the column and row position of any given vertex.

The system variables SURFTAB1 and SURFTAB2 control the density (or resolution) of the 3D mesh. Specifically, the system variable SURFTAB1 controls the N-direction of a polygon mesh. An example is the resolution of the lamp shade created by the RULESURF command.

Consider the lamp base. Both SURFTAB1 and SURFTAB2 come into play because both M and N vertices are applied by the REVSURF command.

If you increase the values of these two system variables, the appearance of 3D models may improve. But the model will require more time to generate on the screen. The HIDE command will also consume more time. If you decrease the numbers excessively, the model will generate quickly on the screen, but the 3D model may not adequately represent your design.

——— NOTE: ———

3D meshes can be edited using the PEDIT command. You can also EXPLODE a mesh.

Questions

1. What is the purpose of the REVSURF command?

   CREATE REVOLVED SURFACE AROUND CENTER AXIS

2. Describe the use of the RULESURF command.

   CREATES RULED SURFACE BY PICKING 2 CURVES

3. How are User Coordinate Systems beneficial when using the REVSURF and RULESURF commands?

   ASSITS IN PLACING ITEMS

4. Explain the purpose of the SURFTAB1 and SURFTAB2 system variables.

   SPEC DENSITY OF MESH

5. What are the consequences of entering high values for the SURFTAB1 and SURFTAB2 variables?

   BETTER CONCISE VIEWS

6. What are the consequences of entering low values for SURFTAB1 and SURFTAB2?

   QUICK REGENS

7. In AutoCAD terms, 3D polygon meshes are made up of what?

   VERTICES OF COLOMNS & ROWS

Problems

1. Using the 3D facilities covered in this unit, create each of the following 3D models. Approximate all sizes. Use REVSURF to create PRB41-1 and PRB41-4 and RULESURF to create PRB41-2 and PRB41-3. Also, use the 3DPROTO prototype drawing.

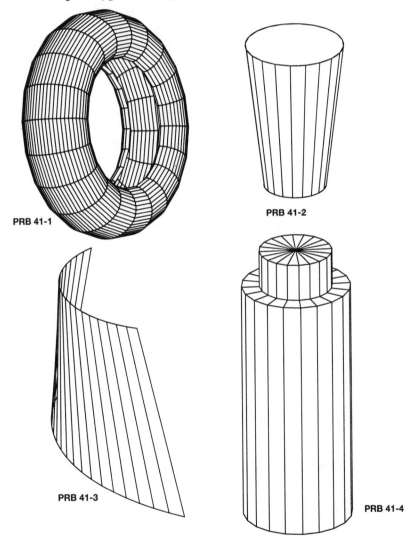

PRB 41-1

PRB 41-2

PRB 41-3

PRB 41-4

2. Refer to VISUAL.DWG and description contained on the optional *Applying AutoCAD* Diskette. Load VISUAL.DWG and review its contents. Apply it to the development of a new 3D model.

3. Refer to 3DPORT.DWG contained on the optional *Applying AutoCAD* Diskette. Load the file and review the model orientation in each viewport. Move from viewport to viewport and change the orientation and magnification of each view.

Unit 42

Advanced 3D Wireframe Modeling

■ OBJECTIVE:

To practice the 3D modeling capabilities of the TABSURF, EDGESURF, and 3DMESH commands

AutoCAD's TABSURF command enables you to create a polygon mesh representing a tabulated surface defined by a *path* (profile) and *direction vector*. The EDGESURF command lets you construct a *Coons surface patch* from four adjoining edges. The most basic of the 3D-specific commands is 3DMESH. It enables you to define a 3D polygon mesh by specifying its size (in terms of *M* and *N*) and the location of each vertex in the mesh.

The following shows basic 3D models created with each of these three commands.

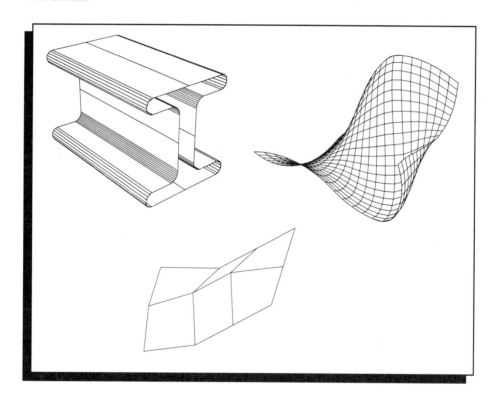

Let's create each of these 3D objects.

■ *TABSURF Command*

REF 169-170
TUT 219

We'll use the TABSURF command to construct the I-beam shown above.

1. Start AutoCAD and begin a new drawing named **I-BEAM** using the prototype drawing named 3DPROTO.

2. Using either the **UCS** or the **DDUCS** command, make **RSIDE** the current UCS.

3. Using the **PLINE** command and Arc and Line options, approximate the following figure. It represents one-quarter of the I-beam profile. (See the following note.)

——— NOTE: ———

It's important to use the PLINE rather than the LINE and ARC commands so that AutoCAD will treat the profile as a single entity.

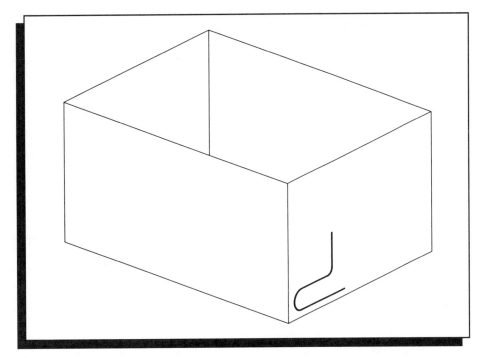

4. Complete the I-beam profile so that it looks like the one in the next illustration.

HINT:

After creating one-quarter of the object, mirror it to complete half of the object. Then mirror that to complete the entire object.

5. Make **TOP** the current UCS and make **OBJ2** the current layer.

6. Beginning at the RSIDE UCS as shown in the following illustration, draw a line approximately 3 units long.

HINT:

Turn on the Snap mode. It should already be set to 0.5 unit. Monitor the line's length at the coordinate display.

The line will provide the *direction vector* for use with the TABSURF command.

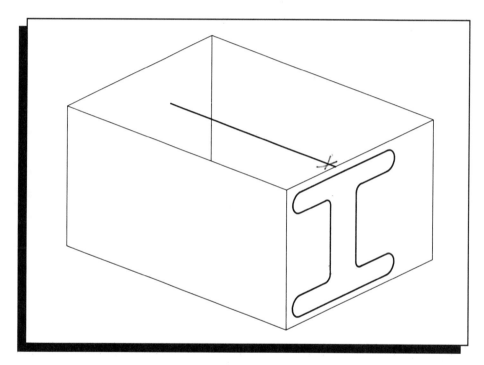

7 Make **3DOBJ** the current layer.

8 Enter the **SURFTAB1** system variable and enter **8**.

NOTE:

System variable SURFTAB1 controls the density of the tabulated surface.

REF 169-170

9 Enter the **TABSURF** command or pick the **Draw** pull-down menu and pick **3D Surfaces** and **Tabulated Surface**.

10 In reply to "Select path curve:" pick a point on the lower right quadrant of the I-beam profile.

HINT:

You may need to turn off the Snap mode.

11 Pick a point on the line in reply to "Select direction vector:". The point *must* be closer to the right endpoint of the line than the left endpoint in order for the tabulated surface to extend in the desired direction.

One-quarter of the I-beam should appear.

12 Complete the remaining parts of the I-beam using the TABSURF command. (See the following hint.)

HINT:

Complete the parts in a clockwise direction—lower left quadrant, upper left, then upper right. Otherwise, a previously created polygon mesh may interfere with the selection of new points.

13 Freeze layers **BOX** and **OBJ2**.

14 Enter the **DVIEW** command, select the entire model, issue the **Distance** option, and pick a point.

As discussed in Unit 40, this creates a perspective projection of your 3D model.

15 Enter the DVIEW **Hide** option.

Your 3D model of the I-beam should look similar to the one found at the beginning of this unit.

16 Enter **QSAVE** to save your work.

EDGESURF Command

REF 172
TUT 215-218

The EDGESURF command is used to construct a *Coons surface patch*. A Coons patch is a 3D surface mesh interpolated (approximated) between four adjoining edges. Coons surface patches are used to define the topology of complex, irregular surfaces such as land formations and manufactured products such as car bodies.

Let's apply the EDGESURF command to the creation of a topological figure similar to the one shown at the beginning of this unit.

1 Using the 3DPROTO prototype drawing, begin a new drawing named **CONTOUR**.

2 Make **OBJ2** the current layer.

3 Using the **LINE** command, draw four vertical lines directly on top of the existing four vertical edges of the 3D box.

The line entities will permit you to snap to the corners of the box during the construction of the Coons patch.

NOTE:

If you used the OSNAP command, set it to NONE.

4 Make **3DOBJ** the current layer.

5 Make **FRONT** the current UCS.

6 Using the **PLINE** command and Arc option, approximate the construction of Polyline A as shown in the following illustration.

NOTE:

When picking the first and last points of the Polyline, use the NEArest object snap mode. This will snap these points onto the vertical line. If you do not do this, the Polyline endpoints will not meet accurately. If they do not meet, the EDGESURF command will not work.

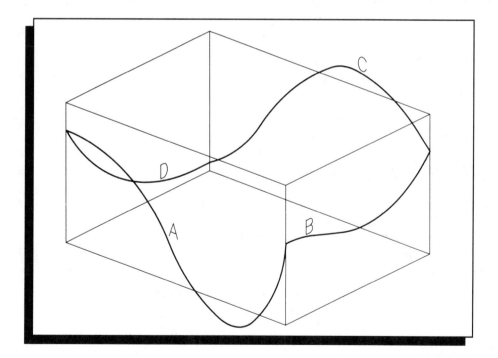

7 Make **RSIDE** the current UCS.

8 Approximate the construction of Polyline B as shown in the previous illustration. Use the ENDpoint and NEArest object snap modes for the first and last endpoints of the Polyline.

9 Make **BACK** the current UCS and construct Polyline C using the same procedure described in the preceding step.

10 Make **LSIDE** the current UCS and construct Polyline D. Use the ENDpoint object snap mode to connect Polyline D to Polyline A.

11 Freeze layers **BOX** and **OBJ2**.

12 Enter the **EDGESURF** command.

13 In reply to "Select edge 1:" pick a point on Polyline A and near corner 1. (Refer to the following illustration.)

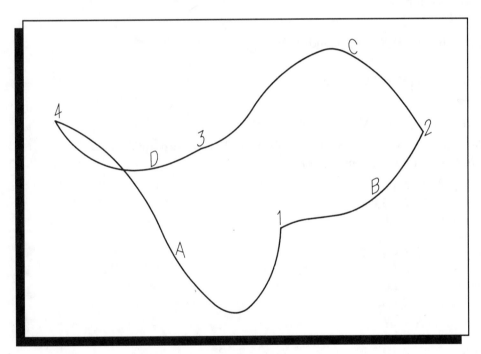

NOTE:

When you select Polyline A, it is important that you pick a point on the Polyline that is near corner 1. The same is true when you select the remaining three Polylines.

14 In reply to "Select edge 2:" pick a point on Polyline B and near corner 2.

15 Select Polylines C and D in the same fashion.

A contour should appear similar to the one shown at the beginning of this unit.

16 Enter the **HIDE** command.

17 View the contour from various orientations in space.

18 Enter **QSAVE** to save your work.

3DMESH Command

The 3DMESH command produces a 3D polygon mesh.

1 Begin a new drawing named **3DMESH** using the 3DPROTO prototype drawing.

2 Enter the **3DMESH** command.

3 Enter **4** in reply to "Mesh M size:".

4 Enter **3** in reply to "Mesh N size:".

5 Enter the following in reply to the series of "Vertex" prompts. Be sure to include the decimal points.

Vertex (0, 0): **5,4,0.2**
Vertex (0, 1): **5,4.5,0.3**
Vertex (0, 2): **5,5,0.3**
Vertex (1, 0): **5.5,4,0**
Vertex (1, 1): **5.5,4.5,0.2**
Vertex (1, 2): **5.5,5,0**
Vertex (2, 0): **6,4,0**
Vertex (2, 1): **6,4.5,0.2**
Vertex (2, 2): **6,5,0**
Vertex (3, 0): **6.5,4,0**
Vertex (3, 1): **6.5,4.5,0**
Vertex (3, 2): **6.5,5,0**

Your mesh should look similar to the one at the beginning of this unit.

6 If the mesh does not appear, **ZOOM** All or Extents.

As you can see, specifying even a small three-dimensional polygon mesh is very tedious. The 3DMESH command is meant to be used primarily with AutoLISP and not in the fashion presented above.

7 Freeze layer **BOX**.

____ NOTE: ____

Similar to 3DMESH is the PFACE command. PFACE produces a polygon mesh of arbitrary topology called a *polyface mesh*.

REF 165-166

Editing 3D Polygon Meshes _____

The vertices of the mesh can be edited with the PEDIT command in a manner similar to editing a Polyline.

1 Enter the **PEDIT** command, pick the mesh, and enter the **Edit** vertex option.

An "X" should appear at one corner of the mesh.

2 Press **RETURN** four times. This will move the "X" to four consecutive vertices.

3 Enter the **M**ove option and pick a new location for the vertex.

4 Enter e**X**it twice to exit the PEDIT command.

Types of Mesh Surfaces _____

REF 248-249

3D polygon meshes can be viewed in any one of these surface types.

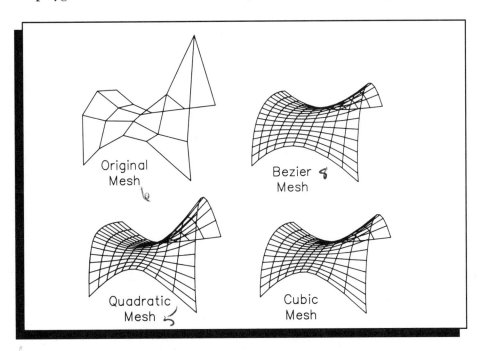

393

Let's create one of them from our original mesh. First, we must specify the mesh type.

1 Enter the **SURFTYPE** system variable.

NOTE:

A SURFTYPE value of 6 specifies the cubic B-spline surface, and a value of 8 specifies the Bezier surface.

2 Enter **5** for the new value. This specifies the quadratic B-spline surface.

3 Enter the **PEDIT** command, pick the mesh, and enter the Smooth surface option.

The 3D polygon mesh should change to a quadratic B-spline surface.

NOTE:

System variables SURFU and SURFV control the accuracy of the surface approximation by changing the surface density in the M and N directions.

4 Enter the eXit option to exit the PEDIT command.

5 Enter **END** to save your work and exit AutoCAD.

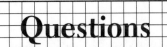

Questions

1. Describe the steps in using the TABSURF command.

   SELECT PATH & SELECT DIRECTION

2. In connection with the TABSURF command, what is the purpose of the direction vector?

   SPEC DIRECTION & LENGTH OF SURFACE

3. Describe the EDGESURF command.

   DEVELOP COONS SURFACE PATCH MESH BETWEEN FOUR EDGES WHICH YOU PICK

4. How are User Coordinate Systems used in conjunction with the EDGESURF command?

   ASSIST IN PLACING THE MESH ENTITIES

5. Why is use of the 3DMESH command not generally recommended for even the simplest 3D meshes?

   TIME CONSUMING, ERROR PRONE

Problems

Using the commands and techniques presented in this unit, construct the following 3D models. Approximate all sizes.

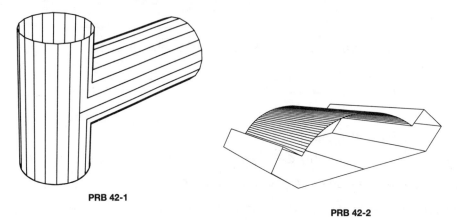

PRB 42-1

PRB 42-2

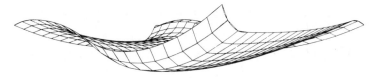

PRB 42-3

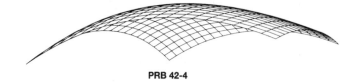

PRB 42-4

Unit 43 Creating and Editing 3D Primitives

■ OBJECTIVE:

To practice creating and editing 3D primitives

With AutoCAD, you can create basic objects from predefined shapes called primitives. You can edit these and other 3D objects using the ALIGN, ROTATE3D, and MIRROR3D commands.

■ *3D Objects Dialogue Box* _____

The 3D Objects dialogue box offers a selection of predefined 3D wireframe primitives.

> 1 Start AutoCAD and begin a new drawing named **EDIT3D** using the 3DPROTO prototype drawing.

_____ NOTE: _____

Check to make certain that the WCS is the current UCS.

> 2 Select the **Draw** pull-down menu and pick **3D Surfaces** and **3D Objects....**

EXTR 13

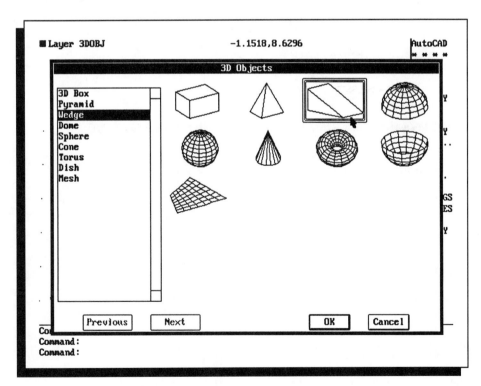

> 3 Pick the wedge image tile as shown in the previous illustration.

EXTR 19-20

HINT:

You can double click on the wedge image tile or you can pick it once and pick the OK button.

4 In reply to "Corner of wedge:" pick point 1 as shown in the following illustration. (Snap should be on.)

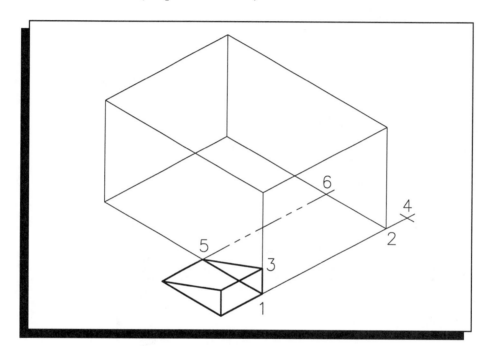

5 Enter **1.5** for the length, **1** for the width, and **0.5** for the height, but do not yet enter a rotation angle.

6 Move the crosshairs and notice that you are able to rotate the wedge around the Z axis.

The Z axis is perpendicular to the current UCS.

7 Enter **180** for the rotation angle.

This will rotate the wedge 180 degrees counterclockwise. The wedge should appear as pictured in the previous illustration.

ALIGN Command

EXTR 138-139

The ALIGN command enables you to move objects in 3D space by specifying three source points and three destination points.

1 Enter the **ALIGN** command, select the wedge primitive, and press **RETURN**.

Reference

2 Pick point 1 (see previous illustration) for the first source point.

3 Pick point 2 for the first destination point.

4 Use object snap to pick point 3 for the second source point.

5 Pick point 4 for the second destination point. Point 4 is located ½ unit from point 2 in the positive Y direction.

6 Pick points 5 and 6 for the third source and destination points, respectively.

The wedge should move and rotate as shown in the following illustration.

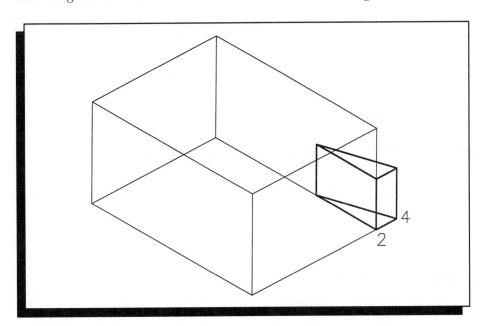

7 Enter **R** for REDRAW.

ROTATE3D Command

EXTR 141-143

The ROTATE3D command permits you to rotate an object around an arbitrary 3D axis.

1 Enter **ROTATE3D**, select the wedge, and press **RETURN**.

AutoCAD presents you with several options for defining the axis of rotation. Notice that "2points" is the default setting.

2 Pick points 2 and 4.

③ Enter **90** for the rotation angle.

The wedge should rotate as shown in the following illustration.

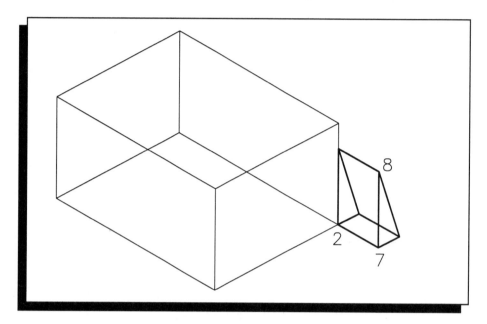

MIRROR3D Command

EXTR 140-141

You can mirror 3D objects around an arbitrary plane with the MIRROR3D command.

① Enter **MIRROR3D**, select the wedge, and press **RETURN**.

You should see several options for defining the plane. Notice that "3points" is the default setting.

② Pick points 2, 7, and 8 to define the plane, and do not delete the old object.

The mirrored object should appear.

③ Freeze layer **BOX** and remove hidden lines.

Your drawing should look very similar to the one in the following illustration.

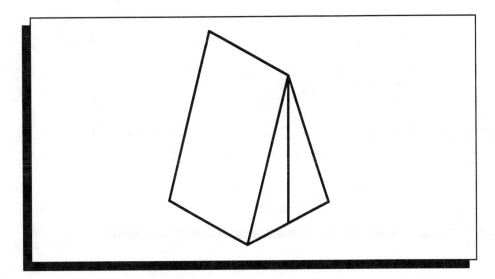

Other 3D Primitives

EXTR 14-19

1 Select the **Draw** pull-down menu and pick **3D Surfaces** and **3D Objects...**.

HINT: If "3D Objects..." was the last item you picked from the Draw pull-down menu, pick "Draw" twice.

2 Pick the 3D box image tile and pick a point (anywhere) in reply to "Corner of box:".

EXTR 14-15

3 Enter **2** for the length.

——— NOTE: ———

At this point, you could create a cube by entering C for Cube.

4 Enter **1** for the width, **0.75** for the height, and **15** for the rotation angle.

5 Remove hidden lines.

The object should appear similar to the box in the following illustration.

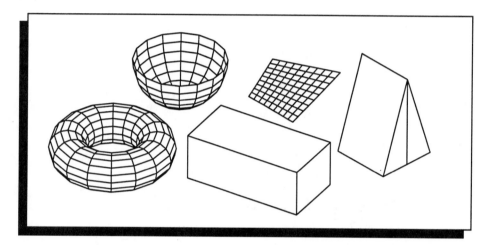

Note, however, that your 3D box may appear different because the viewpoint may be different.

1 Display the **3D Objects** dialogue box by picking the **Draw** pull-down menu twice.

2 Select the torus image tile (donut-shaped object), pick a center point (anywhere), and enter **1** for the radius of the torus.

EXTR 19

The torus radius is the distance from the center of the torus to the center of the tube.

3 Enter **0.3** for the tube radius.

4 Accept the next two default values.

These values specify the density of the wireframe mesh used to create and display the torus.

5 Remove hidden lines.

The torus should appear similar to the one in the previous illustration.

1 Display the **3D Objects** dialogue box.

2 Select the dish image tile.

EXTR 16

3 Pick a center point (anywhere) and enter **0.75** for the radius.

Reference

4 Accept the next two default values.

5 Remove hidden lines.

A dish should appear.

1 Display the **3D Objects** dialogue box once again.

2 Select the mesh image tile.

EXTR 16

3 Pick four points to form a polygon of any size and shape.

4 Enter **10** for both the M size and the N size.

—— NOTE: ——

Refer to the end of Unit 41 for an explanation of M and N vertices.

5 Remove hidden lines.

6 Experiment with the remaining primitives on your own.

7 Practice moving, rotating, and mirroring the objects using the ALIGN, ROTATE3D, and MIRROR3D commands.

8 Enter **END** to save your work and exit AutoCAD.

Questions

1. Name at least five 3D wireframe primitives that you can create using the 3D Objects dialogue box.

   TORUS, DOME, SPHERE, 3-D BOX, CONE

2. Explain how you can move and rotate a 3D object using the ALIGN command.

   USE Align, PiCK OBJ, ENTER 3 SOURCE pts and 3 DESTINATION Pts

3. Briefly state the purpose of the ROTATE3D command.

   Rotate OBJ AROUND 3D AXIS

4. Give the purpose of the MIRROR3D command.

   MIRROR 3D OBJ AROUND an ARBiTRARy pLANE

5. When creating a torus, you must specify the torus radius and tube radius values. What is the difference between these two values?

   TUBE RADiUs is RADiUs OF TUbE TORUS RADiUs is FROM CEN OF touRUS to CENtEr of TUbE

6. After selecting the mesh image tile from the 3D Objects dialogue box, what must you enter to create a 3D mesh?

   FouR Points to FORM polyGON and VAJUES

404

Problems

1. Create the following 3D object. Make it 2.5 units long by 1 unit wide by 0.5 unit high, and rotate it -90 degrees.

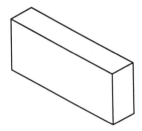

2. Using either the ALIGN or the ROTATE3D command, reorient the previous object so that it looks like the one in the following illustration.

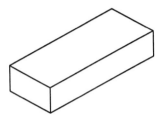

3. Apply MIRROR3D to the previous object to create the following object.

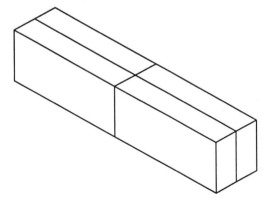

AUTOCAD® AT WORK

AutoCAD Streamlines Radar Assembly Planning

In 1986, the Hughes Radar Systems Group (RSG) set out to design a computer system to improve its assembly planning process. To fit their specifications, system designers needed a CAD program with a low per-seat cost that would run on Sun engineering workstations. But they were also looking for a program they could interface with Oracle Corporation's relational database management software. What they found was AutoCAD.

AutoCAD, with its open architecture and built-in AutoLISP programming language, allowed Hughes software engineers to interface the program to an Oracle database at the core of their automated planning system, called IMPIS. Using custom-built SunView windows, assembly planners enter key pieces of information which are used to extract data from the Oracle database. This data is then automatically passed to AutoCAD and inserted into the assembly instruction. A typical assembly instruction spans 25 pages and includes diagrams, parts and tools lists, as well as detailed instructions.

"The main benefit of AutoCAD and the AutoLISP interface was that it allowed us to automate much of the planning process," says IMPIS project engineer Brant Jones. "A number of tedious tasks, such as lettering and page formatting, that the planner used to do manually are now done automatically."

AutoCAD also lends itself well to IMPIS's networked workstation environment. Because AutoCAD processing takes place on individual workstations, the graphics-intensive IMPIS system runs much faster than if the processing took place on a central host computer. Assembly planners, consequently, have much quicker access to drawings. Jones says that IMPIS makes assembly planners 35 percent more productive than when they used pencils and paper.

IMPIS has also given assembly planners what many consider an even greater benefit: a boost in quality. "What the assembly planners really like about IMPIS is that the quality of the planning is vastly superior to what it was when created manually," Jones says. "They really like working on the system and especially enjoy working with AutoCAD."

Reference

■ OBJECTIVE:

To shade and render 3D models using the SHADE and RENDER commands

AutoCAD offers two basic options for producing shaded views of your 3D work. SHADE produces a quick shaded view of a 3D model, while RENDER produces a higher quality rendering.

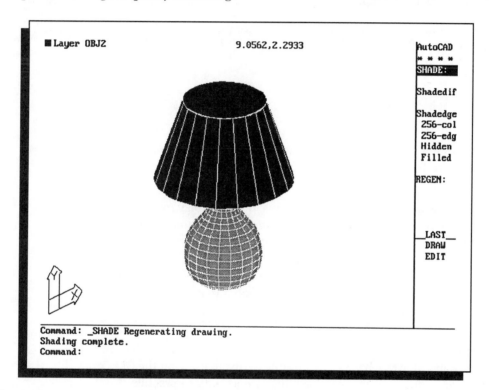

```
■ Layer OBJ2                    9.0562,2.2933            AutoCAD
                                                        * * * *
                                                        SHADE:

                                                        Shadedif

                                                        Shadedge
                                                         256-col
                                                         256-edg
                                                         Hidden
                                                         Filled

                                                        REGEN:



                                                         _LAST_
                                                         DRAW
                                                         EDIT

Command: _SHADE Regenerating drawing.
Shading complete.
Command:
```

SHADE Command _____

REF 299-301

You can quickly shade any 3D object in the current viewport using the SHADE command.

1 Start AutoCAD and open the drawing you created in Unit 41 named **LAMP**.

2 Enter **SHADE** or select **Shade** from the **Render** pull-down menu.

AutoCAD gives the percentage complete as it performs its shading calculations. When the calculations are complete, AutoCAD should display a shaded view of the lamp, as shown in the previous illustration.

NOTE:

The SHADEDGE and SHADEDIF system variables allow you to control the shade style and lighting. However, most AutoCAD users seldom change their values.

REF 300

RENDER Command

REND 29, 108

The RENDER command allows you to produce higher quality shaded views of 3D models using AVE Render (also called AutoCAD Render). AVE stands for AutoCAD Visualization Extension.

1 Enter **RENDER** or pick **Render** from the **Render** pull-down menu.

REND 74

This initializes the AVE Render program.

If AutoCAD does not render the lamp and instead you receive the message "Please reconfigure RENDER" or "AVE_RENDER is not yet configured," skip to the following section, titled "Configuring Render."

As AutoCAD performs its rendering calculations, it will display messages about its progress. After several seconds or minutes—depending on the speed of the computer—AutoCAD will render the lamp.

NOTE:

If AutoCAD does not render the lamp, it is possible that your computer does not contain adequate system memory.

The flat surfaces you see (called facets) improve as you increase the values of the SURFTAB1 and SURFTAB2 system variables prior to creating the 3D objects. In the following unit, you will have the opportunity to practice smooth shading, which smoothes the facets and produces a higher quality rendering.

2 After AutoCAD renders the lamp, press any key to return to the AutoCAD graphics screen.

Configuring Render

REND 6
INST 100-103

When trying to render a 3D object, you may receive the message "Please reconfigure RENDER" or "AVE_RENDER is not yet configured." RENDER, also called AVE_RENDER, is the AutoCAD rendering program that enables AutoCAD to render 3D models.

If you receive either of the previous messages, you will need to follow the configuration instructions. The following steps assume you are using a standard VGA display.

If you did not receive either of the previous messages, but you want to reconfigure the rendering display, skip to the following section, titled "RCONFIG Command."

1 In reply to "Select rendering display device:" select option **1**, AutoCAD's configured P386 ADI combined display/rendering driver.

NOTE:

> If you have installed a protected-mode ADI rendering display, select option 2 and ignore the following steps. Refer to page 100 in the *AutoCAD Interface, Installation, and Performance Guide* for instructions.

INST 100

If you selected option 1, AutoCAD will give you the opportunity to do a detailed configuration of the rendering features.

2 For now, accept the **No** default setting.

Depending on the rendering device you selected, AutoCAD may give the option of rendering to a viewport. If you are using a VGA display, you will not be given this option.

If you have a hard copy output device capable of producing renderings, . . .

3 . . . select the option that matches your rendering device. If you are uncertain, select option **1**, "None (Null rendering device)."

If you are using a VGA display, AutoCAD will use the full screen to render the lamp. The flat surfaces you see (called facets) improve as you increase the values of the SURFTAB1 and SURFTAB2 system variables prior to creating the 3D objects.

NOTE:

> If AutoCAD does not render the lamp, it is possible that your computer does not contain adequate system memory.

4 After AutoCAD renders the lamp, press any key to return to the AutoCAD graphics screen.

RCONFIG Command

REND 107
INST 103-104

The RCONFIG command permits you to reconfigure AutoCAD Render.

1 Enter the **RCONFIG** command.

AutoCAD will display the current rendering device configuration.

2 Press **RETURN**.

3 Enter option **2**, "Configure rendering device."

AutoCAD will display the current rendering display.

4 Enter **Yes** in reply to "Do you want to select a different one?"

5 Execute Steps 1 and 2 in the previous section, titled "Configuring Render."

After you complete Step 2, continue with Step 6 below.

6 Press **RETURN** if you haven't already, and enter **3**, "Configure hard copy rendering device."

AutoCAD will display the current hard copy rendering device.

7 Enter **Yes** in reply to "Do you want to select a different one?"

8 Select the option that matches your hard copy rendering device. If you are uncertain, select option **1**, "None (Null rendering device)."

9 After you are finished configuring the hard copy rendering device, enter **0** to exit the configuration menu.

10 Enter **Yes** if you want to keep the configuration changes.

Statistics Dialogue Box

The Statistics dialogue box displays details about the last rendering. You can save this information in a file, but you cannot change it.

1 Enter **STATS** or select **Statistics...** from the **Render** pull-down menu.

REND 140-141

410

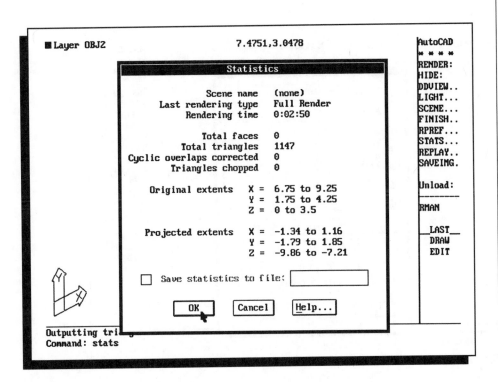

REND 166-167

2 Review the information and pick **OK**.

Save Image Dialogue Box

Using the Save Image dialogue box, you can save a rendering as a TGA, TIFF, GIF, or RND file. Certain other graphics programs are capable of reading, displaying, and printing these file types.

TGA   32-bit RGBA Truevision version 2.0 format

TIFF   32-bit RGBA Tagged Image File Format

GIF   CompuServe image format with a GIF file extension

RND   Autodesk scanline-data-oriented file format

1 Enter the **SAVEIMG** command or pick the **Render** pull-down menu and pick **Files** and **Save Image....**

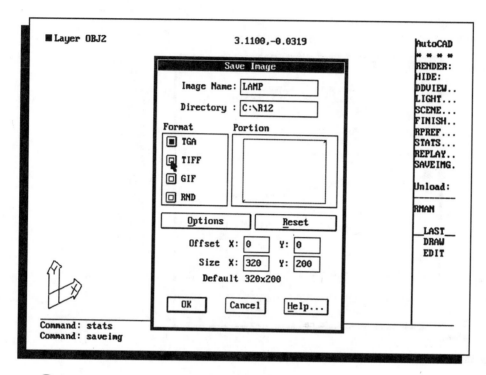

■ Layer OBJ2   3.1100,-0.0319

Save Image

Image Name: LAMP

Directory : C:\R12

Format   Portion
■ TGA
☐ TIFF
☐ GIF
☐ RND

Options   Reset

Offset X: 0   Y: 0
Size X: 320   Y: 200
Default 320x200

OK   Cancel   Help...

AutoCAD
** ** ** **
RENDER:
HIDE:
DDVIEW..
LIGHT...
SCENE...
FINISH..
RPREF...
STATS...
REPLAY..
SAVEIMG.

Unload:

RMAN

LAST
DRAW
EDIT

Command: stats
Command: saveimg

2 Pick the **TIFF** radio button and pick the **OK** button.

AutoCAD will create a file named LAMP.TIF.

3 Using the **FILES** command, locate this file.

Replay Dialogue Box

REND 110-111

You can display TGA, TIFF, GIF, and RND files using the Replay dialogue box.

1 Enter the **REPLAY** command or pick the **Render** pull-down menu and pick **Files** and **Replay Image...**.

REND 110-115,
162-163

The Replay version of the standard Files dialogue box should appear.

2 In the Pattern edit box, change *.tga to ***.TIF** and press **RETURN**.

"LAMP" should appear in the Files list box as shown in the following illustration.

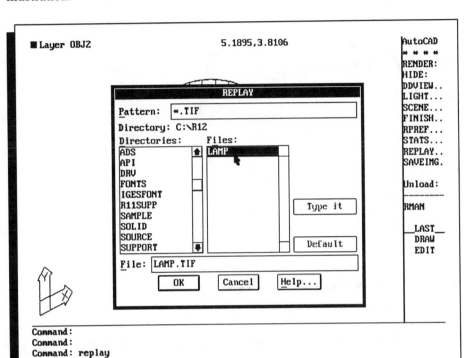

3 Double click on **LAMP**.

This will display the Image Specifications dialogue box.

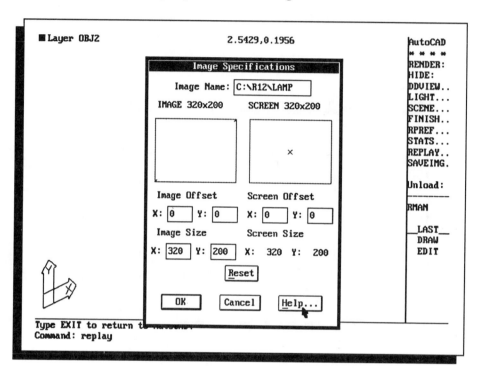

④ Pick the **Help...** button if you want to read about this dialogue box.

⑤ Pick **OK**.

AutoCAD will read the LAMP.TIF file and display it.

Unloading/Loading Render

It is possible to load and unload the AVE Render program. If you want to continue to use AutoCAD after your rendering tasks are complete, you should unload AVE Render. Unloading will restore memory, which improves system performance. After you unload Render, you have the option of reloading it.

Since AVE Render is already loaded, let's unload it.

① Enter (**xunload** "**averendr**") exactly as you see it here. Include the parentheses.

The XUNLOAD command removes AutoCAD ADS (AutoCAD Development System ™) programs, such as AVE Render, from memory.

HINT: You can also unload AVE Render by selecting "Unload Render" from the Render pull-down menu.

Let's reload AVE Render.

② Enter (**xload "averendr"**) exactly as you see it here.

AutoCAD will reload AVE Render. Issuing the RENDER command would also load AVE Render, but it would also produce a rendering, whether you want it or not.

As a result of reloading the Render program, you may need to configure the rendering devices.

③ Enter **END** to save any changes you may have made and exit AutoCAD.

Questions

1. When would it be practical to use the SHADE command rather than the RENDER command?

   FOR QUICK VIEWS

2. When you use SHADE, what system variables control the shade style and lighting?

   SHADEEDGE & SHADEDIF

3. What does AVE stand for?

   AutoCAD VISUALIZATION EXTENSION

4. How do you initialize (start) the AVE Render program?

   TYPE RENDER OR USE PULL DOWN

5. When you configure or reconfigure Render, what two hardware devices does AutoCAD allow you to configure?

   DISPLAY OR HARDCOPY DEVICES

6. What is the purpose of the RCONFIG command?

to RECONFIGURE RENDER

7. What is the purpose of the Statistics dialogue box?

Lists Details about RENDER, Time Etc

8. What file formats can you create using the Save Image dialogue box?

TGA, TIFF, RND & GiF

9. What is the purpose of the Replay dialogue box?

DisplAys TGA, TiFF, RND & GiF Files

10. What must you enter at the keyboard to unload AVE Render?

TYPE XUNLOAD "AVRENDR"

Problems

1. Shade and render THREE-D2.DWG from Unit 40.

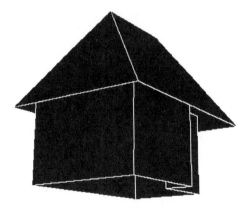

THREE-D2.DWG

2. Create a GIF file of the rendering of THREE-D2.DWG. Name it THREE-D2.GIF.

3. Display the THREE-D2.GIF rendering in AutoCAD.

4. Shade and render I-BEAM.DWG from Unit 42.

I-BEAM.DWG

5. Display statistics on the rendering of the I-beam.

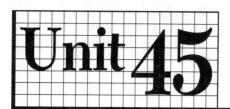 **Advanced Rendering**

■ **OBJECTIVE:**

To change rendering settings and create smooth shaded renderings

AVE Render options enable you to change the appearance of renderings. Instead of views with visible facets, you can create smooth shaded renderings. You can also adjust the lighting and apply surface finishes to objects.

Rendering Preferences Dialogue Box _____

REND 116-129

You can change the appearance of a rendering using the Rendering Preferences dialogue box.

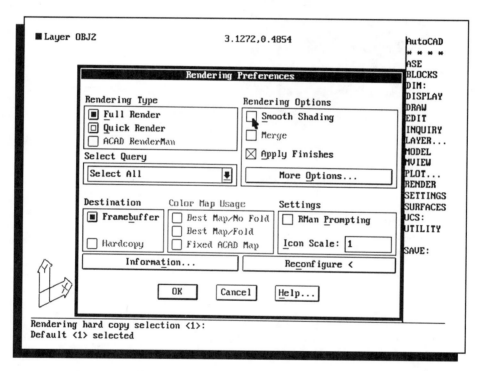

Start AutoCAD and open the drawing you created in Unit 41 named **LAMP**.

Enter **RPREF** or pick **Preferences...** from the **Render** pull-down menu.

The Rendering Preferences dialogue box (see the previous illustration) should appear.

_____ NOTE: _____

If you are using Render for the first time, you must configure it. In most cases, you can accept each of the default values presented to you. Refer to Unit 44 if you need specific instructions on how to proceed.

REND 6
INST 100-102

	Reference

3 Check the **Smooth Shading** option located in the upper right corner and pick **OK**.

REND 118-119

4 Enter **RENDER** or select **Render** from the **Render** pull-down menu.

REND 108

The "Smooth Shading" option causes AutoCAD to blend the facets and produce a smooth shaded rendering of the lamp. Note, however, that the smooth shading takes longer to compute because rendering is compute intensive. As the quality of the rendering increases, so does the time to produce the rendering.

5 Press any key to make the rendering disappear.

6 Redisplay the **Rendering Preferences** dialogue box.

Focus your attention on the "Rendering Type" area located in the upper left corner of the dialogue box. The "Full Render" default setting displays a 3D polygon-generated shaded image. It produces the best image quality, but it usually takes longer than the "Quick Render" option. "Quick Render" uses a Gouraud shading technique that involves horizontal bands called scanlines.

REND 117

7 Pick the **Quick Render** radio button, pick **OK**, and reissue the **RENDER** command.

The rendering may appear similar to the previous rendering, yet the two differ.

8 Press any key and then redisplay the **Rendering Preferences** dialogue box.

9 Pick the **Full Render** radio button.

10 Pick the **More Options...** button.

REND 124-129

This selection displays a set of less frequently used options.

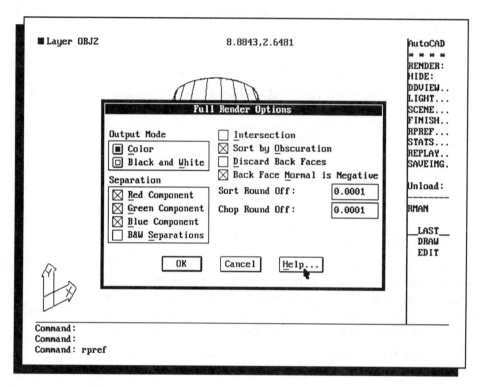

11 Pick the **Help...** button and review the information about this dialogue box.

12 Pick the **OK** button; pick **OK** again.

Here's a summary of other options in the Rendering Preferences dialogue box.

Apply Finishes	Applies predefined surface finishes (see the following section, titled "Finishes Dialogue Box")
Select Query	Before rendering, allows you to select individual objects instead of the entire screen
Destination	Permits you to specify the output destination of the rendering
Color Map Usage	If viewport rendering is allowed, this controls color mapping
Settings	"RMan Prompting" refers to the optional Autodesk RenderMan software; "Icon Scale" controls the sizes of the light and finish blocks
Information...	Displays information about AVE Render
Reconfigure	Allows you to reconfigure the rendering devices

13 Pick the **OK** button to exit the Rendering Preferences dialogue box.

Reference

REND 78-80

REND 78-90

Finishes Dialogue Box

You can define and attach surface finishes to entities using the Finishes dialogue box. For example, you can make the surface of an object appear either shiny or dull.

1 Enter the **FINISH** command or pick **Finishes...** from the **Render** pull-down menu.

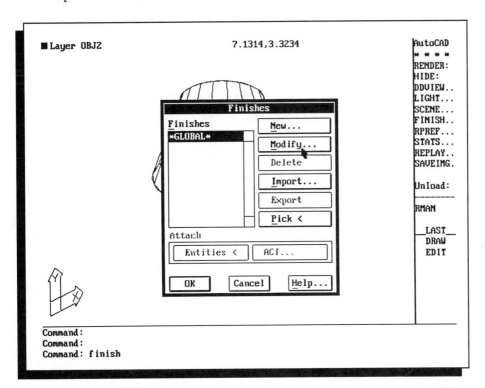

Entities without a surface finish attached to them use the default *GLOBAL* finish.

2 Pick the **Modify...** button.

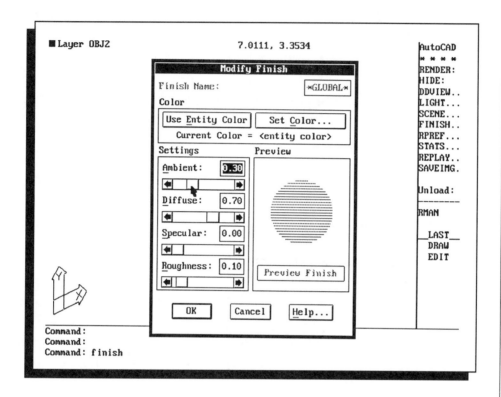

REND 80-83

The Modify Finish subdialogue box permits you to change the Ambient, Diffuse, and Specular values defined for the *GLOBAL* finish. Also included in the dialogue box is "Roughness."

③ Pick the **Help...** button and review the meaning of each of these terms and pick **OK** when you're finished.

④ Using the slider bars, increase (considerably) the values for both **Ambient** and **Specular** and pick the **OK** button; pick **OK** again.

⑤ Enter **RENDER**.

The model of the lamp should be brighter (due to the increased ambient light) with a more reflective, mirror-like surface.

NOTE:

If you are using a VGA display, changes to the surface finish will be less noticeable than if you are using a more sophisticated display subsystem.

⑥ Redisplay the **Finishes** dialogue box and pick the **Help...** button to review the other parts of the dialogue box.

⑦ Pick the **OK** button; pick **OK** again.

Lights Dialogue Box _____

You can control several types of lighting with the Lights dialogue box.

First, let's save the current view.

1 Enter the **VIEW** command and save a view named **VIEW1**.

This will allow us to return to this view later in the exercise.

2 Enter the **LIGHT** command or pick **Lights...** from the **Render** pull-down menu.

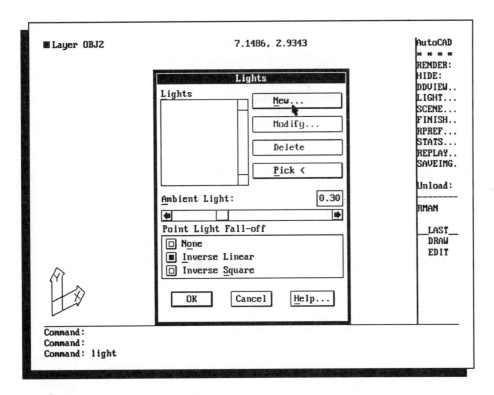

3 Pick the **New...** button.

4 Pick the **Distant Light** radio button in the New Light Type subdialogue box and pick **OK**.

This will cause AutoCAD to display the "New Distant Light" subdialogue box. AutoCAD now expects you to name the new light.

5 Enter **BRIGHT** for the name of the light and pick **OK**; pick **OK** again.

AutoCAD will insert a light block on the plan view of the WCS. Because its location is in line with the current viewpoint, it may appear as a line.

⑥ Enter the **PLAN** command and press **RETURN** to accept the current UCS.

This should provide you with a better view of the light block location and angle.

⑦ Enter the **U** command to undo the last operation.

⑧ Enter the **PLAN** command and, this time, opt for the **W**orld Coordinate System.

You should see a view of the drawing similar to the one in the following illustration.

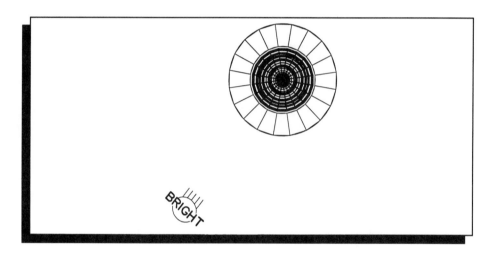

Let's move the light to a new location.

⑨ Enter the **LIGHT** command or select **Lights...** from the **Render** pull-down menu.

⑩ Select **BRIGHT** from the Lights list box (if it is not already selected) and pick the **Modify...** button.

⑪ Pick the **Modify** button in the Modify Distant Light subdialogue box.

The dialogue box will disappear temporarily and AutoCAD will display the graphics screen. In the "Command:" prompt area, AutoCAD will request a light target.

⑫ Press **RETURN** to accept the "current" light target.

Let's specify a point using the X/Y/Z point filter method.

⑬ Enter **.xy** and pick a point anywhere in the upper left corner of the screen.

Reference

14 Enter –1 for the Z value.

The Modify Distant Light dialogue box will reappear.

15 Pick **OK**; pick **OK** again.

16 With the **VIEW** command, restore **VIEW1**.

17 Enter **RENDER**.

AutoCAD will consider the new light as it renders the lamp.

18 Enter the **PLAN** command and choose the current UCS.

Notice the new location of the light.

19 Enter **U**.

Scenes Dialogue Box

REND 136-137

The Scenes dialogue box produces a list of saved scenes. A scene is similar to a named view, but a scene can contain one or more light sources.

1 Enter the **SCENE** command or pick **Scenes...** from the **Render** pull-down menu.

REND 136-139

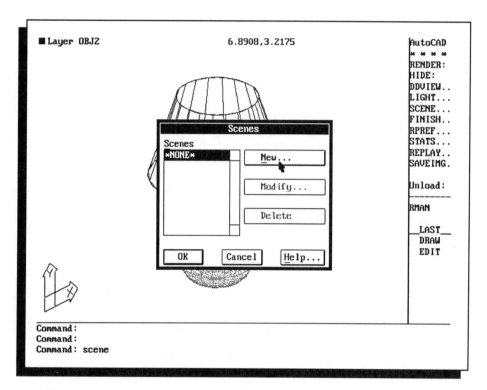

```
■ Layer OBJ2                    6.8908,3.2175              AutoCAD
                                                          ** ** ** **
                                                          RENDER:
                                                          HIDE:
                                                          DDVIEW..
                                                          LIGHT...
                                                          SCENE...
                    ┌──────────── Scenes ────────────┐    FINISH..
                    │                                │    RPREF...
          Scenes    │                                │    STATS...
          ┌─────────────────┐  ┌─────────────┐       │    REPLAY..
          │*NONE*           ▓│  │   New...    │       │    SAVEIMG.
          │                 ░│  └─────────────┘       │
          │                 ░│                        │    Unload:
          │                 ░│  ┌─────────────┐       │    ─────────
          │                 ░│  │  Modify...  │       │    RMAN
          │                 ░│  └─────────────┘       │
          │                 ░│                        │    _LAST_
          │                 ░│  ┌─────────────┐       │    DRAW
          │                 ░│  │   Delete    │       │    EDIT
          └─────────────────┘  └─────────────┘       │
          │ ┌──────┐  ┌────────┐  ┌────────┐ │        │
          │ │  OK  │  │ Cancel │  │ Help...│ │        │
          │ └──────┘  └────────┘  └────────┘ │        │
          └─────────────────────────────────┘        │

          ↑
          │
          └→

Command:
Command:
Command: scene
```

2 Pick the **New...** button.

The New Scene subdialogue box will expect you to name the scene.

3 Enter **SCENE1** and pick **OK**.

"SCENE1" should appear in the Scenes list box, indicating that you have created a new scene. AutoCAD will use the selected scene the next time you issue the RENDER command.

4 Pick **OK**.

5 Enter **END** to save your work and exit AutoCAD.

Questions

1. Why does smooth shading require more computer processing time than faceted shading?

   TO BLEND FACEts

2. In the Modify Finish subdialogue box, what do Ambient and Specular represent?

   Ambient Controls Ambient Light
   SPECULAR Control SHininESS

3. On what coordinate system does AutoCAD insert light blocks?

   WORLD CooRD System

4. When viewing the plan view of the WCS, how can you move the light icon in the X, Y, and Z directions?

   By using LiGHT DiAlog Boy , moDiFy,
   AND Picking Points

5. What does a scene contain that a saved view does not contain?

   SOURCES of LiGHT

Problems

1. Create a smooth rendering of the drawing named EDIT3D.DWG that you created in Unit 43. You may choose to make each of the objects a different color.

2. After changing the Ambient, Diffuse, Specular, and Roughness values, smooth render EDIT3D.DWG.

3. In the same drawing, create and insert a "distant light." After moving the light block in the X, Y, and Z directions, render the drawing. Produce a new scene using the new light.

Unit 46 Region Modeling

■ OBJECTIVE:

To practice AutoCAD's Region Modeler commands

You can produce closed 2D areas known as *regions* using AutoCAD's Region Modeler. Regions are the result of combining two or more 2D entities, which involves the Boolean union, subtraction, and intersection operations. Boolean operations are available in certain solid modeling systems, such as AutoCAD's optional Advanced Modeling Extension™ (AME™) solid modeling software. The Region Modeler commands, in fact, are a subset of the AME commands.

EXTR 39-102

■ *SOLIDIFY Command*

EXTR 69

The SOLIDIFY command changes one or more 2D entities into a region. It is possible to solidify Circle, Ellipse, Trace, Donut, 2D Polyline, and 2D Solid entities. However, these entities cannot contain a thickness.

Let's create an object resembling a bicycle sprocket guard manufactured from sheet metal.

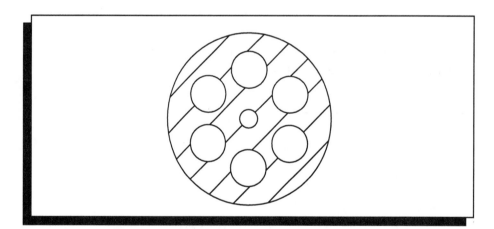

1. Start AutoCAD and begin a new drawing named **REGION**.

2. Set Snap at **1** unit, the default value.

3. Create a new layer named **OBJ**, assign the color red to it, and make it the current layer.

4. Draw a circle 7 units in diameter.

5. Enter the **SOLIDIFY** command or pick **Solidify** from the **Model** pull-down menu.

If you have only the Region Modeler software installed on the computer's hard disk, AutoCAD will load it and execute the SOLIDIFY command. If so, . . .

6 . . . skip to Step 8.

If both the Region Modeler and AME are installed on the computer's hard disk, AutoCAD will display the message "Autoload Region/<AME>." If so, . . .

7 . . . enter **R** (for Autoload Region).

This will initialize the Region Modeler.

NOTE:

If AutoCAD does not load the Region Modeler, your computer may not contain adequate system memory.

8 Select the circle and press **RETURN**.

AutoCAD will hatch the circle, indicating that it is now a region. A basic region, such as this, is called a region primitive.

SOLLIST Command

EXTR 70-72

SOLLIST displays database information about regions.

1 Enter **SOLLIST** or select the **Model** pull-down menu and pick **Inquiry** and **List Objects**.

2 Press **RETURN** to accept the <Object> default.

3 Pick the region and press **RETURN**.

Details on the region should appear. Notice "Material = MILD STEEL" and "Render type = CSG." The material type has no purpose in regions. It exists only to provide compatibility with AME. CSG stands for Construction Solid Geometry, a kind of solid modeler that offers Boolean operations.

NOTE:

SOLLIST offers the Tree option, which displays the definition of a region's CSG tree. The Tree option is applicable when a region has been created using one or more Boolean operations. When AME is configured, the Edge and Face options are available, which display basic information about edges and faces of a solid object.

SOLSUB Command

The SOLSUB command creates a composite region by subtracting the area of one set of 2D entities or regions from another set. A composite region is the result of applying one or more Boolean operations, such as a SOLSUB subtraction.

1 Create a **1.5** diameter circle. Make its center **2** units upward vertically from the center of the large circle.

HINT: With Snap on, move the crosshairs 2 units upward from the center of the large circle.

2 Array the circle 360 degrees as shown in the previous illustration.

3 At the center of the large circle, create a **0.75** unit diameter circle.

4 Enter the **SOLSUB** command or pick **Subtract** from the **Model** pull-down menu.

5 In reply to "Source objects... Select objects:" pick the region primitive and press **RETURN**.

6 In reply to the next prompt, pick all seven of the smaller circles and press **RETURN**.

AutoCAD will subtract the areas of the seven circles from the region primitive and rehatch the object to reflect the new composite region. The large circle is called the region's *outer loop*. The smaller circles are called the *inner loops*.

7 Enter the **SOLLIST** command and the Tree option.

8 Pick the composite region and press **RETURN**.

This displays details about each element of the region's CSG tree. The CSG tree is a hierarchy resulting from one or more Boolean operations. AutoCAD uses the CSG tree to remember the hierarchical order of the Boolean operations. AutoCAD rebuilds the CSG tree each time you edit a composite region.

SOLAREA Command

SOLAREA is similar to the AREA command.

1 Enter the **SOLAREA** command or select the **Model** pull-down menu and pick **Inquiry** and **Area Calc**.

2️⃣ Select the composite region and press **RETURN**.

SOLAREA should calculate the surface area of the region as 27.43985 square centimeters. It is possible to calculate the area of similar geometry using the AREA command, but it would be a more difficult task.

SOLVAR Command

This command allows you to review and set the Region Modeler system variables.

1️⃣ To review the system variables, enter **SOLVAR** and **?**.

Let's change the area units.

2️⃣ Enter **SOLAREAU** and **SQ IN**.

3️⃣ Recalculate the area of the composite region using the **SOLAREA** command.

The region should contain 4.253185 square inches of surface area. This means that if you were actually to manufacture the sprocket guard, it would use this amount of sheet metal, plus waste. You could calculate the waste by subtracting the sprocket guard from a square piece of sheet metal.

SOLCHP Command

Use the SOLCHP command to edit a region primitive. The region primitive can be a part of a composite region.

1️⃣ Enter **SOLCHP**, pick the outer circle, and press **RETURN** after AutoCAD makes the selection.

As you can see by the listed options, you can use SOLCHP to perform several operations. A brief description of each is listed here.

Color	Change primitive color
Delete	Erase primitive
Evaluate	Reevaluate composite region
Instance	Copy primitive
Move	Move primitive
Next	Select another primitive in composite
Pick	Pick another primitive
Replace	Replace selected primitive with another region
Size	Change dimensions of selected primitive

2️⃣ Enter **S** (for Size).

A temporary Motion Coordinate System (MCS) icon should appear. For now, ignore this icon because it is not important when changing the size of this region primitive.

③ Enter 3 for the circle radius and enter **X** (for eXit).

AutoCAD will evaluate the CSG tree and update the composite region to reflect the new size of the primitive.

SOLMASSP Command

EXTR 73-76

The SOLMASSP command calculates the engineering properties of a region.

① Enter **SOLMASSP**, select the composite region, and press **RETURN**.

AutoCAD will display information about the region, including the area, perimeter, bounding box, centroid, moments of inertia, product of inertia, radii of gyration, and principal moments.

② Enter **Yes** in reply to "Write to a file?"

③ When the File dialogue box appears, pick the **OK** button.

This will create a file named REGION.MPR.

④ Review the contents of the file and return to AutoCAD.

SOLMESH and SOLWIRE Commands

SOLMESH displays regions as Pface meshes, a requirement if you want to apply the SHADE command. SOLWIRE performs the opposite function by changing a Pface mesh back to a wireframe representation.

① Enter **SOLMESH** or select the **Model** pull-down menu and pick **Display** and **Mesh**.

EXTR 75

② Pick the composite region and press **RETURN**.

Your composite region should now look like the one in the following illustration.

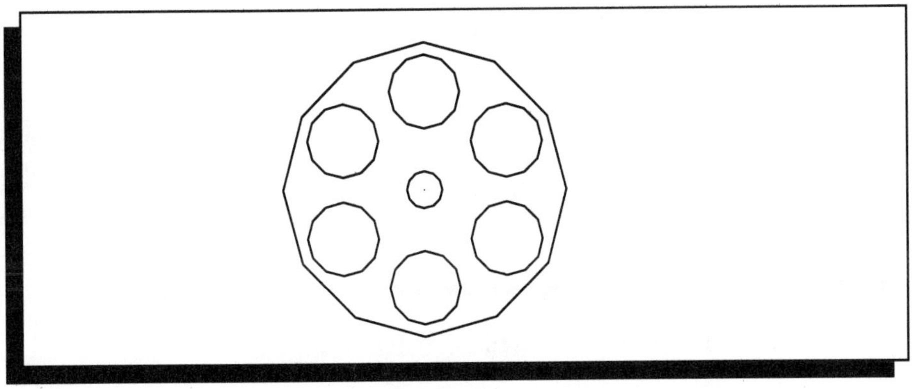

3 Enter the **SOLLIST** command, press **RETURN** to accept the <Object> default, select the region, and press **RETURN**.

Notice that "Representation = PMESH."

4 Enter the **SHADE** command.

AutoCAD will shade the region.

5 Enter **REGEN** to remove the shading.

6 Enter **SOLWIRE** or select the **Model** pull-down menu and pick **Display** and **Wireframe**.

EXTR 85

7 Pick the composite region and press **RETURN**.

The region should now appear as it did before.

SOLUNION Command

EXTR 84

Use the SOLUNION command to create a composite region by combining the area of two or more 2D entities or regions.

1 Set Snap at **0.25** and draw the following rectangle using a Polyline. Approximate its size and location.

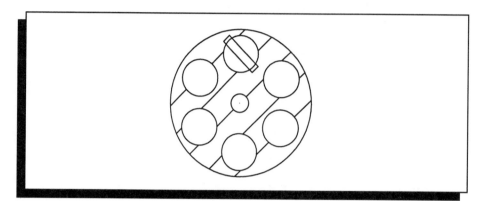

2. Enter the **SOLIDIFY** command, pick the Polyline, and press **RETURN**.

3. Array the new region primitive so that it appears in the other five circles.

4. Enter the **SOLUNION** command or pick **Union** from the **Model** pull-down menu.

5. Pick the composite region as well as the six region primitives, and press **RETURN**.

AutoCAD will combine the regions to create a new composite region.

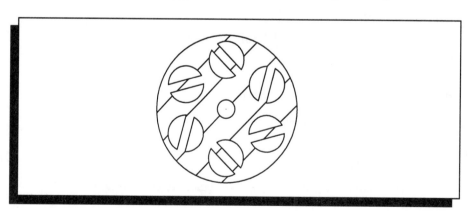

Other Region Modeler Commands

AutoCAD makes available other Region Modeler commands.

1. Experiment with the following commands on your own.

SOLINT   Creates a composite region from the intersection of two or more objects

(continued)

EXTR 63-86

SOLSEP	Separates a composite region into its constituent parts
SOLMOVE	Moves and rotates a region according to a motion description code
SOLUCS	Aligns the UCS with the face or edge of an existing region
SOLPURGE	Removes unnecessary region modeling information, reducing disk space and system memory requirements
SOLFEAT	Creates an AutoCAD entity from the face or edge of an existing region

_____ NOTE: _____

To display a dialogue box related to the Region Modeler, enter DDSOLVAR or pick the Model pull-down menu and pick Setup and "Variables...".

2 Enter **END** to save your work and exit AutoCAD.

■ *Advanced Modeling Extension*™ _____

AME 1-18

You can apply the commands and Boolean concepts you've learned in this unit to solid modeling with AME. In addition, you can produce solid models from your regions by giving them thickness. For example, you could use the SOLEXT AME command to produce the following object.

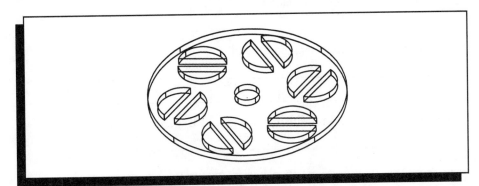

Units on the Advanced Modeling Extension are contained in the optional *Applying AutoCAD Guide to AME*™ available from Macmillan/McGraw-Hill's Glencoe Division. If you have this supplement, now is the most appropriate time to work through the units contained in it. After you have completed the units in the AME supplement, return to this work-text and continue with Unit 47.

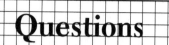

Questions

1. What type of region does the SOLIDIFY command create?

   _____

   _____

2. Describe a composite region.

   _____

   _____

   _____

3. With what command could you create a region by subtracting one object from another?

   _____

4. What is the name of the hierarchy that AutoCAD creates to remember the order of Boolean operations?

   _____

   _____

5. What is the purpose of the SOLMASSP command?

   _____

   _____

6. What command changes a region to a Pface mesh?

   _____

7. Explain the purpose of the SOLUNION command.

   _____

   _____

8. Is it possible to create AME solid models from regions? Explain.

   _____

   _____

Problems

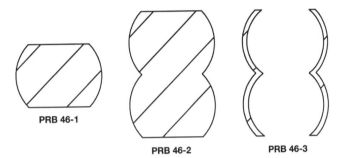

PRB 46-1

PRB 46-2

PRB 46-3

1. Using a circle and rectangular polyline, create PRB 46-1 as a composite region.

2. Calculate the area (in square inches) of PRB 46-1. 3.173234 sq in.

3. From PRB 46-1, create PRB 46-2.

4. Display the CSG tree for PRB 46-2.

5. From PRB 46-2, create PRB 46-3.

6. Display the engineering properties of PRB 46-3.

7. Shade PRB 46-3.

AUTOCAD® AT WORK

Efficient Cultural Center Design with AutoCAD

Based on a story provided by Autodesk, Inc.

This town-like oasis under construction at Lake Genezareth, Israel, includes dining, library, entertainment, theatre and art exhibit areas. It was designed in Denmark, with the aid of project consultants in Israel. Throughout the design process, AutoCAD, AutoShade Version 2 with Autodesk Renderman, and Autodesk 3D Studio all played important roles. These software packages allowed the architectural firm to generate realistic 3D images of building exteriors and interiors, eliminating the need for most physical models and allowing productive long-distance communications with both the customer and builder. The 3D capabilities also enabled the designers to visualize and solve complicated design problems associated with creating an all-in-one traditional theatre, cinema, concert hall, and conference room.

Unit 47 — Viewports in Paper Space

Reference

■ OBJECTIVE:

To apply viewports in paper space using the TILEMODE system variable and the MVIEW, PSPACE, MSPACE, and VPLAYER commands

AutoCAD allows you to work in model space and in *paper space*. Most AutoCAD drafting and design work is done in model space. In fact, all AutoCAD work prior to AutoCAD Release 11 was done in model space. Paper space is used to lay out, annotate, and plot two or more views of your work.

Viewports can be applied to both model space and paper space. This unit focuses on the application of viewports in paper space and its relationship to model space. Unit 18 concentrates solely on the use of viewports in model space and covers the VPORTS command.

■ *TILEMODE System Variable* _____

REF 268-269
EXTR 26-27

TILEMODE is a system variable that you must turn off in order to use paper space. To demonstrate the effect of TILEMODE, we will first prepare to create a simple 3D mechanical object.

1 Start AutoCAD and begin a new drawing named **PSPACE**.

2 Prepare the drawing file for a scale of 1 inch = 1 inch and an 11-inch × 8.5-inch sheet.

HINT:

In the AutoCAD graphics screen, 11 inches should align with the X-axis and 8.5 inches should align with the Y-axis. If necessary, refer to Unit 21 for help with preparing a new drawing. Be sure to Zoom All after setting the Limits.

3 Establish the following settings.

Units	Use default (decimal) units
Grid	Off
Snap	0.5 units
Layers	OBJ (Set color 5-blue and continuous linetype)
	BORDER (Set color 2-yellow and continuous linetype)
	VPORTS (Set color 6-magenta and continuous linetype)
	Make VPORTS the current layer
Text Style	Make a new text style named ROMANS using the Roman Simplex font. Use the default text style settings.

4 Enter **TILEMODE** and **0** (off).

The following should appear.

```
Entering Paper space.  Use MVIEW to insert Model space viewports.
Regenerating drawing.
```

The following paper space icon should replace the standard coordinate system icon. The paper space icon is present whenever paper space is present. The coordinate system icon is present whenever model space is present.

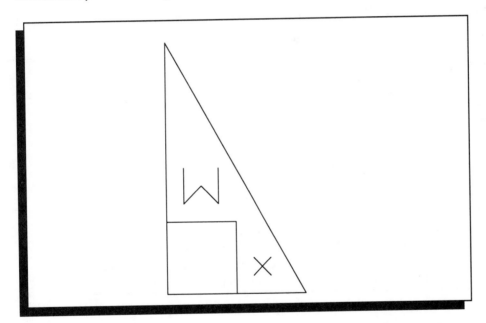

5 Use the **LIMITS** command to enter the same limits you entered in Step 2 and **ZOOM** All.

The limits you have set in paper space should now be the same as the limits set in model space.

MVIEW Command ————————————————————

REF 301-303

The MVIEW command is used to establish and control viewports in paper space.

1 Enter the **MVIEW** command or select the **View** pull-down menu and pick **Mview** and **Create Viewport**.

The following should appear.

```
ON/OFF/Hideplot/Fit/2/3/4/Restore/<First Point>:
```

2 Enter **4** to create four viewports and enter **Fit**.

AutoCAD will fit four viewports in the available graphics area. The viewport entities are contained on layer VPORTS.

MSPACE Command

REF 308

The MSPACE command permits you to switch to model space.

1 Enter **MSPACE**. (See following hint.)

HINT:
The command alias MS is defined for MSPACE. Therefore, just enter MS.

Model space should now be present with coordinate system icons in each of the four viewports.

NOTE:
If the MVIEW command is issued in model space, AutoCAD switches to paper space for the duration of the MVIEW command.

2 Enter **MVIEW**.

Notice that AutoCAD switches to paper space.

3 Cancel the MVIEW command by pressing **CTRL C**.

Notice that AutoCAD returns to model space.

4 Make **OBJ** the current layer.

5 Set the value of the **THICKNESS** system variable to **1**.

6 Make the upper left viewport the current viewport by picking a point inside it.

7 In the upper left viewport, draw the following object. Approximate the size and shape of the object.

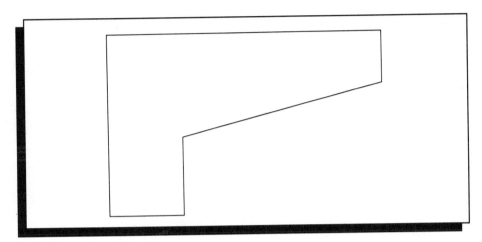

Four Individual Views

Using AutoCAD's viewpoint facilities, let's create four different views of the solid object.

1 Make current the lower left viewport by picking a point inside the viewport.

2 Enter the **DDVPOINT** command and view the object from the front.

HINT:
Set the height angle to 0.

3 Enter **ZOOM** and 1.

4 Make current the lower right viewport.

5 Enter **DDVPOINT** and view the object from the right side.

HINT:
Set both the rotation angle and the height angle to 0.

6 Enter **ZOOM** and 1.

7 Make current the upper right viewport and view the object from above, in front, and to the right.

⑧ Enter **ZOOM** and **1**.

The screen should look similar to the following.

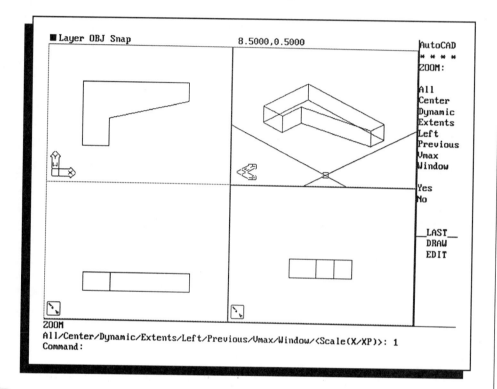

PSPACE Command

The PSPACE command is similar to the MSPACE command. Its purpose is to switch from model space to paper space.

① Enter **PS**, the PSPACE command alias.

Notice that little appears to change except for the coordinate system icons. However, when in paper space, you are not able to edit entities created in model space. Likewise, when you are in model space, you can not edit entities created in paper space.

② Attempt to select the object in any one of the four viewports.

As you can see, you cannot select it because it was created in model space.

③ Draw a short line in one of the four viewports, enter **MSPACE**, and attempt to erase the line.

④ Enter **PSPACE** and erase the line.

Editing Viewports in Paper Space —————————

Viewports in paper space are treated much like other AutoCAD entities. For example, you can edit viewports.

1 Enter the **UNDO** command and **Mark** option.

2 Enter the **MOVE** command, select one of the lines that make up one of the four viewports, and move the viewport a short distance toward the center of the screen.

3 Enter the **ERASE** command, select one of the lines that make up another viewport, and press **RETURN**.

4 Enter the **SCALE** command, select one of the viewports, and enter **0.75** for the scale factor.

5 Enter the **MSPACE** command.

6 Attempt to move, erase, or scale a viewport.

As you can see, viewports in paper space can be moved and even erased, but not in model space. Only the views themselves can be edited in model space. In summary, paper space is used to arrange views and embellish them for plotting (you will do this in the following section), while model space is used to construct and modify entities that make up the 3D model or drawing.

7 Enter **UNDO** and **B**ack option.

You should have returned to the point where you entered UNDO Mark.

Plotting Multiple Viewports —————————

One of the greatest benefits of paper space is multiple viewport plotting.

1 Freeze layer **VPORTS** and make **BORDER** the current layer.

The lines which make up the viewports should now be invisible.

2 Enter **MSPACE**.

The viewport lines are invisible in model space also, but notice the current viewport is outlined.

3 Pick each of the four viewports.

4 Enter **PSPACE** and draw a border and title block similar to those in the following illustration.

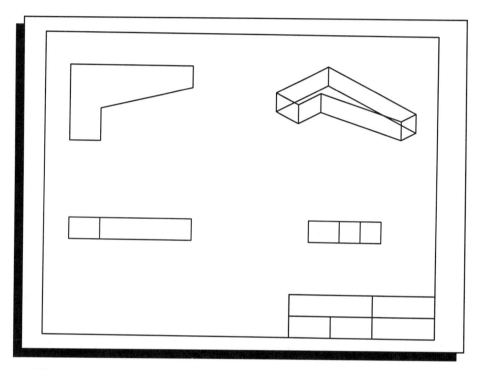

5 Using the PLOT command, plot the drawing at a scale of 1 = 1.

HINT:
Select the Limits radio button after entering the PLOT command. Refer to Units 34 and 35 for help with other plotter settings.

It is quite possible the current position of the border and views did not plot perfectly. Regardless, make adjustments to the location of the border, title block, and views by following these steps.

1 Thaw layer **VPORTS** and move individual viewports accordingly. It is normal for them to overlap one another.

2 Edit the size and location of the border and title block if necessary.

3 Freeze layer **VPORTS** and replot your work.

MVIEW Hideplot Option

The MVIEW Hideplot option is used to perform hidden line removal on selected views.

1 First, thaw layer **VPORTS**.

2 Enter the **MVIEW** command and **H**ideplot option.

3 Enter **On**, select the upper right viewport, and press **RETURN**.

4 Freeze layer **VPORTS** and replot your work.

AutoCAD should have performed a hidden line removal on the upper right view. If it didn't . . .

5 . . . plot the drawing again.

VPLAYER Command

REF 333-336

The VPLAYER command enables you to control the visibility of layers within individual viewports. For example, you may choose to freeze layer OBJ in one viewport, but not in the other viewports. As with other paper space-related commands, TILEMODE must be set to 0 in order to use VPLAYER.

1 Enter **MSPACE** and then make current the upper right viewport.

2 Enter **VPLAYER** and **F**reeze option.

3 Enter **OBJ** and press **RETURN** to accept the (current viewport) default. Press **RETURN** again.

The 3D view contained in the upper right viewport should disappear.

4 Enter **PSPACE**, and plot your work.

Everything will plot except for the object contained on layer OBJ in the upper right viewport.

5 Enter **MSPACE** and make the upper right viewport active if it is not already.

6 Enter the **VPLAYER** command and **T**haw option, and enter **OBJ** and press **RETURN** to accept the default. Press **RETURN** again.

The 3D view contained in the upper right viewport should again be visible.

7 Enter **END** to save your work and exit AutoCAD.

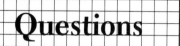

Questions

1. Describe the difference between TILEMODE Off (0) and TILEMODE On (1).

   _____

   _____

   _____

2. Explain the difference between model space and paper space.

   _____

   _____

   _____

3. Give the primary purpose of the MVIEW command.

   _____

   _____

4. Describe the use of the MSPACE and PSPACE commands.

   _____

   _____

5. Explain why you may want to edit viewports in paper space.

   _____

   _____

6. The MVIEW Hideplot option permits you to do what?

   _____

   _____

7. What is the primary purpose of the VPLAYER command?

   _____

   _____

8. What is the main benefit of paper space when plotting?

   _____

   _____

Problems

1. Using the commands and features related to paper space, create multiple views of the following solid object. Dimension the 2D views in paper space. Create a border and title block, and plot the multiple views on a single sheet.

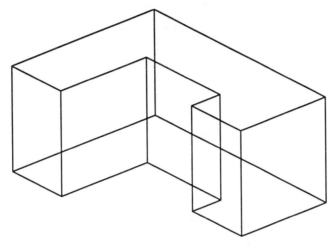

PRB 47-1

2. Create a left side profile view of the above object. The view should contain hidden lines.

Unit 48 External References

Reference

REF 413-422

■ OBJECTIVE:

To apply AutoCAD's external reference feature using the XREF and XBIND commands

External references (also called Xrefs) provide you the option of inserting drawings into your current drawing, similar to inserting a drawing as a Block. However, Xrefs do not become part of the drawing. Instead, the Xrefs are loaded automatically each time the drawing file is loaded. In addition to viewing the Xref, you can make use of the Xref entities by, for example, snapping to them.

External references are helpful if you want to view the assembly of individual components as a master drawing. Xrefs are particularly useful when working with other AutoCAD users in a network environment.

Applying External References

Drawing files must be available to apply external references. Therefore, let's create files to use in the following sections.

1 Start AutoCAD and begin a new drawing named **PTSITE**.

2 Using the **DDUNITS** command, pick architectural units. Pick **0'-0"** for the precision, and accept the remaining default settings.

3 Using the **LIMITS** command, set the following drawing limits:

Lower left corner: **0,0**
Upper right corner: **80',60'**

The upper right corner is based on a scale of $^1/_8'' = 1'$ on a standard A size sheet. The active drawing area on the sheet will be $10'' = 7.5''$.

4 Zoom All.

5 Set the Grid at 10' and Snap at 2'.

6 Enter **QSAVE** to save the prototype drawing.

Using the new prototype drawing, let's create new drawing files.

1 Begin a new drawing named **PROPERTY**.

HINT:

Be sure to specify the PTSITE prototype drawing when creating PROPERTY.

2 Create and make current a new layer named **PROPERTY**. Assign the color red to it.

Most property lines are not a perfect rectangle. However, to keep things simple, follow the next step.

3 Draw a rectangular property line using the **PLINE** command. Make it almost as large as possible (76′ × 56′), but stay inside the drawing limits.

4 Enter **QSAVE** to save your work.

5 Using the PTSITE prototype drawing, begin a new drawing named **BLDG**.

6 Create and make current a new layer named **BLDG**. Assign the color yellow to it.

7 Approximate the following building outline using a Polyline. Allow space for trees and shrubs around the building, but do not draw any at this time.

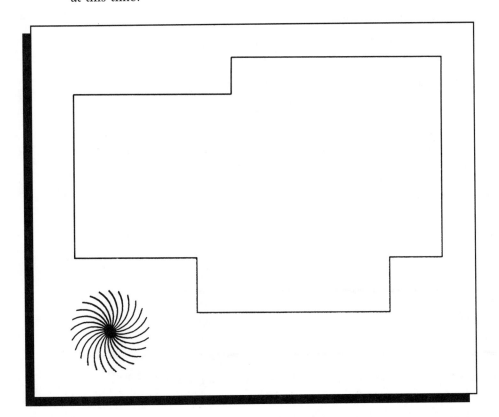

8 Enter **QSAVE** to save your work.

⑨ Create a third drawing using the PTSITE prototype drawing. Name it **LDSCAPE**.

⑩ Create and make current a new layer named **TREES**, and assign the color green to it.

⑪ Create a simplified representation of a tree as shown in the previous illustration. Approximate the size and shape of the tree.

HINT:
Use the ARC and ARRAY commands to create the tree.

⑫ Create a Block of the tree. Name it **TREE** and use the tree's center as the insertion base point.

The screen should currently be blank.

⑬ Enter **QSAVE** to save your work.

XREF Command

REF 414-420

The XREF command is used to attach one or more drawing files to a drawing.

① Enter the **XREFCTL** system variable and enter **I**.

This will cause AutoCAD to create an ASCII log file of Xref activity.

Suppose you are a landscape architect responsible for completing a landscape design for the building contained in BLDG.DWG. Because you are working on a tight schedule and the customer would like to see a proposed landscape design, you must deliver a preliminary design even though the design of the building is not yet stable.

② Enter the **XREF** command.

The following options should appear.

```
?/Bind/Detach/Path/Reload/<Attach>:
```

③ Press **RETURN** to accept the Attach default setting and enter **BLDG**.

Move the crosshairs and notice the BLDG drawing appears to be inserting, as if you were using the INSERT command.

④ Enter **0,0** for the insertion base point and accept the remaining default settings.

The BLDG drawing should now be present.

5 Enter the **LIST** command, select the building, and press **RETURN**.

Listing information about an entity tells whether or not it belongs to an Xref. Notice "External reference" appears in the listing.

We are going to place several trees around the house, inside the property line. Therefore, it would be important to see the property line so that none of the trees extend outside the property line.

6 Enter **XREF**, press **RETURN** to accept the Attach default setting, and enter **PROPERTY**.

7 Enter **0,0** for the insertion base point and accept the remaining default settings.

The property line should now be present.

NOTE:

As a reminder, these new entities are for reference only; they do not become part of your drawing. However, they stay attached to the drawing—even between editing sessions—until they are detached. Also, the drawing file does not increase in size.

8 Enter the **SH** command and press **RETURN**.

9 Enter **DIR *.XLG** to locate the file named **LDSCAPE.XLG**.

10 Use the DOS **TYPE** or **MORE** command to list the contents of **LDSCAPE.XLG**.

HINT: You may need to change to the directory that contains the LDSCAPE drawing. At the DOS prompt, enter either TYPE LDSCAPE.XLG or MORE < LDSCAPE.XLG.

This is an ASCII log file that AutoCAD creates to maintain a log of Xref activity. You may choose to delete it if it consumes disk space that you need to use. Also, you can set the XREFCTL system variable back to 0 to avoid creating logs in the future.

11 If you haven't already, enter **EXIT** to return to the AutoCAD graphics screen.

12 Enter the **INSERT** command and insert the Block named **TREE** contained in the current drawing.

13 Place the tree close to the east side of the building, and accept the default settings.

451

14 Place several other trees (of various sizes) around the building.

15 Enter **QSAVE** to save your work.

Changing an Xref _____

Suppose the customer asks the building architect to expand the east side of the building.

1 Open the **BLDG** drawing.

2 Using the **STRETCH** command, stretch the east part of the building 10′ to the east.

3 Enter **QSAVE** to save your work.

The BLDG drawing has changed. Must the building architect notify the landscape architect of the change? Suppose the landscape architect loads LDSCAPE to continue working on it.

4 Open **LDSCAPE**.

The latest change in the BLDG drawing is reflected in the LDSCAPE drawing, as shown in the following illustration. As you can see, the trees now interfere with the building. Having constant access to the most up-to-date version of a drawing is the primary benefit of an Xref.

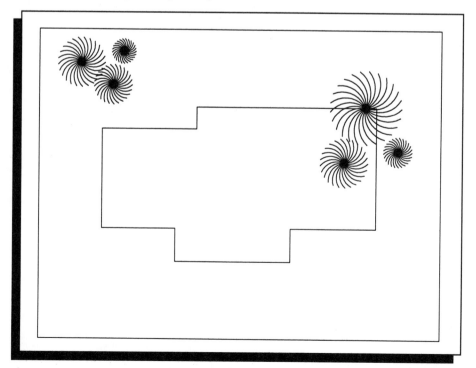

Reference

5 Move the tree(s) away from the building.

Xrefs can be particularly useful when working with others on a project.

Xref Layers ──────────────────

1 Display a listing of layers.

Notice LDSCAPE now contains two additional layers as a result of attaching the two Xrefs. Each of the new layer names is preceded by its parent Xref drawing file name and separated by the | (vertical bar) character. You can control the visibility, color, and linetype of the Xref layers, but the changes are discarded when you end the drawing.

2 Freeze layer **BLDG|BLDG**, and change the color of layer **PROPERTY|PROPERTY**.

3 Enter **QSAVE** to save your work.

4 Open **LDSCAPE** again and notice that the changes made to the layers were not permanent.

XREF Options ──────────────────

XREF offers several options.

1 Enter the **XREF ?** option and press **RETURN**.   REF 415

This will list the Xrefs in the current drawing.

2 Enter the **XREF D**etach option and enter **PROPERTY**.   REF 416

The property line should disappear because the PROPERTY Xref is no longer attached to the drawing.

3 Enter **U** to undo your last operation.

4 Enter **UNDO** and **M**ark.

5 Enter the **XREF B**ind option and enter **PROPERTY**.   REF 415-416

The PROPERTY Xref is now a permanent part of the drawing.

6 Enter **LIST**, select the property line, and press **RETURN**.

"External reference" no longer appears because the property line is no longer a part of the Xref, but rather is a permanent part of the drawing.

NOTE:

In the future, you may not want to bind the entire Xref. If so, use the XBIND command to bind only a part of an Xref. See the following section, titled "XBIND Command," for more information.

7 Enter **UNDO** and **B**ack.

PROPERTY.DWG is an Xref once again.

The XREF Reload option reloads any Xref you have attached to the current drawing. This permits you to load the most up-to-date version of the Xref, without reopening the current drawing.

The XREF Path option allows you to edit the path (in case it were to change) that indicates the location of the Xref.

REF 416-417

XBIND Command

REF 422

The XBIND command permits you to permanently bind a subset of Xref's dependent symbols to the current drawing. Dependent symbols are named items contained in the Xref, such as Blocks and Layers.

1 Enter the **XBIND** command.

The following dependent symbol options should appear.

```
Block/Dimstyle/LAyer/LType/Style:
```

2 Enter the **LA**yer option.

3 Enter **BLDG|BLDG**.

This dependent symbol becomes a permanent part of the drawing.

4 Create a listing of layers.

AutoCAD should have renamed the dependent layer BLDG|BLDG to BLDG0BLDG.

5 Pick **Cancel** or enter **CTRL C** to return to the "Command:" prompt.

6 Enter **END** to save your work and exit AutoCAD.

Questions

1. What is the primary benefit of using external references (Xrefs)?

2. What is the function of the following XREF command options?

   ? _____

   Bind _____

   Detach _____

   Path _____

   Reload _____

   Attach _____

3. XREF Attach is similar to using what common AutoCAD command?

4. What command tells whether or not a given entity belongs to an Xref?

5. What information is contained in an AutoCAD XLG file? _____

6. Describe the purpose of the XBIND command. _____

Problem

This problem works best as a small group activity, involving two to four individuals. The group should identify a project. Make it simple, otherwise it may be difficult to organize. The project should involve several components which fit together. Each individual on the project should be responsible for completing one or more different components. The project leader must coordinate the effort and be responsible for completing the final assembly made up of the individual component drawings.

While a network would aid greatly in the completion of this project, it can be done using individual AutoCAD stations. However, all individuals working on the project must copy their component drawings to a single location (disk and directory) and make them available to others.

 **Unit 49** An Internal Peek at AutoCAD's Menus

■ OBJECTIVE:

To examine and understand the contents of AutoCAD's menu file ACAD.MNU

This unit concentrates on the components which make up the ACAD.MNU file. It reviews the file in its raw form: the parts you don't see when you're at the AutoCAD graphics screen. Later, you will learn to modify and create your own menu, one as simple or as sophisticated as you'd like.

The following steps do not require a word processor or text editor, but it is desirable to use one. In a later exercise (when you actually create a custom menu), a word processor or text editor is highly recommended.

The Raw Menu _____

1 Start your computer system and obtain the DOS prompt
(*e.g.*, C> or C:\>).

2 Change to the directory that contains the AutoCAD ACAD.MNU file.

HINT:
ACAD.MNU contains the accessible source code of your screen menu. This file is contained in the AutoCAD disk directory called SUPPORT. See Appendix C for details on changing directories and Appendix B for details on copying files.

3 Before proceeding, make a backup copy of ACAD.MNU.

4 Using either the DOS **TYPE** or **MORE** command, list the contents of **ACAD.MNU**.

Example: C:\ACAD\SUPPORT>**TYPE ACAD.MNU** (and press **RETURN**)

Example: C:\ACAD\SUPPORT>**MORE < ACAD.MNU** (and press **RETURN**)

HINT:
If you use the TYPE command, the file will scroll off the screen before you can read it. To stop the scrolling, quickly press CTRL S. To resume scrolling, press any key.

You can press CTRL C to start over. Function key F3 reenters your last entry at the DOS prompt.

5 Review the first portion of the file.

The screen should contain information similar to the following.

```
***Comment

          Copyright (C) 1986-1992 by Autodesk, Inc.
          Version 1.0 for Release 12 (6/1/92)

          Permission to use, copy, modify, and distribute this software
          for any purpose and without fee is hereby granted, provided
          that the above copyright notice appears in all copies and that
          both that copyright notice and this permission notice appear in
          all supporting documentation.

          THIS SOFTWARE IS PROVIDED "AS IS" WITHOUT EXPRESS OR IMPLIED
          WARRANTY.  ALL IMPLIED WARRANTIES OF FITNESS FOR ANY PARTICULAR
          PURPOSE AND OF MERCHANTABILITY ARE HEREBY DISCLAIMED.


***BUTTONS1
;
$p0=*
^C^C
^B
^O
^G
^D
^E
^T

***BUTTONS2
$p0=*

***AUX1
;
$p0=*
^C^C
^B
^O
^G
^D
^E
^T

***AUX2
$p0=*

***POP0
[Osnap]
[Center] _center
[Endpoint] _endp
[Insert] _ins
[Intersection] _int
[Midpoint] _mid
[Nearest] _nea
[Node] _nod
[Perpendicular] _per
[Quadrant] _qua
[Tangent] _tan
```

The ASCII file ACAD.MNU contains as many as 6227 lines of code. Much of the code consists of AutoCAD's standard and pull-down menu items. Many examples, such as $S = SOLIDS, are contained in this unit.

Individual Menu Elements

AutoCAD uses several special characters in ACAD.MNU. Each of them performs a specific function.

1 Attempt to locate each of the following components in ACAD.MNU.

HINT: Consider viewing ACAD.MNU using a word processor or text editor. Use the text Find or Search capability if it is an available option.

***BUTTONS1	—specifies a buttons menu for the buttons on a mouse or digitizer cursor control
***SCREEN	—specifies a screen menu
***TABLET1	—specifies tablet menu area 1
***icon	—an icon menu is declared by providing a ***icon item in the menu file
***POP2	—pull-down menu sections are defined using ***POP1, ***POP2, etc.
**poly	—specifies a submenu; poly can be any characters, such as SOLIDS
$S = RENDER	—means to activate submenu **RENDER
$S =	—means to restore the last menu
$p0 = *	—causes pull-down POP0 to appear
$I = fonts1	—here, the "$I = " item addresses the **fonts1 icon menu
$I = *	—this special menu item displays the current icon menu and allows you to make a selection from it
[BLOCK:]	—the text enclosed by brackets will appear in the screen menu; in this particular case, the item "BLOCK:" will appear in the screen menu
[acad(Cone)]	—this addresses the cone slide image contained in the acad slide library for display as an icon
SI	—short for Single; causes the command to execute immediately and does not allow for further object selection interaction
AUTO	—also AU; during object selection, the use of Auto enables you to apply the Window and Crossing options without the need to enter them
;	—issues a RETURN
' (apostrophe)	—specifies transparent command entry

_ (underscore)	—serves no specific function unless you are translating the menu to a foreign language
^M	—presses the RETURN key
^I	—presses the TAB key
->	—as a prefix, indicates that the pull-down or cursor menu has a submenu
<-	—as a prefix, indicates that the pull-down or cursor menu is the last in the submenu
<-<-. . .	—as a prefix, indicates that the pull-down or cursor menu item is the last in a submenu; each "<-" terminates a parent menu
\	—the backslash will stop the computer, and the computer will expect input from the user
(a space)	—an empty space is the same as pressing the space bar
+	—menu item continues on next line
~	—displays prompt in half-tone, disabling the menu item
--	—dashes display a separator line between pull-down and cursor menu items
*^C^C	—when placed at the beginning of a menu item, causes menu item to repeat
^	—this character (called a caret) will automatically press the CTRL key
^C	—this will issue a cancel, the same as pressing CTRL C
^O	—this will activate the CTRL and O keys the same as if you were to press CTRL O to toggle the Ortho mode; ^O is used in the BUTTONS menu to assign button #6 to this function
^D	—toggles coordinates display
^E	—toggles isometric plane
^B	—toggles snap on and off
^G	—toggles grid on and off
^T	—toggles tablet mode on and of
^Q	—toggles printer echo on and off

Menu Items

These individual components are combined to create menu items (sometimes referred to as macros) that perform specific AutoCAD functions. For example, [Redo]^C^C_redo will display Redo in the standard screen menu, will issue cancel twice, and will enter the REDO command.

1 Examine closely each of the following menu items from the ACAD.MNU file.

$S = OSNAPB   —activates the
                                                   **OSNAPB submenu

***POP5	—specifies the fifth (Modify) pull-down menu
[DRAW]$S = X $S = DR	—displays "DRAW" in the screen menu; activates the **X submenu and the **DR submenu
[* * * *]$S = OSNAPB	—displays "* * * *" in the screen menu; activates the **OSNAPB submenu
[ZOOM:]'_ZOOM	—displays "ZOOM:" in the screen menu; enters the ZOOM command transparently
[ERASE:]^C^C_ERASE	—displays "ERASE:" in the menu; issues cancel; issues cancel again; enters the ERASE command
[drag]$S = X $S = PARC drag	—displays "drag" in the menu; activates the **X submenu and the **PARC submenu; enters drag
[3-point:]^C^_CARC \\DRAG	—displays "3-point:" in the menu; issues cancel; issues cancel again; issues the ARC command and space bar; pauses for user input; pauses for user input again; enters drag

[Finishes...]^C^C$S = X $S = RENDER finish   —displays "Finishes..." in the menu; issues cancel; issues cancel again; activates the **X submenu; activates the **RENDER submenu; enters finish (This item is found in the Render pull-down menu.)

^C^C$I = FONTS1 $I = *   —issues cancel; issues cancel again; addresses the **FONTS1 icon menu; displays the current icon menu and allows you to make a selection from it

[acad(romans,Roman Simplex)]'_style romans romans —addresses the romans slide image from the acad slide library; displays "Roman Simplex" in the list box; issues the STYLE command transparently; enters "romans"; enters "romans" again

② Attempt to locate each of the previous menu items in the ACAD.MNU file. Print the pages on which they appear.

③ Start AutoCAD.

④ Referring to the hardcopy printouts, locate each of the above menu items in the graphics screen and pick each of them. Compare the printouts to how they function.

⑤ Enter **QUIT** to exit AutoCAD.

⑥ Locate the file named **ACAD.MNX** contained in the SUPPORT directory.

Note the file ACAD.MNX contained with the other AutoCAD system files. This file is ACAD.MNU in its compiled form. The compiled .MNX file is compact and fast. AutoCAD uses this file to display the screen menus. You are unable to review and edit the contents of compiled menu files such as ACAD.MNX. Therefore ACAD.MNU is made available.

Questions

Describe what each of the following menu items will do.

1. [DIM:]^C^C_DIM

   Causes Dim to Repeat

2. [Dimstyle]_DIMSTYLE

3. [HELP]$S = '_HELP

4. **LINE 3

5. [New...]^C^C_new

6. [Window]_WINDOW

7. [Center, Diameter]^C^C_circle;_diameter

8. [S,E,D:]^C^C_ARC _E _D DRAG

9. [done];

Problems

1. Print a portion of the ACAD.MNU file and then start AutoCAD. Experiment with different command and submenu sequences and attempt to locate the sequences on the ACAD.MNU printout.

2. Locate items in the ACAD.MNU printout that you cannot fully visualize. Attempt to find the corresponding item in the standard or pull-down screen menus and execute it.

AUTOCAD® AT WORK

*Before the Bulldozers Roll**

How does civil construction affect the government? The best time to find out is before work begins. In Denver, Colorado, 4D Imaging is making preconstruction visualization a reality through the use of computer-aided rendering, imaging, and animation.

One of the company's projects involved the creation of visual representations of a proposed I-25 highway Interchange. AutoCAD's 3D modeling commands were used to create cantilever piers, slope pavings, bridge abutments, and other 3D elements. The final output was a highly accurate 3D rendered model of the existing highway site and proposed interchange, showing four flyover ramps, a submerged portion of the new E-470 beltway, a relocated frontage road, and a full 3D topography of the site.

Another project involved the creation of a 3D model to evaluate design, and market the concept of a toll plaza to investors in a highway project.

Data was gathered from five engineering firms, each working on various portions of the project. Cross-sectional modeling code was used to generate the road surface from control line and template data. Other 3D elements were developed using parametric LISP routines.

Once completed, the AutoCAD model was translated to rendering and animation software. An animation was scripted to simulate a motorist's perspective of the tollbooth while driving down the highway, pulling up to the booth, looking at the tollbooth operator, and leaving. The finished animation was output to 1″ video tape.

A third project involved visualization of a portion of the proposed flyover interchange at 6th Avenue and I-25 in Denver. Working from a scanned photograph of the existing interchange, a 3D AutoCAD model of the cantilever piers and bridge section was created. The model was then

matched to the existing photo and saved as a raster file with the AutoCAD vectors composited over the photo.

Using the vectors as outlined information, realistic colors, textures, and shadows were painted in to simulate what the highway would look like prior to construction.

A fourth project involved an innovative design for a grade separation between Speer Boulevard and three of the busiest intersections in the city of Denver.

Working with an engineering firm, 4D created photo-realistic renderings of the company's proposed design solution. Photo simulations were created from the plan and profile drawings. After design changes the final images were digitally film recorded to 4″ × 5″ transparencies. The city plans to use this type of photo simulation for future projects.

*Excerpted from *CADENCE*, June 1990, copyright © 1990, Ariel Communications, Inc.

 **Creating Custom Menus**

■ OBJECTIVE:

To create an AutoCAD screen and pull-down menu and to apply the MENU command

This unit involves the development of AutoCAD menus. It uses a simple approach to creating menus and does not require a word processor or text editor, although using one is recommended.

AutoCAD users can create screen and pull-down menus which can include a wide range of AutoCAD commands. Users can develop custom "macros," which automatically execute any series of inputs. For example, a simple two-item macro can enter ZOOM Previous in one step, thereby minimizing input from the user. Sophisticated macros can activate numerous AutoCAD commands and functions in a single step.

Everything that you can enter at the keyboard can be entered automatically using macros. Thus, you have the flexibility to develop a menu at any level of sophistication.

Developing a Screen Menu ―――――――――――

Let's develop a short and simple screen menu named SIMPLE1.MNU.

1 Start the computer and obtain the DOS prompt, *e.g.,* C:\>.

HINT:
If you have a word processor or text editor, use it. Create a new file and name it SIMPLE1.MNU, and then skip to Step 3.

2 If you don't have access to a word processor or text editor, type the following after the DOS prompt: **COPY CON:SIMPLE1.MNU** and press **RETURN**. If you are storing on A drive, then specify A: (*e.g.,* COPY CON:A:SIMPLE1.MNU).

You have just begun a new file named SIMPLE1.MNU.

――――――― NOTE: ―――――――
Your only editing capability is your backspace key, so be very careful. If you make a mistake you cannot correct, you must start over.

Your cursor should now be at the beginning of the next line.

③ Begin typing the contents of the following menu. Type it *exactly* as shown. You can use either upper- or lowercase letters for the information after the second bracket.

See also the optional *Applying AutoCAD Diskette*

```
***SCREEN
[  A]
[SIMPLE]
[ MENU]


[LINE]^C^Cline
[ERAS L]^C^Cerase L
[ZOOM W]^C^Czoom W
[TEXT]^C^Ctext
[*Cancel]^C^C
```

←— 2 blank lines here

If you are using the COPY CON method, press the F6 function key and press RETURN. If you're using a word processor or text editor, save the file in ASCII format.

④ When you're finished, immediately make a backup copy of this file.

⑤ If you haven't done so already, make this file easily accessible while in AutoCAD by copying it to the appropriate (*e.g.*, ACAD) directory.

⑥ Start AutoCAD.

The standard ACAD.MNU items should be on the screen, as usual.

MENU Command

REF 100-101

① Enter the **MENU** command.

② Locate and select **SIMPLE1**. (If SIMPLE1.MNU is contained in a directory other than the default directory, you must specify the directory.)

The new SIMPLE1 menu should appear.

AutoCAD automatically compiles the file and loads the compiled MNX file. Therefore, the file SIMPLE1.MNX now exists also.

③ Select each of the commands to see whether they work.

NOTE:

You also have full access to all other AutoCAD commands. Just type them. Notice, however, that the tablet, pull-down, and buttons menus are no longer available because they are defined in ACAD.MNU.

4 If you have a mouse or cursor control with more than one button, try each of them. Also, attempt to use the pull-down and tablet menus.

5 Enter **MENU** again and locate and select ACAD.MNU.

All menus should be available once again.

———— NOTE: ————

The UNDEFINE and REDEFINE commands are also available. The UNDEFINE command will delete the built-in definition of an AutoCAD command. This lets you create entirely new command definitions using the existing AutoCAD command names. If you want to restore the original built-in definition of the AutoCAD command, use the REDEFINE command.

CUST 36-37

6 Enter **QUIT** to exit AutoCAD.

Developing a Pull-Down Menu ————

Let's create a simple pull-down menu named PULL.MNU.

1 Store the following in a file named **PULL.MNU**. Skip the first line so that the line above ***POP1 is blank.

See also
the optional
Applying
AutoCAD
Diskette

```
***POP1
[Construct]
[Line]^C^CLINE
[Circle]^C^CCIRCLE
[Arc]^C^CARC
[--]
[->Display]
  [Pan]'PAN
  [->Zoom]
    [Window]^C^CZOOM W
    [Previous]^C^CZOOM P
    [All]^C^CZOOM A
    [Extents]^C^CZOOM E
```

2 Make a backup copy of the file.

3 Start AutoCAD, enter **Menu** and locate and select **PULL.MNU**.

4 Select the new **Construct** pull-down menu and try each of the selections.

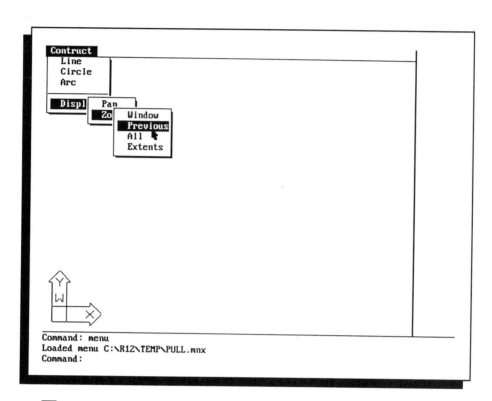

```
Contruct
   Line
   Circle
   Arc

   Displ  Pan
         Zo   Window
              Previous
              All
              Extents
```

Command: menu
Loaded menu C:\R12\TEMP\PULL.mnx
Command:

5 Enter **QUIT** to exit AutoCAD.

Questions

1. Briefly define an AutoCAD macro.

   _____

   _____

2. Why are custom macros useful?

   _____

   _____

3. The INSERT command can be included in a macro like any other command. In conjunction with a drawing name, how could this be useful?

   _____

   _____

4. State one useful application for developing a new AutoCAD macro, and write this macro below.

   _____

   _____

   _____

5. What AutoCAD command allows you to load a new menu?

   _____

6. What is the file extension for a noncompiled menu file? A compiled menu file?

   _____

7. What is the difference between a compiled and a noncompiled menu file?

   _____

8. What menu item specification must precede the contents of a screen menu? Pull-down menu?

   _____

1. Create the following screen menu and name it SECOND.MNU. Enter it exactly as you see it. After starting AutoCAD, load the SECOND menu and execute each of its commands to see whether and how they work. If any of the commands do not work, edit SECOND.MNU. You'll need to use a word processor or a text editor. If available, refer to the optional *Applying AutoCAD* Diskette.

```
***SCREEN
[LINE]^c^cline
[ERAS W]^c^cerase w
[ZOOM W]^c^czoom w
[ZOOM P]^c^czoom p
[Comp S]^c^cstyle comp complex;;;;;;;
[His Name]^c^ctext 6,2 .2 0 John Doe;;Mechanical Engineer;
[My Name]^c^ctext s comp 6,3 .2 0;
[FLIPSNAP]^b
[ARCH U]^c^cunits 4;;;;;;graphscr

[FLIP T]textscr
[*Cancel*]^c^c
```

2. Copy and rename SECOND.MNU by entering COPY SECOND.MNU SECOND2.MNU. Modify SECOND2.MNU so that it looks exactly like the one below. You'll need to use a word processor or a text editor. If available, refer to the optional *Applying AutoCAD* Diskette.

```
**SECOND2
[LINE]^c^cline $S=ZZZ
[ERAS W]^c^cerase w
[ZOOM W]^c^czoom w
[ZOOM P]^c^czoom p
[COMP S]^c^cstyle comp complex;;;;;;;
[His Name]^c^ctext 6,2 .2 0 John Doe;;Mechanical Engineer;
[My Name]^c^ctext s comp 6,3 .2 0;
[FLIPSNAP]^b
[ARCH U]^c^cunits 4;;;;;;graphscr
[FLIP T]textscr
[*Cancel*]^c^c
[LAST MNU]$S=
[ROOT PG]$S=S
```

Note to Student: Place 8 blank lines here—before you continue with the next menu item on the following page.

```
**ZZZ
[End Pt]end
[Cen Pt]cen
[Nearest]near
[More]$S=OSNAPB
```

If you attempt to use the menu in its current form, certain items will not function properly. Make a copy of the AutoCAD standard menu, ACAD.MNU, and rename it ACAD2.MNU. You can do this in a single step by entering COPY ACAD.MNU ACAD2.MNU.

Add the contents of SECOND2.MNU near the beginning of ACAD2.MNU as shown on the following page.

Add the [Sample]$S = SECOND2 item near the top of the root page of the screen menu. (See page 473.) The root page portion begins at approximately the 590th line of the menu.

HINT:

To perform this operation, use the word processor's "text merge," "file read," or "cut and paste" capability.

```
***Comment
```

```
            Copyright (C) 1986-1992 by Autodesk, Inc.
            Version 1.0 for Release 12 (6/1/92)

            Permission to use, copy, modify, and distribute this software
            for any purpose and without fee is hereby granted, provided
            that the above copyright notice appears in all copies and that
            both that copyright notice and this permission notice appear in
            all supporting documentation.

            THIS SOFTWARE IS PROVIDED "AS IS" WITHOUT EXPRESS OR IMPLIED
            WARRANTY.  ALL IMPLIED WARRANTIES OF FITNESS FOR ANY PARTICULAR
            PURPOSE AND OF MERCHANTABILITY ARE HEREBY DISCLAIMED.
```

```
**SECOND2
[LINE]^c^cline $S=ZZZ
[ERAS W]^c^cerase w
[ZOOM W]^c^czoom w
[ZOOM P]^c^czoom p
[COMP S]^c^cstyle comp complex;;;;;;;
[His Name]^c^ctext 6,2 .2 0 John Doe;;Mechanical Engineer;
[My Name]^c^ctext s comp 6,3 .2 0;
[FLIPSNAP]^b
[ARCH U]^c^cunits 4;;;;;;graphscr
[FLIP T]textscr
[*Cancel*]^c^c
[LAST MNU]$S=
[ROOT PG]$S=S
```

8 blank
lines here ←

```
**ZZZ
[End Pt]end
[Cen Pt]cen
[Nearest]near
[More]$S=OSNAPB
```

6 blank
lines here ←

```
***BUTTONS1
;
$pØ=*
^C^C
^B
^O
^G
^D
^E
^T

**vporti
[Tiled Viewport Layout]
[acad(vport-1,Single)]^C^C(ai_tiledvp 1 nil)
[acad(vport-3v,Three: Vertical)]^C^C(ai_tiledvp 3 "V")
[acad(vport-3h,Three: Horizontal)vp3h]^C^C(ai_tiledvp 3 "H")
[acad(vport-4,Four:  Equal)]^C^C(ai_tiledvp 4 nil)
[acad(vport-2v,Two:   Vertical)]^C^C(ai_tiledvp 2 "V")
[acad(vport-3r,Three: Right)]^C^C(ai_tiledvp 3 "R")
[acad(vport-3l,Three: Left)]^C^C(ai_tiledvp 3 "L")
[acad(vport-4l,Four:  Left)]^C^C(ai_tiledvp 4 "L")
[acad(vport-2h,Two:   Horizontal)]^C^C(ai_tiledvp 2 "H")
[acad(vport-3a,Three: Above)]^C^C(ai_tiledvp 3 "A")
[acad(vport-3b,Three: Below)]^C^C(ai_tiledvp 3 "B")
[acad(vport-4r,Four:  Right)]^C^C(ai_tiledvp 4 "R")

**Comment

     Begin AutoCAD Screen Menus

***SCREEN
**S
[AutoCAD]^C^C^P(ai_rootmenus) ^P
[* * * *]$S=OSNAPB
[ Sample]$S=SECOND2 ←
[ASE]^C^C^P(ai_aseinit_chk) ^P
[BLOCKS]$S=X $S=BL
[DIM:]^C^C DIM
[DISPLAY]$S=X $S=DS
[DRAW]$S=X $S=DR
```

After completing the above, start AutoCAD and load ACAD2.MNU. See whether each menu item works properly and be sure to select the new item called Sample.

Also, be sure to experiment with the LINE item from the Sample submenu, and then pick each of its submenu items, including "More."

3. Develop a custom pull-down menu. Make the menu as sophisticated as you'd like.

AUTOCAD® AT WORK

Learning AutoCAD Was No Pipe Dream

Losing his job turned out to be lucky for one piping designer. During the period when he wasn't working, Gene Dorn learned to use AutoCAD, and this opened up a new set of opportunities.

Today Gene Dorn works for Kaiser Engineers Hanford Company in Richland, Washington. There he use AutoCAD to design piping systems for such facilities as research laboratories and treatment plants for nuclear waste. Gene learned drafting in high school and worked on a board for years. Although he was very interested in computer-aided drafting, he never seemed to have the time to learn it.

A few years ago, the company he was working for faced some hard times, and many workers were laid off. Gene was one of them. While he was looking for another job, he learned that Westinghouse and the Washington State Employment Service had teamed up to offer retraining courses to workers like himself. One of the courses was on AutoCAD.

Gene wasted no time in signing up, and before long he had learned enough to apply for jobs requiring an AutoCAD background. Finally, Gene got the job at Hanford, and he believes that knowing AutoCAD was the deciding factor.

Gene plays an important role in helping reduce the effects of toxins in the environment. He designs holding tanks and other storage modules in which liquid wastes are held until the treatment plants he is also helping design are finished. Layering, arraying, stretching, and copying are a few of the commands he finds useful. For example, small lengths of pipe can be drawn and then stretched to fit the desired area. Valves and other pipe fittings can then be copied to wherever they are needed. He also uses powerful programs written in AutoLISP, saving time and eliminating repetition.

Gene's story is one example of how employers and the government can work together to retrain displaced workers. Today's increasingly computerized and automated workforce needs these skilled employees.

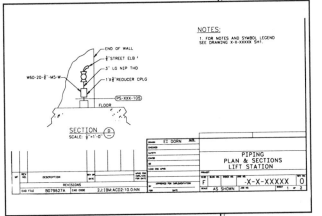

 **Creating Tablet Menus**

■ OBJECTIVE:

To apply tablet menu development, the TABLET command, and the tablet configuration steps

This unit focuses on creating tablet menus and configuring a digitizing tablet for use with a tablet menu. You must, of course, have a digitizing tablet to complete this unit.

As you may know, part of your digitizing tablet allows for *screen menu* pointing. This enables you to select screen menu items with your pointing device instead of typing them in. Other areas of the digitizing tablet can be designated for *tablet menus*, enabling you to enter a wide variety of AutoCAD commands and functions quickly and conveniently.

Developing a Tablet Menu _____

INST 32-35
CUST 98-99
REF 56-58

The first step in designing a new tablet menu is to ask yourself what you would like to include in the menu. The best way to answer this question is to sketch the tablet menu overlay on paper so that you gain some sense of the placement of each menu component. After the sketch is refined to your liking, you can use it in developing the actual menu file. In this unit, an example tablet menu overlay has been provided. Later, after you've learned the procedures, you'll be able to design your own.

The example on the next page is a relatively simple but functional tablet menu overlay. Let's use it as the model for the following steps.

1 Make an enlarged photocopy of the tablet menu overlay so that it comes close to fitting your digitizing tablet. If your copier doesn't have enlargement capability, you may use the overlay at its existing size.

See also the optional Applying AutoCAD Diskette.

_____ NOTE: _____

The overlay must not extend outside the active area on the digitizer. For instance, if the active area is $11'' \times 11''$, then the overlay must not be larger than $11'' \times 11''$.

Next, let's create the menu file that holds the menu items. Notice how these menu items correspond to the items on the tablet menu overlay, starting with tablet menu 1.

2 Using COPY CON or better yet, a word processor or text editor, enter the items on pages 476-477. Name the file **FIRSTTAB.MNU**. Be sure to enter the items exactly as shown and press **RETURN** after each entry.

See also the optional Applying AutoCAD Diskette.

_____ NOTE: _____

The Buttons Menu is for a three-button cursor control.

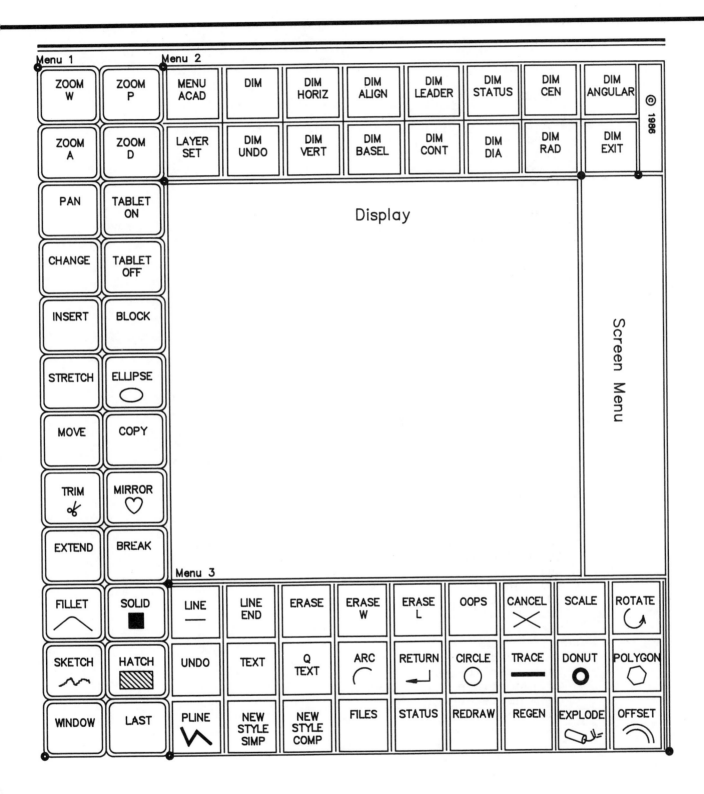

```
***BUTTONS
;
^C^CREDRAW

***TABLET1
^C^Czoom w
^C^Czoom p
^C^Czoom a
^C^Czoom d
^C^Cpan
^C^Ctablet on
^C^Cchange
^C^Ctablet off
^C^Cinsert
^C^Cblock
^C^Cstretch
^C^Cellipse
^C^Cmove
^C^Ccopy
^C^Ctrim
^C^Cmirror
^C^Cextend
^C^Cbreak
^C^Cfillet
^C^Csolid
^C^Csketch
^C^Chatch
window
last

***TABLET2
^C^Cmenu acad
^C^Cdim
^C^Cdim horizontal
^C^Cdim aligned
^C^Cdim leader
^C^Cdim status
^C^Cdim center
^C^Cdim angular
^C^Clayer set
undo
^C^Cdim vertical
^C^Cdim baseline
^C^Cdim continue
^C^Cdim diameter
^C^Cdim radius
^C^C
```

```
***TABLET3
^C^Cline
^C^Cline end
^C^Cerase
^C^Cerase w
^C^Cerase l
^C^Coops
^C^C
^C^Cscale
^C^Crotate
^C^Cundo
^C^Ctext
^C^Cqtext
^C^Carc
;
^C^Ccircle
^C^Ctrace
^C^Cdonut
^C^Cpolygon
^C^Cpline
^C^Cstyle simp simplex;;;;;;;
^C^Cstyle comp complex;;;;;;;
^C^Cfiles
^C^Cstatus
^C^Credraw
^C^Cregen
^C^Cexplode
^C^Coffset
```

③ Be sure to store the menu contents, and then copy the file to the main directory containing the AutoCAD system files, if it is not there already.

④ Make a backup copy of the file.

TABLET Command

REF 93-99

① Secure the menu overlay to the digitizer tablet with tape.

————— NOTE: —————

Be sure that all of the overlay is inside the active pointing area of the digitizing tablet. If it is not, tablet configuration will not work.

② Start AutoCAD.

③ Enter the **TABLET** command, and then enter the Configuration (**CFG**) option.

You should see the following on the screen.

```
Enter number of tablet menus desired (Ø-4) <Ø>:
```

---

④ Enter **3**.

You should now have the following on the screen.

```
Digitize upper left corner of menu area 1:
```

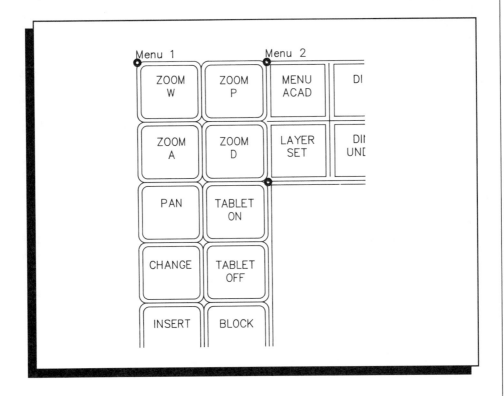

5 Locate the upper left corner of menu 1, shown in the previous illustration, and pick that point. (The point is indicated on the overlay by a small donut.)

NOTE:

In this particular overlay, menu 1 is comprised of the first two columns.

6 Pick the lower left corner of menu 1 (also indicated by a small donut) . . .

7 . . . and the lower right corner of menu 1 (the small donut two cells to the right of the preceding point).

You have just defined the boundaries of menu 1.

8 Enter **2** for the number of columns in menu 1 . . .

9 . . . and **12** for the number of rows in menu 1.

Now AutoCAD knows the exact size and location of all twenty-four cells in tablet menu 1.

AutoCAD should now be prompting you for the upper left corner of menu 2.

10 Locate menu 2 and its upper left corner, and pick that point.

NOTE:

Menu 2 is comprised of the upper two rows, beginning with the cell called MENU ACAD. Menu 2 consists of 8 columns and 2 rows.

11 Proceed exactly as you did with menu 1 until you are finished with menu 2. Be sure you select the rightmost donut when picking the lower right corner of menu 2.

12 Proceed with menu 3. It contains 9 columns and 3 rows.

After you are finished, you should see the following on the screen.

```
Do you want to respecify the screen pointing area? <N>
```

13 Reply with a **Yes**.

14 Digitize the lower left and the upper right corners of the display pointing area (the square area bounded by the three menus).

You are now finished with the tablet configuration. All of the changes have been stored in the file named ACAD.CFG.

Note that the right portion of the overlay has been left open for selecting screen menu items.

Loading the Menu File

REF 100-101

Now let's load the tablet menu called FIRSTTAB.MNU.

1 Enter the **MENU** command and locate and select **FIRSTTAB**.

HINT:

If FIRSTTAB.MNU is stored in a subdirectory, specify the name of the subdirectory.

If you correctly completed the above steps, you should now have full access to the new tablet menu. Ignore the items contained in the standard screen menu area.

2 Experiment with the tablet menu by picking each of the cells on the overlay, but do not yet pick the item named MENU ACAD located in the upper left corner.

3 To bring back the standard ACAD.MNU, pick the tablet menu item called **MENU ACAD** or enter the **MENU** command and enter **ACAD**.

You should no longer have access to the tablet menu.

Combining Menus

Now let's combine FIRSTTAB.MNU with our SIMPLE1.MNU screen menu and create a new file named MERGE.MNU. This will provide us with access to both a screen and a tablet menu.

NOTE:

This process will require a word processor or text editor with a "read in," "insert," or "cut and paste" capability.

1 Bring up the contents of SIMPLE1.MNU with a word processor.

2 Using the capabilities of the word processor, insert (read in) the entire contents of FIRSTTAB.MNU. Place it at the end of SIMPLE1.MNU.

3 Store all in a new file called MERGE.MNU.

See also the optional Applying AutoCAD Diskette.

The contents of the file should now look very similar to the following.

```
***SCREEN                        ***TABLET2
[   A]                           ^C^Cmenu acad
[SIMPLE]                         ^C^Cdim
[ MENU]                          ^C^Cdim horizontal
                                 ^C^Cdim aligned
                                 ^C^Cdim leader
[LINE]^C^Cline                   ^C^Cdim status
[ERAS L]^C^CERASE L              ^C^Cdim center
[ZOOM W]^C^Czoom W               ^C^Cdim angular
[TEXT]^C^Ctext                   ^C^Clayer set
[*Cancel*]^C^C                   undo
                                 ^C^Cdim vertical
                                 ^C^Cdim baseline
***BUTTONS                       ^C^Cdim continue
;                                ^C^Cdim diameter
^C^CREDRAW                       ^C^Cdim radius
                                 ^C^C
***TABLET1
^C^Czoom w                       ***TABLET3
^C^Czoom p                       ^C^Cline
^C^Czoom a                       ^C^Cline end
^C^Czoom d                       ^C^Cerase
^C^Cpan                          ^C^Cerase w
^C^Ctablet on                    ^C^Cerase l
^C^Cchange                       ^C^Coops
^C^Ctablet off                   ^C^C
^C^Cinsert                       ^C^Cscale
^C^Cblock                        ^C^Crotate
^C^Cstretch                      ^C^Cundo
^C^Cellipse                      ^C^Ctext
^C^Cmove                         ^C^Cqtext
^C^Ccopy                         ^C^Carc
^C^Ctrim                         
^C^Cmirror                       ;
^C^Cextend                       ^C^Ccircle
^C^Cbreak                        ^C^Ctrace
^C^Cfillet                       ^C^Cdonut
^C^Csolid                        ^C^Cpolygon
^C^Csketch                       ^C^Cpline
^C^Chatch                        ^C^Cstyle simp simplex;;;;;;;
window                           ^C^Cstyle comp complex;;;;;;;
last                             ^C^Cfiles
                                 ^C^Cstatus
                                 ^C^Credraw
                                 ^C^Cregen
                                 ^C^Cexplode
                                 ^C^Coffset
```

Now let's try it out.

1 Start AutoCAD if you haven't already.

NOTE:

Make sure the MERGE.MNU file is accessible by AutoCAD.

2 Enter the **MENU** command and locate and select MERGE.

You should now have access to the screen, buttons, and tablet menu commands and functions.

3 Enter **QUIT** to exit AutoCAD.

AUTOCAD® AT WORK

*Designing Cams with AutoCAD**

Commercial Cam Machine (Camco) Division of Emerson Electric Company manufactures mechanical intermittent motion devices that use cam technology as their basis for operation. A cam is a mechanical device which typically operates in a rotary fashion and contains information on displacement, velocity, and acceleration for transmission to a secondary mechanical member. A cam can be thought of as a read-only memory (ROM) mechanical device.

Camco has long been involved in computer-aided design and manufacturing for its products. It began using mainframe systems in the mid-1960s. In 1984 the company added AutoCAD, primarily as a learning tool for moving data from one system to another.

Soon, however, a new application was discovered. "We recognized that the DXF file closely matched the numeric data we transmitted to machine tools for the production of cams," says Josef Mang, vice president of engineering. "Suddenly all the pieces fell into place."

By passing machine data through a postprocessor and transmitting it to AutoCAD via the DXF format, Camco could edit machine data graphically. It was a simple project to reverse the process and turn graphics data into machine instructions. So AutoCAD moved from the status of a learning tool to that of a production tool.

How is Camco using AutoCAD as a production tool? "We have written LISP routines that are general in nature and of potential value to other AutoCAD users," notes Mang. "Since Camco's primary product is the mechanical cam, a routine to draw a simple straight line cam was one of the first routines we wrote.

"Camco customers are a diverse group, from automotive giants with large CAD/CAM installations to small machine shops with only one or two engineers and no CAD. All of these customers need accurate engineering drawings for their work, but their format requirements are quite different. AutoCAD can satisfy their requirements without much additional work.

"In design work, the ability to explore various options without redrawing the items you don't plan to change is a major time saver. Most design work consists of 80 percent redraw and 20 percent original work."

While the full impact of all savings has not yet been realized, Camco is already seeing some major savings, and the company is pleased with Auto-CAD. As Mang notes, "While there are a number of low cost microCAD systems on the market, none offers us as much flexibility as AutoCAD."

*Based on a story in *CADENCE* magazine, Vol 2, No. 1.

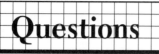

Questions

1. What AutoCAD command and command option are used to configure a digitizing tablet?

   _____

2. Explain the purpose of tablet configuration.

   _____

   _____

   _____

   _____

3. What is the minimum and maximum number of tablet menus that can be included on a digitizing tablet?

   _____

4. Briefly describe the process of combining the FIRSTTAB.MNU tablet menu with the SIMPLE1.MNU screen menu.

   _____

   _____

   _____

   _____

5. What command is used to load a tablet menu file?

   _____

Problems

1. Develop a new tablet menu and include a symbol library into one section of the menu. Use the previously created library called LIB1.DWG or create a new one. The following example should help you get started. It is contained on the optional *Applying AutoCAD* Diskette under the name TAB2.MNU. Name the menu file TAB2.MNU.

```
***TABLET1
^C^Cinsert LIB1 ^C
^C^Cinsert TSAW drag \drag \drag
^C^Cinsert DRILLP drag \drag \drag
^C^Cinsert JOINT drag \drag \drag

***TABLET2
^C^Cline
^C^Cerase
^C^Czoom w
```

2. Develop a new tablet menu using the steps outlined in this unit. Make the menu as sophisticated and powerful as possible. Utilize, as much as possible, AutoCAD's macro development capability.

Configuring and Customizing AutoCAD's Tablet Menu

■ OBJECTIVE:

To configure and customize the standard AutoCAD tablet menu

This unit steps you through the process of configuring AutoCAD's tablet menu. Also, you learn to develop tablet menu area 1, located at the top of the tablet menu. Covered are techniques for positioning new AutoCAD command macros and symbol libraries in this area of the tablet menu. The AutoCAD tablet menu template (overlay) is shown below.

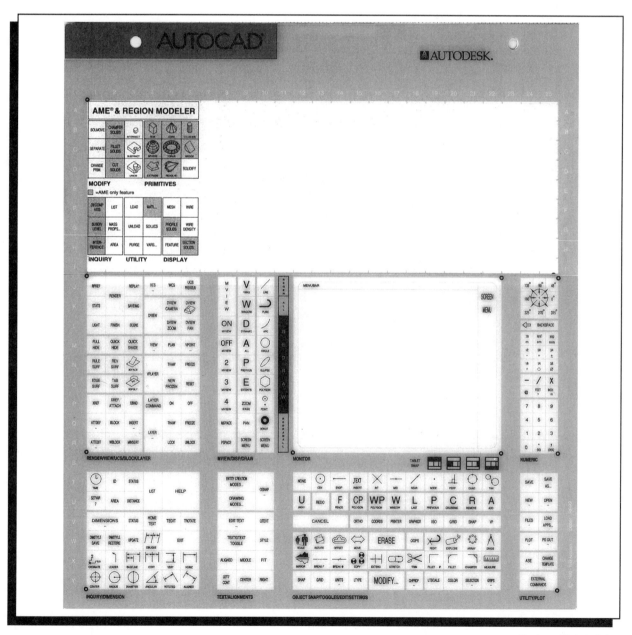

Courtesy of Autodesk, Inc.

The AME™ items, located at the top left, are contained on an optional card which fits under the plastic template. The top right area has been reserved for you to customize. If the optional AME card is not used, a total of 225 cells becomes available. This entire area is referred to as tablet menu area 1.

There is more than one way to develop menu area 1. We will use a basic method which allows you to follow each step of the development easily. This method also shows you how the other portions of the tablet menu were designed.

A word processor or text editor is required to complete the steps in the section titled "Writing the Code."

Configuring the Standard Tablet Menu _____

REF 98-99

Be sure the tablet menu overlay is securely fastened to the digitizing tablet.

1   Start AutoCAD.

2   From the standard screen menu, select **SETTINGS, next, TABLET:**, and then **Config**. If a tablet menu was previously configured, select **Re-Cfg** instead of config.

Use of these screen menu picks simplifies the tablet configuration process.

3   As AutoCAD now requests, digitize the upper left corner of menu area 1 as shown in the following illustration.

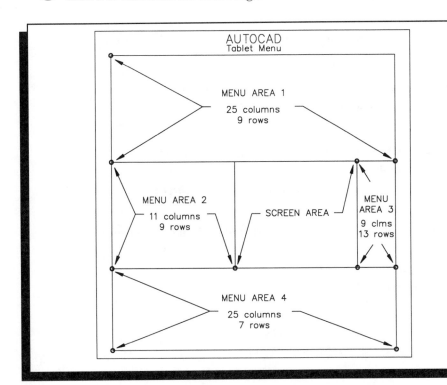

HINT:
See pages 559-561 of the *AutoCAD Reference Manual* for additional information on the standard tablet menu.

REF 559-561
INST 32-35

4 Pick each of the remaining corners as instructed by AutoCAD. Be precise.

Notice that AutoCAD enters the following column and row numbers for you automatically. All you need to do is define the menu areas with your pointing device.

Menu Area	Columns	Rows
1	25	9
2	11	9
3	9	13
4	25	7

When finished, this information is stored in the ACAD.CFG file, and the "Command:" prompt reappears.

5 Pick several items from the tablet menu to make sure it is configured properly.

Customizing the Tablet Menu _____

See also
the optional
Applying
AutoCAD
Diskette

Let's create the rectangular shape of area number 1.

1 Load the AutoCAD tablet menu template drawing named **TABLET**.

HINT:
TABLET.DWG is contained in the AutoCAD directory named SAMPLE. Be sure to create a backup of this file prior to loading it.

As a sidenote, notice that TABLET.DWG uses the Xref facility (covered in Unit 48) to reference several files.

2 After the template generates on the screen, enter the **FILL** command and turn it **Off**.

3 Create and make current a new layer named **MENU** and assign the color **green** to it.

4 Zoom in on menu area 1.

5 Enter the **PLINE** command and trace the outline of the menu area 1 as shown below.

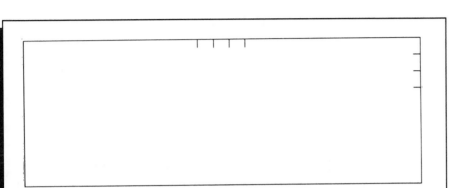

6 Add four short vertical lines beginning at column 12, as shown, and add three short horizontal lines beginning at row A. Zoom closely to these areas prior to drawing the lines.

7 Create a Block named **FRAME** and enter **0,0** for the insertion base point. Select each of the lines and the Polyline outline you created.

8 Enter the **WBLOCK** command, and enter **FRAME** for the file name. Also, enter **FRAME** for the Block name.

9 Do not save your work in the TABLET drawing.

Designing Area Number 1

You now have a drawing file, FRAME.DWG, that matches the size of tablet area number 1. Let's open this file and add command macros and symbols. When finished, you will be able to plot FRAME.DWG and position it under the template's transparent area 1.

1 Open FRAME.DWG.

The rectangular menu area identical to the one in the preceding illustration should appear.

2 Enter **ZOOM** Extents, and then enter **ZOOM 0.95x**.

3 Use the short horizontal and vertical lines to create the following nine cells.

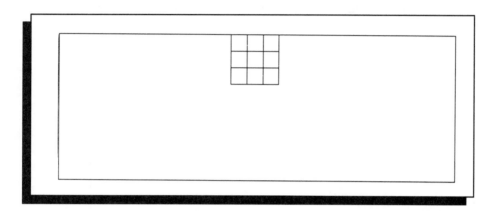

HINT:
The EXTEND and TRIM commands will help you construct the nine cells as quickly as possible.

Now, let's bring in the symbol library named LIB1.DWG created in Unit 30 and place each of the tools in the nine cells.

4 Using the **DDINSERT** command, insert **LIB1**, but be sure to cancel when the "Insertion point:" prompt appears.

5 Perform a Block listing to review the Block definitions now contained in the current drawing.

6 Place each of the tool symbols as shown here. You will probably need to reduce their size; try 0.15 unit.

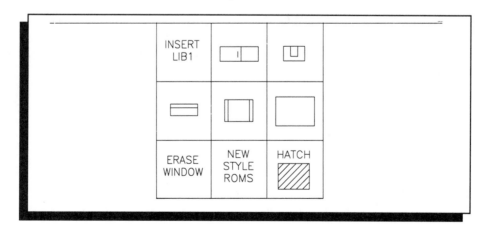

7 Place the text in the cells as shown above, and include a small hatch pattern under the word HATCH.

⑧ **ZOOM** All and plot the drawing.

⑨ After plotting, trim around the menu area with a knife or scissors and secure the menu under the template.

Writing the Code

This part becomes a bit more involved and requires a word processor or text editor.

① Locate the file ACAD.MNU found in the AutoCAD SUPPORT directory. Make a copy of it, and rename it **ACAD3.MNU**.

② Load your favorite word processor or text editor and bring up the ACAD3.MNU text file.

③ Using the Find or Search capability, locate the item ***TABLET1 in the file.

HINT: ***TABLET1 can also be located by paging through the file until you find it. It begins on approximately the 4741st line.

After you locate ***TABLET1 in the file, notice the similar items (A-1 through A-25, B-1 through B-25, and so on) that follow it. The first part of this section is shown below.

```
***TABLET1
[A-1]
[A-2]
[A-3]
[A-4]
[A-5]
```

This is where you enter the macros which correspond with the items in menu area 1. Likewise, each of these numbers corresponds with cells in menu area 1. To illustrate this, the upper middle portion of area 1 is shown below.

A–12	A–13	A–14
B–12	B–13	B–14
C–12	C–13	C–14

The numbering sequence of the cells begins at the upper left corner of the tablet menu and proceeds to the right. Tablet area 1 contains 225 cells arranged into 25 columns and 9 rows.

 Type the menu items over the numbers as shown on the following page. Notice how their placement corresponds directly to the cells in the upper middle portion of tablet area 1.

_____ NOTE: _____

On the following page, code was omitted where you see blank lines. This was to conserve space on the page.

***TABLET1
[A-1]
[A-2]
[A-3]
[A-4]
[A-5]
[A-6]
[A-7]
[A-8]
[A-9]
[A-10]
[A-11]
^C^CINSERT LIB1;^C
^C^CINSERT TSAW DRAG \DRAG \DRAG
^C^CINSERT DRILLP DRAG \DRAG \DRAG
[A-15]
[A-16]
[A-17]
[A-18]
[A-19]
[A-20]
[A-21]
[A-22]
[A-23]
[A-24]
[A-25]

[B-11]
^C^CINSERT JOINT DRAG \DRAG \DRAG
^C^CINSERT PLANER DRAG \DRAG \DRAG
^C^CINSERT BENCH DRAG \DRAG \DRAG
[B-15]
[B-16]
[B-17]
[B-18]
[B-19]
[B-20]
[B-21]
[B-22]
[B-23]
[B-24]
[B-25]

[C-11]
^C^CERASE W
^C^CSTYLE ROMS ROMANS;;;;;;;
^C^CHATCH
[C-15]
[C-16]
[C-17]
[C-18]
[C-19]
[C-20]
[C-21]
[C-22]
[C-23]
[C-24]
[C-25]

5 Save your changes in the ACAD3.MNU file and exit your word processor or text editor.

6 Copy ACAD3.MNU and LIB1.DWG to the main AutoCAD directory.

Using the New Menu

1 Start AutoCAD and load the **ACAD3** menu.

2 Pick the new tablet menu item called **INSERT LIB1**.

This item, as you may have noticed when you typed the macro, inserts the small symbol library, LIB1, into the current drawing.

3 Pick each of the tool symbols and place them one at a time.

4 Pick the remaining three menu items and notice what each of them does.

This should give you a taste of what can be developed with a tablet menu.

Questions

1. How are the four standard tablet areas defined when configuring the tablet menu?

2. What is the purpose of the AutoCAD tablet menu area 1?

3. What is the benefit of customizing the tablet menu?

4. Explain the numbering sequence of cells contained in tablet menus.

5. Explain why a word processor or text editor is required to modify the file ACAD.MNU.

Problems

1. Experiment with different portions of the AutoCAD tablet menu areas 2, 3, and 4 to discover how these menus were designed.

2. Place additional menu items in menu area 1. Categorize the items in area 1 so that related items are grouped together. You may wish to add headings above each group of related items.

Exploring AutoLISP®

■ OBJECTIVE:

To explore AutoLISP applications and capabilities by loading and invoking several AutoLISP programs

AutoLISP is AutoCAD's version of the LISP programming language. AutoLISP is embedded into AutoCAD so that AutoLISP functions can be applied at any time. LISP, short for LISt Processing, is a powerful programming language often associated with artificial intelligence (AI) applications.

AutoLISP provides programmers with a powerful, high level language well suited to graphic applications. For instance, AutoLISP can be used to write a program for expediting the creation of a staircase in a building. If properly written, the program would prompt you for the distance between the upper and lower floors, ask you for the size and/or number of steps (risers and treads), and automatically draw the detailed staircase for you.

AutoLISP programs, also called functions and routines, can be stored and used in at least two different formats:

1) as a file containing an .LSP file extension

2) as a screen or tablet menu item

Lengthy and sophisticated AutoLISP routines are most often stored as AutoLISP files (with the .LSP extension), while shorter and simpler lines of AutoLISP code are typically stored as menu items.

AutoLISP Example

Let's take a look at an AutoLISP program.

1 Start your computer system, but do not proceed into AutoCAD at this time.

2 Using the DOS **CD** (Change Directory) command, change to the directory containing the AutoCAD system files, if you are not already there.

3 Using the DOS **DIR**ectory command, locate the file named 3DARRAY.LSP. Try the AutoCAD SUPPORT directory.

This is an AutoLISP file. Let's review its contents.

4 At the DOS prompt, enter **MORE < 3DARRAY.LSP**. Or, you may choose to enter **TYPE 3DARRAY.LSP**, but be ready to press the **CTRL** and **S** keys to stop the scrolling.

496

Below is the first portion of 3DARRAY.LSP.

```
;;;    3DARRAY.LSP
;;;
;;;    Copyright (C) 1987-1992 by Autodesk, Inc.
;;;
;;;    Permission to use, copy, modify, and distribute this software
;;;    for any purpose and without fee is hereby granted, provided
;;;    that the above copyright notice appears in all copies and that
;;;    both that copyright notice and this permission notice appear in
;;;    all supporting documentation.
;;;
;;;    THIS SOFTWARE IS PROVIDED "AS IS" WITHOUT EXPRESS OR IMPLIED
;;;    WARRANTY.  ALL IMPLIED WARRANTIES OF FITNESS FOR ANY PARTICULAR
;;;    PURPOSE AND OF MERCHANTABILITY ARE HEREBY DISCLAIMED.
;;;
;;;    Functions included:
;;;        1) Rectangular ARRAYS (rows, columns & levels)
;;;        2) Circular ARRAYS around any axis
;;;
;;;    All are loaded by: (load "3darray")
;;;
;;;    And run by:
;;;        Command: 3darray
;;;                 Select objects:
;;;                 Rectangular or Polar array (R/P): (select type of array)
;;;********************************************************************
;;; ===================================================================
;;; ===================== load-time error checking ====================
;;;

  (defun ai_abort (app msg)
     (defun *error* (s)
        (if old_error (setq *error* old_error))
        (princ)
     )
     (if msg
       (alert (strcat " Application error: "
                      app
                      " \n\n  "
                      msg
                      "  \n"
                )
        )
      )
    )
    (exit)
  )

;;; Check to see if AI_UTILS is loaded, If not, try to find it,
;;; and then try to load it.
;;;
;;; If it can't be found or it can't be loaded, then abort the
;;; loading of this file immediately, preserving the (autoload)
;;; stub function.
```

The beginning of many AutoLISP programs includes statements explaining the purpose of the program. For example, notice the statements contained at the beginning of 3DARRAY.LSP.

Now that you have seen the contents of 3DARRAY.LSP, let's load it into AutoCAD.

497

Loading/Invoking AutoLISP Files _____

AutoLISP files, such as 3DARRAY.LSP, can be loaded and invoked by entering the AutoLISP load function at the "Command:" prompt. The file 3DARRAY.LSP—as well as 3D.LSP and MVSETUP.LSP—should be contained in the AutoCAD SUPPORT directory.

1 Start AutoCAD.

2 At the "Command:" prompt, enter the following exactly as you see it, including the parentheses. (You may use upper- or lowercase letters.) Be sure to press **RETURN**.

(load "3darray")

If the program loads properly, you will receive the message "3DARRAY loaded," and you will have access to a new command called 3DARRAY. If you receive an error message, refer to the following section titled "AutoLISP Error Messages" in this unit.

3 Enter **3DARRAY** using upper- or lowercase letters.

4 In reply to "Select objects:" cancel (press **CTRL C**), because no entities are available to select.

5 Create a 3D box 1 unit cube in size and select a viewpoint that is above, in front, and to the right of the object.

6 Enter **ZOOM** and 1 to reduce the current zoom magnification.

7 Enter **3DARRAY**, select the object, and choose to perform a rectangular array.

8 Enter **5** for the number rows, **4** for the number of columns, and **3** for the number of levels. Specify a distance of 1.4 between the rows, columns, and levels, as you would using the ARRAY command.

The 3D array should generate on the screen.

9 Enter the **HIDE** command.

Your screen should look similar to the following.

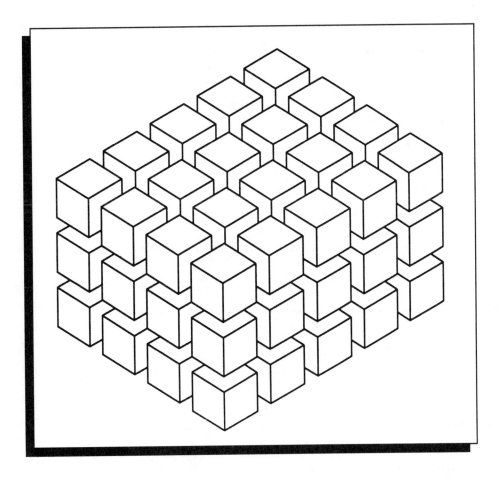

As indicated in the first part of this unit, AutoLISP code can be stored as screen or tablet menu items, instead of .LSP files. These menu items are stored in a menu file, such as ACAD.MNU, and invoked by picking the corresponding item from the screen or tablet menu. Most of AutoCAD's AutoLISP menu items are stored in the file ACADR12.LSP, located in the SUPPORT directory. This procedure is covered in the following unit.

Additional AutoLISP Examples

You (or your school or your business) should have access to the AutoLISP that comes with AutoCAD. These files should be contained in the AutoCAD directories named SAMPLE and SUPPORT. They provide examples of good programming practice, and they illustrate the vast power and capability of AutoLISP.

1 Review the AutoLISP files contained in the SAMPLE and SUPPORT directories.

The AutoLISP files contained in the SAMPLE directory are shown here.

AVE_XMPL.LSP	ALIAS.LSP	ATTREDEF.LSP	BMAKE.LSP	CHROMA.LSP
CL.LSP	DDTYPE.LSP	DELLAYER.LSP	WBLKSOL.LSP	DLGTEST.LSP
EDGE.LSP	EP.LSP	FACT.LSP	FCOPY.LSP	FPLOT.LSP
FPRINT.LSP	GP.LSP	JULIAN.LSP	MFACE.LSP	PROJECT.LSP
RPOLY.LSP	SPIRAL.LSP	SQR.LSP	TABLES.LSP	XDATA.LSP
XPLODE.LSP	XREFCLIP.LSP	HOLE.LSP	STLSUP.LSP	SOLMAINT.LSP

The AutoLISP files contained in the SUPPORT directory are shown here.

3D.LSP	ACADR12.LSP	ASCTEXT.LSP	DDATTDEF.LSP	DDATTEXT.LSP
DDCHPROP.LSP	DDGRIPS.LSP	DDINSERT.LSP	DDMODIFY.LSP	DDOSNAP.LSP
DDRENAME.LSP	DDSELECT.LSP	DDUNITS.LSP	DDVIEW.LSP	FILTER.LSP
APPLOAD.LSP	MVSETUP.LSP	PLUD.LSP	ASCOMMON.LSP	AI_UTILS.LSP
DDPTYPE.LSP	DDUCSP.LSP	DDVPOINT.LSP	3DARRAY.LSP	DLINE.LSP
CHTEXT.LSP	RMAN_DCL.LSP	PTEXT.LSP	DDSOLPRM.LSP	

Among these files are excellent utilities for use with AutoCAD. Brief descriptions of many of them are presented in the following unit. Let's review two of the utilities now.

DELLAYER.LSP Utility

DELLAYER.LSP, contained in the SAMPLE directory, permits you to erase all entities on a specified layer.

1. If you departed from AutoCAD, return to it now.

2. Erase everything on the screen, enter the **PLAN** command, and press **RETURN**.

3. In preparation for applying the DELLAYER.LSP utility, create a new layer named **OBJ**, assign color red to it, and place a couple of entities on it.

4. Set layer **0** and place a couple of entities on it, too.

5. At the "Command:" prompt, enter the following in upper- or lowercase letters—including the parentheses—and press **RETURN**.

(load "sample/dellayer")

HINT: If you receive the message "error: LOAD failed," the DELLAYER.LSP file may not be contained in the default directory. If so, refer to the following examples.

(load "dellayer")
or
(load "lsp/dellayer")

The above directories may be substituted with other directory names.

If you receive a different error message, review the section "AutoLISP Error Messages," later in this unit.

If the file loaded properly, you will receive the message "C:DELLAYER."

6 To use this AutoLISP program, enter **DELLAYER** at the "Command:" prompt.

7 In reply to "Layer(s) to delete:" enter **OBJ**.

8 Press **RETURN** to accept the next prompt.

All entities contained on OBJ should automatically erase. As stated earlier, this is the purpose of the DELLAYER.LSP utility.

ASCTEXT.LSP Utility

ASCTEXT.LSP, contained in the SUPPORT directory, is another useful AutoLISP routine supplied with AutoCAD. It enables you to insert any ASCII text file into a drawing file. Therefore lengthy notes and specifications can be created and edited with a word processor, then later inserted into AutoCAD.

1 Enter **(load "asctext")** as you see it here.

If the file does not load, refer to the previous hint.

You will receive the message "ASCTEXT loaded" when the file loads properly.

2 Enter **ASCTEXT** to invoke the file.

3 Select any ASCII text file currently on disk.

HINT:

You may create a new ASCII text file for use with ASCTEXT.LSP. Use a word processor, text editor, or the "COPY CON" method described near the beginning of Unit 50. Additionally, the AutoCAD file ACAD.MSG and batch files, such as AUTOEXEC.BAT and ACAD386.BAT, are ASCII text files and can be used here. Menu files, such as SIMPLE1.MNU, are also ASCII text files. However, avoid using large files such as ACAD.MNU, README.DOC, and ACAD.HLP because of the time they will require to generate on the screen. Be sure to specify the location of the file.

4 Answer the remaining prompts on your own. They are self-explanatory.

The file you specify will generate on the screen in the current text style. As with normal AutoCAD text, each line of text is treated as a single entity and can be altered using the CHANGE command.

As you can see, AutoLISP programs, such as the two utilities explained here, provide additional power and capability for users of AutoCAD. Thousands of AutoLISP routines have been developed—and many sold commercially—to fulfill a wide range of drafting, design, and engineering needs.

5 Using the **SH** command, display the contents of the ASCTEXT.LSP and DELLAYER.LSP files using the DOS **MORE** or **TYPE** command.

Load AutoLISP and ADS Files Dialogue Box

This dialogue box enables you to load an AutoLISP or ADS file by selecting it.

NOTE:

The AutoCAD Development System™ (ADS) is a C-language programming environment for creating sophisticated AutoCAD programs. ADS programs are loaded by and called from AutoLISP.

1 Enter the **APPLOAD** command or select **Applications...** from the **File** pull-down menu.

The following dialogue box should appear.

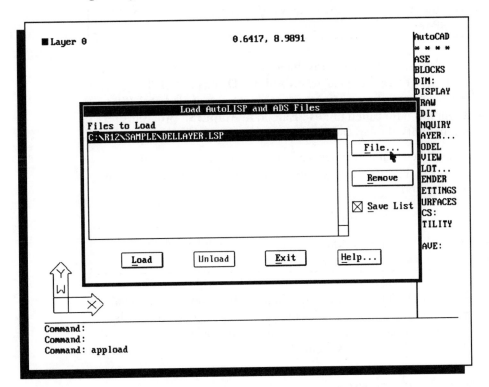

```
 ■ Layer 0                      0.6417, 8.9891          AutoCAD
                                                        * * * *
                                                        ASE
                                                        BLOCKS
                                                        DIM:
                                                        DISPLAY
        ┌──────── Load AutoLISP and ADS Files ──────┐  RAW
        │ Files to Load                              │  DIT
        │ C:\R12\SAMPLE\DELLAYER.LSP                 │  NQUIRY
        │                                            │  AYER...
        │                              ┌─ File... ─┐ │  ODEL
        │                              └──────────┘  │  VIEW
        │                                            │  LOT...
        │                              ┌─ Remove ──┐ │  ENDER
        │                              └──────────┘  │  ETTINGS
        │                              ⊠ Save List   │  URFACES
        │                                            │  CS:
        │                                            │  TILITY
        │                                            │
        │  ┌─ Load ─┐ ┌─ Unload ─┐ ┌─ Exit ─┐ ┌─ Help... ─┐ AVE:
        │  └───────┘  └─────────┘  └────────┘ └──────────┘  │
        └────────────────────────────────────────────┘
  Command:
  Command:
  Command: appload
```

② Pick the **File...** button.

③ Pick a file from the SAMPLE or SUPPORT directory and pick the **OK** button.

The file should appear in the list box.

④ Pick the **Load** button to load the file.

This will load the AutoLISP program as if you had used the AutoLISP "load" command.

AutoLISP Error Messages

At one time or another, you may receive one of many error messages. Here are three examples.

Insufficient node space

Insufficient string space

LOAD failed

NOTE:

Appendix D of the *AutoLISP Programmer's Reference* provides a complete list of AutoLISP-related error messages.

You may receive the error messages "insufficient node space" or "insufficient string space." These messages appear when AutoCAD runs out of "heap" space. The heap is an area of memory set aside for storage of all AutoLISP functions and symbols (also called nodes). Elaborate AutoLISP programs require greater amounts of heap and stack space.

The stack is also an area of memory set aside by AutoLISP. Stack holds function arguments and partial results; the deeper you "nest" functions, the more stack space is used.

NOTE:

Chapter 5 of the *AutoLISP Programmer's Reference* provides details on the use of heap and stack and memory management.

The error message "LOAD failed" appears when the file named in the load function can not be found, or the user does not have read access to the file. This message will also appear when the file name is misspelled or the incorrect file location (directory) is specified.

Recovering Node Space

If you are in need of additional node space, you can undefine a previously loaded AutoLISP program. For example, once you have loaded and used ASCTEXT.LSP, you can enter the following at the "Command:" prompt.

(setq asctext nil)

This will recover the node space taken by ASCTEXT.LSP and will make it available to other AutoLISP programs and routines.

 Enter (**setq asctext nil**).

Additional space should now be available.

2 Enter **QUIT** to exit AutoCAD.

Questions

1. What is AutoLISP?

   _____

   _____

2. Name two applications for AutoLISP.

   _____

   _____

3. What file extension do AutoLISP programs use?

   _____

4. Why is the amount of heap space important when loading AutoLISP programs?

   _____

   _____

5. What specific purpose does the ASCTEXT.LSP program serve?

   _____

   _____

6. How would you load the file named PROJECT.LSP?

   _____

7. Explain the purpose of the APPLOAD command.

   _____

   _____

Problem

Load and invoke each of the AutoLISP programs supplied with AutoCAD.

AUTOCAD® AT WORK

Job Training Partnership Act Does AutoCAD

I was approached last year about teaching an AutoCAD Release 11 course for the Job Training Partnership Act (JTPA) Programs. This is a federally funded program that helps prepare "economically handicapped" people for jobs in today's workplace.

Although I had been teaching professionals at an Authorized Training Center (for AutoCAD) for about four years, I really had no idea how a JTPA group might compare. I admit that I had some doubts about the chance for their success. I am proud to say I was wrong.

Potential students were tested extensively, and only twelve students were admitted into the program. The students that were selected had to be willing to commit to eighteen weeks of training. The class began at 9:00 A.M. and ended by 4:00 P.M. For the students, this was as tough as having a regular job.

After teaching drafting on the boards for about five weeks, I gave these students the option of going to the computer to do a section view problem or doing it manually. The jump to the CAD systems was immediate. I could have just stacked the drafting boards in the corner at that time.

Enthusiasm soared as I helped the students unfold the mystery of computer-aided drafting. It was tough to stay up with them. With the aid of handouts, a technical drawing book, and *Applying AutoCAD*, my students were attacking the assignments at an accelerated pace.

I have worked on many other CAD systems over the last seven years, and I have found AutoCAD to be the most user-friendly program on the market. The ability to start drawing with little aid helps encourage people to begin. After having only three days of training on the system, my students were already producing drawings. Before the course ended, the students were creating their own menus and slide library files. They were even programming with AutoLISP!

Upon completion of the course, the students were assisted in finding employment. One placement agency had an evaluation test for AutoCAD on which students from my class blatantly outscored AutoCAD users of two years.

This story was contributed by Donnia M. Tabor-Hanson. Ms. Tabor-Hanson is the owner/proprietor of CAD by Designing Trends, a consulting firm assisting in placement, drafting work, customization, and industrial training. Ms. Tabor-Hanson is also a part-time instructor at Pellissippi State Technical Community College and has been an AutoCAD instructor for six years.

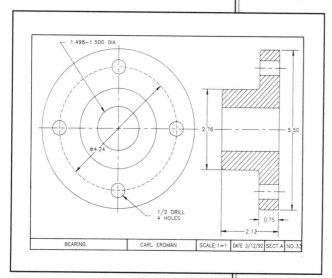

Unit 54 — Easing into AutoLISP® Programming*

Reference

■ OBJECTIVE:

To practice fundamental AutoLISP programming techniques and to create new AutoLISP files and AutoCAD commands

The significance of AutoLISP embedded into AutoCAD has captured the interest of many. This unit will introduce AutoLISP programming so that you can decide whether or not it's for you. Like many others, you may remain satisfied with applying the power of already-developed AutoLISP programs. On the other hand, you may find AutoLISP programming very intriguing and challenging.

If you enjoy programming, you should continue with the unit following this one and then explore and learn other AutoLISP commands and functions on your own. Someday, you may be in a position to serve the AutoLISP programming needs of the AutoCAD industry.

AutoLISP Arithmetic ———————————————————

LISP 74-76

As illustrated in the previous unit, AutoLISP functions, such as (load " "), can be entered directly at the "Command:" prompt. Let's enter an AutoLISP arithmetric expression.

1 Start AutoCAD.

2 At the "Command:" prompt, type (* 5 6) and press **RETURN**.

The number 30 should appear at the bottom of the screen because $5 \times 6 = 30$.

3 Enter (/ 15 3).

You should receive 5 because $15 \div 3 = 5$.

4 Try (+ 25 4).

Did 29 appear?

Setq Function ———————————————————

LISP 147-148

The setq function is used to assign values to a variable.

1 Type (**setq A 10**) and press **RETURN**. ("A" can be typed in upper- or lowercase.)

The value of variable A is now 10.

*ACKNOWLEDGMENT: Some of the basic principles presented here are from the *CADalyst Journal* AutoLISP tutorial series printed in Vol. 3, No. 2 and Vol. 3, No. 3.

2 Enter (setq B (– 20 4)).

Notice the parentheses.

The variable B now holds the value of 16.

3 To list the value of A, enter !A.

Did 10 appear?

4 Enter !B.

Let's try something a bit more complex.

5 Enter (setq CAT (– B A)).

Now CAT is equal to the value of B minus the value of A.

Let's try one more.

6 Enter (setq DOG (* (* 2 CAT)(/ A 5))).

The variable DOG is now equal to 24.

NOTE:

The number of left parentheses must equal the number of right parentheses. If they are not equal, you will receive a message such as 1>. This means you lack one right parenthesis. Add one by typing another right parenthesis and pressing RETURN.

Storing AutoLISP Routines as a File

AutoLISP code can be stored in a .LSP file and subsequently loaded and invoked at any time. The routines executed in the previous unit are good examples. Let's store the above functions to illustrate this capability.

1 Create a new file with a word processor or text editor and store the following exactly as you see it. You may use the "COPY CON" method to create the file, as outlined at the beginning of Unit 50. Name the file **FIRST.LSP**.

```
(defun c:FIRST ()
(setq a 10)
(setq b (- 20 4))
(setq cat (- b a))
(setq dog (* (* 2 cat)(/ a 5)))
)
```

See also the optional Applying AutoCAD Diskette.

Notice the AutoLISP function defun. The defun function allows you to define a new function or AutoCAD command and use it to invoke the AutoLISP file. Once loaded, the above program can be invoked by entering FIRST at the "Command:" prompt.

2 At the "Command:" prompt, enter (**load "first"**) or use the **Load AutoLISP and ADS Files** dialogue box.

"C:FIRST" should appear.

HINT:

If the FIRST.LSP file is contained in a directory under the main AutoCAD directory, specify the path when entering the load function. For example, enter (load "user/first") where USER is the name of the directory. Notice the slash mark (not a backslash).

3 Enter **FIRST**, now a new AutoCAD command, to invoke the program.

The number 24 should appear.

NOTE:

The preceding code could also be stored without the defun function. Also, setq can be entered just once, as shown. It would look like this:

```
(setq
a 10
b (- 20 4)
cat (- b a)
dog (* (* 2 cat)(/ a 5))
)
```

Entering (load "first") would then load and invoke the routine in one step.

Storing AutoLISP Routines as a Menu Item

AutoLISP routines can also be stored and invoked as menu items. As a standard screen menu item, the routine would look like this:

```
[FIRST]^C^C+
(setq a 10)+
(setq b (- 20 4))+
(setq cat (- b a))+
(setq dog (* (* 2 cat)(/ a 5)))
```

FIRST would appear in the screen menu. Notice that menu items such as ^C can be mixed with AutoLISP functions. Also note the + (plus) signs at the end of each line of code. This connects the code so that AutoCAD treats it all as a single line.

1 Using a word processor, add the preceding routine to your SIMPLE1.MNU screen menu (created in Unit 50). Store everything in a new file named SIMPLE2.MNU and try it out.

The first portion of SIMPLE2.MNU should now look like this:

```
***SCREEN
[  A]
[SIMPLE]
[ MENU]


[LINE]^C^Cline
[ERAS L]^C^CERASE L
[ZOOM W]^C^Czoom W
[TEXT]^C^Ctext
[*Cancel*]^C^C

[FIRST]^C^C+
(setq a 1Ø)+
(setq b (- 2Ø 4))+
(setq cat (- b a))+
(setq dog (* (* 2 cat)(/ a 5)))
```

As a tablet menu item, the routine would look like this:

```
^C^C+
(setq a 1Ø)+
(setq b (- 2Ø 4))+
(setq cat (- b a))+
(setq dog (* (* 2 cat)(/ a 5)))
```

List Function

LISP 130

Setq by itself can assign only one value to a variable. The list function can be used to string together multiple values, such as X and Y coordinates, to form a point. Setq, used with list, can then assign a list of coordinates to a single variable. Let's step through an example.

1 Type (setq fish (list 7 6)) and press RETURN.

Did (7 6) appear on the screen? This is now the value of fish.

2 Enter !fish.

(7 6) should appear again.

3 Enter the **LINE** command and pick a point near the lower left corner of your screen.

4 In reply to "To point:", enter **!fish**.

A line should appear.

5 Press **RETURN**.

HINT:

This function is especially valuable when you need to reach a point off the screen. For instance, if the upper right corner of the screen is 15,10 and the LINE command has been issued, you can reach point 25,20 (or any point for that matter) if a variable is assigned to that point. You just enter the variable preceded by the ! as you did in the fish example. Let's try it.

1 Enter (**setq trout (list 35 28**)).

2 Enter the **LINE** command and pick a point anywhere on the screen.

3 In reply to "To point:", enter **!trout**.

Did a line appear? Does it look as though it runs off the screen? It should.

4 Press **RETURN** and enter **ZOOM** Extents.

You should now see the endpoint 35,28 of the line.

Car Function ⸻

LISP 94

The car function is used to obtain the first item in a list, such as the X-coordinate. So, what would be the car of fish? Let's enter it.

1 Type (**car fish**) and press **RETURN**.

The value 7 should appear.

Cadr Function

Cadr is like car, only cadr gives you everything *except* the first item of a list—the Y-coordinate, in this case.

1 Enter (**cadr fish**).

The value 6 should appear.

So now you see we can obtain either the X- or Y-coordinate from a list.

Combining Several Functions

We can also assign a new variable to a set of coordinates that contains the cadr of fish (the Y-coordinate) and 0 as the X-coordinate.

First, we must create a new list containing 0 and the cadr of fish. Then we need to use setq to assign the new list to a variable (we'll call it bird). Therefore . . .

1 . . . enter (**setq bird (list 0 (cadr fish)))**.

You should receive (0 6).

2 Try a similar function using car and 0 (for the Y-coordinate). Use **bug** for the variable name.

You should receive (7 0).

Did you enter (setq bug (list (car fish) 0))? You should have.

3 Enter **!bird** and then enter **!bug**.

The values (0 6) and (7 0) should return.

The preceding steps gave you a taste of basic AutoLISP programming. The next unit will pick up from here and will apply most of the preceding AutoLISP programming techniques.

Few AutoCAD users will write sophisticated AutoLISP programs. Typically, drafting, design, and engineering professionals do not have the time nor the interest to learn AutoLISP fully. They are likely to seek ready-made AutoLISP programs, such as those presented in the following sections.

AutoLISP and 3D

The AutoCAD file 3D.LSP creates several 3D objects including a box, cone, dish, dome, mesh, pyramid, sphere, torus, wedge, and a basic 3D mesh.

1 Enter (**load "3d"**) at the "Command:" prompt or use the **Load AutoLISP and ADS Files** dialogue box.

"3D Objects loaded." should appear.

② Enter **3D**.

The following should appear.

`Box/Cone/DIsh/DOme/Mesh/Pyramid/Sphere/Torus/Wedge:`

---

③ Enter the **B**ox option.

④ Pick any point in reply to "Corner of box:".

⑤ Enter **3** for the length, **2** for the width, **4** for the height, and **0** for the rotation angle.

⑥ View the object from above, in front, and to the right.

⑦ The remaining AutoLISP 3D command options are self-explanatory; so experiment with each of them on your own, but remain at the current viewpoint.

HINT: You can enter 3D at the "Command:" prompt the same as any AutoCAD command and then reenter it by pressing either the space bar or RETURN. Unit 43 contains the 3D Objects dialogue box that provides an illustration of each option.

AutoLISP Programming Examples

Several AutoLISP programs are supplied with AutoCAD, as explained in the previous unit. They are good examples of AutoLISP programming techniques, so you are encouraged to review them. The following provides brief descriptions of many of the AutoLISP files distributed with AutoCAD.

These files are among those provided in AutoCAD's SUPPORT directory:

3D.LSP creates various three-dimensional objects, including a pyramid, box, cone, dome/dish, wedge, torus, and a 3D mesh.

3DARRAY.LSP creates 3D rectangular arrays (by specifying rows, columns, and levels) and polar arrays around a desired axis.

ASCTEXT.LSP (covered fully in Unit 53) inserts ASCII text files into AutoCAD drawings.

CHTEXT.LSP provides basic editing of text entities.

DLINE.LSP permits you to draw continuous double lines using arcs and straight-line segments.

MVSETUP.LSP sets the drawing units and limits of a new drawing based on the paper size and drawing scale.

PTEXT.LSP assists you with inserting and editing a paragraph of text.

These files are among those provided in AutoCAD's SUPPORT directory:

ALIAS.LSP displays a list of command aliases located in the ACAD.PGP file.

ATTREDEF.LSP lets you redefine a Block and update the Attributes associated with any previous insertions of that Block.

CHROMA.LSP displays a chromatic palette style Color Selection dialogue box.

CL.LSP constructs a pair of center lines through the center of a circle.

DELLAYER.LSP (covered fully in Unit 53) erases all entities on a specified layer.

EDGE.LSP lets you interactively change the visibility of the edges of a 3D Face.

EP.LSP lets you enter a coordinate by prompting for each required value.

FACT.LSP illustrates the use of recursion to compute the factorial of an integer.

FCOPY.LSP takes the names of two ASCII text files and copies the first into the second.

FPLOT.LSP generates a 3D polygon mesh.

FPRINT.LSP lists an ASCII text file on the screen.

HOLE.LSP is a sample AME2 routine that allows feature-based creation of countersinks and counterbores.

MFACE.LSP (similar to the AutoCAD PFACE command) permits you to locate the vertices of the perimeter of a face. It then automatically generates the necessary faces.

PROJECT.LSP, consisting of two routines, implements a limited, flat projection of 3D wireframe models onto the current UCS.

RPOLY.LSP refines a random polygon by replacing its vertices with the midpoints of its edges.

SPIRAL.LSP constructs a 2D spiral.

SQR.LSP implements a square root function.

STLSUP.LSP is a sample AME 2 routine that allows automatic creation of common stereolithography support structures.

TABLES.LSP contains a number of functions that exercise AutoLISP's Tblnext and Tblsearch features.

WBLKSOL.LSP is a sample AME 2 routine that allows you to WBLOCK a solid without losing the entity handles.

XDATA.LSP lets you attach extended entity data to an entity in your drawing.

XPLODE.LSP enables you to control the color, layer, and linetype of the component entities of an exploded object.

XREFCLIP.LSP permits you to insert an Xref and clip it; that is, to indicate only the information inside a specified rectangular.

Refer to Appendix A of the *AutoLISP Programmer's Reference* for more information about these programs.

AUTOCAD® AT WORK

*Digitizing 50 Years of Data**

Highland Park, Texas, is located slightly north of bustling downtown Dallas and is known for its lovely homes and affluent population. The town has a geographic area of 2.5 square miles and a population of about 9,000.

The town's public work infrastructure was built primarily during the 1920s and 1930s. The original mapping system consisted of five sets of maps dating back to 1931. Each set was made up of 97 section maps for water, sanitary sewer, storm sewer, street lights, and paving detail. Town engineer James B. Dower was faced with the task of bringing these maps, which had not been changed since 1951, up to date.

He determined that computer-based mapping would be the best solution, and AutoCAD was chosen as the software. A local company, Laser Data-Images, manually digitized the old maps for use in AutoCAD. Laser Data-Images provided a composite map made up of each of the five sets of 97 detail maps. "The resulting map was very clean and accurate and is now a complete working copy," says Dower. "We have since made one thorough update of the electronic maps to include changes and fixtures not clearly shown on the originals and have now placed these maps in service."

Dower is very pleased with the new system. Updating the maps is easy, and new maps can be created from the base map files. "Given the success we've had with our new electronic mapping system, I'd strongly recommend that other municipalities consider implementing such a system."

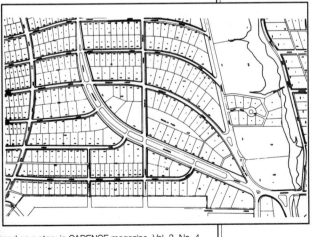

ased on a story in CADENCE magazine, Vol. 3, No. 4.

Questions

1. What will be returned if (* 4 5) is entered at the "Command:" prompt?

   _____

2. Explain the purpose of the setq function.

   _____

   _____

3. If the value of variable XYZ is 129.5, what will be returned when !XYZ is entered?

   _____

4. How do you load and invoke an AutoLISP file named RED.LSP that contains (defun C:RED ()?

   _____

5. What purpose do the car and cadr functions serve?

   _____

   _____

6. What is the purpose of the list function?

   _____

   _____

7. The plus sign (+) is used in screen and tablet macros. What is its purpose?

   _____

   _____

Problems

Using the setq, list, car, cadr, and defun functions, create new AutoLISP routines. Load and invoke them using the steps outlined in this unit.

Unit 55 — Applying AutoLISP® Programming Techniques

■ OBJECTIVE:

To introduce and combine several AutoLISP functions and apply them to the development of a new program, and to apply parametric programming techniques

This unit continues the lesson begun in the preceding unit. The techniques you have learned so far, as well as a few new ones, will be applied.

■ *Applying Our Knowledge*

Let's apply several AutoLISP functions to the creation of a border line for a drawing. At this point, we'll step through the process. Later, we'll store the function as a routine and add the routine to the screen menu called SIMPLE2.MNU.

We'll use the setq, list, car, and cadr functions to define a rectangular border for a 36″ × 24″ sheet. In order to place the border 1″ from the outer edge of the sheet, we'll use an upper left corner of 34″,22″.

1 Start AutoCAD.

Let's begin by assigning a variable to each corner of the border. We'll call the lower left corner variable LL, the lower right variable LR, and so on.

2 Enter (**setq LL (list 0 0)**).

That takes care of the lower left corner. Now, for the upper right corner . . .

3 . . . enter (**setq UR (list 34 22)**).

Now let's utilize car and cadr for the remaining two corners.

4 Enter (**setq LR (list (car UR)(cadr LL)))**.

5 Enter (**setq UL (list (car LL)(cadr UR)))**.

Let's try out the new variables.

6 One at a time enter **!LL**, then enter **!UR**, then **!LR**, and last **!UL**.

The correct coordinates for each corner should appear.

Using the LIMITS and LINE commands, and the above variables, let's establish the new border format.

7 Enter the **LIMITS** command.

8 In reply to "Lower left corner" enter **!LL**.

517

⑨ In reply to "Upper right corner" enter **!UR**.

①⓪ **ZOOM** All.

①① Set the grid to **1** unit.

①② Enter the **LINE** command and enter **!LL** for the first point.

①③ For the second point, enter **!LR**; for the third point, **!UR**; for the fourth point, **!UL**; and then close by entering **C**.

This is all very neat, but it took a lot of steps. Let's combine all the steps into a single routine and store it.

Creating a New Routine

① Using a text editor or word processor, load the SIMPLE2.MNU file. (You will store this file as SIMPLE3.MNU in Step 3.)

② Insert the following as shown on the next page.

```
[34x22]^C^C+
(setq LL (list Ø Ø))+
(setq UR (list 34 22))+
(setq LR (list (car UR)(cadr LL)))+
(setq UL (list (car LL)(cadr UR)));+
limits !LL !UR zoom a grid 1;+
line !LL !LR !UR !UL c
```

Notice the [34 × 22] followed by two cancels and a plus sign. 34 × 22 will appear as a menu item in the screen menu. The two cancels will cancel any command that may currently be executing. The plus signs connect the routine elements so they are treated as a continuous line of code. The two semicolons are present to issue RETURN at the appropriate times.

The file contents should now look like the list on the following page.

See also the optional Applying AutoCAD Diskette.

```
***SCREEN
[  A]
[SIMPLE]
[ MENU]


[LINE]^C^Cline
[ERAS L]^C^Cerase L
[ZOOM W]^C^Czoom W
[TEXT]^C^Ctext
[*Cancel*]^C^C

[FIRST]^C^C+
(setq a 1Ø)+
(setq b (- 2Ø 4))+
(setq cat (- b a))+
(setq dog (* (* 2 cat)(/ a 5)))

[34x22]^C^C+
(setq LL (list Ø Ø))+
(setq UR (list 34 22))+
(setq LR (list (car UR)(cadr LL)))+
(setq UL (list (car LL)(cadr UR)));+
limits !LL !UR zoom a grid 1;+
line !LL !LR !UR !UL c
```

3 Store the contents in a new file named SIMPLE3.MNU.

4 Begin a new drawing. (Name it anything).

5 Enter the **MENU** command, and locate and select **SIMPLE3**.

6 Pick the **34 × 22** menu item.

The following should automatically appear on the screen. If it doesn't, the routine probably contains a bug. If so, . . .

7 . . . edit SIMPLE3.MNU so that it is identical to the one above, reload the menu, and select the 34 × 22 item again.

```
Command: (setq LL (list Ø Ø))(setq UR (list 34 22))(setq LR (list (car UR)
(cadr LL)))(setq UL (list (car LL)(cadr UR)))
(Ø 22)

Command: limits
ON/OFF/<Lower left corner> <Ø.ØØØØ,Ø.ØØØØ>: !LL
Upper right corner <34.ØØØØ,22.ØØØØ>: !UR
Command: zoom
All/Center/Dynamic/Extents/Left/Previous/Window/<Scale(X)>: a Regenerating
drawing.

Command: grid
Grid spacing (X) or ON/OFF/Snap/Aspect <1.ØØØØ>: 1

Command: line From point: !LL
To point: !LR
To point: !UR
To point: !UL
To point: c
```

If the routine works properly, congratulations!

AutoLISP Command Function

The AutoLISP command function executes standard AutoCAD commands from within AutoLISP. In the [34 × 22] routine, let's change the LIMITS, ZOOM, GRID, and LINE commands to the format below using the AutoLISP command function.

1 Make changes to SIMPLE3.MNU so that it contains the following. (It will be stored in a new file named SIMPLE4.MNU.)

```
[34x22]^C^C+
(setq LL (list Ø Ø))+
(setq UR (list 34 22))+
(setq LR (list (car UR)(cadr LL)))+
(setq UL (list (car LL)(cadr UR)))+
(command "LIMITS" LL UR)+
(command "ZOOM" "A")+
(command "GRID" "1")+
(command "LINE" LL LR UR UL LL "")
```

Notice how the AutoCAD commands and command options are enclosed by double quotes ("). The two consecutive double quotes ("") are equivalent to pressing the space bar.

2 Store your changes in a new file named SIMPLE4.MNU.

3 Begin a new drawing (name it anything) and try SIMPLE4.MNU.

Reference

See also
the optional
Applying
AutoCAD
Diskette.

520

The Routine in File Format _____

Let's convert our routine to an AutoLISP file and add explanatory remarks in the file.

1 With a word processor or text editor, create a new file and enter the following. Type it exactly as you see it here, and name the file **34 × 22.LSP**. (See the following hint.)

```
;       This routine establishes drawing limits
;       for a 34" x 22" format (36" x 24" paper size)
;       and draws a border line.
;

(defun C:34x22 ()
    (setq LL (list Ø Ø))
    (setq UR (list 34 22))
    (setq LR (list (car UR)(cadr LL)))
    (setq UL (list (car LL)(cadr UR)))

    (command "LIMITS" LL UR)           ; sets drawing limits
    (command "ZOOM" "A")               ; zooms all
    (command "GRID" "1")               ; sets grid
    (command "LINE" LL LR UR UL LL "")
    )
```

HINT: _____

If your word processor or text editor can write a portion of a file to disk, then write to disk the [34 × 22] routine from the SIMPLE4.MNU file. Name the new file 34 × 22.LSP. This will save you some retyping.

See also the optional Applying AutoCAD Diskette.

Notice the semicolons (;) in the above routine. These allow you to include explanatory remarks. This documentation is valuable to other users of the routine.

As you can see, the first line of the macro, [34 × 22]^C^C+, has been removed. All of the plus signs have also been taken out since they are no longer needed. The lines containing the setq and command functions have been indented for better readability.

Also notice the inclusion of the AutoLISP defun function and the right parenthesis at the program's last line. This right parenthesis evens the number of left and right parentheses. And, in conjunction with the left parenthesis in front of defun, the right parenthesis encloses the function.

2 Begin a new drawing. Name it anything.

③ Load the file by entering (**load** "**34 × 22**") or use the **Load AutoLISP and ADS Files** dialogue box.

④ Invoke the file by entering **34 × 22**.

Other AutoLISP Functions

Here is a list of other commonly used AutoLISP functions. Experiment with them and discover ways of incorporating them into the 34 × 22.LSP file and others.

setvar   — sets an AutoCAD system variable to a given value and returns that value. The variable name must be enclosed in double quotes.
Example: (setvar "CHAMFERA" 1.5)
This would set the first chamfer distance to 1.5.

getvar   — retrieves the value of an AutoCAD system variable. The variable name must be enclosed in double quotes.
Example: (getvar "CHAMFERA")
This would return 1.5 assuming the first chamfer distance specified most recently was 1.5.

getpoint — pauses for user input of a point. You may specify a point by pointing or by typing a coordinate in the current units format.
Example: (setq xyz (getpoint "Where? "))

getreal   — pauses for user input of a real number.
Example: (setq sf (getreal "Scale factor: "))

getdist   — pauses for user input of a distance. You may specify a distance by typing a number in AutoCAD's current units format, or you may enter the distance by pointing to two locations on the screen.
Example: (setq dist (getdist "How far "))

getstring — pauses for user input of a string.
Example: (setq str (getstring "Your name? "))

distance   — returns the distance between two points.
Example: (distance '(1 1) '(1 3))
This would return 2.

You are encouraged to further explore AutoLISP's potential. Review the *AutoLISP Programmer's Reference* supplied with your AutoCAD package and experiment with the AutoLISP functions outlined in the manual.

Parametric Programming

The AutoCAD INSERT command lets you insert Blocks at any height and width. An architectural window symbol, for example, may be inserted into an elevation drawing at 0.6 on the X axis and 0.9 on the Y axis. *Parametrics* function in a very similar fashion, but with far more flexibility and sophistication.

Unlike Blocks, interior and exterior dimensions of parametrics-based objects remain variable. This enables you to specify not only the height and width of an object, but also different sizes of geometry inside the object.

Consider a bicycle design. With parametrics, all elements that make up the frame can be adjusted to user-specified sizes. The wheels and tires can be another size, the sprockets yet another, and so on. This reduces the potentially large number of variations of a design to just one, because each variation shares the same basic geometry. Hence, parametrics reduces the number of files and the amount of disk storage space, while increasing flexibility and speed.

The following door and window variations were created using a parametric routine called DWELEV.LSP, written by Bruce Chase of ASG (Sausalito, CA).

The DWELEV.LSP code is printed on the following pages.

```
;Simple parametric DOOR/WINDOW ELEVATION drawing program

; Copywritten by Bruce R Chase, Chase Systems.
; May be copied for non-commercial use.


(setq hpi (* pi 0.5))
(defun d_wel (pl x y off / tp)       ;draws the rectang & offsets
    (command "pline" pl "w" 0.0 0.0
        (setq tp (polar pl angl x))
        (setq tp (polar tp (+ angl hpi) y))
                (polar tp (- angl pi)  x)
        "cl"
    )
    (setq e (entlast))
    (if off (command "offset" "t"
            (cons (entlast)(list pl))
            (polar (polar pl angl off)(+ angl hpi) off) ""))
    (setq ee (entlast))
)


(defun d_we2 (spt offbase offside offtop x y numx numy sx sy offin trim /
             pl p2 p3 p4 xx yy e ee)
    (d_wel spt x y (if trim (* -1 trim) nil))          ; base d/w w\trim
    (if (and numx numy)(progn                    ; set base of panels
        (setq pl (polar
                    (if offside (polar spt angl offside) spt)
                    (+ angl hpi)
                    (if offbase offbase 0.0)))
    (d_wel pl                                         ; build panels
        (setq xx (if numy (/ (- x offside offside (* (- numy 1) sy)) numy) x))
        (setq yy (if numy (/ (- y offtop  offbase (* (- numx 1) sx)) numx) y))
        (if offin offin nil)                      ; raised panel or glass trim
     )
    (command "array" e ee "" "R" numx numy  pl      ; array the base panel
          (polar (polar pl angl (+ sy xx))
                        (+ angl hpi)(+ sx yy))))
))
)




(defun drwdr2 (spt xx x / tp)                         ; getdist or default program
  (terpri)(terpri)
  (prompt (strcat xx " <"))
  (princ (rtos x (getvar "lunits")(getvar "luprec")))
  (if (Null (setq tp (if spt (getdist spt ">: ")(getdist ">: ")))) x tp)
)
(defun d_we3 ()
  (while (null (setq spt (getpoint "\n \nLower left corner of door/window: "))))
     (setq angl (if (null
          (setq tp (getorient spt "\nBase angle of door/window <0.0>: ")))
          0.0 tp))
)
```

(continued on next page)

```
(defun c:dwelev ( / spt offbase offside offtop        ; gather all the info
                    x y numx numy sx sy offin trim tp angl)
    (d_we3)
    (setq x (drwdr2 spt "Width of door/window" 36.0))
    (setq y (drwdr2 spt "Height of door/window" 80.0))
    (setq trim (if (zerop (setq tp (drwdr2 spt "Trim width" 0.0))) nil tp))

    (if (setq numy (getint "\nNumber of panels rows <none>: "))(progn
        (setq numx (if (null (setq numx
                (getint "\nNumber of panel columns <1>: "))) 1 numx))
        (setq offbase (drwdr2 spt "Bottom rail width" 10.0))
        (setq offtop  (drwdr2 spt "Top rail width"     6.0))
        (setq offside (drwdr2 spt "Side rail width"    4.0))
        (if (> numx 1)(setq sx
                (drwdr2 nil "Spacing between panel rows" 1.0)))
        (if (> numy 1)(setq sy
                (drwdr2 nil "Spacing between panel columns"   1.0)))
        (setq offin   (if (zerop
        (setq tp (drwdr2 nil "Offset distance for raised panel"  0)))
                          nil tp))
    ))
    (d_we2 spt offbase offside offtop x y numx numy sx sy offin trim)
(princ)
)
(prompt "\nCommand: DWELEV \n")


(c:dwelev)              ;call up program with this command
                        ;or use within another procedure with actual sizes:

;(progn (d_we3)
;       -------- spt offbase offside offtop    x     y    numx numy sx  sy  offin trim----
;       (d_we2 spt 10.0    4.0      6.0     40.0 84.0   2    4   2.0 3.0 1.5    4.0)
;)
```

Let's create and use the DWELEV.LSP routine.

1 Using a word processor or text editor, accurately enter this AutoLISP routine and store it using the name **DWELEV.LSP**.

HINT: This file is available on the optional *Applying AutoCAD* Diskette, available from Glencoe.

2 Start AutoCAD and begin a new drawing named **PARAMET**.

Let's first establish an architectural working environment based on a scale of ¼″ = 1′ and a C-size (18″ × 24″) sheet.

3 Enter the **DDUNITS** command and select architectural units. Accept the remaining default settings.

Reference

See also the optional Applying AutoCAD Diskette.

④ Enter the **LIMITS** command and enter **0,0** for the lower left limit and **88′,64′** for the upper right limit.

The upper right limit is based on a plotting area on the sheet of 22″ × 16″.

⑤ **Zoom All** and set Snap and Grid at **2′**.

⑥ At the "Command:" prompt, enter (**load "DWELEV"**), or use the **Load AutoLISP and ADS Files** dialogue box.

This loads the routine and automatically enters the new DWELEV command created by the program.

——— NOTE: ———

If the routine does not appear to load, compare your program code to the DWELEV.LSP code printed in this unit. They *must* be identical. Also, be sure the program is contained in the directory you specify. For instance, if it is contained in a subdirectory named CHAD, enter (load "CHAD/DWELEV").

The rest is mostly self-explanatory because the program employs easy-to-understand prompts. However, . . .

⑦ . . . use the following as a guide as you enter your responses.

Lower left corner of door/window: *(Pick a point at any location.)*
Base angle of door/window <0.0>: *(Press **RETURN**.)*
Width of door/window <3′>: **4′**
Height of door/window <6′-8″>: *(Press **RETURN**.)*
Trim width <0″>: **1.5″**
Number of panel rows <none>: **4**
Number of panel columns <1>: **2**
Bottom rail width <10″>: **8″**
Top rail width <6″>: *(Press **RETURN**.)*
Side rail width <4″>: **5″**
Spacing between panel rows <1″>: **2″**
Spacing between panel columns <1″>: **3″**
Offset distance for raised panel <0″: **1″**

Notice the commands that automatically enter as the door develops on the screen. You may want to print this information (by pressing CTRL Q) and compare it with the AutoLISP code.

⑧ Zoom in on the door and examine it.

Your door should look identical to the following.

You can also create windows using DWELEV.LSP. Just specify 0 in reply to the "number of panel rows and columns." Two or more windows can be linked together (using COPY or ARRAY) to create casement style windows (shown earlier).

⑨ Create additional doors and windows by entering **DWELEV** at the "Command:" prompt, and enter **END** when you are finished.

The DWELEV.LSP routine is intentionally basic. This makes it easier for you to understand its operation. If you are an accomplished programmer, you may choose to embellish the routine by including doorknobs, window molding, and other details normally included on door and window symbology.

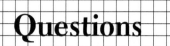

Questions

1. Explain the purpose of the AutoLISP "command" function.

   _____

   _____

2. If AutoLISP programs or routines are not stored as files, in what form are they stored and how are they invoked?

   _____

   _____

3. For what reason are semicolons used in AutoLISP routines?

   _____

   _____

4. Briefly explain the purpose of the following functions:

   getvar _____

   _____

   getpoint _____

   _____

   distance _____

   _____

5. Explain the benefits of applying parametric programming techniques.

   _____

   _____

   _____

Problems

1. Combine several AutoCAD commands and AutoLISP functions to create powerful and useful routines.

2. On your own, learn other AutoLISP functions, such as getreal and distance, and develop them into new AutoLISP routines.

3. Using DWELEV.LSP and AutoCAD commands, create an architectural elevation drawing similar to the one here. This elevation, minus doors and windows, is available in the ELEV.DWG file contained on the optional *Applying AutoCAD* Diskette.

PRB 55-1

AUTOCAD® AT WORK

*Parametric Packaging**

You have probably eaten or used at least one thing that has been in contact with a Ropak container. Ropak Corporation is a leading international manufacturer of plastic packaging and handling products for foods, coatings, and manufacturing materials. As part of its service, Ropak integrates all the functions of design, engineering, tooling, production, and even decoration of the manufactured product. The company's in-house development group works directly with customers to modify existing products for specific uses and to design unique solutions to specialized packaging problems. To provide these services quickly and efficiently, Ropak uses AutoCAD and the Synthesis parametric design package (from Synthesis, Inc.).

Like many manufacturers, Ropak produces products with a large number of variations on similar parts or assembly packages. "Family of parts" products used to require extensive and repetitive redesign efforts for any variations in specifications. With Synthesis, however, an engineer can set up a spec sheet with the design parameters of a particular product. Then, when a small modification is required, a trainee can enter variables, and the program will automatically produce modified drawings that are fully documented and ready to use in the manufacturing process.

Ropak's redesign of a fish roe (eggs) container is an example of their capabilities. The container is used to transport roe from the Pacific Northwest to the Far East. For a variety of reasons, the basic container needed to be redesigned. The improved version satisfied the customer's needs by featuring a slightly domed lid and a revised bottom to accommodate the lid for secure stacking. Redesigning the three parts making up the new container took four days. According to Ropak design engineer David Bailey, this work would have taken about three weeks just a couple of years ago.

Ropak considers the AutoCAD/Synthesis design tool to be a vital part of its effort to compete and grow in the world's marketplace. AutoCAD and Synthesis have added a whole new dimension to Ropak's manufacturing process by allowing it to increase productivity and dramatically increase its ability to serve the customer.

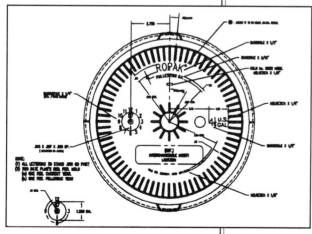

*Based on a story in CADENCE magazine, Vol. 3, No. 5.

Unit 56 Digitizing Hardcopy Drawings

Reference

REF 420-421

■ OBJECTIVE:

To input a hardcopy drawing into AutoCAD using the TABLET command

The intent of this unit is to step through the process of digitizing. Note that you must have a digitizing tablet connected to your CAD system in order to complete this unit.

There will be times, especially in a business environment, when you'll wish your hand-completed drawings were stored in AutoCAD. Suppose your firm has recently implemented CAD. All of your previous drawings were completed by hand and you need to revise one or more of them. As you know, it's very time-consuming to redraw them by hand.

Fortunately, most CAD systems, including AutoCAD, offer a method of transferring those drawings onto disk. It is not always practical to digitize drawings, but it is often faster than starting the drawings from scratch.

■ *Setting Up* _____

Since you may not have easy access to a simple drawing not yet in AutoCAD, let's digitize the previously created drawing DIMEN2. This drawing was completed during the dimensioning exercise (Unit 23) and is shown on the next page.

_____ NOTE: _____

If you do not have a hard copy of DIMEN2, plot the drawing now or make a photocopy of the drawing on the next page.

1 Start AutoCAD and begin a new drawing named **DIGIT**. To save time in establishing the drawing settings, you can use DIMEN2 as the prototype drawing.

If you choose not to use DIMEN2 as the prototype drawing, you will need to set each of the drawing parameters, such as the units, limits, etc., to correspond with the DIMEN2 drawing in Unit 24.

2 When the drawing appears, erase it.

_____ NOTE: _____

Be sure the snap resolution is set at 6″ and is turned on. Also be sure to display the entire drawing area by entering ZOOM All.

3 Make **OBJ** the current layer, if it is not already.

4 Using drafting tape, fasten the drawing called DIMEN2 onto the center of your digitizing tablet.

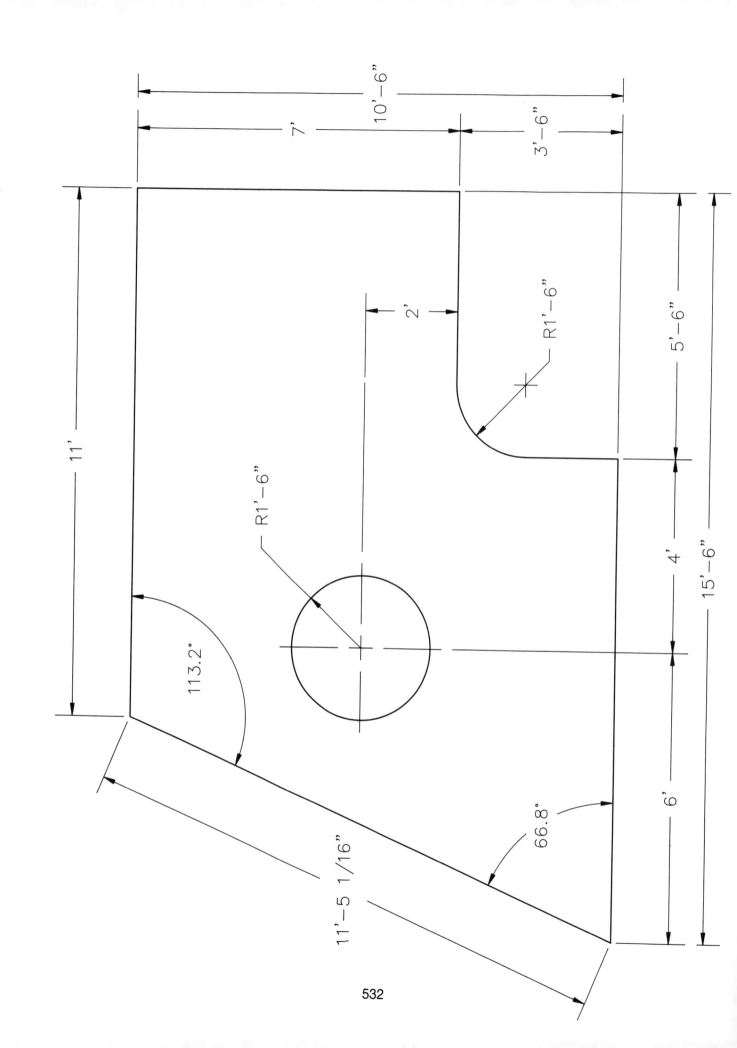

Calibrating the Drawing —————————————

Now, let's calibrate your drawing using the TABLET command.

1 Enter the **TABLET** command and select the **CAL**ibrate option.

REF 95-97

We need to identify at least two known (absolute) points on the drawing. Let's call the lower left corner of the object absolute point 6′,6′.

2 In reply to "Digitize point #1:" pick this point (be precise) and enter the coordinates **6′,6′**.

———————— NOTE: ————————
Crosshairs will not appear on the screen when you pick the point.

Now we need to pick a second known point. Let's choose the corner located 10′ to the right of the first point.

3 Pick this point and enter **16′,6′** for the coordinates.

4 Press **RETURN** to end.

You have just calibrated the drawing and AutoCAD can now size the drawing according to this calibration.

Note that the word "Tablet" now appears in the status line. This means the Tablet mode is on. The Tablet mode can be toggled on and off with a function key, usually F10.

5 Toggle Tablet mode on and off and notice the difference in the position of the crosshairs.

6 Toggle Tablet mode off.

Digitizing the Drawing —————————————

Let's begin to trace (digitize) the drawing by doing the object outline. Let's start at the lower left corner of the object, point 6′,6′.

1 Enter the **LINE** command, and make certain that Snap is on.

2 Turn on the Tablet mode with the function key and digitize (pick) point 6′,6′.

Whenever you digitize points from the drawing, the Tablet mode *must be on*. Whenever you select commands from the screen or pull-down menus, the Tablet mode must be turned *off*.

3 With the Tablet mode on, digitize the next corner point, working counterclockwise.

This should complete the first line segment.

4 When digitizing the third point, ignore the fillet and pick the approximate location of the corner. With Snap on, your selection of the corner will be accurate. The fillet will be inserted later.

5 Continue around the object until you close the polygon.

6 Using the **FILLET** command, specify a fillet radius of 1′6″ and place the fillet at the proper location. Remember to turn Tablet off if you want to use the screen menu.

7 Using the **CIRCLE** command, place the circle. (See the following hint.)

8 Set the layer called DIM.

9 Using AutoCAD's dimensioning commands, fully dimension the object with Tablet mode off.

You're finished.

10 Enter **END** to save your work and to exit AutoCAD.

Questions

1. What command and command option are used to calibrate a drawing to be digitized?

2. Why is the calibration process necessary?

3. Briefly explain the process of calibrating a drawing to be digitized.

4. Why is the snap resolution important when digitizing?

5. Describe when the Tablet mode should be turned on and when it should be turned off.

6. If you have a mouse, explain whether or not you can digitize a drawing using only a conventional mouse.

Problems

Obtain two hand-completed drawings and digitize each.

NOTE:

It is possible to digitize drawings that are larger than your digitizing tablet. Simply move the drawing into the active area on the tablet and recalibrate.

AUTOCAD® AT WORK

Making the Deserts Bloom with Micro-Based CAD

The problem is basic: central and southern Arizona need water, for agriculture and industry as well as people. The water in the rivers of Arizona's deserts has all been spoken for, and rainfall barely makes a dent in the area's hot, dry climate. One of Arizona's largest cities, Tucson, has pumped out so much of its groundwater for agriculture and municipal use that the land on which Tucson sits is literally sinking.

To help resolve the water imbalance the Bureau of Reclamation, a branch of the United States Department of the Interior, is building the long-planned Central Arizona Project (CAP). Administered by the Bureau's Arizona Projects Office (APO), CAP's goal is a major one—to bring water from the Colorado River (whose water supply is renewed yearly by rainfall and melted snow) to the Arizona desert. The project involves creating a 335-mile network of open canals, tunnels, pipe siphons, and pumping plants to form a water conveyance system. Two new dams and two renovated dams will serve as facilities for water conservation and flood control.

To increase efficiency and productivity on this huge project, the APO's engineers, technicians, and drafters are using microcomputers and Auto-CAD software. Drawings can be created faster and changed more easily with AutoCAD than with manual methods. Furthermore, because the system can be easily customized, APO was able to create menus specific to Bureau tasks as well as build libraries of commonly used shapes and title blocks. Such customization has helped users become productive more quickly and has ensured that drawings met or exceeded all Bureau of Reclamation standards.

APO staffers aren't just automating drafting tasks, however; they're also integrating the micro-based CAD system into all parts of their project. A good example is the tract map. This map shows the land through which a canal, pipeline, or other structure is going to pass and indicates which land needs to be acquired. The land must be fully surveyed and described, and precision is crucial. The information collected in the field is processed on the Bureau's Cyber mainframe computer in Denver, Colorado, and then turned into a drawing.

Previously, it took 1 1/2 to 2 weeks just for a person to draft the location of the canal or the roadway and determine how much land would have to be bought. Now this information is fed from the host Cyber system in Denver straight into AutoCAD through the AutoLISP programming language to create the tract map. Total turnaround time is 3 1/2 minutes.

Rob Toy, Chief of the Engineering and Microcomputer Support Branch, says micro-based CAD's capabilities were substantially greater than had been expected. "With Auto-CAD," he says, "we're achieving 90% of what we had anticipated from a mainframe CAD system, at 10% of the price. The system is really putting data processing at the fingertips of the people that should be using it, not ADP Support Services, not my branch, but the users—the engineers and technicians."

EXCAVATIONS

Courtesy of U.S. Dept. of Interior and Autodesk, Inc.

Unit 57 — Importing and Exporting Files

Reference

■ OBJECTIVE:

To practice importing and exporting DXF, IGES, and PostScript (EPS) files

Standard file formats are important for moving graphics from one system to another. This unit steps through the translation process using three industry standard formats: DXF, IGES, and PostScript.

Drawing (DWG) files created with one version of AutoCAD are compatible with other versions. For example, if you create a drawing file with the DOS 386 version, you can read the file into the Macintosh or Sun SPARCstation versions of AutoCAD without translating the file into DXF or IGES formats.

AutoCAD also permits you to read (import) and write (export) PostScript files. PostScript is a popular language used by desktop publishing, illustration, and presentation programs.

■ *DXF* _____

CUST 241-278

The DXF file format is the de facto standard for translating files from one microCAD system, such as AutoCAD, to another, such as VersaCAD. Autodesk, Inc., makers of AutoCAD, created the DXF format, also referred to as a drawing interchange file format. DXF files can be translated to other DXF compatible CAD systems or submitted to programs for specialized applications. For example, certain manufacturing software uses DXF files to generate tool path code for computer numerically controlled (CNC) mills and lathes.

■ *DXFOUT Command* _____

CUST 242

You can generate a drawing interchange (DXF) file from an existing drawing by means of the DXFOUT command.

1 Start AutoCAD and open a simple drawing, such as DIMEN2.DWG.

2 Enter the **DXFOUT** command or select the **File** pull-down menu and pick **Import/Export** and **DXF Out....**

3 Pick the **OK** button to accept the DIMEN2 drawing.

AutoCAD gives you the option of entering decimal places of accuracy. A high number produces a more accurate file, although the file size increases. If you enter E (for Entities), you can select a set of objects to translate instead of the entire drawing. If you enter B (for Binary), AutoCAD creates a binary DXF file instead of an ASCII text file.

4 Press **RETURN** in reply to accept the default value.

The translation may take a while, especially with complex drawings. When the "Command:" prompt returns, the translation is complete.

5 Enter the **SH** command and press **RETURN** again.

6 Perform a **DIR**ectory listing of the directory containing the new DXF file.

How much larger than the DWG file is the DXF file?

7 Using the DOS **TYPE** or **MORE** command, review the contents of your new ASCII DXF file.

—————— NOTE: ——————

If you use the TYPE command, press CTRL S to stop the scrolling of the screen. Press CTRL C to cancel.

The beginning of your DXF ASCII text file should look similar to the following.

```
         Ø
SECTION
         2
HEADER
         9
$ACADVER
         1
AC1ØØ9
         9
$INSBASE
        1Ø
Ø.Ø
        2Ø
Ø.Ø
        3Ø
Ø.Ø
         9
$EXTMIN
        1Ø
```

8 Enter **EXIT** to return to AutoCAD.

Reference

CUST 277-278

Binary DXF Files

Binary DXF files contain all of the information in an ASCII DXF file, but are much more compact. Their file size is approximately 25 percent smaller and they can be written and read by AutoCAD about five times faster.

1 Enter **DXFOUT**.

2 Slightly modify the name of the new file so it does not overwrite the DXF file you created earlier and pick the **OK** button.

3 At the next prompt, enter **Binary**.

Notice that the file is created much faster than the ASCII DXF file.

4 Using the DOS **DIR** command, compare the size of the ASCII DXF file with the binary DXF file.

The binary DXF file should be at least 25 percent smaller. Also, binary DXF files preserve all of the floating-point accuracy in the data base. ASCII DXF files, instead, increase in size as you increase the decimal places of accuracy.

DXFIN Command

CUST 242-243

Both ASCII and binary DXF files can be converted to an AutoCAD drawing (DWG) file by means of the DXFIN command.

1 Begin a new drawing named **FRESH**.

2 Enter the **DXFIN** command or select the **File** pull-down menu and pick **Import/Export** and **DXF In**....

3 Select a DXF file currently on disk. If one is not available that you want to convert to a DWG format, select one of the DXF files you just created. Omit the DXF extension.

The DXF file will generate on the screen as it is translated into a DWG format. When complete, FRESH.DWG (your current drawing) will be the new DWG file created from the DXF file.

See also
the optional
Applying
AutoCAD
Diskette.

4 Enter **QSAVE** if you want to save the new drawing.

IGES

IGES stands for the Initial Graphics Exchange Specification. IGES is an industry standard approved by the American National Standards Institute (ANSI) for interchange of graphic files between small and large-scale CAD systems.

Translating files from one CAD system to another using IGES is useful. However, each CAD system has its uniquenesses. Consequently, certain characteristics, such as layers, Blocks, linetypes, colors, text, and dimensions, are potential problem areas as a result of the translation.

For example, some CAD systems use numbers for layer names and do not accept names such as OBJ or DIM. If an AutoCAD drawing file is translated to a system using layer numbers, all of the AutoCAD layers' names will be changed to numbers. These types of problems are also present when translating files using the DXF file format.

IGESOUT Command

You can generate an IGES interchange file from an existing AutoCAD drawing file by means of the IGESOUT command.

1 Open any drawing you have on disk, but avoid using a complex drawing.

2 Enter the **IGESOUT** command or select the **File** pull-down menu and pick **Import/Export** and **IGES Out...**.

3 Accept the suggested filename and pick the **OK** button.

The translation may take a while (maybe even several minutes) depending upon the size and complexity of the drawing. Be patient.

The IGES file will have the same file name as the current drawing, but with an IGS file extension.

When the "Command:" prompt returns, the IGES translation is complete.

4 Enter the **SH** command and then **RETURN**.

5 With the **DIR** command, review the directory containing the new IGES file.

6 With the DOS **MORE** or **TYPE** command, display the contents of the new IGES file.

The format and contents of the beginning of your IGES file should look similar to the following.

```
IGES file generated from an AutoCAD drawing by the IGES         S0000001
translator from Autodesk, Inc., translator version IGESOUT-3.04. S0000002
,,18HC:\R12\TEMP\DIMEN2,22HC:\R12\TEMP\DIMEN2.IGS,10HAutoCAD-12,12HIGESOG0000001
UT-3.04,32,38,6,99,15,18HC:\R12\TEMP\DIMEN2,1.0,1,4HINCH,32767,3.2767D1,G0000002
13H920921.101947,3.6D-7,360.0,13HTerry Wohlers,19H Wohlers Associates,6,G0000003
0;                                                               G0000004
       304       1       1       2              00000200D0000001
       304                       1       2      BORDER     D0000002
       304       2       1       2              00000200D0000003
       304                       1       2      BORDER2    D0000004
       304       3       1       2              00000200D0000005
       304                       1       2      BORDERX2   D0000006
       304       4       1       4              00000200D0000007
       304                       1       2      CENTER2    D0000008
       304       5       1       4              00000200D0000009
       304                       1       2      CENTERX2   D0000010
       304       6       1       2              00000200D0000011
       304                       1       2      DASHDOT    D0000012
```

7 Enter **EXIT** to return to AutoCAD.

IGESIN Command

CUST 281–282

An IGES interchange file can be converted into an AutoCAD drawing by means of the IGESIN command.

1 Begin a new drawing named **TRANS**.

2 Enter the **IGESIN** command or select the **File** pull-down menu and pick **Import/Export** and **IGES In....**

3 Select an IGES file currently on disk. If one is not available that you want translated into a DWG format, select the IGES file you just created. Omit the IGS extension.

The translation can take a while, so be patient. Eventually, it will generate on the screen. When the translation is complete, the "Command:" prompt will return. TRANS.DWG (the current drawing) is the new DWG file created from the IGES file.

4 Enter **QSAVE** if you want to save the drawing.

See also the optional Applying AutoCAD Diskette.

PSOUT Command

The PSOUT command allows you to output a PostScript (EPS) file.

1 Open the drawing named **LAMP**.

2 Enter the **PSOUT** command or select the **File** pull-down menu and pick **Import/Export** and **PostScript Out...**.

3 Pick the **OK** button to accept the LAMP name.

4 Press **RETURN** to accept the Display default setting.

The PostScript file you're creating can include a screen preview for desktop publishing programs. You can select either the EPSI or TIFF format.

5 For now, press **RETURN** to accept the "None" default setting.

6 Press **RETURN** to accept "Inches" and press **RETURN** again to accept "Fit."

7 Specify **A** for the output size.

AutoCAD will create the EPS file.

8 Check to see if the file exists using the **FILES** or **SH** command.

PSIN Command

The PSIN command permits you to import PostScript images.

1 Begin a new drawing named **POST**.

2 Enter **PSIN** or select the **Files** pull-down menu and pick **Import/Export** and **PostScript In...**.

3 Select an EPS file currently on disk. If one is not available, select the **LAMP.EPS** file you just created.

4 Press **RETURN** to accept the "0,0,0" insertion point.

5 In reply to "Scale Factor:" drag the crosshairs to the right until the box fills most of the screen and pick a point.

See also the optional Applying AutoCAD Diskette.

The LAMP drawing should appear.

 View the lamp from a different angle in space.

Notice that it is now a flat image instead of a 3D model. That's because PostScript does not recognize 3D entities.

AutoCAD offers the PSDRAG command to control the appearance of a PostScript image as you are dragging it into position using the PSIN command. The PSQUALITY system variable is available if you want to adjust the rendering quality of PostScript images. The PSFILL command allows you to fill 3D Polyline outlines using a PostScript fill pattern. The patterns are defined in the AutoCAD PostScript Support File (ACAD.PSF).

 Enter **QUIT** to exit AutoCAD. Do not save your work.

AUTOCAD® AT WORK

*Parametrics and AutoCAD Speed Engine Design**

If there were a real magic wand, Joe Schubeck of Eagle Engine Manufacturing would swear that its name was AutoCAD. Schubeck and his small group of technicians produce an aluminum V-8 engine for use in top fuel dragsters completely designed with AutoCAD and Synthesis, a parametric processor that works with AutoCAD.

Depending on the fuel used, the Eagle Engine can put out as much as 3,000 horsepower. Besides delivering colossal horsepower, the engine is designed to be configurable by the user. It allows interchangeable cylinders and sleeves on five-inch centers. The heads are even designed to allow from one to three spark plugs per cylinder. This flexibility lets one racer build on the basic engine block for top fuel racing while another builds on it for tractor pulls. No longer are drag racers locked into one winning design.

With Synthesis, Eagle Engine Manufacturing can make a part from the drawing and check out the formulas for that part in the dynamometer room or on the strip. When satisfied with the part, the company can use the original formulas modified with Synthesis, to make a similar part without having to bench test it.

Another advantage of Synthesis is its ability to tighten tolerances. By running a DXF file through Synthesis, a user can specify tolerances up to sixteen decimal places.

Schubeck's biggest goal for his engine is to power a top fuel dragster past the 300 mph mark in a quarter-mile. Considering the Eagle's advantages over other competition, that goal seems easily attainable.

*Based on a story in CADENCE magazine, Vol. 3, No. 3.

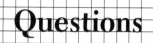

Questions

1. What is a DXF file and what is its purpose?

   _____

   _____

2. What is IGES and what is the purpose of an IGES file?

   _____

   _____

3. Explain the purpose of the DXFOUT command.

   _____

   _____

4. Explain the advantages of using binary DXF files instead of ASCII DXF files.

   _____

   _____

   _____

5. Explain the purpose of the DXFIN command.

   _____

   _____

6. Explain the purpose of the IGESOUT command.

   _____

   _____

7. Explain the purpose of the IGESIN command.

   _____

   _____

8. What are the potential problem areas associated with translating DXF and IGES files from one CAD system to another?

   _____

   _____

9. With what commands do you import and export PostScript files?

   _____

   _____

Problems

1. With AutoCAD drawings, create DXF and IGES files using the facilities provided by AutoCAD. After the translations are complete, review the contents of the DXF and IGES files.

2. If you have access to another CAD system, load the above DXF or IGES files into that system. (Note: The CAD system must have a facility similar to AutoCAD's DXFIN or IGESIN.) If you are successful, review characteristics of the drawings, such as layers, colors, linetypes, Blocks, text, and dimensions. Note the differences between the CAD systems.

3. Create or obtain DXF and IGES files from another CAD system and import them into AutoCAD. Note the differences between AutoCAD and the systems used to create the files you imported into AutoCAD. If available, refer to the optional *Applying AutoCAD* Diskette.

4. Create an EPS file from any one of the drawing files you have created in the past.

5. Obtain or create an EPS file from another program and import it into AutoCAD. If available, refer to the optional *Applying AutoCAD* Diskette.

Unit 58 Lights, Camera, ...

Reference

■ OBJECTIVE:

To develop a slide show as a script file and to create a slide library

The purpose of this unit is to develop a slide show by making slides and including them in a script file. Though it may sound complicated, it is really very simple. A word processor or text editor is recommended for creation of sophisticated slide shows and script files.

The following is an example of a script file. It's nothing more than an ASCII text file with an .SCR file extension. You can execute a script when you start AutoCAD or from within AutoCAD using the SCRIPT command.

CUST 101-108

```
UNITS 4 4 1 0 0 N
LIMITS 0,0 15',10'
ZOOM A
GRID 1'
SNAP ON
```

*See also
the optional
Applying
AutoCAD
Diskette.*

With earlier versions of AutoCAD, users used script files, such as the one above, to store drawing parameters and settings to expedite the setup process. The use of prototype drawings has largely replaced this practice.

Script files can be used for other purposes too. A common application is for showing a continuous sequence of drawings, a sort of electronic flipchart. AutoCAD calls this a slide show.

■ *MSLIDE Command* _____

CUST 105

We must first create slides to include in the script. Slides are created from existing drawings using the MSLIDE command (short for Make Slide). Let's open a couple of drawings, such as THREE-D and DIMEN, and create slides from each.

1　Start AutoCAD and begin a new drawing named **SLIDE**.

2　Using the **DDINSERT** command, insert the drawing named THREE-D. Enter **0,0** for the insertion point and accept the remaining default settings. (You may need to zoom in on the drawing.).

3　View the drawing from any point in space and enter **HIDE** or **SHADE**.

4　Enter the **MSLIDE** command and give the slide file the same name as the drawing file (**THREE-D**). Do not specify the extension, .SLD. AutoCAD does that for you.

— NOTE: —

The new slide file has a file extension of .SLD (THREE-D.SLD). This type of file cannot be edited. Drawing files used to create slides remain untouched and can be edited.

5 Erase the THREE-D drawing so that the screen is blank.

6 Insert the **DIMEN** drawing.

7 With the **PLAN** command, create the plan view of the current UCS.

8 With the **MSLIDE** command, create another slide. Name it **DIMEN**.

VSLIDE Command ————————————————

CUST 105

Let's apply the VSLIDE (View Slide) command to look at the first slide we created.

1 Enter **VSLIDE**, select **THREE-D**, and pick **OK**.

The THREE-D slide should appear on the screen.

2 To restore the original screen, enter **R** (for REDRAW).

3 If you'd like to make additional slides from other drawings, create them now.

Creating the Script File ————————————

Now let's create the script file (slide show). It's going to be a short one!

1 If you have not done so yet, obtain the DOS prompt (*e.g.,* C:\ACAD>).

2 Begin a new file using the COPY CON method as shown below. Name the file **SHOW.SCR**, and be sure to specify the appropriate drive if necessary. Feel free to create the file using a word processor or text editor.

COPY CON:SHOW.SCR (press **RETURN**)

See also the optional Applying AutoCAD Diskette.

ELEV —
ELEVAT —
FELEV —
IBEAM
LAMP — —
LAMP2
RIM —
THREED —

HOUSE
3D HOUS
RIM
THREED —
LAMP —
ROOFFRM
DIMEN —
ELEVAT
ELEV —

③ Now type the following. Be sure to specify the appropriate drive if the slides reside on a drive or directory other than the default drive or directory. If you make a mistake, backspace or start over.

```
VSLIDE THREE-D
DELAY 1000
VSLIDE DIMEN
DELAY 500
REDRAW
```

④ Press the **F6** function key and **RETURN** to save the file.

NOTE:

If you've created additional slides, you must of course include them also.

You have just created a simple slide show stored as a script file. The DELAY command tells AutoCAD to hold the slide on the screen for X number of milliseconds. Although computers run at different speeds, 1000 milliseconds is approximately a one-second delay.

CUST 103

Showtime

Now let's try the slide show.

① At the "Command:" prompt, enter the **SCRIPT** command, and select **SHOW**.

CUST 102-103

AutoCAD will display each slide on the screen.

② To repeat the slide show, enter the **RSCRIPT** command.

CUST 104

This command can be included at the end of the script file to automatically repeat the slide show.

NOTE:

CTRL C or the backspace key will interrupt a running script. This allows you to issue other AutoCAD commands. If you wish to return to the script, enter the RESUME command.

CUST 103

③ Create new slides from other drawings and include them in your SHOW.SCR file. Include the RSCRIPT command at the end of the script.

④ Run the revised slide show.

Reference

548

Creating Slide Libraries _____

The slide library facility lets you store slide files in a single file, similar to filling a carousel tray of 35-mm slides. Once the slide library is complete, you can use it in conjunction with a slide show. The individual slide files need not be present.

_____ **NOTE:** _____

Icon menus require the use of slide libraries. See Unit 59 for details.

1 Identify slide files you would like to group in a slide library. Choose or create 3 or 4 for now.

2 Locate the AutoCAD file named SLIDELIB.EXE (contained in the SUPPORT directory) and copy it to the directory containing the slide files. Make this the current directory.

3 At the DOS prompt, enter **SLIDELIB FIRST** to create a slide library file named FIRST.SLB.

This will start the SLIDELIB.EXE program (which *must* be located in the current directory), and a copyright statement should appear on the screen.

4 At the blinking cursor, type the first slide file name (with or without the .SLD file extension), in upper or lower case letters, and then press **RETURN**.

5 Enter each of the remaining slide file names.

6 When you are finished, press the **F6** function key and then press **RETURN**.

The new slide library file (FIRST.SLB) will be stored in the current directory. It contains images of the slide files you entered.

Viewing Slides from the Slide Library _____

1 At the "Command:" prompt, enter the **VSLIDE** command and pick the **Type it** button from the dialogue box.

2 In reply to "Slide file:" type the slide library name followed by one of the slide file names (for example, **FIRST(DIMEN)**) and press **RETURN**.

The slide image should appear. Try another.

3 Enter **QUIT** to exit AutoCAD.

If you are interested in taking further advantage of the slide library facility, combine a slide library with a script file to create a slide show.

Unit 59 applies slide libraries to the creation of icon menus.

Questions

1. Briefly describe the purpose of each of the following commands.

   MSLIDE _____

   VSLIDE _____

   SCRIPT _____

   RSCRIPT _____

   DELAY _____

   RESUME _____

2. Describe the purpose of an AutoCAD script file.

   _____

   _____

3. What is the file extension of a script file?

   _____

4. What does the number following the DELAY command indicate?

   _____

   _____

5. Is it more practical to store a drawing setup in a script file or in a prototype drawing? Explain why.

   _____

   _____

   _____

   _____

Problems

1. Create a dozen or so slides of previously created drawings. Include them in a slide show stored as a script file. Run the show.
2. Develop a script file that includes several AutoCAD commands. Make it as sophisticated as possible. When you're finished, print the file so that you can work out the bugs as you run it.
3. Refer to EXAMPLE.SLB and instructions contained on the optional *Applying AutoCAD* Diskette.
4. Refer to DISKSHOW.SCR and instructions contained on the optional *Applying AutoCAD* Diskette.

Unit 59 Icon Menus

■ OBJECTIVE:

To develop an icon menu using the slide library facility in connection with the icon menu creation procedures.

Small pictures, called icons, can be used to create menus and symbol libraries. For example, you can use icons to make it easier for you to use the Blocks you've created. Instead of having to remember Block names or referring to hard copy, you can access icon menus (that represent your Blocks) on the screen. This enables you to easily review and choose the Blocks, and it eliminates the need to enter the INSERT or DDINSERT command and the Block name repeatedly.

—— NOTE: ——

This unit requires knowledge of AutoCAD's ACAD.MNU menu, presented in Units 49-51. It also requires a text editor or word processor.

■ *Sampling an Icon Menu*

CUST 94-98

Below is an icon menu for choosing text fonts. Let's experiment with it.

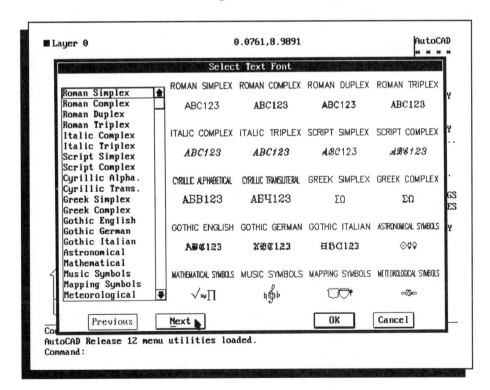

1 Start AutoCAD.

2 Select the **Draw** pull-down menu and pick **Text** and **Select Style...**.

The Select Text Font dialogue box should appear. This is an example of an icon menu.

3 Pick the **Next** button.

This enables you to display more than one page of icons. If a third page existed the "Next" button would be available for you to pick.

Without the use of icons, the selection of a new font would not be as easy.

4 Pick the **Previous** button and pick **Cancel**.

Let's step through the process of creating an icon menu.

Creating the Slide Library

First we must create a slide library. Before we can do this, however, we must identify (or create) several Blocks to include in the slide library. As an example, let's use the small symbol library of Blocks from Unit 30. They are printed here for your reference.

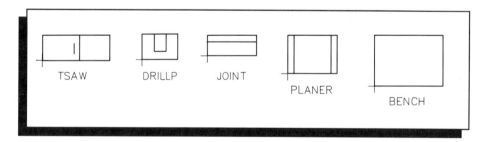

These five Blocks will later become the icons.

1 Using the DOS **MD** command, make a new directory named **WORK** in the main AutoCAD directory.

2 Locate the file named LIB1.DWG you created in Unit 30. (It should contain the five Blocks shown above.) If this file does not exist, or you cannot find it, skip to Step 4.

3 Copy the file **LIB1.DWG** to the **WORK** directory, rename it to **TOOLS.DWG**, and open it. Skip to Step 7.

4 Begin a new drawing named **TOOLS** in the **WORK** directory.

⑤ Create each of the five items shown in the preceding illustration at any convenient size and store each of them as a Block using the names shown. (Refer to Unit 29 if you don't remember how to create Blocks.)

———— NOTE: ————

When creating the new Blocks, be sure to specify the proper insertion base points as indicated.

⑥ Insert each of the five Blocks at any location on the screen.

⑦ Using the **MSLIDE** command, produce a slide of each Block. (First, read the following hint.) Use the Block name for the slide name and store the slides in the **WORK** directory.

HINT:
Using the ZOOM command, make each Block as large as possible on the display before creating the slide. If you don't, the icon may appear too small.

⑧ After you are confident you have five slide files that correspond with the five Blocks, copy the **SLIDELIB.EXE** file from the AutoCAD **SUPPORT** directory to the **WORK** directory.

⑨ Using the procedure outlined in the section titled "Creating Slide Libraries" (in the previous unit), create a slide library named **TOOLS**.

HINT:
You will enter the following:

```
SLIDELIB TOOLS
TSAW
DRILLP
JOINT
PLANER
BENCH
```

If you use the "COPY CON" method, press the F6 function key and RETURN to save the file. If you make a mistake or want to change a slide in the slide library, you must recreate the slide library from scratch.

You should now have a slide library file named TOOLS.SLB stored in the directory named WORK.

Creating the Icon Menu

The steps in creating an icon menu involve the alteration of AutoCAD's source menu ACAD.MNU. This requires the use of a text editor or a word processor.

1 Locate the ACAD.MNU file found in the AutoCAD SUPPORT directory.

NOTE:

Be sure you have a backup copy of this file before you proceed further.

2 Copy ACAD.MNU to the WORK directory and rename it ACAD4.MNU.

3 Display the contents of ACAD4.MNU with a text editor or word processor.

4 Place the following (exactly as you see it here) just prior to the buttons menu in ACAD4.MNU.

See also
the optional
Applying
AutoCAD
Diskette.

```
***icon
**tools
[Select Tool]
[tools(tsaw,Table Saw)]^cinsert tsaw \\\\
[tools(drillp,Drill Press)]^cinsert drillp \\\\
[tools(joint,Jointer)]^cinsert joint \\\\
[tools(planer,Surface Planer)]^cinsert planer \\\\
[tools(bench,Work Bench)]^cinsert bench \\\\
```

Each of the five consistently structured menu items will do the following: (1) display the slide image as an icon on the screen, (2) display the symbol name in the list box, (3) allow you to choose it, and (4) insert the Block you chose.

If you want to learn more about the specific components within these menu items, review Unit 49.

5 Store this information in **ACAD4.MNU**, but do not exit yet.

Making the Icon Menu Accessible

It is possible to access an icon menu using the screen, pull-down, or tablet menu. In any case, you must add a new menu item in ACAD4.MNU.

1 Near the beginning of the ACAD4.MNU file, find the ***POP2 menu item. It contains the Assist pull-down menu.

② Enter the following as the last line in ***POP2. Insert it on the empty line following the item "[Calculator]'cal."

```
[Tools...]^c^cinsert tools ^c$i=tools $i=*
```

This will display "Tools..." at the bottom of the Assist pull-down menu. In addition, it will insert the five block definitions contained in TOOLS.DWG. Any graphics that may be contained in TOOLS.DWG will not insert because a "Cancel" is automatically issued at the "Insertion point:" step of the INSERT command. The last part of the macro addresses the tools icon menu and displays it on the screen.

———— NOTE: ————

You have the freedom to include this menu item elsewhere in the pull-down menus, or in a screen or tablet menu.

③ Store the new information in ACAD4.MNU.

④ Make a backup copy of the revised ACAD4.MNU.

Make sure the revised ACAD4.MNU is contained in the WORK directory. Be certain TOOLS.DWG is also located in this directory.

Using the Icon Menu ————————————————

① Begin a new drawing named **JOB** in the **WORK** directory.

② Enter the **MENU** command and select the **ACAD4.MNU** menu file from the **WORK** directory.

③ Select the **Assist** pull-down menu.

You should see the new "Tools..." item at the bottom of the menu.

④ Pick the **Tools...** item.

The new icon menu should appear.

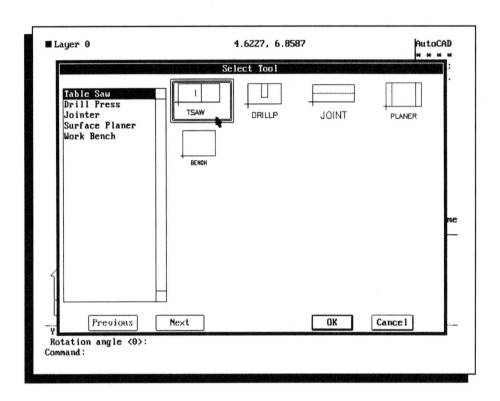

If the icon menu does not appear, a typing error may exist in the information you inserted into ACAD4.MNU. Review the file and make necessary corrections.

5 If the icon menu appeared as shown, select one of the tools, and place it on the screen.

6 Select and place the remaining tools.

_____ NOTE: _____

An icon menu can be of any length, although AutoCAD can display only up to 20 icons at one time. If you include more than 20 icon slides in the icon menu, AutoCAD will make the "Next..." and "Previous..." buttons available to you.

7 Enter **END** to save your work and exit AutoCAD.

When preparing slides for use in icon menus, keep them simple. Complex icons take longer to display on the screen and their complexity may confuse more than they communicate.

Questions

1. Why are icon menus beneficial?

   _____

   _____

2. Name at least one rule you should consider before creating slides for use in an icon menu.

   _____

   _____

3. From what type of files does the slide library facility create a slide library file?

   _____

4. In what AutoCAD file should you enter the icon menu information necessary for displaying the icon menu on the screen?

   _____

5. The ***icon menu item specifies what?

   _____

6. Explain the following: [Tools...]^c^cinsert tools ^c$i=tools $i=*.

   _____

   _____

7. Suppose you want to include 50 selections in an icon menu. How do you go about it when AutoCAD can only display 20 selections?

   _____

   _____

Problem

First, group several Blocks and create a slide of each. Second, create a slide library using the slide files. Third, use the slide library to create an icon menu. Use the steps outlined in this unit to complete this problem.

AUTOCAD® AT WORK

A Technical Illustrator's Story*

Dick Clark is an Engineering Specialist at NEC Information Systems, Inc. He creates illustrations for use in maintenance/repair manuals and user manuals. While he started his career using pencils, templates, and Leroy pens, today his main drawing tool is AutoCAD.

Dick works closely with the hardware technical writers during the writing of maintenance guides for both field and depot level. His main task is creating the Illustrated Parts Breakdown (IPB) for these guides. Since usable master drawings are seldom available, this process often means dismantling a complex piece of computer equipment or peripheral hardware down to the component and base assembly level to obtain the parts to be drawn and also to understand the assembly/reassembly process that is to be shown. Complex electromechanical assemblies and subassemblies are reduced to the Smallest Replaceable Unit (SRU) level and technically illustrated for the generation of the IPB. Each object is measured prior to drawing, and the final drawing is appropriately scaled to match those dimensions.

To create national or local advertisements, data sheets, and brochures, Dick works with the marketing staff to provide technically correct drawings.

Dick does most of his drawing in isometric and 3D views on AutoCAD. For prints, he first plots the drawing, then has the plot photographically reduced to an 8½″ × 11″ size. When incorporating these drawings into manuals, the photoreduced plot is digitized back into an Interleaf publishing system, using a scanner. This technique provides a very high-resolution image in that proper photo reduction improves apparent (but not actual) resolution, allowing the scanner to digitize the image to its maximum potential. Interleaf then incorporates the image with documentation to produce brochures or booklets.

The technical illustrator can wear many hats, from company space planner to advertisement production. One of Dick's special projects is the design of NEC's show booth. In addition to playing with booth layout, he provides a detailed presentation image of it. "My day is not always filled up entirely with production drawings," says Dick, "but if you're doing something new and challenging, and you love drawing, it's a joy. 'Can it be done?' is my favorite professional question."

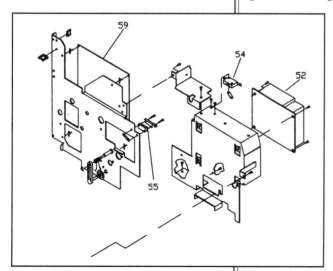

*Based on a story in CADENCE magazine, Vol. 3, No. 8.

Optional Problems

INTRODUCTION

The following problems are provided to give you additional practice with AutoCAD. These problems will help you to expand your knowledge and ability, and they will offer you new and challenging experiences with the system.

The problems range from simple to advanced, and they encompass a variety of disciplines. They have been sequenced from simple to advanced, but your instructor may ask you to complete the problems in a different order.

Regardless of the type of problem, the key to successful completion is: **plan before beginning**. Review previously learned commands and techniques and ask yourself how they can best be applied to your problem. For example, when laying out rectangular objects, plan to utilize the Grid, Snap, and Ortho features. When drawing lines of specific lengths and angles, consider using relative and polar methods of specifying endpoints. Plan how to use COPY, MIRROR, and ARRAY to simplify and speed your work.

As you discover new and easier methods of creating drawings, apply these methods when solving the problems. Since there is usually more than one way to complete a drawing, experiment with alternative methods. Discuss these alternatives with other users and create strategies for efficient completion of the problems.

Remember, there is no substitute for practice. The expertise you gain will equal the time you spend on the system. Set aside blocks of time to work with AutoCAD, think through your approach, and enjoy this fascinating technology!

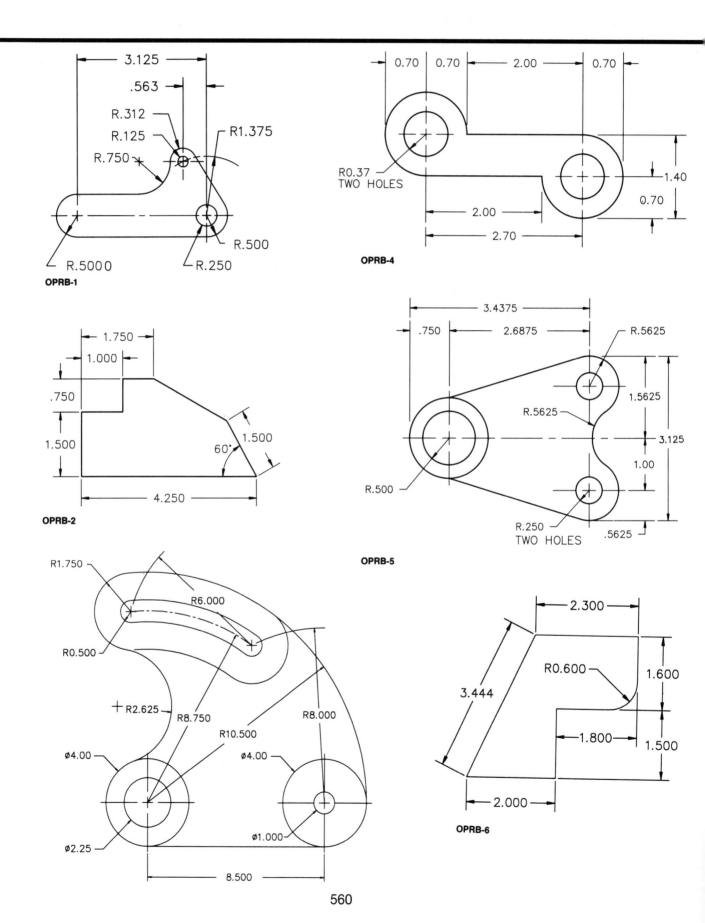

OPRB-1

OPRB-2

OPRB-4

OPRB-5

OPRB-6

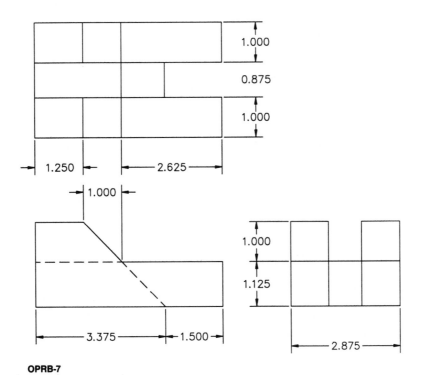

OPRB-7

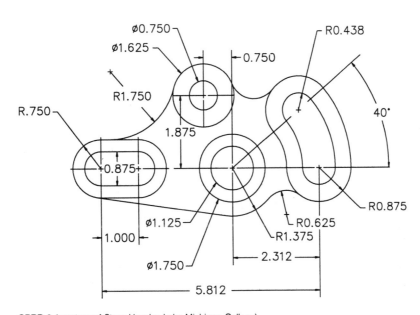

OPRB-8 (courtesy of Steve Huycke, Lake Michigan College)

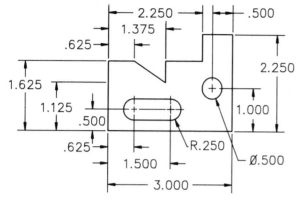

OPRB-9

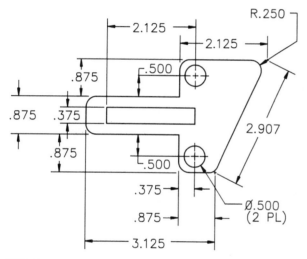

OPRB-10

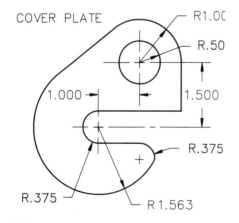

COVER PLATE

OPRB-11

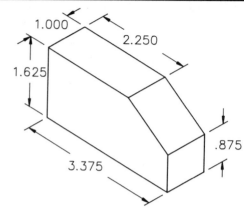

OPRB-12

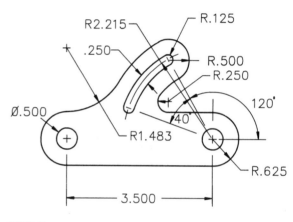

OPRB-13

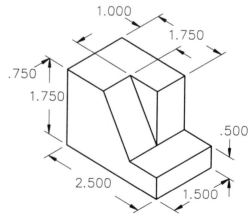

OPRB-14

Note: Consider drawing orthographic views of the isometric drawings on this and the following pages.

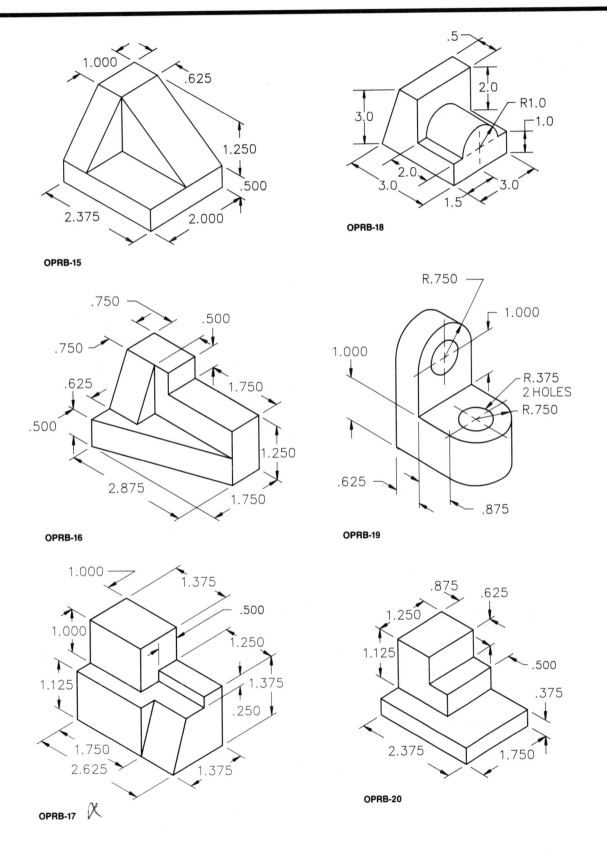

1.000
.625
1.250
.500
2.375
2.000

OPRB-15

.5
2.0
R1.0
3.0
1.0
2.0
3.0
3.0
1.5

OPRB-18

.750
.500
.750
.625
1.750
.500
1.250
2.875
1.750

OPRB-16

R.750
1.000
1.000
R.375
2 HOLES
R.750
.625
.875

OPRB-19

1.000
1.375
.500
1.000
1.250
1.125
1.375
.250
1.750
2.625
1.375

OPRB-17

.875
.625
1.250
1.125
.500
.375
2.375
1.750

OPRB-20

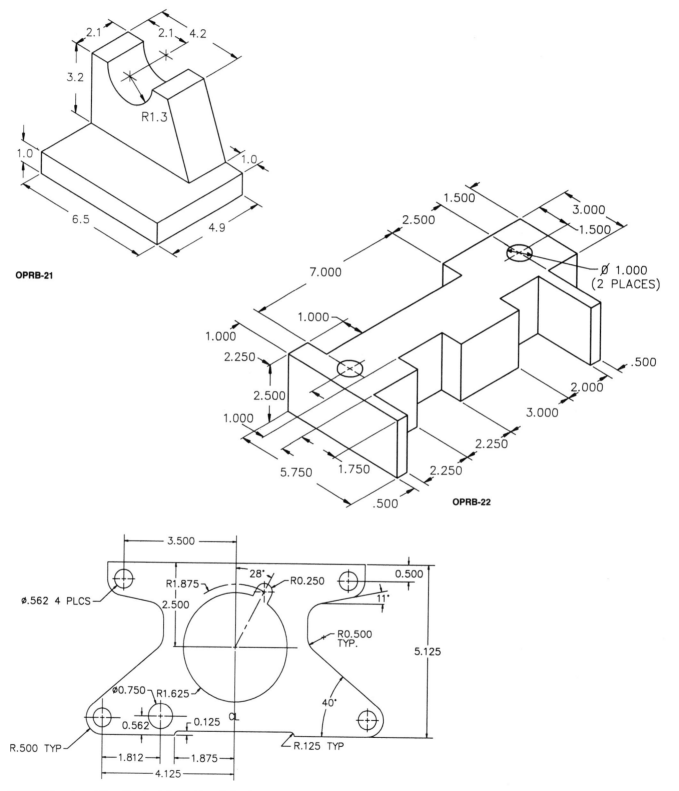

OPRB-21

Ø 1.000
(2 PLACES)

OPRB-22

ø.562 4 PLCS

R1.875

28°   R0.250

2.500

R0.500
TYP.

11°

0.500

5.125

ø0.750   R1.625

0.562   0.125

40°

R.500 TYP

R.125 TYP

1.812   1.875

4.125

OPRB-23 (courtesy of Steve Huycke, Lake Michigan College)

The following are introductory dimensioning problems. Use the dimensioning feature illustrated at the top of each problem to dimension the object shown below it.

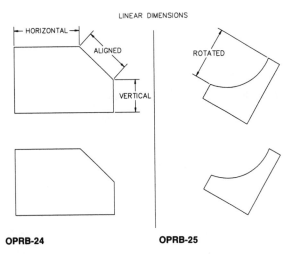

OPRB-24   OPRB-25

(courtesy of Julie H. Wickert, Austin Community College)

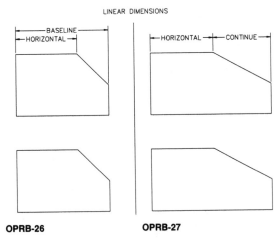

OPRB-26   OPRB-27

(courtesy of Julie H. Wickert, Austin Community College)

ANGULAR DIMENSIONS

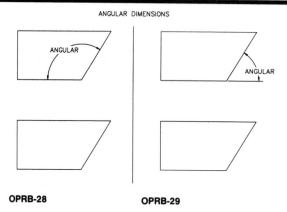

OPRB-28   **OPRB-29**

(courtesy of Julie H. Wickert, Austin Community College)

RADIAL DIMENSIONS

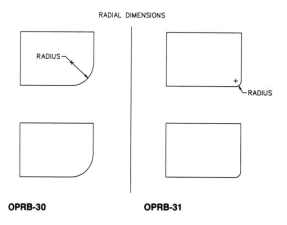

OPRB-30   **OPRB-31**

(courtesy of Julie H. Wickert, Austin Community College)

DIAMETER DIMENSIONS

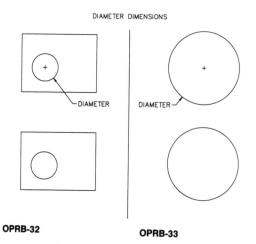

OPRB-32   **OPRB-33**

(courtesy of Julie H. Wickert, Austin Community College)

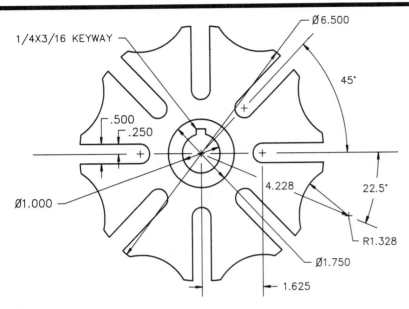

OPRB-34

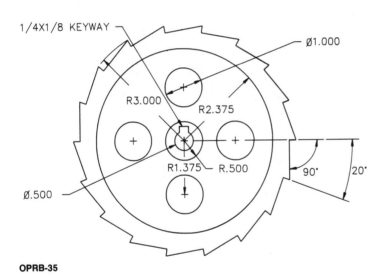

OPRB-35

Ø143

120°

6.5 → R6.5
Ø41.0
R13.0 → Ø8.0
R6.5
R36.5
R13.0
R51
PARALLEL
R13.0
Ø127

UNLESS OTHERWISE SPECIFIED
ALL DIMENSIONS ARE IN MILLIMETERS

OPRB-37 (from the textbook *Drafting Fundamentals*
by Scott, Foy, and Schwendau)

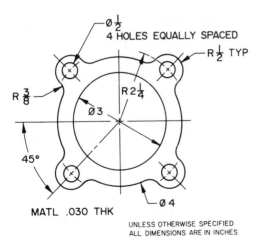

OPRB-36 (from the textbook *Drafting Fundamentals*
by Scott, Foy, and Schwendau)

567

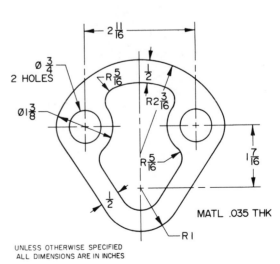

OPRB-38 (from the textbook *Drafting Fundamentals*
by Scott, Foy, and Schwendau)

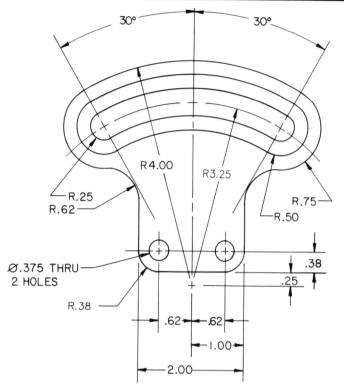

OPRB-39 (from the textbook *Drafting Fundamentals*
by Scott, Foy, and Schwendau)

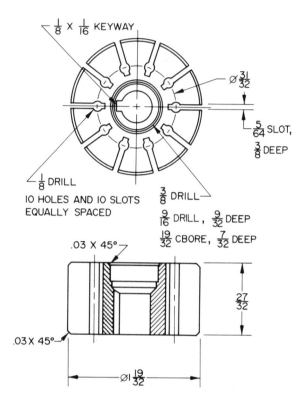

OPRB-41 (from the textbook *Drafting Fundamentals*
by Scott, Foy, and Schwendau)

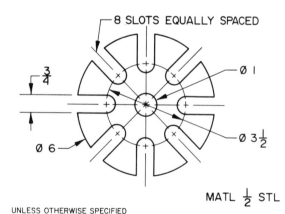

UNLESS OTHERWISE SPECIFIED
ALL DIMENSIONS ARE IN INCHES

REF. ANSI Y14.5M – 1982

OPRB-40 (from the textbook *Drafting Fundamentals*
by Scott, Foy, and Schwendau)

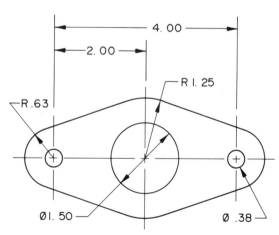

MATL .06 ASBESTOS

REF. ANSI Y14.5M – 1982

UNLESS OTHERWISE SPECIFIED
ALL DIMENSIONS ARE IN INCHES

OPRB-42 (from the textbook *Drafting Fundamentals*
by Scott, Foy, and Schwendau)

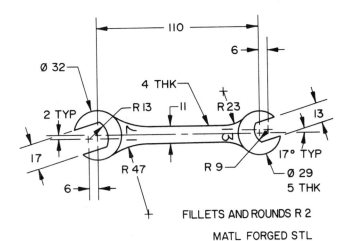

2 TYP
Ø 32
R 13
4 THK
11
R 23
6
110
17
R 47
6
R 9
17° TYP
13
Ø 29
5 THK

FILLETS AND ROUNDS R 2

MATL FORGED STL

UNLESS OTHERWISE SPECIFIED
ALL DIMENSIONS ARE IN MILLIMETERS   REF. ANSI Y14.5M-1982

OPRB-43 (from the textbook *Drafting Fundamentals*
by Scott, Foy, and Schwendau)

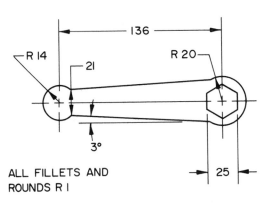

R 14
21
R 20
136
3°
25

ALL FILLETS AND
ROUNDS R 1

MATL 4 MM GALVANIZED STL

REF. ANSI Y14.5M-1982   UNLESS OTHERWISE SPECIFIED
ALL DIMENSIONS ARE IN MILLIMETERS

OPRB-45 (from the textbook *Drafting Fundamentals*
by Scott, Foy, and Schwendau)

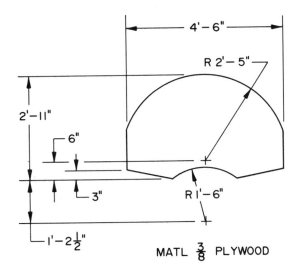

4'-6"
R 2'-5"
2'-11"
6"
3"
R 1'-6"
1'-2½"

MATL ⅜ PLYWOOD

OPRB-44 (from the textbook *Drafting Fundamentals*
by Scott, Foy, and Schwendau)

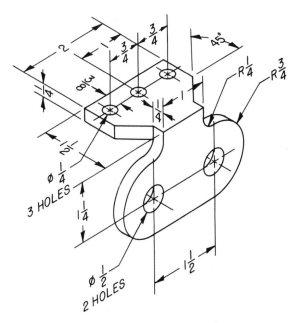

OPRB-46 (from the textbook *Drafting Fundamentals*
by Scott, Foy, and Schwendau)

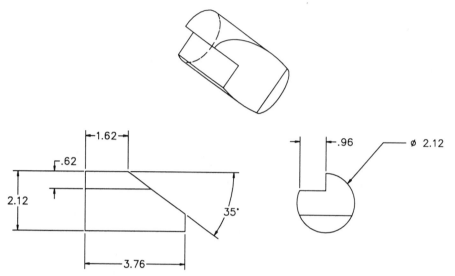

OPRB-47 (courtesy of John F. Kirk, Kirk & Associates)

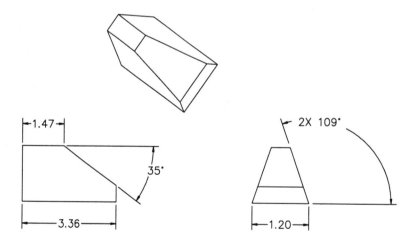

OPRB-48 (courtesy of John F. Kirk, Kirk & Associates)

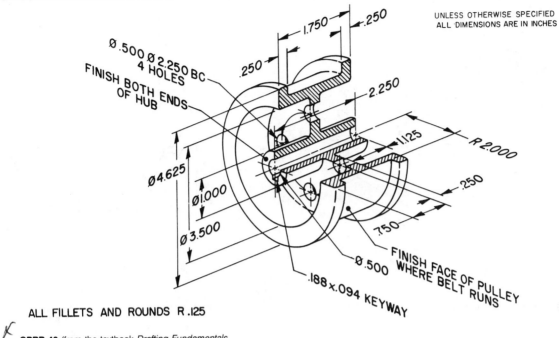

UNLESS OTHERWISE SPECIFIED
ALL DIMENSIONS ARE IN INCHES

Ø .500 Ø 2.250 BC
4 HOLES
FINISH BOTH ENDS
OF HUB

1.750   .250

.250

2.250

1125

R 2.000

.250

Ø 4.625

Ø 1.000

.750

Ø 3.500

Ø .500

FINISH FACE OF PULLEY
WHERE BELT RUNS

.188 x .094 KEYWAY

ALL FILLETS AND ROUNDS R .125

OPRB-49 (from the textbook *Drafting Fundamentals*
by Scott, Foy, and Schwendau)

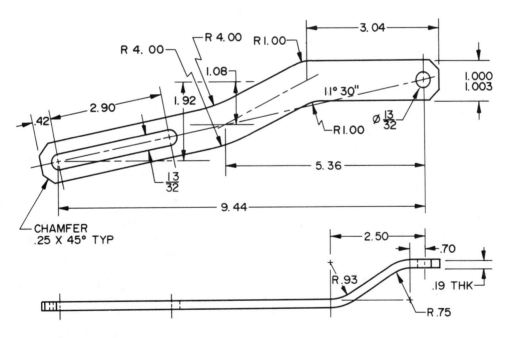

R 4.00

R 4.00   R 1.00

3.04

1.08

1.92

2.90

11° 30"

1.000
1.003

.42

R 1.00

Ø 13/32

13/32

5.36

9.44

CHAMFER
.25 X 45° TYP

2.50

.70

R .93

.19 THK

R .75

OPRB-50 (from the textbook *Drafting Fundamentals*
by Scott, Foy, and Schwendau)

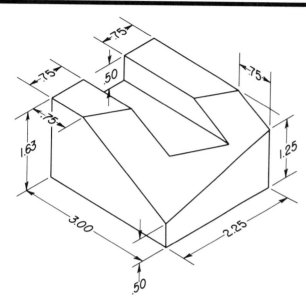

OPRB-51 (from the textbook *Drafting Fundamentals* by Scott, Foy, and Schwendau)

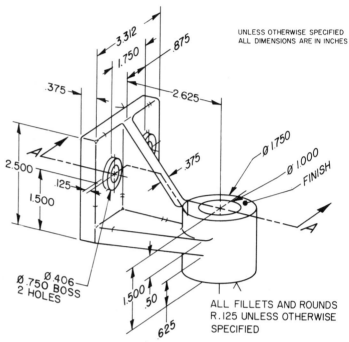

UNLESS OTHERWISE SPECIFIED
ALL DIMENSIONS ARE IN INCHES

ALL FILLETS AND ROUNDS
R.125 UNLESS OTHERWISE
SPECIFIED

OPRB-53 (from the textbook *Drafting Fundamentals* by Scott, Foy, and Schwendau)

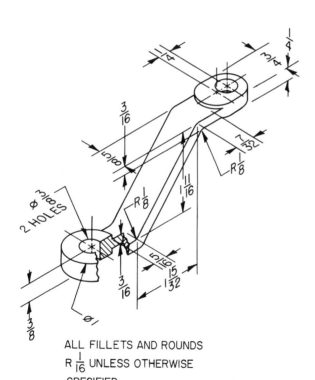

ALL FILLETS AND ROUNDS
R $\frac{1}{16}$ UNLESS OTHERWISE
SPECIFIED

OPRB-52 (from the textbook *Drafting Fundamentals* by Scott, Foy, and Schwendau)

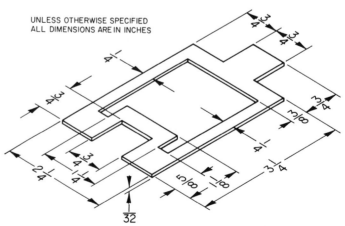

UNLESS OTHERWISE SPECIFIED
ALL DIMENSIONS ARE IN INCHES

OPRB-54 (from the textbook *Drafting Fundamentals* by Scott, Foy, and Schwendau)

572

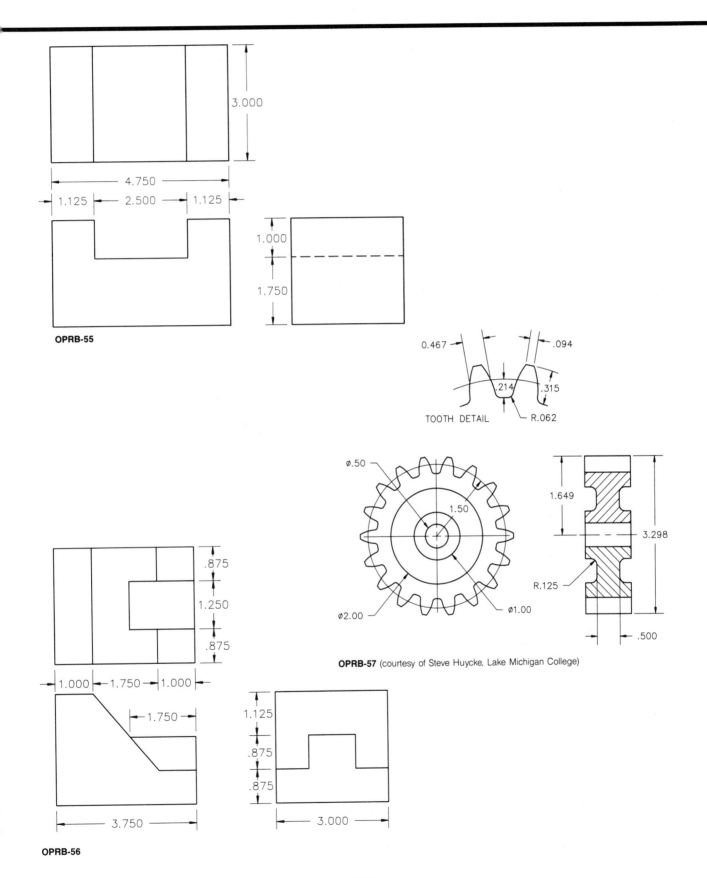

OPRB-55

TOOTH DETAIL — R.062

OPRB-57 (courtesy of Steve Huycke, Lake Michigan College)

OPRB-56

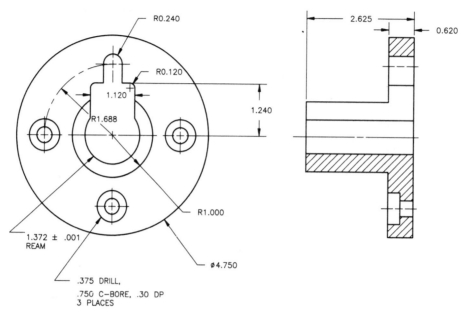

R0.240

R0.120

1.120

1.240

R1.688

R1.000

1.372 ± .001
REAM

Ø4.750

.375 DRILL,
.750 C-BORE, .30 DP
3 PLACES

2.625

0.620

OPRB-58 (courtesy of Steve Huycke, Lake Michigan College)

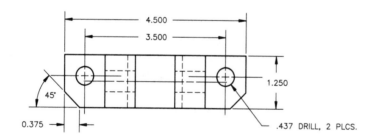

4.500

3.500

45°

0.375

1.250

.437 DRILL, 2 PLCS.

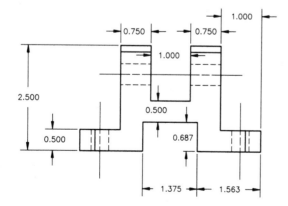

1.000

0.750

0.750

1.000

2.500

0.500

0.500

0.687

1.375

1.563

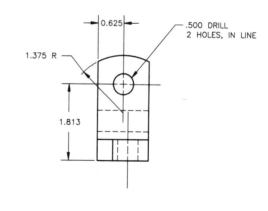

0.625

.500 DRILL
2 HOLES, IN LINE

1.375 R

1.813

OPRB-59 (courtesy of Steve Huycke, Lake Michigan College)

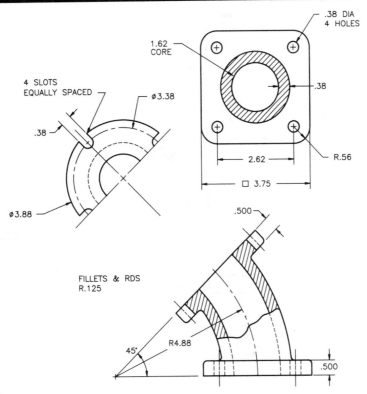

OPRB-60 (courtesy of Steve Huycke, Lake Michigan College)

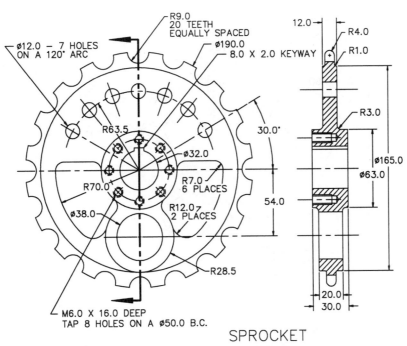

SPROCKET

OPRB-61 (courtesy of Alan Fitzell, Central Peel Secondary School)

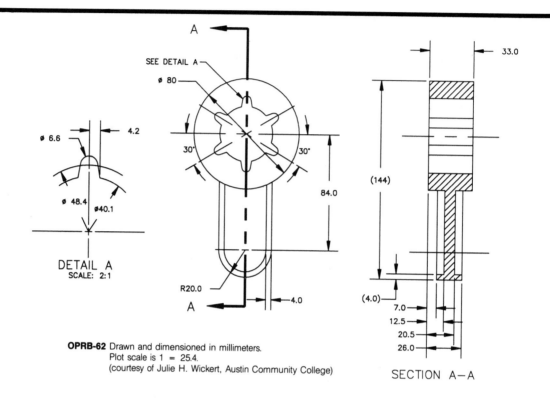

DETAIL A
SCALE: 2:1

SECTION A—A

OPRB-62 Drawn and dimensioned in millimeters.
Plot scale is 1 = 25.4.
(courtesy of Julie H. Wickert, Austin Community College)

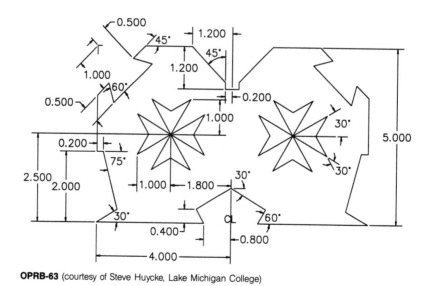

OPRB-63 (courtesy of Steve Huycke, Lake Michigan College)

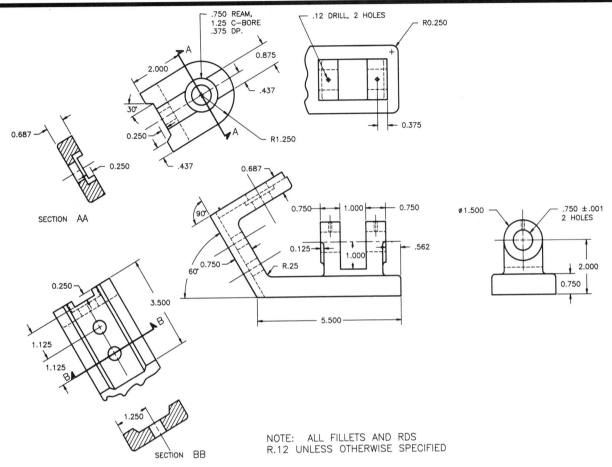

NOTE: ALL FILLETS AND RDS
R.12 UNLESS OTHERWISE SPECIFIED

OPRB-64 (courtesy of Steve Huycke, Lake Michigan College)

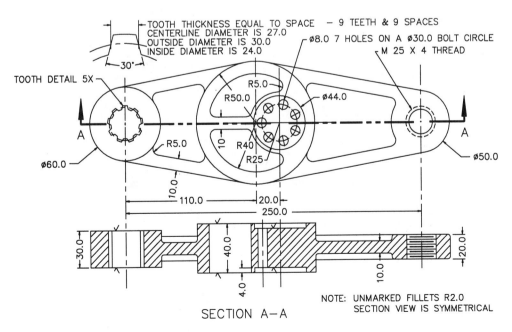

TOOTH THICKNESS EQUAL TO SPACE – 9 TEETH & 9 SPACES
CENTERLINE DIAMETER IS 27.0
OUTSIDE DIAMETER IS 30.0
INSIDE DIAMETER IS 24.0

Ø8.0 7 HOLES ON A Ø30.0 BOLT CIRCLE

M 25 X 4 THREAD

NOTE: UNMARKED FILLETS R2.0
SECTION VIEW IS SYMMETRICAL

SECTION A–A

OPRB-65 (courtesy of Alan Fitzell, Central Peel Secondary School)

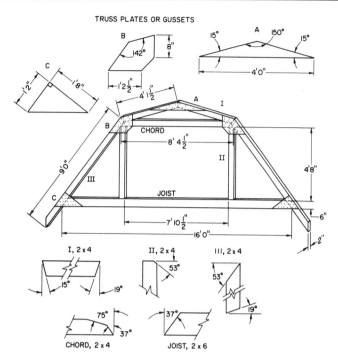

TRUSS PLATES OR GUSSETS

OPRB-66 (from the textbook *Drafting Fundamentals* by Scott, Foy, and Schwendau)

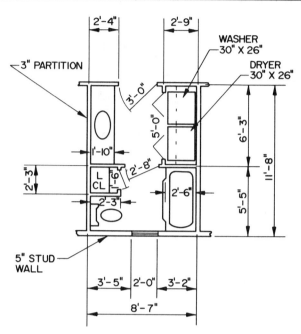

OPRB-68 (from the textbook *Drafting Fundamentals* by Scott, Foy, and Schwendau)

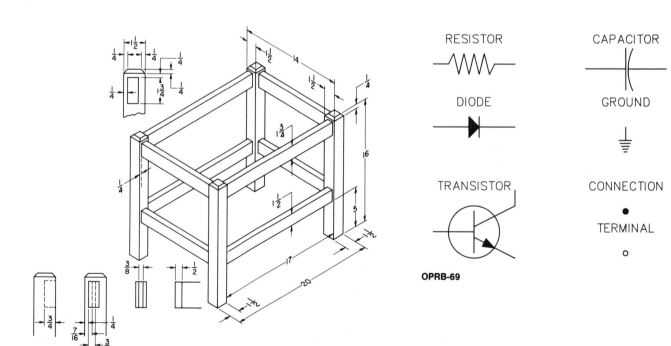

OPRB-67 (from the textbook *Drafting Fundamentals* by Scott, Foy, and Schwendau)

RESISTOR

DIODE

TRANSISTOR

OPRB-69

CAPACITOR

GROUND

CONNECTION

TERMINAL

OPRB-70 (courtesy of Dan Cowell and Ron Weseloh, Red Bud High School)

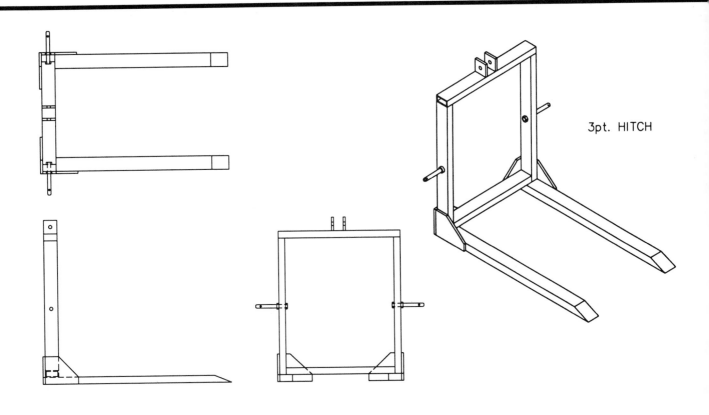

3pt. HITCH

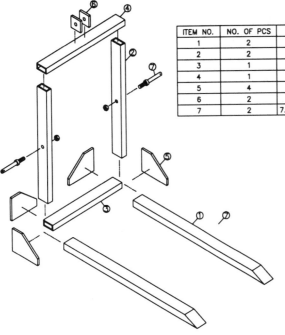

ITEM NO.	NO. OF PCS	SIZE	DESCRIPTION
1	2	42.75	1/8-1.5-3 TUBING
2	2	30	1/8-1.5-3 TUBING
3	1	22.5	1/8-1.5-3 TUBING
4	1	25.5	1/8-1.5-3 TUBING
5	4	3/8-6-8	ANGLE BRACES
6	2	1/2-3-3	UPPER ARM SUPPORTS
7	2	7.25 - 3/4 HEX. NUT	PIN HITCH—STANDARD PART

OPRB-71 (courtesy of Craig Pelate and Ron Weseloh, Red Bud High School)

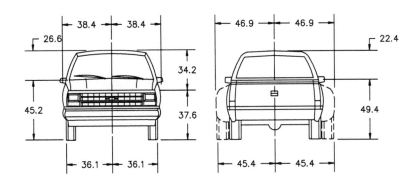

Scale: 1" = 3'

OPRB-72

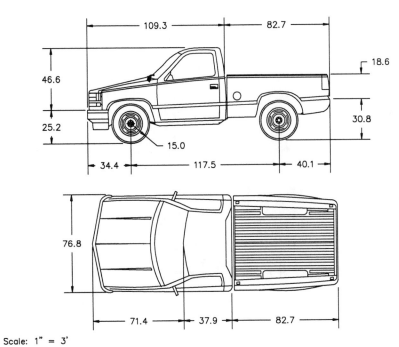

Scale: 1" = 3'

OPRB-73

Approximate the missing dimensions.

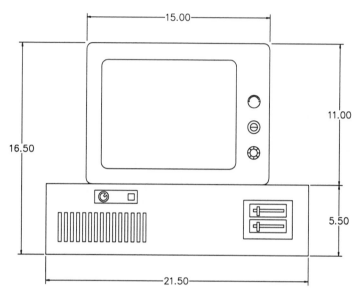

OPRB-74 (courtesy of Dan Myers, Informance Computer Services)

ASEA IRB-2000 industrial robot. Approximate all dimensions.

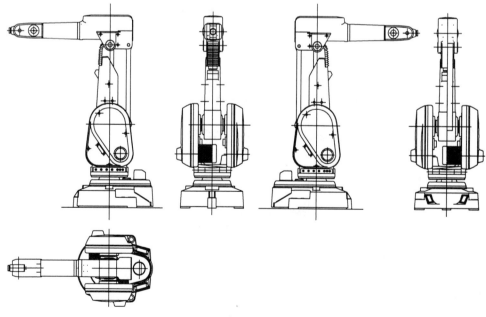

OPRB-75 (courtesy of ESAB Automation)

Approximate all dimensions.

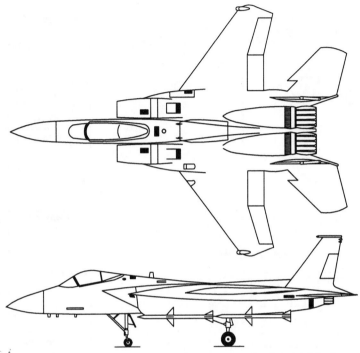

OPRB-76 (courtesy of Matt Melliere and Ronald Weseloh, Red Bud High School)

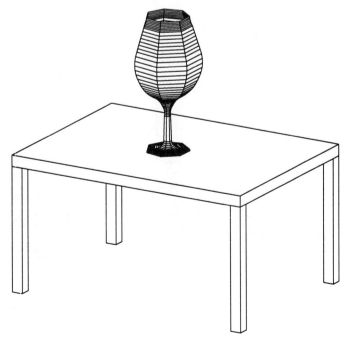

OPRB-77

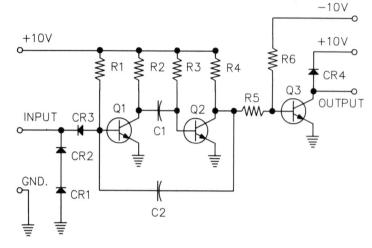

OPRB-78

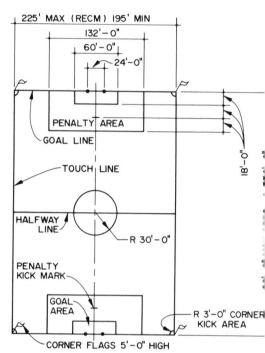

OPRB-80 (from the textbook *Drafting Fundamentals* by Scott, Foy, and Schwendau)

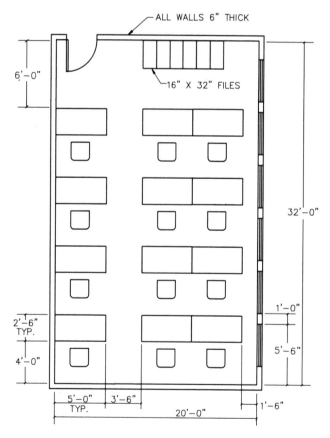

OPRB-79

HIGH SCHOOL 84'-0"

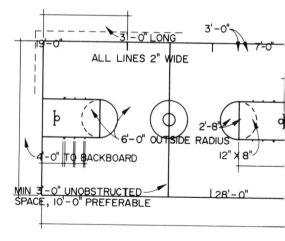

OPRB-81 (from the textbook *Drafting Fundamentals* by Scott, Foy, and Schwendau)

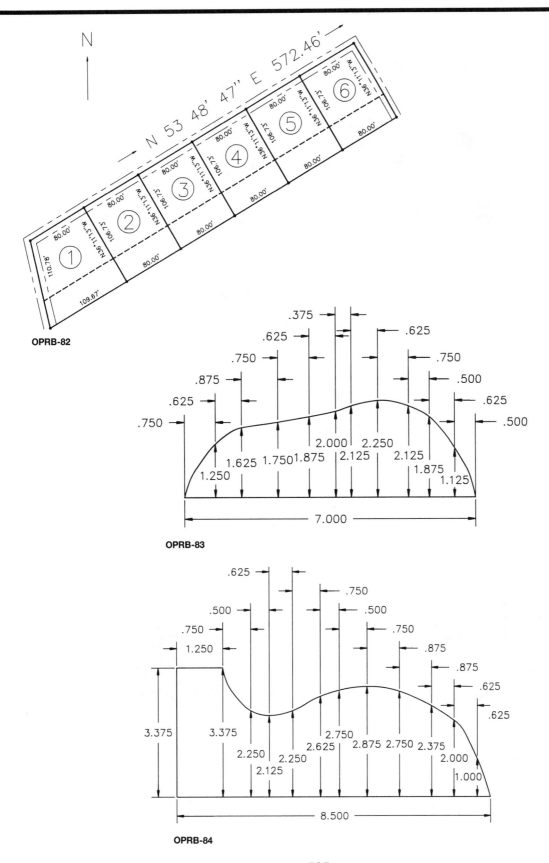

OPRB-82

OPRB-83

OPRB-84

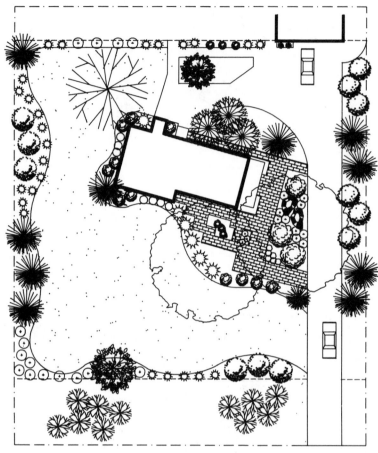

OPRB-85 (courtesy of Mill Brothers Landscape and Nursery, Inc.
Created using LANDCADD software with AutoCAD.)

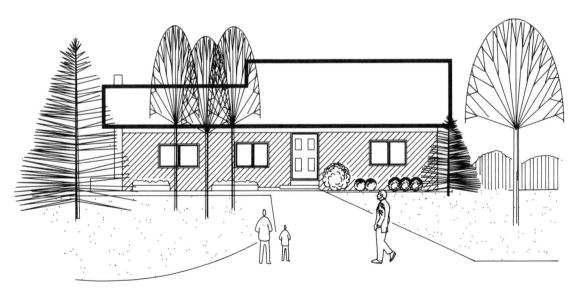

OPRB-86 (courtesy of Mill Brothers Landscape and Nursery, Inc.
Created using LANDCADD software with AutoCAD.)

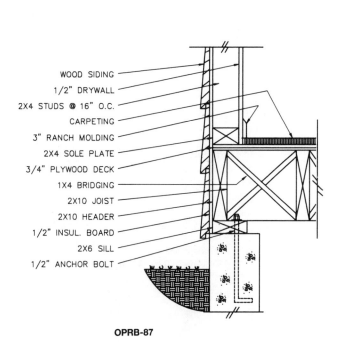

WOOD SIDING
1/2" DRYWALL
2X4 STUDS @ 16" O.C.
CARPETING
3" RANCH MOLDING
2X4 SOLE PLATE
3/4" PLYWOOD DECK
1X4 BRIDGING
2X10 JOIST
2X10 HEADER
1/2" INSUL. BOARD
2X6 SILL
1/2" ANCHOR BOLT

OPRB-87

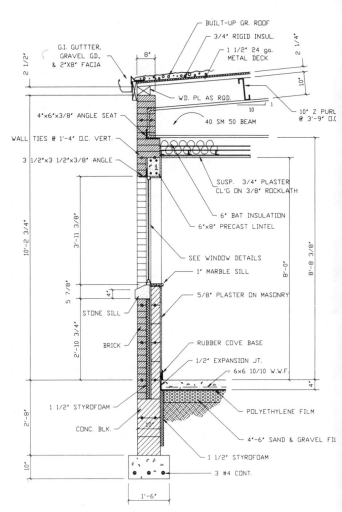

OPRB-88 (courtesy of Paul Driscoll)

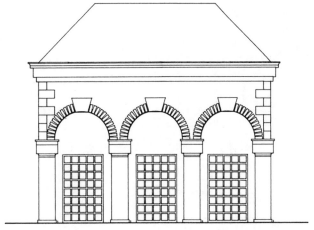

OPRB-89 (courtesy of Robb and Brenner, Architects/Planners)

587

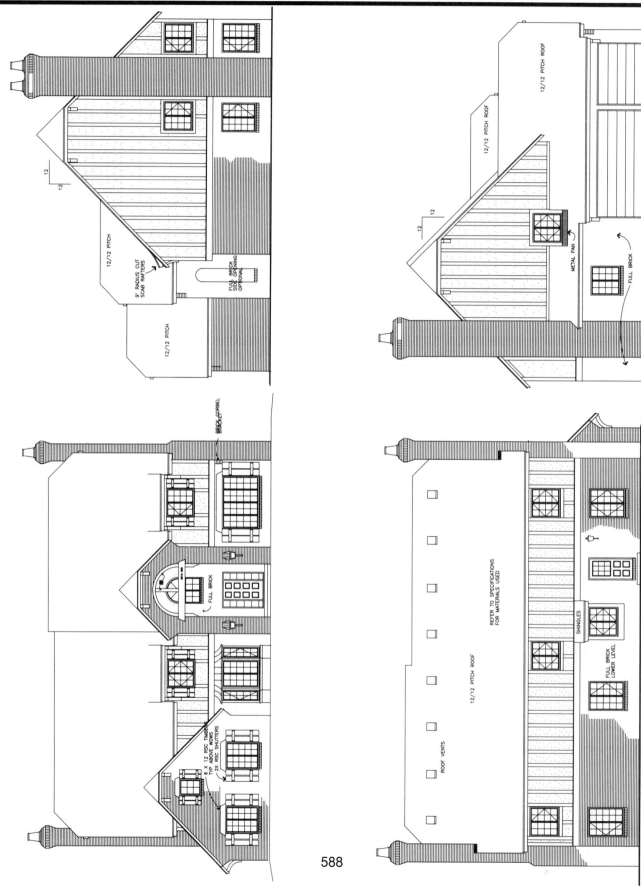

588

OPRB-90 (courtesy of Rodger A. Brooks, Architect)

Appendix A: Formatting Diskettes

Before the computer can accept a new diskette for any type of file storage, you must first format it. To format a new diskette, you must locate the DOS directory (or DOS diskette) containing the file called FORMAT.COM.

1 Change to the DOS directory using the CD (Change Directory) command, or insert the DOS diskette containing FORMAT.COM into the computer. (See Appendix C for instructions on the CD command.)

2 To review the contents of the DOS diskette or directory, type **DIR** (short for Directory) and press **RETURN**.

HINT:
To stop the scrolling, press CTRL S. To resume scrolling, press any key.

The directory should look similar to the following. Yours may differ, depending on the specific version of DOS you are using.

```
ADAPT     COM     21778 12-05-88   12:00p
ASSIGN    COM      6399 04-09-91    5:00a
BASIC     COM      3532 10-03-88   12:00p
BASICA    COM      3532 10-03-88   12:00p
COMMAND   COM     47845 04-09-91    5:00a
DISKCOMP  COM     10652 04-09-91    5:00a
DISKCOPY  COM     11793 04-09-91    5:00a
DOSKEY    COM      5883 04-09-91    5:00a
DOSSHELL  COM      4623 04-09-91    5:00a
EDIT      COM       413 04-09-91    5:00a
FORMAT    COM     32911 04-09-91    5:00a
FORMAT!   COM     13675 10-03-88   12:00p
GRAFTABL  COM     11205 04-09-91    5:00a
GRAPHICS  COM     19694 04-09-91    5:00a
KEYB      COM     14986 04-09-91    5:00a
KEYB33    COM     10974 10-03-88   12:00p
LOADFIX   COM      1131 04-09-91    5:00a
MIRROR    COM     18169 04-09-91    5:00a
MODE      COM     23537 04-09-91    5:00a
MODE33    COM     15188 10-03-88   12:00p
MORE      COM      2618 04-09-91    5:00a
MOUSE     COM      8957 04-28-86    4:43p
MSHERC    COM      6934 04-09-91    5:00a
MSMOUSE   COM      4764 01-08-85   12:19p
REBOOTB   COM        77 06-01-88   12:00p
SCRNSAV2  COM      1538 09-01-88    9:12p
SETCLOCK  COM      3715 10-03-88   12:00p
SYS       COM     13440 04-09-91    5:00a
TEST      COM      2592 09-30-88   12:00p
TREE      COM      6901 04-09-91    5:00a
```

You should see the FORMAT.COM file. If FORMAT.COM is contained on the disk, you can now format a new diskette.

3 Place a new diskette in an open drive (preferably drive A) in the computer.

CAUTION:
BE CAREFUL THAT YOU DO NOT ACCIDENTALLY FORMAT THE HARD DISK INSTEAD OF THE FLOPPY DISKETTE. Formatting a hard disk will permanently erase its contents.

4 After the DOS prompt (*e.g.*, C:\> or C>), type FORMAT in either upper or lower case letters. Note the example below.

C:\>FORMAT A: (press **RETURN**)

The preceding would use the FORMAT.COM file from the C drive and would format the diskette contained in drive A. If necessary, replace "C" and "A" with the appropriate drives.

5 Follow the instructions given by the computer until the format process is complete.

6 Remove the formatted diskette from the computer and place it in its sleeve.

7 Print your name, the date, and any other pertinent information on a self-stick label. Place the label on the newly formatted diskette.

The diskette is now ready for storing data such as backup copies of AutoCAD drawing files.

Let's format another diskette, but this time let's place the DOS System on the diskette. The diskette can then be used for booting (starting) the computer system.

1 Place another new diskette in the computer.

NOTE:
As before, the FORMAT.COM file must be in the computer before you can format new diskettes.

② This time enter the FORMAT command followed by a /S. Note the example below.

C:\>**FORMAT A:/S** (press **RETURN**)

The above will format the diskette contained in drive A and will also place the DOS System on the diskette.

NOTE:

The DOS System is comprised of three files: the visible COMMAND.COM file and two invisible (hidden) files. These three files allow you to start the computer system, to use the *internal* DOS commands, such as DIR, COPY, DEL and REN, and to run application programs such as AutoCAD.

③ Follow the instructions given by the computer until the format process is complete.

④ Enter **DIR** to review the contents of the newly formatted diskette. Note the example below:

C:\>**DIR A:** (press **RETURN**)

The above entry will display the contents of drive A.

The COMMAND.COM file should be contained on the newly formatted diskette.

NOTE:

If you plan to use your diskette only for storing data such as drawing files, then do not use the /S option because it occupies storage space on the diskette.

Appendix B: Commonly Used DOS Commands

DOS commands used frequently are FORMAT, DIRectory, COPY, REName, DELete (or ERASE), MORE, TYPE, DISKCOPY, and CHKDSK (Checkdisk). FORMAT was covered in Appendix A. This appendix lets you practice the others so that you can effectively manage all AutoCAD files. (Additional DOS commands are discussed in other appendices. Refer to the index.)

DIR, COPY, REN, DEL, and TYPE are *internal* DOS commands. These internal commands can be entered at any time at the DOS prompt (*e.g.*, C:\>). You can also enter DIR, DEL, and TYPE at AutoCAD's "Command:" prompt.

DIR

The DIR command allows you to view the "table of contents" of the current directory. DIR also gives you the size of each file and the date and time each was created.

There are three different ways of using the DIR command. The simplest is to enter DIR. A second method is to type /P after the DIR, like this: DIR/P. The third way is to type /W after DIR, like this: DIR/W. Let's try the DIR command.

1. Start (boot) the computer system.

2. After the DOS prompt (*e.g.*, C:\> or C>), type **DIR** and press **RETURN**. Press CTRL S to stop the scrolling, and press any key to resume scrolling.

That's all there is to it.

Note each column in the directory and the information each provides. Also note the file names and their extensions. The file extension indicates the type of file. A list of AutoCAD related file extensions and their meanings is provided below.

File extension	Meaning
.AC$	AutoCAD temporary drawing file
.ADS	ADS applications file
.ADT	Audit report file
.BAK	AutoCAD backup file*
.BAS	DOS BASIC file (file written in the BASIC language)

*This file type does *not* serve as a true backup file. AutoCAD automatically creates the .BAK file each time you edit a drawing file. The .BAK file stores the drawing as it was prior to editing. Thus the .BAK file does not contain the latest version of the drawing but rather the one prior to it. Only the .DWG file contains the latest version of your work.

.BAT	DOS batch file
.BDF	VESA font file
.BKN	Emergency backup file incremented sequentially to next unique name
.CFG	AutoCAD configuration file
.COM	DOS command file
.DCC	Dialogue color control file
.DCE	Dialogue box error report file
.DCL	Dialogue Control Language description file
.DOC	Documentation update file
.DWG	AutoCAD drawing file
.DXB	Binary drawing interchange file
.DXF	Drawing interchange file
.DXX	Attribute extract file in DXF format
.EPS	Encapsulated PostScript file
.ERR	Report file of errors when AutoCAD crashes
.EXE	Execution file
.EXP	ADS executable file
.FLM	AutoShade filmroll file
.HDX	AutoCAD help index file
.HLP	AutoCAD help file
.IGS	IGES interchange file
.LIN	AutoCAD linetype library file
.LSP	AutoLISP® program file
.MAT	AME™ materials file
.MID	Diskette identification file
.MNU	AutoCAD menu source file (in noncompiled ASCII form)
.MNX	AutoCAD compiled menu file
.MSG	AutoCAD message file
.OLD	Old (original) version of a converted .DWG file
.PAT	AutoCAD hatch pattern library file
.PCP	Plot configuration parameters file
.PFB	PostScript font file
.PGP	AutoCAD program parameters file
.PLT	Plot output file
.PS	PostScript file
.PSF	PostScript support file
.PWD	Login file
.SCR	AutoCAD command script file
.SHP	AutoCAD shape or font source file (in noncompiled ASCII form)
.SHX	AutoCAD compiled shape or font file
.SLB	AutoCAD slide library file
.SLD	AutoCAD slide file
.TXT	Attribute extract or template file in CDF/SDF format
.UNT	AutoCAD units file
.XLG	External references log file
.XMX	External message file

③ Next, select a directory that contains more than one screenful of directory information.

④ Enter **DIR/P** (P is for Pause) and press **RETURN**.

As you can see, the /P option causes the computer to pause after it displays a screenful of information.

⑤ Enter **DIR/W** (W is for Wide) and press **RETURN**.

The /W option displays the information in wide format. However, it omits the date and time information.

COPY

The COPY command allows you to copy files from one directory to another. A common use of the COPY command is to make backup copies of drawing files.

① Using the COPY command, copy a file (of your choice) from a hard disk directory to a diskette. Note the example below.

C>**COPY HOUSE.DWG A:** (press **RETURN**)

The above entry will copy the file named HOUSE.DWG from the current directory of drive C to drive A. When using the COPY command, be sure to specify the correct drives depending upon where the files reside and where the files are being copied.

② Perform a **DIR**ectory to make sure the file was copied.

③ This time, copy all *drawing* files from drive A to the current hard disk directory. Note the example below.

C>**COPY A:*.DWG** (press **RETURN**)

This entry will copy all drawing files from drive A and place them on the current drive C directory. Be sure to specify the correct drive.

④ Copy *all* files from the current directory to drive A. Note the example below.

C>**COPY *.* A:** (press **RETURN**)

This entry will copy all files from the current drive C directory and place them on the current drive A directory.

REN

The REName command allows you to change the name of any of your files.

① Rename one of the files you copied using the REN command. Note the example below.

C>**REN A:HOUSE.DWG HUT.DWG** (press **RETURN**)

This entry will find the file on drive A named HOUSE.DWG and rename it HUT.DWG.

② Perform a **DIR**ectory to make sure the file name was changed.

That's all there is to the REN command.

DEL (ERASE)

The DEL (ERASE) command allows you to do exactly that: delete a file. Before using this command, be sure you don't need the file you are about to erase. Once you've erased a file, it's almost impossible to get it back.

① DELete the file you renamed. Note the examples below.

C>**DEL A:HUT.DWG** (press **RETURN**)
C>**DEL \ACAD\ACAD.MSG** (press **RETURN**)

The first entry would delete the file located on drive A named HUT.DWG. The second entry would delete the file ACAD.MSG contained in the \ACAD directory.

② Enter **DIR** to see whether the file was deleted.

——— NOTE: ———

If you erase a file by mistake, it is difficult to restore it. Utility programs that contain an "unerase" feature are available for purchase. One example is PC Tools Deluxe by Central Point Software (Beaverton, OR).

TYPE

The TYPE command is used to review the contents of a standard ASCII (text) file. An example of this file type is the standard AutoCAD screen menu, ACAD.MNU. Other examples include the AutoCAD help file ACAD.HLP, an AUTOEXEC.BAT file, and any .LSP (AutoLISP) file. Let's use the TYPE command with one of these files.

1 Display the contents of the ACAD.HLP file using the TYPE command. Note the example here. (ACAD.HLP is contained in the SUPPORT directory.)

C>**TYPE ACAD.HLP** (press **RETURN**)

CTRL S will stop the scrolling of the information. Press any key to resume scrolling. Press CTRL C to cancel.

2 Experiment with the TYPE command by displaying the contents of other ASCII files.

MORE

The MORE command is an improved version of the TYPE command. The DOS file MORE.COM must be available in order to use MORE.

1 Enter the **MORE** command to display the contents of ACAD.HLP. Notice the use of the less-than (<) sign.

C>**MORE<ACAD.HLP** (press **RETURN**)

2 Press any key to obtain more information. (Press the **CTRL** and **C** keys if/when you want to cancel.)

DISKCOPY

The DISKCOPY command allows you to produce a "carbon copy" of an entire diskette. This command is used only for copying diskettes. If a hard disk drive letter (such as E) is specified, an error message is displayed. The DOS file DISKCOPY.COM must be available.

1 Enter the DISKCOPY command to make a copy of a diskette. Follow the instructions given by the computer. Note the example below.

C>**DISKCOPY A: A:** (press **RETURN**)

The above example will copy everything from the first diskette you place in drive A to the second diskette you place in drive A. When the copying process is complete, the two diskettes will be identical.

CAUTION:

The DISKCOPY command will erase everything on the target diskette as it copies new information onto it. Therefore be sure the target diskette is either blank or contains files you no longer need.

CHKDSK

The CHKDSK command allows you to check for bad sectors or damaged disks. The CHKDSK.COM file must be available.

1 Enter the **CHKDSK** command. Note the example below.

C>**CHKDSK** (press **RETURN**)

This entry will provide information on drive C.

```
61212672 bytes total disk space
  143360 bytes in 9 hidden files
   98304 bytes in 38 directories
51511296 bytes in 1274 user files
 9459712 bytes available on disk

    2048 bytes in each allocation unit
   29889 total allocation units on disk
    4619 available allocation units on disk

  655360 total bytes memory
  553856 bytes free
```

If your disk does not pass inspection, the computer will tell you what's wrong with it.

CHKDSK can also be used with the /F option as in: C>CHKDSK /F. This option creates files of lost clusters on the disk. These files can then be deleted to create additional free space on the disk.

In summary, the DIR, COPY, REN, DEL, and TYPE commands are available at any time when the DOS prompt is on the screen. The FORMAT, MORE, DISKCOPY, and CHKDSK commands require specific files resident in the computer before these commands can be used. Those file names are FORMAT.COM, MORE.COM, DISKCOPY.COM, and CHKDSK.COM, and they are part of the DOS set of files.

Appendix C: Using the Hard Disk

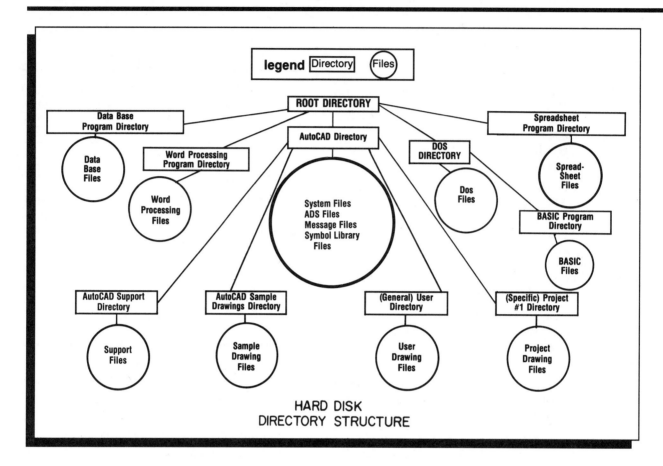

HARD DISK
DIRECTORY STRUCTURE

Hard Disk Organization

A directory is a collection of related files. The diagram above shows a sample directory structure for the hard disk. Notice that all the directories (sometimes called subdirectories) grow from the root directory, like branches on a tree. That's why it is called a tree-structured (also hierarchical) directory system. Note the AutoCAD directory and the files and directories contained within it.

It is important to have a tree structure similar to the one here. The benefits of such a structure include proper categorization of files, faster retrieval of files, and better overall organization of the system.

Keep the AutoCAD directory clean of user drawing files. Use the AutoCAD directory mainly for the files illustrated above; otherwise it will grow large and cumbersome to effectively use. User drawing files can be stored in a subdirectory within the AutoCAD directory, as shown above. You may even want to devote subdirectories to AutoLISP files, menu files, symbol libraries, and prototype drawings. In any case, attempt to keep directories small (i.e., fewer than 75 files).

Store all backup files on a separate disk or tape backup system. That way, if files are lost or damaged or if the hard disk crashes, you will have a copy of the files.

To create and use a directory system, such as the one in the diagram, you need to use the DOS commands CD, MD, and RD.

CD

The CD (Change Directory) command allows you to change to a different directory. For instance, if you are currently in the root directory (\), you can move to the AutoCAD directory (\ACAD) by entering CD ACAD at the command prompt. In this example, ACAD is the name of the AutoCAD directory.

1   Obtain the DOS prompt (e.g., C:\> or C>).

2   Enter CD ACAD in upper or lower case letters. Note the example here.

C>**CD ACAD** (press **RETURN**)

NOTE:

Replace "ACAD" with the name given to your Auto-CAD directory (such as R12) if it is different than ACAD. Also, if the CD command does not work for you, then your system may not contain the named AutoCAD directory. If so, go to the section called "MD" and return to this section after you have created new directories.

Specifying Directory Paths

Whenever you want to change to a (sub)directory that is not contained within the current directory, you must specify a search path. For example, suppose you are in the spreadsheet program directory (see diagram on the previous page) and want to change to the AutoCAD directory. You would enter the following:

C>**CD \ACAD** (press **RETURN**)

This will take you to the ACAD directory even if you are several directories (levels) below the root directory. The backslash specifies the root directory. Therefore the computer will begin its search at the root directory.

The backslash can also be specified by itself in conjunction with the CD command. This changes to the root directory from any other directory. For example:

C>**CD ** (press **RETURN**)

Suppose you don't need to return to the root directory but want to move up one directory level. Here's how to do it.

C>**CD ..**

The two periods specify the parent directory of the current directory. For example, if you are currently in the Project #1 directory (see diagram), the above entry will take you to the AutoCAD directory.

You can go through several directory levels in one step. For instance, if you need to change to the SAMPLE directory (Sample Drawing files), you can do this in one step even if you are currently in the root directory. The path specification would look like this:

C>**CD \ACAD\SAMPLE** (press **RETURN**)

NOTE:

The backslash preceding ACAD is not necessary unless you are in a directory other than the root directory.

The above entry gives the path to the SAMPLE directory, which is contained in the ACAD directory. Note the backslash between the two directory names. This is mandatory when specifying paths such as this.

Here's an example of specifying a path with the COPY command:

C>**COPY \ACAD\SAMPLE\SHUTTLE.DWG A:** (press **RETURN**)

This will find SHUTTLE.DWG in the SAMPLE directory and will copy it to drive A.

Here's another example:

C>**COPY A:NEW.MNU \ACAD** (press **RETURN**)

This will copy NEW.MNU from drive A to the ACAD directory, which resides on drive C.

Here's one more example:

C>**COPY \ACAD\SAMPLE\ENGINE.DWG \ACAD\USER** (press **RETURN**)

This will find ENGINE.DWG in the SAMPLE directory and will copy it to the USER directory, which is contained in the ACAD directory.

DOS Command Prompt

Your computer can be configured to display the current directory at the DOS command prompt. This is recommended because it helps you monitor the current directory. DOS commands work the same whether the computer is configured this way.

If the current directory is the root directory, the DOS prompt may look like this:

C:\>

If the current directory is ACAD, the DOS prompt would look like this:

C:\ACAD>

If you are in a directory within ACAD, such as the SAMPLE directory, the prompt would look like this:

C:\ACAD\SAMPLE>

To configure the computer so the DOS prompt displays the current directory, enter **PROMPT=PG** at the DOS prompt. This entry can be made automatic by including it in an AUTOEXEC.BAT file. See the following appendix for details on how to create an AUTOEXEC.BAT file.

MD

The MD (Make Directory) command allows you to create new directories. While it works with floppy diskettes, the MD command is intended mainly for use with the hard disk. Quickly read through the following steps, including the hint, before you execute the steps.

1 If you are not in the root directory (or if you're not sure), enter **CD**.

2 Enter **MD WP**. (WP is short for word processor.)

You have just created a new directory named WP.

3 Enter **DIR**.

You should see the new WP directory.

4 Enter **CD WP**.

The current directory should now be WP. To prove it, . . .

5 . . . enter **DIR**.

Let's create a new directory inside the WP directory.

1 Enter **MD USER**.

2 Enter **DIR** to see if USER is present.

3 Enter **CD USER**.

The current directory should be USER.

4 Enter **CD ..** to move up to the WP directory.

5 Enter **DIR** to see if you are in fact in WP.

The new USER directory should appear as an item in WP.

RD

The RD (Remove Directory) command is as simple as the MD command.

1 If the current directory is not WP, change to the WP directory using the CD command.

2 Enter **RD USER**.

3 Enter **DIR** to see if the USER directory was removed from WP.

Let's also remove the WP directory.

4 Enter **CD ..** to move to WP's parent directory, which in this case is the root directory. This is necessary because you cannot remove a directory while it is the current directory.

5 Enter **RD WP**.

6 Enter **DIR**.

The WP directory should be gone.

Appendix D: Using Batch Files to Start AutoCAD

This appendix describes alternatives for loading AutoCAD and provides ideas for enhancing AutoCAD's performance.

____ NOTE: ____

Installation of the AutoCAD software should be complete prior to using this appendix. See the *AutoCAD Interface, Installation, and Performance Guide* for details on installing AutoCAD and for details on loading AutoCAD for optimum performance. When creating hard disk directories, see Appendix C for instructions.

Loading AutoCAD

1 Using the CD command, change to the directory containing the AutoCAD system files. (This directory is often named ACAD, but it may be named something else, such as R12.)

HINT: ____
See Appendix C if you do not know how to use the CD (Change Directory) command.

2 Type **ACAD386** to invoke the ACAD386.BAT batch file, and press **RETURN**.

AutoCAD should appear on the screen. See the following section titled "ACAD386.BAT File" for more information about this file.

Automatic Loading of AutoCAD

The contents of an AUTOEXEC.BAT file are executed step-by-step, automatically, when the computer is turned on or when it is restarted. Use of an AUTOEXEC.BAT file can, therefore, provide automatic loading of AutoCAD or other programs. Here is an example of a simple AUTOEXEC.BAT file.

```
DATE
TIME
PROMPT = $P$G
CD ACAD
ACAD386
```

If the computer contains a clock/calendar, the DATE and TIME can be omitted and substituted, if necessary, with the command required by the clock/calendar.

Here are the steps for creating an AUTOEXEC.BAT file with the above contents. Be sure you are in the root directory before you begin. Do not enter the following if an AUTOEXEC.BAT already exists.

1 At the DOS prompt (*e.g.,* C>), type **COPY CON:AUTOEXEC.BAT** and press **RETURN**. (Use upper or lower case letters.)

____ NOTE: ____

DOS treats upper and lower case letters identically. The examples here are in uppercase letters simply for readability and consistency.

2 Type **DATE** and press **RETURN**.

3 Type **TIME** and press **RETURN**.

4 Type **PROMPT = PG** and press **RETURN**.

5 Type **CD ACAD** and press **RETURN**.

6 Type **ACAD386** and press **RETURN**.

7 Press the **F6** function key and press **RETURN**.

The creation of the AUTOEXEC.BAT file is now complete.

8 Restart the computer system by pressing **CTRL ALT DEL** simultaneously, or turn the computer off and then on.

Expanded AUTOEXEC.BAT Files

Here is another example of an AUTOEXEC.BAT file. As you can see, it contains many more DOS functions and, consequently, is more powerful than the one described earlier. (Storing this file will erase the one you created previously.)

1 At the DOS prompt, enter **COPY CON:AUTOEXEC.BAT** and press **RETURN**.

Enter the following. Be sure to press **RETURN** after each line.

> **ECHO OFF**
> **DATE**
> **TIME**
> **PROMPT = PG**
> **PATH C:\;C:\DOS**
> **ECHO ON**
> **CLS**
> **DIR/W**
> **PAUSE: Press CTRL C to EXIT to DOS**
>   **root directory, or ...**
> **CD ACAD**
> **CLS**
> **ACAD386**

 Press the **F6** function key and **RETURN**.

 Test the file by entering **AUTOEXEC**. This activates the AUTOEXEC.BAT file the same as restarting the computer.

Let's examine closely the contents of the file.

"ECHO OFF" prevents the computer from echoing the text to the screen during the execution of AUTOEXEC.BAT. The functions following it, therefore, will be invisible to the user.

"PROMPT = PG" displays the current directory in the DOS prompt. For example, if the current directory is ACAD, the DOS prompt would look like this: C:\ACAD>. (See Appendix C, the section titled "DOS Command Prompt," for more information.)

"PATH C:\;C:\DOS" sets the default search path. This provides the computer with one or more directories to

search in case it cannot locate a file in the current directory. In the previous example, the computer will first search the current directory. Then it will look in the root directory and then in the DOS directory. Generally, you should keep the search path short. Otherwise, the computer will spend unnecessary search time.

"ECHO ON" allows the display of text on the screen. Thus, what follows in the batch file will display.

"CLS" clears the display screen.

"DIR/W" will automatically display the root directory on the screen in wide format.

"PAUSE" is a DOS subcommand that temporarily stops the computer. In other words, it suspends the system processing. It also displays the message "Strike a key when ready . . .". In this particular example, PAUSE is used not only to stop the computer, but also to display another message, "Press CTRL C to EXIT to DOS root directory, or . . .". If you choose to press CTRL C, the batch process terminates and you exit to the DOS root directory. Or, if you want to continue, you can strike a key when ready and the AUTOEXEC.BAT file continues.

"CD ACAD" is used to change to the ACAD directory.

"CLS" clears the screen once more.

"ACAD386" starts the AutoCAD batch file.

Batch Files

Your computer system can contain only one AUTOEXEC.BAT file. However, numerous other batch files (with a BAT file extension) can exist. Like AUTOEXEC.BAT, a batch file contains one or more commands that DOS executes one at a time. Batch files are ASCII text files and are created using the procedure described earlier. A text editor or word processer is recommended for creating lengthy batch files.

You may want to include the previously described functions in a batch file other than AUTOEXEC.BAT, particularly if you use the computer for applications other than AutoCAD.

ACAD386.BAT File

The batch file ACAD386.BAT ships with AutoCAD
Release 12. The file contains the following lines.

```
SET ACAD=C:\ACAD\SUPPORT;C:\ACAD\FONTS;C:\ACAD\ADS
SET ACADCFG=C:\ACAD
SET ACADDRV=C:\ACAD\DRV
C:\ACAD\ACAD %1 %2
```

Normally, you would use this file by entering "ACAD386"
to start AutoCAD, if the main AutoCAD directory is
named ACAD and is located in drive C's root directory. If
you choose to use another AutoCAD directory name, such
as R12, you need to edit the file contents as indicated
below.

```
SET ACAD=C:\R12\SUPPORT;C:\R12\FONTS;C:\R12\ADS
SET ACADCFG=C:\R12
SET ACADDRV=C:\R12\DRV
C:\R12\ACAD %1 %2
```

Furthermore, you could give the batch file a shorter
name, such as GO.BAT. Then you could execute the batch
file by entering GO.

The SET command contained in the ACAD386.BAT
file sets the search path for AutoCAD environment
variables ACAD, ACADDRV, and ACADCFG. The "SET
ACAD . . ." statement tells AutoCAD where to find the
support, font, and ADS files. "SET ACADCFG . . ." tells
AutoCAD where to find the hardware configuration files.
"SET ACADDRV . . ." enables AutoCAD to find the
protected-mode ADI drivers.

The "1%" and "2%" items allow parameters for drawing
and script files. For example, entering "ACAD386 CAR
BEGIN" would set the default drawing name to
CAR.DWG and would run a script named BEGIN.SCR.

CONFIG.SYS

When the computer is started, DOS automatically looks
for the CONFIG.SYS file. This is an ASCII text file which
contains important configuration parameters. If the file
does not exist, DOS assumes default values for the
configuration parameters.

There are parameters you can specify in this file that can
affect AutoCAD. To edit an existing CONFIG.SYS file,
use a word processor or text editor.

Let's use the COPY CON method for creating a new
CONFIG.SYS file. However, if this file already exists, do
not complete the following steps.

1 While in the root directory, type
COPY CON:CONFIG.SYS at the DOS prompt
and press **RETURN**.

2 Type **FILES = 40** and press **RETURN**.

3 Press the **F6** function key and press **RETURN**.

When you start the computer, DOS will automatically set
this parameter.

DOS limits the number of files a program can have open
at once. AutoCAD often needs to access several files
simultaneously, and it can sometimes exceed the DOS
limit on open files. Increasing the value of "files" in the
CONFIG.SYS file will increase the DOS open-files limit.
A value of 40 is recommended as a starting point.

Appendix E: Configuring AutoCAD

This appendix covers the procedure for configuring the AutoCAD software to work with different types of hardware components. For instance, if you want to change from using a mouse to using a digitizer, you must tell AutoCAD about the new device. Otherwise, the device will not work. Also, when you first install the AutoCAD software, you must step through the entire configuration procedure.

Configuring AutoCAD

1 Start AutoCAD.

2 Enter the **CONFIG** command or pick **Configure** from the **File** pull-down menu.

The current hardware configuration, if one exists, will appear.

3 If the following configuration menu is not present, press **RETURN** until it appears.

```
Configuration menu

    Ø.   Exit to drawing editor
    1.   Show current configuration
    2.   Allow detailed configuration

    3.   Configure video display
    4.   Configure digitizer
    5.   Configure plotter
    6.   Configure system console
    7.   Configure operating parameters

Enter selection <Ø>:
```

As you can see, this menu enables you to configure hardware and other operating parameters. Let's configure the input (pointing) device, such as a mouse or digitizer.

4 Enter **4** for "Configure digitizer."

If one is already configured, AutoCAD will ask whether you want to configure a different one.

5 Enter **Y** for "yes."

AutoCAD will display the list of options as shown below.

```
Available digitizers:

     1.    None
     2.    ADI digitizer (Real Mode)
     3.    Calcomp 2500 and 9100 Series ADI 4.2 - by Autodesk
     4.    GTCO Digi-Pad (Types 5 & 5A) <obsolete> ADI 4.2 - by Autodesk
     5.    Hitachi HICOMSCAN HDG Series ADI 4.2 - by Autodesk
     6.    Kurta IS/1, Series I <obsolete> ADI 4.2 - by Autodesk
     7.    Kurta XLC, Series II and III <obsolete>, IS/3 ADI 4.2 - by Autodesk
     8.    Logitech Logimouse ADI 4.2 - by Autodesk
     9.    Microsoft Mouse Driver ADI 4.2 - by Autodesk
    10.    Numonics 2200 <obsolete> ADI 4.2 - by Autodesk
    11.    Summagraphics MM Series v2.0, ADI 4.2 - by Autodesk
    12.    Summagraphics MicroGrid v1.0 (Series II or later) ADI 4.2 - by Autodesk

Select device number or ? to repeat list <9>:
```

6 Enter the number of the device you want to configure.

The remaining prompts are unique to the device you select. Answer them as best you can. If necessary, consult the *Interface, Installation, and Performance Guide* for details on specific hardware components supported by AutoCAD.

7 Complete the digitizer configuration until the "Configuration menu" reappears.

8 Enter **7** to configure the operating parameters.

The following options should appear.

9 Experiment with each option.

10 Enter **0** to exit to the configuration menu.

11 Experiment with the remaining options on your own.

12 Before exiting, check the current configuration by entering **1**.

13 If the current configuration is not correct, make the proper changes now.

14 Enter **0** to return to AutoCAD. Save your configuration changes *only* if you had intended to change them.

```
Configure operating parameters

     0.    Exit to configuration menu
     1.    Alarm on error
     2.    Initial drawing setup
     3.    Default plot file name
     4.    Plot spooler directory
     5.    Placement of temporary files
     6.    Network node name
     7.    Automatic-save feature
     8.    Full-time CRC validation
     9.    Automatic Audit after IGESIN, DXFIN, or DXBIN
    10.    Select Release 11 hidden line removal algorithm
    11.    Login name
    12.    Server authorization and file locking

Enter selection <0>:
```

Appendix F: AutoCAD Management Tips

The use and maintenance of CAD systems entail considerations not found in traditional methods of drafting, design, and engineering. For example, with CAD, disk files must be stored properly for subsequent revision and plotting, and backup files must be produced regularly. If considerations such as these are overlooked or not taken seriously, the CAD system may not meet your expectations. Files will get lost, drawings will have to be redrawn, and users will become frustrated.

Whether you are an AutoCAD user or manager, the following information will help you maintain organization while creating and using AutoCAD files. If the system is properly managed, you should seldom have to create the same drawing twice.

The implementation of the system is an evolving process and does not usually occur quickly. Therefore, refer back to this appendix as you become more familiar with AutoCAD.

Key Management Considerations

Listed here is a sampling of the questions you should ask yourself when installing and organizing AutoCAD. They are intended to help guide your thinking, from a management perspective, as you become familiar with the various components of AutoCAD.

• What hard disk directories must I create to accommodate the AutoCAD software?

• How can I best categorize the files so that each directory does not grow to more than 75 files total?

• If I plan to install three or more AutoCAD stations, should I centralize the storage of user-created files and plotting by using a network and file server?

After AutoCAD is in place and you are familiar with the system, you will create many new files. The following questions address the efficiency by which these files are created and stored.

• Are there prototype drawings (or existing drawings) on file that may serve as a starting point for my new drawing?

• Where should my drawing file be stored, what should it be named, and how can I and others easily locate it in the future?

• Are there predefined libraries of symbols and details that I can use while I develop my drawing?

• Is a custom screen, tablet, or icon menu available that would lend itself to my drawing application?

• Are AutoLISP® routines available that would help me perform certain drafting operations more easily?

• As I create the drawings, am I using time-saving techniques, such as freezing layers and using the QTEXT command?

If you feel uncomfortable about your answers to these questions, there is probably room for improvement. The following is provided to help you organize and manage your CAD system more effectively.

NOTE:

Generally, the following applies to all AutoCAD users and files. However, there are inevitable differences among users (backgrounds/interests), drawing applications, and the specific hardware and software which make up the system. Take these differences into consideration.

AutoCAD System Manager

One person (possibly two, but no more) in the organization should have the responsibility for managing the system and overseeing its use. This person should be the resident CAD authority and should answer questions and provide directions to other users of the system. The manager should oversee the components of the system, including software, documentation, and hardware. The manager should work with the AutoCAD users to establish procedural standards for use with the system.

Software/Documentation

FILE MANAGEMENT — Know where files are located and the purpose of each. Understand which ones are AutoCAD system files and which are not. Create a system for making backup files, and back up regularly. Emphasize this to all users. Delete "junk" files.

PROTOTYPE DRAWINGS — Create a simple system for the development, storage, and retrieval of AutoCAD prototype drawings. Allow for ongoing correction and development of each prototype drawing. Store the prototype drawings in a directory dedicated to prototype drawings so they are accessible by other users.

Document the contents of each prototype drawing by printing the drawing status information, layer listing, text styles, LTSCALE, status of the dimensioning variables and other relevant information. On the first page of this information, write the name of the prototype drawing, its location, sheet size, and plot scale. Keep this information in a three-ring binder (or similar holder) for future reference by other users.

USER DRAWING FILES — Store these in separate hard disk directories. (See the hard disk structure found in Appendix C.) When creating a drawing, place drawing components on the proper layers. Assign standard colors, linetypes, and line thicknesses to the standard layer names. Make a backup copy of the drawing and store it on a separate disk or tape backup system. Plot the drawings most likely to be used by others and store them in a three-ring binder or similar holder for future reference.

SYMBOL LIBRARIES — Develop a system for ongoing library development. (See Unit 30 for details on creating symbol libraries.) Make the libraries available to others and plot the symbol library drawing file. Place the library drawing on the wall near the system(s) or in a binder. Encourage users to contribute to the libraries.

MENU FILES — Develop, set up, and make available custom screen, tablet and icon menu files and tablet overlays. (See Units 50-52 and 59 for details on creating screen, tablet, and icon menus.) Store the menus in a directory dedicated to menus so they are accessible to others.

AUTOCAD UPGRADES — Handle the acquisition and installation of AutoCAD software upgrades. Inform users of the new features and changes contained in the new software. Coordinate upgrade training.

AUTOCAD THIRD-PARTY SOFTWARE — Handle the acquisition and installation of third-party software developed for specific application and utility purposes. Inform users of its availability and use.

Hardware

Oversee the use and maintenance of all hardware components which make up the system. Consider hardware upgrades as user and software requirements change.

Procedural Standards

Develop clear and practical standards within your organization to minimize inconsistency and confusion. For example, each prototype drawing should have a standard set of drawing layers, with a specific color and linetype dedicated to each layer. A layer called DIM could be reserved for all dimensions and could always be shown in the color 2 (yellow) with a continuous linetype. Then, when plotting, color 2 could be assigned to pen 2, which could be a 0.3-mm black pen. That way, whenever dimensions are on a drawing, they'll be yellow on the screen and will be plotted with a 0.3-mm black pen. Furthermore, assign a specific pen to each stall on your pen plotter and make this information available to others. This will avoid confusion and improve consistency in all plotting within your organization. Develop similar standards for other AutoCAD-related practices.

In summary, take seriously the management of your AutoCAD system. Set up subsystems so that users can contribute to the system's ongoing development. Encourage users to experiment and to be creative by making software and hardware available to them. Make a team effort out of learning, developing, and managing the AutoCAD system so that everyone can learn and benefit from its tremendous power and capability.

Appendix G: Paper-Scale-Limits Sample Relationships

	SHEET SIZE (X × Y)	Approximate DRAWING AREA (X × Y)	SCALE	UPPER RIGHT LIMIT (X,Y) (LOWER LEFT LIMIT IS 0,0)
ARCHITECT'S SCALE	A: 12″ × 9″	10″ × 8″	⅛″ = 1′	80′,64′
	B: 18″ × 12″	16″ × 11″	½″ = 1′	32′,22′
	C: 24″ × 18″	22″ × 16″	¼″ = 1′	88′,64′
	D: 36″ × 24″	34″ × 22″	3″ = 1′	11.3′,7.3′
	E: 48″ × 36″	46″ × 34″	1″ = 1′	46′,34′
CIVIL ENGINEER'S SCALE	A: 12″ × 9″	10″ × 8″	1″ = 200′	2000′,1600′
	B: 18″ × 12″	16″ × 11″	1″ = 50′	800′,550′
	C: 24″ × 18″	22″ × 16″	1″ = 10′	220′,160′
	D: 36″ × 24″	34″ × 22″	1″ = 300′	10,200′,6600′
	E: 48″ × 36″	46″ × 34″	1″ = 20′	920′,680′
MECHANICAL ENGINEER'S SCALE	A: 11″ × 8½″	9″ × 7″	1″ = 2″	18″,14″
	B: 17″ × 11″	15″ × 10″	2″ = 1″	7.5″,5″
	C: 22″ × 17″	20″ × 15″	1″ = 1″	20″,15″
	D: 34″ × 22″	32″ × 20″	1″ = 1.5″	48″,30″
	E: 44″ × 34″	42″ × 32″	3″ = 1″	14″,10.6″
METRIC SCALE	A: 279 mm × 216 mm (11″ × 8½″)	229 mm × 178 mm (9″ × 7″)	1 mm = 5 mm	1145, 890
	B: 432 mm × 279 mm (17″ × 11″)	381 mm × 254 mm (15″ × 10″)	1 mm = 20 mm	7620, 5080
	C: 55.9 cm × 43.2 cm (22″ × 17″)	50.8 cm × 38.1 cm (20″ × 15″)	1 cm = 10 cm	508, 381
	D: 86.4 cm × 55.9 cm (34″ × 22″)	81.3 cm × 50.8 cm (32″ × 20″)	2 cm = 1 cm	40.5, 25.5
	E: 111.8 cm × 86.4 cm (44″ × 34″)	106.7 cm × 81.3 cm (42″ × 32″)	1 cm = 2 cm	213, 163

NOTE: 1″ = 25.4 mm

Appendix H: Standard Text Fonts

AutoCAD is supplied with several text fonts. You can use the STYLE command to apply expansion, compression, or obliquing to any of these fonts, thereby tailoring the characters to your needs. (See Unit 20 for details about the STYLE command.) You can draw characters of any desired height using any of the fonts.

The fonts supplied with AutoCAD are the following:

TXT
This is the standard AutoCAD text font. It is very simple and will generate quickly on the screen.

MONOTXT
This is identical to the TXT font but is monospaced, whereas TXT is proportionally spaced.

ROMANS
This is a "simplex" roman font drawn by means of many short line segments. It produces smoother-looking characters than those of the TXT font but takes longer to generate on the screen.

ROMAND
This font is similar to the ROMANS font. Instead of single stroke, it uses a double stroke technique to produce darker, thicker characters.

ROMANC
Complex roman font using double stroke and serifs

ROMANT
Triplex roman font using triple stroke and serifs

ITALLICC
Complex intalic font using double stroke and serifs

ITALICT
Triplex italic font using triple stroke and serifs

SCRIPTS
Single stroke, simplex script font

SCRIPTC
Double stroke complex script font

GREEKS
Single stroke, simplex Greek font using sans serif

GREEKC
Double stroke, complex Greek font with serifs

GOTHICE
Gothic English font

GOTHICG
Gothic German font

GOTHICI
Gothic Italian font

CYRILLIC
Cyrillic—alphabetical

CYRILTLC
Cyrillic—transliteration

SYASTRO
Astronomical symbols

SYMAP
Mapping symbols

SYMATH
Mathematical symbols

SYMETEO
Meterological symbols

SYMUSIC
Music symbols

Samples of 22 fonts are shown in this appendix. With the exception of MONOTXT, each font's characters are proportionally spaced. Hence, the space needed for the letter "i" is narrower than that for the letter "m."

Each font resides in a separate disk file with a name such as TXT.SHX. This is the "compiled" form of the font, for direct use by AutoCAD. Another file, with a name such as TXT.SHP, is supplied as well for some of the fonts. This file type contains the symbolic description of the font's characters and is not normally needed by AutoCAD. The ".SHP" files are provided as examples for those users who might want to define their own text fonts. If you wish to do this, see Chapter 5 of the *AutoCAD Customization Manual*.

!"#$%&'()*+,-./01234567
89:;<=>?@ABCDEFGHIJKLMNO
PQRSTUVWXYZ[\]^_'abcdefg
hijklmnopqrstuvwxyz{|}~°±ø

TXT font

! "#$%&'()*+,-./01234567
89:;<=>?@ABCDEFGHIJKLMNO
PQRSTUVWXYZ[\]^_'abcdefg
hijklmnopqrstuvwxyz{|}~°±ø

MONOTXT font

!"#$%&'()*+,-./01234567
89:;<=>?@ABCDEFGHIJKLMNO
PQRSTUVWXYZ[\]^_'abcdefg
hijklmnopqrstuvwxyz{|}~°±ø

ROMANS font

!"#$%&'()*+,-./01234567
89:;<=>?@ABCDEFGHIJKLMNO
PQRSTUVWXYZ[\]^_'abcdefg
hijklmnopqrstuvwxyz{|}~°±ø

ROMAND font

!"#$%&'()*+,-./01234567
89:;<=>?@ABCDEFGHIJKLMNO
PQRSTUVWXYZ[\]^_'abcdefg
hijklmnopqrstuvwxyz{|}~°±ø

ROMANC font

!"#$%&'()*+,-./01234567
89:;<=>?@ABCDEFGHIJKLMNO
PQRSTUVWXYZ[\]^_'abcdefg
hijklmnopqrstuvwxyz{|}~°±ø

ROMANT font

!"#$%&'()*+,-./01234567
89:;<=>?@ABCDEFGHIJKLMNO
PQRSTUVWXYZ[\]^_'abcdefg
hijklmnopqrstuvwxyz{|}~°±ø

ITALICC font

!"#$%&'()*+,-./01234567
89:;<=>?@ABCDEFGHIJKLMNO
PQRSTUVWXYZ[\]^_'abcdefg
hijklmnopqrstuvwxyz{|}~°±ø

ITALICT font

!"#$%&'()*+,-./01234567
89:;<=>?@ABCDEFGHIJKLMNO
PQRSTUVWXYZ[\]^_'abcdefg
hijklmnopqrstuvwxyz{|}~°±ø

SCRIPTS font

!"#$%&'()*+,-./01234567
89:;<=>?@ABCDEFGHIJKLMNO
PQRSTUVWXYZ[\]^_'abcdefg
hijklmnopqrstuvwxyz{|}~°±ø

SCRIPTC font

!"#$%&'()*+,-./01234567
89:;<=>?@ABXΔEΦΓHIϑKΛMNO
ΠΘΡΣΤΥΩΞΨZ[\]^_'αβχδεφγ
ηιδκλμνοπϑρστυ∈ωξψζ{|}~°±ø

GREEKS font

!"#$%&'()*+,-./01234567
89:;<=>?@ABXΔEΦΓHIϑKΛMNO
ΠΘΡΣΤΥΩΞΨZ[\]^_'αβχδεφγ
ηιδκλμνοπϑρστυ∈ωξψζ{|}~°±ø

GREEKC font

!"#$%&'()*+,-./01234567
89:;<=>?@ABCDEFGHIJKLMNO
PQRSTUVWXYZ[\]^_'abcdefg
hijklmnopqrstuvwxyz{|}~˙±∅

GOTHICE font

!"#$%&'()*+,-./01234567
89:;<=>?@ABCDEFGHIJKLMNO
PQRSTUVWXYZ[\]^_'abcdefg
hijklmnopqrstuvwxyz{|}~˙±∅

GOTHICG font

!"#$%&'()*+,-./01234567
89:;<=>?@ABCDEFGHIJKLMNO
PQRSTUVWXYZ[\]^_'abcdefg
hijklmnopqrstuvwxyz{|}~˙±∅

GOTHICI font

!"#$%&'()*+,-./01234567
89:;ю=я?@АБВГДЕЖЗИЙКЛМНО
ПРСТУФХЦЧШЩЪЫЬЭЮЯабвгдеж
зийклмнопрстуфхцчшщъыьэ˙±∅

CYRILLIC font

!"#$%&'()*+,-./01234567
89:;ю=я?@АБЧДЕФГХИЩКЛМНО
ПЦРСТУВШЖЙЗЬЫЪЮЭЯабчдефг
хищклмнопцрстувшжйзьыьэ˙±∅

CYRILTLC font

!"#$%&'()*+,-./01234567
89:;<=>?@☉♀♁⊕♂♃♄♅Ψ♆☽⚸⚹♈♉
♊♋♌♍♎♏♐♑♒♓⚳⚴≈[\]^_'⚶"∪⊃
∈→↑←↓∂∇~˙`⚵§†‡∃ℒ®©{|}~˙±∅

SYASTRO font

!"#$%&'()*+,-./01234567
89:;<=>?@

SYMAP font

!"#$%&'()*+,-./01234567
89:;<=>?@ℵ'∥|±∓×·÷=≠≡<>≦
≧∝~√∪⊃∩∈→↑[\]^_'←↓∂∇√∫∮
∞§†‡∋ΠΣ()[]{}⟨⟩√√≈≅{|}~˙±∅

SYMATH font

!"#$%&'()*+,-./01234567
89:;<=>?@

SYMETEO font

!"#$%&'()*+,-./01234567
89:;<=>?@

SYMUSIC font

Appendix I: Standard Hatch Patterns

Shown here are the standard hatch patterns supplied in the file ACAD.PAT.

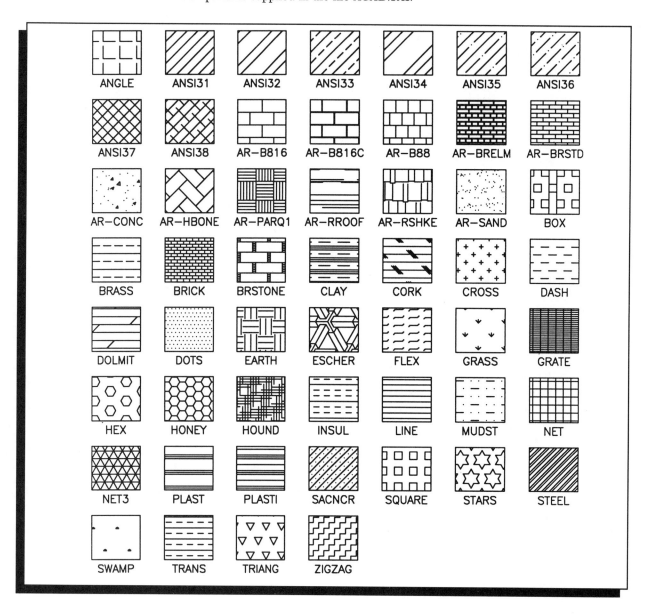

Appendix J: AutoCAD Command Glossary

Brief descriptions of all AutoCAD commands are listed here. For the locations of more detailed descriptions and instructions on how they are applied, refer to the index.

Some commands can be used transparently (that is, used while another command is in progress) by preceding the command name with an apostrophe. Such commands are listed here with an apostrophe.

'ABOUT
Purpose
Displays a dialogue box with the AutoCAD version and serial numbers, and a scrolling window with the text of the ACAD.MSG file and other information.

'APERTURE
Purpose
Controls the size of the object snap target box.

ARC
Purpose
Draws an arc of any size.
Options

A	Included angle
C	Center point
D	Starting direction
E	Endpoint
L	Length of chord
R	Radius
RETURN	(as reply to Start point) sets start point and direction as end of last Line or Arc

AREA
Purpose
Computes the area of a polygon, polyline, or circle.
Options

A	Sets Add mode
S	Sets Subtract mode
E	Computes area of a selected circle or polyline

ARRAY
Purpose
Makes multiple copies of selected objects in a rectangular or circular pattern.
Options

P	Polar (circular) array
R	Rectangular array

ATTDEF
Purpose
Creates an Attribute Definition entity for textual information to be associated with a Block Definition.
Options

I	Controls Attribute visibility
C	Controls constant/variable mode
V	Controls verify mode
P	Controls preset mode

'ATTDISP
Purpose
Controls the visibility of Attribute entities on a global basis.
Options

ON	Makes all Attributes visible
OFF	Makes all Attributes invisible
N	Normal: visibility set individually

ATTEDIT
Purpose
Permits editing of Attributes.

ATTEXT
Purpose
Extracts Attribute data from a drawing.
Options

C	CDF comma-delimited format extract
D	DXF format extract
S	SDF format extract
E	Extracts attributes from selected entities

AUDIT
Purpose
Invokes drawing integrity audit.
Options

Y	Fixes errors encountered
N	Reports, but does not fix, errors encountered

'BASE
Purpose
Specifies origin for subsequent insertion into another drawing.

BHATCH
Purpose
Fills an automatically defined boundary with a hatch pattern through the use of dialogue boxes; allows previewing and repeated adjustments without starting over each time.

'BLIPMODE

Purpose
Controls display of marker blips for point selection.
Options
ON   Enables temporary marker blips
OFF   Disables temporary marker blips

BLOCK

Purpose
Forms a compound object from a group of entities.
Option
?   Lists specified names of defined Blocks

BPOLY

Purpose
Creates a Polyline of a closed boundary.

BREAK

Purpose
Erases part of an object, or splits it into two objects.
Option
F   Respecifies first point

CHAMFER

Purpose
Creates a chamfer at the intersection of two lines.
Options
D   Sets chamfer distances
P   Chamfers an entire Polyline

CHANGE

Purpose
Alters the location, size, orientation, or other properties of selected objects.
Options
P   Changes common properties of objects
C   Color
E   Elevation
LA   Layer
LT   Linetype
T   Thickness

CHPROP

Purpose
Modifies properties of selection objects.
Options
C   Color
LA   Layer
LT   Linetype
T   Thickness

CIRCLE

Purpose
Draws a circle of any size.
Options
2P   Specifies by 2 endpoints of diameter
3P   Specifies by 3 points on circumference
D   Enters diameter instead of radius
R   Enters radius (default)
TTR   Specifies by two tangent points and radius

'COLOR

Purpose
Establishes the color for subsequently drawn objects.
Options
number   Sets entity color number
name   Sets entity color to standard color name
BYBLOCK   Sets floating entity color
BYLAYER   Uses layer's color for entities

COMPILE

Purpose
Compiles shape and font files.

CONFIG

Purpose
Displays options in the text window to reconfigure the video display, digitizer, plotter, and operating parameters.

COPY

Purpose
Draws a copy of selected objects.
Option
M   Makes multiple copies of the selected objects

DBLIST

Purpose
Lists database information for every entity in the drawing.

DDATTDEF

Purpose
Displays a dialogue box that creates an Attribute Definition entity for textual information to be associated with a Block Definition.

DDATTE

Purpose
Allows Attribute editing via a dialogue box.

DDATTEXT

Purpose
Displays a dialogue box that extracts data from a drawing. Available formats are DXF, CDF, SDF, or selected entities.

DDCHPROP

Purpose

Displays a dialogue box that modifies the color, layer, linetype, and thickness of selected objects.

DDEDIT

Purpose

Allows Text and Attribute Definition editing via a dialogue box.

'DDEMODES

Purpose

Sets entity properties (current layer, linetype, elevation, thickness, and text style) via a dialogue box.

'DDGRIPS

Purpose

Allows you to enable grips and set their colors and size via a dialogue box.

'DDIM

Purpose

Controls dimensioning through a series of dialogue boxes.

DDINSERT

Purpose

Displays a dialogue box that inserts a copy of a previously drawn part or a drawing file into a drawing, and lets you set an insertion point, scale, rotate, or explode the part.

'DDLMODES

Purpose

Sets layer properties (New, Current, Rename, On/Off, Thaw/Freeze, Unlock/Lock, Current Viewport, New Viewport, Color, Linetype, Filters) via a dialogue box.

'DDOSNAP

Purpose

Displays a dialogue box for setting running osnaps for the Endpoint, Midpoint, Center, Node, Quadrant, Intersection, Insertion, Tangent, Nearest, and Quick object snap modes; lets you set the size of the cross-hair target box aperture.

'DDRMODES

Purpose

Sets drawing aids via a dialogue box.

DDRENAME

Purpose

Displays a dialogue box that renames text styles, layers, linetypes, Blocks, views, User Coordinate Systems, viewport configurations, and dimension styles.

'DDSELECT

Purpose

Displays a dialogue box that sets entity selection modes, the size of the pickbox, and the entity sort method.

DDUCS

Purpose

Displays a dialogue box for control of the current User Coordinate System in the current space.

'DDUNITS

Purpose

Displays a dialogue box that sets coordinate and angle display formats and precision.

'DELAY

Purpose

Delays execution of the next command for a specified time. (Used with command scripts.)

DIM

Purpose

Invokes Dimensioning mode, permitting many dimension notations to be added to a drawing.

DIM1

Purpose

Allows one dimension notation to be added to a drawing, then returns to normal Command mode.

'DIST

Purpose

Finds distance between two points.

DIVIDE

Purpose

Places markers along a selected object, dividing it into a specified number of equal parts.

Option

B   Uses specified Block as marker

DOUGHNUT (or DONUT)

Purpose

Draws rings with specified inside and outside diameters.

'DRAGMODE

Purpose

Allows control of the dynamic specification (dragging) feature for all appropriate commands.

Options

ON   Honors "DRAG" requests when applicable

OFF   Ignores "DRAG" requests

A   Sets "Auto" mode: drags whenever possible

DTEXT

Purpose

Draws text items dynamically.

Options

See TEXT command for options

DVIEW

Purpose

Defines parallel or visual perspective views dyamically.

Options

CA	Selects the camera angle relative to the target; see below for suboption
CL	Sets front and back clipping planes
D	Sets camera-to-target distance, turns on perspective
H	Removes hidden lines on the selection set
OFF	Turns perspective off
PA	Pans drawing across the screen
PO	Specifies the camera and target points
TA	Rotates the target point around the camera; see below for suboption
TW	Twists the view around your line of sight
U	Undoes a DVIEW subcommand
X	Exits the DVIEW command

Camera and Target Suboption

T	Toggles angle options between X-Y plane and X-Y plane from X axis

DXBIN

Purpose

Inserts specially coded binary files into a drawing.

DXFIN

Purpose

Loads a drawing interchange file.

DXFOUT

Purpose

Writes a drawing interchange file.

Options

B	Writes binary DXF file
E	Outputs selected entities only
(0-16)	Floating point precision

EDGESURF

Purpose

Constructs a 3D polygon mesh approximating a Coons surface patch (a bicubic surface interpolated between four adjoining edges).

ELEV

Purpose

Sets elevation and extrusion thickness for subsequently drawn entities. (Used in 3D visualizations.)

ELLIPSE

Purpose

Draws ellipses using any of several specifications.

Options

C	Specifies center point rather than first axis endpoint
R	Specifies eccentricity via rotation rather than second axis
I	Draws isometric circle in current isoplane

END

Purpose

Exits AutoCAD after saving the drawing.

ERASE

Purpose

Erases entities from the drawing.

EXPLODE

Purpose

Shatters a Block or Polyline into its constituent parts.

EXTEND

Purpose

Lengthens a Line, Arc, or Polyline to meet another object.

Option

U	Undoes last extension

'FILES

Purpose

Displays a dialogue box that performs disk file-utility tasks.

'FILL

Purpose

Controls whether Solids, Traces, and wide Polylines are automatically filled on the screen and the plot output.

Options

ON	Solids, Traces, and wide Polylines filled
OFF	Solids, Traces, and wide Polylines outlined

FILLET

Purpose

Constructs an arc of specified radius between two lines, arcs, or circles.

Options

P	Fillets an entire Polyline
R	Sets fillet radius

FILMROLL

Purpose

Generates a file for rendering by AutoShade.

'GRAPHSCR

Purpose

Flips to the graphics display on single-screen systems. Used in command scripts and menus.

'GRID

Purpose

Displays a grid of dots, at desired spacing, on the screen.

Options

ON	Turns grid on
OFF	Turns grid off
S	Locks grid spacing to Snap resolution
A	Sets grid aspect (differing X-Y spacings)
number	Sets grid spacing (0 = use snap spacing)
numberX	Sets spacing to multiple of snap spacing

HANDLES

Purpose

Assigns a unique, permanent number to each entity in a drawing.

Options

| ON | Assigns handles to all entities and sets system variable HANDLES to 1 |
| DESTROY | Discards all entity handles |

HATCH

Purpose

Performs cross-hatching and pattern-filling

Options

name	Uses hatch pattern name from library file
*name	Hatch pattern is made up of individual line entities, and is not a Block
U	Uses simple user-defined hatch pattern
?	Lists selected names of available hatch patterns

"NAME" AND "U" can be followed by a comma and a hatch style from the following list:

I	Ignores internal structure
N	Normal style: turns hatch lines off and on when internal structure is encountered
O	Hatches outermost portion only

'HELP (or '?)

Purpose

Displays a list of valid commands and data entry options or obtains help for a specific command or prompt.

HIDE

Purpose

Regenerates a 3D visualization with hidden lines removed.

'ID

Purpose

Displays the coordinates of a specified point.

IGESIN

Purpose

Loads an IGES interchange file.

IGESOUT

Purpose

Writes an IGES interchange file.

INSERT

Purpose

Inserts a copy of a previously drawn part (object) into the current drawing.

Options

fname	Loads "fname" as a Block
fname=f	Creates Block "fname" from file "f"
*name	Retains individual part entities
C	(As reply to X scale prompt) specifies scale via two points (Corner specification of scale)
XYZ	(As reply to X scale prompt) readies Insert for X, Y, and Z scales
~	Displays a File dialogue box
?	Lists names of defined Blocks

'ISOPLANE

Purpose

Selects the plane of an isometric grid to be the current plane for an orthogonal drawing.

Options

L	Left plane
R	Right plane
T	Top plane
RETURN	Toggle to next plane

'LAYER

Purpose

Creates named drawing layers and assigns color and linetype properties to those layers.

Options

C a	Sets specified layers to color "a"
F a,b	Freezes layers "a" and "b"
L t	Sets specified layers to linetype "t"
LO a	Locks layer "a"
M a	Makes layer "a" the current layer, creating it if necessary
N a,b	Creates new layers "a" and "b"
ON a,b	Turns on layers "a" and "b"
OFF a,b	Turns off layers "a" and "b"
S a	Sets current layer to existing layer "a"
T a,b	Thaws layers "a" and "b"
?	Lists specified layers and their associated colors, linetypes, and visibility
U a	Unlocks layer "a"

'LIMITS

Purpose
Changes the drawing boundaries and controls checking of those boundaries for the current space.
Options

2 points	Sets lower-left/upper-right drawing limits
ON	Enables limits checking
OFF	Disables limits checking

LINE

Purpose
Draws straight lines of any length.
Options

RETURN	(As reply to "From point:") starts at end of previous Line or Arc
C	(As reply to "To point:") closes polygon
U	(As reply to "To point:") undoes segment

'LINETYPE

Purpose
Defines linetypes (sequences of alternating line segments and spaces), loads them from libraries, and sets the linetypes for subsequently drawn objects.
Options

?	Lists a linetype library
C	Creates a linetype definition
L	Loads a linetype definition
S	Sets current entity linetype

Set Suboptions:

name	Sets entity linetype by name
BYBLOCK	Sets floating entity linetype
BYLAYER	Uses layer's linetype for entities
?	Lists specified loaded linetypes

LIST

Purpose
Lists database information for selected objects.

LOAD

Purpose
Loads a file of user-defined Shapes to be used with the Shape command.
Option

?	Lists the names of loaded Shape files

'LTSCALE

Purpose
Sets scale factor to be applied to all linetypes within the drawing.

MEASURE

Purpose
Places markers at specified intervals along a selected object.
Option

B	Uses specified Block as marker

MENU

Purpose
Loads a file of commands into the menu areas (screen, pull-down, tablet, and button).

MINSERT

Purpose
Inserts multiple copies of a Block in a rectangular pattern.
Options

fname	Loads "fname" and forms a rectangular array of the resulting Block
fname = f	Creates Block "fname" from file "f" and forms a rectangular array
?	Lists names of defined Blocks
C	(As reply to X scale prompt) specifies scale via two points (Corner specification of scale)
XYZ	(As reply to X scale prompt) readies MINSERT for X, Y, and Z scales
-	Displays a File dialogue box

MIRROR

Purpose
Reflects designated entities about a user-specified axis.

MOVE

Purpose
Moves designated entities to another location.

MOVE

Purpose
Moves designated entities to another location.

MSLIDE

Purpose
Makes a slide file from the current display.

MSPACE

Purpose
Switches to model space.

MULTIPLE

Purpose
Causes the next command to repeat until canceled.

MVIEW
Purpose
Creates and controls viewports.
Options

ON	Turns selected viewport(s) on; causes model to be regenerated in the selected viewport(s)
OFF	Turns selected viewport(s) off; causes model not to be displayed in the selected viewport(s)
Hideplot	Causes hidden lines to be removed in selected viewport(s) during paper space plotting
Fit	Creates a single viewport to fit the current paper space view
2	Creates two viewports in specified area or fit to the current paper space view (see below for suboptions)
3	Creates three viewports in specified area or fit to the current paper space view (see below for suboptions)
4	Creates four equal viewports in specified area or fit to the current paper space view
Restore	Translates viewport configurations saved with the VPORTS command into individual viewport entities in paper space
<point>	Creates a new viewport within the area specified by two points

Suboptions for "2"

Horizontal	Creates a horizontal division between two new viewports
Vertical	Creates a vertical division between two new viewports (default selection)

Suboptions for "3"

Above	Specifies placement of larger viewport above the other two
Below	Specifies placement of larger viewport below the other two
Horizontal	Splits area into thirds based on a horizontal division
Left	Specifies placement of larger viewport to the left of the other two
Right	Specifies placement of larger viewport to the right of the other two
Vertical	Splits the area into thirds based on a vertical division

NEW
Purpose
Creates a new drawing.

OFFSET
Purpose
Allows the creation of offset curves and parallel lines.
Options

number	Specifies offset distance
T	Through: allows specification of a point through which the offset curve is to pass

OOPS
Purpose
Restores erased entities.

OPEN
Purpose
Opens an existing drawing.

'ORTHO
Purpose
Constrains drawings so that only lines aligned with the grid can be entered.
Options

ON	Forces lines to horizontal or vertical
OFF	Does not constrain lines

'OSNAP
Purpose
Enables points to be precisely located on reference points of existing objects.
Options

CEN	Center of Arc or Circle
END	Closest endpoint of Arc or Line
INS	Insertion point of Text/Block/Shape
INT	Intersection of Line/Arc/Circle
MID	Midpoint of Arc or Line
NEA	Nearest point of Arc/Circle/Line/Point
NOD	Node (point)
NON	None (off)
PER	Perpendicular to Arc/Line/Circle
QUA	Quadrant point of Arc or Circle
QUI	Quick mode (first find, not closest)
TAN	Tangent to Arc or Circle

'PAN
Purpose
Moves the display window.

PEDIT

Purpose

Permits editing of 2D polylines.

Options

C	Closes an open Polyline
D	Decurves, or returns a spline curve to its control frame
E	Edits vertices (see below for suboptions)
F	Fits curve to Polyline
J	Joins to Polyline
L	Toggles linetype generation to be either a continuous pattern at vertices, or with dashes generated at the start and end of vertices
O	Opens a closed Polyline
S	Uses the polyline vertices as the frame for a spline curve (type set by SPLINETYPE)
U	Undoes one editing operation
W	Sets uniform width for Polyline
X	Exits PEDIT command

Suboptions for "E"

B	Sets first vertex for Break
G	Go (performs Break or Straighten operation)
I	Inserts new vertex after current one
M	Moves current vertex
N	Makes next vertex current
P	Makes previous vertex current
R	Regenerates the Polyline
S	Sets first vertex for Straighten
T	Sets tangent direction for current vertex
W	Sets new width for following segment
X	Exits vertex editing, or cancels Break/Straighten

PEDIT (3D)

Purpose

Permits editing of 3D polylines.

Options

C	Closes an open Polyline
D	Decurves, or returns a spline curve to its control frame
E	Edits vertices (see below for suboptions)
O	Opens a closed Polyline
S	Uses the polyline vertices as the frame for a spline curve (type set by SPLINETYPE)
U	Undoes one editing operation
X	Exits PEDIT command

Suboptions for "E"

B	Sets first vertex for Break
G	Go (performs Break or Straighten operation)
I	Inserts new vertex after current one
M	Moves current vertex

N	Makes next vertex current
P	Makes previous vertex current
R	Regenerates the Polyline
S	Sets first vertex for Straighten
X	Exits vertex editing, or cancels Break/Straighten

PEDIT (Mesh)

Purpose

Permits editing of 3D polygon meshes.

Options

D	Desmooth—restores original mesh
E	Edits mesh vertices (see below for suboptions)
M	Opens (or closes) the mesh in the "M" direction
N	Opens (or closes) the mesh in the "N" direction
S	Fits a smooth surface as defined by SURFTYPE
U	Undoes one editing operation
X	Exits PEDIT command

Suboptions for "E"

D	Moves down to previous vertext in "M" direction
L	Moves left to previous vertex in "N" direction
M	Repositions marked vertex
N	Moves to next vertex
P	Moves to previous vertex
R	Moves right to next vertex in "N" direction
RE	Redisplays the polygon mesh
U	Moves up to next vertext in "M" direction
X	Exits vertex editing

PFACE

Purpose

Creates a 3D mesh of arbitrary complexity and surface characteristics.

PLAN

Purpose

Puts the display in Plan view (Vpoint 0,0,1) relative to either the current USC, a specified UCS, or the World Coordinate System.

Options

C	Establishes a plan view of the current UCS
U	Establishes a plan view of the specified UCS
W	Establishes a plan view of the World Coordinate System

PLINE
Purpose
Draws two-dimensional polylines.
Options
H	Sets new half-width
U	Undoes previous segment
RETURN	Exits PLINE command

In line mode:
A	Switches to arc mode
C	Closes with straight segment
L	Segment length (continues previous segment)

In arc mode:
A	Included angle
CE	Center point
CL	Closes with arc segment
D	Starting direction
L	Chord length, or switches to line mode
R	Radius
S	Second point of three-point arc

PLOT
Purpose
Plots a drawing to a plotting device or a file. (The CMDDIA system variable controls whether you use the dialogue boxes or the command line to plot.)

POINT
Purpose
Draws single points.

POLYGON
Purpose
Draws regular polygons with the specified number of sides.
Options
E	Specifies polygon by showing one edge
C	Circumscribes around circle
I	Inscribes within circle

PSDRAG
Purpose
Controls the appearance of an imported PostScript image that is being dragged into place by the PSIN command.
Options
0	Only the image's bounding box is displayed as you drag it into place
1	The rendered PostScript image is displayed as you drag it into place

PSFILL
Purpose
Fills 2D Polyline outlines with PostScript fill patterns defined in the AutoCAD PostScript support file (ACAD.PSF).

PSIN
Purpose
Imports Encapsulated PostScript (EPS) files.

PSOUT
Purpose
Exports the current view of your drawing to an Encapsulated PostScript (EPS) file.

PSPACE
Purpose
Switches to paper space.

PURGE
Purpose
Removes unused Blocks, text styles, layers, linetypes, and dimension styles from the drawing.
Options
A	Purges all unused named objects
B	Purges unused Blocks
D	Purges unused dimstyles
LA	Purges unused layers
LT	Purges unused linetypes
SH	Purges unused shape files
ST	Purges unused text styles

QSAVE
Purpose
Saves the drawing without requesting a filename.

QTEXT
Purpose
Enables Text entities to be identified without drawing the text detail.
Options
ON	Quick text mode on
OFF	Quick text mode off

QUIT
Purpose
Exits AutoCAD.

RECOVER
Purpose
Attempts to recover damaged or corrupted drawings.

REDEFINE
Purpose
Restores a built-in command deleted by UNDEFINE.

REDO
Purpose
Reverses the previous command if the previous command was U or UNDO.

'REDRAW
Purpose
Refreshes or cleans up the current viewport.

'REDRAWALL
Purpose
Redraws all viewports.

REGEN
Purpose
Regenerates the current viewport.

REGENALL
Purpose
Regenerates all viewports.

'REGENAUTO
Purpose
Controls automatic regeneration performed by other commands.
Options
ON   Allows automatic regens
OFF   Prevents automatic regens

REINIT
Purpose
Allows the I/O ports, digitizer, display, plotter, and PGP file to be reinitialized.

RENAME
Purpose
Changes the name associated with text styles, layers, linetypes, Blocks, views, User Coordinate Systems, viewport configurations, and dimension styles.
Options

B	Renames Block
D	Renames dimension style
LA	Renames layer
LT	Renames linetype
S	Renames text style
U	Renames UCS
VI	Renames view
VP	Renames viewport configuration

'RESUME
Purpose
Resumes an interrupted command script.

REVSURF
Purpose
Creates a 3D polygon mesh approximating a surface of revolution, by rotating a curve around a selected axis.

ROTATE
Purpose
Rotates existing objects.
Option
R   Rotates with respect to reference angle

RSCRIPT
Purpose
Restarts a command script from the beginning.

RULESURF
Purpose
Creates a 3D polygon mesh approximating a ruled surface between two curves.

SAVE
Purpose
Requests a filename and saves the drawing.

SAVEAS
Purpose
Same as SAVE, but also renames the current drawing.

SCALE
Purpose
Alters the size of existing objects.
Option
R   Resizes with respect to reference size

'SCRIPT
Purpose
Executes a command script.

SELECT
Purpose
Groups objects into a selection set for use in subsequent commands.

'SETVAR
Purpose
Allows you to display or change the value of system variables.
Option
?   Lists specified system variables

SH
Purpose
Allows access to internal operating-system commands.

SHADE
Purpose
Shades model in the current viewport.

SHAPE
Purpose
Draws predefined shapes.
Option
?   Lists available Shape names

SHELL
Purpose
Allows access to other programs while running AutoCAD.

SKETCH

Purpose

Permits freehand sketching.

Options

C	Connect: restarts SKETCH at endpoint
E	Erases (backs up over) temporary lines
P	Raises/lowers sketching pen
Q	Discards temporary lines, exits SKETCH
R	Records temporary lines, remains in SKETCH
X	Records temporary lines, exits SKETCH
.	Draws line to current point

'SNAP

Purpose

Specifies a round-off interval for digitizer point entry so that entities can be placed at precise locations easily.

Options

number	Sets snap alignment resolution
ON	Aligns designated points
OFF	Does not align designated points
A	Sets aspect (differing X-Y spacings)
R	Rotates snap grid
S	Selects style

Suboptions for "S"

Standard	Sets snap with the regular rectangular type of grid
Isometric	Sets snap to assist in creating two-dimensional drawings that represent 3D objects

SOLID

Purpose

Draws filled-in polygons.

'STATUS

Purpose

Displays drawing statistics and modes.

STRETCH

Purpose

Allows you to move a portion of a drawing while retaining connections to other parts of the drawing.

'STYLE

Purpose

Creates named text styles, with user-selected combinations of font, mirroring, obliquing, and horizontal scaling.

Option

?	Lists specified currently defined text styles

TABLET

Purpose

Aligns the digitizing tablet with coordinates of a paper drawing to copy it accurately with AutoCAD.

Options

ON	Turns Tablet mode on
OFF	Turns Tablet mode off
CAL	Calibrates tablet for use in the current space
CFG	Configures tablet menus, point area

TABSURF

Purpose

Creates a polygon mesh approximating a general tabulated surface defined by a path and a direction vector.

TEXT

Purpose

Draws text characters of any size, with selected styles.

Options

J	Prompts for justification options
S	Lists or selects text style
A	Aligns text between two points, with style-specified width factor; AutoCAD computes appropriate height
C	Centers text horizontally
F	Fits text between two points, with specified height; AutoCAD computes an appropriate width factor
M	Centers text horizontally and vertically
R	Right-justifies text
BL	Bottom Left
BC	Bottom Center
BR	Bottom Right
ML	Middle Left
MC	Middle Center
MR	Middle Right
TL	Top Left
TC	Top Center
TR	Top Right

'TEXTSCR

Purpose

Flips to the text display on single-screen systems. Used in command scripts and menus.

'TIME

Purpose

Displays drawing creation and update times, and permits control of an elapsed timer.

Options

D	Displays current times
ON	Starts user elapsed timer
OFF	Stops user elapsed timer
R	Resets user elapsed timer

TRACE
Purpose
Draws solid lines of specified width.

TREESTAT
Purpose
Displays information on the drawing's current spatial index, such as number and depth of nodes in the drawing's database. (Use with the TREEDEPTH system variable setting to fine-tune performance for large drawings.)

TRIM
Purpose
Erases the portions of selected entities that cross a specified boundary.
Option

U	Undoes last trim operation

U
Purpose
Reverses the effect of the previous command.

UCS
Purpose
Defines or modifies the current User Coordinate System.
Options

D	Deletes one or more saved coordinate systems
E	Sets a UCS with the same extrusion direction as that of the selected entity
O	Shifts the origin of the current coordinate system
P	Restores the previous UCS
R	Restores a previously saved UCS
S	Saves the current UCS
V	Establishes a new UCS whose Z axis is parallel to the current viewing direction
W	Sets the current UCS equal to the World Coordinate System
X	Rotates the current UCS around the X axis
Y	Rotates the current UCS around the Y axis
Z	Rotates the current UCS around the Z axis
AZ	Defines a UCS using an origin point and a point on the positive portion of the Z axis
3	Defines a UCS using an origin point, a point on the positive portion of the X axis, and a point on the positive Y-portion of the XY plane
?	Lists specified saved coordinate systems

UCSICON
Purpose
Controls visibility and placement of the User Coordinate System icon.
Options

A	Changes settings in all active viewports
N	Displays the icon at the lower-left corner of the viewport
OR	Displays the icon at the origin of the current UCS if possible
OFF	Disables the coordinate system icon
ON	Enables the coordinate system icon

UNDEFINE
Purpose
Deletes the definition of a built-in AutoCAD command.

UNDO
Purpose
Reverses the effect of multiple commands, and provides control over the undo facility.
Options

number	Undoes the "number" most recent commands
A	Auto: controls treatment of menu items as UNDO Groups
B	Back: undoes back to previous UNDO Mark
C	Control: enables/disables the UNDO feature (see below for suboptions)
E	End: terminates an UNDO Group
G	Group: begins sequence to be treated as one command
M	Mark: places marker in UNDO file (for Back)

Suboptions for "C"

All	Enables the full UNDO feature
None	Disables U and UNDO entirely, and discards any previous UNDO information saved earlier in the editing session
One	Limits U and UNDO to a single operation

'UNITS
Purpose
Selects coordinate and angle display formats and precision.

'VIEW

Purpose

Saves the current graphics display and space as a Named View, or restores a saved view and space to the display.

Options

D	Deletes named view
R	Restores named view to screen
S	Saves current display as named view
W	Saves specified window as named view
?	Lists specified named views

VIEWPORTS (or VPORTS)

Purpose

Divides the AutoCAD graphics display into multiple viewports, each of which can contain a different view of the current drawing.

Options

D	Deletes a saved viewport configuration
J	Joins (merges) two viewports
R	Restores a saved viewport configuration
S	Saves the current viewport configuration
SI	Displays a single viewport filling the entire graphics area
2	Divides the current viewport into two viewports
3	Divides the current viewport into three viewports
4	Divides the current viewport into four viewports
?	Lists the current and saved viewport configurations

VIEWRES

Purpose

Allows you to control the precision and speed of Circle and Arc drawing on the monitor by specifying the number of sides in a Circle.

VPLAYER

Purpose

Sets viewport visibility for new and existing layers.

Options

?	Lists layers frozen in a selected viewport
Freeze	Freeze specified layers in selected viewport(s)
Thaw	Thaws specified layers in selected viewport(s)
Reset	Resets specified layers to their default visibility
Newfrz	Creates new layers that are frozen in all viewports
Vpvisdflt	Sets the default viewport visibility for existing layers

VPOINT

Purpose

Selects the viewpoint for a 3D visualization.

Options

R	Selects viewpoint via two rotation angles
RETURN	Selects viewpoint via compass & axes tripod
x,y,z	Specifies viewpoint

VSLIDE

Purpose

Displays a previously created slide file.

Options

file	Views slide
*file	Preloads slide, next VSLIDE will view

WBLOCK

Purpose

Writes selected entities to a disk file.

Options

name	Writes specified Block definition
=	Block name same as filename
*	Writes entire drawing
(blank)	Writes selected objects

XBIND

Purpose

Permanently adds a selected subset of an Xref's dependent symbols to your drawing.

Options

Block	Adds a Block
Dimstyle	Adds a dimstyle
Layer	Adds a layer
Ltype	Adds a linetype
Style	Adds a style

XREF

Purpose

Allows you to work with other AutoCAD drawings without adding them permanently to your drawing and without altering their contents.

Options

Attach	Attaches a new Xref or inserts a copy of an Xref that you've already attached. Also updates the display of an externally referenced drawing currently being edited by another person
Bind	Makes an Xref a permanent part of your drawing
Detach	Removes an Xref from your drawing
Path	Allows you to view and edit the filename that AutoCAD uses when loading a particular Xref
Reload	Updates one or more Xrefs at any time, including the display of an externally referenced drawing currently being edited by another person, without leaving and reentering AutoCAD
?	Lists Xrefs in your drawing and the drawing associated with each one

'ZOOM

Purpose

Enlarges or reduces the display of the drawing.

Options

number	Multiplier from original scale
numberX	Multiplier from current scale
numberXP	Scale relative to paper space
A	All
C	Center
D	Dynamic PAN/ZOOM
E	Extents
L	Lower-left corner
P	Previous
V	Virtual screen maximum
W	Window

3DFACE

Purpose

Draws 3D plane sections.

Option

I	Makes the following edge invisible

3DMESH

Purpose

Defines a 3D polygon mesh by specifying its size (in terms of "M" and "N") and the location of each vertex in the mesh.

3DPOLY

Purpose

Creates a 3D polyline.

Options

C	Closes the polyline back to the first point
U	Undoes the last segment entered
RETURN	Exits 3DPOLY command

Dimensioning Commands

ALIGNED

Purpose

Generates a linear dimension with the dimension line parallel to the specified extension line origin points. This permits you to align the dimensioning notation with the object.

ANGULAR

Purpose

Generates an arc to show the angle between two nonparallel lines or three specified points.

BASELINE

Purpose

Continues a linear dimension from the baseline (first extension line) of the previous or selected dimension.

CENTER

Purpose

Draws a Circle/Arc center mark or center lines.

CONTINUE

Purpose

Continues a linear dimension from the second extension line of the previous or selected dimension. In effect, this breaks one long dimension into shorter segments that add up to the total measurement.

DIAMETER

Purpose

Dimension the diameter of a circle or arc.

EXIT

Purpose

Returns to the normal Command mode.

HOMETEXT

Purpose

Restores the text of an associative Dimension to its default (home) location if you've moved it.

HORIZONTAL

Purpose

Generates a linear dimension with a horizontal dimension line.

LEADER

Purpose

Draws a line or sequence of lines (similar to the normal LINE command) for controlled placement of dimension text. Useful mostly for radius and diameter dimensioning.

NEWTEXT

Purpose

Changes the text of existing associative Dimensions.

OBLIQUE

Purpose

Adjusts obliquing angle of a linear associative dimension's extension lines.

ORDINATE

Purpose

Creates ordinate point associative dimensions.

OVERRIDE

Purpose

Overrides a subset of the dimension variable settings associated with a selected dimension entity.

RADIUS

Purpose

Dimensions the radius of a circle or arc, with an optional center mark or center lines.

REDRAW

Purpose

Redraws the entire display, erasing any marker blips that were present (just like the normal REDRAW command).

RESTORE

Purpose

Restores a specified dimension style by name or selection.

ROTATE

Purpose

Generates a linear dimension with the dimension line drawn at a specified angle.

SAVE

Purpose

Saves a group of dimension variables as a named dimension style.

STATUS

Purpose

Displays all dimensioning variables and their current values.

STYLE

Purpose

Switches to a new text style.

TROTATE

Purpose

Allows specification of a rotation angle for the text items of several associative dimensions at one time.

UNDO

Purpose

Undoes any changes made by the most recent dimensioning command.

UPDATE

Purpose

Updates existing associative Dimension entities to use the current settings of the dimension variables, the current text style, and the current DDUNITS (or UNITS) settings.

VARIABLES

Purpose

Lists the settings of dimension variables associated with a particular dimension style.

VERTICAL

Purpose

Generates a linear dimension with a vertical dimension line.

Appendix K: AutoCAD System Variables

Listed in this appendix are all AutoCAD system variables and their meanings. You can change all but read-only system variables at the "Command:" prompt using either the SETVAR command or AutoLISP's getvar and setvar functions. AutoCAD saves certain system variables in the configuration file ACAD.CFG, as indicated in the following. These settings apply to all drawings that you create and edit. AutoCAD saves other system variables in the drawing itself.

ACADPREFIX
Type: String
Meaning:
The directory path, if any, specified by the ACAD environment variable, with path separators appended if necessary (read-only).

ACADVER
Type: String
Meaning:
The AutoCAD version number, which can have values such as "12" or "12a" (read-only). (Note that this differs from the DXF file $ACADVER header variable, which contains the drawing database level number.)

AFLAGS
Type: Integer
Meaning:
Attribute flags code for ATTDEF command (sum of the following):
0	No Attribute mode selected
1	Invisible
2	Constant
4	Verify
8	Preset

ANGBASE
Type: Real
Saved in: Drawing
Meaning:
Angle 0 direction (with respect to the current UCS).

ANGDIR
Type: Integer
Saved in: Drawing
Meaning:
0	Counterclockwise (with respect to the current UCS)
1	Clockwise angles (with respect to the current UCS).

APERTURE
Type: Integer
Saved in: ACAD.CFG
Meaning:
Object snap target height, in pixels (default value = 10).

AREA
Type: Real
Meaning:
Last area computed by AREA, LIST, or DBLIST (read-only).

ATTDIA
Type: Integer
Saved in: Drawing
Meaning:
Controls the use of dialogue box with the INSERT command.
0	Causes the INSERT command to issue prompts
1	Causes the INSERT command to use a dialogue box for entry of Attribute values

ATTMODE
Type: Integer
Saved in: Drawing
Meaning:
Attribute display mode.
0	Off
1	Normal
2	On

ATTREQ
Type: Integer
Saved in: Drawing
Meaning:
Controls the use of prompts for values of Attributes.
0	Assumes defaults for the values of all Attributes during insert of Blocks
1	Enables prompts (or dialogue box) for Attribute values, as selected by ATTDIA

AUDITCTL
Type: Integer
Saved in: ACAD.CFG
Meaning:
Controls whether an .ADT log file (audit report file) is created.
0	Disables (or prevents) the writing of .ADT log files
1	Enables the writing of .ADT log files by the AUDIT command

AUNITS
Type: Integer
Saved in: Drawing
Meaning:
Controls angular units mode.
0	Decimal degrees
1	Degrees/minutes/seconds
2	Grads
3	Radians
4	Surveyor's units

AUPREC
Type: Integer
Saved in: Drawing
Meaning:
Angular units decimal places.

BACKZ
Type: Integer
Saved in: Drawing
Meaning:
Back clipping plane offset from the target plane for the current viewport, in drawing units (read-only). Meaningful only if the Back clipping bit in VIEWMODE is on. (The distance of the back clipping plane from the camera point can be found be subtracting BACKZ from the camera-to-target distance.)

BLIPMODE
Type: Integer
Saved in: Drawing
Meaning:
Marker blips.
1	On
2	Off

CDATE
Type: Real
Meaning:
Calendar date/time (read-only).

CECOLOR
Type: String
Saved in: Drawing
Meaning:
Sets the color for new entities.

CELTYPE
Type: String
Saved in: Drawing
Meaning:
Sets the linetype for new entities.

CHAMFERA
Type: Real
Saved in: Drawing
Meaning:
Sets the first chamfer distance.

CHAMFERB
Type: Real
Saved in: Drawing
Meaning:
Sets the second chamfer distance.

CIRCLERAD
Type: Real
Meaning:
Sets the default circle radius.
0	No default
number	Sets default

CLAYER
Type: String
Saved in: Drawing
Meaning:
Sets the current layer.

CMDACTIVE
Type: Integer
Meaning:
Bit-code that indicates whether an ordinary command, transparent command, script, or dialogue box is active (read-only). It is the sum of the following:
1	Ordinary command is active
2	Ordinary command and a transparent command are active
4	Script is active
8	Dialogue box is active

CMDDIA
Type: Integer
Saved in: ACAD.CFG
Meaning:
Controls the use of dialogue boxes with the PLOT command.
0	Don't use dialogue boxes for PLOT command
1	Use dialogue boxes for PLOT command

CMDECHO
Type: Integer
Meaning:
Controls echo of prompts and input when the AutoLISP (command) function is used.
0	Echo is off
1	Echo is on

CMDNAMES

Type: String
Meaning:
Displays in English the name of the command (and transparent command) that is currently active.

COORDS

Type: Integer
Saved in: Drawing
Meaning:
Controls updating and display of coordinate display.

0	Coordinate display is updated on point picks only
1	Display of absolute coordinates is continuously updated
2	Distance and angle from last point are displayed when a distance or angle is requested

CVPORT

Type: Integer
Saved in: Drawing
Meaning:
The identification number of the current viewport.

DATE

Type: Real
Meaning:
Julian date/time (read-only).

DBMOD

Type: Integer
Meaning:
Bit-code that indicates the drawing modification status (read-only). It is the sum of the following:

1	Entity database modified
2	Symbol table modified
4	Database variable modified
8	Window modified
16	View modified

DIASTAT

Type: Integer
Meaning:
Dialogue box exit status (read-only).

0	The most recent dialogue box was exited via "CANCEL"
1	The most recent dialogue box was exited via "OK"

DIMxxx

Type: Assorted
Saved in: Drawing
Meaning:
All the dimensioning variables are also accessible as system variables. See Chapter 11 of the *AutoCAD Reference Manual* for descriptions of these variables.

DISTANCE

Type: Real
Meaning:
Distance computed by DIST command (read-only).

DONUTID

Type: Real
Meaning:
Default donut inside diameter (can be zero).

DONUTOD

Type: Real
Meaning:
Default donut outside diameter. (Must be nonzero. If DONUTID is larger than DONUTOD, the two values are swapped by the next command.)

DRAGMODE

Type: Integer
Saved in: Drawing
Meaning:
Controls dragging feature.

0	No dragging
1	On if requested
2	Auto

DRAGP1

Type: Integer
Saved in: ACAD.CFG
Meaning:
Regen-drag input sampling rate (default value = 10).

DRAGP2

Type: Integer
Saved in: ACAD.CFG
Meaning:
Fast-drag input sampling rate (default value = 25).

DWGCODEPAGE

Type: String
Saved in: Drawing (header)
Meaning:
Drawing code page. This variable is set to the system code page when a new drawing is created, but otherwise AutoCAD doesn't maintain it. It should reflect the code page of the drawing and you can set it to any of the values used by the SYSCODEPAGE system variable or "undefined."

DWGNAME

Type: String
Meaning:
Drawing name as entered by the user (read-only). If the drawing hasn't been named yet, DWGNAME reports that it is "unnamed." If the user specified a drive/directory prefix, it is included as well.

DWGPREFIX

Type: String
Meaning:
Drive/directory prefix for drawing (read-only).

DWGTITLED

Type: Integer
Meaning:
Bit-code that indicates whether the current drawing has been named (read-only).

0   The drawing has not been named
1   The drawing has been named

DWGWRITE

Type: Integer
Meaning:
Controls the initial state of the read-only toggle in the OPEN command's "Open Drawing" standard file dialogue box.

0   Opens the drawing for reading only
1   Opens the drawing for reading and writing (default)

ELEVATION

Type: Real
Saved in: Drawing
Meaning:
Current 3D elevation, relative to the current UCS for the current space.

ERRNO

Type: Integer
Meaning:
Code for errors caused by on-line programs such as AutoLISP and ADS applications.

EXPERT

Type: Integer
Meaning:
Controls the issuance of certain "Are you sure?" prompts, as indicated below:

0   Issues all prompts normally (default)
1   Suppresses "About to regen, proceed?" and "Really want to turn the current layer off?"
2   Suppresses the preceding prompts and BLOCK's "Block already defined. Redefine it?" and SAVE/WBLOCK's "A drawing with this name already exists. Overwrite it?"
3   Suppresses the preceding prompts and those issued by LINETYPE if you try to load a linetype that's already loaded or create a new linetype in a file that already defines it

4   Suppresses the preceding prompts and those issued by "UCS Save" and "VPORTS Save" if the name you supply already exists
5   Suppresses the preceding prompts and those issued by "DIM SAVE" and "DIM OVERRIDE" if the dimension style name you supply already exists (the entries are redefined)

(When a prompt is suppressed by EXPERT, the operation in question is performed as though you had responded "Y" to the prompt. In the future, values greater than 5 may be used to suppress additional safety prompts. The setting of EXPERT can affect scripts, menu macros, AutoLISP, and the command functions.)

EXTMAX

Type: 3D point
Saved in: Drawing
Meaning:
Upper-right point of drawing extents. Expands outward as new objects are drawn, shrinks only by ZOOM All or ZOOM Extents. Reported in World coordinates for the current space (read-only).

EXTMIN

Type: 3D point
Saved in: Drawing
Meaning:
Lower-left point of drawing extents. Expands outward as new objects are drawn, shrinks only by ZOOM All or ZOOM Extents. Reported in World coordinates for the current space (read-only).

FILEDIA

Type: Integer
Saved in: ACAD.CFG
Meaning:
Controls use of file dialogue boxes.

0   Don't use file dialogue boxes unless requested via ~ (tilde)
1   Use file dialogue boxes if possible

FILLETRAD

Type: Real
Saved in: Drawing
Meaning:
Fillet radius.

FILLMODE

Type: Integer
Saved in: Drawing
Meaning:
Controls fill mode.

0   Off
1   On

FRONTZ

Type: Real
Saved in: Drawing
Meaning:
Front clipping plane offset from the target plane for the current viewport, in drawing units (read-only).
Meaningful only if the front clipping bit in VIEWMODE is On and the Front clip not at eye bit is also On. The distance of the front clipping plane from the camera point can be found by subtracting FRONTZ from the camera-to-target distance.

GRIDMODE

Type: Integer
Saved in: Drawing
Meaning:
Controls use of grid.
1	Grid on for current viewport
2	Grid off for current viewport

GRIDUNIT

Type: 2D point
Saved in: Drawing
Meaning:
Grid spacing for current viewport, X and Y.

GRIPBLOCK

Type: Integer
Saved in: ACAD.CFG
Meaning:
Controls the assignment of grips in Blocks.
0	Assigns grip only to the insertion point of the Block (default)
1	Assigns grips to entities within the block

GRIPCOLOR

Type: Integer (1-255)
Saved in: ACAD.CFG
Meaning:
Color of nonselected grips; drawing as a box outline (default value = 5).

GRIPHOT

Type: Integer (1-255)
Saved in: ACAD.CFG
Meaning:
Color of selected grips; drawn as a filled box (default value = 1).

GRIPS

Type: Integer
Saved in: ACAD.CFG
Meaning:
Allows the use of selection set grips for the Stretch, Move, Rotate, Scale, and Mirror modes.
0	Disables grips
1	Enables grips (default)

(To adjust the size of the grips, use the GRIPSIZE variable. To adjust the effective pick area used by the graphics cursor when you snap to a grip, use the GRIPSIZE system variable.)

GRIPSIZE

Type: Integer (1-255)
Saved in: ACAD.CFG
Meaning:
The size in pixels of the box drawn to display the grip (default value = 3).

HANDLES

Type: Integer
Saved in: Drawing
Meaning:
Enables/disables entity handles (read-only).
0	Disables entity handles
1	Enables entity handles

HIGHLIGHT

Type: Integer
Meaning:
Object selection highlighting.
0	Off
1	On

(HIGHLIGHT does not affect objects selected with grips.)

HPANG

Type: Real
Meaning:
Default hatch pattern angle.

HPDOUBLE

Type: Integer
Meaning:
Default hatch pattern doubling for "U" user-defined patterns.
0	Disables doubling
1	Enables doubling

HPNAME
Type: String
Meaning:
Default hatch pattern name. Up to 34 characters, no spaces allowed. Returns " " if there is no default. Enter . (period) to set no default.

HPSCALE
Type: Real
Meaning:
Default hatch pattern scale factor (must be nonzero).

HPSPACE
Type: Real
Meaning:
Default hatch pattern line spacing for "U" user-defined simple patterns (must be nonzero).

INSBASE
Type: 3D point
Saved in: Drawing
Meaning:
Insertion base point (set by BASE command) expressed in UCS coordinates for the current space.

INSNAME
Type: String
Meaning:
Default block name for DDINSERT or INSERT. The name must conform to symbol naming conventions. Returns " " if there is no default. Enter . (period) to set no default.

LASTANGLE
Type: Real
Meaning:
The end angle of the last arc entered, relative to the XY plane of the current UCS for the current space (read-only).

LASTPOINT
Type: 3D point
Meaning:
The last point entered, expressed in UCS coordinates for the current space. Referenced by @ during keyboard entry.

LENSLENGTH
Type: Real
Saved in: Drawing
Meaning:
Length of the lens (in millimeters) used in perspective viewing, for the current viewport (read-only).

LIMCHECK
Type: Integer
Saved in: Drawing
Meaning:
Limits checking for the current space.
0   Off
1   On

LIMMAX
Type: 2D point
Saved in: Drawing
Meaning:
Upper-right drawing limits for the current space, expressed in World coordinates.

LIMMIN
Type: 2D point
Saved in: Drawing
Meaning:
Lower-left drawing limits for the current space, expressed in World coordinates.

LOGINNAME
Type: String
Meaning:
Displays the user's name as configured or input when AutoCAD is loaded (read-only).

LTSCALE
Type: Real
Saved in: Drawing
Meaning:
Global linetype scale factor.

LUNITS
Type: Integer
Saved in: Drawing
Meaning:
Linear units mode.
1   Scientific
2   Decimal
3   Engineering
4   Architectural
5   Fractional

LUPREC
Type: Integer
Saved in: Drawing
Meaning:
Linear units decimal places or denominator.

MACROTRACE

Type: Integer
Meaning:
Debugging tool for DIESEL expressions (see the
AutoCAD Customization Manual for details).

0	Disables MACROTRACE (default)
1	Displays an evaluation of all DIESEL expressions in the command line area, including an evaluation of expressions used in menus and the status line

MAXACTVP

Type: Integer
Meaning:
Maximum number of viewports to regenerate at one time.

MAXSORT

Type: Integer
Saved in: ACAD.CFG
Meaning:
Maximum number of symbol/file names to be sorted by listing commands. If the total number of items exceeds this number, then none of the items are sorted (default value = 200)

MENUCTL

Type: Integer
Saved in: ACAD.CFG
Meaning:
Controls the page switching of the screen menu.

0	Screen menu doesn't switch pages in response to keyboard command entry
1	Screen menu switches pages in response to keyboard command entry (default)

MENUECHO

Type: Integer
Meaning:
Menu echo/prompt control bits (sum of the following):

0	All menu items and system prompts are displayed (default)
1	Suppresses echo of menu items (^P in a menu item toggles echoing)
2	Suppresses printing of system prompts during menu
4	Disables ^P toggle of menu echoing
8	Debugging aid for DIESEL macros; prints input/output strings

MENUNAME

Type: String
Saved in: Drawing
Meaning:
The name of the currently loaded menu file. Includes a drive/path prefix if you entered it (read-only).

MIRRTEXT

Type: Integer
Saved in: Drawing
Meaning:
Controls mirroring of text.

0	MIRROR command retains text direction
nonzero	MIRROR command reflects text

MODEMACRO

Type: String
Meaning:
Allows you to display a text string in the status line, such as the name of the current drawing, time/date stamp, or special modes. You can use MODEMACRO to display a simple string of text, or use special text strings written in the DIESEL macro language to have AutoCAD evaluate the macro from time to time and base the status line on user-selected conditions. See the *AutoCAD Customization Manual* for details.

OFFSETDIST

Type: Real
Meaning:
Sets the default offset distance. If you enter a negative value, it defaults to Through mode.

ORTHOMODE

Type: Integer
Saved in: Drawing
Meaning:
Controls Ortho mode.

0	Off
1	On

OSMODE

Type: Integer
Saved in: Drawing
Meaning:
Sets object snap modes using the following bit codes. To specify more than one osnap, enter the sum of their values. For example, entering 3 specifies the Endpoint (1) and Midpoint (2) osnaps.

0	NONe
1	ENDpoint
2	MIDpoint
4	CENter
8	NODe
16	QUAdrant
32	INTersection
64	INSertion
128	PERpendicular
256	TANgent
512	NEArest
1024	QUIck

PDMODE
Type: Integer
Saved in: Drawing
Meaning:
Point entity display mode.

PDSIZE
Type: Real
Saved in: Drawing
Meaning:
Point entity display size.

PERIMETER
Type: Real
Meaning:
Perimeter computed by AREA, LIST, or DBLIST (read-only).

PFACEVMAX
Type: Integer
Meaning:
Maximum number of vertices per face (read-only).

PICKADD
Type: Integer
Saved in: ACAD.CFG
Meaning:
Controls additive selection of entities.

0   Disables PICKADD. The most recently selected entities become the selection set. Previously selected entities are removed from the selection set. (You can add more entities to the selection set, however, by holding down the SHIFT key while selecting the entities.)

1   Enables PICKADD. Each entity you select, either individually or by windowing, is added to the current selection set. To remove entities from the selection set, hold down the SHIFT key while selecting. (default)

PICKAUTO
Type: Integer
Saved in: ACAD.CFG
Meaning:
Controls automatic windowing when the "Select objects:" prompt appears.

0   Disables PICKAUTO

1   Allows you to draw a selection window (or crossing window) automatically at the "Select objects:" prompt (default)

PICKBOX
Type: Integer
Saved in: ACAD.CFG
Meaning:
Object selection target height, in pixels.

PICKDRAG
Type: Integer
Saved in: ACAD.CFG
Meaning:
Controls the method of drawing a selection window.

0   You draw the selection window by clicking the mouse at one corner, and then at the other corner (default)

1   You draw the selection window by clicking at one corner, holding down the mouse button, dragging, and releasing the mouse button at the other corner

PICKFIRST
Type: Integer
Saved in: ACAD.CFG
Meaning:
Controls the method of entity selection so that you can select objects first, and then use an edit/inquiry command.

0   Disables PICKFIRST

1   Enables PICKFIRST (default)

PLATFORM
Type: String
Meaning:
Read-only message that indicates which version of AutoCAD is in use.

PLINEGEN
Type: Integer
Saved in: Drawing
Meaning:
Sets the linetype pattern generation around the vertices of a 2D Polyline.

0   Polylines are generated with the linetype to start and end with a dash at each vertex

1   Linetype is generated in a continuous pattern around the vertices of the Polyline

PLINEGEN doesn't apply to Polylines with tapered segments.

PLINEWID
Type: Real
Saved in: Drawing
Meaning:
Default polyline width (can be zero).

PLOTID
Type: String
Saved in: ACAD.CFG
Meaning:
Changes the default plotter, based on its assigned description.

PLOTTER

Type: Integer
Saved in: ACAD.CFG
Meaning:
Changes the default plotter, based on its assigned integer (0-maximum configured). You can create up to 29 configurations.

POLYSIDES

Type: Integer
Meaning:
Default number of sides for the POLYGON command. The range is 3-1024.

POPUPS

Type: Integer
Meaning:
Reports the availability of dialogue boxes, the menu bar, pull-down menus, and icon menus for the currently configured display driver (read-only).

0   Features are not available
1   Features are available

PSLTSCALE

Type: Integer
Saved in: Drawing
Meaning:
Controls paper space linetype scaling.

0   No special linetype scaling
1   Viewport scaling governs linetype scaling

PSPROLOG

Type: String
Saved in: ACAD.CFG
Meaning:
Assigns a name for a prologue section to be read from the ACAD.PSF file when using the PSOUT command. (See the *AutoCAD Customization Manual* for details.)

PSQUALITY

Type: Integer
Saved in: ACAD.CFG
Meaning:
Controls the rendering quality of PostScript images and whether they are drawn as filled objects or as outlines.

0   Disables PostScript image generation
nonzero   Enables PostScript image generation

(A positive setting sets the number of pixels per AutoCAD drawing unit for the PostScript resolution; a negative setting sets the number of pixels per drawing unit, but uses the absolute value and causes AutoCAD to show the PostScript paths as outlines.)

QTEXTMODE

Type: Integer
Saved in: Drawing
Meaning:
Controls quick text mode.

0   Off
1   On

REGENMODE

Type: Integer
Saved in: Drawing
Meaning:
Reports status of REGENAUTO.

0   Off
1   On

RE-INIT

Type: Integer
Meaning:
Reinitializes the I/O ports, digitizer, display, plotter, and ACAD.PGP file using the following bit codes. To specify more than one reinitialization, enter the sum of their values.

1   Digitizer port reinitialization
2   Plotter port reinitialization
4   Digitizer reinitialization
8   Display reinitialization
16   PGP file reinitialization (reload)

SAVEFILE

Type: String
Saved in: ACAD.CFG
Meaning:
Current Autosave filename (read-only).

SAVENAME

Type: String
Meaning:
The filename you save the drawing to (read-only).

SAVETIME

Type: Integer
Saved in: ACAD.CFG
Meaning:
Automatic save interval, in minutes (or 0 to disable automatic saves). The SAVETIME timer starts as soon as you make a change to a drawing, and is reset and restarts by a manual SAVE, SAVEAS, or QSAVE. The current drawing is saved to AUTO.SV$.

SCREENBOXES
Type: Integer
Saved in: ACAD.CFG
Meaning:
The number of boxes in the screen menu area of the graphics area (read-only).
0   Screen menu is disabled

(On platforms that permit the AutoCAD graphics window to be resized or the screen menu to be reconfigured during an editing session, the value of this variable might change during the editing session.)

SCREENMODE
Type: Integer
Saved in: ACAD.CFG
Meaning:
A (read-only) bit code indicating the graphics/text state of the AutoCAD display. It is the sum of the following bit values:
0   Text screen is displayed
1   Graphics mode is displayed
2   Dual-screen display configuration

SCREENSIZE
Type: 2D point
Meaning:
Current viewport size in pixels, X and Y (read-only).

SHADEDGE
Type: Integer
Saved in: Drawing
Meaning:
Controls shading of faces and edges.
0   Faces shaded, edges not highlighted
1   Faces shaded, edges drawn in background color
2   Faces not filled, edges in entity color
3   Faces in entity color, edges in background color

SHADEDIF
Type: Integer
Saved in: Drawing
Meaning:
Ratio of diffuse reflective light to ambient light (in percent of diffuse reflective light).

SHPNAME
Type: String
Meaning:
Default shape name. Must conform to symbol naming conventions. If no default is set, it returns a " ". Enter . (period) to set no default.

SKETCHINC
Type: Real
Saved in: Drawing
Meaning:
SKETCH record increment.

SKPOLY
Type: Integer
Saved in: Drawing
Meaning:
Controls type of line generated by SKETCH.
0   Lines generated
1   Polylines generated

SNAPANG
Type: Real
Saved in: Drawing
Meaning:
Snap/grid rotation angle (UCS-relative) for the current viewport.

SNAPBASE
Type: 2D point
Saved in: Drawing
Meaning:
Snap/grid origin point for the current viewport (in UCS X,Y coordinates).

SNAPISOPAIR
Type: Integer
Saved in: Drawing
Meaning:
Current isometric plane for the current viewport.
0   Left
1   Top
2   Right

SNAPMODE
Type: Integer
Saved in: Drawing
Meaning:
Controls snap for current viewport.
0   Off
1   On

SNAPSTYL
Type: Integer
Saved in: Drawing
Meaning:
Snap style for current viewport.
0   Standard
1   Isometric

SNAPUNIT

Type: 2D point
Saved in: Drawing
Meaning:
Snap spacing for current viewport, X and Y.

SORTENTS

Type: Integer
Saved in: ACAD.CFG
Meaning:
Controls the display of entity sort order operations using the following codes. To select more than one, enter the sum of their codes. (The default, 96, specifies sort operations for plotting and PostScript output.)

0	Disables SORTENTS
1	Sort for object selection
2	Sort for object snap
4	Sort for redraws
8	Sort for MSLIDE slide creation
16	Sort for REGENs
32	Sort for plotting
64	Sort for PostScript output

SPLFRAME

Type: Integer
Saved in: Drawing
Meaning:
Controls display of spline surfaces.

0	Does not display the control polygon for spline fit Polylines; displays the fit surface of a polygon mesh, not the defining mesh; does not display the invisible edges of 3D Faces
1	Displays the control polygon for spline fit Polylines; displays only the defining mesh of a surface fit polygon mesh (the fit surface is not displayed); displays invisible edges of 3D Faces

SPLINESEGS

Type: Integer
Saved in: Drawing
Meaning:
The number of line segments to be generated for each spline patch.

SPLINETYPE

Type: Integer
Saved in: Drawing
Meaning:
The type of line segments to be generated by PEDIT Spline.

5	Quadratic B-spline
6	Cubic B-spline

SURFTAB1

Type: Integer
Saved in: Drawing
Meaning:
Number of tabulations to be generated for RULESURF and TABSURF. Also mesh density in the M direction for REVSURF and EDGESURF.

SURFTAB2

Type: Integer
Saved in: Drawing
Meaning:
Mesh density in the N direction for REVSURF and EDGESURF.

SURFTYPE

Type: Integer
Saved in: Drawing
Meaning:
Type of surface fitting to be performed by PEDIT Smooth.

5	Quadratic B-spline
6	Cubic B-spline
8	Bezier surface

SURFU

Type: Integer
Saved in: Drawing
Meaning:
Surface density in the M direction.

SURFV

Type: Integer
Saved in: Drawing
Meaning:
Surface density in the N direction.

SYSCODEPAGE

Type: String
Saved in: Drawing
Meaning:
Indicates the system code page specified in ACAD.XMF (read-only). Codes are as follows:

ASCII	dos863	iso8859-4
dos437	dos864	iso8859-5
dos850	dos865	iso8859-6
dos852	dos869	iso8859-7
dos855	dos932	iso8859-8
dos857	iso8859-1	iso8859-9
dos860	iso8859-2	mac-roman
dos861	iso8859-3	

TABMODE
Type: Integer
Meaning:
Controls the use of Tablet mode.
0   Disables Tablet mode
1   Enables Tablet mode

TARGET
Type: 3D point
Saved in: Drawing
Meaning:
Location (in UCS coordinates) of the target (look-at) point for the current viewport (read-only).

TDCREATE
Type: Real
Saved in: Drawing
Meaning:
Time and date of drawing creation (read-only).

TDINDWG
Type: Real
Saved in: Drawing
Meaning:
Total editing time (read only).

TDUPDATE
Type: Real
Saved in: Drawing
Meaning:
Time and date of last update/save (read-only).

TDUSRTIMER
Type: Real
Saved in: Drawing
Meaning:
User elapsed timer (read-only).

TEMPPREFIX
Type: String
Meaning:
Contains the directory name (if any) configured for placement of temporary files, with a path separator appended if necessary (read-only).

TEXTEVAL
Type: Integer
Meaning:
Controls how text strings and Attribute values are evaluated by AutoCAD.
0   All responses are taken literally
1   Text starting with "(" or "!" is evaluated as an AutoLISP expression, as for nontextual input. (Note that the DTEXT command takes all input literally, regardless of the setting of TEXTEVAL.)

TEXTSIZE
Type: Real
Saved in: Drawing
Meaning:
The default height for new Text entities drawn with the current text style (meaningless if the style has a fixed height).

TEXTSTYLE
Type: String
Saved in: Drawing
Meaning:
Contains the name of the current text style.

THICKNESS
Type: Real
Saved in: Drawing
Meaning:
Current 3D thickness.

TILEMODE
Type: Integer
Saved in: Drawing
Meaning:
0   Enables paper space and Viewport entities (uses MVIEW)
1   Release 10 compatibility mode (uses VPORTS)

TRACEWID
Type: Real
Saved in: Drawing
Meaning:
Default trace width.

TREEDEPTH
Type: Integer
Saved in: Drawing
Meaning:
A 4-digit (maximum) code that specifies the number of times the tree-structured spatial index may divide into branches, hence affecting the speed in which AutoCAD searches the database before completing an action. The first two digits refer to the depth of the model space nodes, and the second two digits refer to the depth of paper space nodes. Use a positive setting for 3D drawings and a negative setting for 2D drawings.

UCSFOLLOW

Type: Integer
Saved in: Drawing
Meaning:
Controls how UCS changes affect the current view.

0   UCS change does not affect the view
1   Any UCS change causes an automatic change to plan view of the new UCS (in the current viewport)

The setting of UCSFOLLOW is maintained separately for both spaces and can be accessed in either space, but the setting is ignored while in paper space (it is always treated as if set to 0).

UCSICON

Type: Integer
Saved in: Drawing
Meaning:
The coordinate system icon bit-code for the current viewport (sum of the following):

1   On (icon display enabled)
2   Origin (if icon display is enabled, the icon floats to the UCS origin if possible)

UCSNAME

Type: String
Saved in: Drawing
Meaning:
Name of the current coordinate system for the current space. Returns a null string if the current UCS is unnamed (read-only).

UCSORG

Type: 3D point
Saved in: Drawing
Meaning:
The origin point of the current coordinate system for the current space, in World coordinates (read-only).

UCSXDIR

Type: 3D point
Saved in: Drawing
Meaning:
The X-direction of the current UCS for the current space (read-only).

UCSYDIR

Type: 3D point
Saved in: Drawing
Meaning:
The Y-direction of the current UCS for the current space (read-only).

UNDOCTL

Type: Integer
Meaning:
A (read-only) code indicating the state of the UNDO feature. It is the sum of the following values:

1   Set if UNDO is enabled
2   Set if only one command can be undone
4   Set if Auto-group mode is enabled
8   Set if a group is currently active

UNDOMARKS

Type: Integer
Meaning:
The (read-only) number of marks that have been placed in the UNDO control stream by the UNDO command's Mark option. The Mark and Back options are unavailable if a group is currently active.

UNITMODE

Type: Integer
Saved in: Drawing
Meaning:
Controls display mode for fractional, feet and inches, and surveyor's angles

0   Displays as previously set
1   Displays in input format

USERI1-5

Type: Integer
Saved in: Drawing
Meaning:
Five variables for storage and retrieval of integer values. Intended for use by third-party developers.

USERR1-5

Type: Real
Saved in: Drawing
Meaning:
Five variables for storage and retrieval of real numbers. Intended for use by third-party developers.

USERS1-5

Type: String
Meaning:
Five variables for storage and retrieval of text string data. Accepts strings with embedded blanks. To discard the existing text string, enter ".". The maximum string length is platform-dependent, and can be as low as 460 characters. Intended for use by third-party developers.

VIEWCTR

Type: 2D point
Saved in: Drawing
Meaning:
Center of view in current viewport, expressed in UCS coordinates (read-only).

VIEWDIR

Type: 3D vector
Saved in: Drawing
Meaning:
The current viewport's viewing direction expressed in UCS coordinates. This describes the camera point as a 3D offset from the TARGET point (read-only).

VIEWMODE

Type: Integer
Saved in: Drawing
Meaning:
Viewing mode bit-code for the current viewport (read-only). The value is the sum of the following:

1	Perspective view active
2	Front clipping on
4	Back clipping on
8	UCS follow mode on
16	Front clip not at eye

If on, the front clip distance (FRONTZ) determines the front clipping plane. If off, FRONTZ is ignored and the front clipping plane is set to pass through the camera point. This flag is ignored if the front clipping bit (2) is off.

VIEWSIZE

Type: Real
Saved in: Drawing
Meaning:
Height of view in current viewport, expressed in drawing units (read-only).

VIEWTWIST

Type: Real
Saved in: Drawing
Meaning:
View twist angle for the current viewport (read-only).

VISRETAIN

Type: Integer
Saved in: Drawing
Meaning:
Determines precedence of current drawing's On/Off, Freeze/Thaw, color, and linetype settings for Xref-dependent layers over Xref's layer definition

0	Settings in current drawing take precedence
1	Settings in current drawing do not take precedence (default)

VSMAX

Type: 3D point
Meaning:
The upper-right corner of the current viewport's virtual screen, expressed in UCS coordinates (read-only).

VSMIN

Type: 3D point
Meaning:
The lower-left corner of the current viewport's virtual screen, expressed in UCS coordinates (read-only).

WORLDUCS

Type: Integer
Meaning:
Reports whether current UCS is the same as the World Coordinate System (read-only).

0	Current UCS is not the same as the World Coordinate System
1	Current UCS is the same as the World Coordinate System

WORLDVIEW

Type: Integer
Saved in: Drawing
Meaning:
DVIEW and VPOINT command input is relative to the current UCS.

1	Current UCS is changed to the WCS for the duration of a DVIEW or VPOINT command (default)

XREFCTL

Type: Integer
Saved in: ACAD.CFG
Meaning:
Controls whether .XLG files (external reference log files) are written.

0	Xref log (.XLG) files are not written
1	Xref log (.XLG) files are written

Index